# THE FANTASY WORLDS OF
# IRWIN ALLEN

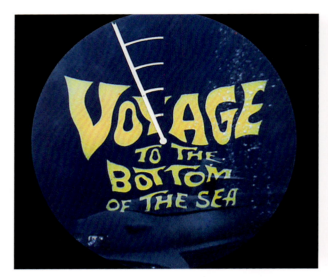

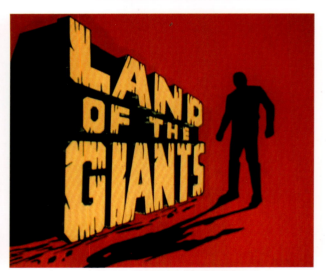

# THE FANTASY WORLDS OF IRWIN ALLEN

## JEFF BOND

Foreword by Bill Mumy

Design by Jason Adam

**TITAN** BOOKS

THE FANTASY WORLDS OF IRWIN ALLEN®
ISBN: 9781835411360

First edition: October 2024

10 9 8 7 6 5 4 3 2 1

Published by Titan Books
A division of Titan Publishing Group Ltd
144 Southwark St, London SE1 0UP

www.titanbooks.com

Author: Jeff Bond
Designed by Jason Adam
Editor: John Michlig

Special Thanks to: Joe Sikoryak, Matthew Abrams

All text and original material in this book is © 2024 Legendary Pictures, LLC. Licensed by Synthesis Entertainment. All Rights Reserved.

The Fantasy Worlds of Irwin Allen® is a registered trademark of Synthesis Entertainment.

No similarity between any of the names, characters, persons, and/or institutions in this book with those of any living or dead person or institution is intended, and any such similarity that may exist is purely coincidental.

Did you enjoy this book? We love to hear from our readers. Please e-mail us at: readerfeedback@titanemail.com or write to Reader Feedback at the above address.

To receive advance information, news, competitions, and exclusive offers online, please sign up for the Titan newsletter on our website: www.titanbooks.com

No part of this publication may be reproduced, stored in a retrieval system, or transmitted, in any form or by any means without the prior written permission of the publisher, nor be otherwise circulated in any form of binding or cover other than that in which it is published and without a similar condition being imposed on the subsequent purchaser.

A CIP catalogue record for this title is available from the British Library.

Printed in China

To Logan Bond, my own little Will Robinson—
here's what I was into when I was your age.


And to Sheila Mathews Allen, whose loving interest
in protecting her husband's legacy made this book possible.

# CONTENTS

ix    FOREWORD
       *By Bill Mumy*

1    INTRODUCTION

2    **CHAPTER 1**
     **THE IRWIN ALLEN SHOW**
       – *Hollywood Merry-Go-Round*
       – *The Sea Around Us*

22    **CHAPTER 2**
     **THE MISUNDERSTOOD HERO**
       – *Dangerous Mission*
       – *The Animal World*

46    **CHAPTER 3**
     **IN THE FOOTSTEPS OF DEMILLE**
       – *The Story of Mankind*
       – *The Big Circus*

78    **CHAPTER 4**
     **THE TOY BOX**
       – *The Lost World*
       – *Voyage to the Bottom of the Sea*
       – *Five Weeks in a Balloon*

130    **CHAPTER 5**
     **MOVIES ON TV**
       – *Tales of Edgar Allan Poe*
       – *Voyage to the Bottom of the Sea*

178    **CHAPTER 6**
     **SPACE FAMILY ROBINSON**
       – *Lost in Space*

254    **CHAPTER 7**
     **THREE RING CIRCUS**
       – *The Time Tunnel*

294    **CHAPTER 8**
     **UNDERFOOT**
       – *Land of the Giants*

328    **CHAPTER 9**
     **THE SHOWS THAT NEVER WERE**
       – *The Man from the 25th Century*
       – *City Beneath the Sea*

374    **CHAPTER 10**
     **VOYAGE TO THE TOP OF THE BOX OFFICE**
       – *The Poseidon Adventure*

418    **CHAPTER 11**
     **NOVEL SOLUTION**
       – *The Towering Inferno*

456    **CHAPTER 12**
     **THE MASTER OF DISASTER**
       – *Viva Knievel!*
       – *The Return of Captain Nemo*

486    **CHAPTER 13**
     **BAD BUZZ**
       – *The Swarm*

520    **CHAPTER 14**
     **SEQUELS AND VOLCANOES**
       – *Beyond the Poseidon Adventure*
       – *When Time Ran Out...*

552    **CHAPTER 15**
     **IRWIN IN WONDERLAND**
       – *Alice in Wonderland*
       – *Pinocchio*

584    **CHAPTER 16**
     **LIFE AFTER DEATH**

**OPPOSITE**
Guy Williams, June Lockhart, and Mark Goddard in an early CBS publicity still from Irwin Allen's TV series *Lost in Space*.

# FOREWORD

## By Bill Mumy

During the years I worked for him—and for several more beyond—Irwin Allen was larger than life. Hugely successful and instantly recognizable, he stood out from everyone else. Irwin was one of the last of the "old-time Hollywood producers" who had been a part of showbiz since the Golden Age. His talent and tenacity helped him earn the title "The Master of Disaster"—thanks to a string of hits, both in television and feature films, that stretched for more than two decades.

Although many considered Irwin a complicated man, in many ways, he was really just a big kid. He liked the kinds of things that kids like: dinosaurs, the circus, outer space, deep-sea exploration, time travel, and alien worlds. He loved to play in arenas where the imagination could soar unbridled. Since I was just a kid when I knew and worked for him, he and I got along fine.

Physically, Irwin was quite a bold and colorful character. He always wore bright-colored sweaters, usually yellow or pink. Although he grew up in New York City, he spoke in a Kennedyesque Boston accent. He wore thick glasses, but by far his most distinguishable feature was the bird's nest of black hair that rested on top of his head. It was one of the great wonders of the modern world. Everyone at 20th Century Fox studios talked about Irwin's coiffe, *sotto voce* behind his back. It wasn't a toupee—but it wasn't a comb-over either. It was kind of a "comb up and over and around." Rumor was that he had had it especially designed by the legendary hairstylist, Jay Sebring. I can't imagine the process he must have undertaken before leaving his home and heading to the studio every day to get that strange floating dark mass of tresses—that seemingly came together from every possible direction—into place. But looking back on it, I truly respect him for doing it, because it was always perfect. Just like his productions.

Irwin was famous for assembling excellence. His casts, his sets, his props, his special effects, and his composers were always impressive. Irwin Allen productions were spectacular studio events. As far as the cast and crew were concerned, they were difficult and oftimes dangerous undertakings, but they created an indelible impression on audiences.

Irwin is remembered, as he should be, mainly as a producer, but I don't think he gets enough credit for his abilities as a director—although in this regard he was often unintentionally comical.

I can't help but laugh when I recall my experiences on the Fox lot making the original *Lost in Space* pilot with Irwin at the helm. It was a totally positive environment shot on several soundstages with multiple fantastic sets. However, regardless of whether I was filming a master scene with explosives and six fellow cast

**OPPOSITE**
The once and future Will: Maxwell Jenkins and Bill Mumy on the set of Netflix's 2018 *Lost in Space* series.

members (along with a chimpanzee in a furry hat) on a supposedly imposing alien planet, or we were shooting a quiet two-shot in the interior of the Jupiter 2, Irwin always communicated his direction to the cast through a bullhorn.

To this day, I can still hear him yelling "ACTION!" and "CUT!" at the top of his lungs through that bullhorn.

He also used to bang on a metal pail with a small hammer to cue us all to "LURCH," as he called it, from one side of the frame to the other. Irwin liked noise and he made a lot of it. Yes, it was absurd, but in the end the results turned out wonderfully. I personally wish Irwin had continued to direct more episodes of *Lost in Space* beyond the pilot. But he didn't. He was always moving forward and always had several projects in pre-production that he was focused on.

The Fox lot was a busy and magical place in the 1960s. Every soundstage was full with a variety of projects ranging from the prime time soap opera, *Peyton Place*, to sci-fi fantasy films like *Fantastic Voyage* and *Planet of the Apes*.

There were a lot of television shows filmed at Fox back then: *Batman, The Green Hornet, Daniel Boone, Julia,* and *12 O'Clock High,* just to name a few. But the "big man on campus" was unquestionably Irwin Allen. At one time he had no less than three television series being filmed simultaneously on the Fox studio grounds.

My personal impression of him was that, as nice as he could be to his "stars" (as he called them), he could be very tough on his crews—particularly his directors. Every day after lunch, he would show up on our stage and approach whatever setup we were working on. He'd stand there without saying anything with a somewhat dour expression on his round bespectacled face and tap his watch. It meant, "Time is money." After properly intimidating whoever was currently directing the episode being shot, Irwin would depart and repeat the procedure on the surrounding soundstages where his other shows were filming. Everyone snapped to attention when Irwin was around.

He liked to surround himself with "yes men"—chief among them was Paul Zastupnevich (or, "Paul Z" as we used to call him). Paul was Irwin's costume designer and designed all of our wardrobe on *Lost in Space*. He also designed many of our "monsters." But Paul was also Irwin's personal assistant and, in that regard, he was devoted. Irwin appreciated loyalty, that's for sure. He often hired the same actors, writers, and directors again and again. It was kind of a "stock company."

Irwin's office was both impressive and intimidating. When you entered he was often seated behind a huge dark desk that sat on a raised platform. This was designed so that Irwin was on a higher level than everyone else.

His office was always filled with panoply of very cool storyboards and wardrobe or set sketches for multiple projects that were either currently in production or in development. Irwin's inner sanctum was also a place where he kept merchandise from his shows. I made it a habit to visit Irwin often, because, when I did, he would always give me a *Lost in Space* model kit or a Mattel laser rifle. Of course, on each occasion the budget-conscious Irwin would always say, "You may have *one*, Billy."

I worked for Irwin from the age of ten till the age of fourteen. I rarely saw him after we finished filming *Lost in Space*. Whenever I was working or auditioning at the Fox lot I made sure to pay him a visit and say hello. I repeated that routine when Irwin moved to Warner Bros.

However, when he was at Fox, Irwin's offices were many and they were impressive. His name was on a golden plaque outside the building. His first office at Warner Bros. was even bigger. But the last time I saw Irwin, his office had been reduced to a trailer parked near the exit gate.

Irwin Allen's career was like a rollercoaster. It went up and up—reaching incredible heights. But, at the end, it came back down to earth. As far as he was concerned, it didn't matter. Irwin enjoyed the ride. Every minute of it.

Because riding rollercoasters is what kids like to do.

# ACKNOWLEDGEMENTS

Special thanks to Kevin Burns and Jon Jashni of Synthesis Entertainment for their incredible support and inspiration throughout this project, and to publisher and uber-mensch Taylor White for his patience and support; to Jason Adam for his gorgeous design work; to Derek Thielges and Trent Bullard of Prometheus; to Ron Hamill for enduring six months of searching and scanning countless photos and documents from the Irwin Allen archives; for the invaluable contributions of Gene Kozicki of the Visual Effects Society; Greg Jein and Lou Zutavern for their insight and access to materials on many of the miniatures and props from the Irwin Allen productions; William Creber for his memories and materials; to Sally Queen, Greg Nicotero, Bill George, and Bob Burns for their help and support; to Herman Rush, George Jensen, Roy Alexander, Ron Croci, and Joe Musso for their wonderful recollections of working with Allen; to Frank Winspur, Daren R. Dochterman, and Doug Diamond; to Bill Cotter for his help and suggestions for the manuscript; Mike Clark (for photos of the modified Seaview from *The Return of Captain Nemo*); and John Antonellis (for photos of his amazing Chariot reconstruction). Thanks to Lukas Kendall for his inspiration and help moving this project to completion. Thanks to Irwin Allen himself, whose painstaking record-keeping and stewardship of his own materials made this book possible, and whose inspiration to this particular child of the 1960s made it necessary. And finally, thanks to Sheila Mathews Allen, who lovingly preserved and catalogued Allen's materials and who worked diligently for years after her husband's passing to keep the legacy and memory of Irwin Allen alive.

**OPPOSITE**
Gene Hackman in a scene from Allen's disaster movie *The Poseidon Adventure*.

# INTRODUCTION

This book is an attempt to quantify Irwin Allen's life and career. In a way, Allen himself made that job easier—he lived and breathed show business, slept very little, and seemed to spend every waking hour either at work on his film and television projects or socializing with the movie stars that would populate them.

Orson Welles once said that Hollywood was "the biggest electric train set any boy ever had." Irwin Allen was no Orson Welles, but there's probably no one else who better embodied Welles' famous quote than Allen did. Most of us who grew up on his career either owned or wanted Irwin Allen toys when we were kids—the Remco Seaview, the Remco *Lost in Space* Robot, and Mattel Roto-Jet weapon set that actually wound up as props on *Lost in Space*; the Aurora Flying Sub and Spindrift model kits. As kids we had to envy Allen and his technicians because we knew that those were giant models—toys—of the Seaview, the Jupiter 2, and the Flying Sub on our TV screens, and we knew or grew to learn that it was somebody's job to put those beautiful models through their paces during filming—to play with giant submarines and flying saucers all day.

Allen was the guy who organized all this play, and like a lot of his fans he never really grew up.

Episode guides and making-of books about Irwin Allen's TV shows have been written, biographies have been attempted, but I'd never seen a book that got across the visual impact and fun that Irwin Allen's TV shows and movies projected at their best. When I met producer Kevin Burns almost 20 years ago and discovered that he was the custodian of Irwin Allen's legacy—the man who'd made the documentary *The Fantasy Worlds of Irwin Allen* and entertained me and others on a recreation of the Jupiter 2 while filming another documentary, *Lost in Space Forever*—I started bugging him about the idea of some kind of "Art of Irwin Allen" book. My friend Taylor White, another custodian of Hollywood fantasy with his Creature Features store and publishing enterprise, started bugging Kevin along with me, and eventually we got this project rolling in late 2015. Kevin gave us access to a storage facility that holds every piece of paper, every memo and letter, and every piece of artwork that ever sat on Irwin Allen's desk or was pinned to his office wall, going back to around 1945. With Allen archivist Ron Hamill I spent the first six months of 2016 going through that incredible treasure trove of artifacts.

Kevin also gave me access to all of his raw interview transcripts from the 1995 *The Fantasy Worlds of Irwin Allen* documentary (all the interview quotes noted as from 1995 are sourced from the interviews done for the documentary) and numerous other materials, including the incredible production paintings and photographs seen inside. I personally pulled hundreds of storyboard drawings and art direction sketches from folders inside the boxes in the Irwin Allen archives, and met with some of the brilliant craftsmen who helped preserve and restore many of the original miniatures used on Allen's TV shows and movies, to find photographs and even take new photos of models from *Voyage to the Bottom of the Sea* and *Lost in Space* showing them as they look today.

Irwin Allen relied on and championed some of the finest production artists and illustrators in the business to visualize, plan, sell, and promote his projects, so I tried to track down as many of these people as possible to get their recollections of working with Allen—people like production designer William Creber and production illustrators Joe Musso (who provided a treasure trove of stories about Allen), Dan Goozee, George Jensen, and Roy Alexander (who supplied some striking production artwork from *Lost in Space*). I also spoke with Allen's longtime agent and friend Herman Rush, who had some excellent insight into Allen's television productions.

Kevin Burns suggested we call this book *The Fantasy Worlds of Irwin Allen*. Fantasy is an excellent catch-all term for what Allen did, as he worked in various genres including science fiction and his "disaster movie" cycle. But, given our title, we've placed the focus on the unusual. In our judgment Allen's theatrical disaster movies had the outsized scope and impact to qualify as fantasy, but we've devoted less attention to his "mini" disaster movies for television like *Fire!* and *Cave-In*. Similarly, you'll find more about *The Return of Captain Nemo* (Allen's last produced science fiction project) and a number of TV projects he never completed than you will about his short-lived *Code Red* TV show about firefighters. We have, however, devoted lengthy chapters to Allen's more colorful early movie productions—his two documentaries, *The Sea Around Us* and *The Animal World*; *The Big Circus*, *The Lost World*, *Voyage to the Bottom of the Sea*, and *Five Weeks in a Balloon*; his TV shows *Voyage to the Bottom of the Sea*, *Lost in Space*, *The Time Tunnel*, and *Land of the Giants*; his TV movie *City Beneath the Sea*; and of course his disaster movies, *The Poseidon Adventure*, *The Towering Inferno*, *The Swarm*, *Beyond the Poseidon Adventure*, and *When Time Ran Out...*

There's a very human story here of a driven man who fought for independence and creative control while finding a nurturing home inside the Hollywood studio system—a man who built his greatest success at a studio that never fully trusted him with a director's bullhorn. A man who jumped ship to a rival studio where he was given carte blanche to do whatever he wanted—only to find that the studio system that he thrived in was dying and that the special effects-driven mega-productions that he virtually invented were now surpassing the thrills that he could deliver himself. It's the story of a man who never grew up, a man who we read about and remember because part of us, too, will never grow up. So this book is for the 10-year-old inside us that still thrills to the words "created by Irwin Allen."

—Jeff Bond
February 4, 2018

**OPPOSITE**
Scenes from Allen's productions including (clockwise from top left) *Lost in Space*, *The Poseidon Adventure*, *The Towering Inferno*, *The Lost World*, *Land of the Giants*, and *The Time Tunnel*.

# BEING A MAN WHO BELIEVES IN GOD, I DECIDED THAT THE CREATION OF THE WORLD WAS FOUNDED ON A DIVINE PLAN.

**IRWIN ALLEN**

# THE IRWIN ALLEN SHOW

*Young Irwin Allen's evolution from fan, to agent, to Oscar-winning movie producer*

**OPPOSITE**
Irwin Allen atop the overturned hull of the Poseidon, during the filming of *Beyond the Poseidon Adventure* in 1979.

If you were a kid growing up in the 1960s, there were a few names that produced an immediate charge of adrenaline the second you saw them on your TV screen: Ray Harryhausen. George Pal. Hanna-Barbera. But the one who produced the most consistent excitement, the one who visited your living room on a weekly basis, was Irwin Allen. Like a circus impresario from the future (a character type that Allen may have invented), Irwin Allen's name was an ironclad guarantee of glass-nosed super submarines, smack-talking robots, jet packs, rampaging giants, slithering dinosaurs, underground time machines, fusion-powered flying saucers, and a minimum of two spark-scattering explosions per hour.

Irwin Allen is probably best-known as the "Master of Disaster"—the producer and creative prime mover behind *The Poseidon Adventure* and *The Towering Inferno*, two disaster blockbusters that launched a cycle of "jeopardy/survival" thrillers that included *Earthquake, The Hindenburg, Rollercoaster, Meteor,* and the *Airport* films. But Allen had forged a successful B-movie career, working for RKO, Warner Bros., and 20th Century Fox, creating a brand name for himself that helped him launch his career in television.

Allen's television series—*Voyage to the Bottom of the Sea, Lost in Space, The Time Tunnel,* and *Land of the Giants*—were appointment viewing for kids, both in their original network runs from 1964 to 1970, and in syndicated reruns from the 1970s through the 1980s, with many of the programs available for viewing five days a week just before dinner time. His early movies—*The Story of Mankind, The Lost World, Voyage to the Bottom of the Sea,* and *Five Weeks in a Balloon*—were staples of the syndicated movie packages local stations ran each day, too.

There was a branding consistency to Allen's product that was apparent even to a kid: the stylized title logos and animated title sequences of the TV shows; the way actors like David Hedison and John Crawford would pop up in different roles in his shows and movies; the

What is *Die Hard* if not *The Towering Inferno* with a hostage situation thrown in? What is James Cameron's *The Abyss* if not the grandest episode of *Voyage to the Bottom of the Sea* ever? Allen's disaster movies laid the groundwork for the escapist, special effects-packed summer blockbusters that would dominate movie theaters for decades after the release of *The Poseidon Adventure*—but Allen himself couldn't adapt to the high tech, modern movie era he all but invented.

Allen was, for kids of the 1960s, a kind of gateway drug, priming them for the genre-dominated world that came in the wake of *Star Wars*. Before Spielberg and Lucas turned their childhood science fiction dreams (some inspired by Allen) into big screen movies, before filmmakers like J.J. Abrams and Guillermo del Toro proudly wore the label of "monster kids" and made movies out of their own childhood obsessions, Irwin Allen became a mogul based on his own childhood literary and movie fascinations—Jules Verne, King Kong, Buck Rogers, and Tom Swift. But Allen did it before it was cool.

"I was a buff and turned it into a career," the producer said in a 1969 interview.

Irwin Allen was born Irwin Grinovit in New York City on June 12, 1916. He was the youngest of four boys, a circumstance that, along with the hardship of the Great Depression, forced Irwin into self-reliance at an early age. Irwin Grinovit was well-read, excited by Nick Carter detective stories, travel writer Richard Haliburton, the Tom Swift juvenile science fiction adventure series, and the classic works of Jules Verne and H.G. Wells.

elaborate miniature effects and catchy theme music. So when Allen made the prototypical disaster movie, *The Poseidon Adventure,* in 1972, it may have stunned adult audiences and critics—but to 12 year-olds, Allen's name on the *Poseidon* poster was no surprise—this seemed like exactly the sort of thing the guy who made *Voyage to the Bottom of the Sea* would do.

After Allen made his magnum opus, 1974's *The Towering Inferno*, he reached the peak of his power and influence—and rapidly squandered it after being lured from his longtime home at 20th Century Fox to Warner Bros., where he was granted a palatial office in a building named after him. While Steven Spielberg's *Jaws* and George Lucas's *Star Wars* were changing the landscape of movie blockbusters, Allen was toiling away on *The Swarm*, a movie about killer bees.

He was mystified by the success of *Star Wars*—a movie with "no stars and no love story"—yet if you loved *Star Wars* with its bantering comedy team of robots and triumphant John Williams score, a part of you had to be flashing back to the antics of *Lost in Space*'s Dr. Smith and the Robot, and the brassy space music Williams wrote for that TV series, which would become a template for his *Star Wars* scores. Spielberg would hire Allen's veteran special effects men to create the miniature effects for his WWII comedy *1941*, and he made his own salutes to Allen's TV ideas with *seaQuest DSV* (a redo of *Voyage to the Bottom of the Sea*) and *Earth 2* (about a family lost on an alien planet, just like the Robinsons in *Lost in Space*).

But in other ways he was an atypical nerd, compared to that particular genus as it's known today. For one thing, he was active in and enthusiastic about sports—he cited writer Paul Gallico, author of the novel *The Poseidon Adventure* was based on, as a "childhood hero," due to Gallico's work as a sports writer. Irwin ran cross country track and managed a neighborhood baseball team, and loved Frank Merriwell, the lead character of a series of juvenile sports hero books, who excelled in college sports while solving campus mysteries.

Irwin also ate up the writings of Horatio Alger, another young adult series about hardscrabble poor kids who pull themselves up by their bootstraps from poverty and into "middle class security." Irwin, according to his older cousin, Al Gail, enthusiastically took Alger's philosophy to heart very early on. "You know this phrase of pulling yourself up, by your own bootstraps—that was Irwin," Gail said. "'Cause he never had any help, from the very beginning to his eventual success. He did it all on his own." While Gail insisted Irwin had "very supportive, very loving parents," both would die before Irwin was 22 years old.

Irwin and Al Gail both had early ambitions to be writers. "I guess it was the excitement, the adventure, the creativity of the writers, and, we always sought to emulate them if possible," Gail said in 1995. "We all wanted to be writers in those days, and many of us became writers. In his high school days [Irwin] wrote a column for the high school newspaper. He did some

**LEFT**
Infant Irwin Grinovit with his father, circa 1916.

**ABOVE**
Irwin Grinovit at his cousin Al Gail's stomping grounds at Coney Island.

freelance work on some local newspapers. He was always interested in writing, advertising, publicity, all the writing fields."

Another summer job that Irwin took on, reportedly at around age 16, was as a barker for a Skee-Ball alley at a carnival—a gig that ignited a lifelong fascination with circuses. Irwin also loved setting out from his home in the Bronx and visiting his cousin who lived at Coney Island, home to a sprawling amusement park and a great view of another of young Irwin's fascinations: the ocean.

"We'd sit on the beach, and we'd look at some of these tremendous ocean liners, coming from Europe into New York harbor," Gail recalled. "We'd say, 'some day,' 'cause then it was just a wild dream—who could afford that kind of a luxury of traveling on this ocean steamer? But he said some day we'll make it, and we'll do all those things—you'll see."

Irwin was disappointed when his cousin went away to college at the University of Alabama and his family couldn't afford to pay for Irwin to join him. Instead, Allen went to night school at the University of Columbia, where he studied journalism and advertising, eventually getting work at an agency and doing advertising and promotion for Greenwich Village nightclubs. Irwin had not yet completed his degree when Al Gail graduated and joined him in New York, where the two young men began a professional relationship that would last for over four decades. Irwin had a keen sense for promotion—he was able to communicate his own infectious enthusiasm for the projects he worked on. That, and the young man's eye for detail, would serve him very well in later years. But, despite his knack for the work, both Irwin and his cousin found the New York advertising world "a dead end," according to Gail.

Irwin's love of adventure literature and colorful journalism was one side of him, but he had an equal fascination with the movies, movie stars, and radio. Irwin and Gail had a cousin in Los Angeles, and on a whim both young men decided to drive across the country and check out opportunities in Los Angeles and Hollywood. It took very little time for the two men to realize that Irwin was in his element. Any ambitions to finish his degree were forgotten as Irwin's salesman instincts kicked in and the young man found himself selling his most important product: himself.

Irwin Grinovit didn't sound like the name of a popular newspaper columnist or a hot young disc jockey, fields that Irwin was eager to explore.

"It's an old family name and, it was a difficult name," Gail said in 1995. "It was a harsh name and people had trouble remembering [it]. So when we came out here we decided to change it to something that's more easily spoken and remembered, and we came up with Irwin Allen, which came trippingly [off] the tongue."

The newly minted Irwin Allen, along with his cousin, landed jobs at a Los Angeles entertainment magazine called *Key*, where Gail wrote a column and Allen sold advertising.

"We were always a team," Gail recalled. "He did what he did best and I did what I did best. I was basically a writer, and he was a presenter, and a talker, salesman, and very creative on his own—and also a writer."

Irwin was angling for a night disc jockey job at a Los Angeles radio station, and the young man's mind was already on branding. Allen had written Hollywood news and gossip pieces for *Key* and he eventually parlayed his growing connections and knowledge of the industry into a 15-minute daily radio show called *Hollywood Merry-Go-Round*.

This would become one of the longest-running radio programs in the Los Angeles area, airing from 1941 to 1946 on KMTR/570 and continuing after KMTR was bought out and switched to KLAC/570 from 1946 to 1952. Allen had a newspaper column, "Inside Hollywood," syndicated in over 30 papers. He was singled out in a *Hollywood Reporter* column ("On the Air") in 1944 for "something of a record in the consistent and excellent broadcasting of Hollywood movie news." Allen had been doing his KMTR daily radio show, *The Hollywood Merry-Go-Round,* for five years and had interviewed a thousand Hollywood personalities. He was particularly industrious at working with, promoting and retaining his sponsors, sometimes ruffling the feathers of Hollywood stars like Claudette Colbert and Loretta Young and their agents when he involved them, willingly or unwillingly, in commercial tie-ins with his advertisers.

One of Allen's associates on his radio show was announcer Dick Tufeld, who Allen would rehire two decades later to narrate his television show *Lost in Space* and provide the voice for the show's robot. Another announcer followed Tufeld—Steve Allen, who would later become a pioneering television talk show host.

In 1995 Allen recalled Irwin Allen's approach to radio broadcasting:

> He actually stood up, leaning on a desk with his script papers and notes in front of him, and he had his own little bi-bi-bi-bi-bip, dot- and dash- machine—'Flash! Beverly Hills! Bi-bi-bi-bi! This is Irwin Allen with an exclusive report,' and he would give exclusive reports. And then at the end of it I would say, 'Thank you Irwin, and we'll see you again next Tuesday.' And I never forgot cause he was the only man I ever knew who stood up while doing that kind of show. Maybe he couldn't afford a chair—I never thought of that before. Of course, people like Bob Hope had been standing up in front of twelve microphones with scripts in their hands, but this was not what he was doing—his papers were down on the desk, but he disdained sitting. It gave him more energy, I guess, to tell America the latest about Hollywood from an erect position. So that was our first relationship. We didn't get to know each other well until some years later.

By 1947 Irwin Allen's ratings gave him an audience of 400,000 per day, and the following year the show began broadcasting nationally. Allen had introduced a quiz show element to the program, having guests identify movies after listening to a few seconds of audio clips from the respective films, and the gimmick encouraged other radio stations across the country to pick up *Hollywood*

*Merry-Go-Round*. KLAC quickly took advantage of the show's popularity by launching a television version on KLAC-TV Channel 13, and Allen and cousin Al Gail found themselves working together on a television series. Allen struggled to add enough bells and whistles to keep the attention of a television audience, eventually switching up with a newly named but ultimately very similar program called *Irwin Allen's Hollywood Party* in 1949. But Allen's early foray into TV broadcasting wouldn't have the staying power of his radio work.

One job that helped give Allen some stability was a stint at the Orsatti Agency, where he represented authors and worked to package and sell their works. Allen had his advertising experience from New York and, while it wasn't as glamorous as radio and television, the job allowed him to put food on the table and ultimately it would be his entryway into the one Hollywood playground Allen hadn't yet been able to enter—the movies.

From his first days at the company, Allen showed that he wasn't exactly the typical Hollywood agent. Victor and Ernest Orsatti had founded the agency (Victor's son Kendall Orsatti was head of the Screen Actors Guild for many years).

**ABOVE**
Allen (left) with guests Ann Rutherford, Chester Conklin, and Marie Windsor on his *Hollywood Merry-Go-Round* program.

**OPPOSITE**
Irwin Allen mans the mike at his KMTR radio show, circa 1942.

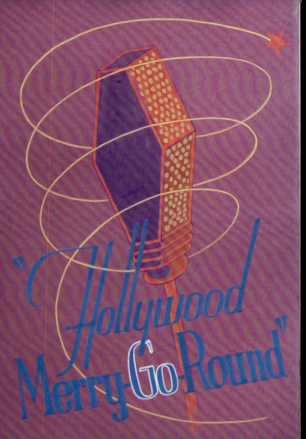

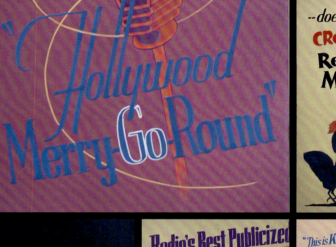
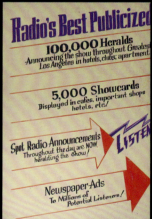
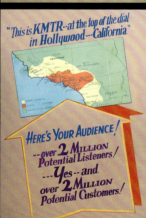

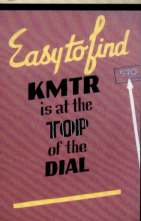
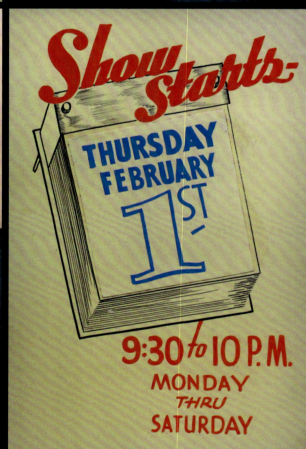

Allen's *Hollywood Merry-Go-Round* radio show had become the longest-running radio program in Hollywood. Allen often wrote his own press releases and tirelessly promoted the show, boasting (truthfully) that the program had never been without a sponsor. He broke movie casting news and interviewed stars, familiarizing himself with and sometimes befriending numerous Tinseltown power players and serving as master of ceremonies at over a hundred movie premieres. Allen was becoming a fixture around "the business"—but he wanted to be *in* the business, and his agency continued to be the best avenue for achieving that end.

The biggest deal of Allen's career—the one he had written Rex Beach about—involved a script called "It's Only Money."

"One day he had a script that he liked, and he decided to see if could package it—that is, get a director, a star, and backing from one of the studios," Al Gail recalled in 1995.

"Packaging" has been a staple of the movie business for so long that it is taken for granted—but Allen was one of the people who helped invent the process. He would buy novels, short stories, and other literary properties, have a screenplay written based on the work, sign a director, cast actors, and then sell the entire package to a studio. In the coming years, this approach would help shift power away from the studios, which were already declining in their influence due to other factors. Talent agencies would quickly move in to fill that power vacuum and wield immense influence on the movie-making process.

As Gail explained, Allen quickly used the leverage he had in packaging properties to put himself in the position of being a movie producer, beginning with *It's Only Money*. "We ended up at RKO, and the director was Irving Cummings, Sr., who was a very well known director in those days."

The project would become a movie called *Double Dynamite*, and the stars were Frank Sinatra, sex goddess Jane Russell, and Groucho Marx. Sinatra played a down-on-his-luck bank teller who gets involved with gangsters and becomes suspected of embezzlement; Groucho played a wisecracking waiter who tries to get Sinatra out of the jam; Russell was the girl the crooner-cum-banker wanted to marry.

Jane Russell was the protege of famous billionaire Howard Hughes. Hughes had bought the studio in 1948, just as Allen was gearing up production on *It's Only Money*, and he had suggested (or more likely ordered) Russell for the film's female lead. Russell's fame rested squarely on Hughes' exploitation of her legendary bust-line in the lurid western *The Outlaw*. Frank Sinatra was an up-and-coming star groomed by RKO, and MGM's Louis B. Mayer expressed enough interest in the crooner that he and Hughes agreed to split Sinatra's contract. Groucho Marx, meanwhile, was an aging comedian with little left in the way of a movie career—but he did have a burgeoning career on radio with his game show *You Bet Your Life*.

In a 1976 speech at a dinner honoring Groucho, Allen recalled that the movie marked an important transition between Marx's famous look from the Marx Bros. movies

**ABOVE**
Allen (center, inside host box) on his television *Hollywood Merry-Go-Round* game show with guests including Richard Arlen (far left), and on the far right, Jackie Coogan and Roddy McDowall.

**OPPOSITE**
Pages from a promotional booklet for *Hollywood Merry-Go-Round*. Some of this nearly 70-year-old artwork is missing elements that were glued onto the backgrounds.

Ernest Orsatti's wife was opera singer Inez Gormley. Years after she met Allen, Gormley told production illustrator Joe Musso about Irwin Allen's unusual approach to making deals at the agency:

> Irwin had all these little toy animals on his desk, the kind you wind up and they walk and jump around. Irwin would go in for a meeting and close the door with these different agents for different stars, and you'd hear him winding up these toy animals. We're in there trying to figure out whether he was going to make the deal or not, and he's got all these agents playing with his toy animals. We knew he was going to amount to something, but we didn't know what. But he put all these deals together by getting these people to play with his toy animals.

Allen wasn't just selling projects to talent and vice versa. He was selling himself and his own child-like enthusiasm.

One of Allen's clients was Rex Beach, known for a series of Jack London-like adventure novels set in the Alaskan wilderness—books that Allen had read and loved as a young boy. In 1945 he got the rights to Beach's *The World in His Arms* and sold it to Universal-International, and later handled all of Beach's literary properties as well as those by Ben Hecht, P.G. Wodehouse, and others. Beach was in declining health and living in Florida while Allen represented him and Allen corresponded with the author often. In October '47 Allen wrote Beach and told him "I'm working on the biggest deal of my career," and asked Beach for an autographed photo so he could frame it and display it in his office (Beach would die two years later).

By 1948, after three years with Orsatti, Allen resigned to form The Irwin Allen Agency, with offices in Hollywood and New York. Allen's company represented "story properties for picture sale" and intended to "serve as consultant and aid for independent picture producers in the planning of productions."

to his familiar appearance as a television personality in later years. In the famed Marx Bros. movies such as *Duck Soup* and *A Day at the Races*, Groucho wore a stylized mustache that was painted on with black shoe polish, a holdover from the performer's vaudeville days. But two days before shooting, Groucho announced that he would no longer wear the shoe-polish mustache on film.

"This was a calamity on the order of World War II," Allen stated. "Groucho without a mustache was totally unrecognizable as Groucho." Marx fully intended to establish himself onscreen clean-shaven—but Howard Hughes wouldn't have it. "That gentleman advised me by endless midnight telephone calls and mysterious messengers that Groucho without a mustache was unacceptable! No mustache, no movie." Both men were adamant, but according to Allen, he convinced Groucho with a four a.m. phone call to compromise by growing a real mustache. Marx agreed, and he maintained the now-familiar look from the making of Allen's movie throughout the remainder of his career.

Allen was finally doing what he wanted, making movies. But *It's Only Money* would become an inauspicious debut. By 1948 Sinatra (who Allen later described as "a terrible little man") had infuriated both Hughes and Louis Mayer. Between RKO and MGM there were two Sinatra vehicles in the can—*It's Only Money* and MGM's *On the Town*, which co-starred Gene Kelly. Hughes and Mayer decided to hold back both films and reduce Sinatra to second-billing. *It's Only Money* would become a vehicle for Jane Russell. Hughes retitled the picture *Double Dynamite*, a not-so-subtle reference to Russell's physical charms, and he held back release of the movie until 1951. By this point Sinatra was billed third, behind Russell and Groucho, and some posters for the movie showed only Russell and Groucho.

Allen never received an onscreen credit for his producing chores or for his help in shepherding the work from the page to the screen. It would be director Irving Cummings' last movie after a 30-year career in Hollywood. But the project did decent box office business, and, better yet, it hooked Allen up with the man who would become his best friend—Groucho Marx.

On paper the bespectacled and already balding publicity man, literary agent, and ex gossip columnist, and the famously lecherous, witheringly-witted Groucho might have seemed like an odd match. But Groucho and Irwin had one tremendous personal characteristic in common: *schadenfreude*. Costume designer Paul Zaztupnevich, who would work closely with Allen in later years, described the relationship in 1995: "He and Groucho used to say the crumbling of clay feet was always music to their ears. If a competitor had a project that bombed out, they would chortle with glee."

Being pals with Groucho Marx wasn't such a bad calling card, and when Allen launched his *Hollywood Merry-Go-Round* show for television in 1949, Groucho would be a guest along with numerous other celebrities, as Allen used his television platform to network and form friendships with more Hollywood players. Groucho returned the favor years later, putting Allen on his TV show *You Bet Your Life* as a guest.

**ABOVE**

*The Double Dynamite* theatrical poster, with Jane Russell and Groucho Marx. Their costar Frank Sinatra is conspicuously absent.

Allen on his late 1940s variety program *The Irwin Allen Show*, with guests including actress and Howard Hughes protege Faith Domergue (front row, second from right).

While Allen's first movie project at RKO hadn't put the producer's name up in lights, RKO's mercurial Howard Hughes liked Allen, and Hughes and the burgeoning producer enjoyed socializing at Hughes' haunts all over town. RKO was far from the heydays of *King Kong* (1933) and *Citizen Kane* (1941)—it had been cranking out B-movies for a number of years, including a series of Dick Tracy crime adventures. Hughes' takeover in 1948 had alienated the studio's other executives, sending many of them (including Dore Schary) packing. Allen's ability to navigate the troubled waters at the studio and stay on Hughes' good side would serve him well later in his years at 20th Century Fox.

Well before *Double Dynamite* opened, Allen earned his first on-screen, associate producer credit (with Irving Cummings as producer) on a Robert Mitchum thriller, *Where Danger Lives*, with a screenplay by Charles Bennett and co-starring veteran actor Claude Rains as well as Faith Domergue, another ingenue that Hughes was trying to mold into a star. As a fan of detective fiction and a film buff, Allen was thrilled to be working with Mitchum and Bennett, who had scripted the early Alfred Hitchcock thrillers *The Man Who Knew Too Much, The 39 Steps,* and others. Allen would remember Bennett when he began producing his own projects.

Allen recruited Groucho for another comedy, *A Girl In Every Port*, this time with William Bendix and Marie Wilson, and he was busy funneling an assortment of movie projects through the RKO pipeline, including a suspense tale initially titled *The Glacier Story*. With his movie work taking up the bulk of his time, Allen finally gave up his radio and TV show hosting gigs and moved full time into the movie business.

Amid the various dramas, westerns, and gumshoe thrillers Allen was developing, one oddball project stood out—one that harkened back to the young Allen's fascination with the ocean, and one that revealed a new Irwin Allen skill-set that would serve him well in later years: the ability to juggle thousands of feet of stock footage into a usable—and inexpensive—narrative.

Allen had glommed onto marine biologist Rachel Carson's 1951 best-seller *The Sea Around Us*, a non-fiction look at the world's oceans and sea life from the distant past to its possible future. This was not the sort of thing RKO or Howard Hughes normally embraced, but Allen was passionate about the project and threw his organizational skills into an efficient, elaborate operation designed to get the movie made with minimal production costs.

Howard Hughes had clearly demonstrated during his management of RKO that his primary interest was action—crime and war movies. A documentary project would be a hard sell to Hughes, but Hughes' own reckless management of the studio soon gave Allen an unexpected opportunity to pitch *The Sea Around Us* to a much more sympathetic ear. With RKO's stockholders revolting against Hughes, the billionaire made a deal to sell the studio to a firm in Chicago, and Chicago theater owner Sherrill Corwin wound up head of production at the studio for a scant three months. During that time Allen pitched *The Sea Around Us* to Corwin, citing the

**ABOVE**

Robert Mitchum and Faith Domergue in a publicity still for *Where Danger Lives*.

Poster for *Where Danger Lives*.

Allen (left) with Claude Rains (center) and Robert Mitchum. Allen would recruit Rains for later projects such as *The Lost World*.

movie as a shoo-in to win the Academy Award for Best Documentary Feature—after all, the book was a best-seller and an award-winning title.

In the meantime the government had uncovered what they considered to be ties between the Chicago firm taking over RKO and organized crime—and consequently put a stop to the deal. Corwin was out at RKO and Hughes was back in—but Corwin had already greenlit *The Sea Around Us* and the production went forward.

Allen's first job was to convince the book's reluctant author to allow the studio to handle the property. "He had a lot of trouble getting an okay from Rachel Carson, the writer," Al Gail remembered in 1995. "She didn't want to do anything in Hollywood with it. But he flew to New York, saw her with her agents and attorneys, and told her pretty much what he had in mind, and she was satisfied that he wouldn't desecrate it."

Carson, in fact, not only embraced the project in its early stages, but she also gave Allen quite a bit of assistance despite her age and health problems. Making the film proved to be one of the most gigantic bookkeeping chores in Hollywood history.

"First we broke down the various categories contained in Miss Carson's Book," Allen said in publicity materials for the film in 1953. "There were 75 categories of subject matter. Next we started writing letters to all kinds of people and places for the film. In all, we contacted exactly 2,341 persons." RKO assigned one of their editors, George Swink, to assist Allen and eventually supervise the editing of the entire picture, a mammoth and critical responsibility. Swink would become one of Allen's longest-serving and most loyal associates.

Allen and his staff (sometimes with the help of Rachel Carson) contacted numerous institutions requesting film for the project, including Narragansett Marine Laboratory in Rhode Island, the Marine Biological Laboratory of the Florida State University, Bermuda Biological Station for Research, the Lerner Marine Laboratory in Florida, the Dept. of Oceanography of A&M College of Texas, McGill University Dept. of Zoology in Montreal, the University of Washington in Seattle, the Harvard Museum of Comparative Zoology, Princeton University, and the Woods Hole Oceanographic Institute, among numerous others.

Carson corresponded extensively with Allen and actually made inquiries and requests for footage on Allen's behalf to various oceanographers and filmmakers in 1952; Allen and his staff eventually catalogued 1,622,362 feet of film.

"It took us more than 300 hours to look at all the films before we actually began work on the picture," Allen said in 1953. "Our big problem was color. We received the film, all 16 millimeter, in at least 20 different color processes—some bad, some good. Then we made the final prints in Technicolor. If we had made this from scratch it would have cost us four and a half million dollars. This way we brought it in for a little over $300,000."

**ABOVE**
Allen on the RKO lot with Groucho Marx (middle) and Groucho's agent brother, Gummo (left).

Poster art for *A Girl in Every Port*.

**OPPOSITE**
Allen and an assistant in a publicity still, combing through footage for *The Sea Around Us*. Not pictured: the movie's actual supervising editor, George Swink.

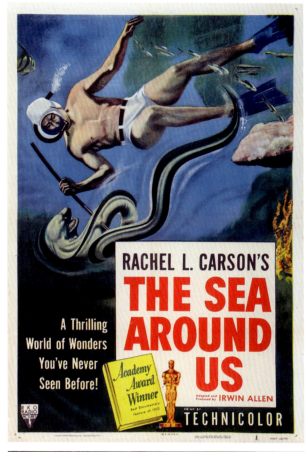

**ABOVE**
Theatrical poster for *The Sea Around Us*.

**OPPOSITE**
Allen surrounds himself with motivational materials to keep himself on task during the making of *The Sea Around Us*.

Well before its official release in June of 1953, *The Sea Around Us* was already garnering enthusiasm from both critics and marine scientists, some of whom had participated in obtaining footage for Allen with some degree of skepticism about what the final product might be. A review by Edwin Martin described the movie as "61 minutes of entrancing excitement that could well represent a peak in the field of informative entertainment." In December of 1952 the USC Chancellor wrote Allen to say that, "The picture is little short of amazing and will open up an entirely new world to the tens of thousands who are fortunate enough to see it. I wish you every success." The head of USC's Zoology Dept., W.E. Martin, added, "A few weeks ago someone wrote in *The Los Angeles Times* about the forthcoming 'Sea Around Us' and expressed some doubt that the movie could match the beautiful prose of Rachel Carson. I think you have done it or approached it very closely."

A piece in *The New York Times* earlier that winter noted the religious element Allen brought to the project—not unusual for the pious 1950s, when Biblical epics were the equivalent of today's action blockbusters:

> Only the concept of the creation of the world, with which Miss Carson began her book, was created in the studio. The question which bothered Mr. Allen was this: In the creation of the world should the picture go along with the theory of evolution or the doctrine of Divine creation. "Miss Carson went down the middle in her book," Mr. Allen said, "and that left it up to me. Being a man who believes in God, I decided that the creation of the world was founded on a divine plan."

Allen's interpretation of that plan would eventually create friction between the production and Carson. In January, 1953, after seeing the finished film, an angry Carson wrote RKO:

> I find that a number of the errors in the original script, pointed out in my memorandum of November 10, remain uncorrected. These are misstatements of scientific facts with which I cannot allow my name to be associated.

Carson was particularly bothered by Allen's apocalyptic denouement, which depicted the eventual "drowning of the world" after the melting of the polar icecaps.

> The section on polar ice and the consequences of its melting has no basis in fact. The script bases its sensational threat of the "drowning of the world" on the 100-foot rise of sea level that would follow the eventual melting of all the ice in the polar caps. As I have said in my book and in my earlier memorandum, the 100-foot rise described would bring the sea only to the Appalachians on the East Coast, with comparable effects on other shores and continents. No continent, and no island of moderate size and elevation, would be threatened with drowning. Furthermore, the sea would rise so gradually that no individual would observe a marked change in his own lifetime. This is an extremely serious and damaging error, and the climax of the film rests on it.

Allen struck back with a memo to Peter Enecht of RKO on January 28, 1953, stating his opinion that the production had fulfilled its legal obligation to Carson by submitting

the final script to her and making most of the changes she requested:

> Do we want to please Miss Carson by making these costly changes in the hope that she will cooperate publicity and promotion-wise? This is apparently hopeless because Miss Carson has never had any intention of doing anything actively to help promote the picture. I understand that she has seen very few motion pictures during her lifetime and that she has some unexplained objection to pictures in general.

Allen went on to address Carson's objections in detail, noting the epilogue about the "drowning of the world":

> There are countless theories on the part of both science and religion as to how the world will end… we made no statement of fact regarding the end of the world. We took the safest possible position and posed the question—"is this the way the world will end?" Neither the large group of scientists, which viewed the picture for accuracy, nor the members of the church council, which viewed it for church approval, had any objections whatsoever to this particular scene.

RKO had no plans to change the film to mollify the author. Allen's project had squeaked through the studio on the strength of its low costs, and Allen's use of the term "costly changes" in his memo was a rhetorical masterstroke. He was already beginning to realize that *The Sea Around Us* was shaping up to be a critical success, and that the positive publicity it was generating could make the film into a money-maker for RKO.

*The Sea Around Us* may seem primitive today—and its bloody scenes of whaling operations and divers spearing sting rays may seem at odds with a documentary ostensibly designed to generate a sense of curiosity and wonder about the natural world—but Allen was far ahead of the curve in anticipating a fascination with the oceans, undersea life, and undersea cinematography, beating Jacques-Yves Cousteau's 1956 documentary *The Silent World* into theaters by several years.

Irwin Allen had pitched *The Sea Around Us* to RKO as a potential Oscar winner, and well before it went into wide release his words were beginning to sound prophetic. A UP article by Aline Mosby nailed it down: "One of Hollywood's hottest candidates for an Oscar is an inexpensive movie version of a textbook that stars the sea and wasn't even filmed in Hollywood."

Allen had produced, directed, written the narration for and supervised the editing of *The Sea Around Us*—unlike his collaborative work on his previous features at RKO, *The Sea Around Us* was all Irwin Allen.

On March 19th, 1953, Allen's prediction about the movie came true, and he accepted the Academy Award for Best Documentary Feature for *The Sea Around Us*, moving in one night from a B-movie producer to an Oscar-winning filmmaker.

"RKO producer Irwin Allen holds the distinction of winning the Academy Award with his first movie," Vernon Scott wrote in the *L.A. Daily News*. It was a bit

**LEFT AND OPPOSITE**
Lobby artwork created for *The Sea Around Us*.

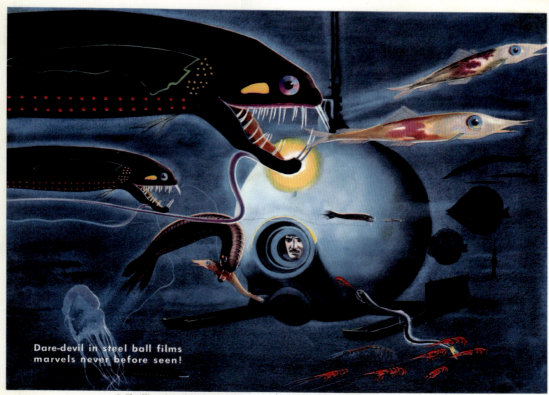

of an exaggeration, since Allen had his name on at least two other RKO productions, but Allen wasn't complaining. "Everyone said I was crazy when I announced I was going to make a picture from Rachel Carlson's best-seller," he told Scott in the article. "But that book topped the best-seller list for 70 weeks. How could I lose?"

Allen's Oscar for *The Sea Around Us* had an impact on another producer working with RKO: Walt Disney. "RKO took Disney in when they wanted to do *Snow White* and no other studio wanted to touch Walt," Joe Musso points out today. RKO successfully distributed Disney's animated features, including *Pinocchio, Dumbo, Bambi* and others. By 1950 Disney had partnered with RKO on a series of live action adventures made in England that would include *Treasure Island, Robin Hood, The Sword and the Rose,* and *Rob Roy*.

Disney had started a series of "True Life Adventure" nature documentary shorts in 1948, winning Academy awards for several of them. Disney wanted to expand the approach to feature-length documentaries, especially after he saw Allen walk away with the Feature Length Documentary Oscar in 1953. But Hughes wanted more action movies like *Robin Hood* and *Treasure Island*. Disney ended his arrangement with RKO and formed Buena Vista Pictures to make live action movies—*Rob Roy* would be the last live action film produced under the agreement with Hughes' studio. The next year, Disney's feature-length *The Living Desert* won the Best Documentary Feature Academy Award. Irwin Allen had beaten both Disney and Jacques Cousteau to the punch, helping to pave the way for work that Disney and Cousteau would later be far better known for than Allen.

But Allen's Oscar win was pivotal. He could return to RKO as an Academy Award-winning filmmaker, instantly minted as Hollywood royalty with all the clout that implied.

It was time to start making Irwin Allen movies.

**ABOVE**
Allen accepts the Best Documentary Feature Academy Award for *The Sea Around Us* from Jean Hersholt.

Allen heads the table at a congratulatory dinner after his Oscar win.

**OPPOSITE**
Detail of lobby card artwork for *The Sea Around Us*.

> **MAN HAS BEEN AROUND ONLY A MILLION YEARS. IN TELLING THE STORY OF LIFE, THIS IS ONLY A SNAP OF THE FINGERS. MAN DOESN'T MEAN A DAMN THING.**
>
> **IRWIN ALLEN**

# THE MISUNDERSTOOD HERO

*A last,* **DANGEROUS MISSION** *at RKO and Allen's first independent production,* **THE ANIMAL WORLD**

## DANGEROUS MISSION

Well before the debut of *The Sea Around Us*, Irwin Allen had a pipeline of potential projects for RKO on his desk. He intended to keep his personal and professional relationship with Groucho Marx going with the comedy *Time For Elizabeth*, which would have been a technicolor picture with Groucho based on a stage play. Always on the lookout for unusual promotion strategies, Allen believed Marx would consider touring with the stage production to drum up interest before the release of the potential film. Allen also wrote RKO's Edmund Grainger that he had a list of "33 scripts and novels which I have read since our first meeting as possible projects."

Only one of these projects would reach completion at RKO under Allen's stewardship. Allen had begun development *The Glacier Story*, based on a novel by James Edminston, in 1951. A cat-and-mouse suspense thriller set in and around Glacier National Park in Montana, *The Glacier Story* involved a former Marine, Matt Hallett, who has secretly been assigned to protect a woman named Louise Graham, the witness of a gangland murder. Allen had written a treatment as early as December, 1951, and a little over a year later, he recommended in a memo to Edmund Grainger that the studio purchase Edminston's novel. Allen noted that the story would require, "a good deal of work. However, by correcting these faults, by the use of a semi-documentary technique, and by the utilization of mountain climbing film which might be secured in the same manner as we did on *The Sea Around Us* this should make an exciting commercial movie...that could and should be made with two stars for around $500,000."

Allen's experience in gathering stock footage for *The Sea Around Us* gave him a leg up on *The Glacier Story*, and by February 1953 he had assembled documentary footage that would become a key component for the film's ambitious action.

**OPPOSITE**
Allen shows the animators how it's done in this publicity photo—the lion's share of *The Animal World*'s stop-motion work was done by Ray Harryhausen, who didn't figure in any P.R. photos.

"Tomorrow I will run for you the 16mm film shot in Montana which is intended to serve as a blueprint for our 2nd Unit operation," he wrote Grainger. "In addition I will run some of the stock footage (fires, etc.) as well as a commercial short showing the production values of the park."

That same month, Allen assigned writer W.R. Burnett, a screenwriter and author of the crime novel *Little Caesar*, to work on the *Glacier Story* script. The studio produced a report on the subsequent screenplay that noted:

> This is sheer, unadulterated commercial corn dressed up in Technicolor and possibly 3D. It's an outdoor, wild-west show set in a beautiful, breath-taking, mountainous background of which the public has seen very little. Every attempt should be made to maintain the "outdoor elements" involved for actually this is, in truth, a western, set in modern dress, with the overtones of a "whodunit melodrama." This combination appears to be highly commercial and most certainly should be maintained.

To retain the western vibe, Allen and RKO hired a veteran—if not past his prime—director of dozens of westerns from the 1920s on: Louis King, whose best-known picture was likely 1945's *Thunderhead, Son of Flicka*. Allen no doubt had ambitions to direct himself, but at this point, with *The Sea Around Us* still in production, he had no leverage to even inquire about directing at RKO.

After a few more script polishes (and a rushed comparison requested by the studio to the similar script to *Second Chance*, which RKO would release the same year), Allen was scouting locations and preparing the film for a release in Technicolor and 3-D, with a new title: *Dangerous Mission*.

With its setting at a famous national landmark, plus intrigue and scenes inside a lavish resort lodge, *Dangerous Mission* seemed an early stab at something like Hitchcock's *North by Northwest*. In fact, along with *Second Chance*, the movie was part of a brief cycle of 3-D outdoor thrillers that included *His Kind of Woman* and the 20th Century Fox Marilyn Monroe vehicle *Niagara*. Allen cast a smoldering, young Piper Laurie as his female lead. Laurie was being groomed by Universal as a rival for Monroe, but the actress would quickly become frustrated with these kinds of parts and eventually leave Hollywood for New York.

Allen's male co-stars weren't nearly as temperamental. Victor Mature played the ex-Marine and undercover police officer Matt Hallett. Mature already had a reputation by 1953 as one of the most easygoing stars in Hollywood, a man who never took his acting ability or career seriously for a moment and happily cashed his checks while he relaxed in the role of a musclebound man's man. To counter Mature, Allen cast Vincent Price as Paul Adams, an affable photographer who happens to be a contract killer stalking Piper Laurie's character.

**ABOVE**
Allen on the set of his KLAC-TV show with actors Francis Lederer (left), Vincent Price (center, behind camera), Don DeFore (second from right), and Cecil Kellaway (far right). Allen would subsequently employ Price on many of his future film and television projects.

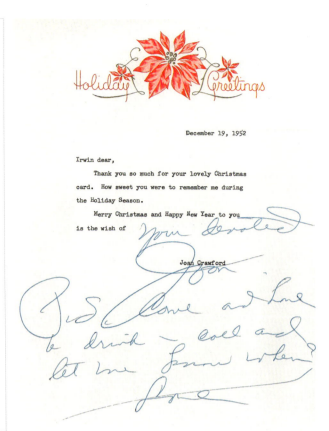

**RIGHT**

Letters between Irwin Allen and Hollywood legend Joan Crawford, part of a correspondence that took place between 1948 and 1952.

Price was not yet typecast as a horror movie star—that would begin a month after the release of *Dangerous Mission*, with Price's starring role in another 3-D thriller, *House of Wax*. He was, however, already well known for villainous roles, everything from the Invisible Man (in *The Invisible Man Returns* and a cameo at the end of *Abbott and Costello Meet Frankenstein*) to Cardinal Richelieu in the 1948 *The Three Musketeers*. It wouldn't have been difficult for audiences to peg Price as the villain in *Dangerous Mission* (particularly since the posters showed Price stomping on the fingers of hero Mature as Mature and Laurie cling desperately to a cliff). But one of the interesting things about *Dangerous Mission* is the way Price almost convinces you that he's a nice guy and Mature very nearly convinces you he's a heel.

Critics at the time pointed out Mature's role as "the misunderstood hero"—already a cliched staple of melodrama, particularly female-driven "weepers." The misunderstood hero was someone who, over the course of the story, alienates and drives away the other characters, seemingly out of selfishness and cruelty, but who is actually making secret sacrifices for the greater good. The moment we're shown that Mature's character keeps a revolver in the glove box of his car we're manipulated into thinking that he may be the assassin sent to kill Piper Laurie. In some amusing scenes early in the film, Mature and Price vie for the affections of Laurie, and one almost feels sorry for Price's character as Mature gleefully cock-blocks him.

The "Misunderstood Hero" would become a familiar character archetype in Allen's subsequent films— Mature would play one again in *The Big Circus*, Walter Pidgeon's Admiral Nelson in *Voyage to the Bottom of the Sea* would become probably the best-known example, and Stuart Whitman's Commander Matthews in *City Beneath the Sea* might be the most extreme. How this character type related to Allen himself is another question—Allen was always driven, and tended to shut himself off from associates emotionally, all while demonstrating remarkable loyalty and steadfastness in his professional relationships.

Harry Harris, who would work with Allen on many of his later television productions, said in 1995:

> I don't think you can describe him in one word. He had a fantastic imagination. He had a major ego. He was a man who built a wall in front of him so nobody could really tell what he was like. He was a little too complicated. I would have to say one word—he was an original.

Also in 1995, Al Gail said:

> He would make a lot of snap decisions—many times they were correct and, sometimes they were not. He had instant dislikes and likes when he met new people. Now, once he accepted someone, as part of his team, they had in effect a job for life. He's the only one I know who never had fired one person in the thirty-forty years of his film activity. They were loyal to him and he was loyal to them. In times when things were slow he often carried them on, from his own pocket. He liked people around that he knew and trusted, and, that was his philosophy.

Allen would cast Victor Mature again after *Dangerous Mission*, and employ Vincent Price numerous times over the next decade, and he would begin to accrue a core group of collaborators both behind and in front of

27

**ABOVE**
Production sketches for the glacier fissure action climax of *Dangerous Mission*.

**RIGHT TOP**
Production sketch for the moody, film noir opening scene of *Dangerous Mission*.

**RIGHT BOTTOM**
Production sketch for Victor Mature's scaling of a burning, electrified utility pole in *Dangerous Mission*.

**OPPOSITE**
Set design artwork for *Dangerous Mission*.

the camera as he completed his next few film projects. Those collaborators quickly discovered that Irwin Allen's life—even his social life—was his work.

Al Gail continued:

> He was a workaholic. In fact, I cannot recall when he had his last vacation, or if he ever had a vacation. His vacation was his work, and he paid enormous attention to every little detail. In the office, he would check the mail that was going out to make sure it was addressed properly. He's very meticulous. And if genius is paying attention to detail, he had it.

Harry Harris agreed that Allen's life was his work—Allen was drawn to the glamour and excitement of the movies, and he strove to make that integral to both his professional and personal life. "He was very movie star conscious," Harris said in 1995. "He wanted to be a great

29

**LEFT**
Photos from some of *Dangerous Mission*'s location work and its glacier crevasse climax.

**OPPOSITE**
The cliffhanging poster art for *Dangerous Mission*, which unfortunately spoils the identity of the villain.

movie producer. He wanted to be a part of Hollywood in a major way. His whole life was making movies—that's all he cared about."

Allen cultivated friendships, and sometimes more, with movie stars. Between his radio work, his work as an agent packaging talent together with projects, and his burgeoning career as a movie producer, he had actors, writers and directors around him at all times—it was only natural that his social life would involve people in the movie business, and at times the line between business and pleasure became blurred. A series of letters between Allen and famed actress Joan Crawford, the subject of the recent television series *Feud: Bette and Joan*, showed Crawford perusing and critiquing movie scripts sent to her by Allen, inviting the producer over for drinks, and thanking him for gifts to her four children over a period between 1948 and 1952.

In fact, Crawford had her children write Allen thank-you letters for various Christmas and birthday presents in which they refer to Allen as "Uncle Irwin," indicating that Allen was a common enough presence in the Crawford household to be considered a family member. Allen's archives also include letters to Crawford's *Feud* rival Bette Davis, although these were purely business-oriented. Neither Crawford nor Davis ever appeared in an Irwin Allen production.

*Dangerous Mission* is probably most notable for the way it demonstrated Allen's attraction to outsized action and low budget production gloss, all exaggerated by its status as a 3-D movie experience. An early sequence features an avalanche with a large group of characters trapped in a lodge, with sections of the interior collapsing and people scattering and shielding themselves in panic. Immediately afterward, a loose electrical line traps the group inside the lodge and Mature's character is forced to scale the power pole while sparks shower around him and pull the line loose. These scenes foreshadow the kind of action Allen would feature in his disaster movies, and they called for large scale physical effects, stunt work, and design.

Allen began working with art directors Albert S. D'Agostino and Walter Keller to design the avalanche and power line sequence as well as the climactic glacier pursuit, a mix of location photography and studio filming, with characters pursuing each other across the surface of a glacier and plummeting dozens of feet into crevasses. Allen broadened the movie's production values with some very well chosen and vivid stock footage of a forest fire—scenes that critics noted had very little to do with the movie's plot, but nonetheless added visual value for audiences to experience in 3D.

Between the ambitious action and the competitive banter between Mature's and Price's characters, *Dangerous Mission* is a fast-paced, entertaining film, and the first dramatic picture to bear Allen's credit as sole producer.

# THE ANIMAL WORLD

By the time *Dangerous Mission* hit theaters, Allen was already flying on the critical acclaim and Oscar win for *The Sea Around Us*. It didn't hurt that the low budget documentary turned out to be one of the most profitable movies ever produced by RKO. Allen's methods and focus in his subsequent projects would reflect his new status as an Oscar-winning filmmaker. He immediately launched plans for a follow-up documentary project: *The Animal World*, which would not only cover all the dry land nature footage opportunities missed by *The Sea Around Us*, but would also look at the formation of the Earth itself and the giant creatures of the Mesozoic Era, the dinosaurs.

Allen spent the remaining part of 1953 tying up his responsibilities at RKO while putting together a deal for his own production company, with *The Animal World* as his calling card to other studios. In February, 1954, Allen wrote:

> …Both RKO and United Artists have voluntarily offered to finance the picture. …Have asked that they hold this offer in reserve until such time as I can complete, what I hope will be total private financing. The official name of the company is now Windsor Productions and our official insignia will be a little red and black crown and Old English printing of the name. I closed the deal this morning with Technicolor to handle the making of the negative and the release prints and am currently finishing the story line on which the picture will be based.

Allen even discussed the possibility of famed broadcast journalist Edward R. Murrow narrating the film. "I know he was very much impressed with the success of *The Sea Around Us* and by the fact that it had won not only the Academy Award but some 31 additional awards."

*The Animal World* was two-and-a-half years in production. Allen stated he wrote the story in the hopes of reproducing the success of *The Sea Around Us*—and just as he had with *The Sea Around Us*, Allen placed science side by side with religion when he wrote the script.

**ABOVE**
Publicity photo showing Allen with production sketches and schedule for *The Animal World*.

**OPPOSITE**
Color booklet that Allen and his staff created to pitch *The Animal World* project.

**FOLLOWING**
Pitch artwork for *The Animal World*, linking it to the Oscar-winning *The Sea Around Us*.

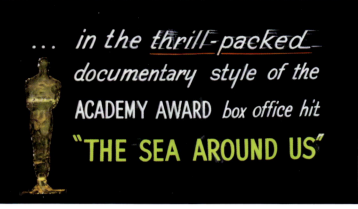

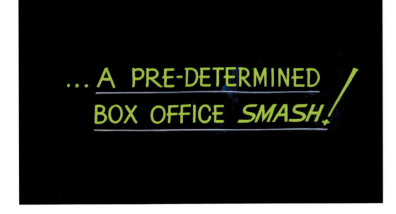
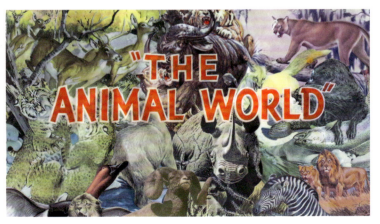

"In writing such a story, one has to be very careful that we don't overstep the bounds of propriety where science and religion are concerned," he said in publicity materials for the film. "After I had written the story, we submitted it to the National Council of the Churches of Christ." The council's only objection was Allen's description of humans as animals too, but Allen's point that humans were "animals with a soul" seemed to silence their objections. In a February, 1955 *New York Times* feature on filming sequences for the film at the Museum of Natural History, Allen explained how at least one controversial scientific issue would be skirted by the production:

> We don't use the word "evolution." We hope to walk a very thin line. On one hand we want the scientists to say this film is right and accurate, and yet we don't want to have the church picketing the film.

Allen started with a 32-page storyline from which a 174-page screenplay was written—around 50 pages longer than a typical screenplay.

> We determined that it was possible to get almost any kind of film described in the story and in the screenplay, with the exception of the dinosaurs as obviously there are no dinosaurs, so we worked backwards. We determined how much we wanted in the way of dinosaur material. I came to New York and consulted with the paleontologists at the Museum of Natural History. They took me through their dinosaur material and finally I shot three or four hundred stills of dinosaurs.

To wrangle the required footage of animals in their natural environment, Allen and his staff sent out 8,000 letters looking for specific film from governments, colleges, aquariums, and zoos. Unlike on *The Sea Around Us*, Allen claimed that the production convinced numerous agencies and individuals to shoot footage specifically for *The Animal World*. Allen said in publicity interviews:

> An average film shoots 300–500 thousand feet of film. *The Animal World* gathered 3,262,830 feet. We don't believe any picture ever made exposed that much footage. During production we had as many as 27 units shooting somewhere throughout the world, expressly for us. If we had to outfit the safaris and pay for the film, this picture would have cost close to six million dollars. Many institutes of science charged us only actual cost, and this coupled with all the film we shot, represents the three million two hundred thousand feet of film we exposed.

Inspired by the popularity of *The Sea Around Us*, nature documentarians and researchers around the world jumped at the chance to contribute footage for the picture.

> We had a correspondence with someone in the African hemisphere and this fellow in his over-enthusiasm to help us get film, bought an ad in the newspaper and reproduced our letter. Consequently, we had hundreds and hundreds of letters from people down there and they created quite a problem when they started shipping us film without permission. We paid hundreds and hundreds of dollars in shipping costs, duty and so on from Africa.

**LEFT**
Storyboard sketches for the introductory, non-dinosaur scenes of *The Animal World*.

**OPPOSITE**
Allen and his crew shooting at the Museum of Natural History in New York City.

Skeletons from New York Museum

Animated Brontosaurus

According to Allen, Prince Rainier of Monaco, a big game hunter who owned his own zoo, offered to shoot film for the production but then got involved in his legendary romance with movie star Grace Kelly, "...so we lost our cameraman."

With all of the assembled footage, the first cut of *The Animal World* ran four hours.

In March, 1954, *Variety* reported that Allen was seeking a distribution deal for *The Animal World* with RKO, and had set up his "indie unit" Windsor Productions and appointed Ernest Scanlon as general consultant. Allen's wooing of his old B-movie studio alma mater was short-lived, and by summer he was looking into a deal with one of the majors: Warner Bros.

*The Animal World* was already becoming a talked-about project in Hollywood and Allen's reputation as an up-and-coming producer (no doubt talked up by Allen himself) was attracting a great deal of attention around town. Allen's friend at Columbia Records, Goddard Lieberson, wrote Allen in 1954 and jokingly asked:

> Do you own THE ANIMAL WORLD by now? I don't mean the story, I mean the world itself!

Allen wrote back:

> Just returned from darkest Africa (Pasadena after dark), to find your letter. Yes, I now own the world (see enclosed leases on Abyssinia).

In September Allen met with Warners VPs Ben Kalmeson and Mort Blumenstock about *The Animal World* and quickly worked out a deal. He wrote in a ltter that month:

> You may have read in the public press of the formation of my new independent company, Windsor Productions, Inc., and about my entering into a contract with Warner Bros. Pictures, Inc. to distribute *The Animal World*. This motion picture...will trace the fabulous and exciting history of animals and will use, as the source of its story line, the Bible, recorded history, folk-lore, fable and fantasy. It will also document the fascinating relationship of man and beast.

*The New York Times* did a February, 1955 feature on Allen filming sequences for the movie at the Museum of Natural History. "You know, before I made the documentary *The Sea Around Us*, I had made pictures with the Marx Brothers," Allen said, exaggerating just a little. "Now if you can figure out the connection between Harpo and a dinosaur, you're a better man than I. But here I am, and happy about it. I plan to stay with documentary making."

Allen's seven-day shoot at the Museum of Natural History was a publicity boon, although he was careful to note that the Museum was not officially endorsing the movie. In production interviews for the film, he told the story of a representative of the Screen Actors Guild visiting the production at the museum shoot:

> I was sitting in the chair waiting for the next camera set up, and he was standing directly under this enormous

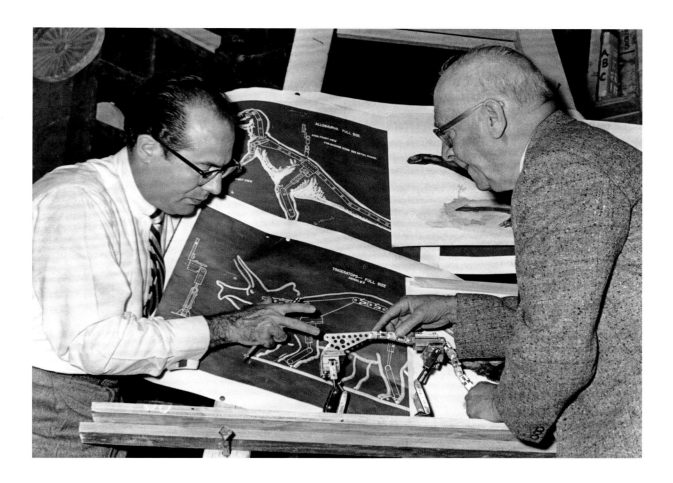

70-foot long fossil skeleton. He said to me, "Mr. Allen?" I said, "Yes, may I help you?" and he said, "I'm with the Screen Actors Guild and am just here to safeguard the interests of our members. We want to make sure that everybody who works for you is a member." I pointed to the monstrous skeleton and said, "Him?" He turned a blank and incredulous look at me and said, "Is he the only one?" I said, "Yes, he's the only actor in the picture."

Later Allen told *The New York World-Telegram*:

I love to make pictures without actors. No temperament, and they're always on time in the morning because they're the only actors you can lock away at night.

Allen did eventually hire an actor to play a primitive man on a soundstage in a scene depicting the creation of the first bow and arrow.

We got a wonderful actor with a huge hairy set of arms to pull the bow and indicate the first form of hunting. It was great until in the dailies, we saw a blue tattoo on the arm of "The First Man" which said, "John Loves Mary."

Allen brought in the American Humane Association as consultants, as well as Dr. Charles L. Camp, former director of the University of California Museum of Paleontology, the "leading Vertebrate Paleontologist" on the West Coast. While the compilation of real-life animal footage for the movie was a mammoth undertaking, the centerpiece of the film's publicity was a 12-minute sequence of stop-motion animation that would show, in color for the first time on motion picture screens, dinosaurs of the Mesozoic Era.

Allen explained to *The New York Times*:

Under the supervision of Charles L. Camp we started off by photographing the paintings of Charles Knight, who is the world's most famous painter of the dinosaur period. We built to scale a number of large model dinosaurs from our own paintings which were also full scale. In other words, if the model dinosaur was going to be three feet long and approximately a foot and a half high, we had a painting made exactly that size.

The paintings were made by none other than Willis O'Brien, the famed stop-motion animator who had brought King Kong to life in RKO's 1933 monster hit.

O'Brien wrote Allen in November of 1954: "I have designed for you four production sketches at a cost of $100." O'Brien also intended to make five 16" x 30" production sketches as well as mechanical drawings in the same size "representing the same animals. I understand that you intend to show these painted production sketches to some Professor of Paleontology of your choice for the purpose of getting his approval as to relative size, color, shape and general scientific accuracy."

O'Brien intended to charge $250 for these remaining conceptual sketches and offered his availability at meetings to offer advice and explain the workings of the intended models.

Willis O'Brien's name was legendary, and just a few years before working on *The Animal World* he had won an Oscar for special effects for another movie about a

**OPPOSITE**
Storyboard sketches for the transition from the Museum of Natural History to the stop-motion dinosaur footage.

**ABOVE**
Allen and stop motion animator Willis O'Brien (right) confer over the dinosaur model schematics and interior armatures for *The Animal World*.

giant gorilla, 1949's *Mighty Joe Young.* But the esteemed animator had been virtually unemployed since then, with several ambitious projects falling through after years of frustrating development. He took on *The Animal World* despite the fact that the simple "table top" animation—with no process work or composites to combine the small dinosaur models with human actors or other live action elements—was far from the ambitious, technically challenging work O'Brien had striven for in his career.

O'Brien's protege and animation assistant on *Mighty Joe Young,* Ray Harryhausen, had already established a budding solo career with *The Beast from 20,000 Fathoms* and was preparing the giant octopus feature *It Came From Beneath the Sea* when O'Brien brought him in to do the actual hands-on animation on *The Animal World.*

Allen was more than happy to trumpet the contributions of both men.

"The dinosaur animation is by Willis O'Brien who, incidentally was the animator of *The Lost World*—the grandaddy of all dinosaur pictures," Allen said in *The New York Times,* referring to O'Brien's 1925 silent classic. "O'Brien was our supervising animator on the picture. We should also mention that Ray Harryhausen was the actual animator."

According to Allen, he suggested shooting the dinosaurs with two stop-motion cameras, which O'Brien and Harryhausen initially resisted—but since the dinosaur animation didn't have to be synchronized with any live action elements, shooting with two cameras wasn't problematic.

"When we did stop-frame photography, shooting one frame at a time, we weren't getting one frame, we were getting two, one from each camera angle," Allen continued. "This gave us an opportunity of intercutting properly without making new setups. This is the first time to my knowledge, that dinosaurs were ever shot in color and on a big screen."

Under O'Brien's supervision, Harryhausen worked 73 days to produce 12 minutes of footage, a typical output for stop-motion work. To match some of the graphic footage of real-life animals stalking and killing prey in the film, Allen had O'Brien and Harryhausen create some gruesome dinosaur combat, and some of the gorier shots were actually pared down after test screenings. Harryhausen's work was intercut, sometimes quite effectively, with mechanical puppets in the sequence.

Unlike his work at RKO, where Allen toiled behind the scenes and relatively anonymously as a studio producer, *The Animal World* showed Allen placing himself dead center where publicity for the project was concerned. Looking at photos of Allen at RKO, you saw a movie fan beaming over getting in photos with Robert Mitchum and Groucho Marx. But the star of *The Animal World* was Irwin Allen himself, and he's at the forefront of virtually every behind-the-scenes publicity photo from the film, showing off his breakdown of the project's complex schedule, shooting footage of dinosaur skeletons at the Museum of Natural History, and working with

**ABOVE**
Allen lines up a shot of early man skulls at New York's Museum of Natural History.

Allen examines a dinosaur sculpture with animator Willis O'Brien (left), sculptor Pasqual Manuelli (right) and editor/post production supervisor George Swink (far right).

**OPPOSITE**
Taking a light reading for the tyrannosaurus/triceratops table-top dinosaur animation setup.

technicians on the elaborate, articulated dinosaur puppets built for the project. Several shots show him conferring with Willis O'Brien about the dinosaur models and animation setups, and some even show Allen seemingly manipulating some of the animation models himself, giving the casual viewer the impression that the producer-director might have executed a few of the stop-motion shots to show O'Brien and Harryhausen just how it was done.

Harryhausen later pointed out that all of the shots of Allen and other technicians gathered about the stop-motion setups were staged for publicity purposes—Harryhausen executed the animated sequences in his customary fashion, working alone.

While Allen could not exactly be hands-on with the exacting, solitary stop-motion work, he was heavily involved in the shooting of the mechanical puppet work.

"For the dinosaur shoot we built a cliff on the back lot and used large model dinosaurs that had to be mechanically operated by six men," he pointed out. "There was a low camera angle shooting up against the sky and you could see this fantastic cliff towering a hundred or two hundred feet high. At the top were tiny palm trees and these enormous monsters towering over them fighting. In their fight and hysteria they dislodged the edge of the precipice which came crashing down to a raging torrent below."

Allen and his effects crew used detergent to give the water a very convincing sense of scale for the sequence. Some of the lower-angle shots of the dinosaurs, particularly the long-necked "brontosaurus" (shown eating a cave man in a hypothetical shot that opened the sequence), were shot against the Hollywood Hills that loom behind the Warner Bros. lot in Burbank.

"During one fight scene between dinosaurs the cameramen accidentally caught two Navy jets flying in the background of the shot," Allen said.

Sixty men worked for a month to create the climactic earthquake sequence, which shows the Cretaceous landscape under blood-red skies as volcanos erupt and fissures in the earth open to swallow the terrified dinosaurs. The landscape was mounted on a large table with breakaway sections, with dinosaur models in positions to interact with miniature fire and water in a sequence that took eight days to complete. After dividing the sequence between Jurassic animals (the brontosaurus, stegosaurus and two fighting, meat-eating ceratosaurs) and Cretaceous (a T-Rex and triceratops), Allen and the animators made the best use of their expensive animation models by showing all the creatures from both eras dying in the conflagration.

In gearing up for the film's release, Allen exercised what would become his customary, detailed oversight over publicity and promotion, but he also began to explore

**ABOVE**
Allen and technicians filming one of the mechanical dinosaur puppets used for closeup shots.

**OPPOSITE**
The vivid stop-motion dinosaur sequences in *The Animal World*, as depicted in the popular View-Master photo set.

a new area that demonstrated his growing marketing expertise: merchandising.

Noting how Willis O'Brien and the production's sculptors and prop makers had created the movie's dinosaurs by basing them closely on famed painter Charles Knight's paintings of prehistoric life at the Museum of Natural History, Allen stated that a toy manufacturer had plans to mass produce replicas of the dinosaurs for kids—"The first time such a thing has been done," Allen said. The Marx Toy company launched their original line of plastic dinosaurs in 1955, around a year before *The Animal World* was released, although there is no indication that they ever had discussions with Allen about the project, and there's no record of any set of dinosaur toys from Allen's movie being released. Allen also had mockups of a jigsaw puzzle based on the dinosaur sequence from the movie and a record album created, but neither went into production.

The one well-known piece of merchandise that did come out of the movie was the 1956 View-Master reel set "Battle of the Monsters." The set showed still, stereoscopic images of the dinosaur models and animation set-ups from the movie, and was released in May, 1956 to coincide with the movie release, and sold for one dollar. The set remained in the View-Master lineup well into the 1970s.

Throughout many of his publicity interviews for *The Animal World*, Allen took every opportunity to remind the press that he was an official F.O.G.—Friend of Groucho. Even in the production notes released for the film, Allen made mention of Groucho Marx:

> Groucho is my best friend and I made Groucho's last two pictures—I suppose Groucho might say that he drove me frantic and that I finally had to get away from actors, and dove off the deep end into *The Sea Around Us*.

While at work on the film he told a New York World-Telegram writer, "This is a far cry from Groucho. Some nights I dream of being chased by dinosaurs but Groucho protects me." After the film's release, he said to *The New York Herald Tribune*, "After being around Groucho, I was glad to get to dinosaurs. The dinosaurs aren't so hysterical."

Groucho too reportedly inserted himself into the proceedings on *The Animal World*. At Allen's Windsor Productions the producer had his secretary answer the phone by saying, "This is *The Animal World*" during production. Groucho Marx would call once or twice a day and respond to the secretary by saying, "This is an unemployed gorilla, is the Head Keeper in?" or "Well, this is a wolf, will you be my cub?'"

Before the release of the film, Allen called in a favor from Marx, asking him to have *The Animal World*'s technical advisor, paleontologist Dr. Charles L. Camp, on Groucho's *You Bet Your Life* TV show.

Allen was 39 years old at the release of *The Animal World*. The second documentary was a success, though not as as big a hit as *The Sea Around Us*. While it earned a citation from the American Humane Association for creating

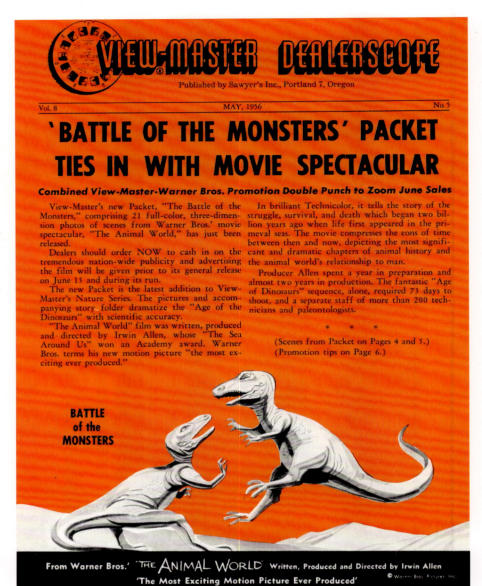

"[A] cultural and exciting milestone in expanding public knowledge and sympathetic understanding of the animal world," and the color dinosaur footage was groundbreaking, the bulk of the movie wasn't radically different from the feature length nature documentaries Disney had been producing since 1953.

After declaring himself to be a "documentary filmmaker" who was happy to no longer have to work with actors, Irwin Allen would quickly do an about-face and make a dramatic motion picture with a "cast of thousands"—although most of those thousands would exist only as stock footage.

**ABOVE**

Promotional flyer for View-Master's "Battle of the Monsters" packet, one of Allen's first pieces of movie merchandising.

**OPPOSITE**

Although they occupied only a fraction of the film's running time, the stop-motion dinosaurs became the main selling point in promotional materials for *The Animal World*.

> **TELLING HISTORY ON THE SCREEN CAN BE LIKE A BAD JOKE TOLD TWICE. YOU FIRST HAVE TO FIND A GIMMICK.**
>
> **IRWIN ALLEN**

# IN THE FOOTSTEPS OF DeMILLE

*Allen directs* **THE STORY OF MANKIND** *and explores a childhood obsession on* **THE BIG CIRCUS**

**OPPOSITE**
Irwin Allen on the set of
*The Big Circus* (1959).

## THE STORY OF MANKIND

It's strangely appropriate that, on what may have been the biggest night of his life at the 1953 Academy Awards, Irwin Allen sat in the audience clutching his Oscar for *The Sea Around Us* and watched legendary director Cecil B. DeMille win the Best Picture Oscar for his circus epic *The Greatest Show On Earth*. DeMille was in many ways a model for Irwin Allen: a larger than life personality who produced larger than life movies, a popular artist who thrived on spectacle and sensationalism. For Allen, watching DeMille make the most spectacular movie ever made about the circus—Irwin Grinovit's childhood obsession—must have been inspiring. And after leaving documentaries behind, Allen's next two movie projects—*The Story of Mankind* and *The Big Circus*—would be heavily inspired by DeMille.

Like *The Sea Around Us* and *The Animal World*, T*he Story of Mankind* sprang from a non-fiction source—Hendrik Van Loon's book, which Allen's newly formed Cambridge Productions bought the rights to in March, 1955 for $22,500. *The Story of Mankind* was a Newberry Medal award winner, a history of human civilization with illustrations by the author, that had sold 23 million copies. Production notes for the film stated that, "…only *Gone With the Wind* and the Bible have been read by more people."

Allen once again bet on the cost-effective use of stock footage to depict famous moments in world history, moments that, conveniently enough, had been filmed by earlier movie producers and were now sitting in storage at Warner Bros., waiting for Allen to use them. But this time Allen didn't have a documentary approach in mind—*The Story of Mankind* would be a full-blown fantasy, with mankind put on trial by a heavenly tribunal for developing a dangerous "gamma bomb" that could destroy the earth. Part historical pageant, part *It's A Wonderful Life*, part *A Matter of Life and Death*, the movie would be Allen's first step into fantasy and one of his last steps into comedy.

Before he began making *The Story of Mankind*, Allen had to convince Warner Bros. that the project was worth doing. Director Harry Harris, who worked on many of Allen's later television projects, related an anecdote he heard from Allen's associate producer and post

production manager (and *The Sea Around Us* editor) George Swink.

"There was a guy that was head of Warners that [Irwin] was trying to get to and he couldn't get to him," Harris said in 1995. "Irwin found out the man never flew in an airplane. He only took the train between New York and L.A., and he knew he had to change trains in Chicago. One way or another he found out where that man was, bunked on that train. Irwin flew to New York, got on the train, got in there, met the man and by the time the train pulled into Los Angeles he went to Warner Brothers and made the picture. I think George used to loan him his car, when he would go out on a meeting, cause Irwin didn't have a car."

Allen had a new motivation to make *The Story of Mankind*. While he had supervised every aspect of *The Sea Around Us* and *The Animal World*, essentially directing both pictures, he had yet to fulfill the traditional duties of a motion picture director—directing actors and working off a script with a fictional narrative. *The Story of Mankind* would allow him to do just that, beginning a struggle for Allen to stay in the director's chair that would last for the rest of his career.

With the deal at Warner Bros. made, Allen and his staff did more than three years of research, filling more than a complete room at Warner Bros. Allen and Charles Bennett, who'd written *Dangerous Mission*, worked on the script, based very loosely on Van Loon's book.

"There have been 400 or more giants of history in all fields," Allen told *The Los Angeles Times* in November, 1956. "Our big problem has been to bring them down to some 50, asking about each: Was what he or she did lasting—and how long did it last? Telling history on the screen can be like a bad joke told twice. You first have to find a handle, a gimmick."

The Gamma Bomb and tribunal was Allen's gimmick, one that would allow for a sprawling, epic story—the original running time for the film was to be three hours, putting Allen squarely in the footprints of Cecil B. DeMille and his epics.

With its trial format, the movie would take on the form of a series of vignettes, each designed to illustrate the good or bad side of mankind, with The Spirit of Man (personified by smooth Ronald Colman, in his last screen role) put on trial in the heavenly firmament by the devious Mr. Scratch (Vincent Price). Allen and Bennett had at least one spot-on instinct: by placing the Devil (in the form of a none-too-subtle stand-in named "Mr. Scratch") as a central character, they could provide an entertainingly cynical counterpoint to what threatened to be a too-saintly and boring catalogue of historical events. But as a 1957 *Sunday News* article pointed out, Scratch turned out to be almost too good a character:

> Allen rigged up a chart for the proposed trial, adding to the red line when the devil scored a round, lengthening the white band when mankind proved itself worthy. The bad so far outdistanced the good that Irwin was obliged to abolish some of the knaves and scrounge around for some do-gooders.

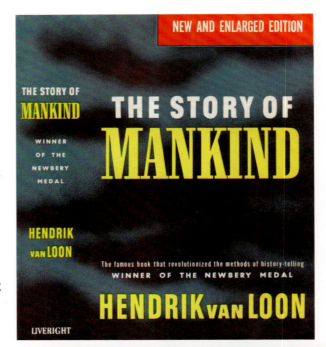

**ABOVE**

Hendrik van Loon's book, *The Story of Mankind*—loosely adapted by Allen and screenwriter Charles Bennett for the film.

Vincent Price and John Carradine (right) as Egyptian Pharaoh Khufu.

**OPPOSITE**

In a publicity photo, Allen confers about set designs for *The Story of Mankind* with Hedy Lamarr, who plays Joan of Arc in the film.

**ABOVE**
Storyboard sketches for the Egyptian and trial sequence with John Carradine's character of Khufu.

**LEFT**
Vincent Price's Devil presents some of Leonardo da Vinci's weaponry inventions to the tribunal.

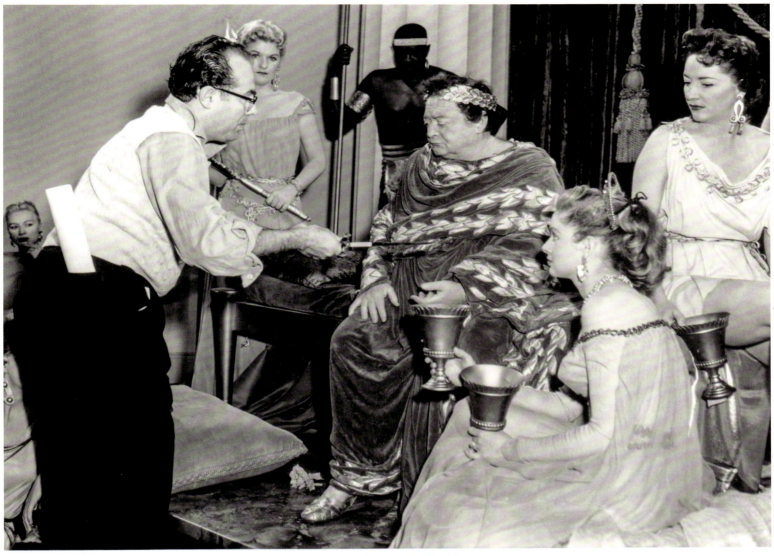

**ABOVE**
Allen with Peter Lorre (middle, as Roman Emperor Nero) on the set of *The Story of Mankind*.

Peter Lorre as Nero—already part of Allen's recurring company of familiar actors.

With a host of famous historical characters to play, the project quickly became an exercise in stunt casting, and Allen worked overtime to attract big name stars to the production.

"We started by paying them the compliment of playing a big part in history, and then telling them we're not paying too much," the producer noted at the time.

Most of the stars worked for one day at $2,500 apiece. Allen cast numerous past and future colleagues in the film, from his best friend Groucho Marx (as Dutch Governor Peter Minuit, who swindles the local "Indian" tribes out of Manhattan Island for $24) to Peter Lorre (as Roman Emperor Nero).

Hedy Lamaar came out of retirement to play Joan of Arc, flying from her home in Texas and, according to *Mirror-News* columnist Erskine Johnson, given "two vitamin shots" by a doctor before climbing on a horse to lead her army in battle.

Allen reportedly cast a young Dennis Hopper as Napoleon because he thought the actor resembled portraits of Napoleon as a young man. Other members of the "cast of 50 stars" included Don Megowan and Nancy Miller as Adam and Eve, Charles Coburn as Hippocrates,

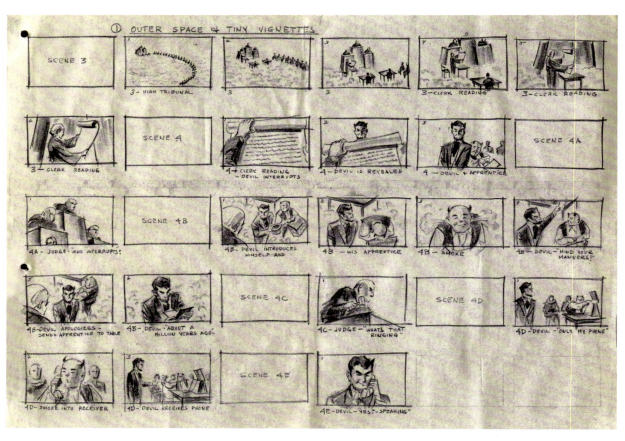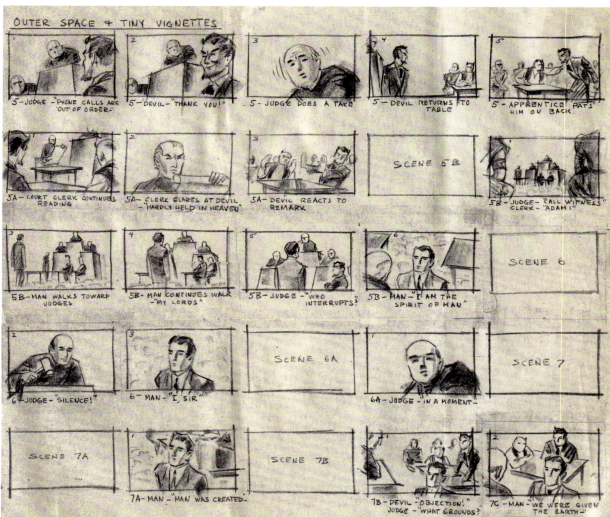

**LEFT**
Storyboard sketches for the opening scenes and introduction of Vincent Price's character of the Devil for *The Story of Mankind*.

**OPPOSITE**
The impressive "cosmic tribunal" set for the trial of humanity in *The Story of Mankind*.

55

**ABOVE**
Allen's pal Groucho Marx (seen here with his then-wife Eden Hartford [middle] and Abraham Sofaer [right] in a scene lampooning the legendary purchase of Manhattan from Native American tribes.

Vincent Price as Mr. Scratch (left) and Ronald Colman, in his final screen role, as the Spirit of Man (right).

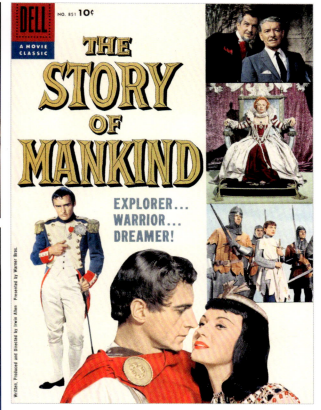

**ABOVE**
Dell's comic book tie-in for *The Story of Mankind*.

**RIGHT**
Establishing shot of the courtroom, and the entrances of Vincent Price and Ronald Colman in *The Story of Mankind*.

Virginia Mayo as Cleopatra, Cesar Romero as the Spanish envoy to Queen Elizabeth (Agnes Moorehead), Reginald Gardiner as Shakespeare, and Harpo Marx as Isaac Newton. Chico Marx also appeared as a monk, marking *The Story of Mankind* as the first movie to feature The Marx Brothers without putting them in any scenes together.

45 sets, from the 18,000 square foot "outer space" courtroom set to Queen Elizabeth's court, Marie Antoinette's court, Nero's palace, Leonardo Da Vinci's study and Napoleon's house at Versailles, were constructed on sound stages at Warner Bros. Art director Art Loel supervised construction, consulting with historical experts on the details. Allen even noted that real constellations were built into the outer space backdrop for the courtroom set.

As Allen filmed his all-star cast, the movie began earning comparisons to another project—Mike Todd's *Around the World in 80 Days*, which had drummed up a lot of publicity through its own cast of major stars. Philip K. Scheuer in the Nov. 9, 1956 *LA Times* compared the production to *Around the World in 80 Days* (noting that Cesar Romero was cast in both *Around the World* and *The Story of Mankind*), and the following spring, as shooting completed, *Newsweek* repeated the comparison, noting:

> Last week, Irwin Allen, producer and director of Warner Brothers' *The Story of Mankind*, had finished shooting on the most pretentious-sounding movie in recent history. Allen, a roundish, 40-year-old former movie columnist and actors' agent, has been profitably inspired on other occasions. Walt Disney's successes inspired him to make *The Animal World* and he also cashed in on Rachel Carson's best seller, *The Sea Around Us*.

*The Story of Mankind*'s title may have sounded pretentious, but Allen and Charles Bennett had more or less produced a comedy, as the casting of the Marx Brothers confirmed. Allen's research and his staff's painstaking documentation of the Warner Bros. stock footage library had kept costs on the production low, but at three hours, it was too long (no one would get away with a three-hour comedy until Stanley Kramer's 1963 epic *It's A Mad, Mad, Mad, Mad World*), and Warner Bros. had Allen cut it down to 100 minutes.

No movie starring Vincent Price as the Devil can truly be bad, but *The Story of Mankind* didn't exactly burnish Allen's growing credentials as a filmmaker. As a comedy it was half-hearted, as history it was half-serious, and Ronald Colman at the end of his career was no match for Vincent Price in his prime. Price effortlessly propelled the film with his fiendish good humor, often outmaneuvering the Spirit of Man, particularly when Colman whitewashes the settlement of the New World and Scratch points out the slaughter of native Americans and the blight of slavery.

When a court announcer heralds the arrival of Philip of Spain to Queen Elizabeth's court, the mellifluous, radio-trained voice belonged to Allen himself, beginning a habit of Allen's of stepping in to provide off-camera vocals for radio announcers and other unseen characters in his later movies and TV shows.

The opening of the movie (after Paul Sawtell's score highlights every movie star name with an orchestral flourish) is a brazen knock-off of the opening of Frank Capra's *It's A Wonderful Life*, with two angels in the form of blinking stars in the firmament gossiping about mankind's latest folly. The film's "heavenly tribunal" scenes hearkened back to Michael Powell and Emeric Pressburger's 1946 fantasy *A Matter of Life and Death*, otherwise known as *Stairway to Heaven*.

Reviews for the movie were tough, and for the first time Allen's ingenious and thrifty use of stock footage brought him in for criticism, as reviewers pointed out that the scenes shot by Allen were done on small sets that rarely matched the grandeur of the historical epics whose footage they were supposed to fit into. Still, at 100 minutes, Warners could book enough showings that *The Story of Mankind* could make money. And Allen was happy with the outcome.

"He liked it," Al Gail said in 1995. "I liked it. We felt, naturally, that some of the reviews were unfair, but the film did fairly well. No blockbuster. But for the type of thing it was it did fairly well."

**LEFT & OPPOSITE**
Theatrical poster art for *The Story of Mankind*.

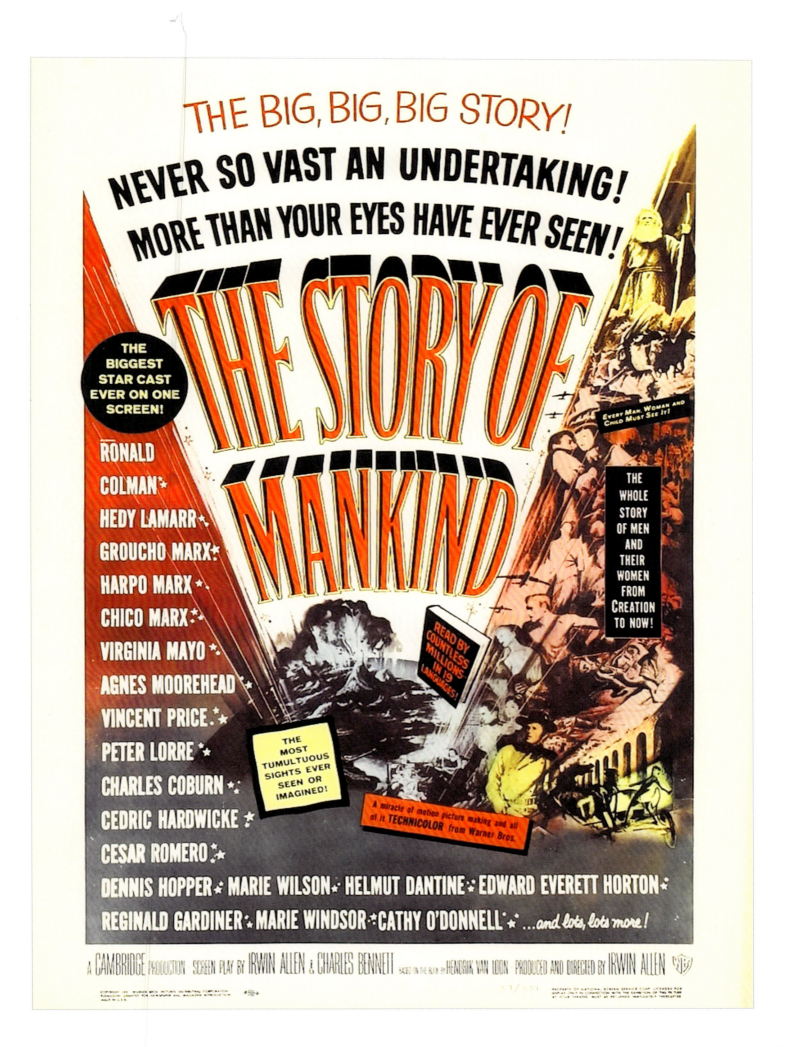

# THE BIG CIRCUS

*The Story of Mankind* had given Irwin Allen a taste of what it might be like to make an epic. Now he would proceed to make four widescreen spectaculars in four years, and he began by revisiting his lifelong love of carnivals and the Big Top in 1959's *The Big Circus*.

Inspired by the success of DeMille's *The Greatest Show on Earth*, Allen had dictated an idea for a circus movie just after winning the Oscar for *The Sea Around Us*. While wrapping up production on *The Story of Mankind* in 1957, he embarked on a 23,000 mile tour of America, a kind of mythic quest to determine what American audiences were looking for in a movie—and to determine if *The Big Circus* was it.

Allen said in 1959:

> What it amounted to was a personal poll of exhibitors. I saw the heads of theater chains and the owners of neighborhood houses, showed them the brochure, told them the story, the cast I had in mind, my production and exploitation ideas, and asked them, "Can you sell a picture like this? Do you want it?" I contend that if Hollywood would make exhibitor polls a regular prerequisite of production it would save itself millions of dollars and make additional millions by tailoring pictures to the demand and broadening the market.

Allen's tour marked the beginning of the producer's close relationship with and deep understanding of national film exhibitors and how to woo them. Thereafter Allen would personally oversee every detail of his projects' presentation to film exhibitors, engineering showy, offbeat publicity events across the country, bringing a touch of Hollywood to middle America while taking care to bring exhibitors to Hollywood, wine and dine them, and ensure that they would greet anything with the name Irwin Allen on it with enthusiasm.

To produce *The Big Circus*, Allen's Irwin Allen Productions teamed with Allied Artist Pictures. Allied Artists had been Monogram Pictures, producers of low budget serials and pulp movies throughout the 1940s and early 1950s. Steve Broidy had run the studio since 1945, and he'd been joined by Walter Mirisch around the same period. Mirisch convinced Broidy to upgrade the studio's image, aiming to make "B-plus" pictures instead of B-movies, and by 1953 the studio's name was changed to Allied Artists Pictures Corporation. Despite that move and a few respectable hits, the studio throughout the 1950s was still largely known for

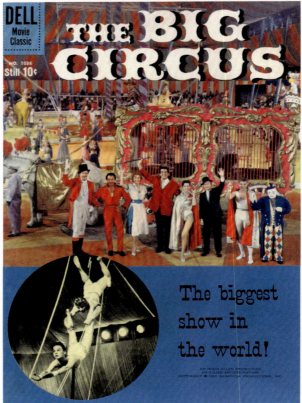

**ABOVE**
On the set of *The Big Circus* (L to R): *Variety* columnist Army Archerd, Victor Mature, Irwin Allen, Rhonda Fleming, and Peter Lorre.

Dell's comic book adaptation of the movie.

**OPPOSITE**
Theatrical poster art for *The Big Circus*.

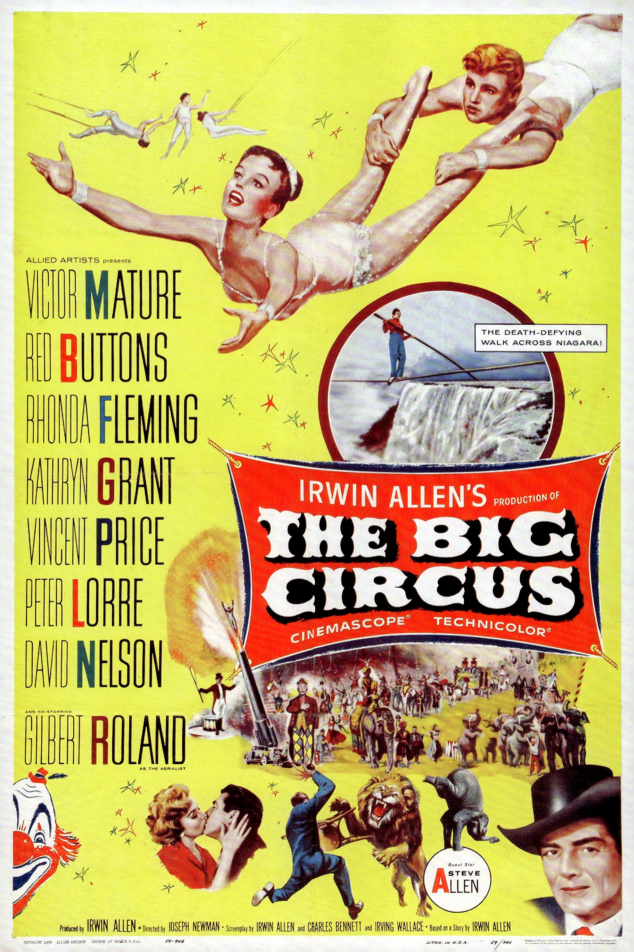

exploitative horror and sci-fi movies: *World Without End, Attack of the Crab Monsters, The Giant Behemoth, Not of This Earth*, and *Attack of the 50-Foot Woman*. Almost all of these were low budget, black and white programmers, while Allen's *The Big Circus* would be a widescreen, full color epic.

*The Big Circus*' screenplay (by Allen, Charles Bennett and screenwriter/novelist Irving Wallace) told the tale of debt-ridden circus impresario Hank Whirling (Victor Mature), whose traveling circus is saddled with banker Randy Sherman (Red Buttons), who is assigned to stick with Whirling to safeguard a large bank loan intended to keep the circus in business. Also along to dog (and flirt with) Whirling is a reluctant Madison Avenue press agent, Helen Harrison (Rhonda Fleming), who needles Whirling while the circus chief deals with various crises among his stable of stars as well as what seems to be a mysterious saboteur in their midst.

Allen wrote the part of Whirling specifically for his *Dangerous Mission* star Mature, citing the veteran actor as "one of the most colorful personalities in pictures." Kathryn Grant, who was Bing Crosby's considerably younger wife, played Whirling's spunky daughter Helen, a budding trapeze artist, while veteran Golden Age star Gilbert Roland played trapeze superstar Zach Colino.

Fleming's casting fulfilled a prophecy Allen had made to the actress back when he was doing one of his radio programs. Appearing on the program when she was still using the name Marilyn Lewis, Fleming was told by Allen that she would be a big star someday and that he would be a movie producer and put her in one of his pictures.

Peter Lorre, who'd had a small role in *The Story of Mankind*, was originally hired to play the "sleazy bank official" character that would ultimately be played by Red Buttons. Buttons and Lorre agreed early in production to switch roles—but circumstances in the script put Buttons' character in the position of having to do Lorre's clown act.

"You see," Lorre said, "In this way the clown is me, but all my pratfalls are done by Red. This part of it was my idea. And after they shot my clown act, Red was limping for two days." Circus clown Bobby Kaye coached Red Buttons through his clown routine.

Mature was famous for fighting lions in *Samson and Delilah* and in Fox's *Demetrius and the Gladiators,* and Allen arranged for Mature to do it again when a saboteur sets a lion loose inside the circus tent in the movie. While the press materials touted Mature's training for the scene (and had Mature complaining to Allen, "What is it about me and lions anyway?"), in all three cases the actor was doubled by a stunt man and got nowhere near the real king of the beasts. Trainer Mel Koontz trained the lion for the scene.

*The Big Circus* also reunited Mature with his *Dangerous Mission* costar Vincent Price, who this time played the much more sympathetic role of circus announcer— and unofficial cheerleader—Hans Hagenfeld. Allen reportedly reedited the film to give Vincent Price's character a larger role.

**ABOVE**
Concept paintings for the Whirling Circus arrival at a downtown bank for the film's opening.
(Art by Stan Johnson)

Whirling's arrival at the bank he owes money to at the beginning of *The Big Circus*.

**ABOVE**
Allen with Vincent Price, who plays the Whirling Circus ringmaster.

**RIGHT**
Red Buttons (right) in the first of many roles for Irwin Allen, as a bank supervisor drafted into clowning at the circus (with Kathryn Grant, left).

Vincent Price at the center of the Big Top.

"Actors never know what goes on in the cutting room, and they dread it," Price said in press for the film. "I dread it myself. This time I was lucky. But some pretty terrible things have happened to me in the cutting room, too." Price apparently relished the opportunity to be the centerpiece of Allen's lavish production. "Every actor must be a ham at heart. Some of us underplay, we try to project the subtlest nuances; before the camera we don't dare as a rule to rant. But how we love it when we get the chance!"

After telegraphing his villain with the casting of Vincent Price in *Dangerous Mission*, Allen cannily littered *The Big Circus* with red herrings like Price and Peter Lorre, both known for villainous roles, while holding off the revelation that clean-cut David Nelson (then known for his role on the popular sitcom *The Adventures of Ozzie and Harriet*) was the plot's mystery saboteur until the final moments. After he saw the completed film, Allen gave Nelson star billing along with the movie's veteran actors.

"I changed his billing, because in *The Big Circus* his personality comes through with the candlepower of a born star's, and because of his growing popularity on TV," Allen said, predicting that David would become as famous as his pop star brother Ricky Nelson.

To create the scope of the lavish Whirling Circus, Allen combined equipment from five small circuses: the Yankee Patterson, Camel Bros., Arthur Bros., Jimmy Wood, and Jungleland. Allen got the Flying Alexanders from Ringling Bros. Barnum & Bailey Circus, as well as Hugo Zacchini, the 29-year-old "human cannonball." The Ronnie Lewis Trio, high ladder balance artists, were from the Polack Bros. Circus; Dick Walker and his lions were from Jungleland of Thousand Oaks, CA; other acts included Tex Carr and his Chimpanzees, Dick Perg's Movieland Seals from Pacific Ocean Park; Chester Hayes, stilt-walker, and popular kids' TV show star Bozo the Clown. Famed clown Emmett Kelly's services were offered but turned down.

**PREVIOUS**
Concept painting for the title sequence circus parade.

**ABOVE**
The title sequence opening circus parade.

**LEFT**
Emmett Kelly's agent offers the famous clown's services to Allen for *The Big Circus*. For whatever reason, Allen declined the offer.

**OPPOSITE**
Design painting for the three-ring circus tent interior, prominently featuring "Irwin Orange."

The full-sized interior circus tent set, shot on a soundstage at MGM.

**ABOVE & OPPOSITE**
Set concept paintings for *The Big Circus*.

Allen hired Barbett (Vanderclude Broadway) as circus production manager and technical adviser. Barbette was an aerial choreographer for Ringling and later the Polack Circus—he staged the movie's opening and closing circus parade and supervised the trapeze training for the film's actors.

Allen moved the production into MGM because of the needed soundstage size for the interior circus tent scenes. Metro's Lot 3 housed the largest circus set ever built at 18 acres: six pavilion-sized tents, another six smaller ones totaling 120,000 square yards of canvas; 40 circus wagons, eight animal cages, 12 trailers, and two railroad cars, and 20,000 square feet of ground covered with nine tons of sawdust. Art director Al D'Agostino and set decorator Bob Priestley lined Metro Stage 30 with 35,000 yards of canvas striped coral and gray, all of which had to be fireproofed because of the heat of the klieg lights that raised temperatures to 100 degrees at the ceiling. The full crowd and circus parade scenes were shot over a period of three days.

Demonstrating an ingenious strategy for getting the press on his side, Allen rounded up entertainment journalist pals James Bacon of AP, Joe Hyams of *The New York Herald Tribune*, Erskine Johnson of NEA syndicate, Army Archerd of *Daily Variety*, and syndicated columnist Earl Wilson. It was doubtful any of these influential figures were going to write anything bad about a movie they co-starred in.

During production of *The Big Circus*, Allen added some important collaborators to his "inner circle," people he would return to on numerous future projects.

He hired Winton C. Hoch as cinematographer on the complex project. Hoch was a three-time Oscar-winner (for *The Quiet Man*, *She Wore A Yellow Ribbon* and 1948's *Joan of Arc*) whose work went back until at least the mid-1930s. He was an uncredited Technicolor consultant on *Gone With the Wind*, shot numerous John Wayne films including *The Searchers*, and the same year he began working with Allen on *The Big Circus*, Hoch also shot one of the most demanding and bravura visual effects spectaculars of all time, Disney's *Darby O'Gill and the Little People*. Allen recognized Hoch's experience and technical prowess, which he needed on *The Big Circus*. Hoch would later shoot Allen's features *The Lost World, Voyage to the Bottom of the Sea* and *Five Weeks in a Balloon* and the first two seasons of the *Voyage to the Bottom of the Sea* TV series, *Lost in Space*'s pilot episode "No Place To Hide," as well as three season two episodes of the series, and the entire one-season episode run of *The Time Tunnel*.

Perhaps more important even than Hoch was the man who would become the movie's costume designer, Paul Zastupnevich. Nicknamed "Paul Z" because of his seemingly unpronounceable name (actor and comedian Red Buttons said of Zastupnevich, "That's not a name, that's an epidemic."), Zastupnevich would design costumes for all of Allen's later projects and become the producer's unofficial art department supervisor, longtime personal assistant, and sometimes whipping boy. Outspoken and wryly funny, Zastupnevich developed an intimate, sometimes frustrating working relationship with Irwin Allen over the next three decades, helping to supervise the details for the notoriously picky producer not only on his entertainment projects but also for Allen's living arrangements, his eventual wedding—even his funeral.

"I was supposed to be there only three weeks," Zastupnevich said in 1995. "I ended up with Irwin approximately thirty-two years. I'm like the proverbial man who came to dinner—I never left."

Nevertheless, it wasn't originally Allen's idea to hire Paul Zastupnevich. Zastupnevich had designed costumes for Rhonda Fleming on her previous picture and the actress wanted him to follow her onto *The Big Circus*, so Allen met with him in November, 1958. Zastupnevich recalls:

> Rhonda Fleming had arranged for me to see Irwin. She wanted me to do her wardrobe. And I remember walking into the office with my presentation folder, and he was so smitten with the presentation he didn't care what was inside of it. My presentation was so outstanding as far as he was concerned, he said "it has showmanship." I thought that he gave it to me basically on my merits but later I learned that Rhonda Fleming put a gun to his head and said, "Either he does the clothes, or I don't do the picture."

Zastupnevich never forgot the key word from Allen at the meeting—Showmanship:

> He surrounded himself with the best of people. And he went for talent. Even if they were unknowns or, if they had been on the top and had slipped a little, his premise was, get a familiar face and put it in the production. So throughout all the years that I was with him, I saw him apply all of these principles.

Zastupnevich was under no delusions that *The Big Circus* was anything more than Allen's attempt to make his own version of DeMille's *The Greatest Show On Earth*:

> He imitated. When we were doing *The Big Circus*, he envisioned himself as Cecile B. DeMille because Cecile B. DeMille had done *The Greatest Show On Earth*. We went through phases. We went through the Selznick phase. We went through the Disney phase. The DeMille phase.

The key difference between Allen and DeMille in 1959 was that Allen still didn't have a reputation as a film director, despite—or perhaps because of—his work on *The Story of Mankind*. While he developed and micromanaged nearly every aspect of the production, Allen had to hand over directorial duties on *The Big Circus* to Joseph M. Newman, a reliable hand at B-movies. Newman's best-known movie was probably the 1955 science fiction thriller *This Island Earth*—but famed sci-fi director Jack Arnold (*The Incredible Shrinking Man*, *The Creature from the Black Lagoon*) wound up reshooting about half of that film and was responsible for much of its atmosphere and appeal.

**ABOVE**

The Misunderstood Hero: Circus owner Hank Whirling (Victor Mature, standing) gives some tough love to broken trapeze artist Zach Colino (Gilbert Roland).

Colino performs his trapeze act inside Allen's color-drenched circus tent.

**OPPOSITE**

Allen goes over the script with his stars on the set of *The Big Circus*.

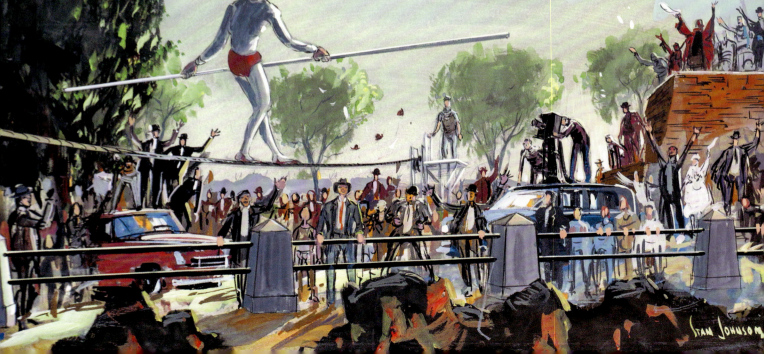

**OPPOSITE**
Production paintings for Gilbert Roland's climactic tightrope walk across Niagara Falls. (Top by Mentor Huebner, bottom by Stan Johnson)

**ABOVE**
Whirling watches as Colino tightrope walks over Niagara Falls at the climax of *The Big Circus*.

Newman would have a similar, albeit less publicized, experience on *The Big Circus*, as actor Red Buttons recalled in 1995:

> That was my first encounter with Irwin—*The Big Circus*. And he was kind of co-directing the picture and that kind of disturbed me a little bit, having two directors going at the same time. The director would say cut, print, and Irwin would get in there and then you had to do another shot. But that came out of Irwin's enthusiasm.

Victor Mature came onto *The Big Circus* as a silent partner (paperwork lists the movie as a coproduction of Allen's Saratoga and Vic Mature Productions), with the actor not only adding his star power, but his own money to the project. But Mature wore the mantle of co-producer as lightly as he did that of movie star.

When Mature suffered a family tragedy in early March of 1959, the production gave the star three days off and Allen had flowers sent to his house. An appreciative Mature wrote the production, "In view of the fact that you granted me permission to be absent for three days during the employment period referred to in my employment agreement for THE BIG CIRCUS, I agree to render services without compensation..."

Nevertheless, Mature managed to retain his trademark irascibility, as Paul Zastupnevich remembered:

> Victor Mature, at that time, was always chasing his stars. While I was in the fitting room one day Rhonda says, "If Victor ever comes in when I'm in the dressing room with you, don't leave. Never leave me alone with him." She says, "I want you to stick to me like glue." It was so funny because all through the production, Victor would be glaring at me. Finally there was one scene where there wasn't anything I could do about it, he was on the float with Rhonda Fleming, he bent over and he gave Rhonda a big kiss and then he turned around and stuck his tongue out at me, and he said, "You can't do a damn thing about it this time!"

Allen and his screenwriters made Mature's character wittier and more likable than his *Dangerous Mission* bodyguard, but Hank Whirling still fit into the "misunderstood hero" mold, particularly later in the movie as he appears to cruelly goad the tragic figure of Gilbert Roland's trapeze walker forward to complete a climactic tightrope walk across Niagara Falls, after the man loses his wife in a train accident.

Years later, appearing on an episode of *The Merv Griffin Show*, Allen talked about learning an important lesson about screenwriting while working on the Gilbert Roland plot-line with Charles Bennett and Irving Wallace:

> Originally Gilbert Rolland was going to walk across Niagara Falls on page eight. And of course it didn't really make any sense because nobody knew who Gilbert Rolland was in terms of the picture. But someone suggested if you put him on Niagara Falls on page 88, and put him through some terrible calamities—his wife is killed on 75, he loses three children on 62, he gets hungry on 53, then on 88 when he crosses the falls, everyone's with him, and it's that simple.

Mature's character was crucial to the trapeze artist's semi-tragic arc. Only near the end of the movie does Whirling make the viewer understand that he's trying to restore the proud trapeze artist's confidence, and Mature does a brilliant job of giving Whirling just enough natural arrogance that the audience believes he might be enough of a bully to treat Roland's character so badly.

Allen, too, could be distant and perplexing, and Paul Zastupnevich, several years after Allen's eventual death in 1991, would not hesitate to psychoanalyze the man he spent more than three decades working for. Zastupnevich's take conflicts with that of Allen's cousin, Al Gail, in terms of Allen's childhood and family history.

"He never really had a childhood as far as I can figure," Zastupnevich said in 1995. "He loved circuses. I think he was just a boy trying to be a boy—he was just trying to be a young boy again…because he did lose his parents when he was so young."

Zastupnevich claims he saw Allen's lighter side too, although even that, he claims, was mixed with a Machiavellian bent. "He loved to be mischievous too, he loved to get the upper hand of you. And he was devious too. He plotted people against one another. That's how he got a lot of things done."

Red Buttons, who would work with Allen on and off for almost as long as Zastupnevich, said that Allen's sense of humor was highly underrated. In fact, a number of people who worked with him over the years insisted that Allen had no sense of humor whatsoever—but it's possible they just didn't get the man.

Buttons on how he originally was cast in *The Big Circus*:

> I met Irwin Allen at the close of '58, somewhere around December. He was casting *The Big Circus*, and he was looking for somebody to play the banker, the young banker in that movie. At that time my agent was Martin Baum, of GAC. He had just gotten me signed. I had just finished a movie with Glenn Ford at MGM, called *Imitation General*, which was an imitation movie. We met at one of the big hotels for lunch, and my agent was really selling me a mile a minute about how big I am, how popular I am, how everybody knows me, how everybody loves me. I mean I can't go anywhere where people don't recognize me. And as we were talking and talking and talking, and, Irwin just listening and nodding, a busboy comes over the table and says to my agent, "Mr. Buttons, can I have your autograph?" Well, after we all got up from collapsing on the floor, Irwin Allen turned to my agent and said, "Red, you got the job." That's the first time I met him and that was the first indication I got that there was a real, silent, sense of humor to Irwin Allen, which, maybe a lotta people didn't recognize, because he was so intense about things.

With *The Big Circus* nearing completion and his eye as always on promotion, Allen reached back to another acquaintance from his radio days—his former announcer, Steve Allen.

By the time *The Big Circus* was in production, Steve Allen had been the star of *The Tonight Show*, laying the

groundwork for Johnny Carson, Ernie Kovacs, Jay Leno, David Letterman, and all the other "kings of late night" that would follow, and he had transitioned to a Sunday night variety show, *The Steve Allen Show*.

Allen wrote Steve Allen on February 9, 1959:

> Just talked with Jules Greene in New York and with Mick Vanoff here on the Coast. I explained to both of them that I am most anxious to have you in my picture, THE BIG CIRCUS, currently shooting at Metro. I was so anxious to have you in the picture that you will notice on the enclosed pages of the script your name, which, of course, was written in long ago. Hope you can do this for old times' sake. It is very important to me and the timing is just perfect if you can do it for me this week.

Allen intended to get the high profile TV host into his movie as a cameo, hoping that Steve Allen's name and presence would drum up additional publicity for *The Big Circus* and that Allen in turn might book some of the stars of the movie on his variety show.

Steve Allen recollected that when Irwin called, the variety show host was competing with no less than Ed Sullivan on Sunday night television:

> Ed Sullivan and I were opposite each other on Sunday nights at eight o'clock—he was on CBS, I was on NBC. And Irwin had done this exciting film about a big circus indeed, and he got the idea that it should be kicked off in that way so he just called our office and guaranteed to deliver a number of stars who were in this film, and it all worked out to our mutual satisfaction. And I think there's a scene where I play what we call a cameo. In fact, back in those days, because I was busy with television, I was doing so many cameos, I thought about going to Italy and changing

**ABOVE**

A sweeping aerial shot descends toward Whirling's circus early in the movie.

Irwin Allen's former announcer, Steve Allen, in his cameo appearance in *The Big Circus*.

my name to Cameo Vignette, and coming back as a big Italian star but that didn't work out.

Allen's plan to use the variety show host quickly ran into some pushback from NBC. Allen received a wire from the network's Jules Green on Octobter 2, 1959:

> ...We do not permit the use of Steve Allen's name in connection with advertising *The Big Circus* since he is on the screen for only a few seconds; may we have your assurance on this point.

Allen did not respond, and Allied Artists PR director Sandy Abrahams backed him up in a memo a month later:

> Jack Sattinger informs me that there is nothing in [Steve] Allen's contract which would prohibit us from using his name. I know that you certainly did not put him in the picture to be a "mystery guest," but because you felt that his name gave us a box office plus...we certainly aren't going to reprint the poster and lobby displays, etc., nor do I think you are going to remake the main title which bills him.

Steve Allen's name and cameo remained in the picture and Allen also promoted the movie on Groucho Marx's *You Bet Your Life* TV show.

The movie opened in late June of 1959 and earned some enthusiastic reviews. *Boxoffice* magazine, admittedly a publication geared more toward promotion than film criticism, raved that *The Big Circus* was...

> ...Literally an exploiter's dream. The first and deepest bow for the picture's overall attractiveness must be taken by Allen...surprisingly impressive production values, atmosphere and backgrounds. On the scrivening front, Allen's work was comparably praiseworthy, albeit the intelligentsia—real and would be—may opine that the screenplay undertakes to cover too much territory and is loaded with schmaltz and corn. So what? It's the kind of schmaltz and corn that the average ticket-buyer will gobble up and ask for more.

*Variety* was equally enthusiastic:

> A rousingly lavish film, stocked with tinted elephants, snarling lions and three rings of handsome production. Photographically, the picture is, or comes close to being, the finest CinemaScope film yet made.

*The Hollywood Reporter* noted the convincing nature of the process shots that had Gilbert Roland seemingly walking over Niagara Falls:

> Robert R. Hoag's technical effects for this perilous walk over the crashing rapids brought a spontaneous round of applause from the preview audience.

Today, *The Big Circus* languishes as one of Irwin Allen's least-well-known productions—which is a pity, because it's probably his most well-rounded film prior to *The Poseidon Adventure*.

It's also the only one of his early works that is entirely out of the mainstream of interest that unites Allen's

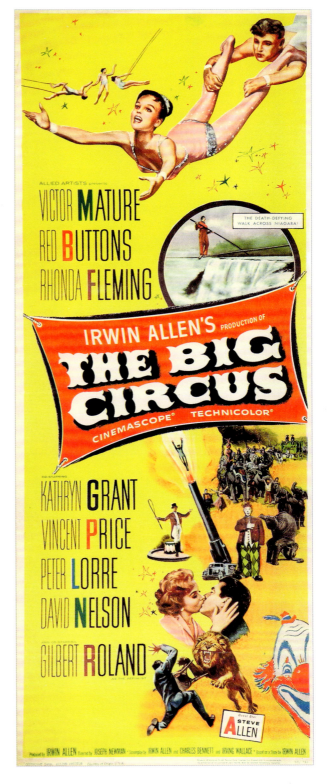

**RIGHT**
A rare 14" x 36" insert poster for *The Big Circus*.

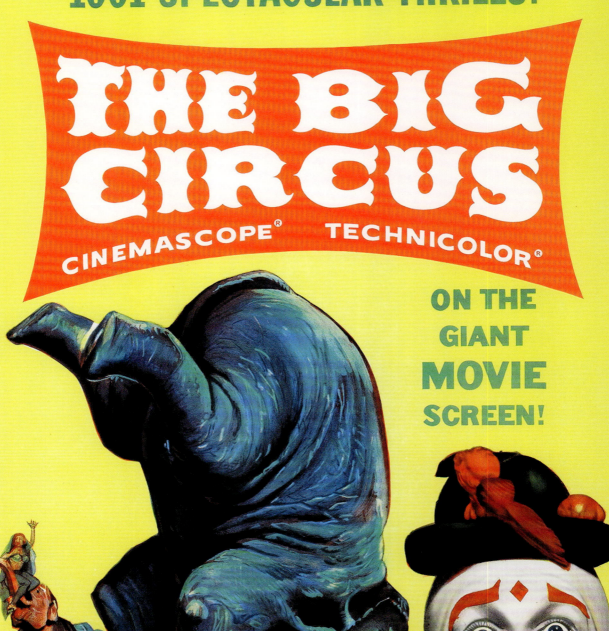

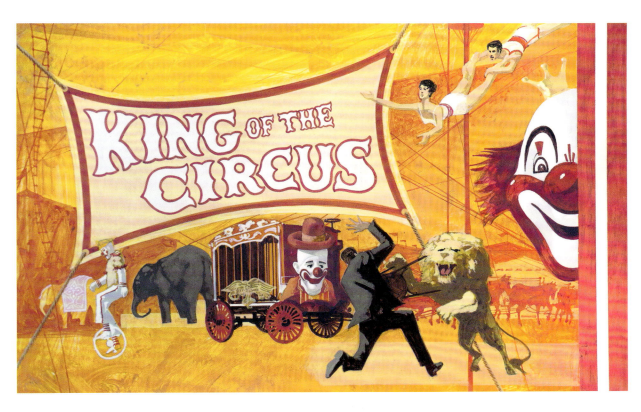

fans—it is not science fiction or fantasy, not set in the future, and doesn't feature harrowing pyrotechnics. But taken on its own terms, it's surprisingly entertaining and it constructs a fantasy world all its own. The screenplay by Allen, Bennett, and Wallace is fast-paced and amusing, allowing the movie to coast for the first 30 minutes on the interplay between the smug Mature and the apoplectic Red Buttons character. Allen's production gloss is at its height, with a mammoth opening parade of elephants dyed in primary colors, acrobats and clowns (including one with a goldfish bowl filled with fish covering his head), all inside the production's immense, orange-and-grey-striped circus tent interior with its bright yellow floor, three orange rings and openings for rows of klieg lights overhead.

Allen opens the film with a series of explosions and dire newspaper headlines flying at the audience (something he would redo virtually verbatim for his *Voyage to the Bottom of the Sea* feature a few years later). After the fast and funny introduction of Victor Mature's circus impresario and his fiscal problems, a stunning aerial shot swooping down on the massive circus tent being raised plummets the audience into the middle of the action.

After a half hour of conditioning the audience to a character-based comedy, Allen and his screenwriters jolt viewers with an escaped lion that Mature has to handle by himself in order to distract the beast from the other members of the circus and press. When the saboteur sets a hay fire that panics the circus animals and forces Mature to save the day again, Allen again demonstrates his skill at staging fire gags and stunts with a white-knuckle POV shot of a jeep driving directly into the fire and smashing through the flaming hay bales.

Allen may have started *The Big Circus* with the idea of capitalizing on the success of DeMille's *The Greatest Show On Earth*, but in this case he achieved the very rare goal of bettering his inspiration. DeMille's movie has long been submitted as the chief argument against the Academy Awards as arbiters of movie art, and as possibly the worst movie ever to win the Oscar for Best Picture. Allen's film achieves almost all the spectacle that DeMille's did (the big exception is the train wreck pivotal to both films—DeMille's was a centerpiece and one of the great miniature effects spectacles in the movies, while Allen's largely takes place off screen)—but Allen's movie is far more light on its feet, entirely without DeMille's heavy-handed pretension, funnier and more entertaining.

It was also undeniably cheaper—but for Allen, *The Big Circus* was an expensive picture, with a budget that swelled from $1,370,772 to $1,493,869, money that probably cut into its potential profits for Allen's production company, as well as for Allied Artists and Warner Bros., which distributed the film.

Nevertheless, Allen had achieved a dream with a colorful salute to his childhood obsession, the circus. One letter about the production he kept was from a circus performer, Tom O. Inabinette, who wrote Allen on July 17, 1959:

> I thought your office might like to know that in the opinion of quite a few professional Circus people your recent picture, *The Big Circus*, is very good, some say it is the best Circus picture they have seen.

*The Big Circus* was Allen's first real epic and the producer was thrilled with the achievement.

"Ever since I was in high school I wanted to be a motion picture producer," he said at the time. "Now I'm happy. To me this is still the most exciting business in the world."

**OPPOSITE**
More theatrical poster art for *The Big Circus*.

**ABOVE**
Allen pitched numerous later film and television properties based on circus themes including this *King of the Circus* concept developed for TV in the 1960s.

# "
## SHOOTING STILL CONTINUES ON THE LOST WORLD. BUT IF THEY DON'T SETTLE THE STRIKE SOON, I'LL RUN OUT OF NON-UNION MONSTERS!

**IRWIN ALLEN**

# THE TOY BOX

*Allen finds a home for his widescreen adventures at 20th Century Fox with* **THE LOST WORLD, VOYAGE TO THE BOTTOM OF THE SEA,** *and* **FIVE WEEKS IN A BALLOON**

## THE LOST WORLD

In 1960, Irwin Allen started a series of ambitious projects at 20th Century Fox studios, beginning an almost 15 year period that would define him as a creative talent and make him a household name to a generation of children and teenagers growing up in the 1960s. Turning back to the imaginative literature and movies that had inspired him as a child, Allen set out to film Arthur Conan Doyle's novel *The Lost World*—in what would be a remake of one of the groundbreaking special effects pictures of the silent era, the 1925 adaptation of Conan Doyle's story that had been stop motion animator Willis O'Brien's splashy debut in feature films.

Having worked with O'Brien on *The Animal World*, Allen was eager to bring the venerable animator onboard and promote O'Brien's connection to the 1925 classic. O'Brien was flattered and excited by the opportunity—since *The Animal World*, O'Brien had settled largely for work on low budget monster movies—1957's *The Black Scorpion* and 1959's *The Giant Behemoth*, a cheap knockoff of Ray Harryhausen's earlier *The Beast from 20,000 Fathoms* that showed O'Brien sadly chasing after the success of his onetime protege. By the standards of these movies, a color, Cinemascope project like Allen's *The Lost World*, done at a major studio, had the potential to be the crowning achievement of O'Brien's career.

For Allen, moving onto the storied lot of 20th Century Fox offered a security and talent roster that he'd lacked as an independent filmmaker. Perhaps even more important to Allen was that the studio, then under the supervision of one of its original founders, Spyros Skouras, allowed Allen the opportunity to direct the movie projects he brought onto the lot.

Allen arrived at Fox at a pivotal moment—Skouras was in the final years of his reign (the longest-running of any studio head at Fox) and the studio's resources were already being poured into the mammoth overseas production of *Cleopatra*. With all eyes on the historical epic and what would become its growing financial and publicity travails, Allen and his crew found themselves relatively free of studio oversight—as long as they didn't spend too much money. Fox had also had a recent hit in *Journey to the Center of the Earth*, a Jules Verne adaptation that featured strange locales and dinosaurs, very similar to what Allen had planned for *The Lost World*.

**OPPOSITE**
Poster art for 1960's *The Lost World*, Irwin Allen's first feature at 20th Century Fox and the beginning of a spectacular, decade-long run of movie and television projects made at the studio.

Allen brought many of his collaborators from his early films along to Fox: screenwriter Charles Bennett (who co-wrote the script for *The Lost World* with Allen), cinematographer Winton Hoch, costume designer Paul Zastupnevich (who would do a cameo in the film in a scene at a British zoological society), production illustrator Maurice Zuberano, and composers Paul Sawtell and Bert Shefter. He would draw many of his new stable of talent from Fox. Allen's and Bennett's screenplay followed famed Professor George Edward Challenger, who claims to have discovered a world where prehistoric dinosaurs still live on a remote plateau near the Amazon River in Brazil. Challenger recruits a reporter, Ed Malone, a big game hunter, Lord John Roxton, and two local guides, Manuel Gomez and a man named Costa, as well as Challenger's snooty rival Professor Summerlee, to explore the plateau. On the way they're joined by an adventurous heiress, Jennifer Holmes, whose brother David is reported to have been lost on the plateau during Challenger's first expedition.

Allen began casting *The Lost World* in January of 1959—a process that would take up the entire year. Fox casting director and studio manager Lew Schreiber quickly suggested David Hedison, who was under contract to the studio, for the reporter role. Allen concurred, in a Jan. 6, 1959 studio memo, saying, "He's certainly young enough, clean cut, and has had just enough exposure for good marketing and exploitation." But Allen also suggested Jeffrey Hunter, Earl Holliman, Fess Parker, Cliff Robertson, Robert Wagner, and Robert Stack as alternates, and he wouldn't settle on Hedison until filming was about to begin.

For Challenger, British actor Robert Morley, Burl Ives, Hugh Griffith, and Orson Welles were discussed. Another name brought up was James Mason, who had starred in Fox's *Journey to the Center of the Earth*.

In the same January 6, 1959 memo:

> I remind you that there will be at least seven months between the release date of JOURNEY and THE LOST WORLD ...and while I was originally concerned about having Mason in both pictures, I do not feel that that is now a serious consideration in view of the elapse of time between the two pictures, plus the fact that Mason could play the role of Challenger with a beard. He would be my first choice after Morley.

For the film's female lead, Allen looked at film of Jill St. John in Fox's comedy *The Remarkable Mr. Pennypacker,* and *Holiday For Lovers*. Allen was critical of St. John's weight in the latter picture, an inauspicious sign for what would become an unhappy working relationship between Allen and the actress.

Allen wanted Gilbert Roland, his veteran star from *The Big Circus*, for Gomez. Roland had been an extra in the 1925 version of *The Lost World* and wanted to be in the remake, but his asking price was too high even when he offered to do the role (a far less substantial one than his role in *The Big Circus*) for less. Allen also wanted to bring back David Nelson from *The Big Circus* for the role of Jennifer Holmes's brother.

**ABOVE**
Test shot of Vitina Marcus made during casting for *The Lost World*.

Vitina Marcus in the finished film.

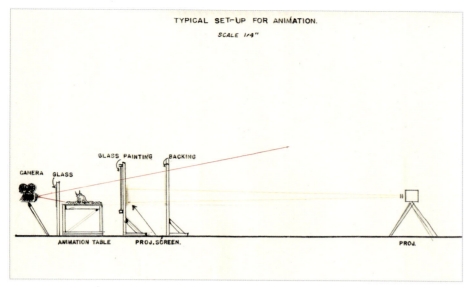

**ABOVE**
Dinosaur sequence sketches by Willis O'Brien, made early in preproduction when stop-motion animation was still being considered to bring the creatures to life on screen.

And he believed he had found the perfect choice for a "native girl" featured in the story.

"The girl's name is Vitina Marcus. I made a color still test of her yesterday and it turned out great. I suggest that Fox might want to take an option on her services or put her under contract." Allen would later cast Marcus as the "Girl from the Green Dimension" in his *Lost in Space* TV series.

Allen and the studio had spent $80,000 for the rights to the Arthur Conan Doyle book. He planned to spend $145,000 on casting, $25,000 in set construction, $100,000 for special effects and $10,000 for photographic effects for a total budget of $840,179.00—considerably less than that of *The Big Circus*.

In September, 1959, Allen wrote Ray Harryhausen in an attempt to bring him onboard the production:

> As you probably have heard, I am going full blast ahead on THE LOST WORLD and I can think of no one I would be more pleased to have associated with me on this project than yourself. Won't you please take a few minutes out and write me and let me know your schedule to the extent of when you could give me 2 or 3 months of your time. I could be willing to juggle my own production problems in order to fit your availability. In the meantime, you have regards from all including your old buddy, Willis O'Brien.

By 1959, after a successful series of low budget science fiction movies, Harryhausen was increasingly in control of his own destiny as a filmmaker and had served as an uncredited associate producer on the color *The 7th Voyage of Sinbad*, a big hit for Columbia. Harryhausen already had his followup, *The 3 Worlds of Gulliver* in production, and he turned Allen down.

The decision over how to bring *The Lost World*'s dinosaurs to life became a thorny issue for the production as studio executives began to pressure Allen to keep costs on the picture down. Fox's special effects department head, L.B. "Bill" Abbott, already had experience employing live lizards—in this case iguanas—for the dinosaur sequences in Fox's *Journey to the Center of the Earth,* and stop motion was known to be a time-consuming, and therefore expensive, process.

On October 16, 1959, Allen sent out a memo requesting a meeting with Abbott, miniature director of photographer Ralph Hammeras (a veteran effects photographer and artist who had worked on everything from the 1925 *The Lost World* to Disney's *20,000 Leagues Under the Sea*) and Willis O'Brien to look at Maurice Zuberano's sketches of the dinosaur sequences:

> The purpose of the meeting is to pool our mutual experience and make at least tentative decisions regarding the most satisfactory and economical method of handling these sequences. (Specifically, whether to use real animals or animation with stop frame photography or build sections of animals and then photograph at high speed).

Allen was also looking into ways of cutting down the actual amount of special effects footage the production would need to generate. On Oct. 28, 1959 he wrote Fox executive Sid Rogell and told him he had negotiated with Warner Bros. for the rights to use outtakes from the dinosaur animation from *The Animal World*: "Highly acceptable dinosaur fight material that we may want to dress up and use for process as seen through thick jungle foliage of animals fighting in THE LOST WORLD." At this stage the movie had not been budgeted, but Allen thought it was possible that the *Animal World* footage "might replace one of the sequences we are currently planning and, hence, save money which would be reflected in our budget. Or we might decide to use it in addition to our own new sequences."

While he was ironing out the details of *The Lost World*, Allen began trying to sell another project. He wrote Chuck Belden at MCA Artists, Ltd. on October 5, 1959:

> Enclosed herewith "Around the World in 80 Days" in a Western setting—THE LAST RIDE WEST. Would appreciate your reading it and then calling me to see if we can't package this as my next project following THE LOST WORLD.

*The Last Ride West* was, in fact, much more similar to what would become MGM's Cinerama epic *How the West Was Won*, which would reach movie screens three years later. Had Belden taken Allen's bait, *The Last Ride West* might have beaten *How the West Was Won* into theaters and hit at the height of the western genre's popularity. But Belden passed and Allen spent the next fifteen years trying, and failing, to get the picture made.

Allen planned to shoot *The Lost World* in 30 days, starting in the first half of February, for a release date in mid July. But by this time, in a decision that proved a devastating blow to Willis O'Brien, Allen and Fox had chosen to drop the idea of using stop-motion animation for the dinosaur sequences and instead employ live animals on miniature sets constructed by Fox prop expert Herb Cheek. In a Jan. 12, 1960 memo from Allen to Fox's Sid Rogell, Allen said:

> It has always been my intention that the special effects shooting involving miniatures and animals be completed prior to the start of principal photography. However, because of the complications involved in preparing these animals, we will not be able to start shooting such miniatures until January 25th.

L.B. Abbott and his department had settled on the use of monitor lizards to play most of the dinosaurs, because of the monitor's large size and aggressive nature. But all of the creatures seen in the film would require foam rubber "makeup appliances" to make them resemble dinosaurs, and other animals were being considered to play some of the script's additional creatures, including a "fire monster" that would menace the characters in an underground cavern at the film's climax.

Allen continued in the Jan. 12 memo:

> I have asked that you be shown the test on the cobra which was shot last Friday. You will quickly see that the cobra is the wrong animal to portray the "fire monster." Our plans call for the use of a Monitor which is being

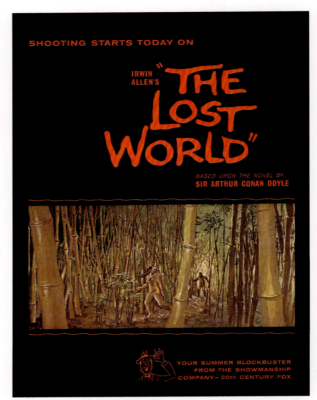

**ABOVE**
Shooting announcement for the movie.

A technician wrangling one of the monitor lizards made up to resemble dinosaurs and filmed on miniature sets for *The Lost World*.

A caiman prepares to battle the dinosaur monitor lizard in a frame from the finished film.

**OPPOSITE**
Some of *The Lost World*'s impressive full-size sets.

shipped to us from India. The Monitor is much more ferocious looking and is of greater girth than the cobra. Only by proper testing of these various animals can we know for certain what we are going to get in the final end result. Therefore, it will take the balance of this week and all of next week to receive all of the animals that will portray monsters in our picture, complete the building of the various appendages to be put on them, complete the miniature sets, test all of the animals in the actual miniature sets, and see these animals on the screen and agree that they are exactly what we want.

A few days later, Allen wrote Rogell about bringing cameraman Winton Hoch in for two days to review the miniature and full-sized sets:

On January 20th we plan to test all of the miniature sets with all of the animals available at that time, dressed in their final form. It is imperative that Winton Hoch sit in on the lighting and supervise such testing in view of the fact that he will be committed to whatever Bill Abbott does with the miniatures.

Allen also wanted Hoch present to review the set-ups on the full-size sets on the same day that the production tested the final miniature sets and animals. "This way, [Hoch's] time can be divided on that day between the big sets and a two hour session of lighting on the final miniatures."

Art directors Duncan Cramer and Walter M. Simonds created 16 sets for the movie, designated as The Vineyard of Choking Vines, Garden of Man-Eating Plants, Grazing Plain of Dinosaurs, Forest of Spider-Webs, Battleground of the Monsters, Cave City of the Cannibals, Volcanic Stairway, Tentacles of Death, Graveyard of the Damned (Cemetery of the Dinosaurs), The Wall of Death, The River of Lava, Cave of the Fire Monster, Altar of Diamonds, Lake of Boiling Lava, Exploding Plateau, and The Hatching of the Dinosaur Eggs.

On January 19, 1960, Allen sent a casting memo to Lew Schrieber urging "we attempt to close as many of the following people this week as possible." At this point, Janet Leigh, Dina Merrill, Terry Moore, Polly Bergen, Jane Powell, and Barbara Eden were under consideration for Jennifer—Jill St. John wasn't on the casting list and Anne Francis' name was, but was crossed out. Gilbert Roland was still the sole name listed for Gomez (the project would lose a nice promotional angle tying the remake into the 1925 film when Roland eventually dropped out). Vitina Marcus and Arlene Martel were up for native girl ("Either one of these girls would be perfect," Allen said). He also suggested Cedric Hardwicke, who he had worked with on *The Story of Mankind*, for Challenger (Hardwicke would later play a similar character in Allen's *Five Weeks in a Balloon*), and David Nelson for David.

Ultimately Claude Rains would play Challenger, Richard Haydn would be cast as Summerlee, Michael Rennie would play Broxton, Jill St. John would be Jennifer Holmes, Fernando Lamas would be Gomez, and the little-known Ray Stricklyn, rather than David Nelson, would play David Holmes.

David Hedison also, finally, made the final cut. Hedison was under exclusive contract to Fox and had just changed his stage name to David from Al Hedison, which he had used on the Fox films *The Enemy Below, The Fly*, and *Son of Robin Hood*. Hedison recalled in 1995:

> I got a wonderful letter, when I was doing an NBC TV series, *Five Fingers*, from a woman who wanted to know if I was related to Al Hedison. She said, "...because you look alike." But she said, "...although I think that you're better looking, Al was a better actor." I think that was quite good.

*The Lost World* wasn't a pleasant experience for Hedison:

> It was one of those pictures that the studio wanted me to do and I felt I had to do, and I didn't want to go on suspension, all that sort of thing. I didn't like the script. I didn't believe in the script. I'd get on the set and I'd see Jill St. John in pink tights holding a poodle. And I was on that film for about eight weeks or so and I was really, truly depressed.

Hedison appreciated Allen's command of the picture's technical effects, but felt frustrated as an actor:

> All the monster stuff and the dinosaurs, all of that worked very well, for that time, and that part of it was great. But the actors were just nothing. I mean even that magnificent actor, Claude Rains, was in it. It was just that there was nothing we could do. It was looking helpless and looking frightened and all that bullshit. It didn't work on the on the written page and it didn't work when I was doing it. When I saw it, I thought, "Oh my God, never again. Never again."

Allen obviously had no issues with Hedison on the set—Hedison was a well-behaved Fox contract player and Allen would be eager to work with the actor again later when he was casting *Voyage to the Bottom of the Sea*. Allen evidently did have problems with Jill St. John, which he later outlined in a memo to Fox casting director Owen MacLean while casting the *Voyage to the Bottom of the Sea* movie:

> You know only too well the bitter experience I had on the last picture in which I was forced to use a girl who neither fit the role, nor had any desire whatsoever to be in the picture. She cost us three days of shooting by actual production department records *[redacted from the memo was "and her sheer bitchiness made every possible attempt to wreck the morale of the company."]* This must not happen again.

What the exact conflict between Allen and St. John was has never been clear; Allen was concerned with her weight, and St. John (who reportedly had a Mensa-level I.Q. of 167) may have been chafing under the typical pressures on Hollywood actresses to look impossibly thin and beautiful at all times.

Costume designer Paul Zastupnevich came to the conclusion, after working with Allen for decades, that the producer/director simply had difficulty relating to women:

> I think basically he was afraid of women. He just didn't know how to cope with them. And he had a way of talking down to women that, women were ready to haul off and hit him. And I still say to this day that he'd have been charged with harassment, vocal harassment, if he were around today with some of the things that he did.

Allen had a much more positive relationship with another budding actress he met during the production: singer and performer Sheila Matthews, who would, a decade and a half later, become Mrs. Irwin Allen. Matthews recalled in 1995:

> We were introduced at a restaurant by a mutual friend and he invited me out to the studio, and he was shooting *Lost World* at the time. So he sat me in his director's chair, and, let me watch the shooting. After about an hour he said you can leave your picture and resume with my secretary. So I did, and I totted off the lot."

Matthews ran into Allen a year later near his office:

> We had a chat, and two weeks later he invited me out to dinner, and my dinner date was at Groucho Marx's house, which was quite interesting, to say the least. So then we started dating.

In marked contrast to Zastupnevich's perspective on Allen, Matthews found the producer gentlemanly, if not downright courtly, with women:

**ABOVE**

Claude Rains (left) as Professor Challenger and Richard Haydn (right) as Summerlee.

Jay Novello (left) as Costa and Fernando Lamas as Gomez.

(l to r) Claude Rains, Michael Rennie, Richard Haydn, Jill St. John, and Ray Stricklyn in Paul Zastupnevich's color-coded costumes.

**ABOVE**
Irwin Allen (left, seated) with the cast of *The Lost World* during a break in filming.

**RIGHT**
Jill St. John and David Hedison in their first scene in *The Lost World*.

**OPPOSITE**
Allen (seated, looking through camera) works with Hedison and St. John next to a set piece designed for compositing into one of the dinosaur sequences.

**ABOVE**
The finished composite, with the actors cowering as lizard dinosaur stand-ins rush into combat.

Some of the vicious on-screen action, as monitor lizard and caiman struggle, bite, and ultimately plummet off a cliff.

By early March, 1960, Allen's plans to shoot *The Lost World* in 30 days were being overturned by a Writers Guild of America strike, which was briefly joined by actors, including some working on Allen's film.

On March 7, Allen boasted in a memo to the studio's Buddy Adler that he had reduced his schedule overage from three days to three quarters of a day. He still promised to bring the movie in on or under schedule and that, "it will be as potential a blockbuster as JOURNEY (even more monsters, excitement, special effects, etc.) and at a fraction of the cost."

Allen also continued to explore marketing ideas for the movie, writing Charles Einfeld, one of Fox's PR men, that, "There must be a toy manufacturer in New York who would be delighted to put out a simple cardboard game called 'Adventures in THE LOST WORLD.'"

By the end of March, Allen was starting to admit defeat regarding his schedule, writing Mike Connolly of *The Hollywood Reporter* to say: "As you predicted, shooting still continues on THE LOST WORLD. But if they don't settle the strike soon, I'll run out of non-union monsters!"

By April 1st, special effects for the picture were wrapped and Allen wrote Fox's Bill Eglinton:

> Just a note of thanks for a most difficult job beautifully done. I refer to the special effects and miniature work on THE LOST WORLD for which you and your department are responsible in such a great way. Bill Abbott contributed efforts above and beyond the call of duty and I am most grateful to him and to you for what now promises to be some of the best special effects, miniature and animal footage ever seen on the screen.

When the film's credits were being assembled, Allen took a stand for his own brand, writing Frank Ferguson on May 11 that, "the credit 'Sir Arthur Conan Doyle's THE LOST WORLD' must in no way affect card b which must read: 'Irwin Allen's Production of...'."

But Allen also stood up for the recognition of his crew, disputing Ted Cain's objection to granting composers Sawtell and Shefter their "composed and conducted by" credit, and arguing for the retention of Production Illustrator Maurice Zuberano's credit, insisting that both Zuberano and the composers had done excellent work and been appropriately credited on Allen's previous productions.

Allen's dedication to his production illustrators was legendary—he had every feature project and television pilot he worked on completely storyboarded.

"We probably hired half the union," Al Gail said of Allen's art department hiring over the years. "We had almost as many sketch artists as Disney, and they worked all the time, because it was so much easier, saved so much time. The director can come in and look at the sketches and see what we have in mind, rather than having to struggle through a script, on one week's notice, and try to figure out all the shots, because they were difficult shots. So it was a tremendous help to them, to have all these sketches." Allen also loved

The very first thing that struck me after I went in to see him in his office that day was that he left his door open, to his secretaries, and that impressed me very much. 'Cause I was a little leery, coming out from New York and meeting producers and things like that. [He was] a very sweet man, a very affectionate person. We were not that young when we met and Irwin had been in Hollywood a long time before me, so... every now and then I'd run into, some of his former lady friends and they all seemed very sweet and very, very nice. I wasn't jealous of them. Actually he didn't give me any reason to be which was nice.

Matthews also had numerous opportunities to watch Allen interact with his famous best friend, Groucho Marx:

They had a very, unusual relationship I think. I feel Groucho was almost like a second father to Irwin. They had a really good time together. Groucho was of course, quite funny and Irwin had his moments too. They really enjoyed each other for many years. I guess we had dinner at Groucho's about three times a week practically. Evidently Groucho figured I was okay, because I don't think we would have been seeing each other if [he hadn't].

**LEFT**
The fiery climax of *The Lost World*.

**ABOVE & OPPOSITE**
Theatrical poster art and trade art for Allen's *The Lost World*

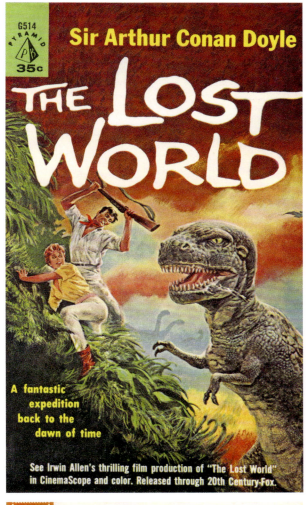

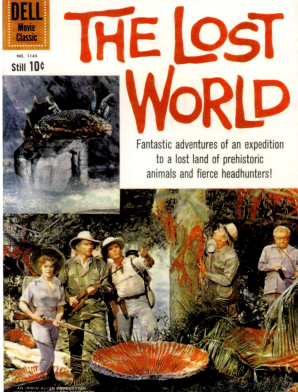

**LEFT**
Dell comic book adaptation of the movie.

Paperback movie tie-in release of Sir Arthur Conan Doyle's classic novel.

**OPPOSITE**
(top) A quad poster for the British release of *The Lost World*; (bottom) and a 22 x 28 half sheet from the U.S. theatrical release.

having production schedules and artwork covering the walls in his office, so he could easily check out the progress of a film or television episode and show off what he was working on to visitors.

Allen continued to beat the publicity drums for *The Lost World* in the run-up to its July 13 opening. When Albert Pickus of the Theatre Owners of America omitted the movie from a list of "eleven big summer box office releases," Allen sent Pickus a telegram pointing out the oversight.

*The Lost World* turned out to be one of Fox's bigger hits of the year, laying the groundwork for a long stint for Allen at the studio. After its release the movie ran for years in local afternoon movie packages for television, its impressive widescreen cinematography smashed down into muddy, pan-and-scan presentations that ironically made the film fit in perfectly with Allen's later science fiction TV shows, all of which repurposed dinosaur footage from *The Lost World* into their episodes.

In more recent high definition presentations available in streaming services and on blu-ray, the movie looks quite impressive, particularly in regards to its big, imaginative sets (like the "dinosaur graveyard" with a pathway leading directly through the gigantic ribs of a long-dead monster) and special effects.

Allen's cast of characters is colorful—literally so in Paul Zastupnevich's color-coordinated wardrobe, which allows viewers to identify each character in long distance shots by what they're wearing. The 90-minute movie takes 30 minutes to get to the Brazilian plateau (depicted via impressive aerial photography), but once there the action rarely lets up from the various dinosaur battles, giant spiders and man-eating plants to the final, nail-biting journey along a narrow cliff ridge past boiling volcanic waters inhabited by the scaly "fire monster."

The animal action, particularly as a monitor lizard wearing a triceratops-like frill battles an alligator-like caiman, is almost shocking to watch today with the reptiles clearly biting each other and even drawing blood. To enhance the action, sound effects editors Harry M. Leonard and E. Clayton Ward drew upon real animal sounds that they altered by changing the pitch and speed of the original recordings; one sound of a bull elephant roar (repeated often in the film and in other Fox productions of the period) was later stretched out by sound effects artist Ben Burtt and used as the familiar engine roar of the TIE fighters in *Star Wars*.

While a success for Irwin Allen, *The Lost World* was nothing less than a tragedy for Willis O'Brien, who never again was able to mount a major film project; his last work was on the animated fire ladder climax for the comedy *It's a Mad, Mad, Mad, Mad World*, which was released in 1963, a year after O'Brien died. O'Brien never received credit for his work on the comedy.

## VOYAGE TO THE BOTTOM OF THE SEA

While working on securing the rights to Arthur Conan Doyle's *The Lost World* novel, Allen wrote literary agent Henry Lester, who had suggested another Conan Doyle work with an underwater theme:

> Thank you for your suggestion regarding the Conan Doyle ocean story. Unfortunately, this would conflict with my next project which is also an undersea picture. I have been developing an original on the subject ever since the success of *The Sea Around Us* and it is now almost ready for production.

The undersea picture was *Voyage to the Bottom of the Sea*, and it would be Allen's most ambitious production yet—although it would ultimately be overshadowed when Allen used its success to launch a series of science fiction TV series at 20th Century Fox.

Allen himself had jumpstarted interest in oceanography with *The Sea Around Us*, and his own interest in Jules Verne no doubt dovetailed with the success of Disney's film adaptation of Verne's *20,000 Leagues Under the Sea* in instigating what would become *Voyage to the Bottom of the Sea*. Just as the Disney film's submarine Nautilus had sparked the imaginations of filmgoers, the U.S. Navy's real-life Nautilus (SSN-571) made headlines in the late 1950s as the world's first nuclear powered submarine, particularly after it became first to travel completely under the North Pole while submerged in August, 1958. Working with Charles Bennett, Allen concocted a story that had an experimental nuclear submarine, a kind of super-Nautilus, saving mankind from a climatic disaster when the Earth's Van Allen radiation belts begin to burn out of control.

To prepare for the production of *Voyage to the Bottom of the Sea*, Allen and his collaborators screened every submarine and naval-themed movie they could get their hands on, including *Submarine Patrol, The Enemy Below, Hell and High Water, Crash Dive, Underwater Warrior, Torpedo Run, Torpedo Boat, Submarine Command, The Sea Around Us, The Caine Mutiny, 20 Thousand Leagues Under the Sea, South Pacific, Beneath the 12-Mile Reef, Boy on a Dolphin, The Sea Hornet, City Beneath the Sea, Underwater!,* and *Up Periscope*.

**ABOVE**
The one-sheet poster art for *Voyage to the Bottom of the Sea*.

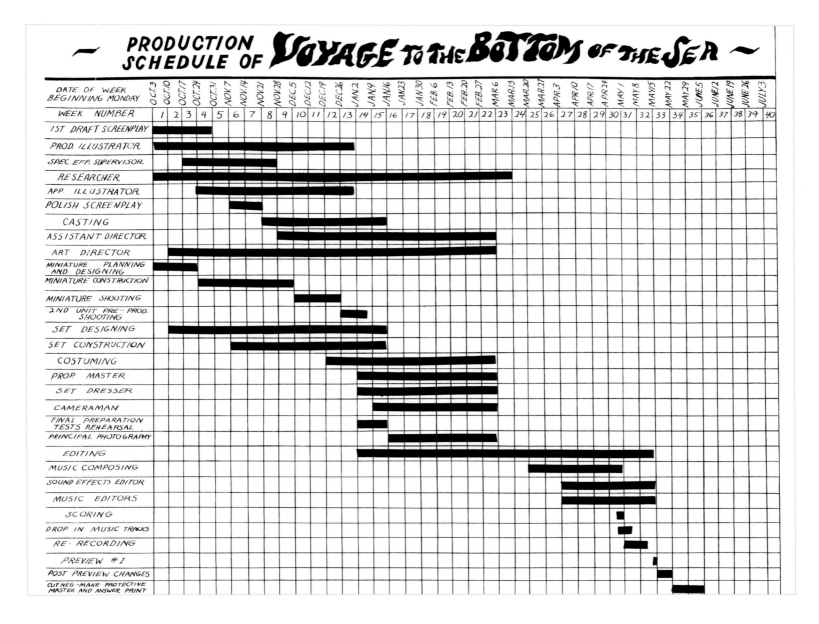

**ABOVE:**
Allen's painstaking production schedule for the *Voyage to the Bottom of the Sea* feature.

After making a deal with Fox to make the movie in September, 1960, Allen wrote Fox's PR chief Charles Einfeld in New York to announce the production:

> This biggest of all spectacular underwater adventure sagas goes into pre-production operations today in order to be before the cameras on January 16 in Cinemascope and Deluxe color and with an international all star cast. ...Please start those great Charlie Einfeld drums beating now for what promises to be a gigantic summer blockbuster to be delivered to you in early June.

Did Allen coin the term "summer blockbuster?" Maybe....

*Voyage to the Bottom of the Sea* boasted challenges that Allen and his team had never confronted before. He and Bennett had created a sometimes confounding central character in Admiral Harriman Nelson, the designer of the experimental nuclear submarine Seaview. Nelson was based on Navy Admiral Hyman George Rickover, who oversaw development of the U.S. Navy's nuclear submarine fleet, beginning with the Nautilus. Rickover was described as "Hyperactive, political, blunt, confrontational, insulting, flamboyant, and an unexcelled workaholic," and Allen and Bennett embraced Rickover's already controversial persona to develop Admiral Nelson as a contradictory figure and a classic "misunderstood hero," so driven to use his mighty atomic submarine to defeat the menace threatening mankind that he's willing to walk over anyone who gets in the way—including the U.S. government, the United Nations, and his own officers and crew.

Allen and Bennett drew from one of the movies they'd used as research—the Humphrey Bogart classic *The Caine Mutiny*, which depicted a naval uprising in reaction to a cruel, vindictive commander played by Bogart. The *Voyage to the Bottom of the Sea* screenplay would have Nelson pushing his own crew to the point of mutiny with his seemingly callous decisions, at one point striking a subordinate who questions his orders.

Allen had to cast the difficult role of Admiral Nelson as well as the rest of the Seaview crew, several important scientists and politicians, and a disruptive castaway taken on by the submarine. The Seaview itself had to be designed and built—not only a series of elaborate interior sets, but miniatures in various scales that had to

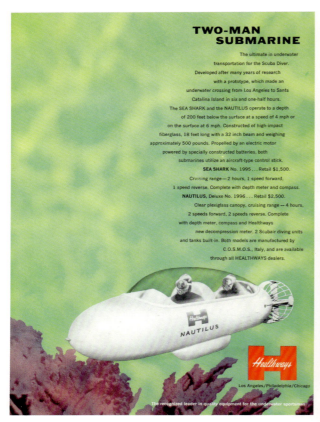

operate convincingly underwater and on the surface of massive water tanks on the Fox lot. The script also called for a sequence at the U.N. in New York and a number of underwater scenes, including one in which the Seaview's scuba divers work to tap a transatlantic cable and encounter a giant squid.

As Allen geared up for production, he began looking for other locations to film the movie's underwater sequences. The director of Florida's Cypress Gardens wrote Allen in September, 1960, about their 165-foot long, 80-foot wide photography tank, assuring him that, "This tank, which appears to the layman to be a very beautiful pool, can be dressed up with sets to accomplish almost any scene above or under the water."

Allen's script also called for the use of a two-man "mini-sub" that Seaview crewman would use to cut the Seaview free from a minefield midway through the movie. Gustav Dalla Valle of Healthways Sporting Goods offered the potential rental of two different two-man submarines to the production. Dalla Valle sent Allen a color brochure of the submarines, of which, the "Nautilus, Deluxe No. 1996" appears to be what would be used in the film, painted orange and with additional control surfaces added to it. The sub was built to operate at up to 200 feet below the surface at a speed of 4 mph— it was 18 feet long with a 32-inch beam, weighed around 500 pounds and was constructed of fiberglass.

On September 30, 1960, Allen noted in a PR memo that Claude Rains had agreed to star in *Voyage to the Bottom of the Sea*, and declared that Admiral Rickover was invited to read the script and serve as technical advisor on the film. He also noted that the Navy had offered cooperation on *Voyage* but later refused because of

**ABOVE LEFT**
An ad featuring the for-rent recreational underwater craft that Allen and his crew modified to create the Seaview's orange mini-sub.

**ABOVE**
The full-size mini-sub prop in the torpedo room set.

The mini-sub recreated in miniature for a sequence of the Seaview trapped in a mine field.

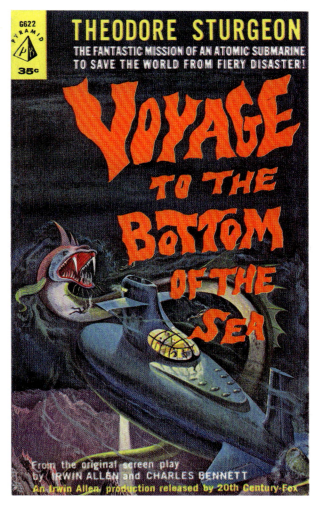

**ABOVE**
Science fiction author Theodore Sturgeon's novelization of *Voyage to the Bottom of the Sea*, released with artwork reflecting an early design of the Seaview.

"mutiny, scientific super yet pseudo secrets [which] may be revealed."

With Rickover out of the picture, Allen wrote Frank McCarthy in October, wondering how far the studio should go in seeking cooperation with the Navy. Allen was still looking for a naval technical advisor who would "have to be a man with atomic submarine experience and who would have to have a knowledge of equipment, procedure, language, etc. relative to atomic submarine service." He told casting director Lew Schreiber:

> Insofar as the "Nelson" role is concerned, I feel that I have a virtual commitment with Claude Rains. He is perfect for the part and I sincerely trust that 20th will so agree. The role was actually written for him and he has already read the script, approved it, and cancelled a Theatre Guild play in order to be available on or about January 16th.

As late as October 12, 1960, Allen was hoping to maintain friendly relations with the U.S. Defense Department and possibly using Navy equipment and advisors on the film.

He wrote Fox's Frank McCarthy:

> However, I believe it is most important for me to stress that, unlike any 20th pictures relating to the Department of Defence [sic] made in the past or in the present, requiring equipment, sets, men, uniforms, stock footage, etc., from the Navy, we are in need of none of these things since our picture will be made here on the lot and all of the equipment and all of the sets will be built by us from scratch. The reason for this is that we are depicting a submarine of the future which does not now exist, that *Voyage to the Bottom of the Sea* is, in fact, a science fiction picture, not one showing the Navy of today.

Allen stressed he was pointing this out to avoid making major story changes to secure cooperation with the Navy when such cooperation wasn't needed.

Allen's script did, however, deal with the launching of nuclear missiles, and the production inquired about getting photos of Polaris missile launch control panels. Allen was informed by Everett Hayes of the Lockheed Missile and Space Division that photographs of the Polaris launch control panel were classified at the time.

Allen hired Fox art director Herman Blumenthal, who had worked on *Journey to the Center of the Earth* and had done some of the early work on *Cleopatra*, for the critical job of supervising the movie's production design. An October 19, 1960 memo from Allen to Blumenthal called for him to review the "over-all schedule of operations as it applies to sketches, designs, miniatures, second unit (in tank or in ocean). Sets for principal photography available January 2nd for inspection." Allen directed Blumenthal to "paint stripes on enemy sub" to differentiate a Naval attack sub from the Seaview (in the final production the "U.N. submarine" remained a realistic black like the Skipjack-class attack sub it was based on).

Allen had a similar order for the mini-sub, requesting a different color from the Seaview and the enemy sub (it was painted orange, a color Fox art director and production designer William Creber later noted was a favorite of Allen's).

Allen also directed Blumenthal to design, and his prop department (headed by Herb Cheek) to "manufacture and rig" four models of the Seaview at 1:192, 1:96, and 1:48 scales, with one 1:24 scale submarine for "surface work only." Total budget authorization was $3,575.00.

The 1:24 scale "surface" model measured 17 feet, making the full size, fictional Seaview submarine about 408 feet in length, just slightly smaller than the USS Triton (SSRN-586), the fifth nuclear submarine built by the navy, a radar picket vessel 447 feet in length.

The 1:48 scale Seaview miniature measured around eight-and-a-half feet in length, and was designed for filming the bulk of underwater shots of the submarine.

The 1:96 submarine was approximately four feet in length; this model would eventually be used in a sequence of a giant octopus attacking the submarine, and it served as a decorative model seen in Admiral Nelson's office and in the Seaview's observation nose.

The smallest miniature, the 1:192 version, was only two feet in size, relatively undetailed, and was not utilized in filming the movie, but it was employed several years later to generate some inexpensive underwater shots for the resulting television series.

The design of the Seaview became one of the most distinctive and beloved science fiction vehicles ever put on film, probably second only to Disney's Nautilus among enthusiasts of movie submarines. Herman Blumenthal worked out the particulars with a lot of input from Allen, evolving the look of the sub from familiar to exotic. An early incarnation of the Seaview was inspired by the Skipjack attack submarine, a teardrop-shaped vessel with a high "conning tower" equipped with a huge, canopy-like glass observation bubble trailing from the rear edge of the tower.

Allen worked out a deal with Pyramid Books to release a novelization of *Voyage to the Bottom of the Sea*'s script early in production, and he provided the publisher with early design sketches of the Skipjack-inspired Seaview design that were consequently used for the cover painting of the novel. Blumenthal and Allen later shifted their design focus for the Seaview backwards to the original Nautilus submarine, with its long hull topped by a streamlined "turtleback" superstructure.

Some early concept paintings of the Seaview had Blumenthal taking a very literal approach to Allen's idea of a "glass-nosed" submarine, with the entire bow of the Seaview being transparent, decks and crew visible from outside—an all but impossible-to-solve technical problem for the production. Blumenthal then refined this shape and gave the Seaview a double decked observation nose with 12 windows and a series of spotlights.

Allen also requested the distinctive "manta ray" fins at the Seaview's bow—according to one story, Allen asked for the fins because he thought the Seaview's nose looked too phallic without them. While they made no sense from a hydrodynamic standpoint, the fins immediately gave the Seaview an unforgettable, futuristic appearance that would make the fictional submarine a compelling character in its own right. An uncredited Bill Creber helped develop the design, leading to a long association with Allen's productions.

Creber was a junior assistant art director at the time who had worked at Fox since late 1954 after being discharged from the Navy. He had considered a career in aerospace at Hughes Aircraft but his father Lewis H. Creber, who had been an art director at Fox since the 1930s, suggested that Bill's drafting skills would be best employed at the studio. Creber's naval experience, technical knowledge and imagination would add a distinctive, believable look to some of the hardware for which Allen's later projects would become famous.

Bill Creber recalls finalizing the look of the Seaview:

**ABOVE**
Early concept paintings of Herman Blumenthal's design for the Seaview.

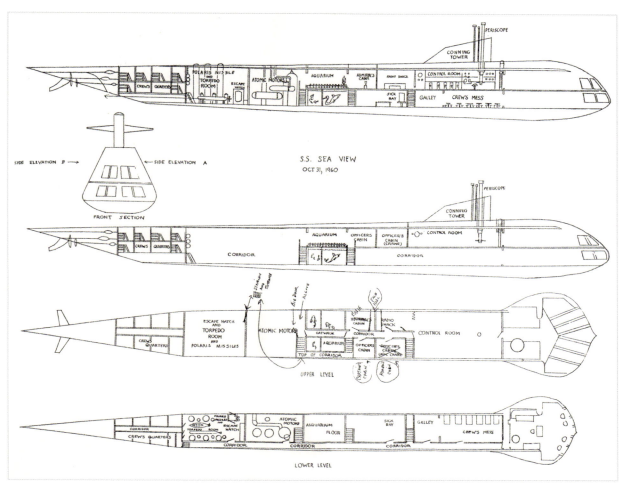

**RIGHT TOP**
Cutaway diagram of the submarine, showing where the film's key sets and action would take place. Although this appears to show an earlier design of the sub with a markedly different stern section, it is dated close to the final blueprints for the sub that clearly show the familiar "cadillac" tail fins on the design.

**RIGHT BOTTOM**
Production painting of the final Seaview design, featuring the manta-finned nose and the Cadillac-influenced tail fins.

The Seaview miniature on film.

**FOLLOWING**
Blumenthal's final design for the Seaview, with a blunt bow, 12 windows, and multiple searchlights. Place markers for the bow manta fins are visible at this stage, although they are much smaller in proportion to the bow hull than the final design, which reduced the multiple searchlights to one large forward light and the number of windows to eight.

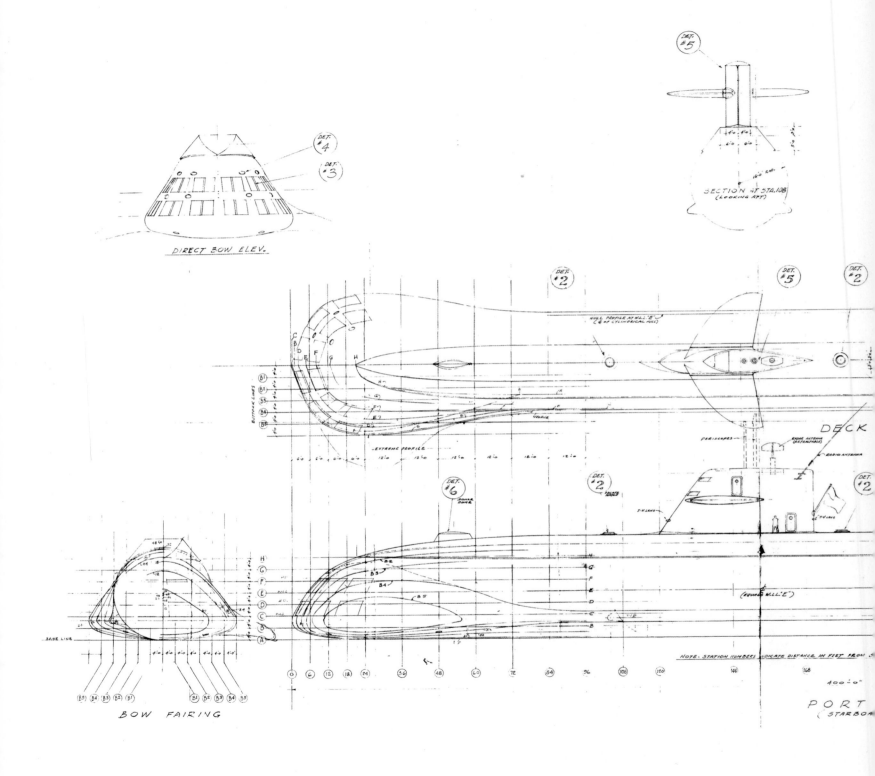

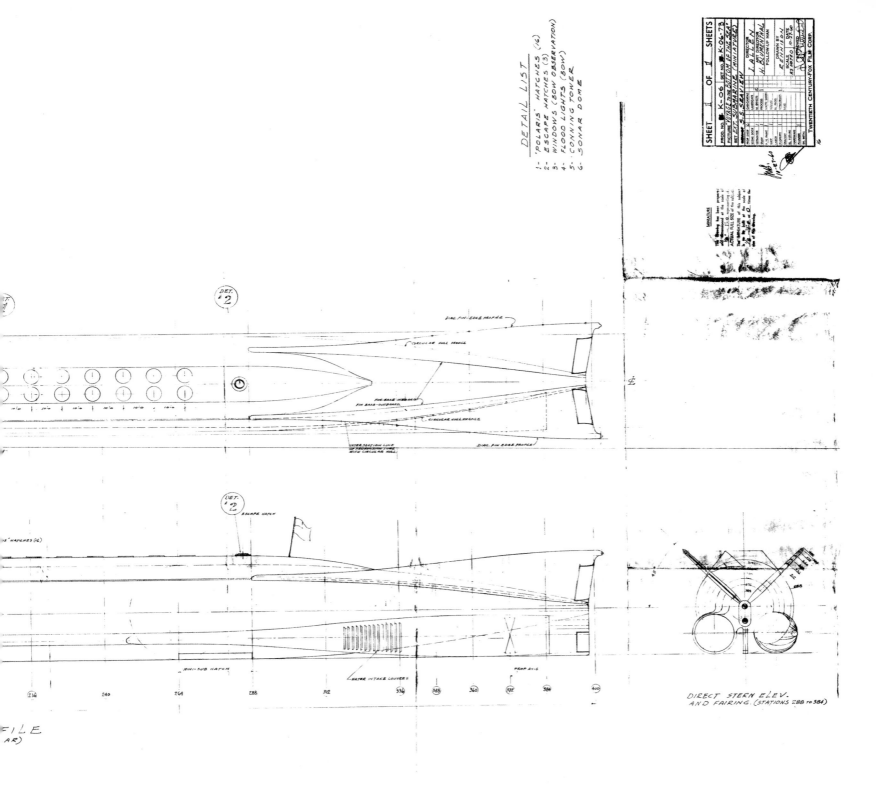

I was an assistant art director and I was assigned to Herman Blumenthal, who was already a mentor. He just assigned me to ramrod the submarine. I had been a draftsman, which was then called a set designer, and I liked to work on a drafting board so I just drew up the submarine knowing the practical sides of it. It was just a big steel tube basically. It would be more free form now but when you design movie sets you almost pretend you have no money. And so you have to think about the practical side of getting it done for as little money as possible, and we had all sorts of different diameter tubing available. Irwin wanted to have windows and the script called for windows, so we developed the front of [the sub].

Creber recalls that Allen took a literally hands-on approach to finalizing the look of the Seaview's distinctive nose:

I had a couple of ideas, and one was a little sleeker and one was like a manta ray. I had the model shop do a couple clay renderings on the front of a tube. So Irwin looked at it and he brought over a couple of his henchmen and his costume designer, Paul Zastupnevich. Irwin took one look at the manta ray thing and reached over at the clay and he says, "I like the idea, everything works, but let's turn the ends down a little." And he just grabbed it and bent the clay, and that's how that look happened.

After Creber and Blumenthal reduced the number of windows on the nose to eight, and changed the multiple searchlights to one large nose-mounted lantern and two below, one under each of the nose's flaring stabilizer fins, the Seaview design was completed.

Allen and Blumenthal were still searching for a convincing look for the interior of the submarine. The production wrote J. Gilbert Baird, manager and sales promotion of Westinghouse Appliances, after Westinghouse had set up interior submarine fittings for a Nautilus exhibition at Pacific Ocean Park, saying, "We are particularly interested in knowing if you have any mock-ups of the interior of a modern atomic submarine...that we could borrow for a brief time to utilize in photography of our picture."

On October 26, 1960, Allen wrote Charles Einfeld and copied Doc Merman, Fox construction supervisor Ivan Martin, Blumenthal, L.B. Abbott, Sol Halprin and Herb Cheek, noting that, "Current schedule calls for shooting miniatures, special effects and stunts during the entire month of December. Principal photography starts on January 16th." The next day Allen wrote Ivan Martin, Jack Martin Smith and Herman Blumenthal after screening *20,000 Leagues Under the Sea*, on which Ivan Martin had worked. Martin suggested that Allen might be able to make use of props from Disney's film:

Will you please be kind enough to follow through on your suggestion regarding both the Disney mechanical shark and the Disney molds from which we plan to make our giant squid. As for the squid molds—it is important that we know as quickly as possible how many actual working arms there will be and whether the head had to be camouflaged, or if portions of it will actually be seen.

The same day Allen wrote Jack Martin Smith after his morning meeting with Allen, Smith, Blumenthal, Ivan Martin, L.B. Abbott and Bill Eglinton:

...All of our undersea miniatures and undersea second units will be shot in tanks here on the lot (the moat and green tanks), and that all of the surface miniatures will be shot on the surface of Sersen Lake.

Sersen Lake was actually a large tank with a sky backing, located on the Fox back lot, that had been used

**ABOVE**
Concept painting of the giant squid encounter and the finished scene on film.

**OPPOSITE**
Storyboard panels of the Seaview's chase with a Skipjack-type U.N. attack submarine.

369. EXT. UNDERWATER – MINIATURE – DAY
LONG SHOT – THE SEAVIEW – MINIATURE – DIVING DEEP SECOND SUB CHANGES DIRECTION, DIVES IN PURSUIT.

371. EXT. UNDERWATER – MINIATURE – DAY
LONG SHOT THE SEAVIEW DIVING PAST VAST UNDERWATER CLIFFS

378. UNDERWATER – MINIATURE – DAY
LONG SHOT AS SEAVIEW VEERS MINIATURE THE TORPEDO EXPLODING AGAINST A TOWERING PINNACLE.

492. EXT. OCEAN SURFACE – MINIATURE – NITE
LONG SHOT – THE SUBMARINE – GLIDING AWAY INTO MOONLIT NITE.

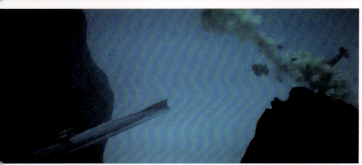

during the filming of *20,000 Leagues Under the Sea*. This tank would be demolished not long after the *Voyage to the Bottom of the Sea* movie completed filming, and a new outdoor tank at the Fox Ranch in Malibu was constructed for the naval battle sequences of *Cleopatra*. This facility was also named Sersen Lake and would later be employed on the *Voyage* television series.

The schedule called for the movie's miniature shoot to start Dec. 5th, and second unit photography to begin on Dec. 26th. "The floor of the tank will be covered with a milk-white, special sand that Ivan Martin is now checking into. The walls will be painted a color that will help the reflecting of lights, to give us the blue-white underwater color we seek."

On October 28, Ivan Martin reported to Allen about the *20,000 Leagues* shark and squid props:

> I have found that the original shark is not available, but the molds for recasting and manufacturing a rubber shark of this type are available at a nominal price. Also, I am able to get from Disneyland one plaster squid tentacle mold and one plaster squid feeler mold of the same scope used in *Twenty Leagues* at a cost of approximately $150.00.

Martin broke down the budget for the two creatures as follows:

> $862 for a manually operated shark; $1,437 for a "radio control, internally powered" shark; $4,600 for a squid with "one feeler and four tentacles, half the size of the 20,000 Leagues squid; $6,382 for the same with a complete squid body, half the size of the 20,000 Leagues squid."

The screenplay opened with a spectacular shot of the Seaview bursting nose-first out of the Arctic ocean, and on October 31 L.B. Abbott wrote Allen with thoughts about how to achieve the shot:

> Opening sequence of picture should be night so that ice and lights in sub can be more properly seen. This will also help the shock value of nose jumping toward sky in opening scene *[Allen didn't use this suggestion, and the breaching scene was instead filmed in daylight]*. Change thinking so that opening shot of sub breaking surface comes directly toward camera instead of moving from right to left. Immediately look into problems relating to the 100 water escape holes surrounding the submarine. Make final decision whether submarine (when burning its way out of the ice) glows red or do we superimpose lightning flash or do we drop it out of the script entirely.

The idea of the sub "burning" through Arctic ice was indeed dropped from the script. Abbott and his crew eventually achieved the shot by rigging the 17 foot Seaview miniature in a pit in one of the studio's water tanks that had been dug to show the sinking of the ocean liner miniature in Fox's 1953 film *Titanic*. The Seaview was mounted on rails at a 30 degree angle and rigged to a pulley system attached to a truck, which accelerated and yanked the sub model out of the water on cue.

Allen broke down the film's miniature shooting in a November 9, 1960 memo:

**LEFT**
The final sub chase sequence miniature work in the film.

**OPPOSITE**
The 8-1/2 foot Seaview miniature and the four foot U.N. sub model being put through their paces by divers in one of Fox's underwater tanks.

The miniature plates and other miniature shooting includes photographing: The ice field from above and beneath the surface of the sea; the minefield from beneath the surface of the sea; Rises and descents of the sub (as seen through the nose of the sub); the enemy sub action (both direct and as seen through the glass nose); the implosion of the enemy sub (same); the movements of the mini-sub through the minefield and its explosion (same); all other miniature plates and other miniatures as designated in the shooting script. Some of these plates will be made with the use of two cameras on a sled. (The need of the two cameras is dictated by the fact that we need to rear-project them on two screens when we shoot process in the interior of the glass nose).

Allen also made mention of an attack on the submarine by a "monster, which then turns to fight a second monster," noting:

> [The creatures] will probably be an octopus and a shark, both dressed to look still more grotesque and weird. We are now checking out the availability and usage of such animals, versus the use of an octopus and a moray eel. As soon as it's been determined which monsters will be used, it will be necessary to immediately purchase them, house them, feed them, and have their dressing designed and ready for shooting on a date to be designated by L.B. Abbott.

Ultimately the idea of the two monsters fighting was dropped and the challenge of "dressing" any aquatic animals into exotic monsters proved too much to overcome. A small octopus was coaxed onto the nose of the four-foot Seaview model, which the animal quickly vacated. Film of the encounter was run backwards to show the octopus apparently leaping onto the bow of the Seaview.

By November 10, Allen announced that the production was eliminating an entire sequence, dubbed "the lost city," to shave the film's budget. Eleven days later Allen wrote Fox art department head Jack Martin Smith about saving $6,000 by reworking a "scene involving the firing of the Polaris missile from beneath the surface of the sea," which had involved the construction of an "Exterior Firing Tube and Side of Sub. Combined with the elimination of the Lost City sequence amounting to over $17,000 in savings. Some of this would be offset by costs on the Control Room and underwater sea floor set which were amounting to more than originally estimated."

Allen got two important responses to his script in later November. The MPAA registered its approval of the screenplay with two exceptions:

> Page 100: The cries of "Fire" are unacceptable under the Code.

> Page 130: We presume that you will avoid unnecessary gruesomeness in the scene in which the shark attacks the woman in the tank.

Allen had also finally employed the services of a Naval technical adviser, Admiral Thomas M. Dykers, a decorated submarine commander who had also worked in film and television as a writer and producer and had

**ABOVE**
Storyboard art for the Seaview's entrance at the opening of *Voyage to the Bottom of the Sea*.

The spectacular reveal as it appeared in the final film.

**ABOVE**
Storyboard art of the Seaview underneath the flaming skies of the Van Allen Belt effect, and the finished miniature and composite effect, created by printing footage of a flame thrower volley into the sky behind the miniature submarine.

**RIGHT**
A sequence from the film of two deep sea "monsters" attacking the Seaview, and each other. Though this was originally planned to be filmed with a shark and octopus "made up" to look like bizarre creatures, it was ultimately accomplished using a small octopus and the four-foot Seaview miniature.

**FOLLOWING**
Concept painting of the sequence.

narrated the submarine TV series *The Silent Service*. Dykers indicated the Navy would likely be unhappy with the script as it stood and his comments were outlined by one of Allen's staff: "The most important suggestion the Admiral made was to change the submarine and its personnel from the Navy to a civilian submarine and civilian personnel."

Dykers said the Navy would object to:

1. The Admiral's relationship to his ship. As an Admiral he shouldn't vie all the orders to be carried out by the Captain. Captain would give orders.

2. The defiance of the United Nations.

3. The Admiral's relationship to his Captain.

4. Women on the submarine. Particularly, the Wave. They would even object to Cathy being a civilian.

5. Mutiny. It is definitely mutiny for the men to leave the submarine. It is not mutiny for the Captain to sincerely believe the Admiral crazy and relieve him of his command.

6. Pentagon is very touchy about the idea that one person could have the ability to fire a missile without authority. This power could be placed in the hands of an irresponsible person - they have set up safe-guards against this ever happening. This is very important to our international relations.

7. Dancing in the mess hall. To portray this as happening on a Navy submarine would make the picture look ridiculous to Navy people.

Dykers also noted that the Navy specifically objected to:

1. Submarine diving in East River in New York. The East River is very shallow and couldn't accommodate a submarine as large as ours.

2. Hand detonator used to set off missile from exterior. This should be explained in more detail.

Dykers explained that by changing the Seaview to a civilian vessel, the production could get away with all the established relationships and situations with very little dialogue changes. But he noted that the Admiral "as a civilian scientist would still be requested by the President to come to the international UN meeting. He would still request the President's approval before firing the missile." Dyker also explained that a civilian ship could still have missiles for scientific research but that the name should be changed from Polaris to something fictitious.

Meanwhile Allen continued to work with Herman Blumenthal on the Seaview's interior sets. A memo to Blumenthal listed several concerns, including that the Seaview corridors...

...must have tubes, pipes, wires, etc. as well as intercoms at specified places (check script and continuity sketches). All sets must have a sense of being crowded. Otherwise we lose the feeling of being on a submarine. We need a

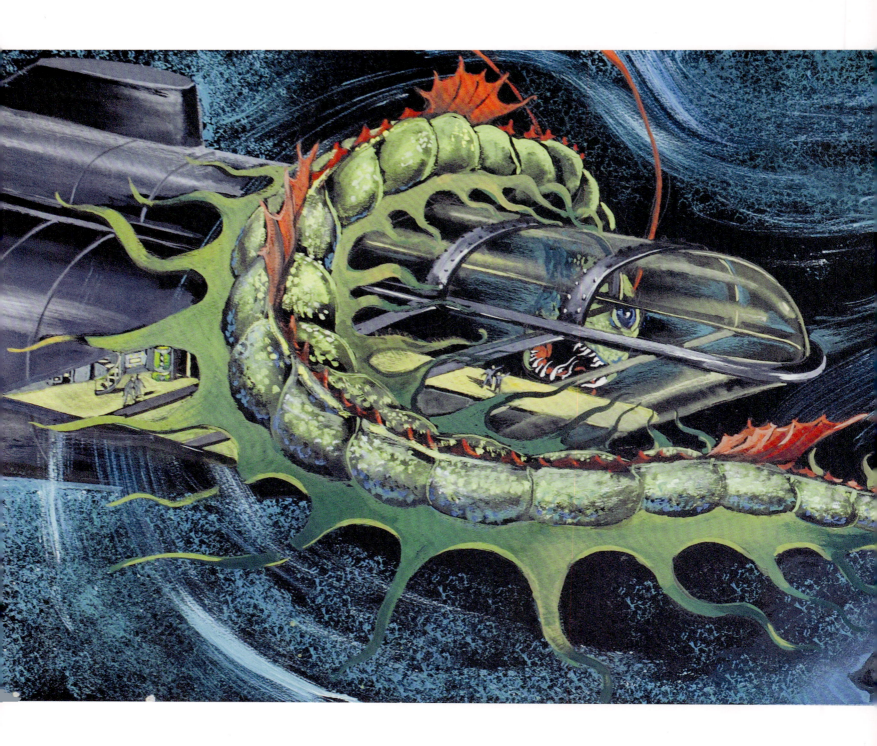

**LEFT**
Set design sketches for the interior of the Seaview.

**OPPOSITE**
Design sketch for the expansive observation nose set, and how it appeared in the final film.

~ OBSERVATION NOSE ~

couple of holes in the ceiling of the control room through which men can appear to disappear into the conning tower up above.

A December 6, 1960 memo from Allen to Doc Merman reported the total budget was not to exceed $1,488,200. Allen noted the dropping of the Lost City sequence and an effect of the Seaview glowing red and that most of the budget cuts had been accomplished in construction.

By December 22, 1960, actor Walter Pidgeon was noted as the choice to play Admiral Nelson (Claude Rains, Franchot Tone, Joseph Cotten, Robert Young, and Dana Andrews were alternate choices); Barbara Eden had the role of Cathy (Anne Francis was also in the running); Robert Sterling was chosen as Captain Crane—Lloyd Bridges (famed for his scuba diver role on TV's *Sea Hunt*), Barry Nelson and Cliff Robertson were also considered. Joan Fontaine was nabbed as Dr. Hiller, a seemingly sympathetic scientist with ulterior motives—Patricia Neal, Maureen O'Hara, and Ida Lupino were also considered for this role. For Nelson's irascible scientist friend Dr. Emery, Peter Lorre was chosen and seemed to be the only one under consideration. Alvarez, the religious zealot refugee who threatens the mission late in the game, had not been cast but Ricardo Montalban, Fernando Lamas of *The Lost World*, John Ireland, and Richard Conte were under consideration.

There were two other interesting notations—a character named Chip Morton was listed with Gene Nelson and Skip Homier as possible actors. The character was evidently eliminated from the movie script but later became a regular on the TV series. Another character, Cookie, was listed—with comedian Don Rickles listed as a possible actor.

The choice of Walter Pidgeon as Nelson was a sore spot for Allen, although after working with Pidgeon on the movie the two men would become lifelong friends. Pidgeon was apparently foisted on Allen by the studio, with the feeling that Claude Rains was too old.

Allen wrote a letter of protest to Fox executives:

> I think there is a serious misunderstanding regarding the suggested casting of Claude Rains in the vitally important role of ADMIRAL NELSON. Bob Goldstein and Lew Schreiber were both told that one of the reasons we wanted certain casting privileges was that we had made a commitment with Claude Rains to play this role and that, in fact, Rains had firmly scheduled such an assignment and had turned down a Theatre Guild offer to play the lead in THE DEVIL'S ADVOCATE. At that time, no objections were made regarding the casting of Rains. The only question raised by Bob Goldstein was whether or not Rains was too old.

Allen went on to point out that Rains' bearded, aged appearance in *The Lost World* was an intentional "caricature" created by makeup and a wig, without which Rains appeared 20 years younger and similar to Admiral Rickover, the developer of the Nautilus on whom the character was based.

> The Claude Rains situation, therefore, can be summed up in the following way:—I think he is perfect for the

**ABOVE**

Introduction of Barbara Eden's Cathy Connors (foreground) and Frankie Avalon's Lt. Danny Romano (originally named Chip Morton, a character relegated to the later TV series).

Eden (right) with Robert Sterling as Captain Crane.

Walter Pidgeon as the Seaview's creator, Admiral Harriman Nelson.

**ABOVE**
Allen shares a laugh with Barbara Eden on the Seaview set.

The Seaview navigates the East River in New York, against the Navy's objections.

Seaview crewmen rock and roll as enemy torpedos explode around the ship—in what would become an action convention on Allen's TV shows.

role; the script was literally written with him in mind; the price is right; he is available, and I made a commitment within which the studio, in effect, indicated they would honor by not objecting to him in the original presentation and by specifically stating that they would give every consideration to any casting we were insisting upon.

By Jan. 24, 1961, *Voyage to the Bottom of the Sea* had its final budget estimate of $1,488,300—around the same as *The Big Circus*. $197,700 went to the cast, $124,000 to sets, $61,785 to miniatures, $16,300 to photographic effects. Joan Fontaine was the highest paid actor at $45,000, closely followed by nominal star Walter Pidgeon at $40,000. Frankie Avalon got $20,000, a bit more than veteran Peter Lorre at $16,000.

Allen continued to work on promotion and merchandising. In late December, 1960, he had written Charles Einfeld about a possible *Voyage to the Bottom of the Sea* board game, enclosing a "dummy" version for Einfeld's inspection. ("Adrian Awan was here the other day as we were completing the game. He expressed great enthusiasm over its potential and felt that your office could make a manufacturer's tie-up.") Although no board game was issued for the film, Milton Bradley did put out a board game tie-in to the later TV series.

In March, 1961, Allen got a commitment from Saks Fifth Avenue to create a window display of "nine giant paintings," miniature models of the interior sets and the 17-foot miniature of the Seaview. Custom-tailored rubber diving suits used in the picture were also made available for display and Allen spoke of a possible promotion with Voit Company, a manufacturer of skin diving equipment, for cross promotion involving photos of Frankie Avalon wearing their diving equipment. The Pyramid books paperback (with a printing of 100,000 copies) and a potential comic book tie-in were also discussed. Allen also mentioned meetings with Henry Blankfort of Revell Toy Co. which he hoped would make a "build-it-yourself submarine kit for a *Voyage to the Bottom of the Sea* sub." Aurora Plastics would eventually release a model kit of the Seaview to tie in to the TV series, a model based on the appearance of the Seaview in the movie.

Allen also mentioned a "noise maker which will be an audio identification of the movie." This foreshadowed the distinctive sonar sound that would eventually be created for the Seaview: "To be more explicit—as per Bill Stutman's excellent suggestion—we will use an odd, identifying sound in the picture depicting either attacking torpedoes, the escaping sub, etc. If this sound is weird and wonderful enough, we are hoping that every kid in America will be mimicking the sound by use of this sound-making toy."

Allen was also hoping to have a hit record with Avalon's recording of the theme song. Avalon did record a song for the movie's title sequence, with lush orchestrations by Paul Sawtell and Bert Shefter, a dreamy tune that was probably not the upbeat pop number Avalon's fans might have hoped for. The singer appeared on Groucho Marx's NBC TV show on June 8th, and the Pyramid paperback and a Dell comic book adaptation also shipped in June. Voit sent scuba diving gear displays to

**LEFT**
Irwin Allen with Robert Stirling as Seaview Captain Lee Crane and Peter Lorre as irascible scientist Dr. Emery.

Allen (left) with a Fox executive and cast members (from l to r) Joan Fontaine, Robert Stirling, Barbara Eden, and Frankie Avalon.

**OPPOSITE**
Allen goes over the script with Avalon in another staged publicity photo.

4000 retailers and Allen began a promotional tour of exhibitors beginning on June 12th. Although the budget had risen to $1,580,000, once *Voyage* launched on July 12, 1961, it went on to gross $7 million for Fox, a handsome return on their investment.

*Voyage to the Bottom of the Sea* still stands up today as an exciting movie from Irwin Allen, one that boasts the strongest drama of any of his early pictures, with Walter Pidgeon's arrogant Harriman Nelson a compelling, sometimes infuriating "misunderstood hero." The miniature effects of the Seaview, particularly the dazzling opening shot of the Seaview bursting through the surface of the Arctic Ocean (heralded by an explosion of newspaper headlines hurtling toward the screen just like the ones at the beginning of *The Big Circus*), a white-knuckle sequence of the Seaview fleeing from a torpedo-firing U.N. attack sub, and a nail-biting scene of the sub becoming mired in a web of explosive mines, are ambitious and still relatively convincing today. The series of climatic disasters and the threat of ever-rising temperatures seems eerily contemporary.

What holds the movie together, however (apart from the constant visual appeal of the sleek, futuristic Seaview submarine) is the dramatic conflict between Pidgeon's Nelson and Robert Sterling's Captain Lee Crane. Allen actually offered the role of Crane to David Hedison, who turned it down; Sterling isn't a terribly interesting performer, but Pidgeon is such a convincing tyrant (even slapping Frankie Avalon's character at one point, almost a decade before the famous soldier-slapping scene in Fox's *Patton*) that it becomes almost understandable when one of the crew appears to attempt to murder the Admiral midway through the film.

Fox's Charles Einfeld announced Allen's next projects two days before the release of *Voyage to the Bottom of the Sea*, stating, "Allen to make five more movies for Fox, starting with *Five Weeks in a Balloon* and *Passage to the End of Space*."

He was off by two movies.

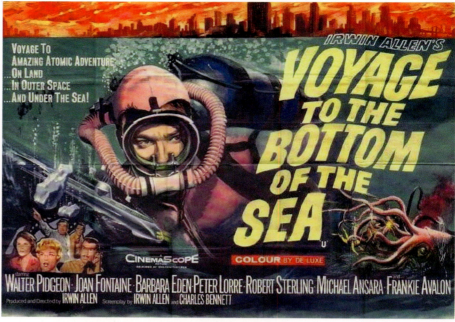

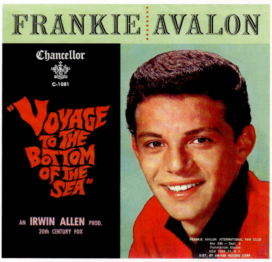

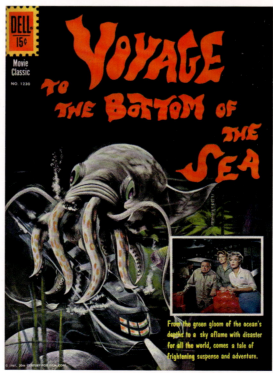

**LEFT**
A quad poster sheet for the British theatrical release of the movie.

Picture sleeve for Frankie Avalon's 45 rpm single of the *Voyage to the Bottom of the Sea* theme song.

Cover for the Dell comic book adaptation of the *Voyage* movie.

**OPPOSITE**
22 x 28 half sheet poster art for the *Voyage* movie.

Allen poses with some "mermaids" for a promotional event for the film.

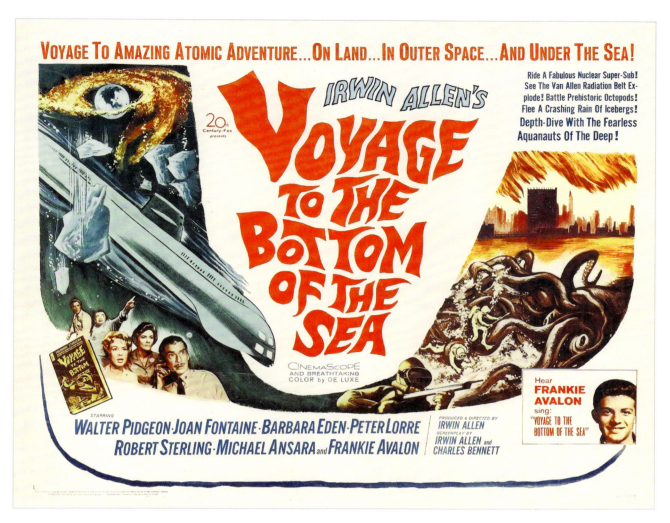

# FIVE WEEKS IN A BALLOON

While attempting to clear the title *Voyage to the Bottom of the Sea* in January, 1960, Irwin Allen wrote to lawyer Fulton Brylawski and added an inquiry over whether Verne's *Five Weeks in a Balloon* was in public domain. It was—in fact another production company had made plans to film it and actually beat Allen's production to movie screens under the title of *Flight of the Lost Balloon*, directed by Nathan Juran. But Allen and Fox successfully forced the competing production to drop references to Jules Verne, so Allen's became the first official movie adaptation of Verne's novel.

Verne's tale follows an explorer, Dr. Samuel Ferguson, his manservant Joe, and a hunter named Richard Kennedy as they use Ferguson's advanced balloon technology to travel across Africa, from Zanzibar to Senegal, encountering various adventures and hardships along the way.

*Voyage to the Bottom of the Sea* had been partially inspired by Verne's *20,000 Leagues Under the Sea* as well as the Walt Disney film adaptation; and, after *The Lost World* and *Voyage*, a Verne adaptation was a natural progression for Allen. But Mike Todd's balloon adventure *Around the World in 80 Days*, another Verne adaptation, was certainly an inspiration, and it showed Allen appearing to chase better-known producers in duplicating their successes, from *The Big Circus* aping *The Greatest Show On Earth* to *Voyage* one-upping *20,000 Leagues*.

*The Lost World* and *Voyage to the Bottom of the Sea* had both been hits, but particularly on the second film, Allen had noted a trend that caused him to begin repeating a mantra that the *Denver Post* reported as, "He's not a producer of science fiction movies." While he had been a lifelong fan of science fiction and fantasy adventures ("I was a buff and turned it into a career," he would tell *Variety* in 1968), Allen did not want his commercial prospects limited by the label.

He told the *Post*:

> My hackles go up when I'm identified with science fiction. I'm a commercial movie maker, and I enjoy making money at my job. I enjoyed making *Voyage to the Bottom of the Sea*, but something happened that I don't want ever to happen again: mature women and teenaged girls stayed away in droves. They stay away from all science fiction films. So remember—*Voyage* was my one venture into that field.

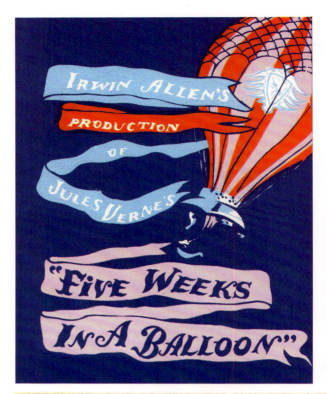

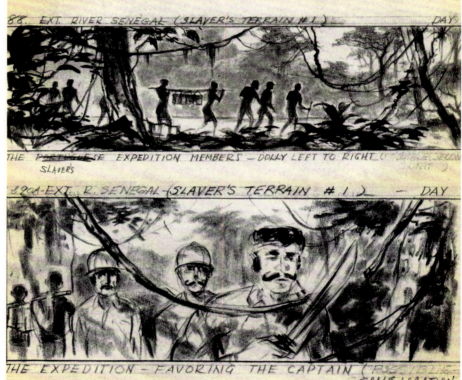

**ABOVE**
Allen's colorful preproduction announcement for *Five Weeks in a Balloon*.

Storyboard art of the slaver expedition that the Jupiter balloon races in the film.

**OPPOSITE**
Another pre-production announcement.

Verne's *Five Weeks in a Balloon* was a straight adventure, and Allen, like Disney with *20,000 Leagues*, produced his adaptation as a period film with no fantasy elements apart from the elaborate design of the balloon itself, the Jupiter. He included two female characters, a hunky, young, crooning costar in the form of Fabian, and an abundance of comedy.

Allen was hoping to get *Five Weeks in a Balloon* out for the 100th anniversary of the book's publication. A British team actually attempted to reproduce the flight described in the novel but made only 400 miles of the trip before it was brought down by weather. Allen was in touch with the balloonists while the film was in production—the balloonist said, "It was easier for Verne to write of such a flight than it was to actually fly it."

Allen faced his own challenges in making the film. He submitted his treatment for the movie to Fox for approval on August 22, 1961. Five days later Charles Einfeld, now VP of the studio, sent out a statement from Fox's new president, Darryl F. Zanuck. Zanuck had replaced Spyros Skouras over the tremendous cost overruns from the still-in-production *Cleopatra*, and was making bold moves to bring Fox's financial house in order:

> I am now engaged in making a study of all scenarios and film projects on the current production schedule. Some projects out of necessity will be postponed and this also applies to certain individual commitments affecting studio personnel. I am not a hachet(sic) man either by instinct or nature. My desire in the long run is to provide more jobs on a permanent basis. During this period of reorganization I seek your sympathetic understanding and patience…

*Five Weeks in a Balloon* required a cast of stars and a great deal of location shooting that Allen planned to accomplish in Hawaii, so he would need the studio's backing to complete the project. Once again Allen worked with screenwriter Charles Bennett, and this time Allen's cousin and longtime associate Al Gail, an assistant producer on his previous three films, contributed to the screenplay as well.

Allen hired Cedric Hardwicke to play the bombastic inventor Fergusson, and brought back Richard Haydn of *The Lost World* to play Fergusson's bickering compatriot and President of the Royal Geographical Institute, Sir Henry Vining. Fabian played Fergusson's manservant, performing a similar function to Frankie Avalon in *Voyage to the Bottom of the Sea*. Allen also brought back Red Buttons of *The Big Circus* to play a reporter along for the trip, Donald O'Shay; Barbara Luna as a slave girl rescued by the adventurers, and Barbara Eden and Peter Lorre from *Voyage* as, respectively, an American school teacher captured by slavers and a comical slave trader.

Allen and his team scouted locations in Maui in November, 1961, noting that the production requirements included "A large truck mounted crane with a minimum of 75' boom. Investigate whether there are bridges, small or large, that would have to be crossed to get to potential sites and if there are, the capacity of weight. Check to see about largest helicopter available (non-military)." The boom would be used to raise and

**RIGHT**

Sir Cedric Hardwicke (left) as Fergusson and Richard Haydn as Sir Henry Vining in *Five Weeks in a Balloon*.

Teen heartthrob Fabian as Jacques, Fergusson's assistant.

(l to r) Red Buttons as reporter Donald O'Shay, Barbara Luna as Makia, a slave girl, and Fabian.

Peter Lorre, in his last appearance in an Allen project, as wily slave trader Ahmed.

**OPPOSITE**

Map artwork of the trajectory of the voyage of the Jupiter, given an intentionally discolored, aged look to add period authenticity.

lower the elaborate gondola of the movie's balloon vehicle, named the Victoria in Verne's novel but dubbed the Jupiter in Allen's production. Designed under the supervision of art director Alfred Ybarra (and Fox art department head Jack Martin Smith), the Jupiter gondola was designed to resemble a unicorn with lanterns illuminating its two eyes. The gondola as constructed by the Fox prop department weighed five tons and had to be transported to different shooting locations (while some establishing shots were filmed in Hawaii, the bulk of the film's outdoor scenes were shot in California); a special permit from the California Highway Patrol was required to move the gondola on local freeways. It was shot at Leo Carillo Beach, the El Centro sand dunes, at Sherwood Forest north of Los Angeles and the Fox ranch.

The gondola had to be constructed to come apart in sections that locked together so that it could be lifted. The Jupiter's internal heating apparatus was designed based on Verne's descriptions in his novel. Dr. Kurt Stehling of NASA visited the set and informed Allen that the principles of heated and cooled gas instead of ballast were already in use in some experimental balloons.

Just as he had with *Voyage to the Bottom of the Sea*, Allen embarked on a nationwide tour of exhibitors to lay the groundwork for the rollout of *Five Weeks in a Balloon* in 1962. Before he was ousted, Fox President Spyros Skouras appeared at Allen's exhibitor seminar for the film, still predicting that *Cleopatra* would earn $250 million worldwide. Allen had invited 1500 exhibitors to the event and announced that Fox had earmarked $1.2 million for advertising and promotion of the movie over five-six weeks.

Allen took pains to point out that the movie would be "sold as a comedy-adventure, rather than science fiction, to attract the teenage girls and mature women." *Variety* described Allen's films as "exploitation" attractions and discussed how smaller, more independent efforts often didn't get the benefit of the studio's advertising and promotion dollars so Allen did a lot of the work himself. The initial print order for the film was upped from 450 to 600 after Allen went on a promotional tour of 11 key cities, speaking to representatives of 5000 theaters, distributing 8000 promotional kits of material and doing 112 interviews. Allen showed movie and television trailers and played records of the film's song.

"The reaction was one of tremendous enthusiasm, not only for the picture itself, but for the sales possibilities made apparent," Allen said at the time. "After all, exhibitors knew very little about the film and they appreciated our concern for their problems and our ideas for its solution. They realized that here was a film made with them in mind."

On January 2, 1962, Allen released a tentative, 22 day shooting schedule starting with the Prime Minister and British Consul scenes on Feb. 14 and 15, travel to Maui for location shooting on Feb. 17 to last through the 24th, studio shooting for the interior balloon scenes on the 26th, with scenes on the Scottish Moors and the Zanzibar slave market to be shot from the 27th and 28th. Shooting between March 1st and the 9th included

**LEFT**
Concept paintings of the Jupiter balloon, gondola, and interior and heating apparatus.

**ABOVE**
The film's opening sequence of the Jupiter navigating cliffs (filmed utilizing miniatures) and landing (via the use of an offscreen crane), and the Jupiter gondola on the ground.

**RIGHT**
Color concept art of The film's opening sequence and later landing at an oasis (bottom).

**LEFT**
Set and location sketches for *Five Weeks in a Balloon*.

**OPPOSITE**
Color production paintings for a storm and a volcano sequence.

124

**OPPOSITE**
Allen promotes *Five Weeks in a Balloon* with a group of actresses cast as harem girls in the picture—including future Mrs. Irwin Allen, Sheila Mathews (to the right of Allen), who had started dating Allen around the time the film was being made.

**RIGHT**
Theatrical poster artwork for *Five Weeks in a Balloon*.

Zanzibar Beach, the consul's courtyard, Sultan's pavilion, Hezak and Timbuktu (all noted as being shot at RKO), and some final scenes in the balloon cabin and gondola. The Zanzibar street scenes, involving a chase through a market bazaar, were shot between March 5th and 9th and required seven stunt performers doubling for Red Buttons, Fabian, Barbara Luna, and other local characters.

The production worked out a calendar of events and locations to occur in the movie between the dates of January 19th and February 21st, with stops at locations representing Tanganyika, north of Lake Victoria, the Congo, S. of Lake Chad, a desert and oasis, Timbuktu, and the Volta River country where the film's climax occurs.

Allen premiered the movie in August at the Denver Theater at the JCRS Shopping Center where Don Piccard, a famous balloonist and technical advisor on the movie, took off in the parking lot to kick off the show. Eden, Lorre, Barbara Eden's husband (and *Voyage to the Bottom of the Sea* costar) Michael Ansara, and the chimpanzee from the film were in attendance. The stars visited cancer patients at the JCRS Hospital and did a junket at the Brown Palace Hotel for the press. Allen had a stilt-walker and harem girls on hand for the 8:30 premiere; earlier Denver Mayor Batterton declared Allen an honorary citizen of Denver.

The late film critic Roger Ebert once formulated a dictum that he called "The Balloon Rule," which said in effect that no good movie has ever featured a hot air balloon. *Five Weeks in a Balloon* at least earned an enthusiastic review from *The Denver Post*, but with a budget of $2,340,000, almost a million dollars more than *Voyage to the Bottom of the Sea*, it was a handsome and good-natured, but ultimately unmemorable comedy-adventure. As the squabbling, stuffy heroes, Cedric Hardwicke and Richard Haydn (who would later have much better luck in Fox's *The Sound of Music*) seem to be recycling schtick from Allen's earlier *The Lost World*. The Jupiter gondola prop is impressive, and shots of it set up as a camp in a nighttime forest look forward to the TV set grandeur of Allen's later *Land of the Giants*.

While Allen took pains to make a colorful travelogue that would appeal more to women than his prior science fiction adventures, he kept his most important female character, the school teacher played by Barbara Eden, offscreen for the first 48 minutes of the film (almost half its length), while introducing Barbara Luna's slave girl character with minimal dialogue much earlier.

With its budget ballooned to almost two and a half million dollars, *Five Weeks in a Balloon* only grossed $1,200,000 in the U.S.

Maybe being a science fiction producer wasn't so bad after all.

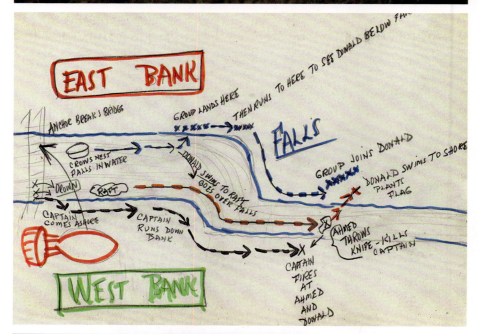

**ABOVE**
Production painting and finished sequence of the Jupiter over Africa.

A diagram outlining the film's action and locations.

**LEFT**
The only remains of the Jupiter today—the attachment point between the balloon and the gondola, rigged with a rotating cuff that would allow the gondola to be separated and dropped during the river bridge sequence.

**RIGHT TOP**
Theatrical poster artwork for *Five Weeks in a Balloon*.

**RIGHT BOTTOM**
Production paintings of the movie's climactic river bridge climax [left] and the finished sequence [right].

129

> **THE ROMANCE OF THE WORLD'S MIGHTIEST UNDERSEA CRAFT PUTS *VOYAGE* PRETTY MUCH IN A CLASS BY ITSELF.**
>
> **IRWIN ALLEN**

# MOVIES ON TV

*Allen launches his television sci-fi empire with one false start (*TALES OF EDGAR ALLAN POE*) and a hit (*VOYAGE TO THE BOTTOM OF THE SEA*)*

In July 25, 1962, Darryl F. Zanuck became President of 20th Century Fox and quickly issued a report:

> The corporation is not in a healthy condition. The decline from prosperity and leadership has been five years in the making. Prompt action to reverse this trend is a necessity. [The years 1958–1961] show a deterioration in all major phases of the company's operations. They reveal losses from the manufacture and distribution of films and films for TV amounting to $66,200,000, including a loss of $40,000,000 in 1961 alone.

Zanuck stated that he expected losses for 1962 to amount to $25 million but expected the turnaround of the company's fortunes to begin:

> Recognition must be taken of the fact that while many assets must be written down, a number of other assets having no book cost, low book cost, or costs greatly reduced by depreciation have value much greater than book.

These included theater circuits in Australia, New Zealand, Rhodesia, Kenya, East and South Africa, realty on Santa Monica Blvd, Western Avenue and Malibu Lake, offices in Manhattan, Atlanta, Buffalo, Dallas, Houston, Indianapolis, L.A., NY, Pittsburgh and Washington, a Minneapolis TV station, De luxe Laboratories, Inc., Fox's library of feature films for television licensing, and its music company holdings. Zanuck recommended these be developed as investments and stated that the company's basic wealth was solid and not in danger of insolvency.

In a development that Irwin Allen surely paid close attention to, Zanuck continued:

> I will ask the directors at this meeting for full authority to organize a complete television department for producing shows for television; to seek out the young and able talent looking for opportunity, and to dedicate this company to a firm policy of making a place for itself in this rich and growing field. No field presents greater opportunity, not only for profits, but for absorption of part of the overhead of manufacturing film for theaters. There is poetic justice in transforming television into a financial aid, and we must adhere to such poetry and such justice.

**OPPOSITE**
Caricature art created by Bob Bentovoja for *Voyage to the Bottom of the Sea* TV series.

Zanuck was still confident that his productions of *The Longest Day* and Fox's *Cleopatra* would "translate from inventory into cash."

Zanuck appointed his son Richard Zanuck as vice president in charge of production (Richard Zanuck later was instrumental in firing his own father from the studio when he took over Fox later in the decade, in one of the greatest Oedipal conflicts ever engaged in Hollywood). Richard Zanuck put producer William Self in charge of television production at the studio. Self had been director of development at CBS and had overseen the launch of *The Twilight Zone* before being lured to Fox, where he would eventually supervise the development of 44 TV shows—which included all of Irwin Allen's programs.

With the studio rocked by the growing financial black hole of *Cleopatra*, Allen and his production group found themselves in an unusual position. While *Five Weeks in a Balloon* had likely lost money for the studio, Allen's production operation wasn't coming under any particularly negative scrutiny from Fox. Allen and his associates kept working on their projects while keeping their heads low.

Al Gail recalled in 1995:

> You never knew, when you came back into work the next day, who was running the studio. They were in bad shape. *Cleopatra* almost knocked them out completely. We'd go out to lunch, we'd never go out the front gate—we'd all climb into [Irwin's] Rolls Royce, and we'd sneak out the back gate and hope none of the executives saw it. They usually didn't. We didn't want any of the current executives to see that we're still on the lot, and we didn't want to remind them because they had no money. And then suddenly someone would say, "Oh what's Irwin Allen doing?" if they happened to spot us. Cause at that time nothing was happening. And it went on that way for weeks until things started to perk up here. And then something happened, and we were back in action again.

While Allen's Rolls Royce was a classic Hollywood affectation—the archetypal symbol of wealth and status for decades in the U.S. and Britain—it should be noted that Allen had purchased his Rolls used, and he and Gail frequently had to push the vehicle to get it started.

The "something" that happened was Allen's concept for a TV series based on *Voyage to the Bottom of the Sea*.

Allen, in the early Sixties, had taken on a new agent: Herman Rush of General Artists Corporation. In Rush's storied career he would eventually help work out the deal to make Norman Lear's classic TV show *All in the Family* and represent and befriend countless famous celebrities and performing artists.

In an interview with the author, Rush said:

> Before I met [Irwin] I never knew him as an individual. I may have known his name as a producer or director and maybe had seen one or two of his films but knew who he was. I was introduced to him and we hit it off, became friends

**ABOVE**
Allen's agent Herman Rush (left) with Allen and a study model of the Flying Sub, as well as artwork for *The Time Tunnel* visible on the wall behind them.

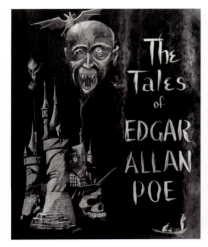
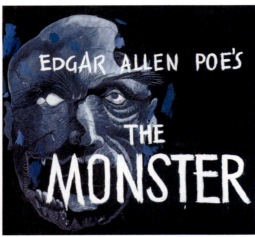

**ABOVE**
Cover of the glossy pitch presentation booklet for *The Tales of Edgar Allan Poe*.

Presentation artwork for the Poe series (with the Freudian slip of misspelling Poe's middle name as "Allen").

and I became his agent, and I guess that was 1961 or close to it. He had a production deal with Fox as a producer and decided he wanted to get involved in television, and my first representation with him was to renegotiate the Fox deal to include television, which we accomplished.

Rush found a kindred spirit in Allen, a former agent himself who reveled in both the creative and business sides of Hollywood:

He was a very gregarious individual. He loved to entertain, he felt very comfortable with performers and other creative individuals—writers, directors, etc. That was his life. Irwin was a workaholic—he was first in the office before anyone else in the morning and the last to leave. He would quickly freshen up and go out to dinner, and most of his dinners included people that would eventually be in pictures and work for him, or have some relationship with the projects he was doing. The weekend was his busy time. I was fortunate—we lived only a few blocks away from each other, and he had more meetings on Saturday and Sunday than he had Monday through Friday.

Even for someone of Rush's experience, Irwin Allen was a unique client:

He covered two bases—he was not only a creative individual, he had a sense of business. So Irwin, unlike many creative individuals back then and today, didn't just turn over the aspects of a business relationship to their agent—Irwin was very active in participating with that discussion and the eventual decisions that were made. He read every contract, he had his input on every clause of every contract, so he combined the business aspect and the creative aspect, and that's sort of unusual. Many times an agent doesn't want to take his client to a meeting—he might say the wrong thing to a network and really shouldn't be involved in negotiation. To the contrary, Irwin was very productive in such meetings: he felt at home and he wasn't afraid to voice his opinion to the other side. His entire life was what he did every day and every day was creating material, executing and implementing that material into television and motion pictures, and the people he surrounded himself were always creative people.

If Allen had had his way, his first TV program would not have been *Voyage to the Bottom of the Sea*. Ever the literary maven, Allen concocted a program concept called *The Tales of Edgar Allan Poe*, and with his usual showmanship worked up a glossy, bound presentation booklet with a mix of gruesome, black and white painted artwork and photographs of props and production charts from Allen's feature films.

The presentation book text read:

THE TALES OF EDGAR ALLAN POE is planned as a weekly, one-hour show presenting the weirdly wonderful world of terror. It is intended for the latest prime time available. The closer to the witching hour the better!

This show will not be an anthology! *Edgar Allan Poe will appear in each segment as a continuing character* playing the role of detective-author and confidant of the new personalities in each show. He will be aided by an assistant who will provide the comedy relief set against the background of terror. Thus, Poe and his aide will be importantly and intimately involved in every episode.

Each episode will be based on, or adapted from, hundreds of Poe's classic stories now in public domain. Their universal appeal is limitless because of the perpetual attraction of all ages to unexplainable mysteries. By dramatizing this rich reservoir of eerie imagination, this series will bring to television an amazing variety of strange and intriguing tales.

A separate page headed "PRODUCTION TECHNIQUE" highlighted Allen's reputation as a technical mastermind, as well as the producer's secret weapon—his art department:

Irwin Allen's special magic of integrating life-like miniatures, trick footage and award-winning opticals should make THE TALES OF EDGAR ALLAN POE the most unusual show on television. Intense attention to detail, evidenced in advance sketching of all key scenes and camera set-ups, makes the Irwin Allen company one of Hollywood's most unusual production teams—cost conscious, highly experienced in all phases of filming and ready to bring new tricks, new flairs and new horizons to television...

While he took pains to declare the *The Tales of Edgar Allan Poe* would not be an anthology show, Allen was clearly banking on the success of CBS' *The Twilight Zone* and likely on William Self's connection to that series, reasoning that the Edgar Allan Poe concept would seem an innovative twist on a format that had already been exploited by shows like *Alfred Hitchcock Presents* and *Thriller*. Allen was correct to emphasize the point that his show would not be an anthology—this would have been truly groundbreaking since no one had done an adult horror series with continuing characters. But Self and Fox didn't take the bait and *The Tales of Edgar Allan Poe* never became anything more than a bound presentation.

Allen and his Cambridge Productions then came up with a proposal to turn the 1961 *Voyage to the Bottom of the Sea* movie into a weekly TV show that would continue the adventures of Admiral Harriman Nelson, Captain Lee Crane, and the submarine Seaview. According to Herman Rush:

Irwin had success with the *Voyage to the Bottom of the Sea* movie and felt it would make a good television series, and he convinced Bill Self and Fox to do it as a series. He had a head start in the fact that they had the models of the ship and other models that they needed of the submarine, so it was a step towards making a presentation to the network and saying, "This is what it's going to look like, this is what we did as a motion picture entity, and now we're going to use these same models and miniatures and do a television series," and that's how we made the sale to ABC.

On June 14, 1963, Fox's Maurice R. Morton sent a memo to Frank Ferguson, Richard Zanuck, and Stan Hough:

William Self has approved the following for *Voyage to the Bottom of the Sea*: Prepare an agreement authorizing General Artists Corporation to act as our exclusive

representative for the above-mentioned hour television series, authorization shall be for a period commencing as of this date and ending with expiration of joint venture deal with Irwin Allen.

A July 16, 1963 Fox memo to Cambridge Productions, Inc. from Maurice R. Morton offered confirmation:

Cambridge and Fox have entered into a joint venture, reached an oral agreement with ABC TV for the development of a story, a pilot script, and should ABC exercise its option the production of a pilot film, and should it exercise its further option, the production of a *Voyage to the Bottom of the Sea* TV series. Agree to employ Allen as writer of the story and pilot script for $12,500 and to produce and direct the pilot for $15,000. Allen was to be paid $1500 per week for producer services. Formal agreement by Allen submitted on July 19, 1963. The agreement required principal photography on the pilot to begin on or before February 28, 1964 and to be financed by Fox. Budgets for the individual episodes were not to exceed $113,050.00.

Early casting ideas for the series included Dana Andrews, Victor Mature, Joseph Cotton, James Whitmore, Richard Carlson, Everett Sloan, Leo Genn, Dan Duryea, Joel McCrea, Leif Ericson, Howard Duff, John Forsythe, Gary Merrill, Sterling Hayden(!), Richard Denning, James Gregory, Forest Tucker, Howard Keel, Carroll O'Connor, James Daly or Richard Basehart for Nelson, and Dewey Martin, Michael Dante, Peter Breck, Robert Lansing,

**ABOVE**
Publicity photo of Richard Basehart as Admiral Harriman Nelson.

**OPPOSITE**
Pages from Allen's presentation book for the *Voyage to the Bottom of the Sea* TV series. The show logo was printed on a mylar overlay through which a photo of the iconic Seaview could be seen.

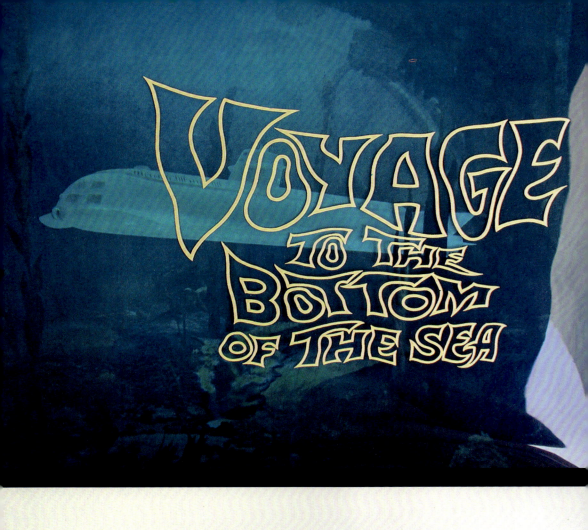

Mission for viewers: sit on the edge of your seat, hold your breath, and enjoy the most unique, most spellbinding television series your senses have ever experienced.... on the **ABC TELEVISION NETWORK**

Don Murray, or Patrick O'Neal for Crane. An ABC sales PR release announced the casting of Richard Basehart as Nelson and David Hedison as Crane in the fall of 1963, shortly before production began in November.

According to Paul Zastupnevich, Basehart was only on Allen's radar because of a former girlfriend. "Before Sheila [Mathews], he was dating a gal by the name of Jodi Desmond. Jodi came from Italy and she knew Basehart." (Desmond had co-written the catchy title song for *Five Weeks in a Balloon*, and Allen would name one of his production companies, Jodi Productions, after her.)

Basehart, after an impressive career in numerous films noir in the U.S., had made *La Strada* in Italy with Federico Fellini and married the Italian actress Valentina Cortese. But Cortese had left Basehart in 1960, moving back to Italy with their young son—and Basehart's previous wife, Stephanie Klein, had died suddenly of a brain tumor. The actor's personal travails and, according to Zastupnevich, his short stature, dogged his career and led to a drinking problem that would occasionally affect Basehart's work on *Voyage to the Bottom of the Sea*. Despite those issues, Basehart was a marvelously expressive, highly intelligent actor who was able to lend gravity to nearly any situation.

"Some of the dialogue that was written for him, by the time he got through saying it, you believed it," Zastupnevich said in 1995. "And it was so trite and so corny. But he was so believable."

It was the presence of Basehart that convinced David Hedison to join the series after turning down the role of Crane in the *Voyage* theatrical film:

> [Irwin] called me for *Voyage to the Bottom of the Sea*—the series. I turned that down. I said, "Irwin I'm grateful that you think of me for this part, but I really feel I'm not right for it and I'm looking for something with a little bit more dimension for an actor." And the guy wouldn't let go. I went to New York. He called me in New York. I went to London and I did a show with Roger Moore—*The Saint*, and I was guesting on that. And Irwin called me in the middle of the night, pursued it. For some reason he wanted me. So finally, after I heard that Richard Basehart was playing the admiral, I was terribly impressed that he got Richard. And I thought, "Well, God, if Richard Basehart can do this, I certainly can."

Hedison quickly discovered, however, that *Voyage* was not going to stretch him as an actor:

> I would say, Irwin, you know, Captain Crane, Admiral Nelson—we should have a background. There should be some sort of humor in the characters, not so grim. I came in with like fifty pages of biography for the character and he would have none of it. He just didn't want to know. He said to me, "David, what do you mean? What do you mean about character? What are you talking about? Do you mean like, for instance, when you're standing there, and you got a cup of coffee in your hands, you're drinking a cup of coffee, then suddenly something hits the sub and the coffee spills all over your pants—is that what you mean?" He just knew that he always wanted the action to be very grim, and very solid and very tense. And that's what he got.

**LEFT**
David Hedison as Captain Lee Crane, the role he'd turned down for Allen's 1961 *Voyage to the Bottom of the Sea* movie but accepted for the TV series.

Theo Marcuse as villain Dr. Gamma—positioned to be the Seaview's Blofeld, but sidelined after the pilot.

**OPPOSITE**
The mysterious Dr. Gamma (silhouetted) plots with fellow international villains against the Seaview—with the four-foot miniature of the sub as a visual aide.

Dr. Gamma's aircraft dive-bombs the Seaview; and the airship miniature as it appears today.

As a TV series, *Voyage to the Bottom of the Sea* presented the opportunity to combine several popular genres: science fiction, the cold war thriller, and the burgeoning spy movie craze kicked off by the James Bond films. Underwater action was still novel and exciting for American viewers, as Lloyd Bridge's popular TV series *Sea Hunt* had proved and Jacques-Yves Cousteau's documentary specials for ABC would soon reinforce. To take advantage of the spy craze, Allen had intended to position a Blofeld-like, exotic, bald-headed villain named Dr. Gamma as a regular nemesis for the Seaview's crew. Played by Theo Marcuse, the character appeared in the *Voyage* television pilot, "Eleven Days to Zero."

In a May 1, 1964 memo, Allen addressed questions submitted by Dwight Houser of ABC regarding the show's "promotable elements":

> The 102-foot submarine "Seaview" and all of the special equipment it includes [the Seaview's length varied in publicity materials, but the 102-foot figure, more the size of a WW II U-boat, was likely a typo]. The 21 permanent Seaview interiors with missile launching tubes, cast and fantastically complex control room, unique glass nose, radio controlled miniatures, etc. ...constantly recurring underwater sequences. Not only sequences in which the Seaview proceeds underwater, but scenes involving underwater fights, monsters, giant denizens of the ocean, etc. The mini-sub, a practical two-man underwater runabout launched from the belly of the Seaview may well prove an interesting and highly promotable Voyage ingredient. The ever-present menace of the redoubtable Dr. Gamma, an internationally powerful master criminal, must be considered...as well as the unique role of the Seaview, the Nelson Institute and the fact that both are cover for the United States' outstanding task force of commando-scientists and counter-espionage agents. It is our opinion that this show stands alone except the broad categorization action-adventure which might apply. We are unique in presenting stunning adventure, high suspense and international intrigue set into a fabric of intensely believable science-fiction. All of this plus the added romance of the world's mightiest undersea craft puts Voyage pretty much in a class by itself.

Despite Allen pointing him out as one of the program's more promotable elements, the villainous Dr. Gamma character became an early casualty of the show's developing concept and was abandoned after the pilot. "There were creative reasons why it was a plus to include that in the series, and there were negative reasons why it was better not to include it in the series and not have the show be compared to James Bond," Herman Rush recalled. "And not to have one single villain but have a series of villains, and that was a creative decision made by Irwin."

Rush, in fact, was intimately involved in all of Allen's television shows and, despite never receiving any official credit, he attended creative development meetings and had input on casting, format, and numerous other decisions in developing Allen's shows. Like Allen had been in his early years, Rush was a "packaging" agent:

I didn't represent writers or producers or directors as individuals, I represented them as elements in a package that I would put together and sell the package to a network. My relationship with all my clients, it was not only business advice but whatever creative input they were willing to take from me, and Irwin included me in all his creative meetings and I participated by agreeing or disagreeing with the creative ideas that were passed around the table at the time.

An ABC sales/promotional memo noted that Allen's *The Lost World* airing on NBC's *Monday Night Movies* attracted a 32.1 share of the audience, ranking it third among all movies in the Monday night series in the 1963–64 season to date. ABC also noted the impact of New York TV airings of *The Fabulous World of Jules Verne* (a 23.7 share) and the 1950s sci-fi thriller *The Atomic Submarine* (26.9 share) when broadcast in early evening time slots, which *Voyage* would be occupying on Monday nights.

*Voyage* replaced *The Outer Limits*, which ABC noted leaned as more adult fare as opposed to *Voyage*'s "true all-family appeal." The network cited *Voyage*'s continuing characters—a first in terms of a major network science fiction program—as opposed to *The Outer Limits*' anthology format. *Voyage* would be facing up against game shows (*To Tell the Truth* and *I've Got a Secret* on CBS) and sitcoms (*Karen* and *Tom, Dick and Mary* on NBC)—making *Voyage* effective counter-programming.

Allen continued to demonstrate his facility for hiring—and retaining—talent behind the camera, and with the veteran technicians and artists at Fox, he brought a formidable technical polish to *Voyage*'s first season. (The show was filmed in black and white due to network reluctance to pay the additional fees for color, despite Allen's and Fox's desire for the program to be broadcast in color.)

Allen retained art director Bill Creber, who had helped refine the design of the Seaview for the theatrical movie, to work on the television series:

> I went on a project outside the studio and when I got back it was like two years later and Irwin called and said I have this pilot, *Voyage to the Bottom of the Sea,* and he said Herman [Blumenthal] doesn't wanna do it. Irwin trusted me I went back to Fox and did the pilot and, and Jack Martin Smith was the head of the department at that time. He said, "I'll keep you on and you can be kind of a utility assistant art director—if something comes along and I think you can handle it I'll let you do the film," and I said great.

L.B. Abbott continued to supervise visual effects on the series, putting the miniature Seaviews through their paces with Ralph Hammeras as cameraman. Howard Lydecker, who with his brother Theodore had established an incredibly high standard for miniature photography and effects sequences in years of work for war pictures and action serials dating back to the 1930s, lent his expertise and the brothers' "Lydecker rig" method of flying miniatures on guide-wires, providing sequences like Dr. Gamma's saucer-shaped bombers attacking the Seaview from the air in the pilot episode,

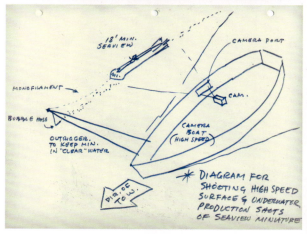

**LEFT**

Color footage of the 17-foot Seaview miniature recycled from the *Voyage* feature for the pilot "Eleven Days to Zero," and black and white shot (tinted blue) of the 8-1/2 foot Seaview filmed for the series' first season.

The 17-foot Seaview miniature on the surface, shot in color for *Voyage*'s pilot episode.

Diagram illustrating the rigging and shooting process for the largest Seaview miniature and the "bubble rig" placed in front of the model, designed to create the illusion of a foamy, ocean wake.

**TOP LEFT**
Henry Kulky (left, standing) with David Hedison as Captain Crane and Chris Connelly (seated) as a Seaview crewman. Kulky died between seasons one and two of *Voyage to the Bottom of the Sea*.

**TOP RIGHT**
Terry Becker as Chief Sharkey, introduced in the second season of the series.

and a flying saucer—portrayed by the miniature from Fox's classic *The Day the Earth Stood Still*—crashing into the ocean in the episode "The Sky Is Falling."

Abbott's technicians also created highly convincing sea monsters for the show, including a rampaging sperm whale for "The Ghost of Moby Dick." In a Dec. 10, 1964 press release promoting the episode, Allen proclaimed:

> It is a battle never before seen on television. We went all out to accomplish reality. Our sub is more than 600 feet long. To make it an even fight, we constructed a whale of equal proportions but one which contains credibility in every ounce of its blubber.

Two months of preproduction time were needed to construct the whale—Allen noted that guest star June Lockhart screamed in real fright when she saw the rough cut of the episode. Abbott created an equally convincing, giant manta ray monster with flapping "wings" for "The Creature" with Leslie Nielsen.

Despite these effects highlights, for the most part new miniature footage was kept to a minimum in the first season, aside from a series of library shots of the Seaview, and Allen took full advantage of footage from the *Voyage* movie to keep costs down. In an ABC promotional interview, Allen stated:

> It would be impossible to obtain the production values for the TV series had it not been for the movie. For example, the three main underwater sections of our Seaview submarine cost more than $400,000 to built—more than most television pilot films in their entirety. Yet when we were ready to make the television pilot we had at our disposal, and in perfect working shape, the intact sections of the control room, the viewing room (the only submarine with a glass nose) and the missile and torpedo room fully equipped with more than two dozen of the latest atomic warhead-carrying missiles.

The debut of the series was strong—30-city Nielsen ratings (a survey of the top local television markets in the country) were #1 for "Eleven Days to Zero": a 19.3 rating and a 37.2 share; "City Beneath the Sea" aired the following week was even higher, with a 22.2 rating, 38.9 share (viewership went up both weeks in the second hour as CBS' competing show *To Tell the Truth* switched to *I've Got A Secret*). NBC's midseason replacement *Karen* and *The Man from U.N.C.L.E.* were by February 1965 offering strong competition—*Karen* took the lead, putting *Voyage* in third place on February 1st (although the show rebounded in its second half hour against *U.N.C.L.E.* and jumped ahead).

National Nielsens were similar albeit more consistent, sticking in the 19-20 range until the final two episodes, "The Secret of the Loch" and "The Condemned," which each rated around 16.5. By March 1965. *The Man from U.N.C.L.E.* was consistently beating *Voyage*'s second half hour and that situation encouraged Allen to add more "James Bond gimmicks" and espionage into the show's second season.

The highest rated 30-city first season episodes were:

| | |
|---|---|
| The Village of Guilt | 26.2 |
| The Sky is Falling | 26.1 |
| The City Beneath the Sea | 25.3 |
| No Way Out | 24.9 |
| Turn Back the Clock | 24.7 |
| The Ghost of Moby Dick | 24.3 |
| Submarine Sunk Here | 23.9 |
| The Last Battle | 23.8 |
| The Fear Makers | 23.7 |
| Mutiny | 23.3 |

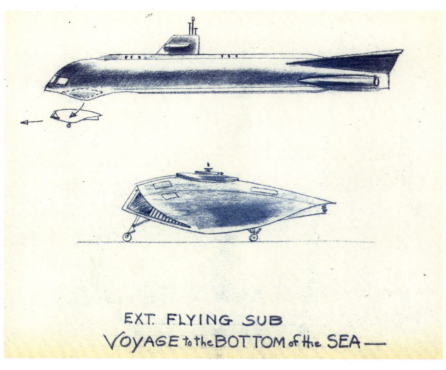

The lowest rated were:

| | |
|---|---|
| The Buccaneer | 19.4 |
| The Exile | 19.0 |
| Long Live the King | 18.9 |
| The Traitor | 17.8 |
| The Condemned | 16.6 |

By 1965, color television sets were becoming the norm across the U.S., and Allen prepared to retool *Voyage to the Bottom of the Sea* to reflect that and bring a more dynamic, attention-grabbing look and feel to the series. In switching to color, the show was playing catchup to some of its network competition.

"If you were shooting a show for NBC, they increased their license fee so that you would shoot it in color, and NBC was a leader in that because RCA color systems was the one that was in use," Herman Rush explained. "*Voyage* was in black and white, we all felt it had long-term value and should be in color. 20th Century Fox felt that way, Bill Self reflected that, Irwin reflected it, and ABC finally agreed to increase the license fee as a contribution towards the increased color costs, and everything after that that Irwin did was in color. It was one of the early shows to go to color and it was not what you would call a four-wall type of show—it was a show about a submarine, a show about the ocean and nature, and color was just a natural way for it to evolve."

Henry Kulky, the ex-wrestler turned actor who played the gruff Chief Curley Jones, had died prior to the end of season 1. To replace him, Terry Becker was brought on as Chief Francis Sharkey in season 2, becoming a popular addition to the crew. It would be Becker who, perhaps against Irwin Allen's wishes, would bring some much-needed humor to the series.

Arguably the show's most exciting new character was not a human being—nor was it even alive. Fox Television PR director Bob Suhosky teased the new addition in an "About the Production" feature:

> In a touch of Jules Verne, producer Allen has made a scientific addition to the Seaview for his second season offering in color. Attached directly under the bow of the submarine is a "Flying Fish"—a vehicle that flies through the air at incredible speeds and submerges to travel under water at great depths. This addition, cites Allen, opens up an entirely new vista of activity for the Seaview's crew, taking them literally out of the water and placing them in the fast-moving space age.

In an August 30, 1965 press release on the Flying Sub, Allen claimed he had a Flying Sub "on the drawing board" for 10 years, and he responded to the claim that the Navy had announced it was researching a sub-plane that would fly to a target area by saying, "I think I'll sue them for plagiarism."

Designed under the supervision of Bill Creber, the "Flying Fish" was quickly designated the Flying Sub before its debut in the second episode of season two—although viewers who stay tuned through the end of the season opener, "Jonah and the Whale," had a view of the vehicle seemingly hovering mysteriously over the ocean in a still photo under the show's end credits.

Creber and his team of illustrators initially designed the vehicle with down-swept "wings" that fit the contours of the manta wing fins around the Seaview's nose—production sketches make the little ship look like it snaps into the bottom of the larger submarine's bow, which fit the early P.R. description of the vehicle being "attached directly under the bow" of the Seaview.

"I had designed it and had a model made of it," Creber recalls. "Irwin handed it back and looked at it and he liked it, but he said, 'Turn it over. Don't you think it

**ABOVE**

The original design sketches of the Flying Sub, showing it oriented upside down to the way it ultimately appeared—apparently so that the vehicle could "plug in" underneath the down-swept contours of the Seaview's bow

**OPPOSITE AND FOLLOWING**

Concept paintings of the Flying Sub, before the ship's distinctive blue trim was developed.

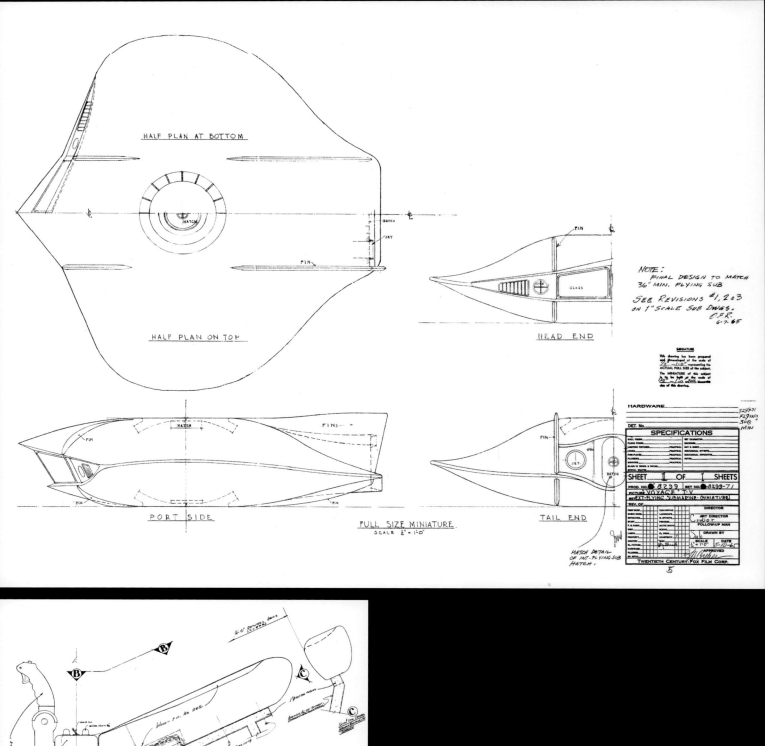
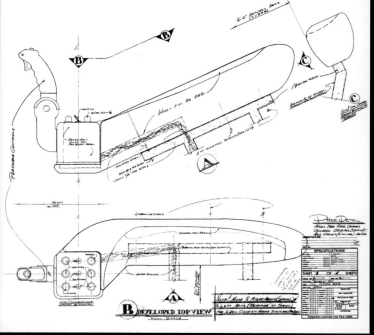

**RIGHT**
Flying Sub launch sequence, showcasing some of the show's most impressive miniature work.

Richard Basehart with the 18″ Flying Sub study model.

**OPPOSITE**
Blueprints for the 36″ Flying Sub miniature. These were closely followed by Aurora Plastics for the development of their plastic Flying Sub model kit; the various production miniatures—9″, 18″ and 36″ in diameter, featured slightly different contours, more tapering wings, and thinner fins.

Blueprints for the distinctive Flying Sub flight controls. Note the instructions to purchase the moveable hand grips—many props like this were created using surplus parts from military aircraft.

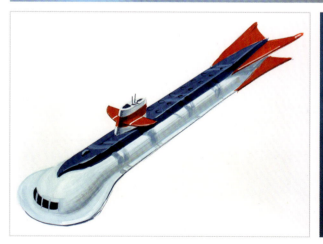

**LEFT**
The 18″ miniature Flying Sub used for launch sequences with the 17 foot Seaview.

One of the 36″ Flying Sub miniatures, made of fiberglass, with an undetailed nose and mirrored glass windshields. Visible on either side of the leading edge of the wings are the "Lyedecker rig" tubes which enclosed cables that the miniature slid along for its flying scenes. Also visible is the metal eyelet between the front windows that was connected to a third cable that would pull the miniature along its flight path.

Concept art for a distinctly patriotic color scheme for the redesigned, season two Seaview.

The redesigned Seaview in footage utilized in the show's memorable "radar screen" title sequence.

**RIGHT**
The Flying Sub in its "Lydecker rig" flight sequences, shot against real clouds as well as against the painted backdrop of the huge Sersen Lake tank at the Fox Ranch.

looks better that way?' And I said, 'whatever you say.' We changed it a little bit and redid the fins the way they were, right side up, so they looked better with that arrangement."

Creber had the Flying Sub miniatures painted bright yellow with blue trim—the same as the Seaview's diving bell and, interestingly, similar to the look of the advanced diving saucers that ocean explorer Jacques-Yves Cousteau had constructed for his ship, the Calypso.

However, Creber says the Calypso wasn't an overt influence. "Irwin liked bright colors anyway, so we just thought underwater stuff was painted that way. The diving bell [set] was painted the same yellow and blue scheme, and that looked good on the stage. We liked industrial safety colors so it wasn't done for any particular artistic reason; it was more of a practical thing."

Like the Seaview, the Flying Sub was produced in varying scales for different purposes, starting with a 9" version that could be shot in conjunction with the 8-1/2 foot underwater Seaview model (and sometimes with giant undersea creatures shown clutching the comparatively tiny craft); an 18" model built for the launch sequences that would show the Flying Sub emerging from the bottom of the 17-foot "surface" Seaview model; and a number of 36"-wide models used for sequences of the vehicle in flight, crashing into and flying out of the ocean, and operating underwater.

Howard Lydecker supervised the flight sequences using the Lydecker rig he and his brother had devised. Two guide wires were strung from a gantry that had a steering wheel-like mount that allowed a technician to adjust the attitude of the flying model as it traveled down the wires from a high point at the gantry down to the ground. The wires entered at the front bulkhead of the Flying Sub miniature (where the little ship's twin headlights, forward windows, and air intake vents were situated) and exited on the upper trailing edge of each wing. When the miniature was flown down the rig, two effects technicians waited at the bottom with a badminton net strung between them to safely catch the vessel before it crashed into the ground.

The same rig was used to fly the 36" miniature from the sky (actually a painted sky backing behind the large Sersen Lake tank at the Fox ranch) down into the ocean—but the first attempt at achieving this exciting sequence failed miserably. Lydecker and Abbott originally arranged to "fly" one of the finished and detailed, three-foot Flying Sub miniatures down into the tank, weighting the craft so that it would have a convincing impact with the water and sink down beneath the waves. However, the Flying Sub's blunt, detailed front end, with its large windows and headlights, caved in completely on impact with the water, ruining the model. Abbott had a new Flying Sub miniature built with a solid, featureless front end, with mirrors added over solid fiberglas to replace the fragile plexiglas windows used in the original model. With the reinforced model, its lack of detail obscured by backlighting, the shot worked perfectly and became one of the most exciting and often-used sequences in the series.

The addition of the Flying Sub also required Bill Creber

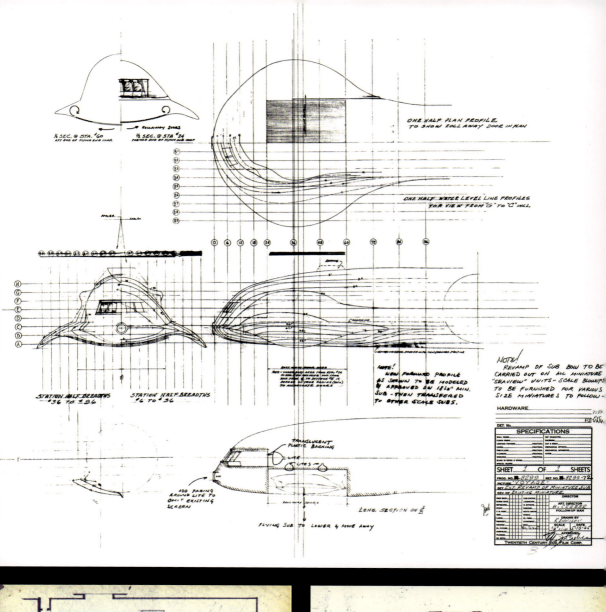

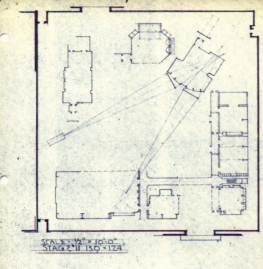

"VOYAGE" USE OF STAGE #11

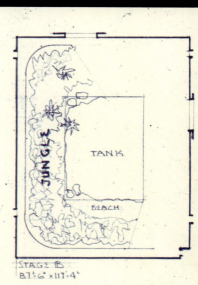

PROPOSED TANK STAGE B

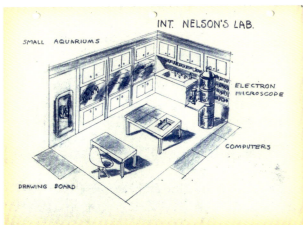
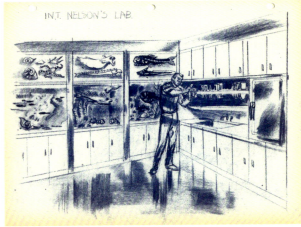
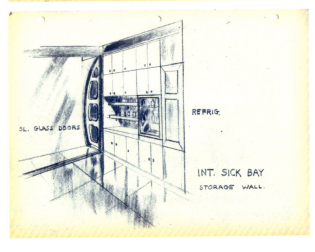
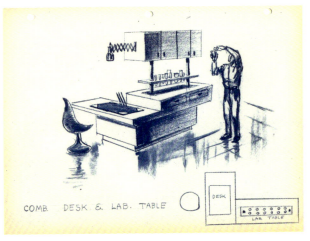

**RIGHT**
Proposed set designs for *Voyage*'s second season. The War Room set was never built.

**OPPOSITE**
Blueprints for the Seaview nose redesign supervised by art director William Creber.

Diagrams of the show's standing Seaview sets on stage 11 at 20th Century Fox and a proposal for a tank on the lot that could be used to shoot both beach and underwater scenes.

to redesign the nose of the Seaview, reducing the double deck of eight windows at the bow to two large, bisected windows, adding two teardrop-shaped sonar bulges to either side of the nose, expanding the bottom of the bow to add room for the Flying Sub berth, and adding double, corrugated sliding doors that would operate during the launch sequences. This ultimately became the most familiar version of the Seaview for television audiences, although stock footage of the first season/movie version of the sub that had been filmed in color continued to be used throughout the series. The Aurora model kit of the sub put out in 1965 and the yellow Remco toy were based on the eight-window, first season look of the sub.

The Flying Sub also required a new interior set where Nelson and/or Crane could be shown piloting the vehicle, and changes to the Seaview control room set to account for an access hatch for the craft near the nose and forward viewing area of the control room.

A March 25, 1965 Fox memo from Allen to Gaston Glass following a meeting about pre-production needs for the new season outlined some of these additions as well as a new underwater tank facility to be built at the studio:

> We have carefully reviewed with you and Jack Smith those additional set requirements and the refurbishing of the old sets to keep faith with our verbal agreement with ABC that *Voyage* would have a new look next year and that all efforts would be made toward a truly COLORFUL look. ...Stage 11 would house all our old sets (as refurbished) as well as all the new contemplated sets. In addition to stage 11, we presented to you blueprints indicating a proper utilization of a tank to either be constructed on our present Stage B or on a stage to be designated by you. This tank could be shared by the studio for its other needs as well as by our two companies and would pay for itself within one season. It would provide surface operations for the first company, underwater operations for both the second unit and the miniature operation as well as provide a lagoon jungle set so badly needed by many of our segments. It would have practical, cost-saving advantages over the use of the moat and green tank. Shooting in the moat, while vital to us for silent, big scope production scenes, is hopeless insofar as sound is concerned and requires, as you well know, expensive looping. Shooting in the green tank has the most serious shortcomings and is virtually impractical for both second unit and miniatures.

Another memo noted that the Observation Nose, Control Room, Missile Room, Admiral's Cabin, Crew's Quarters, Corridors, and Backings housed on Stage B were to be moved; the stock watertight doors, pipe units, missile room panels, Control Room Radar Panel were to be refurbished, and new sets including a War Room & Ward Room, Seaview Laboratory & Aquarium, Sick Bay, Corridors & Stairway, Flying Sub, Nelson Institute Offices, and Changeover Panel for Alternate subs in Control Room were to be constructed.

On April 8, 1965, Allen sent blueprints of Stage 11 to Glass, indicating the proposed layout of the stage with both the old sets and proposed new ones, a budget for relocation of the sets to Stage 11 (another memo indicated the main interior sets would remain on stage 10) and one for repair and refurbishment, one for

**ABOVE**
The 36" Flying Sub miniature operating underwater, footage shot in one of 20th Century Fox's tanks.

The Flying Sub miniature being shoved into its maneuvers by divers in one of the Fox tanks.

**OPPOSITE**
Blueprint for the mechanical spider monster seen in "The Monster's Web" (designated on the blueprints with the earlier title "Web of Destruction"). Note the name of visual effects supervisor Howard Lydecker, who had created miniature effects on film with his brother Theodore since the cliffhanger movie serials of the 1930s. Lydecker's expertise was in rigging miniature aircraft, watercraft, and, when necessary, monsters to move convincingly onscreen, and he supervised the construction of the giant underwater spider miniature so that it could trundle across the ocean floor and attack the Seaview.

Seaview vs. giant sea spider in "The Monster's Web."

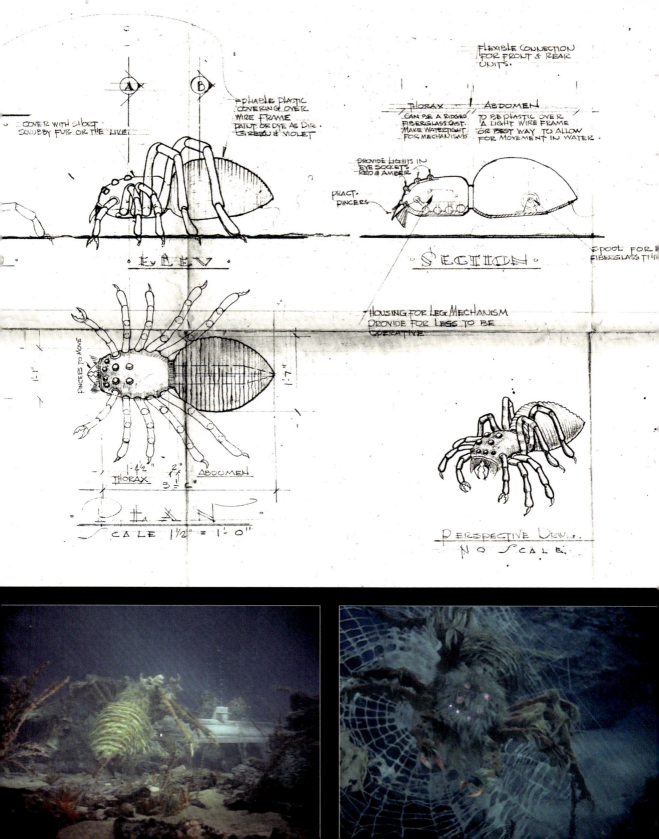

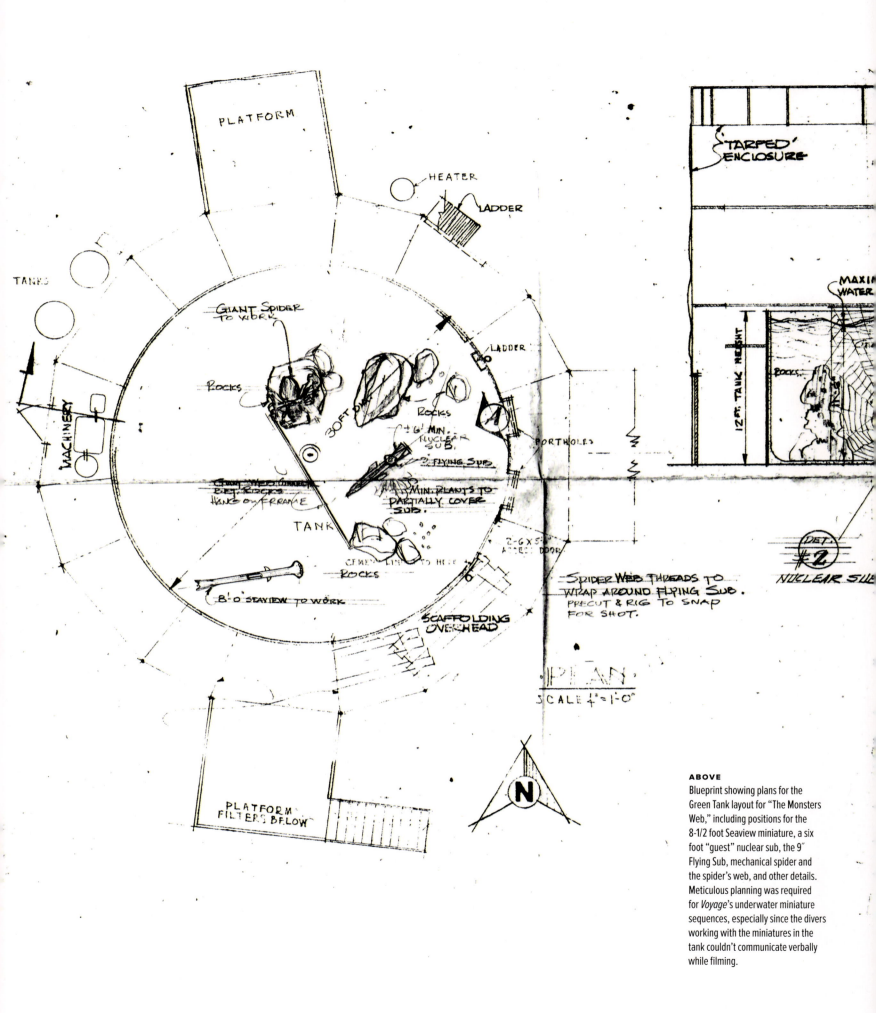

**ABOVE**
Blueprint showing plans for the Green Tank layout for "The Monsters Web," including positions for the 8-1/2 foot Seaview miniature, a six foot "guest" nuclear sub, the 9" Flying Sub, mechanical spider and the spider's web, and other details. Meticulous planning was required for *Voyage*'s underwater miniature sequences, especially since the divers working with the miniatures in the tank couldn't communicate verbally while filming.

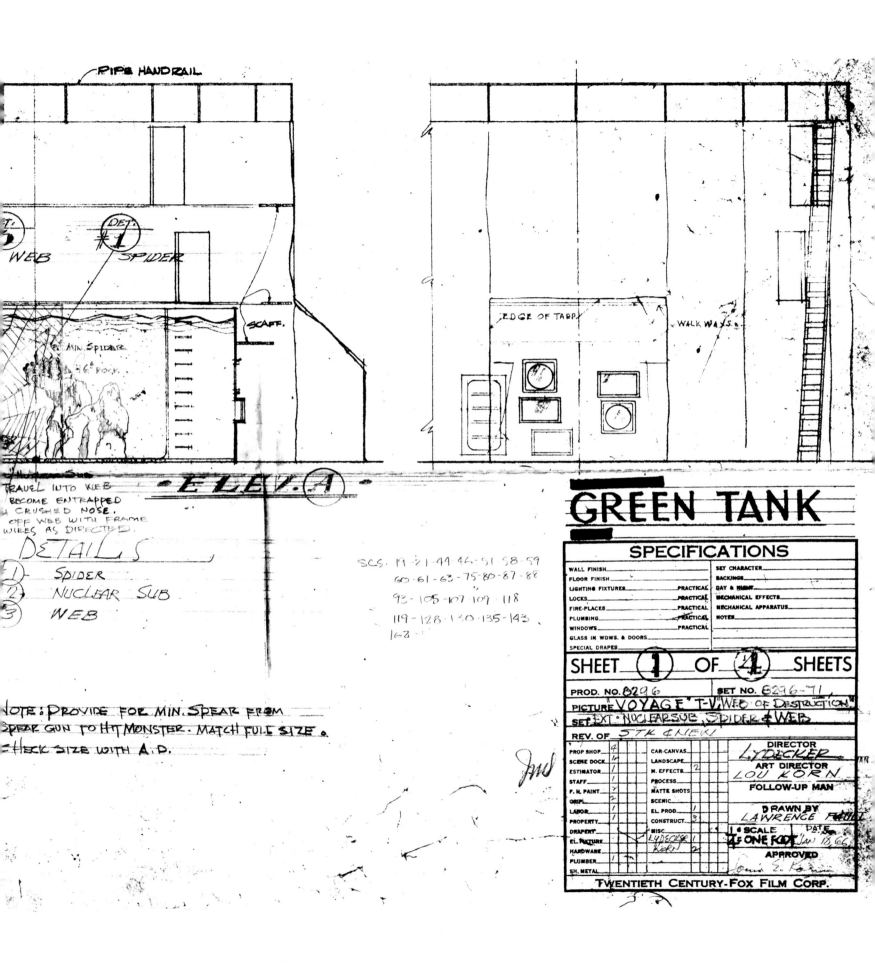

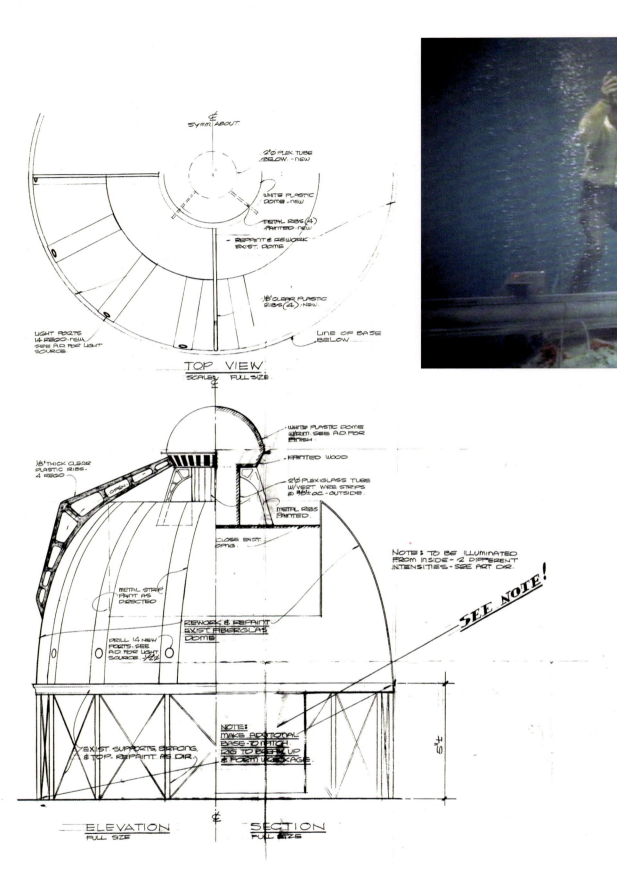

**ABOVE**

The Seaview vs. a guy in a sweater in season two's "Leviathan."

Blueprints for the underwater laboratory seen in "Leviathan" and other episodes.

construction of new sets, and a required new miniature set list. Allen enclosed artwork including the first rendering of the Flying Sub, depicted at the time upside down in orientation compared to the way it would be eventually seen on the series, and without the familiar forward headlamps, vertical stabilizers, and blue trim that would be added later.

The most expensive new set—the War Room/Ward Room, which included a bank of TV monitors and a wall-sized and pivoting world map all budgeted at $15,000—was never constructed. The Flying Sub interior was budgeted at $11,000. In addition to the modifications of the Seaview models to reflect the Flying Sub berth, Allen also wanted new eight-foot and four-foot Seaview miniatures constructed, but these were never built.

An outline of season two's second unit and miniature shooting indicated nine days of miniature photography for the season opener "Jonah and the Whale" (which presumably included numerous library shots of the newly-modified Seaview as well as the Flying Sub). Other episodes requiring new miniature photography were "The Silent Saboteurs" (one day), "The Machines Strike Back" (three days), "Escape from Venice" (three and 1/2 days), "The Phantom Strikes" (one and 1/2 days), "Graveyard of Fear" (five days), "Dead Men's Doubloons" (one day), "The Monster's Web" (three days), "The Menfish" (two days) for a total of 15 days of miniatures/plate shooting for the series. But other episodes like "Leviathan" required still more miniature effects.

The abundant second season underwater action also offered viewers an interesting, if unintended window into the nuts and bolts behind the show's miniature submarine effects. In episodes like "The Menfish" and particularly "Leviathan," distinctly man-like monsters attacked the Seaview—meaning stuntmen, and even actors, would appear directly in the frame with the 8-foot Seaview miniature, menacing and sometimes wrestling with the massive model and giving viewers a graphic idea of exactly what the Seaview really was.

In "Leviathan," actor Liam Sullivan played a scientist whose experimental formula grows him to gigantic size. Wearing the monstrous teeth originally made for the Cyclops monster seen on *Lost in Space*, Sullivan, otherwise just wearing slacks and a sweater, wrestled with the Seaview in what must have been a torturous ordeal, but one that gave a great view of a human being's size *vis-a-vis* the Seaview miniature. In "The Machines Strike Back," a scuba diver can be seen in the middle of the frame, right behind the miniature of a nuclear missile drone submarine, having just sent the miniature along its underwater trajectory. The diver may have been hidden in lower-resolution TV broadcasts, but on the remastered DVD release of the series he is shockingly visible.

**RIGHT**

Remote control missile drone miniature in action in "The Machines Strike Back."

A technician in scuba gear (lower right hand corner) vainly struggles to get out of camera range in a shot that made it on the air from "The Machines Strike Back."

Drone miniature from "The Machines Strike Back."

Allen was determined to deal with the program's ratings competition in season two. An April 26, 1965 memo to Bob Suhosky of Fox PR:

> We should still be concerned with an entire summer of weekly ratings for *Voyage*. *Voyage* has run a poor second to *Man from UNCLE* in the past two Nielsen ratings.

...If you're on the sub, see something new. But get off the sub as much as you can. Use some James Bond gimmicks. Faster pace to show. Inspire performers not to be so square and dull. Move! Girls! Romance! Hit and run kind of thing. Intrigue of an international flavor. Fantastic footage of colorful sea—strange and unusual fish through observation nose window. Swing! Move! Modernization of very stiff guys. Use of discordant music. Shock cutting. More scenes of less duration—people getting hit on head, etc. Go to interesting cities—Rome, Paris—see the world. Dana Wynter.

Other suggestions were to use writers from *The Man from U.N.C.L.E.* and "The swinging set! Youth, music, sex!"

Allen's references to music on the show were reflected in his choice to redo the show's opening title sequence with a new theme by film and TV composer Jerry Goldsmith, who was under contract to Fox at the time. This despite the fact that Paul Sawtell's uniquely memorable first season theme for *Voyage*, arguably the finest piece of composition Sawtell ever produced, was becoming popular in its own right. Goldsmith wrote a strange, Bernard Herrmann-like piece for the series, echoing the famous Seaview sonar ping with a gong-like sound likely derived from an electric guitar, and working his three-note title motif into his score for the second season opener, "Jonah and the Whale," as a theme for the Seaview. Allen apparently hated Goldsmith's theme and dropped it after one episode, reinstating Sawtell's theme, which remained in place through the rest of the show's four-season run. According to Fox music editor Ken Hall, Goldsmith appeared at a Hollywood party after his theme was dropped wearing a sign around his neck that said, "Ban Irwin Allen."

Allen's other suggestion for "people getting hit on head, etc." was embraced by the show's makers to the extent that a French sketch comedy show filmed a bit parodying how often characters on the show, like Del Monroe's hapless Kowalski, found themselves clobbered over the head and "knocked out."

In a PR feature, Allen was eager to point out that season two would abound with romantic possibilities for Nelson and Crane. "We did everything by the book last season, will now unbend a bit. We are humanizing the military men," he said. The show cast female guest stars Ina Balin, Gia Scala, Susan Flannery, Barbara Bouchet, Audrey Dalton, Nancy Hsueh, Delphi Lawrence, and Francoise Rugieri. The romantic opportunities didn't last much longer than season two—in later years David Hedison said that Allen didn't like using female guest stars on *Voyage* because of the cost of hairdressing and makeup and the lost time in filming that those two elements created.

Basehart and Hedison had become popular TV stars after a year of *Voyage*. Basehart had been the kind of respected dramatic actor who might normally turn his nose up at television. When asked about why he took the role in a PR interview, Basehart said:

> I was amazed myself—but the deal he offered was just too good to resist. It came at a time when the last half dozen motion pictures I made weren't satisfying experiences; so

**LEFT**
Barbara Bouchet in season two's "The Left-Handed Man"—one of the second year's unsuccessful stabs at putting more female characters and potential romance on the show.

**OPPOSITE**
In a publicity photo, Allen (left) confers with director Harry Harris about a *Voyage* script.

I'd done a few guest shots, enough to convince me the medium now had possibilities.

In comments that sound tailored for the press, Basehart continued:

We began our second year with a more adventurous approach and some very pretty girls. Episodes got me off the sub and into trouble of various sorts on land. But audiences seem to want the boat.

Basehart then hinted at the problems he would soon be having with the show:

A series is exhausting, can become monotonous to performers and is sometimes limited as to material; but a successful series can make a fortune for those participating in it. ...You cannot disregard the economics involved. If a top series runs for several years, a man can come off a millionaire. I was asked to direct some segments of *Voyage*, but came to the conclusion that directing is a complete job and no one can act and direct at the same time and do justice to both things. Dave Hedison and I carry the weight of the dialogue, so there's a lot of memorizing to be done. There is little time for anything else. I don't watch TV because that's like going to work again and there's no time for seeing movies. Just at first I was bugged by the lack of time to develop themes and study character possibilities; but I've learned to live with it. We try to stay with it until it's as right as it can be made—we knock ourselves out, and sometimes it's backbreaking. I do narration on documentaries sometimes on Saturdays to keep my hand in; I don't want to remain in TV series forever and some day I'll be off to do some stage work.

In a July 18, 1965 feature in *The Chicago Tribune*, Basehart praised the show's technical bells and whistles:

Call us lucky. No other series has ever been handed a million dollars worth of sets and props to work with right from the start. All this is an enormous help to the actor. When the submarine skipper tells me that we're at a depth of 2,400 feet, proceeding at 65 knots on a 70-degree course, I can flick my eyes to the instruments and those are the readings. If the script calls for us to change depth, speed or course, the instruments immediately adjust—even when the camera isn't looking. Maybe the critic who said actors are just tall children was right. If so, us kids in this series should be happy—we've been given the most expensive toys ever made.

The article claimed that Hedison received 9,000 letters from fans, and that 90% of the fan mail was from female viewers between 20-30—a conclusion that butted up against Allen's earlier concerns that the *Voyage* movie had turned off younger females. In fact, *Voyage to the Bottom of the Sea* began a trend later continued by *Star Trek* in drawing female viewers to science fiction, initially by offering attractive male characters that they could relate to. Viewers may have sensed the warm relationship between Basehart and Hedison, despite stories that often had them (under the influence of enemy fear gases or alien mind control) at each other's throats. "Unlike some of the other ones in our other series, our two leads got along famously," Al Gail said

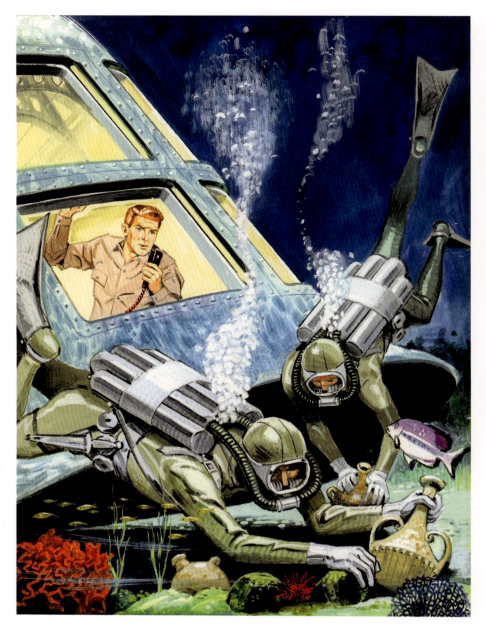

**ABOVE**
Artwork for a *Voyage to the Bottom of the Sea* coloring book.

**ABOVE**
Artwork for the popular *Voyage to the Bottom of the Sea* lunchbox, which was reproduced as a collectible decades after the series went off the air.

in 1995. "Dave Hedison and Richard Basehart never had a disturbing word between them. Because they were not competitors. David recognized Basehart as a fine actor, as an older man, and he never felt competitive. And we made sure that they each had a good role in each episode. So we never had any trouble on that set."

Director Harry Harris shot a dozen episodes of the series. Production illustrator Joe Musso recalled that the crew used to call Harris "Midnight Harry." "He hated that term, but that was his nickname because…they'd always be working 'til midnight."

Harris found Basehart one of the most appealing elements of the show. "The thing I liked the most about *Voyage to the Bottom of the Sea* was Richard Basehart, because he was a fine actor. Richard did the show, and he bitched all the time about doing the show, but he did do well on it and he was a pleasure to work with. I'd read the script and I'd say, 'I wonder how he's gonna play this scene, cause it's kind of corny, and I'd rehearse it and I'd listen to him and God, I believed ever word he said. Richard Basehart made that whole thing come to life. And David Hedison was fun. It was a fun show to work on."

Season two boasted some of *Voyage*'s best episodes, blending fast-paced espionage action with colorful underwater threats. Visually, the show was dazzling, unlike anything American audiences had ever seen, and had to be the centerpiece of conversation in any household with a large color TV set on the nights that it aired. It was, however, already beginning to demonstrate elements that would become irritatingly common, some appearing in almost every episode.

One was the "rock and roll," which had the Seaview out of control or hit by enemy fire or alien forces that would cause the sub to rock back and forth wildly, sending everyone inside staggering from one side of the control room set to the other. Harris remembered:

> There was always something hitting the submarine. So when the submarine got hit or was on the bottom, it would always go one way and the people would go the other way. So you had a five gallon can, and when you hit the can, the camera went one way, the people went the other and all the props went with the people. So by the end of the season, this tin can that I had, it would look like a piece of mangled metal. So at the wrap party, Irwin had it sprayed in gold, and he had the hammer welded to the top of the can, and he gave it to me as a trophy when we finished the season on that show. But that's how that show worked.

Allen's imagination and ingenuity were showcased throughout the season, but the "Jonah and the Whale" episode might have been the best example. Shimon Wincelberg wrote the story. He noted in 1995:

> Irwin always did think in big terms. We needed a set that was the interior of a whale, and there's no way the studio was gonna spring for the money to build it. So Irwin scouted around and he found out there was a set from *Fantastic Voyage*, Saul David's film that was filming at the same time. That was a high budget feature film. And he somehow got the key to the sound stage where that set was stored, and there was nobody there, nobody was using it, and he shot the episode inside the set that represented a human body, and it was just a wonderful effect, and cost next to nothing.

*TV Guide* did a special feature on the episode in October, 1965. "It was a horrible, frightening experience. It gave me goose pimples," Gia Scala said of filming the whale interior sequences. Bill Creber explained how the whale's stomach was created: "The stomach wall was 60 x 60 foot vinyl bags, inflated with low pressure to give a breathing effect. We had a hanging 'uvula' of vinyl and foam-rubber with foam rubber tentacles. Red paint and red and yellow lights completed the effect."

*Variety* reviewed the episode enthusiastically on September 27:

> With much of the action taking place within the huge fish, a good deal of credit goes to special effects, who recreated the interior of the whale realistically and strikingly. It's an auspicious start for another *Voyage* [season].

*The Hollywood Reporter* also raved about the next episode, the spy thriller "Time Bomb":

> Irwin Allen has a strong ratings contender in this one, based on second color show of the semester. In fact, the "Time Bomb" segment was strong enough to have sustained as a feature. Science aspects are believable, and color adds much. Basehart comes through strongly again, with fine assistance from Hedison, Ina Balin portrays a double-crossing spy very effectively. Leith Stevens' scoring lends a big assist to the show.

Despite this effort, *Voyage to the Bottom of the Sea* now faced hit shows on other networks (*Lassie* and *My Favorite Martian* on CBS and Walt Disney on NBC) on Sunday night instead of the game shows and sitcoms it had been up against in its season one Monday night timeslot. In the 30-City Nielsens, "Jonah and the Whale" debuted with a considerably lower rating (14.9) than "Eleven Days to Zero," but its second half hour was up to 18.4 against *Martian* and Disney. CBS' *Lassie* began beating *Voyage* in its first hour, leaving it second over NBC's *Bell Telephone Hour*; but NBC's *Disney's Wonderful World of Color* soon dominated the second half hour, leaving *Voyage* to contest with *My Favorite Martian* for second and third position. "The Phantom Strikes," with Alfred Ryder as the ghost of a WWII German U-boat commander, managed to dominate the full hour on January 16, 1966 and "The Sky's On Fire" accomplished the same feat the next week. Despite its apparent popularity, a quickie sequel episode to "The Phantom Strikes," "The Return of the Phantom," was edged out by *Lassie, My Favorite Martian* and Disney on March 20.

While *Voyage* featured a variety of dramatic, suspense, science fiction, Cold War, and espionage stories in both season one and season two, the show would soon devolve into a repetitive, monster-of-the-week format, and fans have often wondered what accounted for this apart from the pressure on the series to save money (and monster shows weren't necessarily cheap to film).

The production's own analyses of its ratings provides at least part of the answer:

> There is little correlation between monster and non-monster shows. "Escape from Venice" was an excellent show...with a ruinous rating. This bears out the conviction held by Adrian Samish that our shows must stick to the sea and stories relating directly to it.

In fact, the show runners were discovering that as far as *Voyage* went, it didn't matter whether the episodes were good or bad:

**ABOVE**
Gia Scala poses with a detailed schematic of the underwater lab featured in several episodes in this publicity photo for the "Jonah and the Whale" episode.

**LEFT**
Evocative, episode-specific promotional art was often created for the series.

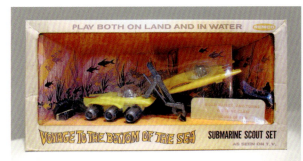

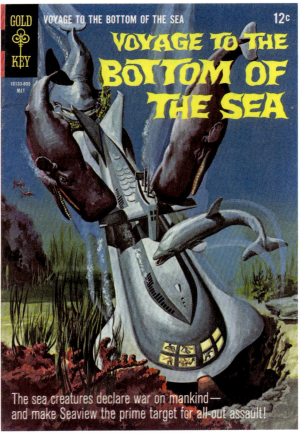

**RIGHT**
Examples of *Voyage* merchandise and product tie-ins to the show including lunchboxes, coloring books, a board game, model kits of the Seaview and Flying Sub produced by Aurora Plastics, and a set of 3D View-Master reels.

There is little correlation between well-written, well-directed, well-produced shows and high ratings. The single exception in two seasons seems to be "Sky Is Falling" which had a peak rating without any other discernible factors influencing it.

Another memo noted that "Christmas is a DISASTER for us. It is strongly urged that we try for a preemption next Christmas." Kids (and probably moms) were the show's core audience, and with them tied up wrapping and opening presents, *Voyage* lost a lot of eyeballs.

Another culprit was the show's competition:

> A comparison of the first two seasons leads to one unmistakable conclusion: *Voyage* did exceptionally well the first season until *UNCLE* came on opposite it. *UNCLE* was—until *Batman*—the best promoted show on television. In the second season *Voyage* did badly until an elaborate promotion campaign was instituted. Within four weeks of that time, ratings soared and have continued to climb. The obvious conclusion is that extensive promotion is the single greatest factor in building and maintaining a rating. A point of illustration: "Graveyard of Fear" currently has the highest rating among the episodes. It is very possible that a large part of that rating is attributable to the fact that the previous week's trailer showed the 200-year-old woman and created great curiosity and anticipation among the audience.

Allen kept his staff working as hard on promoting the series as they were on making it, and his staff of illustrators were instrumental in that effort. production illustrator George Jenson recalls:

> We would do weekly little publicity designs and promotional things for each show that Irwin would send over to the networks. He was constantly promoting his shows and working at selling, so I remember working on for instance a drawing of Rasputin for *Time Tunnel* and something about going back to the Czars of Russian during that period. So we would do these drawings and there would be a little tag line that Al Gail would write, and we would do that as well as storyboards and things.

The second season's top-rated episodes were:

| | |
|---|---|
| Graveyard of Fear | 25.2 |
| The Monster's Web | 23.3 |
| The Phantom Strikes | 21.7 |
| The Shape of Doom | 20.5 |
| Dead Men's Doubloons | 20.1 |
| The Sky's On Fire | 19.7 |
| The Menfish | 19.7 |
| The Mechanical Man | 19.5 |
| The Death Ship | 18.8 |
| ...And Five of Us Are Left | 18.7 |

Many of these shows featured spectacular miniature effects sequences and giant monsters. The lowest-rated second season episodes were:

| | |
|---|---|
| Time Bomb | 15.9 |
| Deadly Creature Below | 15.6 |
| Leviathan | 15.5 |
| The Return of the Phantom | 15.4 |

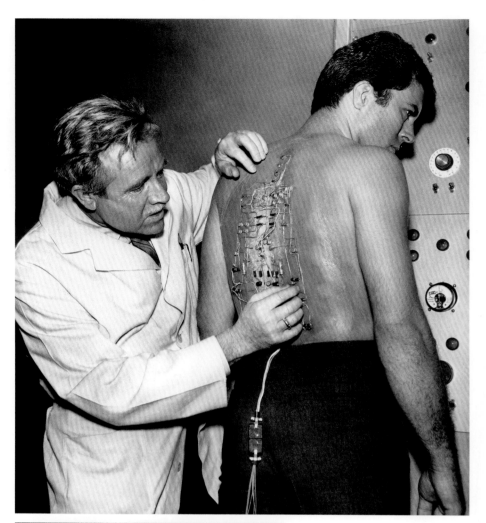

**ABOVE**
Arthur O'Connell and James Darren in season two's "The Mechanical Man,"

**LEFT**
Vitina Marcus and David Hedison in "Turn Back the Clock."

**RIGHT**
The dramatic title sequence from *Voyage to the Bottom of the Sea* season two.

| | |
|---|---|
| The Deadliest Game | 15.2 |
| The Left-Handed Man | 14.9 |
| The Peacemaker | 14.4 |
| Escape From Venice | 13.0 |
| Terror on Dinosaur Island | 13.0 |

"Deadly Creature Below" and "Leviathan" also featured spectacular miniature sequences but suffered low ratings, while "Time Bomb," "The Left-Handed Man," "The Peacemaker" and "Escape From Venice" were espionage/spy action stories, which were quickly abandoned by the series in favor of science fiction.

In 1965 Allen was hard at work launching a second science fiction series, Lost in Space. By 1966 he would soon be stretched thin with three sci-fi shows (Voyage, Space and The Time Tunnel) on the air.

For David Hedison, that wasn't necessarily a bad thing:

> In year one he was concentrating more on the thing we were doing. In year two, thank God, he did have other projects, and he left us alone. And we got some wonderful directors. I remember Leonard Horn and Sutton Roley, and a lot of terrific directors and we all sort of worked together, and Irwin left us alone. I thought year two was especially good, myself. I just thought we had some very good stories. And in year three and four I think is when it began to fall apart.

Negative costs for season two amounted to $4,259,486, with individual episode budgets ranging from a high of $191,747. ("The Return of the Phantom") to $141,240 ("The Shape of Doom")—well above ABC's original agreement for budgets of about $113,000 per episode.

Years later in a 1987 letter to Bud Grant of CBS, Allen explained how he corrected for budget overages by incorporating "one man shows" into his series, particularly Voyage with its isolated submarine setting.

> I explained the concept of the "one man show" interspersed every seven episodes...When we did this on Voyage to the Bottom of the Sea, it solved the problems of controlling overruns on the budgets. The very substantial savings made on these "one man shows" picked up the overages on the balance of the season. It worked like a charm.

It may have worked like a charm, but episodes like "The Death Ship," with Nelson, Crane, and Sharkey creeping around the Seaview with no other cast members in sight, were often torture for viewers.

Allen also plundered stock footage from his own earlier films, both Voyage to the Bottom of the Sea and The Lost World (whenever the show needed dinosaur footage), as well as earlier Fox features like The Enemy Below. He took full advantage of David Hedison's appearances in The Lost World and The Enemy Below, building an entire episode around footage from the latter film and having Hedison and Basehart separated on a Navy destroyer and the submarine it was hunting. He even employed footage of both Hedison and Vitina Marcus from The Lost World in the dinosaur episode "Turn Back the Clock." The show would also ceaselessly reuse the spectacular miniature footage of the Seaview crashing to the ocean bottom, so much so that a Voyage fan website later used "Seaview on the bottom" as part of a Voyage drinking game cue.

Variety's June, 1966 issue showed Voyage ranked as #32 of all network series, but the show was on a steady artistic and ratings decline despite Emmy awards earned by Winton Hoch and L.B. Abbott for the show's visual effects. Allen noted the show's sometimes nit-picky fan mail in a PR article:

> Lost in Space doesn't bring us a lot of mail because that series is quite some time in the future. But on Voyage, things are a little closer to today. Everything is scrutinized by the armchair admiral sitting at home, from the control room of the Seaview, right down to buttons and insignia on uniforms. But I am happy to report that so far we have yet to be caught in a technical error. That's probably because we make sure we're right before we go ahead.

A lot of the "armchair admirals" were women, again belying Allen's prior complaints that women "flee in droves" when they see the label science fiction. The female viewers were as detail-oriented in their critiques as any male sci-fi fan, as seen in this letter:

> I'm afraid there have been too many monsters lately. How can a three thousand year old mummy know anything about how to wreck the Flying Sub or how to open the doors and hatches on the Seaview? Repetition has also set in now. So far the bug-eyed monster in "Deadly Creature Below" has been on three times; there have been three whales of gigantic size that "are the granddaddy of all whales," two themes dealing with the attempted return of the Nazis, three appearances of the creature used in "The Menfish," a couple of giant jellyfish, and three episodes with ancient dinosaurs living in mist-covered seclusions. Why aren't there more episodes like "Hail to the Chief," "Long Live the King," "Silent Saboteurs," "Escape from Venice"' or "Death Watch"?

Fans didn't realize that these "good" Voyage episodes hadn't done as well in the ratings as the monster stories they reviled.

A viewer named Susan Kritzin wrote:

> You definitely lack realism. The setting of the submarine such as Seaview is real, and you should carry out this in your episodes—all of the equipment, even the flying submarine, is actually feasible, but the plot of the individual episodes often misses the boat. This really isn't too bad considering that you run out of material and it is good to use imagination. It is the smaller details that kill me. If you look for actions and phrases used by characters, you realize they are quite redundant. You can count on Crane getting knocked out about 10 times every hour, you can be sure that Nelson will say, What the devil is going on? or What in blazes is happening? and every ten minutes, the good ship loses neutral buoyancy and trim. It is really pathetic to see the sub rock back and forth so often, always with a plentiful amount of sparks and fires. I really think that's poor and so does everyone else.

Kritzin also voiced a common complaint about TV

**RIGHT**
Sharkey gets wrapped up with "The Mummy" in season three, then faces "The Shadow Man" while Captain Crane sits down with Michael Dunn's diminutive, creepy clown in "The Wax Men."

violence at the time, in which characters were knocked out or shot, only to reappear a scene or two later, no worse for the wear:

> By the way, have any of you ever been shot? Or knocked out? Contrary to your examples, someone wounded in the shoulder doesn't galavant around a submarine giving orders, saving the world, etc.

Kritzin maintained her letter was in the spirit of constructive criticism and that *Voyage* remained her favorite TV series.

Noting that they had just finished a book based on characters from *Voyage* (possibly the first TV character "fan fiction"?), viewers Sheila Efrom and Linda Oppenheimer critiqued the show's often (but not always) used designation for the sub, "SSRN Seaview":

> In doing research, we discovered that the letters SSRN were used to classify a radar picket sub at the end of World War II. The other possibility, SSNR could not be found anywhere!

The two women listed some alternate designations—SSGN for Guided Missile Sub, SSBN for Fleet Ballistic Missile Sub, and SSN for Attack Sub.

Some viewers would harshly criticize the show, then inquire whether the production was accepting scripts and where they could be submitted. Several female viewers pushed for more romance for Nelson and Crane.

Camille Lawrence wrote:

> What would save this show from a fate worse than death is this: Romantic interest! Can't you even write that? .

Jean Payne of New York agreed:

> In color the underwater scenes are just beautiful and it is my belief, along with many others that this series should continue on for a number of years. In fact, the only thing wrong with the series is that I do believe you would have more viewers if perhaps a female interest for Captain Crane could be brought in. ...many feel that a girl in the series would make ratings go even higher.

Many viewers agreed with David Hedison that the show's characters needed more dimension:

> The audience doesn't want to see monsters—they want to see MEN!

Roseanne Martin of Maryland wrote:

> What KIND of men have the courage to go down in some sub that usually sinks every week, anyway? ...who do these men work for? You've developed no concrete organization which could serve as a foundation for the show. Get rid of the monsters and build on the naval and marine aspects of the show. I believe in this show—it's got so much potential, Please save it before it's too late.

Roberta Romanoski offered:

Your actors have created some interesting characterizations. I would like to see an increase in episodes that take advantage of this fact, that develop the regular characters' relationships to their fellow crew members and to other people (women as well as men). Give humans equal time with monsters; *Voyage* will benefit from such a balance.

A woman named Edyth Middleton, writing from Columbia Pictures Corporation, summed it up:

The whole meaning of this show has a scope which you have not even scraped the surface of.

An analysis of 13 viewer letters addressed to Irwin Allen noted that all 13 were written by women—half included unfavorable comments regarding the "monsters" while four decried the lack of women and/or romance. Suggested solutions included reducing the percentage of monster segments, cutting down drastically or eliminating the use of stock (i.e., repeated footage from earlier episodes) monsters, or "seek a different visual impact for our monsters. E.g., they should not appear as humans dressed in costumes, but tend more to the 'Shadowman,' 'Plant Men' or 'Heat Monster' concepts."

Regarding the requests for more women and romance, the memo analysis was:

...The letter writers all being women, they are possibly seeking some self-identification on the screen. Our over-all ratings for the past season seem to indicate that the lack of women or romantic interest has not been detrimental to the series. However, an occasional female role could well be a plus value for our female viewers.

"*Voyage* disappointed me a little bit in that it became a monster show," production designer Bill Creber said in 1995. Creber wasn't the only one frustrated by the show's direction.

"It was a very difficult thing for Richard [Basehart]," Hedison said. "Because Richard had always done fine films, worked with good directors for the most part, and suddenly to go in and do work like this, doing a TV series, doing it in six days and working very hard, and I think when he first started it he was very sorry that he didn't—even though he was paid well."

Hedison recalled a cathartic incident that cemented his friendship with Basehart. "I remember once they sent him home, because they figured they were through with him and he went home and had a drink and was getting ready for dinner, but they called him back, because they needed him for another scene. He came back and he was very angry and irritable about it. And he suddenly walked off the set, which I knew was a dangerous thing to do in Hollywood." Hedison recalled that he chased after Basehart and wound up putting his hand through a glass door and injuring himself. "Suddenly everyone's coming to me because I got this blood all over the place. And then Richard comes on the set, and then he sees what happened and saw that I was chasing him and trying to get him. I think that's what sealed our friendship. I could see the pain that he was going through, and it was terrible. And he had a tendency to drink too much, then, and I think that got in

**LEFT**
The Seaview hits the bottom—something the sub managed to do in almost every color episode.

The two-headed hairball from "Deadly Creature Below"—one of *Voyage*'s ubiquitous undersea monsters—seen grasping the 9-inch Flying Sub miniature.

**OPPOSITE**
David Hedison in prosthetic makeup clowns on the set with some Seaview crewmen during filming of season three's "Werewolf."

Richard Basehart and David Hedison pose with their caricature puppets and frequent Irwin Allen guest star Vincent Price during filming of "The Deadly Dolls."

his way. But then towards the end he stopped and he got into Zen, and he didn't drink anymore."

The 1966-67 30-City Nielsen ratings showed the third season opener, "Monster from the Inferno," opening with an unimpressive 15.0/17.0—it was briefly beaten in the second hour as audiences sampled CBS sitcom *It's About Time*. By the next week's "Werewolf," the show was solidly back on top with an 18.7/20.5 rating and first place finish.

The analysis about the show's Christmas fortunes was correct, however—on December 11th and 18th Voyage was destroyed by airings of *A Charlie Brown Christmas* and *How the Grinch Stole Christmas* on CBS, allowing the time travel comedy *It's About Time* to beat *Voyage* in its final half hour both weeks. By the first week in January, however, the show was back on top, suffering only against CBS' annual airing of *The Wizard of Oz* (with the feeble "Shadowman") on February 12th. In national ratings *Lassie* and Disney offered stronger competition, tying or beating *Voyage* on a number of Sundays.

Season three's highest rated episodes were:

| | |
|---|---|
| Thing From Inner Space | 23.1 |
| The Terrible Toys | 22.6 |
| The Mermaid | 21.6 |
| Deadly Waters | 21.5 |
| The Mummy | 21.4 |
| Werewolf | 20.9 |
| Day of Evil | 20.9 |
| Deadly Invasion | 20.5 |
| The Haunted Submarine | 19.9 |
| The Plant Man | 19.7 |
| Death from the Past | 19.4 |

The lowest-rated were:

| | |
|---|---|
| The Deadly Cloud | 18.1 |
| Monster from the Inferno (season opener) | 16.7 |
| Night of Terror | 16.7 |
| Destroy Seaview! | 16.7 |
| The Death Watch | 16.5 |
| The Lost Bomb | 14.7 |
| Shadowman | 13.9 |
| Brand of the Beast | 11.1 |

A memo with "Suggestions for next season's *Voyage*" included ideas for handling an increasingly unhappy Richard Basehart and for addressing some viewer complaints about the series:

— All scripts be written so that Richard Basehart works only in the mornings.
— Never use the same monster twice.
— To all Directors—don't let Basehart act as though everyone else is stupid.
— Instruct Terry Becker that he is not to start examining the script and interpreting it with other actors. If possible, in a diplomatic way, tell him to stay away from Basehart if Basehart has to work in afternoons.
— Consider a different material for our scuba suits as actors find them uncomfortable and impossible to act in…and the repetitive use of scuba suits for our monsters has led to most of our monsters looking man-like and losing some of the shock value that a monster appearance should entail.

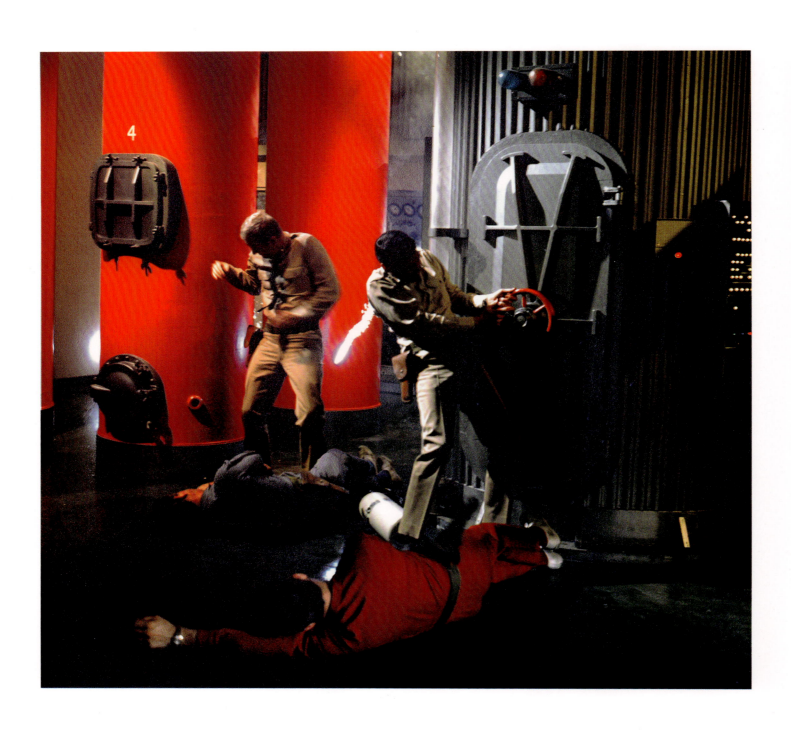

The memo summed up the situation this way:

> Unquestionably, the basic projection of *Voyage* meets with unqualified approval from our writing viewers. It is in peripheral areas that some of the adverse critique is involved with. Criticism relative to characterization of our principals and broader knowledge of their backgrounds is not too valid. The success of the series is NOT based on interpersonal relationships, inner soul-seeking or emotional conflicts. There should be, however, as a secondary theme, some emotional involvement of one or more of our principals relative to the necessity of resolving the basic story conflict. The more fantastic, bizarre, exotic and imaginative our story concepts, effects, sets and visual projection on the screen can be, the more successful the series will be. COMMENTS ON CRITICAL LETTERS: In summary, the above objections stem almost entirely from our lack of budget, making it difficult for us to get off the Seaview, to have adequate second unit underwater sequences, miniatures and occasional female roles.

The man responsible for designing *Voyage*'s numerous monsters—and for frequently sticking them inside scuba diving suits—was costume designer Paul Zastupnevich. An April 9, 1966 feature in *The New York Journal-News* profiled Zastupnevich and his work on the show, noting that he had designed the Creature from the Black Lagoon-like monsters that had appeared in "The Menfish." He told reporter Charles Witbeck:

> These underwater sequences are tricky. You just can't put an actor into a fish costume and throw him into the water. You have to construct a costume so the actor is able to regulate his buoyancy; he must be able to get rid of the necessary weights around his body in a hurry. Secondly, he needs an air hose, because we can't shoot him with a bulky air tank on his back. If the actor used a tank, air bubbles would result and ruin the whole effect. At the moment, we'll probably have the actor work a minute under water and then come up for air.

30 years later, Zastupnevich explained how limited his resources were on the series. "Irwin had to resort to a lot of recycling. He was a very ecologically-minded man. There were a lot of monsters in one show that would end up in another show and in another show, and in another color, and with another outfit on."

"That was also a question of budget," Al Gail added. "You had to make do with what you had, and Paul Zee who did most of that, was great at improvising. He would pull something from here, something from there, and there's a monster. For example we had one show particularly, the Lobster Man, which was quite popular for its time, and he created this walking lobster outfit. Very funny, with little bells running out of the head and everything else. It was one of particularly favorites of mine cause I happened to have written it."

Zastupnevich said that he was often allotted only $250 to make a costume. "Two hundred and fifty dollars to do a fish monster—that's ridiculous, because those fish scales were all done by hand. I would be in the shop gluing on the fish scales myself, showing them what I wanted in order to get it as fast as we could."

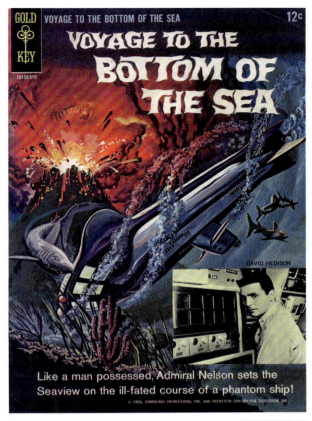

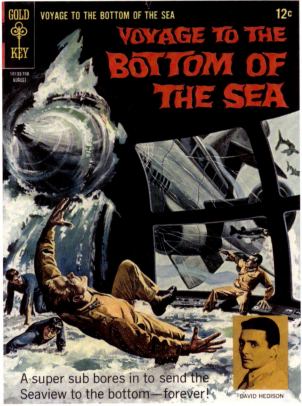

**OPPOSITE**
Bob Dowdell and David Hedison struggle through another of *Voyage*'s numerous action sequences.

**RIGHT**
Covers of Gold Key's 1964 *Voyage* comic book, issues 3 and 9.

"It wouldn't be unusual to see me coming down on the lot, [and in one] hand I would have a monster for *Lost in Space*, in the other one I'd have a monster for *Voyage to the Bottom of the Sea* or *Time Tunnel*. It got to the point where I was doing three shows at the same time, but I was only getting one salary, split among the three shows."

The *Voyage* monsters became so ubiquitous, and their voices so frequently dubbed after the on-set performances were given by stunt men, that actor Don Matheson (who would later star in Allen's *Land of the Giants*) shocked the cast by delivering a real performance inside one of Zastupnevich's monster suits. Allen had put Matheson under contract but hadn't used him since his appearance in an early *Lost in Space* episode, so he decided to give the actor a role in the *Voyage* episode "Deadly Amphibians." He recalled in 1995:

> I was a fish, an amphibian called Proto and I was a cross between a toad and a lizard. My first scene with Richard Basehart and David Hedison, Richard fell down. Because I came out of the floor of the submarine soaking wet—this fish, this apparition appears and Richard's looking at me and he thinks there's a stuntman in there and they're gonna dub—you know, somebody's gonna read the lines offstage. 'Cause no actor's gonna get in that stupid suit and go down in that water and come up. And then I started spouting these lines and I sounded like Cyrano de Bergerac. And Richard said: "God, there's an actor in there!" Then he got a little hysterical and fell down laughing. And he said, and he said, "On top of that, he knows his lines!"

*Voyage* still had some ratings mojo in its fourth season. The highest rated episodes were:

```
Time Lock.....................................21.8
Rescue .......................................19.9
Fatal Cargo...................................19.7
Cave of the Dead..............................18.7
Terror .......................................18.1
Man of Many Faces ............................17.9
Journey with Fear ............................17.6
A Time To Die.................................16.3
```

The lowest season four episodes were:

```
Lobster Man...................................14.2
Secret of the Deep............................14.1
Return of Blackbeard..........................14.0
Savage Jungle.................................13.8
Attack! ......................................13.6
Abominable Snowman ...........................13.3
No Way Back ..................................13.2
The Death Clock ..............................12.8
```

By 1968, though, both Allen and the network felt the series had run its course. David Hedison disagreed. "*Voyage to the Bottom of the Sea* was on the air for four years, had wonderful actors. It could have been on for seven or eight. And I think [Irwin] ruined it, in, in the last year or two, bringing in the fossil man, the rock man, the lobster man, the this man, the that man—it was ludicrous. I mean the show was bound to go off the air. And towards the end I thought this is gonna be the end, and sure enough, boom we were off."

Nevertheless, *Voyage to the Bottom of the Sea* remained for many years the longest-running science fiction show ever broadcast on network television, beating *Star Trek*'s run on NBC by a full year. It formed the cornerstone of what would become an impressive, if somewhat short-lived empire of television programs for Irwin Allen, and it would be a mainstay of TV syndication for years afterward. Syndication package materials for the series stated that *Voyage* pulled a 30+ share of its audience in 45 markets in the last ratings sweep of the 1967–68 season (in Augusta, Birmingham, Houston, and the Lower Rio Grande Valley the show pulled over a 50 share).

The show inspired later underwater adventure shows like *The Man from Atlantis* and Steven Spielberg's *seaQuest DSV*, and the Seaview and Flying Sub remain some of the most iconic sci-fi vehicles ever designed, inspiring countless toys and model kits.

Just as importantly, *Voyage to the Bottom of the Sea* helped establish 20th Century Fox as a production house for hit TV shows, with Irwin Allen bringing production values and special effects normally seen only in motion pictures into American living rooms week in and week out. In the lean years following the disaster of *Cleopatra*, Allen's TV shows, and Fox hits like *Batman* and *Daniel Boone*, it provided a revenue stream for the studio and helped to right what might have been a sinking ship—or submarine.

**OPPOSITE**
*Voyage to the Bottom of the Sea* merchandise on display in Allen's offices at Fox.

# MINIATURE GALLERY
## VOYAGE TO THE BOTTOM OF THE SEA

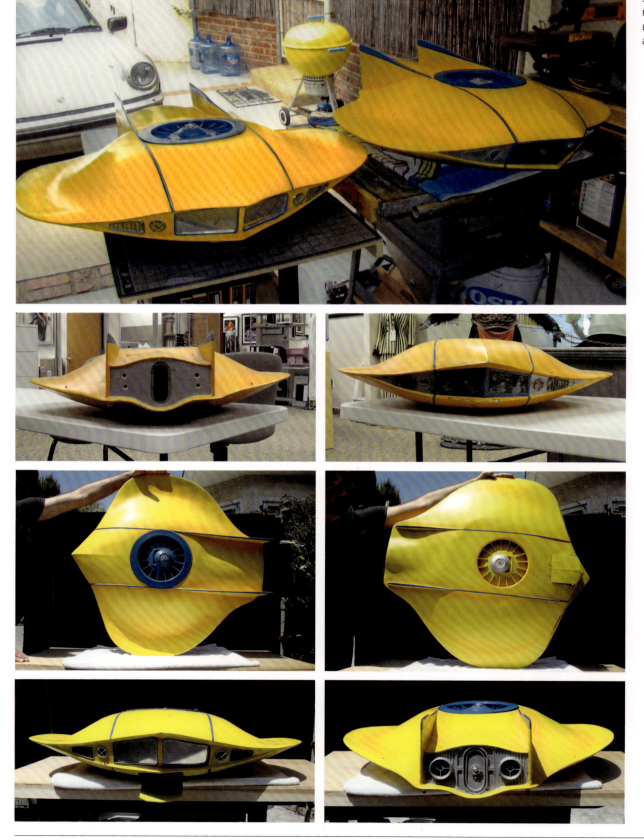

Several of the 36" Flying Sub miniatures, used in both flight and underwater sequences on the show, as they look today.

Special effects outtake of the "landing gear" 36″ Flying Sub miniature, outfitted with retractible landing gear and forward manipulator arms.

# MINIATURE GALLERY
## VOYAGE TO THE BOTTOM OF THE SEA

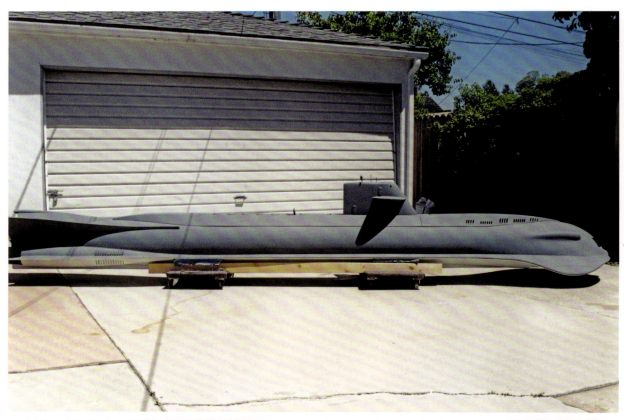

The massive, 17-foot-long Seaview miniature used for the Flying Sub launch sequences and shots of the submarine cruising on the ocean surface, seen during a restoration done by model builder Louis Zutavern in 1995, with modeler John Mauvezin shown for scale.

Special effects outtake of the 17-foot Seaview with the rubber "bubble rig" out of the water and visible in front of the miniature's bow.

The working torpedo miniature and its internal apparatus, used for the 1961 *Voyage to the Bottom of the Sea* movie and throughout the TV show.

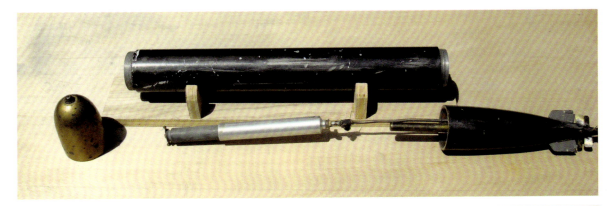

One of the Seaview diving bell miniatures.

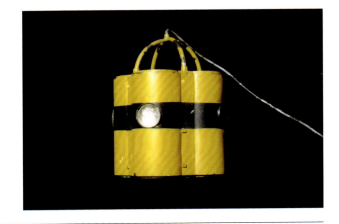

# "
# PRODUCING LOST IN SPACE IS THE FINAL FULFILLMENT OF MY TWENTY YEARS OF MAKING MOTION PICTURE MAGIC.

## IRWIN ALLEN

# SPACE FAMILY ROBINSON

LOST IN SPACE: *from adventure to comedy*

**OPPOSITE**
The cast of *Lost in Space*: (L to R): Mark Goddard as Major Don West, Marta Kristen as Judy Robinson, Billy Mumy as Will Robinson, Angela Cartwright as Penny Robinson, June Lockhart as Maureen Robinson, and Guy Williams as John Robinson.

While promoting *Five Weeks in a Balloon* in 1962, Irwin Allen announced that his next production would be *Passage to the End of Space*, from a screenplay by Charles Bennett, which would involve "11 incompatible persons accidentally fired into the wild blue in the first space transport." Allen cast Barbara Eden as one of the passengers, in what would have been her third role in a row in an Irwin Allen movie. *Passage to the End of Space* was never made—but Allen would apply a very similar concept for two different TV shows, *Lost in Space* and *Land of the Giants*.

*Lost in Space* would become Allen's most popular and iconic television program, and were it not for his later disaster films the show might be the creation for which he is most remembered today. For the first time, Allen left behind his usual assortment of scientists, military men, and the occasional entrepreneur and focused on an American family shot into space, into a strange new world where they would have to rely on their wits, their technology, and on each other to survive. This made *Lost in Space* more character-based than any of Allen's previous projects, and circumstances beyond Allen's control would conspire to make the show even more focused on character than the producer had originally planned.

The basis for the idea was Johann David Wyss' classic novel *The Swiss Family Robinson*, which had been adapted into a hit movie by Walt Disney in 1960 but was still very much in the public domain. Allen had proposed a straight adaptation of the novel to CBS, but the network already had a show about castaways on a desert island— the sitcom *Gilligan's Island*. For Allen, moving the concept in more of a science fiction direction was a natural step.

Herman Rush remembered:

> The concept of *Lost in Space* started out as a *Swiss Family Robinson* project. It was something that Irwin wanted to do and in the process of developing it, it was

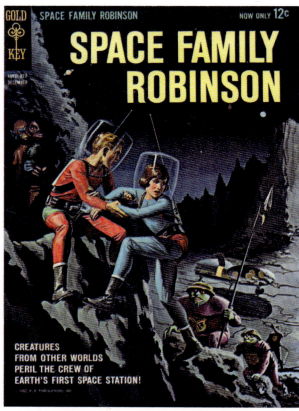

Irwin who said that he would want to take advantage of today's world and technology of space travel and move *The Swiss Family Robinson* into space. We pitched it at CBS when CBS had a relationship and a commitment to Red Skelton's company, which Guy Della-Cioppa ran. CBS said, "We can save everyone a lot of time, if you can find a way, Herman and Irwin, to make a deal with the Red Skelton company—since we have a commitment with them, it would be a step forward to getting *Lost in Space* on the air." We met with them and were compatible and worked the deal out, Guy Della-Cioppa was head of the production entity, and it fulfilled a commitment that CBS had that got *Lost in Space* on the air very quickly that year.

Since Allen had successfully launched *Voyage to the Bottom of the Sea* on ABC, why wouldn't he approach ABC to take on his second series? The reason was a policy at ABC that the network would quickly come to regret, as far as Allen was concerned.

Rush explained:

*Voyage to the Bottom of the Sea* was on ABC, and ABC's programming executive at the time, Edgar Scherick, had a philosophy that they wanted exclusivity on a producer for the first year of his show. Not exclusivity against CBS or NBC; they didn't want [Irwin] to have two shows at the same time the first year. That, for whatever reason, was never included in any contract, but that was the philosophy ABC had at the time. ABC never knew about *Lost in Space* because they never took a meeting and had a very close relationship between all the people I mentioned—Irwin, Scherick, [ABC founding chairman] Leonard Goldenson at the time. Irwin just said, "Look, you can deal with a lot of producers who are limited in what they can do. I'm not limited—I can do two series, I can do three series. I work 20 hours a day." CBS didn't have that concern and Irwin proved he could do two series. But the reason *Lost in Space* went on CBS is because ABC wanted him to wait another year before they would do a second show with him. So they lost *Lost in Space* but they ended up doing *Time Tunnel* and *Land of the Giants* within the following year.

The idea of putting *The Swiss Family Robinson* in space had been floating around more than one orbit in Hollywood in the early 1960s. Western Publications' Gold Key comics produced a comic book called *Space Family Robinson*, created by Del Connell, beginning in late 1962. The second issue, in which a cosmic storm throws the Robinsons and their Space Station One spacecraft into another section of the galaxy, was actually titled "Lost in Space." Western Publications had already engaged in licensing deals with Irwin Allen properties under their Dell Comics label, issuing comic book adaptations of *The Story of Mankind* and *Voyage to the Bottom of the Sea* as well as comics based on TV shows.

Science fiction writer Ib Melchior, who had written and directed the incredibly pulpy but entertaining sci-fi movie *The Angry Red Planet*, had created an outline for a movie he called *Space Family Robinson*. Melchior's concept shared strong similarities with what would become *Lost in Space*, but many of these (the makeup of the family, the idea of a meteor storm—as opposed to the novel's sea storm—shipwrecking the family, etc.)

**LEFT**
Gold Key's *Space Family Robinson* comics, not to be (but often) confused with Irwin Allen's TV series.

**OPPOSITE**
Early concept paintings of what would become the Jupiter 2 on its launch cradle and during lift-off—the "flying saucer" shape and launch cradle concept would survive into the final designs for the series.

derived from the original inspiration of *The Swiss Family Robinson* itself.

Writer Hilda Bohem, wife of Endre Bohem, a producer on the CBS western *Rawhide*, had also developed a concept for a theatrical movie called *Swiss Family 3000*, which was at one point taken to Irwin Allen's partner on *The Big Circus*, Steve Broidy of Allied Artists Motion Pictures. The idea was reportedly developed at the behest of a CBS executive named Bud Groskopf, but like Melchior's idea, *Swiss Family 3000* never got rolling as a movie project. Groskopf did, however, present the idea to people at CBS and, after discovering the similar *Space Family Robinson* comic book concept, optioned the comic series as a possible TV show. That didn't go forward either—CBS was open to the idea of a family in space, but not Bohem's. After seeing the success of *Voyage to the Bottom of the Sea*, however, the network was eager to get into the Irwin Allen business, and once Allen's concept was put in front of them, they proved receptive.

The characters in Allen's show would be Professor John Robinson, an esteemed scientist; his wife; several young children as well as a teenaged daughter; and a pilot and scientist, Major Don West. Over the course of the story the Robinsons would crash-land on an alien planet after their ship is thrown off course by a meteor storm, and discover a dangerous race of giant, cyclops-like monsters. Allen's early ideas for the show had the Robinson family stranded on Mars, and a great deal of research went into exploring, and eventually rejecting, that notion.

On August 3, 1964, Jodi Productions and Van Bernard Productions entered into a Joint Venture Agreement for formation of the venture under the fictitious firm name Space Productions for development of *Space Family Robinson* or *Lost in Space*. The agreement memo broke down three points about the proposed series:

> Standard prologue should be planned for each episode, illuminating the background for the viewer. How the family reached Mars. In essence, an extract from a projected first show for broadcast of approximately one minute, 30 seconds.
>
> Pilot script should be a typical episode about 10 shows into the series, rather than the first story to be broadcast.
>
> Mars as our planet offers more advantages than disadvantages. Accepted fact about Mars should be distorted (air too thin, no water, gravity variation, etc.) Our family should not wear helmets and space suits, or special weighted boots. The creatures they meet, the unusual flora and fauna, the terrain will be sufficient to create the reality of a new world. Against these we should play our people as real as possible, for viewer ease of identification and personal involvement.

The memo went on to say that the pilot should clearly delineate the characters (and that they be likable), show the family's "courage, determination, pioneer spirit," show the "orientation of the wrecked spaceship" as a permanent home with food, water, power, etc.; show examples of the Robinson's ingenuity; "reference leading to suspense potential that beings of human capability may be present on Mars"; reference to hope and possibilities for rescue but with no means of communicating with Earth and "no horror creatures or fearful weird beings in direct conflict." Friendly and benign animals, but "constant suspense of the unknown," plus "brief moments of reflective exposition—father concerned for family, mother courageous just for moments of despair, children full of spirit, Don's excitement scientifically, etc."

An early outline of the pilot story titled "The Lake of the Sun" or "No Place To Hide" and ID'd as "Episode VII" has the Robinsons landing on Mars and depicts John and Don's run-in with a giant cyclops at the weather station—in this version John Robinson (sometimes described as an "old man") tries to communicate with the giant before it attacks, arguing that it might be the last survivor of an extinct race. There's a personality conflict between the more suspicious, survival-oriented Don and the scientifically curious John, one that was papered over in the eventual filmed pilot.

In the story, young daughter Penny wanders off into an "enchanted forest" and is attacked and carried off by a giant, predatory bird, which John engages in an "aerial dogfight" in his rocket belt. The Chariot is referred to as "the amphibian"—other suggested names were the "Rover," Half-Track, Amtrack, Duck, Chariot, Stagecoach, and Phaeton. A scientist, Dr. Lessing, briefed the Robinsons before their trip and monitors some of their activities from Earth. After discovering a castle-like set of ruins (with suggestions to depict or borrow footage from sequences of Atlantis from *Journey to the Center of the Earth*), the Robinsons find a "Jules Verne-like" rocketship with the skeletal remains of three astronauts and a diary that ends with the words, "beware of…"

A later outline had the year stated as 1984 and the Robinsons' mission to Orion, but a solar storm causes them to crash-land on Mars. Teenaged daughter Judy is named Susan, and Don is threatened in the teaser by a "Martian polar bear." The Robinsons use weapons that fire bullets instead of lasers. In this version the crashed spaceship and skeletons hail from 1970.

The Original Robinson family was identified as: Alan (age 6), Penny (12), Billy (16), Susan (18), Judy (mother—"a Maureen O'Hara type"), and John ("an Eddie Albert type"). Plus Don ("a Nick Adams type").

Actors under consideration for Professor Robinson (or "Father Scientist") were Eddie Albert, Michael Rennie, Ronald Reagan(!), Dan O'Herlihy, Cornel Wilde, Joseph Cotten, James Gregory, Richard Carlson, Jose Ferrer, Rod Taylor, Dana Andrews, Barry Nelson, Ray Milland, Lloyd Bridges, Howard Duff, Leif Ericson, Brian Keith, Richard Kiley, James Mason, Leslie Nielsen, James Daly, Forrest Tucker, Warren Stevens, Richard Egan, Arthur Hill, Hugh Beaumont, Richard Anderson, Kevin McCarthy, Ray Milland, Steve Allen, Walter Matthau(!), Lee Marvin, Jack Lord, and Darren McGavin

For Maureen Robinson: June Allyson, Jane Wyatt, Mercedes McCambridge, Joanne Dru, June Lockhart, Dana Wynter, Maureen O'Sullivan, Barbara Billingsley, Jeanne Crain, Phyllis Thaxter, Betty Garrett, Anne

**OPPOSITE**

Concept paintings of the Robinson's spaceship encountering a storm of meteors, approaching Mars, and of the crash site on Mars.

**NEXT PAGE**

Concept painting of the Robinson's tracked exploration vehicle—what would become the Chariot.

185

**ABOVE**
Actors Guy Williams and June Lockhart as John and Maureen Robinson.

Angela Cartwright as Penny Robinson, and Billy Mumy as Will Robinson.

**OPPOSITE**
Concept paintings of the spacecraft passing beneath Saturn's rings and approaching a moon.

Baxter, Audrey Meadows, Rhonda Fleming, Celeste Holm, Kim Hunter, Virginia Mayo, Gene Tierney, and Joan Fontaine were considered, with 40 actresses looked at for the role overall.

Actors considered for Don West (the "Nick Adams type") were, unsurprisingly, Nick Adams, Richard Beymer, Mark Goddard, Clu Gulager, Earl Holliman, Roddy McDowall, Martin Milner, Dean Stockwell, Guy Stockwell, Russ Tamblyn, Guy Williams (obviously considered alongside the much older versions of John Robinson), Kerwin Matthews, Andy Prine, and a young actor named "Bill Shatner." Also in the mix for Major West were Robert Walker, Jr., Robert Conrad, Robert Drivas, Richard Jordan, Tony Bill, Ron Ely, James MacArthur (who'd been in Disney's *The Swiss Family Robinson*), James Darren, Martin Sheen, Burt Reynolds, and James Farentino.

For Judy Robinson: Lyn Loring, Kim Darby, Brooke Bundy, Marta Kristen, Laurel Goodwin, Susan Tyrrell, and over 30 other actresses, mostly unknowns, were considered.

Allen eventually cast Guy Williams, famous for playing TV's Zorro, as John Robinson—but he did so over the network's objections. CBS considered Williams, who was born Armand Joseph Catalano, too "ethnic" for what they had wanted to be an "all-American" lead for Allen's first family in space.

While Allen had hoped to cast Maureen O'Hara as Maureen Robinson (hence the character's name), he had liked June Lockhart for her work on the *Voyage to the Bottom of the Sea* episode "The Ghost of Moby Dick," and her wholesome familiarity from the TV hit *Lassie* made her a strong choice for the Robinson mom.

Fiery method actor Mark Goddard became Major Don West, Icelandic beauty Marta Kristen was cast as eldest daughter Judy, West's potential paramour, and *Make Room For Daddy* costar Angela Cartwright would play the younger daughter, Penny. The pilot's biggest casting coup was young actor Billy Mumy, a veteran of everything from episodes of *The Twilight Zone* to *Alfred Hitchcock Presents* and an incredibly natural, talented performer, perfect to embody the Robinson's genius-level youngest sibling, Will Robinson.

On December 2, 1964, Fox TV production manager Gaston Glass briefed William Self on the "No Place to Hide' budget: estimated at $392,142 based on black and white photography, 12 shootings days by first unit, five by second unit. This was raised to $395,270 after a change of location for the second unit. On December 28, a more detailed budget breakdown listed above the line costs for producer ($19,600), director ($10,500) and cast ($25,000) as well as $19,000 for miniatures, $5,815 for "mechanical effects and snow dressing," $15,112 for Animals and Action Devices (presumably the Chariot), $11,833 in Art Costs, and $8000 in music costs.

A press release from Jim Hardeman of CBS announced the network had ordered the pilot film for the 1965-66 season as a joint venture of Allen's Jodi Productions, Red Skelton's Van Bernard Productions, and Fox Television in

**LEFT**
Early publicity photo of Angela Cartwright as Penny Robinson, Marta Kristen as Judy Robinson, and Billy Mumy as Will Robinson. These season one costumes were never seen in color by viewers as the show would not be broadcast in color until season two.

**OPPOSITE**
Guy Williams and June Lockhart in their season one spacesuits, including John Robinson's rocket belt.

association with CBS, production to start in two weeks. Guy Della-Cioppa was production executive for Van Bernard Productions and William Self was P.E. for Fox.

"No Place To Hide" was the most expensive television pilot ever filmed at the time it was made at Fox. Allen's *Voyage to the Bottom of the Sea* pilot had taken full advantage of the standing sets and miniatures from the *Voyage* movie, as well as the abundant amount of visual effects footage shot for the feature, to reduce its costs. But for "No Place To Hide," an entire new world had to be envisioned, designed, constructed, and filmed. The Robinsons would need a spaceship as well as a fully-functioning, full-sized, convincingly futuristic rover vehicle that could operate in the desert environments the production would shoot in. They would need costumes including space suits, weapons, and at least one monstrous, inhuman adversary, all of which would have to be created from scratch.

Allen released a memo on April 13, 1964 with notes about the Robinson's spaceship, initially called the Pilgrim 1 but eventually designated the Gemini 12 for the pilot:

> [Hull] Material to be of a far-advanced mineral-metal alloy. Extremely light, heat-resistant, shock and stress resistant, many times stronger than steel and lighter than aluminum. Lift off of space ship from other planets—no gantry needed. The three retractable legs will be sufficient support for liftoff.
>
> Observation ports: Main ports in front section of control room. Three super-strength, heat-resistant glass. Total overall dimension: 13′ 6″ wide, 4′ 0″ vertical height. Automatic 'Celestial Guidance' blister located in the center and top of the ship. A 5′ 0″ diameter hemisphere, retractable and protected by a sliding metal door. Manual 'Celestial Guidance' blister—located in the top of the ship, directly in back of the larger center blister. A 3′ 6″ diameter hemisphere, retractable and protected by a sliding metal door.
>
> Propulsion: Ship to be propelled by an electro-magnetic force-field. The attraction or repulsion of the electric charges of other planets and electric fields in outer space will govern the speed or stopping power of the ship. Force-field generated by a self-contained super-magna-pressure steam circuit, powered by a multi-plane, atomic reactor engine.

Art director Bill Creber worked out the design of the saucer-shaped spacecraft and its interior to Allen's specifications. "I'm sure in discussions with Irwin, what he wanted was a saucer and that's what we designed," Creber said in 1995. "I drew it up just as sections of a column, and I realized that it needs some subtlety to it so we added a little bit of curve to the surfaces, and I thought it made it a little bit more appealing."

The ship as designed for the pilot had a single deck and a larger forward window, which was illuminated from behind on some versions of the miniature. For the series, the saucer shape was refined, the forward window was reduced in size, illuminated from within, and equipped with scale human figures, an approach Allen continued from the *Voyage to the Bottom of*

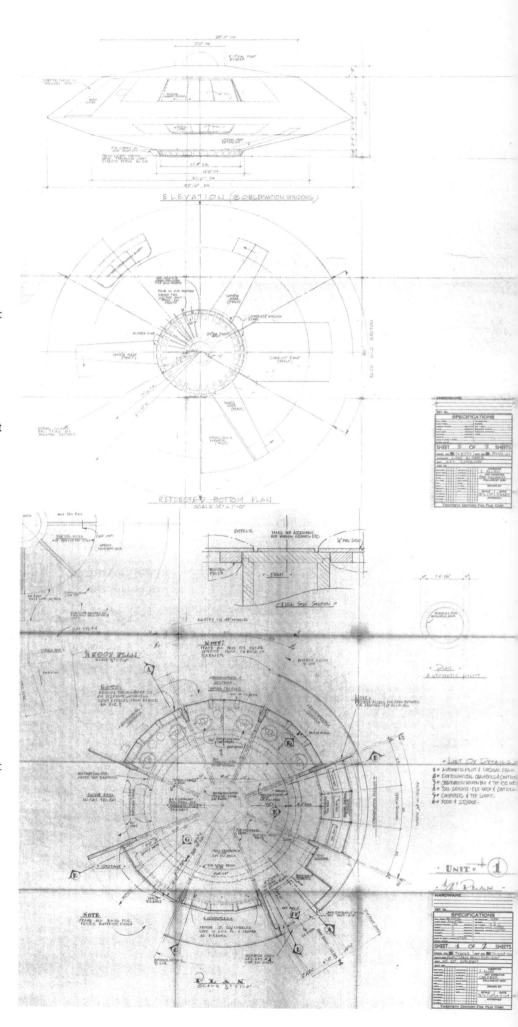

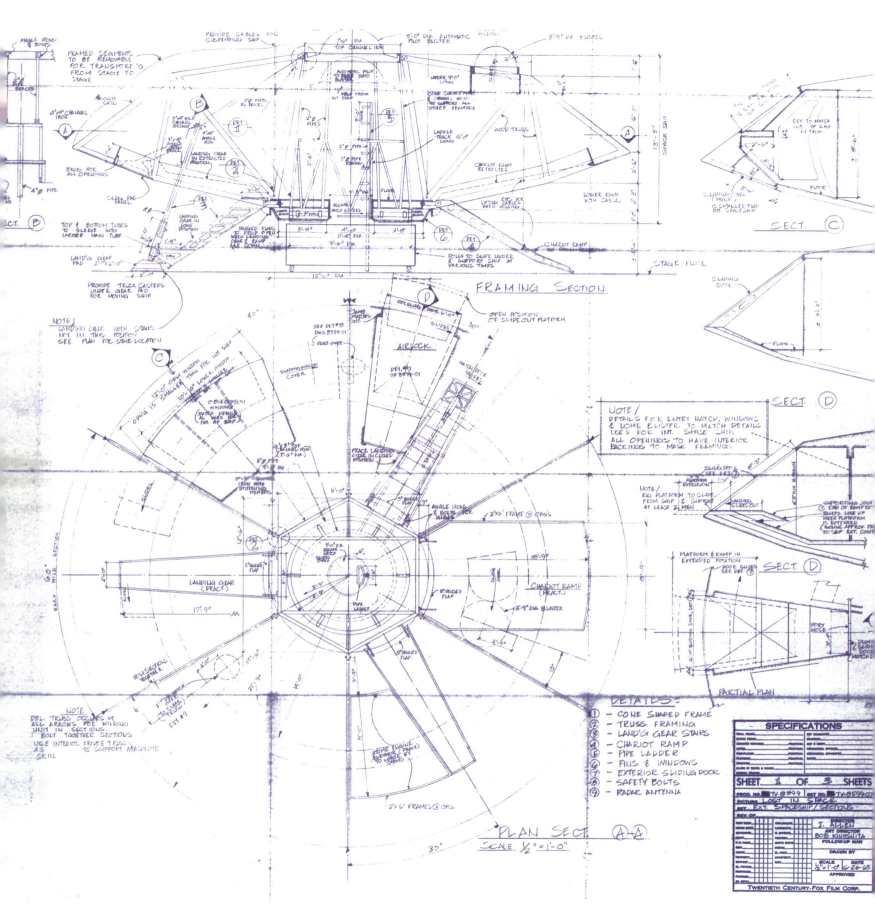

**ABOVE & OPPOSITE**
Construction blueprints for the full size Jupiter 2 spacecraft as it would appear on the series.

*the Sea* Seaview. This gave the viewer an immediate sense of scale and instantly placed the characters in relationship to the vehicle, even in exterior sequences where miniatures were employed. "He wanted windows like the sub in *Voyage to the Bottom of the Sea*, so you know that's the way we worked. The biggest problem was it had to hold the whole crew and it had to be pretty sizable for that reason."

Creber and Robert Kinoshita designed the ship's underside with a nod to both functionality and futurism, with a definite influence, unconscious or not, from *Forbidden Planet*'s C57-D space cruiser. Three landing legs would extend from the bottom of the hull, with steps for the Robinsons to descend. To indicate the generation of the "electro-magnetic force field," Creber had a disc-shaped extension ringed with rectangular, transparent ports and interior lights rigged to create the illusion of a spinning interior light source. "Irwin wanted something moving," Creber says. "Like most things in a movie, the director can have an idea and can insist on it and Irwin always liked blinking lights—he didn't care whether it made sense or not, and he was really into color."

Creber faced an even bigger challenge with the Robinson's rover vehicle, now designated the Chariot, which would have to be constructed in a full-size, operating version that would be able to transport the Robinsons, and in two miniature renditions. "We needed some kind of a lunar vehicle that would appear to work, and I had remembered working on a film up in Mammoth, these Thiokol wide-treaded snow vehicles, and it so happened that I saw an ad or something for one —it was very cheap—it was like twelve hundred dollars or something. We got it and tried it and I think we ended up getting a new one cause that one didn't have the strength and power, and we just put a cab on it."

Illustrator George Jenson was hired by Fox in November of 1964 along with Joe Musso, and Jenson found himself shifted from work on features to Allen's art department during a slowdown at the studio. Jenson would join illustrators Tom Cranham, Roy Alexander and others to work on the Irwin Allen TV shows. Jenson and his fellow illustrators worked under the various art directors that would oversee the design of the television productions, designing some of the most futuristic sets, vehicles and props ever seen on television at the time. "There was Rodger Maus and Bill Creber and Bob Kinoshita," Jenson says. "There wasn't a lot for these guys to draw from—in those days there wasn't that much research for that type of design, and a lot of the great stuff came along later, in *Space Odyssey* and *Star Wars*."

Creber, Howard Lydecker, and assistant director Jack Aldworth took a crew to Red Rock Canyon, north of Los Angeles, in mid-December, 1964, to scout locations for miniature photography of the Robinson spacecraft plummeting toward a crash landing among the bizarre rock formations of an alien planet, and the attack on the Chariot by a towering cyclops creature. The Lydecker brothers had achieved an impressive level of realism on their previous miniature work by shooting outdoors in natural light, and Red Rock Canyon boasted a landscape of small rock columns and peaks that

**LEFT**
The Chariot, on the soundstage at Fox and on display on the lot in 1968.

**RIGHT**
Shooting the operating Chariot vehicle at the Trona Pinnacles.

(Top left) The camera truck used to film the moving background plates for views through the front and rear windshield of the Chariot. The man wearing what appears to be a police chief's hat is L.B. Abbott; Irwin Allen is seated in front of Abbott, nearer the camera, and wearing a light jacket and hat.

scaled perfectly to the spacecraft and rover miniatures that were planned (the Lydeckers had shot miniature effects for the Commander Cody serial *Radar Men from the Moon* there in 1952).

"It was an amazing place—a lot of this stuff was shot out there," Creber said of the location and the show's miniature work. "An interesting phenomenon was that the parts where erosion occurred were miniaturized already. What looked like a 100 foot cliff would be two feet high. So you could scale a miniature right against actual rocks that were really built almost the right size. The crash of the Jupiter was shot out there and [several years later] we shot the full scale ship for *Beneath the Planet of the Apes* there, for raw desert strata."

Since the rover miniatures hadn't been finished yet, Creber and Lydecker brought a 1940s, 1:12 scale automobile miniature and blocked out the cyclops attack just by shooting a man standing over the model car. After the location scouting on December 22, the crew returned to the location the following day to shoot sequences involving the miniature rover and the rocket belt. The prop department constructed dummy versions of Penny Robinson and her pet "Bloop"—a chimpanzee-like creature played by a live chimp—for a sequence in which John Robinson uses his rocket belt to transport Penny and the Bloop out of a canyon after she becomes lost.

The "rocket belt" was a real device created by Bell Aerosystems. Writer Shimon Wincelberg noted in 1995:

> A person could actually fly, twenty or thirty feet, rocket propelled, and I made sure to make the maximum use of that device. I've never seen it used anywhere since and I imagine it must have been much too dangerous, cause you have a guy who has got all this rocket fuel burning right behind his back, and I guess it must have been a problem with fuel running out too soon.

The full size rocket belt scenes, and the bulk of the footage of the full size chariot vehicle, would be shot at Trona Pinnacles near San Bernadino, California, with Jim Haynes driving the Chariot and Bob Courter designated as "Rocket Pilot" along with two unnamed rocket belt engineers.

To create the cyclops, the production cast 260-pound Los Angeles Rams defensive end Lamar Lundy. Costume designer Paul Zastupnevich designed the creature to look like something halfway between animal and vegetable:

> The most fabulous monster that I did was the one-eyed cyclops, and that was made out of palm tree bark. I was walking along the street at Fox and they were trimming the palm trees, and I happened to bend over and pick up part of the bark that had come off, and I played with it and I said, "Gee, this looks so strange and so foreign, it would make a wonderful costume." So I went back to my office and I took a hammer and I pounded it, and made it very flexible, then I sprayed it with some fire retardant and found that it even got softer. I found out there were about three truckloads of palm leaves that they had just gathered up so I had them take it down to the staff shop and I had the paint department process it, and fire proof it, and then we

**ABOVE**
The Gemini 12, with its larger forward windows indicating a single deck layout, on its launch pad as seen in "No Place To Hide."

The 48-foot Jupiter 2 prop constructed with landing gear extended. For this sequence in "Island in the Sky," a mound of soil was built up around the landing gear to create the terrain for the crash landing site. In later episodes a much more flat stage set and a grounded, permanent replica of the Jupiter 2's upper hull was constructed.

The 4-foot miniature of the Jupiter 2, flown on wires in front of a painted sky backdrop at Fox.

**OPPOSITE**
A view of the Gemini 12 crash site set from the pilot, showing the slab-sided construction of the spaceship.

**ABOVE**
*Lost in Space*'s "Debbie the Bloop" rides a prop alien turtle created for the pilot.

**OPPOSITE**
(Clockwise from top) John Robinson in his rocket belt—a real rocket belt developed by Bell Aerosystems, and piloted on location at the Trona Pinnacles near San Bernadino, California by pilot Bob Courter.

The real Bell rocket belt on display today at the Smithsonian Institution in Washington D.C. Photos courtesy Gene Kozicki.

Angela Cartwright, the chimpanzee "Bloop" and Guy Williams on a camera crane in front of a rock formation constructed at Fox—the crane was used to create the illusion of John Robinson flying in his rocket belt for close shots.

got it back up wardrobe and we sewed it over a union suit and we made the cyclops outfit out of that.

After Christmas, another Red Rock Canyon location shooting was scheduled for Sunday, December 27th, with the director and AD, cameraman Gene Polito, Irwin Allen, Bill Creber, production illustrator Maurice Zuberano, and 20 other crew members including two camera operators, two prop makers (Robert Frazier and Sid Jacobs), and an effects man. Shots for both the full-size Chariot and the "rocket belt" were planned, although it's likely these were ultimately done at the Trona Pinnacles. Second unit director Sobey Martin (who would later become a full-fledged director on all four of Allen's TV shows) directed these scenes, as well as the scenes of the Giant attacking the Chariot and menacing John and Don in a cave. Doubles for the cast sat inside the full size chariot for its scenes.

"No Place To Hide" commenced first unit shooting with the cast at Fox on January 6. While the pilot was shooting, the Fox lot was busy with numerous other productions including the Doris Day comedy *Do Not Disturb*, Richard Fleischer's ambitious science fiction thriller *Fantastic Voyage*, the Fox TV series *Peyton Place*, the *Voyage to the Bottom of the Sea* episode "The Saboteur," a pilot for *The Legend of Jesse James*, directed by Don Siegel, the *12 O'Clock High* episode "The Threat" (plus music scoring for the show on Stage 1), and the *Daniel Boone* episode "The Devil's Four."

Meanwhile L.B. Abbott, Ralph Hammeras and Howard Lydecker continued filming miniature effects for "No Place To Hide" in the Lower Moat on the Fox lot, including shots of the rover Chariot entering and leaving the shores of an inland sea, shots of it traversing the ocean surface and being caught in a massive whirlpool.

The first day of first unit shooting on the *Lost in Space* pilot started with the interior of the spaceship and the meteor storm sequence, and the establishing footage for the matte shot of the spaceship and camp with four ostriches, the bloop, a turtle, and the Chariot. Also to be filmed was Will racing off with a laser gun to defend John and Don from the Giant. On the second day the Robinsons were to prepare the Chariot for their journey south only to discover Penny missing, and the sequence of John returning on his rocket pack with Penny and the Bloop.

The third day, January 8, involved shooting at the Fox Moat, with Penny riding an alien turtle and John Robinson arriving in his jet pack (designated as "the scooter" on the schedule). A Chapman Crane was required to lower Robinson, attached to the crane by wires, in the jet pack (this technique was used for any scene of Guy Williams landing or taking off in the jet pack, while the location shots of the real jet pack operating with a pilot were used for wide shots of the jet pack in action).

The same day, the production moved to Stage 15 to shoot the Chariot emerging from the storm and being inspected by John and Don. The day continued with Judy and Don trapped inside a "tomb" in the catacombs of a lost alien city, and John cutting through the wall with his laser gun, their escape, and the earthquake inside

199

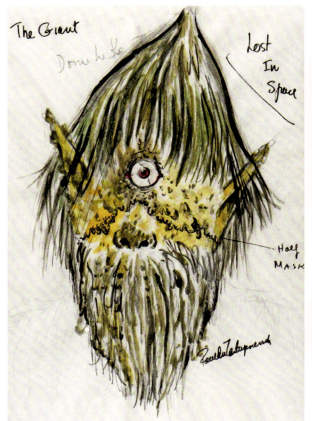

**LEFT**
Costume designer Paul Zastupnevich's original sketch for the cyclops monster seen in "No Place To Hide" (and later incorporated into the first season episode "There Were Giants in the Earth").

The cyclops on location shooting at Red Rock Canyon.

**OPPOSITE**
The cyclops monster with the large scale Chariot miniature, completing the shot blocked out with a miniature car during location shooting.

the ruins. Another scene refers to "finding strange seeds that bloom in Will's pocket"—but it's unclear if this was actually filmed.

On January 11th the crew began filming scenes in the "Underground Communications Center" (later designated Alpha Control) with an Earth TV commentator (played by announcer Don Forbes, who had narrated Allen's *The Sea Around Us* and played TV reporters and commentators in various Allen projects including *A Girl in Every Port* and *The Lost World*) as well as commentators from other nations (Allen's assistant and costume designer Paul Zastupnevich played a Russian commentator) and nearly 50 other military and scientific personnel.

January 12th continued shooting inside the catacombs with Will and Penny locked into a tomb with a horrifying mummy and a reverse angle of John cutting through the wall with his laser.

January 13th shooting entailed John and Don climbing up to the weather station and getting trapped by the Giant on Stage 15. The "enchanted forest" scene involved John in his rocket belt being grabbed out of the air by the Giant, shooting the Giant with his laser gun, and escaping as the Giant falls. This scene was shot but never finished: a detailed miniature of John Robinson and the jet pack were constructed for cyclops actor Lamar Lundy to grab, and a sequence of John buzzing the Giant in his jet pack was filmed using forced perspective of the cyclops and the real rocket belt operator in the air behind him.

The rest of the day involved shooting the president making his announcement to the people of the world, and John and Don checking the weather station instruments and finding the footprints of the Giant on the plateau.

Day seven (January 14th) involved shooting the Chariot breaking down and stopping, and the Robinsons making camp and a camp fire at night on Stage 15.

Day eight (January 15th) was shot at the Moat "equatorial jungle" for the coda of the pilot with the Robinsons setting up camp in a jungle while hidden aliens spy on them. After that the crew shot Will Robinson meeting John and Don after he slays the Giant with his laser pistol.

Day nine (Monday, January 18th) was shot on the spaceship interiors with the Robinson party entering the ship's freezing tubes and being frozen for space travel.

Day 10 involved John and Don hiding from the Giant in a cave and the Giant using a "tree-trunk battering ram" to probe at them, Maureen looking up at the spaceship camp to see John and Penny's arrival via jet pack, and the family searching for Penny before John goes out in the jet pack to find her.

Day 11 was one of the most arduous days for the actors w were placed inside the Chariot on rockers and a gimbal and sprayed with water dump tanks while Don attempts to repair the Chariot's antenna power source in the middle of the whirlpool, with a process screen in the background to play miniature effects of the storm.

**LEFT**
For a sequence shot, but never used in the show, football player Lamar Lundy suited up as the cyclops and played cat and mouse with a miniature of John Robinson flying around him in the rocket belt—and eventually caught.

RIGHT
June Lockhart as Maureen Robinson, preparing to be placed in suspended animation in one of the Jupiter 2's freezing tubes.

The final day of shooting was equally ambitious, with more process shooting of the Robinsons inside the Chariot racing past a balancing rock, developing engine trouble moving through an electrical storm to a cave opening, being attacked by the Giant, and Don emerging from the Chariot roof to fire a laser rifle at the creature.

Once finished, "No Place To Hide" cost almost $600,000, around double the original budget estimate. As a point of comparison, the budgets for the other pilots shot at Fox that February were *The Legend of Jesse James* at $265,000, *Sally & Sam* for $154,000, *The Long Hot Summer* at $325,000, *My Island Family* for $225,000, *Heaven Help Us* for $150,000, *You're Only Young Twice* at $191,000, *Take Her, She's Mine* at $160,000, *Mr. Belvedere* for $168,000, and *Go Fight City Hall* at $156,000. "No Place To Hide" cost almost twice as much as the next most expensive dramatic pilot, and around four times the cost of the more inexpensive comedy pilots.

Fox executives expressed some concerns over the costs, but Allen's pilot seemed worth the money.

Herman Rush explained the studio's attitude:

There were always concerns about the costs no matter what it would be. Most of Irwin's shows that had technology and miniatures and that kind of action were expensive shows. The networks knew that and Fox knew that—Fox supported that, they wanted to be on the cutting edge of that kind of programming, and the networks negotiated the best they could to keep the license fee reasonable and realistic. We used to get in those days something we referred to as breakage, where you had a negotiated license fee in X amount, and then certain items including the extra special effects were added as breakage and you got the license fee plus reimbursement for those additional expenses. So *Lost in Space* and *Voyage to the Bottom of the Sea* were both expensive shows as opposed to doing *Perry Mason* or *Dick Van Dyke*—they broke the walls of the studio down, they did location shooting, and it did increase the costs, and both the network and Fox were supportive of such increases, and they proved to be correct—it not only got them high ratings, it brought longevity to both those series.

"No Place To Hide" was worth the expense, and impressed CBS enough for the network to buy the series for the Fall, 1965 season. By April, Allen and his staff were working on upgrading the pilot sets and miniatures to expand the scope of the spacecraft, now designated the Jupiter 2, turning it from a single deck ship to one that would contain a lower deck and, in later seasons, even reference a third "power core" level. Basic sets would be the Interior Spaceship Control Center and Int. Spaceship Lower Deck, Interior & Exterior Chariot (tracked vehicle would be available to shoot for exterior scenes on the stage and a process mockup chariot would be mounted on a gimbal with a 16-foot process screen behind it). The Exterior Spaceship set would be adjacent to a large blue screen backing for sequences of space walks outside the ship as well as the basic cyclorama set which would also be used to develop other exterior spaces per story requirements. Allen contemplated at least nine different changeovers in the first five segments. The cyclorama set would be available for miniature shooting but Allen noted that stage 7 or 12 could also accommodate the miniatures.

Art director Robert Kinoshita, who had designed Robby the Robot for the 1956 science fiction epic *Forbidden Planet*, worked to upgrade the sets and miniatures after Bill Creber departed for other Fox projects (although Creber would continue to do work for the show from time to time).

An April 14 spaceship design concepts memo called for a one-man elevator...

> ...To service the lower deck, control room and the manual "Celestial Guidance" blister in the ceiling of the control room, powered by a "force-field" platform which is contained in a 42" diameter plastic tube. Atomic engine elevator—an airtight, cable-operated platform, which is actually both the floor of the engine room in the lower deck and a part of the lower portion of the space ship, to be operated by gravity for opening and motorized cables for lifting. [*This was a concept also utilized on the saucer-shaped* Forbidden Planet *spacecraft C-57D*]

The memo also called for a Chariot elevator-ramp, a "drive-on" type of metal ramp for the half-dismantled chariot.

The Jupiter 2 would have:

> ...One main entrance hatch, located in pan, 45 degrees to the right of the main control panels in the control room. Exits to the exterior of the ship will be made thru a tube-like airlock. Escape Hatches—36" diameter hatch with retractable metal ladder located in the center and bottom of the ship on the exterior side, interior side through sliding metal door in the lower extension of the inter-floor elevator. A 30" square hinged door in the sleeve of the retractable manual celestial guidance blister. Gravity in outer space: Interior of the space ship, artificial gravity created by a force field. Exterior of ship, no artificial gravity, crewmen to use magnetic boots when walking on exterior of ship. Set construction: double-hulled like a submarine for protection against air leaks or structural defects and to insulate the inner hull.

Conceptual memos discussed whether the Robinsons would sleep in the suspended animation tubes, on conventional mattresses, whether beds would be multi-use, slide out, etc., and even whether the Robinsons would use "powder baths" (beeswax smoke), or blue light baths for washing and bathing, as well as the idea of concentrated food and an "electro-revitalizer" oven, as well as water recycling and repurification.

One question that continually cropped up after the show became popular was exactly how large the Jupiter 2 was and how it was able to contain multiple leveled living areas, not to mention the Chariot (which at least one script line noted as having to be "assembled," although plans for the full-size ramp that the vehicle could drive down out of the Jupiter 2 were made and a 10-foot miniature with this feature was partially constructed, though never finished or filmed). An April 15, 1965 memo on "Spaceship Dimension Scales" indicated that even the "full-sized" exterior set of the Jupiter 2 was not necessarily meant to be taken at face value as an indication of the spacecraft's size. A notation indicated, "Theoretical overall dimension: 80 feet," almost twice the size of the 48-foot shooting set. Other dimensions listed:

> Full size shooting sets:
> — Interior control room/lower deck—40" diameter;
> — Exterior spaceship in cyclorama set—50" diameter;
> — Miniatures—48" diameter, 13" diameter.

Art director Bill Creber acknowledged that the operating dimensions of the Jupiter 2 were never concrete, nor were they intended to be:

> That question comes up all the time—where did you put the rover vehicle? Where was the space for that? We just went straight forward and did what we could, what was asked of the pilot and solved the script requirements and as it became more obvious that they needed more space, they just added it. We did our budget's worth and it wasn't in the script, and nobody said, "Gee, this thing should be two stories high." It was probably closer to being fanciful than factual. They so conveniently landed on a planet that had oxygen and didn't have the gravity problems and a lot of the things that you would, odds on, encounter. [Irwin] was telling a story I think more about people and their adventures and relationships than he was trying to depict any scientific situation.

The production spent an additional $133,845.00 revising the main deck of the Jupiter 2, constructing the new lower deck, building out the base camp and cyclorama set, repairing and painting the Chariot, and creating special translite backings for views outside the Jupiter 2's viewports. $35,500.00 of this was spent on building a full-sized mockup of the Jupiter 2 mounted on its three extended landing legs, a prop that was to include "a hydraulic ram to activate Celestial Guidance Dome and Manual Guidance dome."

After spending so much money on sets, visual effects and props for the pilot, Allen cannily planned to amortize those expenditures by utilizing the pilot's major visual set pieces throughout four of the first five episodes of the series: "The Reluctant Stowaway,"

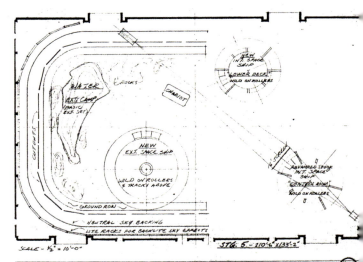

which would depict the Jupiter 2's launch from Earth and its encounter with a meteor storm, "Island in the Sky," which would have John Robinson lost in a spacewalk and the Jupiter 2 crash-landing on an alien planet; "There Were Giants in the Earth," which would show the space family's encounters with the towering cyclops monsters, and "The Hungry Sea," which would show the Robinsons fleeing a deadly heat wave by traversing an inland sea in the Chariot. The episodes, and ensuing ones in the series, would be tied together by "cliff-hangers" right out of classic movie serials, with each episode ending with the Robinsons in some terrifying danger, only to have the action stop and a "To Be Continued...Next Week!" title shown, so that viewers would have to wait until the next week to see the situation resolved.

Shimon Wincelberg, who'd written "No Place To Hide" with Allen, said in 1995:

> I think that was Irwin's idea. And because I had so much material on the first pilot, far more than could possibly be accommodated in one hour, he got the idea of chopping it up and using the special effects and sets we had for the pilot and spreading it out over six episodes, and that worked out very well.

Shimon Wincelberg had set up story elements in "No Place To Hide" that were intended to lay down an ambitious mythology for the series that would trap the Robinsons between battling factions—the primitive cyclops giants and a race of secretive, devious, human-sized aliens, on their new world. Wincelberg's story outline for the pilot indicated, "family remains unaware that their refuge is also occupied by scattered survivors of super-intelligent race, whose civilization has been destroyed by the giants. Living as fugitives, survivors of super-race have become cunning, malevolent, cowardly, treacherous, and clearly intend to deal with these intruders as soon as they can safely get away with it." When the Robinsons discover the underground "lost city" and its catacombs in the pilot, barely glimpsed hieroglyphs on the walls actually spell out this mythology.

Wincelberg also had the Robinsons discovering a wrecked spaceship on the other side of the inland sea: "Dead pilot's log book suggests he had been forced to

**ABOVE**
The full-size Jupiter 2 mockup on the Fox lot.

Stage 5 layout for the standing Jupiter 2 exterior and interior sets.

**RIGHT**
Blueprints for artwork to be discovered within the ruins of an ancient city that would hint at the relationship between the cyclopean giants and an advanced race of aliens on the Robinsons' planet—sophisticated concepts that were dropped in favor of more internalized threats for the space family.

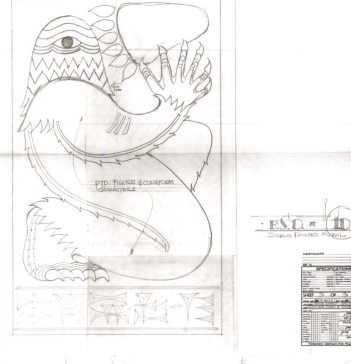
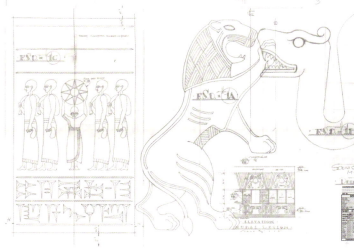

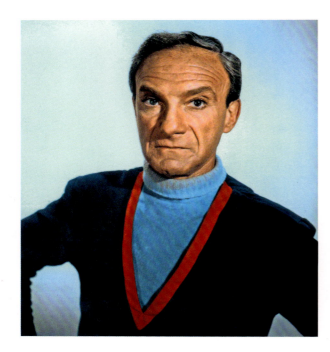

aid in escape of small band of international super-criminals, masterminded by 'The Baron.'" This places the Robinsons between the alien super-intelligent race and the criminals, and after Judy wanders off after a fight with Don she's kidnapped by the Baron and his gang. "Not being equipped with the new super-weapons carried by Don and Robinson, the Baron is forced to employ subterfuge, treachery, blackmail and an assortment of traps, and his primary use for Judy is as bait for capturing the chariot."

At the end of the pilot, as the Robinsons pray near an alien jungle, in thanks for their deliverance from the threats they've faced, two mysterious, bald-headed aliens observe them in secret—presumably members of the devious, super-intelligent race referenced in Wincelberg's outline. However these particular aliens were never seen again in the regular run of the series.

Ultimately, all of the ambitious ideas for the series listed above were dropped, but some of the concepts for a devious antagonist for the Robinsons found their way into the show through another venue. One of the keys to expanding the pilot's action set pieces into full-fledged episodes was the addition of two new characters to the series' concept—characters that would help to radically shift the focus and tone of the show over the next three years.

The first was Dr. Zachary Smith, introduced as a foreign spy who sabotages the Jupiter 2, causing the spacecraft to deviate from its planned course and become lost in space. Shimon Wincelberg recalled that newly hired story editor Anthony Wilson came up with the idea for Smith:

> Smith came in as a virtual afterthought. We were [preparing to go into production on the series] and Tony Wilson [said] why don't we bring in a character somewhat like Long John Silver, who would be kind of a treacherous, hitchhiking fellow traveler whom they couldn't get rid of, and who was full of ideas for mischief and who also formed a relationship where he was more of a father figure for the little boy than the father was, who was pretty straight. And I immediately saw the value of this, and wrote another draft of the script. At first I had kind of an exotic name for Dr. Smith, something like Asgart, a name out of Nordic mythology. I was always doing research in books like that. And again Irwin said "No, call him a straightforward American name," and I called him Dr. Smith, and I think he was right about that.

To play Dr. Smith, Allen originally sought actor Carroll O'Connor, now known for playing the dim-witted, bigoted Archie Bunker on Norman Lear's classic sitcom *All in the Family*, as well as the lead role in the later drama *In the Heat of the Night*. In the 1960s, O'Connor was more of a chameleon-like character actor akin to Peter Ustinov, particularly in his appearances on Allen's shows like *Voyage to the Bottom of the Sea* and later *The Time Tunnel*. But O'Connor didn't want to be tied to a weekly TV series at the time, and eventually Allen turned to actor Jonathan Harris for Smith.

The character brought an instant, ongoing and affordable sense of conflict to the series, which would otherwise have had to continue to provide a variety of expensive, external threats to the Robinsons—monsters, aliens, and natural phenomena. With Smith as a constant foil, these external threats were still introduced, but the focus remained on Smith and the Robinsons and the way these external forces engendered conflict between the stowaway and the space family. Smith started as a menacing character, but Wincelberg originally wrote him as even more dastardly:

> I created a Dr. Smith, who was really kind of a vicious villain, and Irwin didn't okay that and I think he was right. And what we came up with finally was a comic villain. It was two totally different characters, and fortunately we went with the better one.

Jonathan Harris had his own ideas for the character, and if there was perhaps a hint of comic villainy in the show's early episodes, Harris made certain that Smith would become a full-blown comic foil by the time the pilot episode's footage was used up and the series began producing complete episodes.

Harris said in 1995:

> [Smith] was written as a deep-eyed snarling villain, and he bored the shit out of me, because there is no longevity in deep, dark, snarling villainy. And already I started to plan what I was gonna do about that. I did not like that man—Dr. Smith, as written. Because of my expertise and my experience, which is of course *vast*, I knew that in four or five shows he'd be killed off, and then I'd be jobless again, which is very boring. Villainy is easy. I played many villains in my time, and my most successful villains have been comedic villains—and I knew that. So I started to plan what to do. And I began to sneak it in, and Tony Wilson, the story editor, knew what I was up to, and talked to Irwin, and I must say, Irwin not only allowed me to do that but one day said, "Do more." And I did. And the rest as we say is history. I loved that character. I created him, from nothing—he was not on the page. And of all the many myriad characters that I've played in my life, he surely is the favorite.

**LEFT AND OPPOSITE**
Late addition Jonathan Harris as Dr. Zachary Smith, depicted as a dangerous, military spy in early episodes (opposite), and later as a cowardly, buffoonish foil for the Robinsons (left).

206

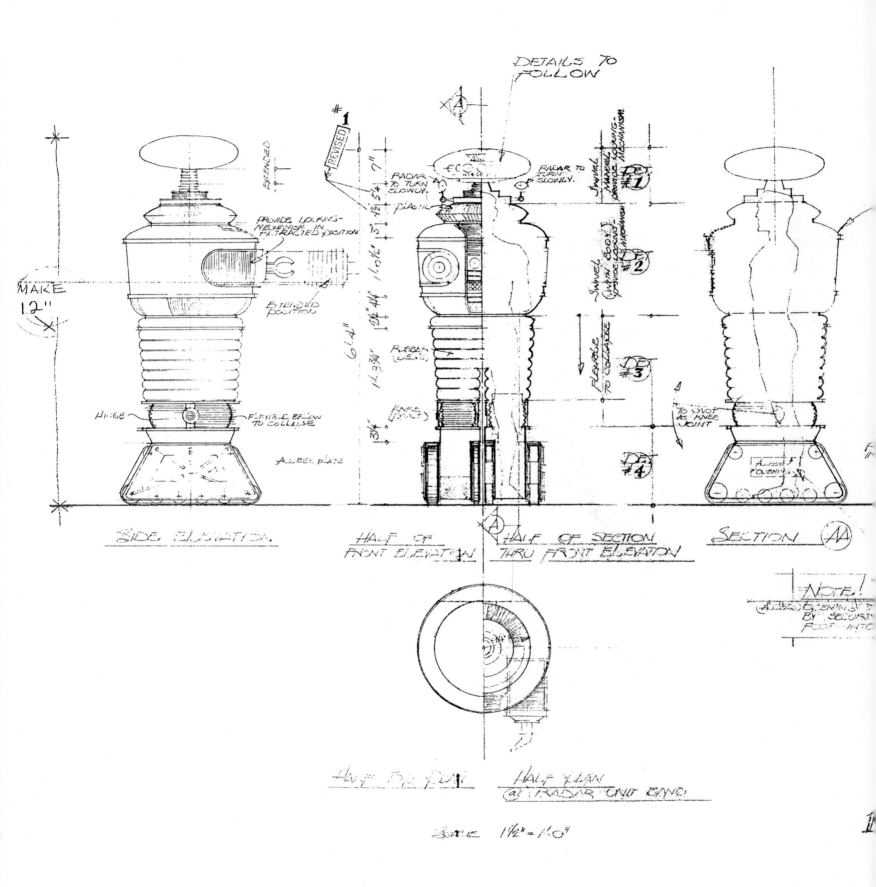

**ABOVE**
Blueprints for the Robinson's "environmental robot," designed by Robert Kinoshita.

From the first few episodes of the show, Smith's relationship with the first suspicious, then sympathetic and loyal Will Robinson character played by Billy Mumy, began to fulfill Anthony Wilson's concept of a "Long John Silver" who would increasingly become a kind of father figure to Will.

Harris recalled:

> I had Billy Mumy to play with, and what fun that was. He was eleven, twelve, something like that, and already a brilliant actor, and it was marvelous to have that relationship. Billy was straight as a die you know, very serious, and I was Christ knows where, from time to time—up in the air flying or, whatever.

The second additional character wasn't human. A tread-mounted, bubble-topped "environmental robot" was designed by Robert Kinoshita, utilizing some of the same design approaches he had incorporated into *Forbidden Planet*'s Robby the Robot (like the extending, accordion-pleated arms, forward torso control panels, and clear upper bubble "head"). The Robot cost $36,000 to construct and reportedly weighed 275 pounds.

Like Smith, the Robot was originally intended as a menacing character, programmed by Smith to sabotage the Jupiter 2 and later to destroy the Robinsons. But, as performed by actor Bob May inside the heavy and uncomfortable Robot suit, and as voiced by announcer Dick Tufeld, the Robot evolved into the third part of an incisive comedy act that included Smith and Will Robinson, with Will the ever-earnest straight man, Smith the bumbling, cowardly and venal foil to the goody-two-shoes Robinsons, and the Robot as a sardonic countermeasure and warden to Smith.

Harris enjoyed the dynamic:

> I say whoever had a straight man called a Robot, in television? Me, and that was marvelous. I decided that the Robot was my alter ego, and was not a robot at all but a person to be dealt with. Then we really took off—the Robot and I. And that's the way I treated him. That was great fun. Bobby [May] was lovely; he had learned all the lines. And it was kind of fun to react to that as a person—a member of the group, rather than a Robot or automaton.

Having somewhat less fun was Bob May himself. With his face covered with black greasepaint so that it would not be visible behind the Robot's clear collar, May sometimes had to walk with the heavy Robot body supported on suspenders over his shoulders. For shots where the Robot's lower treads were visible, a cable pulled the Robot—and May—along the stage floor and sometimes even up the steep incline of the ramp that led into the Jupiter 2, an operation that on at least one occasion caused May and the Robot suit to flip backward and smash down onto the stage floor.

Adding insult to injury, May wasn't initially credited for his work as the Robot. He said in 1995:

> [Irwin] wanted the kids in our audience to believe that that was a real, actual robot. And he did very well by that except for I would say, after the second season at

Christmas time I received a Christmas card from this one child, and the child said, "Dear Mr. May, we love your show, my sister and I, and we think you're just great. Love you, Robot." Now that child knew I was there but also realized it was a robot, too.

By season two, *TV Guide* included a credit for May in its episode synopses, and the jig was up.

May's physical performance as the Robot became increasingly expressive, registering surprise and indignation and even doing double-takes as the character matched wits with Dr. Smith. May often registered emotion simply by raising and lowering the Robot's bubble "head":

> The bubble would be up, for instance and Smith would, come back at it real strong. And the Robot would drop the bubble, as if I would personally inside go, "Oh, he did it to me again. Oh, what am I gonna do?" Or the bubble was down, and an alien came around and it was to the point of saying, "Warning, Warning, Will Robinson!" Well, the bubble would come up, because you needed that stark reaction.

Dick Tufeld's vocal characterization of the Robot became as important to the character as May's physicality. A former radio announcer, Tufeld had run across Allen when both were doing radio work early in their careers, and Allen had hired Tufeld to narrate *Lost in Space*, opening each episode with a voiceover by starting, "As you recall from last week..." But Allen also thought Tufeld's voice might work for the Robot, so Tufeld met the producer at the dialogue looping room at Fox for a test.

Tufeld recalled:

> Irwin says, "Okay, we have a Robot character here." I said, "I presume, Irwin, what you want is a mechanical, robotian, kind of sound." And Irwin patted me on the head and said, "My dear boy, that is exactly what I do *not* want. This is a highly advanced civilization, what I want is a cultured, low key, Alexander Scourby kind of approach" —referring of course to the marvelous New York narrator and actor who's since passed on.

Tufeld then voiced the character in low and measured tones:

> I'm saying, "Warning, warning, it will not compute." And, "Danger, Will Robinson," and "Aliens approaching." And he said, "No, that's not it. Try it again." Finally, after ten minutes, Irwin says to me, "Dick, I appreciate you coming in, we're just not getting this. You're not right for the Robot," he said, "but you're the narrator still in the show," and he said, "I appreciate you coming in." Now I say, "Irwin, before I go, let me try one more thing for you." And now in my best mechanical, robotian kind of sound, I say, "Warning! Warning! It will not compute. Danger, Will Robinson!" and Irwin looks up, and his eyes get wide, and he says, "My God, that's the Alexander Scourby approach I wanted—what the hell took you so long?"

**LEFT**
The Robot, like Jonathan Harris' Dr. Smith, was initially a menacing figure, but as these first season publicity photos (with the Robot showing a distinctly monochromatic color scheme) show, the character quickly evolved into a comic character.

Announcer Dick Tufeld (left), voice of the Robot, and actor Bob May (right) pose with the Robot suit in 1995.

**OPPOSITE**
Behind the scenes shot of the "bermuda shorts" Robot outfit, with actor Bob May wearing only the top part of the Robot costume for greater mobility.

Tufeld would do his vocal work for the series one day a week on the looping stage:

> Bobby May was in the Robot, doing eight hours a day, doing all the Robot lines, and as he talked he pressed a button inside the hands and a light on his chest flashed in synchronization with every syllable. So they would give me loops of Bob's lines, and I had to sync to his dialogue readings. If I was in sync with him, of course then the light flashes were in sync with me.

Although May was initially disappointed that his on-set dialogue readings weren't going to be used, he quickly recognized the tremendous contribution made by Tufeld:

> I had the great fortune of having the best announcer in show business re-dub my voice. He took my phrasing, and my tempo of the dialogue, and put that marvelous voice that he has to it. So it's all those different elements come into it.

As *Lost in Space* geared up for production in the spring and summer of 1965, Allen dealt with several unexpected challenges. Early in the project's life, Fox television executive William Self assigned producer Buck Houghton to work with Allen on the series. With Allen still overseeing *Voyage to the Bottom of the Sea*, Houghton may have been positioned to be the primary producer for *Lost in Space* with Allen in an executive producer position as the show's creator. Self had given Houghton a producer job on Rod Serling's *The Twilight Zone* when both men were at CBS, and Houghton had developed an excellent reputation working on the hit anthology show, where he toiled on some of the series' best-loved episodes.

Post-*Twilight Zone*, however, Houghton had a reputation for butting heads with actors and other producers, and he and Allen would soon be at odds as Houghton sought to bring a hardcore science fiction bearing to *Lost in Space* that was anathema to what Allen, and later the network, wanted.

An April 14, 1965 memo lists Allen and Houghton as producers, with the Robinson spaceship designated "Pilgrim1." The same day Houghton wrote to Allen with a laundry list of suggestions for personnel to be hired for the series. He recommended Lew Rackmil as associate producer because he had worked on the series *Men in Space*. Rackmil recommended Chesley Bonestell, the famed space artist who had created the background paintings of the planets for the prologue of George Pal's *War of the Worlds*, to serve as technical advisor; and special effects man Thol "Si" Symondson, who had worked to rig George Reeves for his flying sequences in *The Adventures of Superman*, for weightless rig work. Houghton listed potential directors, many veterans of *The Twilight Zone*, including Don Medford, Leo Penn, Paul Wendkos, Herschel Dougherty, Robert Butler, Tom Gries, Leonard Horn, Sobey Martin, Joseph Sargent, Dick Donner, and Bernard MacEveety. Houghton then followed up the next day, urging Allen to make a decision on his list and adding the possibilities of Lamont Johnson, David Greene and William A. Graham.

Houghton then added this passive-aggressive conclusion:

**ABOVE**
A stunt man doubles for Guy Williams during an early spacewalk sequence that put both Robinson parents in danger—and raised objections from CBS censors and some viewers.

One of the show's monsters—silly by adult standards, but downright scary for kids.

**RIGHT**
Angela Cartwright and Billy Mumy register terror in the *Lost in Space* pilot under the direction of Irwin Allen. CBS wanted a show about a space family, for families—so putting children in danger immediately set off alarms among the network censors.

This covers everyone that we talked about with the exception of John Peyser with whom I regret to say I would be uncomfortable in these early pictures; it is undoubtedly a blind spot on my part which I will undertake to overcome.

A week later, while making arrangements for Allen to meet director Alex Singer (who would direct "The Derelict" for the series), Houghton noted that Singer knew Louis and Bebe Barron, who had done the electronic music for *Forbidden Planet*, and recommended talking to them. (Although some experimental music effects would be used on the series, Allen hired composer John "Johnny" Williams as well as other experienced, traditional television composers, to provide music for the series)

The next day Houghton urged Allen to hire science fiction writer Arthur C. Clarke (then at work on Stanley Kubrick's *2001: A Space Odyssey*), as a consultant on the series. Houghton continued to work on the series over the summer (an August 7 PR column discusses Allen and mentions "His producer for *Lost in Space* is Buck Houghton, who produced Rod Serling's Emmy-winning *Twilight Zone*"). But by then Allen had had enough and it was clear that his ideas for an adventure-oriented program were at odds with Houghton's pursuit of contributions from artists known for much more sober science fiction.

Allen's agent Herman Rush finally wrote Self on September 1, stating that "Rush, Allen and Self had met and discussed the hiring of Houghton under specified conditions in March of that year and that those conditions had not been met." At this point the decision had been made to remove Houghton from his position, that he would not receive credit and would no longer be producer of the series and that Irwin Allen "has assumed the duties of, and has in fact, always been the producer of *Lost in Space* and that Buck Houghton is no longer connected in any way with the series."

The second challenge Allen faced would have a much greater impact on the show, and it involved the tone and direction the CBS network preferred for the series. Allen and his production team had envisioned *Lost in Space* as a gripping science fiction adventure with monsters and constant threats to the Robinson clan, as the show's "cliff-hanger" endings would indicate week after week. But the fact that the high tension, suspense and even horror seen on the series involved the two youngest members of the Robinson family, Will and Penny, caused deep concern, first from the network's Program Practices Department (colloquially known as the Network Censors), and later from some of CBS' top executives.

As early as December 4, 1964, on the eve of production for the *Lost in Space* pilot, Guy Della-Cioppa of Van Bernard Productions received script notes on the pilot:

> As a prospective early evening program, the following are suggested to lessen the horror-picture impact on young viewers: Please display the freezing process...with perhaps a clouding of the freezing chambers, rather than having the actors assume a gruesome frozen attitude,

suggestive of staring-eyed death.

The memo also suggested the frozen family should have their eyes closed so they "appear unknowing, rather than impotent."

Other notes suggested:

> The GIANT should not depart too far from the human form if it is to suggest a humanoid vegetable.
>
> The FADEOUT should not occur as the child PENNY is menaced by a huge hummingbird.
>
> Suggest that ROBINSON appears to aim his laser gun at the animal to lessen the cliff-hanging aspect of the FADEOUT.
>
> The bird itself should not be too horrible.
>
> Restraint is suggested in the scene of the menacing GIANT and the GIANT's screams.

Over the summer, as the network looked at early episodes, CBS Program Practices' Dorothy Mox wrote William Self about "The Derelict":

> Eliminated a shot of Don using fire extinguisher foam to cool the overheated John and Maureen. Eliminated Will's scene of terror at seeing himself reflected over and over in the glass tiles. The bubble creatures now come from a cauldron set in the floor instead of the reflecting walls.

CBS Chairman William Paley himself was concerned about the show's cliff-hangers, as a June, 21, 1965 memo from Perry Lafferty to Boris Kaplan indicated:

> The Chairman is extremely anxious that the cliff-hangers on *Lost in Space* are done carefully and with an eye to the potential fears of the younger members of the audience. Please relay Mr. Paley's feelings to Mr. Allen so that we won't run into difficulties along this line at some future date.

Also bubbling up were concerns over Gold Key's comic book *Space Family Robinson*, which had adopted the title *Lost in Space* prior to Allen's series going on the air. A June 15 memo from Robert L. Brenner of the legal firm Pacht, Ross, Warne, Bernhard & Sears to Allen said:

> ...Two weeks ago Jack Purcell of CBS Legal took the position that the title *Lost in Space* should be dropped as the series title since one of the comic books in which Hilda Boehm is claiming ownership bears the same title. A meeting was held on Friday, June 11 to attempt to resolve this issue. After discussion of Irwin Allen's prior registration of the *Lost in Space* title Purcell retreated from his position.

The same comic book company had licensed and produced comic books not only for Allen's *Voyage to the Bottom of the Sea*, but also *The Twilight Zone* and other CBS television properties, and both companies wished to retain good relations and continue their mutually beneficial, marketing revenue streams. The Gold Key comic would subsequently become

**ABOVE**
June Lockhart and Guy Williams—forced to be as chaste as Ozzie and Harriet in space to satisfy the network's Standards and Practices department.

The Robinson party tends to a stricken Maureen in the wake of the spacewalk. Two of the show's early cliffhangers left the Robinson parents trapped outside the spacecraft, creating unprecedented tension for younger viewers.

**OPPOSITE**
John and Maureen Robinson are trapped outside the Jupiter 2 airlock as their children watch in horror in "Island in the Sky."

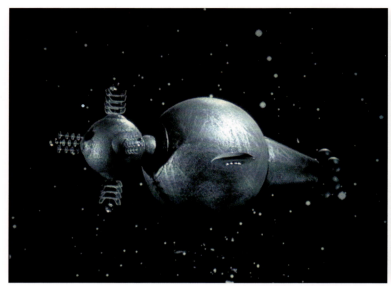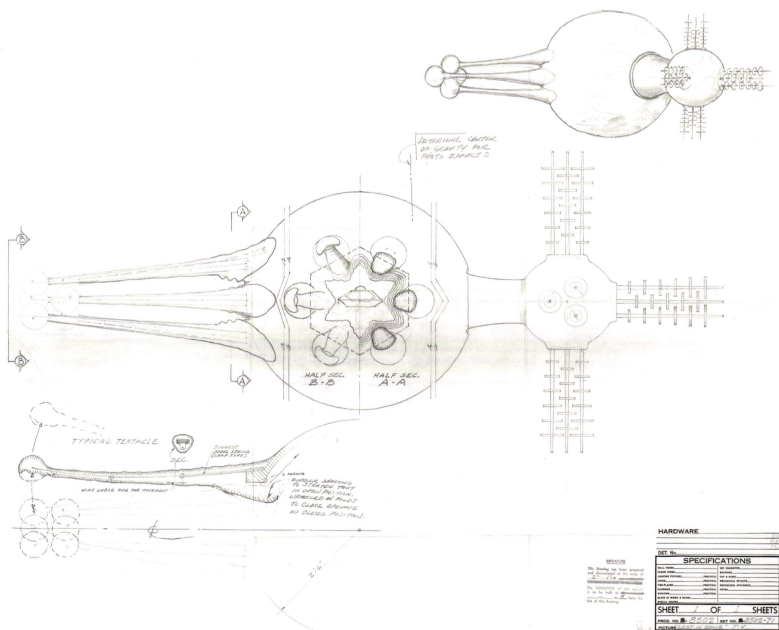

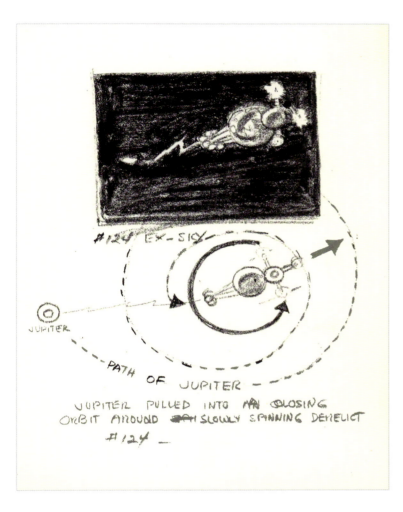

**THIS PAGE**
Storyboard sketches for "The Derelict."

**OPPOSITE**
The Jupiter 2 orbits—and is about to be swallowed up by—a massive alien spaceship in "The Derelict."

The full size Jupiter 2 prop on the remains of the "brain" set from Fox's *Fantastic Voyage*, doubling as the organic interior of the alien spacecraft in "The Derelict."

Blueprints for the "Derelict" spacecraft supervised by art director Robert Kinoshita, indicating that the original concept was for the exterior of the ship to register as a "living" machine with organic, pleated rubber arm joints, and the spherical objects on the ends of the "mouth" stalks were to be eyes.

a kind of official comic book adaptation of Allen's series, and a consistent source of confusion for kids who read the comic (which only vaguely resembled the TV series) and watched the show.

Around the same time Allen was drumming up publicity for the show's September premiere in, among other outlets, a feature in *Variety* on June 1st:

> There is nothing like this show on TV. *Space* will be the first primetime cliffhanger in the history of TV. The whole series is a cliffhanger. We will leave them hanging in space, and resolve it the next week, then get them in worse difficulties that week. This is a show designed for adults, but you couldn't keep the kids away with a baseball bat. So we had damned well better write adult stories to get maximum appeal.

Allen's writers were attempting to strike the medium the producer was aiming for, as Shimon Wincelberg explained in 1995:

> I was not a great reader of science-fiction. I didn't see many science-fiction movies. So I treated it pretty much like *Little House on the Prairie*: a tight family, surrounded by a hostile environment. The emphasis was very much on making it a family story. I think the time slot also had something to do with it.

Al Gail agreed that the show's time slot was the cause of a lot of the network's concerns:

> We always had the seven p.m. spot on Sunday [on *Voyage to the Bottom of the Sea*], which was a family time spot. We could not say hell, or damn, or anything. We couldn't aim a pistol at the camera. We couldn't do anything in those days. You were doing family entertainment. And it appealed to the youngsters, and it appealed to adults who enjoyed science fiction.

CBS' concerns extended even to the marital relationship between Guy Williams' and June Lockhart's characters. There was to be no indication the two were sleeping together, and as the series progressed even simple indications of affection like hugs and kisses were taboo. "In *Lost in Space*, I'm still not allowed to get any more familiar with my husband Guy Williams than a firm and friendly handshake," Lockhart said in a *Staten Island Advance* newspaper feature. "But at least I wear form-fitting silver lame jumpsuits."

Paul Zastupnevich said in 1995:

> June Lockhart and Guy Williams, I mean, supposedly CBS said that mother couldn't touch father, and mother should never be in jeopardy. That's why poor June never could, even when we put her out in space at one time, try to help Guy back into the spaceship, there was quite a bit of clack about that.

When *Lost in Space* finally debuted in mid-September, reviews were mixed, but most critics agreed that Allen's new series was going to find an audience.

In a September 16 review, critic Jerry Coffey said:

> I suspect that a sizable portion of the TV audience—young and old—will find it irresistible. Jonathan Harris as the snickering, cowering villain and the robot practically stole the first show, but the real star of *Lost in Space* is producer Irwin Allen, the special effects master who also is responsible for *Voyage to the Bottom of the Sea*. The space gadgetry and visual effects are something to behold.

*The Hollywood Reporter* agreed:

> Weekly serial, great tongue-in-cheek spoofer, should lure kids like old Saturday matinees, while adults will watch just to hiss the villain or make snide remarks. Producer-creator Irwin Allen has a sure fire hit in this one. The villain of the piece is Jonathan Harris…he sneered, scoffed, scowled and menaced, doing all but twirl mustache. His weekly scenery chewing, emoted so facetiously, is to be awaited.

*The New York Herald Tribune* was less enthusiastic, calling the show, "Childish science fiction in a 'Perils of Pauline' package…The gadgetry, special effects and villainy were pure Grade B hokum." But Donald Freeman of *The San Diego Union* found *Lost in Space*, "…a blend of Buck Rogers and *The Adventures of Ozzie and Harriet*. …a diverting show, expensively produced and grimly, perhaps satirically futuristic."

Nevertheless, CBS' concerns about the program's deliberately scary action found agreement in some important quarters. The National Association for Better Radio and Television cited *Lost in Space* as "highly objectionable for teens and children. Cliff-hanger terror is designed to keep child viewers in a state of alarm from week to week."

An *L.A. Times* column by Hal Humphrey quoted Mrs. Orman Longstreet, former chairman of the LA 10th District PTA's TV-radio committee:

> In an age of space and space technology, a five year-old would not understand this show as fantasy, and my main objection to it is that having hurled a family into orbit without even minimal safety or security precautions the plot first puts the mother into considerable peril and shows her family being worried about her, and then goes on to put the father in mortal danger and leaves him there until the next week!

The show's initial season, shot in moody black and white by cinematographer Gene Polito, registered a relatively sober, if not grim sci-fi/adventure feeling, launching with the spectacular series of episodes built around the pilot footage as well as "The Derelict," with Allen utilizing the spun-fiberglass "brain" set of Fox's *Fantastic Voyage* as the interior of an alien spacecraft. Other episodes like "My Friend, Mr. Nobody" and the two-part "The Keeper" with Michael Rennie became fan favorites that demonstrated the potential for high adventure, drama, and emotion inherent in the series concept.

Another strong early episode, "The Sky Is Falling," had the Robinsons facing down an alien family of space colonists—mutes that the Robinsons struggle

**OPPOSITE**

Michael Rennie threatens the Robinsons in "The Keeper."

Don Matheson as a mute alien in "The Sky Is Falling."

Mercedes McCambridge with Jonathan Harris in "The Space Croppers."

to understand until Will's friendship with the aliens' young son defuses a growing conflict between the two groups. Don Matheson made his first appearance in an Irwin Allen production in the episode, playing the alien father and turning in an impressive, dignified performance:

> I played a mute so I never got to say anything. I had lines, but evidently they were gonna lay them in later—and when Irwin saw the dailies, he said, "The guy is doing it all with his face and his body and his eyes so what do we need dialogue for?" And it was a compliment to me. In fact, he made a point of coming down and telling me that. He said, "We're not going to use your voice or a voice because you conveyed everything without it."

Despite these strong early installments, as early as the sixth episode, "Welcome, Stranger," with Warren Oates as a space cowboy, the show fell into a formula that would last throughout its three-season run, with the Robinsons encountering every manner of "space" personalities—space cowboys, space pirates, space magicians, space hillbillies, space convicts, etc. Veteran actress Mercedes McCambridge, who had been considered to play Maureen Robinson (and would later be infamous for providing the guttural, hideous demon voice for Linda Blair's character in *The Exorcist*), talked about being cast as a space hillbilly in the episode "The Space Croppers," in a March 21, 1966 feature in the *Los Angeles Times*:

> Well, first I cry a little bit. Then I began thinking what I can do with $2,500—doctor bills, clothes and so on—but by the time the money gets to me it will be only 60% of $2,500. So now the ham in me takes over, and I say to myself, "By golly, this will be the damndest hillbilly anybody's ever seen on TV or anywhere else" and I tell my agent to go ahead. Of course, when you see it on the TV screen next week, she'll be like all hillbillies.

As the series moved deeper into its first season, Jonathan Harris' Dr. Smith character and the Robot were already growing in popularity and becoming more and more comic characters. Harris' and Billy Mumy's unusual professionalism (Mumy had a photographic memory that allowed him to memorize lines instantly and then deliver them with flawless timing in every take) also made them the easiest and most efficient characters to film, and Allen and the production staff began to lean on them even more to keep the complicated production on schedule. This did not go unnoticed by the rest of the cast, particularly Guy Williams and June Lockhart, who were gradually being reduced from series leads to supporting characters on their own show.

Shimon Wincelberg, in 1995, took some of the blame for this development:

> I was pretty much out of the loop. But I liked all of them, as people and as actors, and, just thought that, and this is probably my fault—they weren't terribly interesting as characters. And this is why Dr. Smith and Will carried more and more of the weight.

An early magazine profile on Guy Williams underscored

**ABOVE**
A visibly unhappy Mark Goddard models his silver spacesuit for a costume test.

**OPPOSITE**
Mark Goddard, Guy Williams and Billy Mumy on the crash site soundstage set at Fox.

**OPPOSITE**
Caricature by artist Bob Bentovoja created for *TV Weekly* cover.

**RIGHT**
The animated title sequence from *Lost in Space* season 2.

the actor's disappointment with his diminishing role on the series:

> The high hopes he started with, the feelings that this series might be just the thing he had been looking for all these years, faded in an exact ratio to Harris's rise. Perhaps the lowest point in a "lousy" year was the morning a director placed Harris, a master scene thief, in the foreground of a scene written for Guy and June Lockhart. That was the last straw. "I walked off the set and called Irwin. He came down and we reached a compromise."

The feature went on to note that, despite his frustrations, Williams managed his money well and had, "a 16-room, Mediterranean-style villa off Sunset and a healthy stock portfolio." Said one of his directors, "He walks on the set combing his hair. 'Hold it,' he says and we wait. This man is more interested in his hair than his performance." Billy Mumy's nickname for Williams was "The Comb."

Another feature in *The Los Angeles Harold-Examiner* painted a similar portrait of frustration for Mark Goddard: "'This show...' Mark Goddard says. 'I just wish I had more to do. The script writers at least could let me kill a monster.'"

Al Gail recalled in 1995 that the mood on the set soon made *Lost in Space* the last choice for some of the directors Allen worked regularly with:

> There were five, six individual stars, and none of 'em were too happy with what they were getting. You would never know it from what came out, but directors were never in a rush to do that show, cause they knew it was a headache. But then again they could always blame it on the writers, you know and say, "Gee, I didn't write this." But the stars fought for their close-ups.

Dick Tufeld was not one to blame the writers or Irwin Allen:

> The direction that *Lost In Space* took was not necessarily of Irwin's doing. The first year of the show, for example, the scripts were much more sophisticated. They had terrific writers—they always had good writers. The trouble is, CBS, the network, in their own wisdom, and I don't mean to single CBS out because all networks do it, but they got involved in the direction the show went. They determined that they needed more over the top, comedic, outrageous performances from Jonathan, who of course was spectacular in that he provided that. The Robot and Billy Mumy, the kid, became the focus of the show. That wasn't the way the show started, but that's the direction it took, and CBS, as it took that direction, sensed they were on to something. So whether Irwin wanted this show to be over the top that much didn't even matter because that's what CBS wanted. For the show to stay on the air, that's the direction the show had to take. I'm not sure Irwin can be blamed or credited for that.

While Will Robinson and the Robot were hugely popular, by the beginning of season two it was clear that Dr. Smith was the show's breakout character and central focus. Kids had an intense love/hate relationship with Smith, who couldn't help but cause disastrous problems

for the Robinsons and got away with acting out in a way that probably made the average kid feel like a mature adult by comparison. Harris, in fact, was inspired by children's behavior in building his character:

> I like to think that I drew Dr. Smith based on every kid I'd ever known and met. I watch kids—I like kids—and I watch them. And they teach me a lot. I did a lot of stuff as Smith that was absolutely childlike and childish, like nobody would notice how bad I am—kids are that way. Or I'd cover it up or blame somebody else as all kids do, and I think that's where it began. And then I added to it all of my experience playing crazy, strange, eccentric, stylish, stylized, people. I started to do that in my early years on Broadway. And that's really what I was hired to do—I do play strange, off center, characters—they interest me.

Although he was getting the benefit of the new focus on Will Robinson, Smith, and the Robot, Billy Mumy had mixed feelings about the evolution of the show:

> On one hand of course I was pleased to see Will becoming this heroic little guy, and this formidable guy who's taking care of business. I liked having plenty to do. On the other hand, I certainly was aware of the fact that the cast who made the pilot weren't doing what they expected to be doing once we went to series. I kind of felt bad that they weren't getting a lot of work. I don't think *Lost In Space* ever really knew what it was. I mean I always played *Lost In Space* straight. I think that June did. She played it straight but half the time we were playing it for comedy and half the time it was farce.

Mark Goddard had been concerned about working on

**ABOVE**
Guy Williams mugs on the set with "space pirate" Albert Salmi (center) while Billy Mumy stays in character.

**OPPOSITE**
The Robinsons gear up for the comedy-oriented "campy" second season in a PR shot for *Mad Magazine*. The original photo did not feature Jonathan Harris and the Robot; they were digitally composited in later.

the show from the beginning, and after gaining some confidence that he wouldn't be humiliated during the first year, his worst fears were confirmed as the Smith character began to dominate:

> My first concern was doing science-fiction, because science-fiction hadn't been done since the Buck Rogers days in the '30s. So it was that genre. I had done a detective series. I had done a western. And I wasn't sure with science-fiction if we'd be laughed at. When I met Irwin, I went into his office and he had all this stuff all around. He was so organized. It was really something else and he showed me the pictures of the Jupiter 2 and what he wanted to do and he was really very enthusiastic, so I gave it more serious thought. I first told my agent I didn't want to do it, and he said, do it—just do the pilot. Take the money and run. Nobody'll ever see that show. You'll never go on the air. And, he was wrong.

Goddard's worst early moment on the show came from trying on one of Paul Zastupnevich's silver spacesuits:

> When we went to wardrobe and I put on the silver pajamas that we walked in space in—I cried. I cried, and said, "This what it's come to." I didn't know we were walking in space in this. I said, "This is how they're dressing me." It was very cartoonish to me at the time. I had illusions that I was gonna be a serious actor—I'd studied in New York, and I want to do something with more depth to it than I thought this was going to be. I got a look at this silver thing with these big silver boots and… We were on a stairwell there [with my wife] and I just, I cried and she said, "It's okay. You know, we got two kids. You'll be fine. Take care of the kids with this.'"

Goddard managed to plow his ill feelings into his work on the show, and Major West's near-homicidal frustration and loathing of Smith became one of the more reliable and entertaining character dynamics in the series:

> I still played what was real to me. It was that I want to get off this planet. And with me, I'd go to the real things that are happening in life, and I want to get off this show. So that's what I kind of was playing. I was kickin' the dirt and doin' my little "method boost." I never played it for comedy cause it wasn't comedy to me. We had enough of a balance where we had Guy and I doing something serious and Jonathan and the Robot and Billy getting involved in something.

By halfway through season one, both Allen and the network agreed that *Lost in Space* was a success, but Allen felt that CBS was undercutting the show by not asking for enough in ad fees for the hour. He wrote Sal Iannucci of CBS on December 29, 1965:

> We have completed 15 episodes at an average cost of $159,733 per episode. Despite the amortizing of some of the expensive pilot costs by spreading the footage out over the first five episodes of the series, gross income from the series was estimated at only $350,000, out of which we must pay the actors, writers and directors their residuals.

Allen suggested that there were only two possible solutions to the problem—one was to get more

**ABOVE**
Angela Cartwright (right) prepares for a scene with a costume dragon voiced by June Foray in "The Questing Beast."

Publicity shot of Marta Kristen and John Carradine ("The Galaxy Gift").

**OPPSITE**
Allen (left) in his office with a wall chart of progress on *Lost in Space* scripts in 1966.

advertising money for the show and the other was to cut costs, which the producer insisted would jeopardize the quality of the show. Allen recommended that, "CBS re-evaluate the sales price on this show in view of its rating success."

As the show moved into its second season and switched to color, *Lost in Space* was suffering the slings and arrows of an adversary more deadly than any giant cyclops or insidious alien: Fox's own *Batman*, which had launched in January and become a pop culture phenomenon on ABC. *Batman*'s pop art color scheme and parade of big name stars playing bizarre comic book villains only reinforced the phantasmagorical direction *Lost in Space* was headed in. In an interview in *The Buffalo Evening News*, Paul Zastupnevich even argued that the relative levelheadedness of *Lost in Space* vis-a-vis *Batman* gave the Irwin Allen series an advantage:

> We have no doubt about *Lost in Space* surviving against *Batman*. Strange as it may seem, our space villains are quite realistic compared to these comic book characters. We may be far-out, but we do relate to current space ideas.

Interestingly, the *Batman* producers were not dismissive of the Irwin Allen series as their competition. In a Jan. 11, 1967 Houston Chronicle TV feature, *Batman* producer William Dozier said he "is convinced that *Batman* will be with us for a third season—even though the Wednesday ratings battle has been rough against *Lost in Space* and *The Virginian*."

"The second season is just camp," Bill Mumy argued in 1995:

> It's that period of pop art. It's a very short lived period in our American culture. It was when *Batman* was premiering. I think *Laugh-In* was getting ready to come on the air. Everything was these bright, day-glow colors and Andy Warhol was painting soup cans and that was the big rage. That stuff just sticks out like a sore thumb to me.

Guy Williams and June Lockhart obediently chimed in about the show's approach to color in P.R. interviews timed to the beginning of season two. For her part, Lockhart demonstrated a surprising aptitude for scientific analysis:

> Who knows what combinations of light and intensity will be found on strange planets when man is actually able to travel millions of miles into the skies? We know enough about light rays to realize that basic colors as we know them will be the same everywhere in the universe, but the way primary colors are mixed and blended and the textures of the reflecting surfaces are able to bring some surprising results. Irwin Allen is really the only one who knows what outer space looks like.

Williams found a positive spin:

> One of the things I am grateful for is that the series is fun to work on. I actually look forward to getting our scripts on each new episode to find out what adventure Irwin and his writing staff have mapped out for us. I never know whether I'll be sailing 50 feet over the earth in a space belt, wrestling with some outer space monster, battling

**LEFT**
Vitina Marcus as the ultimate space siren, "The Girl from the Green Dimension."

Dennis Patrick (center) as Mr. Keema in "The Golden Man."

wits with Jonathan Harris or just being domestic, in a space-age pioneering way with my television family.

Season two was arguably *Lost in Space* at its silliest, with the introduction of Vitina Marcus in two appearances as the ethereal, floating "Girl from the Green Dimension" with a crush on "pretty, pretty Dr. Smith"; a "Space Circus"; and Smith facing down a menacing space gunslinger lookalike (Harris himself, hilarious in one of his favorite roles on the series) named Zeno in "West of Mars." If the season two shows were entirely lacking in credibility as science fiction, they were often charming fables like "The Thief of Outer Space" (the highest-rated second-season episode), with a magnificent Malachi Throne as a devious interstellar sultan and an equally good Ted Cassidy as his double-crossing slave; or "The Golden Man," with the Robinsons charmed by a too-good-to-be-true, gold-plated alien named Keema (Dennis Patrick)—until Penny learns Keema's sworn enemy, a frog-like, disagreeable creature that the Robinsons have feared, is really the good guy.

Actor Don Matheson returned to the show in another unusual role that probably illustrated the desire to emulate *Batman* better than any other *Lost in Space* episode. In "Revolt of the Androids," Matheson played a superhero-suited android with a killer catchphrase:

> I played a character named Idak—which stood for "instant destroyer and killer." Of course, I had to walk around through the entire episode saying that, "Crush, kill, destroy." I was in clown white silver makeup, with a silver helmet and a blue Superman-type costume, and so I was a super Android. I could lift huge rubber boulders and throw them all over the sound stage. It was fun.

Matheson also recalled that he may have taken his android super powers too seriously during shooting:

> I broke the robot on that show. The only actor that's ever done it—I had to give it a karate chop, little Bobby May was inside of it. I whacked it the way the script called for. I had never whacked it that hard in rehearsal but when the red light goes on and the adrenaline starts pumping, I whacked it and knocked it over, knocked it off the track. And they left it in. Bobby was very unhappy because that was his robot, you know—he was strongly attached to it.

The switch to color inspired a visual upgrade for the show in general, with new props and costumes, begging the question of how the Robinsons, stranded on an alien planet since the beginning of the series, were able to dig up an entirely new wardrobe.

Costume designer Paul Zastupnevich didn't overthink it:

> The purpose of that was that they wanted a change. They'd been in and out of those costumes, continually and it was very difficult. In fact even the silver suits changed. In the very beginning we used what had originally been a fire retardant suit and cut it apart and made a flying suit out of it. And then all of a sudden, twenty-four karat, silver jersey came in, which was more pliable and more movable. They didn't have to be on a leaning board between takes after that. I had leaning boards for June and, and Angela and, Marta because the silver suits were

**RIGHT**

Don Matheson as I.D.A.K. in "Revolt of the Androids."

Jonathan Harris as the cold-blooded gunslinger Zeno in "West of Mars."

**LEFT**
Bill Mumy demonstrates the Mattel Roto-Jet gun, which looked so cool that the show's prop men wound up using it for the Robinsons' laser rifles later in the series.

**OPPOSITE**
Aurora model kit and packaging for the The Robot.

The air-powered Lost in Space Switch-N-Go Playset, Milton Bradley board game and a puzzle.

**LEFT**

Remco's much-coveted *Lost in Space* Robot toy, used to create an army of miniature robots in "The Mechanical Men."

A rare and inaccurate Japanese model kit of the Jupiter 2; the spacecraft wouldn't get a domestic model kit reproduction until the 1990s.

Aurora model kit for the Cyclops.

**OPPOSITE**

Box cover art for the Aurora Plastics Cyclops model kit painted by Mort Kuntsler, who would later create the poster art painting for *The Poseidon Adventure*.

232

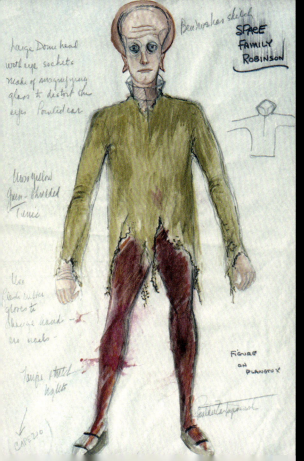

**ABOVE**

Guest star Al Lewis (left) on the set of "Rocket to Earth" with Will, Dr. Smith and the Robot.

"Rocket to Earth" set sketch by Roy Alexander.

Alien monster design sketch by Paul Zastupnevich.

**OPPOSITE**

Color sketches by costume designer Paul Zastupnevich of some of the show's costumes and alien creatures.

so stiff, and so uncomfortable to sit in—and they were hot, too, basically."

Zastupnevich applied his theory about color-coding the actors, which went back at least to *The Lost World*, on the show:

> We changed the colors because basically children, watching the sets, love primary colors, so the colors were always geared so that a kid could associate with them. And each actor or actress had their own particular color—one was in blue, one was in green, one was in orange. This was so that if you saw them in a long shot, you'd [know which character was which]. I color-coded them and tried to keep the colors basically just to them. In some of the main pictures that I did, if I have a leading lady in white, or pink, I never let anyone in the crowd around her wear white or pink. It's a trick from the old days.

Irwin Allen, too, loved bright colors on everything from sets and miniatures to his own wardrobe. Sheila Allen said in 1995:

> Irwin did not want to be surrounded with dull colors. He needed happy colors—colors that made him feel good. If you look back on his early motion pictures—*Big Circus, Five Weeks in a Balloon*. I mean these were, colorful extravaganzas. I guess you could say that they were in a sense gaudy. We lived for quite a few years with orange and green. He called it his Bahama period. He thought Bahama meant orange and green and shutters and things like that. And you couldn't surround him in browns and grays. I must say he did the decorating in our house, and I let him. Some of it was pretty funny. He loved beautiful clothes. He had very handsome things. But he also liked his leisure suits and things like that. They could be unusual colors for men: powder blues and pinks and things like that.

Allen, in fact, had his own distinctive wardrobe, and if you look at the lead characters in projects like *City Beneath the Sea, The Towering Inferno* and *The Swarm*, they're often dressed not unlike Allen would be in real life.

The show's popularity with children led to a number of merchandising deals with toy manufacturers. Aurora Plastics released model kits of the Robot and the Cyclops. Mattel released a "Switch and Go" playset with a plastic Jupiter 2 and a Chariot that moved along a track propelled by compressed air, as well as an elaborate "Roto Jet Gun" that could be reconfigured into a rifle, a carbine, or a pistol. And Remco made a very popular, if misshapen reproduction of the Robot.

The Roto Jet Gun and Robot toys actually became props on the show—the Roto Jet Gun components were lengthened with plastic tubing to make laser rifles for the Robinsons, and the Remco Robot toys appeared as an army of miniature robots in "The Mechanical Men."

Just as *Voyage to the Bottom of the Sea* started getting some blowback from fans as it began to settle into a monster-of-the-week formula, *Lost in Space* got its share of letters over the show's comic direction and the dominance of Dr. Smith over the other characters. In

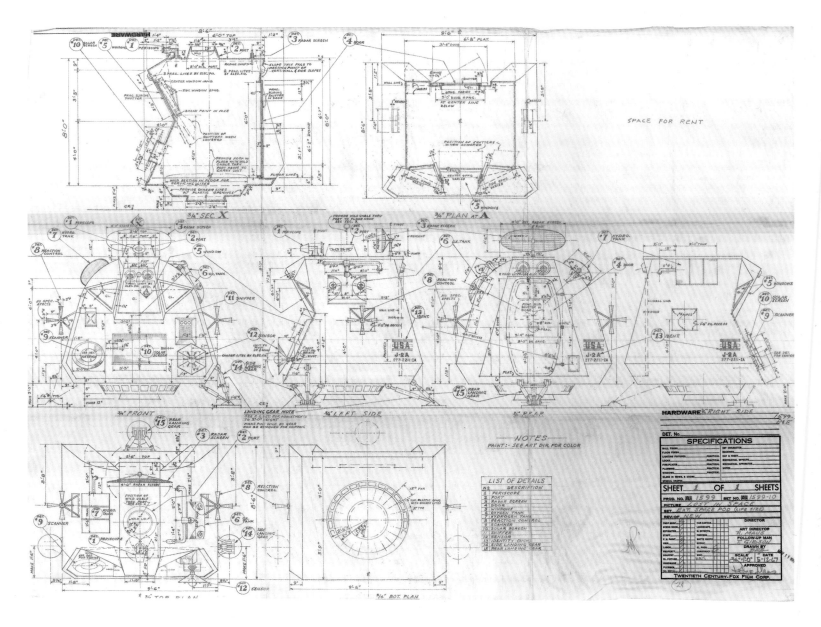

January, 1967, Mary Gaeta of Staten Island wrote:

> I must admit I enjoyed it enormously until you started giving all your star roles to one Jonathan Harris portraying Dr. Smith. ...you have excellent star and acting material in Guy Williams and June Lockhart and the supporting players—when are you going to realize this and utilize their talents...

A production summary of fan letter critiques read:

- Doctor Smith: too much of him and his repetitive chatter. ...feeling was expressed that he be turned back into more of a villain.
- Locale: Get off the planet and back into space; too many alien visitors to this one planet.
- Aliens: Too anthropomorphic in outfit and not science fiction enough; too many so-called "nuts" as guest aliens. Monster aliens described as "silly" rather than frightening; many recognized the repeating of monster suits.
- Cast: More Guy Williams and June Lockhart.
- Action: More wars, fighting and action, more chariot expeditions.

**ABOVE**
Construction blueprints for the third season's Space Pod.

**OPPOSITE**
The Space Pod, lifting off from a planet, in flight, and being tended to by technicians on the sound stage at Fox.

**FOLLOWING**
A collection of Roy Alexander's vivid production artwork for second season episodes including "Rocket to Earth," "Forbidden World," "Mutiny in Space," "Trip Through the Robot," "Prisoners of Space" and others.

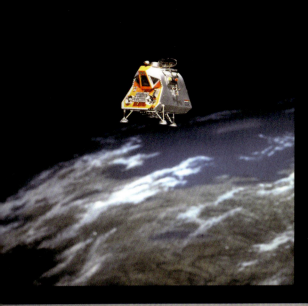

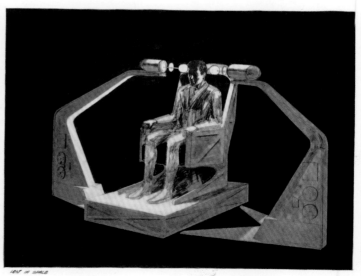

240

LOST IN SPACE

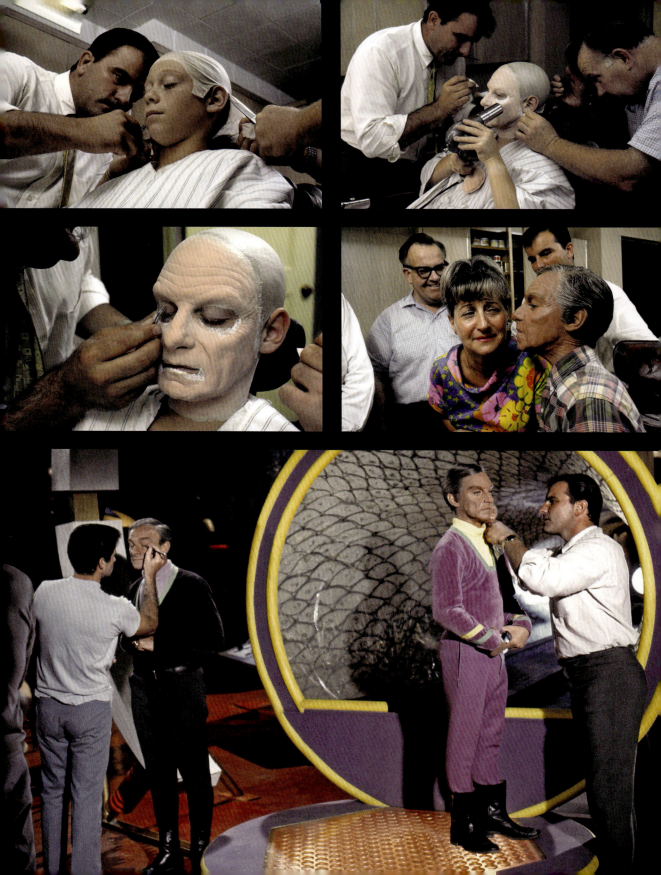

**OPPOSITE AND ABOVE**
Billy Mumy being transformed into a miniature Dr. Smith under the supervision of Fox makeup department head Dan Striepeke (dark hair) and prosthetics specialist John Chambers (with glasses) for "The Space Destructors"—and the final result. Photos by Gene Trindl for a proposed *TV Guide* spread.

Another memo, dated Feb. 27, 1967, from unit production manager William Faralla to Allen recommended:

> ...An informal but very pointed discussion with each member of the cast (separately) re their behavior in the past and what is expected of them next season. Similar discussion with directors that will come in on multiple deals. Commitments should not exceed 6 episodes. Address sketch artist and art director problem. Interview replacements for Kit Carson [*cinematographer Frank G. "Kit" Carson nonetheless remained with the series through the end of its run*]. Angela Cartwright is going to be quite a young lady by the time we open up next season. All writers should be made aware of this. The lack of imagination and the cost of photo effects should be seriously discussed. I still recommend going outside regardless if it can be worked out with the studio. Next season shall we agree to minimize the Dr. Smith contribution in every script.

With *Lost in Space* in its second season, Irwin Allen had three shows on network television—*Space* on CBS, and *Voyage to the Bottom of the Sea* and his new series *The Time Tunnel* on ABC. He had *Land of the Giants* in development and was even proposing a *Buck Rogers* series to NBC (although Allen's project never got off the drawing board, a *Buck Rogers* series ultimately did run on NBC in 1979, produced by Glen Larson). As far as television went, Allen was at the height of his power, and the producer radiated that on the set.

Bill Mumy recalled:

> He was almost like a caricature of a director. You know, megaphones and stuff. You know—CUT! He was an authority. He was the owner, he was the executive producer, he was the creator, he was the director [on the pilot]. He was story by I believe. He had a big ego. You didn't mess around with him. He didn't have any sense of humor. I'm not painting a bleak picture of the guy but he was all business. Every day towards the end of the day he would come down, on the set when we were working, and he would look at his watch—just to make the directors and people aware of the fact that time is money—and he wanted things to go quicker. He was a powerful presence to deal with.

Mumy recalled that Allen was always friendly to the child actor; but, even as Mumy set a remarkable record for attendance and hard work on the set, Allen did send a producer to his house on one of the three days (out of three years of production) that the young actor was missing work to confirm that he was sick.

With all his other commitments, Allen continued to work hard for *Lost in Space*'s place on the network and with advertisers, meeting with sponsors in New York in December, 1966 about *Voyage to the Bottom of the Sea* and *Lost in Space*, with presentations on *The Time Tunnel* and *Land of the Giants* that were enthusiastically received. A report on the meeting noted:

> All of the aforementioned agencies were exposed to the LIS area of the Irwin Allen room and all agreed that LIS was healthy, sure of renewal, and would be a show that they would support.

RIGHT
Jonathan Harris as Dr. Smith and Billy Mumy as Mini-Smith in "The Space Destructors."

According to *Variety*, 20th Century Fox had spent $12 million in TV production per season while *Lost in Space*, *Voyage*, and *The Time Tunnel* were on the air, and Allen used six Fox stages simultaneously through the season with the possibility of three swing stages being added, while also doing location work in Trona, CA for *Space* and *Time Tunnel* and a week in Catalina for *Voyage*. 25 writers were employed and 36 scripts prepped, with a total of 85 people employed on Allen's shows. In 1966 Allen even claimed he had plans to make *Time Tunnel* and *Lost in Space* into feature films sometime in the future.

In March, 1967, Richard Zanuck and William Self approved CBS exercising its option on *Lost in Space* for a third year on the network. But CBS was already requesting cuts in the show's budget. A May 31, 1967 memo from Jack Sontag to William Self suggested that cuts in set construction and special effects were in order:

— Sets: This season they requested $8,452, last season average cost $5,622;
— Miniatures and second unit—this season they requested $5,000, last season average cost $2,889.
— Photo effects: This season they requested $4,600, last season average cost $1,580.
— What we save in these three areas, plus the overhead charge of 15% and Fringe Benefits, should bring the final figure close to $160.000.

With season three, Allen tried to get the series back on firmer footing, with more action and space travel. He even added a Lunar Module-like "Space Pod," designed by third season Art Director Rodger Maus, that would exit from the Jupiter 2 much like the Flying Sub did from the Seaview, allowing individual characters to leave the spacecraft and explore planets on their own.

The percolating first and second season theme music by John Williams was replaced by a more dynamic "countdown" title sequence and a propulsive, adventurous theme by Williams. Episodes like "Hunter's Moon" put Guy Williams on location in a version of *The Most Dangerous Game,* and the weird "space caveman" episode "The Space Primevals" teamed up Smith with Major West on a colorful excursion in the Chariot.

But there were also numerous fairy tale stories like "The Haunted Lighthouse," "Castles in Space," and "Space Beauty," as well as the space biker episode "Collision of Planets" and another hippy freak-out in "The Promised Planet," which put Jonathan Harris in a Prince Valiant wig, doing the Twist with a group of space teenagers.

The show often hired makeup artist John Chambers—who was already busy creating the simian makeups that would win him an Academy Award for Fox's *Planet of the Apes* in 1968. Chambers created a variation on his *Apes* makeup to turn actor Michael Conrad into an ape-like space convict in "Fugitives in Space," and he helped create an army of Dr. Smith androids—and turn Billy Mumy into a creepy miniature Smith—for "The Space Destructors."

**LEFT**

A third season highlight: "The Anti-Matter Man."

A Prince Valiant-wigged Dr. Smith gets freaky while Bill Mumy registers his displeasure in "The Promised Planet."

Marcel Hillaire as the space junkman in the series-ending "Junkyard of Space."

Michael Conrad as Creech, with Jonathan Harris (makeup by John Chambers) in "Fugitives in Space."

The high point of the season, and possibly the series, was *Lost in Space*'s twist on the "evil parallel universe" story, "The Anti-Matter Man," a visually arresting fantasy with a brutal otherworld John Robinson, well-played by Guy Williams, taking the place of the real Professor and attempting to infiltrate the Robinson clan while a suspicious Will Robinson tries to thwart him. Director Sutton Roley and cinematographer Frank Carson worked with art director Frank Barnette to create a nightmare "negative" world on the standing planet set, home to a scarred, vicious Don West and a miserable, embittered black-and-white Robot suspended in chains in a cave.

Bob May recalled in 1995:

> Sutton Roley shot it like you would for a feature, a motion picture, instead of trying to cut corners and do things for television. He made a masterpiece out of different scenes—there was the scene where Will Robinson and the Robot were going across this one area and he had this smoke come off over and it looked like they were just floating, and it was just beautiful. And the work that Mark Goddard did in that, and Guy Williams, God rest his soul. They had to play their double as well as themselves, as anti-matter. It was a brilliant show.

Goddard, too, listed "The Anti-Matter Man" as his favorite of the series:

> Because I was able to play a dark side of me. I was Don West and then I was the other side of Don West where I could wear a beard and had a little scar. I could be vicious. That was my favorite show cause I could let out all that frustration I had. I was going up to somebody that was in a cage and I was poking 'em with fire—I felt good. I was gonna burn up everybody. I was just a terrible mean kind of a guy. Didn't have to be the nice Don West that I always was.

On March 1, 1968, CBS sent a letter to Space Productions with a Notice of Termination for the series. But this news wasn't passed on to the cast and much of the staff, which had been developing scripts for a fourth season. The show wrapped up with a strange, bittersweet and unintended finale: "Junkyard of Space," with the Jupiter 2 following the lost Robot and Space Pod down to an eternally dark planet covered with space debris and run by a silver-faced, half machine "Junk Man" (Austrian actor Marcel Hillaire) who is eager to reduce the Robot and Jupiter 2 to rubble. With its apocalyptic landscape of space garbage and the threat of the Robot and Jupiter 2 being scrapped, the show seemed an almost poetic sendoff to the series and its characters.

Bob May remembered a favorite sequence:

> I loved the scene between the Robot and Will Robinson when the Robot is saying goodbye, and he's gonna put himself into the blast furnace to sacrifice himself for the family, and the touchy-ness of the scene between Will Robinson and the Robot, when they're saying goodbye. It was really nice.

Reportedly, the network demanded more budget cuts for the fourth year, and Allen, rather than incorporate the

**RIGHT**

Angela Cartwright models her mod third season wardrobe.

Judy (Marta Kristen) looks on while Don West (Mark Goddard) attacks the Robot (Bob May) with a screwdriver—a touch of the acerbic relationship between West and the Robot character that was infrequently explored in the series.

247

cuts, elected to discontinue the series after its summer hiatus. But his discussion of the cancellation of the series in an interview in *The Houston Chronicle* at the end of July, 1968 pointed to network dissatisfaction with the show's viewing audience:

> *Lost in Space* had three good happy seasons on CBS and we still had plenty of good scripts. But someone decided according to the "demographics" that the right people, the people who buy the products, were not watching. I don't believe any of that. I don't believe you can test 1,100 people in the United States and determine who's watching anything. *Lost in Space* always had a good rating and I doubt very much if all those people who were watching were either too young or too poor to buy the product.

For the cast of *Lost in Space*, the cancellation of the series was an ugly surprise, particularly for Billy Mumy:

> We were told that we were coming back for the fourth season. So when we finished the third season we were told, "See ya in ten weeks or twelve weeks," and my family and I went to Hawaii and had our little vacation and came back fully expecting to return. And then right around the time we were expecting to get ready to gear back up for the fourth season, I got a call from my agent, Howard Ruben, who said, "Wow, we just found out that we're not coming back. The show's off the air. It's been cancelled." I cried. I really did. I cried. It was very sad to me. I mean in show business, you're used to things ending, moving on. Saying good-bye to people that you've become close with and letting it go. *Lost In Space* was certainly the longest amount of time I'd ever spent working with the same group of people—a little over three years. And, I wasn't prepared to say good-bye, because we didn't get to say good-bye. I never said good-bye to Guy Williams. He was gone. He went to South America. I never saw him again. Never said good-bye. Never said anything to him again. It was sad. But I'm still close with the cast members and that's show biz.

Determined that he wasn't finished with the talent behind the series, Allen proposed a series with Jonathan Harris as part of a traveling circus, and even a half-hour comedy series called *Rodney the Robot*, with the following outline:

> An alien robot lands on Earth and after being short-circuited by the crash, is revived by two Boy Scouts on a camping trip in Death Valley. After they take the robot home, their single father, an electrical engineer, works on Rodney, reviving his various abilities—he scans the *Encyclopedia Brittanica* on their book shelves and immediately absorbs the knowledge. Potential plots included Rodney taking over cooking duties using scans from the recipes of famous world cooks, leading to the family winning a medal for a cake at the county fair; Rodney brilliantly playing the stock market to solve the family's financial woes; Rodney using his analysis to help the local high school football team win the big game; Rodney panicking Washington by proving that the collection of income tax is illegal.

Neither of those ideas took root, but *Lost in Space* thrived in afternoon syndicated reruns, reinforcing its position as an iconic piece of television escapism. Most of the cast went on to other projects, but the constant repeats of the show ensured that they would be forever remembered as the Robinson family, Dr. Smith and the Robot—the first, and most famous, family in outer space.

**OPPOSITE**
Marta Kristen with a purple, talking Llama, rumored to become a series regular in season four—until Jonathan Harris and the other actors rebelled over the idea.

# MINIATURE GALLERY
## LOST IN SPACE

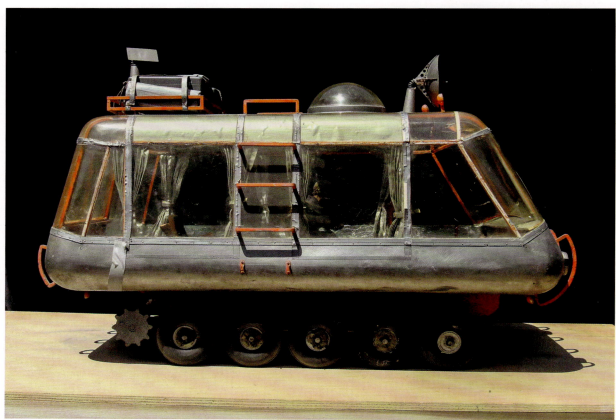

The large, two-foot Chariot miniature used for the sequence of the Cyclops attacking the Chariot.

The miniature figures built to populate the 24-inch Chariot. Springs in the figures' waist joints allowed them to shift realistically as the miniature bounced along. In addition to the Robot, a miniature of the Bell Jet Pack was made for the unused sequence of John Robinson buzzing the Cyclops in his rocket belt.

A Jupiter 2 miniature carved up to be one of the buildings in Irwin Allen's later City Beneath the Sea.

The small, 12-inch Chariot miniature used for the whirlpool sequence. Photo by Ron Hamill.

# MINIATURE GALLERY
## LOST IN SPACE

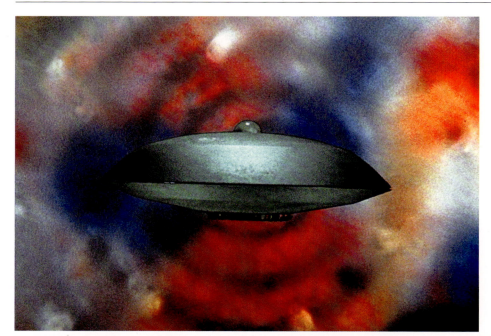

Jupiter 2 miniature shots filmed for season three. The kaleidoscopic upper image is one of the few composite shots of the Jupiter 2; virtually all other shots of the ship in flight were accomplished in camera with the model in front of painted backdrops—even the orbital shots.

The original Space Pod miniature on sale at Profiles in History. Photo by Gene Kozicki.

> **"**
> THERE IS NO LIMIT, EITHER IN SPACE OR TIME, AS TO JUST HOW FAR WE CAN GO WITH THE TIME TUNNEL.
>
> **IRWIN ALLEN**

# THREE RING CIRCUS

*Allen's coup: Three network TV shows, including his favorite:* **THE TIME TUNNEL**

**OPPOSITE**
Darren and Colbert try recreating their zero G tumble through time on the set for this publicity photo.

In 1966, Irwin Allen would have the distinct honor of having three high-profile, expensive series on network television—and his newest entry, The Time Tunnel, would grant Allen something his prior programs hadn't quite managed: critical acclaim.

The production roots of The Time Tunnel went back at least to Allen's The Story of Mankind, which jumped around in time to depict various important junctures in history, and did so economically by utilizing stock footage from Hollywood historical movie epics. The new concept would mix Allen's fascination with history and his love of science fiction and technology, telling the tale of Tony Newman (James Darren) and Doug Philips (Robert Colbert), "Two American scientists… lost in the swirling maze of past and future ages, during the first experiments on America's greatest and most secret project, the Time Tunnel."

The Time Tunnel was a massive underground installation built to send travelers through time, and in the first episode the project's chief personnel, Dr. Heywood Kirk (Whit Bissell), Dr. Raymond Swain (John Zaremba), and Dr. Ann MacGregor (Lee Meriwether) send the eager young Tony Newman into the past and watch as he lands on the ocean liner Titanic, hours before it makes its fateful rendezvous with an iceberg. The team sends Newman's associate and friend, Doug Philips, to retrieve Newman—but they soon discover that they can only shift Newman and Philips into different time eras when they're in trouble, and that they cannot bring the two adventurers back into the complex and the present—leaving the two men "tumbling helplessly somewhere along the infinite corridors of time."

It was an exciting, open-ended concept that promised to rebut all the criticisms that had been lobbed at *Lost in Space* and *Voyage to the Bottom of the Sea* during their early years on the air, and it would become Allen's favorite of all the shows he produced. After its promising debut, however, The Time Tunnel also crashed back to Earth more quickly than any of Allen's other series.

Irwin Allen began developing the *Time Tunnel* concept in 1964, while he was working to get *Voyage to the Bottom of the Sea* on the air. As originally conceived, *The Time Tunnel* would have focused on a single time traveler. Allen was inspired by the success of the David Janssen drama *The Fugitive*, about a man fleeing the law after being accused of a crime he did not commit, who traveled around the country encountering new characters and situations every week. The show had premiered a year earlier on ABC to great acclaim.

From an early outline:

> The concept of THE TIME TUNNEL concerns a man thrust into time, both past and future. He cannot and will not tamper with history as we know it. He must survive against the most bizarre and provocative situations and backgrounds yet devised for a continuing lead on TV. Above all, he will experience dramatic situations with interesting people that he will encounter during his time-adventures.

The outline went on to compare *The Time Tunnel* concept with *The Fugitive*:

> With respect to the success of the ABC series, THE FUGITIVE, we feel this show is an example of the dramatic direction we intend to take. The Fugitive enters a strange town and is immediately caught up in a dramatic story, against a background that has human values, is exciting and is constructively resolved. The Fugitive, who is always faced with the powerful motivation of survival, moves on to another unknown destination in his quest to return to his normal place in life. THE TIME TUNNEL will therefore have all of the successful ingredients of THE FUGITIVE plus those special, fantastic elements of its own.

In the early drafts of the concept, Peter (rather than Doug) Philips was the man lost in time, while Tony Newman, the Time Tunnel's primary inventor, works at the Time Tunnel complex (referred to very rarely with the nickname "Project Tic-Toc") to monitor Philips and try to rescue him, week after week. In a June 30, 1964 inter-office memo to Allen on a *Time Tunnel* presentation, Allen's agent (and uncredited advisor on his shows) Herman Rush suggested the opening end with an explanation:

> Peter Phillips is a man lost in time. Dr. Tony Newman, frustrated by the imperfection of his time tunnel, succeeds only in moving Phillips from one time period to another, constantly missing his target, the present time. Our series that follows concerns the adventures of Phillips, as he travels from one time period to another, and the futile efforts of Newman as he attempts to bring Phillips back to 1964.

Allen and his writers, including Shimon Wincelberg, came up with a number of different story concepts set in different time periods, which Rush read and addressed. A story set in 1927 involved multiple time travelers crossing paths and actually selling journeys through time, which Rush thought too confusing. The concept also involved the characters wearing high-tech rings that would allow them to be tracked through time.

Rush wrote:

> I feel very strongly that there only should be one other time traveler, not many. Therefore, I think your basic theme has to be changed. This is a good story and I don't want to change it completely, but I think that we must eliminate these additional time travelers. Perhaps the girl believes that there might be other time travelers, and when she spots Phillips and his ring, she assumes that he is one of many that are chasing her. You should eliminate the problem she faces, that is, the sale of unauthorized time vistas. This is too complicated. Additionally, if this were true, and time travel conquered, then obviously, Phillips could be saved and brought back. I also suggest that the girl should be left to continue in time, perhaps with Phillips, or, perhaps, Phillips will run into her again in future episodes.

Other story outlines included "The Distant Past—1863," "The Ancient Past—200,000 BC," and "The Future—2065," which involved an adventure in outer space.

On the last outline, Rush commented:

> I find this to be the weakest of the five stories. There basically are no other people in it, there are no other sets, there's no sense of excitement, there's no problem to resolve of any consequence. Additionally, I am personally opposed to incorporating space travel in a series concerning itself with time travel. I think it's difficult enough for the audience to accept time travel, and we should not complicate this with space travel. I think that a future story that takes place in 2000 or 2100 might concern itself with what might happen on this earth, our life, our civilization, or a new civilization in the future. Something with a moral, a warning; perhaps some horrible disaster or war that the world was faced with, or of the conquering of underwater living; the conquering of space travel, or something of this nature, but we should keep it on earth and not make it happen on Mars.

At this point one of the two lead scientists was still to remain behind in the Time Tunnel complex, monitoring the other's status. Rush went on:

> ...Each of these stories, or at least several of them, should include some communication between Phillips and Newman. This should be only when Phillips is in transit. This should be used to develop a relationship between the two, as well as getting the audience to know a little about Newman and his problems, frustrations and guilts.

While the series would initially begin with Phillips and Newman separated, and depict them becoming separated in a few later episodes of the series, the show kept them as a team throughout most of its run, allowing them to discuss the ramifications of each time travel situation with each other rather than always having the "Project Tic-Toc" technicians fill in the blanks for the audience.

On November 17, 1964 Allen wrote a letter to ABC's Edgar J. Scherick regarding a "blueprint of operations" for *The Time Tunnel*: "The time is now ripe to expand on a solid base of operations of which, you know, I am very proud," Allen said, referring to his burgeoning television

**OPPOSITE**
Original presentation artwork, prepared to pitch *The Time Tunnel* to the ABC network.

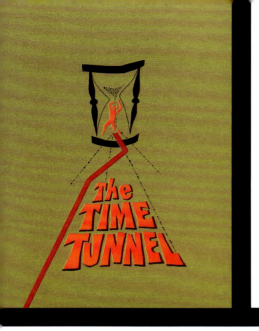

**beyond the known...
into the future!**

**beyond history...
into the past!**

THE TIME TUNNEL takes a young physicist of the 20th Century through the black emptiness of the fourth dimension to the first landing on the moon; back to the crossing of the Delaware with the first Continental Army; then on to the Battle of Midway; back to the French Revolution; down to the center of the Earth; to a thousand present lands; to countless fabled yesterdays; to untold mysterious tomorrows.

**boldly imaginative!
vividly prophetic!
the fantastic future!
the incredible past!**

The spine-tingling reality of Man coursing through the complex of the most ingenious time-warp ever conceived, beyond the mist of all known spacial relationships into the deep mysteries of:

## THE PAST

**PREHISTORIC WORLD**

**RICHARD THE LION HEARTED**

**DAVID AND GOLIATH**

"THE TIME TUNNEL"
AS A SPECTACULAR TELEVISION SERIES
AN IRWIN ALLEN PRODUCTION

## THE FUTURE

**WORLDS OF TOMORROW**

**RETURN OF THE ICE AGE**

**ATTACK OF THE STARS**

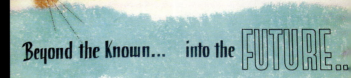

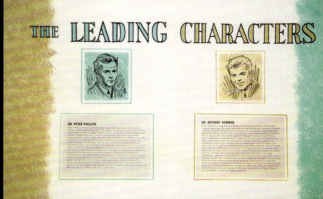

**ABOVE**
Time travelers Doug (Robert Colbert, left) and Tony (James Darren, right) captured by pirates.

**OPPOSITE**
Original presentation artwork, prepared to pitch *The Time Tunnel* to the ABC network.

production operation that now included *Voyage to the Bottom of the Sea* and would soon see the launch of *Lost in Space*. Allen intended for Shimon Wincelberg to be story consultant and write "not less than four of the first thirteen scripts" for *The Time Tunnel*. Allen provided 26 basic episode ideas for Scherick's perusal and added:

> While *The Time Tunnel* was created as a one-hour show, it also beautifully lends itself to a bi-weekly, one-half hour format. In this instance we would end the first half hour segment with a wild and woolly, Perils of Pauline curtain hook to bring the audience back strongly for the concluding segment.

(The half-hour, split story approach would be used two years later in Fox's *Batman* series, while the idea of a cliffhanger ending to the show would be used for both *Lost in Space* and *The Time Tunnel*).

Allen urged Scherick to schedule a meeting in New York with Bill Self and Herman Rush to discuss the possibilities.

The list of specific story proposals read as follows:

Lost Civilization—Tony and Doug find dinosaurs and the ruins of metropolitan skyscrapers, and a human couple under attack from retrogressive semi-humans of this degenerate era.

Atlantis—Tony and Doug save a husband and wife who help them from the cruel citizens of Atlantis, then they in turn save the couple from the inevitable destruction of Atlantis.

The Gladiators—Tony and Doug forced to fight as gladiators in ancient Rome.

Inferno of Terror—Tony and Doug find themselves in an "alien earth-boring machine" plunging toward the center of the earth. They must defeat the aliens and save the planet.

Monster of the Snow—Tony and Doug confront the Abominable Snowmen, actually aliens from a distant galaxy in disguise.

Return of the Ice Age—Tony and Doug wind up in New York a 100 years hence, where city is threatened with glaciers.

When the World Drowned—In 12,000 A.D. the pair confront amphibians, survivors of a cataclysm that has drowned the world and destroyed civilization.

A broader, more general list of story possibilities featured a host of potential historical events to be explored:

> Prehistoric, future events, the eruption of Vesuvius, the building of the Pyramids and burning of Alexandria, the siege of Troy, sacrifices of the Incas, Genghis Kahn, the fall of Rome, the Crusades (Richard the Lion-Hearted), King Arthur's Court, Captain Kidd, Battle of Waterloo, the French Revolution, Joan of Arc, Pancho Villa, Marco Polo, Salem witchcraft trials, Benedict Arnold, Valley Forge, Billy the Kid, the Alamo, the Chicago Fire, Little Big Horn, the San Francisco earthquake, the Hindenberg, Pearl Harbor, D. Day, and the Fall of Berlin (inside Hitler's suicide bunker).

Allen's experience on *The Story of Mankind* had given him great experience at canvasing and organizing libraries of stock footage, and with his staff and those at Fox, the production began to amass an incredible, indexed breakdown of all the historical movie footage available at Fox, which would occupy a cross-referenced, tabbed book four to five inches thick that broke down the footage by period and type of action (battle scenes, crowd scenes, naval action, etc.).

In the early casting discussions for the show, the Philips character, now named Doug, was to be the younger, dashing character trapped in time, and Glen Corbett, Lloyd Bochner, Guy Stockwell, Ben Gazarra, Steve Forrest, and Paul Burke were looked at for the role. Tony Newman was conceived as a more fatherly figure who would remain behind in the Time Tunnel complex and not get mixed up in the show's action. Older character actors like Edmond O'Brien (who would perspire his way through a similar role in Fox's *Fantastic Voyage*), Carroll O'Connor, Richard Carlson, Robert Sterling, Leif Erickson, Richard Kiley, Joseph Cotton, MacDonald Carey, Howard Keel, Hugh Marlowe, and David Wayne were discussed for Newman.

Ultimately the two characters were adjusted so that Tony Newman would be the headstrong and sensitive, younger scientist and Doug Philips the somewhat older and wiser (although still leading-man handsome) character. James Darren (who would be cast as Tony

Newman), like Frankie Avalon of the *Voyage to the Bottom of the Sea* movie and Fabian of *Five Weeks in a Balloon*, was a budding crooner and teen matinee idol who had appeared movies like *Gidget* and *Gidget Goes Hawaiian* before Allen cast him as an android on the *Voyage to the Bottom of the Sea* episode "The Mechanical Man." Robert Colbert (whose name was spelled, and pronounced, the same as late night TV host Stephen Colbert's) had appeared in 200 prior television episodes, dating back to *Bourbon Street Beat* in 1960 and including gigs on *Maverick* (As Brett Maverick's brother Brent) and *Hawaiian Eye*, *77 Sunset Strip*, *The Virginian*, *12 O'Clock High*, *Perry Mason*, *Bonanza* and many others. Colbert would play the manly, level-headed (for the most part) Doug Philips.

Harve Bennett was Vice President of Programming at ABC while Allen was developing the series (Bennett would later be known for taking over the *Star Trek* movie franchise and producing *Star Trek II: The Wrath of Khan* in 1982). In June, 1965, Allen wrote Bennett after ABC had requested paragraphs on the story ideas designated as "Roman Gladiators," "Ivanhoe" and "Captain Cook" as a possible pilot episode for *The Time Tunnel*. Allen and his team preferred the "Roman Gladiators" idea, but the actual pilot story, entitled "Rendezvous with Yesterday," would have Newman and Philips landing on the Titanic in 1912. This would allow Allen and his team to employ footage from Fox's 1953 proto-disaster movie *Titanic*—although after he assigned writer Shimon Wincelberg to the pilot, Allen told Wincelberg specifically not to identify any of the proposed *Titanic* footage in the teleplay because he didn't want the network to know that the series would be saving money by using Fox movie footage.

Unfortunately for Wincelberg, the network insisted on changes to the story. Wincelberg recalled in an October, 1990 interview with Mike Clark in *Starlog*:

> ABC wanted another script because they were still interested in the show. I said I would do it, but Fox said, "No, your name is already associated with the first script." And even though everyone at Fox liked my script, they felt, for tactical reasons, there should be another writer's name on it, and brought in Harold Jack Bloom. I was pretty annoyed at the studio's lack of loyalty after they had been so high on the script. There was still a lot of my stuff left in the final script, mostly involving the establishing of the tunnel and some Titanic material.

One of Wincelberg's Titanic elements involved Doug Philips' father and grandfather being onboard the doomed ocean liner; Harold Jack Bloom removed this storyline, but the idea of one of the time travelers encountering their own parents became part of a later episode, "The Day the Sky Fell In." The final episode credited Allen, Wincelberg and Bloom for the story, but the experience rankled both Allen and Wincelberg (who had annoyed Allen on *Lost in Space* by insisting on using his pen name, S. Bar David, on "The Reluctant Stowaway"), and *The Time Tunnel* pilot would be the last time Allen employed the writer.

Stories on the production of the pilot episode (including one from *The Hollywood Reporter*) credited Harold Jack Bloom without mentioning Wincelberg. Allen expounded enthusiastically about the series concept in the *Reporter* story:

> There is no limit, either in space or time, as to just how far we can go with *The Time Tunnel*. In script form at the moment is a story concerning Halley's Comet and its plunge to earth. We have a story built around Appomattox, Dunkirk, the American Revolution, Columbus' discovery of America, the storming of Troy and the Babylonian revels.

After the falling out with Wincelberg on the Titanic episode, Allen's production nearly ran into another, smaller iceberg owned by MGM. A January 3, 1966 letter from Saul N. Rittenberg of MGM to Allen after reading *The Hollywood Reporter*'s first story about *The Time Tunnel* read:

> You are no doubt aware of our feature entitled *The Time Machine* produced by George Pal about 5 years ago...We feel that your use of the title *Time Tunnel* is in conflict and unfair competition with *The Time Machine* and therefore request that you desist from using the title.

While the threat from the accusations of cribbing from the *Space Family Robinson* comic book had been given serious consideration during the production of *Lost in Space*, neither Allen nor executives at Fox took seriously the idea that MGM and H.G. Wells had a monopoly on the word "time" or the concept of time travel. But Allen's show would be the first to mount a serious, weekly exploration of the idea, and it would ultimately impact other science fiction programs of the period (including *Star Trek*) and inspire later series.

After topping the early season of *Voyage to the Bottom of the Sea* with the impressive pilot for *Lost in Space*, Allen sought to make *The Time Tunnel* his most spectacular television production yet. Art director Bill Creber, working with Rodger Maus and Allen's team of illustrators and storyboard artists, began the process of designing the Tunnel itself with a focus on the look of an hourglass—sometimes turned on its side, sometimes drawn upright. One fascinating illustration shows an upright, hourglass-like machine with stairways and corridors leading inside in Escher-like, Moebius strip trajectories, as if the machine itself is composed of materials that create physics-bending, extra-dimensional shapes. Eventually the hourglass-on-its-side evolved into the massive Time Tunnel seen in the pilot episode, an immense "limbo" set with the Tunnel a series of concentric ovals that (thanks to forced perspective and an incredible Emil Kosa, Jr. matte painting) appear to recede into infinity.

The massive look of the facility began with features built into sound stages at Fox to facilitate studio tours. "They had just built brand new sound stages on the Fox lot along the Avenue of the Stars," Creber says. "They had thought they would have tours and allow the tour groups to watch from a room onto the live shooting sets. So they built these big, windowed rooms overlooking the sound stages without talking to any directors or anybody that was on the sound stages. We got the idea that one of those rooms would be part of the set. So we took the whole sound stage and painted it black, which it

**OPPOSITE**
Early concept design sketches for the Time Tunnel, created under the supervision of art director William Creber.

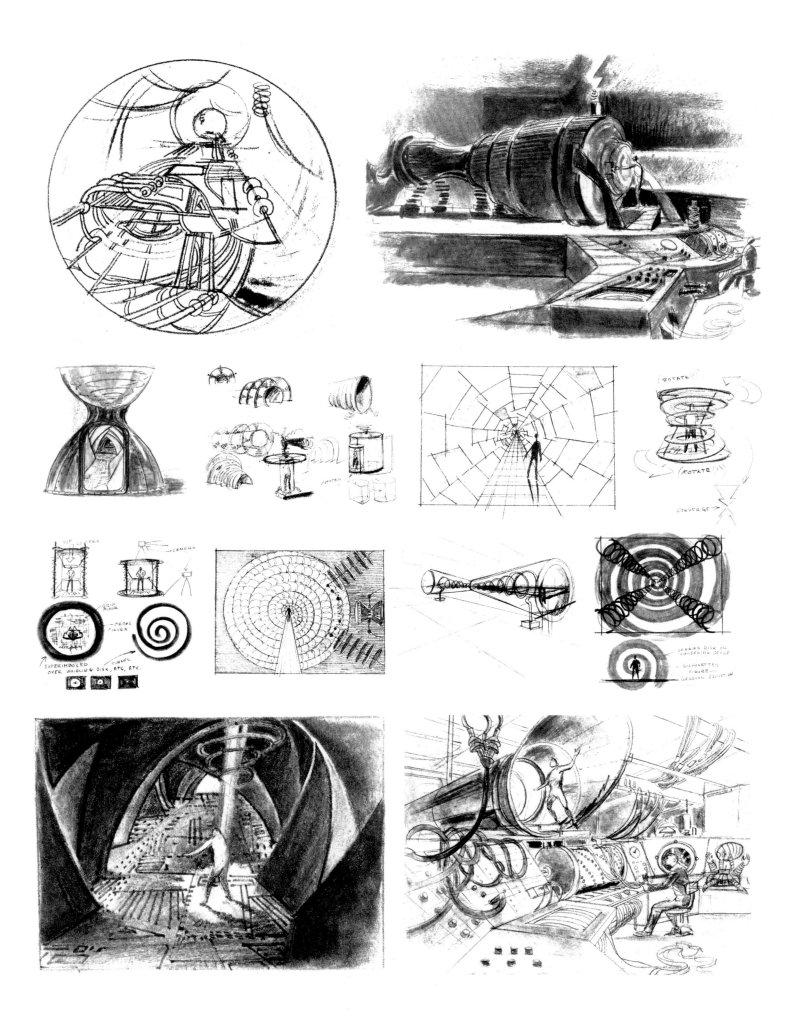

should be anyway. The stages were adjacent so you could walk from one to the other and they had big stage doors to close them off, so it was really one big building. We took over the whole complex for the pilot and went onto the black stage and built a big oval, op-art tunnel in the doorway between stages, so if they wanted to extend it they could. It was all forced perspective and the last part that appeared to be the last 100 feet was a photograph of the actual set that we used to extend the tunnel to infinity—it was about a 5-foot by 7-foot image that made it appear to go on forever."

The massive, gantry-like "power platforms" to the right of the Time Tunnel controls were also part of the odds and ends on the Fox lot. "We had a system of platforms that they seldom used," Creber says. "They were very square and they didn't have the usual fake platform look, they were all square, parallel sections. We built four of those and built them up to about thirty feet high, and with four of them we strung lights on them like Christmas tree lights. They were painted sort of a metallic gray so there was just a little contrast between them and the walls of the soundstage. On the floor we had the insignia and we had some consoles that we probably found in stock, but that was the set—there were no real walls to the set, just stage walls painted black, so the whole set seemed to be in a kind of limbo."

Creber talked about the set in a 1966 issue of *TV Guide*:

> The set fills a complete soundstage at 20th Century-Fox. The infinity segment of the tunnel at the rear goes back an additional 26 feet into another stage, and is built on wheels so that it can be moved into position to join the body of the tunnel or moved back to increase the tunnel's illusion of infinity. The front segment of the tunnel is wired for both lighting and special effects, and can shoot jagged streaks of colored lights and smoke.

The colored lights and smoke, along with Allen's trademark sparking explosions, were part of the effect of the time machine in operation, and the end result of a lot of experimentation, according to Allen in the *TV Guide* story:

> At first we tried a kaleidoscopic effect, lights flashing and whirling. Then we tried using old newsreel shots, blurring them to give the impression of time telescoping, but it looked like dirty soup. We finally went for op art and came up with this tunnel, built at a cost of $84,000, out of Styrofoam, sheets of aluminum, and mostly paint for a *trompe l'oeil* effect. It rests on an enormous concrete base. The consoles and ancillary equipment cost $45,000 and we used war-surplus material. The thing really works. Wheels turn and lights blink. The power towers are made of iron works put together piece by piece like Tinker Toys. They stand 45 feet tall.

Allen filmed the pilot at Fox's main studio lot over a 20-day shooting schedule, with major and second unit photography taking place at California and Arizona location sites. The show's opening would depict a government watchdog, played by Gary Merrill, landing by jet in the Arizona desert and being driven into the hidden Time Tunnel complex through a driveway that magically appears in the desert floor. Once inside he

**ABOVE**
The forced perspective Time Tunnel, so large that the background extended into an additional sound stage at Fox.

**OPPOSITE**
The towering "power platforms" and barely visible observation rooms above them on the massive sound stage holding *The Time Tunnel*'s main set.

views a staggering underground installation descending hundreds of levels below the earth's surface, powered by throbbing atomic reactors, and reachable by a dizzying glass elevator tube descent.

An *American Cinematographer* feature showcased L.B. Abbott's effects for the show (Abbott would win his third Emmy in a row for the effects on *The Time Tunnel*, after nabbing the award for his effects on *Voyage to the Bottom of the Sea* and *Lost in Space* the previous two years). Each episode of the series would begin with Doug Philips and Tony Newman tumbling through a kaleidoscopic vortex, seemingly suspended in space, before landing in a new time period. An IATSE official bulletin from the New York quarterly described the approach Abbott took to show Phillips and Newman plummeting through "the endless corridors of time":

> To symbolize these repeated journeys, Brother Abbott came up with a drum nine feet in diameter, covered with scraps of colored cellophane. A camera with a Kinoptic 9.8mm ultra wide lens was set up close to the surface of the drum and adjusted so that the image photographed would fill the frame as the drum revolved toward it. Subsequently this scene was flipped over to fill the blank half of the frame and the two complimentary images were printed through a "ripple" glass to form the master background scene. To play against this background, scenes were shot of the time travelers suspended by wires in front of a blue screen in such a way that they could be revolved about an axis. The camera, mounted on a crane, was equipped with an image inverter prism before the lens, thus creating the illusion of the actors revolving in the opposite direction. Filmed at 64 frames per second, they seemed to float gracefully end over end.

The shot of the two scientists tumbling through time opened each episode, and was enhanced by John Williams' fluttering, disorienting music, created by having numerous woodwind instruments play overlapping trills. Williams also contributed a dynamic, mechanistic piece of theme music for the show's animated title sequence, one of the most gripping and exciting of Allen's career, opening with a multicolored, kaleidoscopic vortex that coalesces into an hourglass with a stylized human figure helplessly trapped in the sands of time.

A Chicago newspaper story by Dorothy Storck broke down the final costs on "Rendezvous with Yesterday": "The pilot cost a million dollars. It was 35 days in production and had two full time crews." Storck noted the difficulty in pinning down Allen for quotes, and conjured up a fanciful portrait of the man now known for three of the most expensive and colorful programs on network television:

> Ask for an interview with Allen and network press agents blanch. Apparently he dreams his monster dreams alone in his office, surrounded by charts of time and space and limitless bank balances. It is rumored he speaks through two tiny antenna, attached to the middle of his forehead.

On March 14, 1966, an ABC inter-department correspondence from Joseph Schrier to Edgar Scherick broke down the ASI audience test results of *The Time Tunnel* pilot:

**LEFT**
The Time Tunnel main controls and the entryway into the Tunnel

**LEFT BOTTOM**
An experiment with having the Time Tunnel machinery physically interact with the past, in a scene dropped from the pilot.

**OPPOSITE**
Storyboard artwork depicting Doug and Tony's plummet through time, which would open every episode of the series.

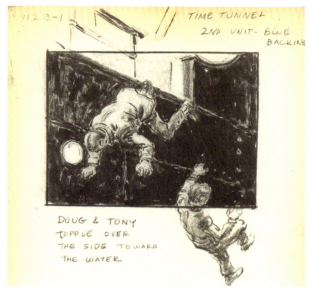

**OPPOSITE**
Preliminary artwork and photography for the power plant view and Time Tunnel reveal.

**RIGHT**
The animated title sequence from *The Time Tunnel*.

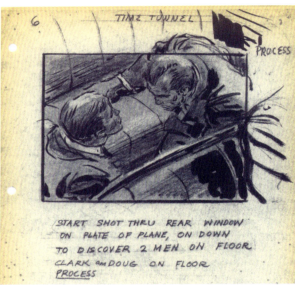

**LEFT**
These storyboards show Allen's meticulous planning, even for something as simple as Doug's conversation with the government official inside their car.

**OPPOSITE**
Storyboards for a view downward into the Time Tunnel facility's massive power plant and the initial view of the Tunnel itself.

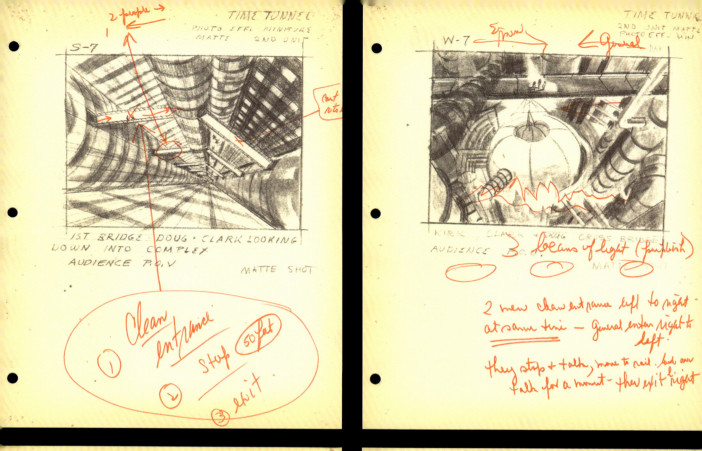

**S-7** — TIME TUNNEL / PHOTO EFF · MINIATURE / MATTE · 2ND UNIT
1ST BRIDGE · DOUG · CLARK LOOKING DOWN INTO COMPLEX
AUDIENCE P.O.V.    MATTE SHOT

2 people →
① Clean entrance
② Stop 50 feet
③ exit

**W-7** — TIME TUNNEL / 2ND UNIT MATTE / PHOTO EFF · MIN · DAY
← General
KIRK · CLARK · DOUG CROSS BRIDGE
AUDIENCE    Beams of light (pinplush)    MATTE SHOT

2 men claw entrance left to right at same time — General enter right to left.
they stop + talk, move to rail, look over talk for a moment — then exit right

**D-16 CONT-A** — TIME TUNNEL / 2ND UNIT MATTE / PHOTO EFF · MINIATURES
PERSONNEL RUSHING ACROSS BRIDGES
Second Camera on high hat!

**8A** FULL SHOT · THE COMPLEX — PHOTO EFF · MIN / MATTE · 2ND UNIT / DAY
THEY ARE DWARFED BY ENORMOUS MACHINERY THAT MAKES UP THE CONTROL AREA AND THE TUNNEL ITSELF
MATTE SHOT

...Somewhat above average for an hour-long drama in most program areas, although neither of the lead characters appeared particularly strong. ...most viewers responded quite favorably to the basic idea of the program which...seemed realistic and believable. Adults tested enjoyed the Titanic premise but many complained about the ending involving a prehistoric monster ("You go too far and make it ridiculous with dinosaurs"). Viewers seemed to prefer Doug Philips ("more mature and intelligent") to Tony Newman, while Newman was viewed as too young to be believable ("Does not exactly give impression of being a doctor of science—immature"). Gaged against its potential competition, *The Time Tunnel* rated above *Daktari* and *The Virginian* but below *The Man from UNCLE*. Recommendations included "continue using story lines that are as 'plausible' to adults as the one in the pilot," i.e. events they can relate to, and create a stronger, more mature personality for Tony Newman.

An April 26, 1966 concept depth research memo from Alan Sacks to Leonard Goldberg of ABC read:

Viewers seem to respond favorably to the basic idea.... it appears the fantastic situations are more acceptable to viewers if the two scientists have no control of their situation—they should not be able to return to the present when they desire or at the will of Time Tunnel personnel. If both scientists were able to return to the present many viewers may find it difficult to see why they would go back into the time machine.

Viewers wanted to see the Time Tunnel machinery in each episode:

The presence of the Time Tunnel would bring the story back to the present and possibly make the fantastic more acceptable. A gradual improvement of the machine—giving the viewer an indication that the plight of the scientists is not hopeless. Viewers did NOT want to see the scientists attempt to change the past and felt they should realize they can never change history. But perhaps some historical mysteries could be explained. Suggested "off-shoots" of major historical events, like having the scientists arrive at Dr. Mudd's house after Lincoln was shot rather than trying to prevent the assassination. Viewers did not want to see stories on other planets which would be too similar to *Lost in Space*. Viewers also felt the year 1968 when the pilot took place was too close to the present and felt the series should be set in the early 1970s or later.

*The Time Tunnel* pilot was selected for a preview showing at the 24th World Science Fiction Convention in Cleveland on Sept. 2-5, where it was presented alongside another science fiction TV series debuting in 1966: Gene Roddenberry's *Star Trek*. As far back as Stephen Whitfield's 1967 book *The Making of Star Trek*, the history of the Cleveland sci-fi convention has been that *Star Trek* received an ovation by the tough-minded crowd of science fiction fans and that Allen's *Time Tunnel* was more or less laughed off the screen (writer Jerry Sohl, who wrote *Star Trek*'s "The Corbomite Maneuver," reported that Allen's name was booed when it appeared on the screen in the credits for *The Time Tunnel*).

An unpublished book by Richard Lynch, *Worldcons of the 1960s*, quoted "a young Cleveland-area fan, Jerry Kaufman (at his first convention), perhaps spoke for many when he commented that, 'you have no idea how funny it was to see 600 stf-fans mocking that thing in front of a hopeful studio agent.'"

But the stated reactions of many of science fiction literature's biggest luminaries, in attendance at the con, were quite different, and Allen was able to trumpet the arrival of *The Time Tunnel* with some stellar endorsements.

John W. Campbell, legendary editor of *Analog*:

One of the best jobs of adult and true science fiction programs I've seen. You've got a science fiction rather than a fantasy approach.

Edgy author Robert Sheckley wrote:

Nicely done; nice effects. I think this concept and series has fine possibilities.

Ace Books editor Donald Wolheim:

The most authentic appearing sets and backgrounds I have ever seen. Unlike so many, this is good science fiction done as it ought to be. I do not usually care for the SF productions on TV, but I was enthralled by this one.

Frederick Pohl wrote:

SF in television has gone a long step forward with *Time Tunnel*. The production is superb, leaving out most of the cliches. The cast acts its parts instead of parodying them, and the story line is highly promising. Bearing in mind that this is adventure SF, not the cerebral kind, it is high quality.

Science fiction historian and critic Sam Moskowitz:

I found the film one of the most convincing presentations of a very difficult theme—time travel—that I have ever seen. The linkage with the space program in making the creation of a time machine a vast project requiring tremendous effort and expenditure, goes a long way toward contributing to this. The pilot story is superbly acted and photographed. The structure of the series' device makes possible unlimited and fascinating story possibilities. I like the maturity of presentation which makes it possible to develop humor, poignancy, adventure, tragedy or the entire gamut of the literary range.

Hugo-nominated illustrator Jack Gaughan:

It is a giant step toward eliminating the "Buck Rogers" stigma from TV science fiction. The sets are impressive and convincing. The story line takes advantage of the almost limitless possibilities of adventure in other times and other places.

A cover piece in *TV Week* by Marian Dern asked "Will *Time Tunnel* Stand the Test of Time?" Even at this point, Allen had a nickname—The King of Special Effects. But

**ABOVE**

Irwin Allen on the set of the *Time Tunnel* pilot with a young Dennis Hopper, playing White Star chairman J. Bruce Ismay. Hopper's scenes were cut from the final episode.

Doug Philips and Senator Clark (Gary Merrill) arrive at the *Time Tunnel* complex in the show's pilot, "Rendezvous with Yesterday."

Dern was another writer stymied by the challenge of getting an interview with Irwin Allen, who now didn't like talking to reporters—reportedly because he didn't like explaining how the special effects for his shows were created.

*Time Tunnel* has some strong plus qualities: the concept is imaginative, with potential for great variety in storyline; the special effects, particularly in color, of the huge underground research lab...all live up to the wildest dreams of what a futuristic lab should look like; the cast is appealing, and competent. There is a *Twilight Zone* quality in the story, a quality that could be developed, along with action-adventure, as the series proceeds. The program has far greater plot potential than either the space suburbanites of *Lost in Space* or the cliche and monster-ridden format of *Voyage*.

When Colbert, interviewed by Dern, enthused about the use of stock footage from Fox historical movies to expand the show's scope, the writer noted:

While this isn't exactly a secret, the publicists would prefer the matter be soft-pedaled. They think the public might feel cheated in terms of fresh, new material.

Darren stated that he suggested doing a storyline about the earth after an atomic war but was told it was too depressing for viewers. When he suggested it take place on another planet, Darren said, "That didn't go over, either." Dern noted that, as reviewed by other outlets, *Lost in Space* and *Voyage to the Bottom of the Sea* had squandered potentially exciting concepts by retreating rapidly into formula, throwbacks to the cliffhanging serials and mad scientist/monster movies of yesteryear:

Only time, excuse the expression, will tell if *Time Tunnel* keeps its potential promise, or descends, as the other series did, into a show about which even a representative of that often referred to "12-year-old mind" was heard to say recently, "It's just too stupid to watch anymore."

Regarding the use of stock footage, the ABC publicists may have been right, as at least one newspaper writer, P.M. Clepper in his column *Tonight's View*, lambasted the show for "tricking" audiences with the Fox movie footage:

Probably the most expensive-looking television show is *The Time Tunnel*. I stress "looking" because it is not the most expensive to produce. *Time Tunnel* slices in scenes from old movies. So far, only one show about the future has been completed. That's because the studio hasn't got as much science fiction footage in its vaults as it has of historical events.

"Irwin used a lot of stock footage—that was one of his trademarks throughout," Paul Zastupnevich said in 1995. "*Story of Mankind* was a picture that was built on outtakes, and stock footage. And *Time Tunnel* was based a lot on stock footage. And we had to match up costumes and tie in things so that they would carry on through. Wherever he could beg borrow or steal, he always did. That was one way of his cutting down the budget. And if we weren't on time he just went down to the set, just rip out a couple a pages, and we were back on schedule."

Costumes were one of the show's—and the lead actors'—biggest challenges. In his *Tele Views* column, Larry Rummel explained that Phillips and Newman wore the same clothes every week because the characters wore those outfits for the expensive pilot shots of them spinning through the time vortex. If they changed clothes every week, the time travel effects shots would have to be refilmed at great expense. James Darren was trapped in a stifling, wool turtleneck sweater that became uncomfortable under the hot stage lights, forcing Paul Zastupnevich to build in a hidden zipper so that Darren could open up the neck and get a little bit of relief between setups.

The show's constant action meant that Darren and Colbert's outfits had to be cleaned and repaired daily to maintain a consistent look. Paul Zastupnevich expounded on the challenges in a January 14, 1967 article in *The Marion Indiana Chronicle*:

> Few people realize the number of costumes needed for a show like ours. If a costume is soiled, a clean duplicate set of apparel must be immediately available. With the lead players, we keep as many as four different copies of each costume on hand. Dressing the extras is a major headache. They keep changing shape. Many times we have fitted clothes to people for a crowd scene, and at the next day's shooting different extras report in. A short, fat man might be replaced by a tall thin one, which means quick alterations. We had a problem in the very first episode deciding what Darren and Colbert would wear to go back to the Titanic. Their outfits had to be generic as they never return to the Time Tunnel headquarters.

Zastupnevich dressed Darren in a turtleneck and Colbert's suit was chosen because the Norfolk jacket "has repeated itself as a perennial masculine favorite. In this way they rarely seem completely out of place." For an episode set on Devil's Island, research showed the prisoners wearing suits of red and white stripes, but just before shooting, a producer decided that the outfits might look ridiculous to viewers. "I whipped the outfit off the actor, rushed off to tint it charcoal gray, hand-dried it with hot irons—and got the actor in the set with two minutes to spare."

An ABC press release trumpeted the show's attention to historical authenticity:

> Allen's credo is accuracy at any cost and he leaves no stone unturned to assure realistic portrayals of historical events. Allen founded his own research department in 1954. Today, it is one of the finest in the entertainment industry, run by Elizabeth Emanuel. The research library has 25,000 "volumes of every description" and Emanuel is assisted in research by five other women. "Mr. Allen is a stickler for making his motion pictures and television series as realistic and accurate as humanly possible. He realized years ago that there are millions of television viewers who do know the difference. That's why he formed his own research department to authenticate the word of his writing staff."

Emanuel pointed out one instance in the pilot where historical accuracy trumped commonplace wisdom:

**ABOVE**
Irwin Allen on the set of the *Time Tunnel* pilot, with guest star Michael Rennie as the captain of the Titanic.

**RIGHT**

Tony Newman (right) confronts himself as a young boy (Sheldon Golomb) while Doug Philips looks on in "The Day the Sky Fell In."

Joe Maross as General Custer in "Massacre."

Robert Colbert, Paul Carr (background) as Paris, and Dee Hartford as Helen of Troy in the wild "Revenge of the Gods."

We have a scene where the Titanic hits an iceberg on its maiden voyage and begins to sink. The question was whether the ship's band played "Nearer My God to Thee" as is mentioned in virtually every treatise written on the subject. We found no documented evidence that it did, and as insurance we made a call to a survivor of the Titanic now living in Denver. She affirmed that it did not.

Emanuel also noted that an episode involving Custer's Last Stand had the General fighting without his famous long golden hairdo—"It's a historical fact that General Custer had his locks shorn almost to a crewcut just before he went into his last battle."

Another ABC press release quoted Allen as saying, "I have always disliked the limitations of time. Clocks annoy me, and I have never worn a wristwatch." This directly conflicts with tales—confirmed by James Darren—of Allen stalking onto his TV show's sets and pointing to his wristwatch to remind the crew that "time is money" (maybe it was a pocket watch?), but it made for a catchy PR quote for the series.

> The key to my shows is escape. I firmly believe that audiences occasionally like to get completely away from the here and now, and science fiction offers that escape. It also offers a basis for speculation, since today's science fiction is rapidly becoming science fact. How many times have you wondered how history might have been changed if some major event had been forestalled—if Lincoln had not gone to Ford's Theater, or if Columbus' fleet had gone down in the mid-Atlantic? In *The Time Tunnel* we dabble with history, to see what might happen if someone with knowledge of the consequences tried to change the course of events. We can't change history—but that's not to say that our two young scientists won't be tempted to try.

In fact, *The Time Tunnel* differed completely from the way time travel was depicted on shows like *The Twilight Zone* and later on *Star Trek*, where several episodes were designed around characters' desperate attempts to prevent history from being changed. On *The Time Tunnel*, there was an underlying assumption, sometimes worked out in fascinating ways, that Philips and Newman were already a part of history, and numerous early episodes has the two scientists desperately trying to warn people in the past about upcoming events that only they knew about. There are even suggestions that the two time travelers are part of some hidden pattern affecting the overall thrust of history. In an interview with TV critic Rex Polier, Allen said:

> We created something we call "shadows of time." Great world-shaking events have shadow areas. In these areas things happen. We can find no explanations for them. Man knows little about time. Time, some say, is stationary and all of time exists in time. Some say you can cut a cake but it never disappears.

James Darren said in the piece:

> Aside from the effect of simply breaking through the fourth dimension, some of the situations in The Time Tunnel are downright spooky. In one story the character I play finds himself at Pearl Harbor right before the attack in

which he lost his father. He seeks him out, and when they meet they are both the same age. Then he sees and talks to himself at the age of seven. A similar thing occurs when the two men are projected forward to join a space flight to the moon. One of the men back at the Time Tunnel, watching their movements on a detector screen, sees himself aboard the craft—years in the future. That's what I mean by spooky.

Colbert had his own philosophical theories about how stories in the show might transpire:

It seems to me that with the ability to move about in time, even death could be overcome in some instances. If one of the characters were to be killed in some future time period, why couldn't he be brought back to life by moving the clock back a day or two? I was a little skeptical when the series was first offered to me because science fiction can so easily become incredible to an adult viewer. But seeing the finished pilot film erased all my doubts. I'm sure that children will enjoy the show, and it will attract adults too.

After *The Time Tunnel* was previewed, Allen found himself the recipient of a number of enthusiastic fan letters from an unusual source: fellow film and television producers.

Malvin Wald at Ivan Tors Films, Inc., wrote Allen:

I have had two entertainment delights in the past few weeks. One was seeing the feature picture *Fantastic Voyage*. The other was seeing the preview last night of your first air show on *Time Tunnel*. ...they both aroused the emotions of excitement and curiosity from the very beginning and gripped me to the very end. ...you performed the function of a creative producer—or perhaps a better word is showman. There are very few television shows on the air that have me hooked. I'm afraid *Time Tunnel* has now become one of them.

David Levy of Filmways and *The Addams Family:*

I saw your opening *Time Tunnel* show and I thought it was one of the best of the new breed. The production values were most impressive and I thought the script and direction were top flight. You scored your own triple play.

Larry Auerbach of William Morris:

I don't normally write fan letters, but having watched the first two episodes of "Time Tunnel," I've now become a big fan. I believe the quality, production, and performance are just great. If my own personal rating service, which involves my three kids and their friends, has any validity, you've got a big hit.

Jack Brodsky of Columbia Pictures:

I simply had to write to tell you that *Time Tunnel* is one of the best things to come along on television in years, and certainly is head and shoulders above anything else on the screen this year.

Stan Shpetner of Shpetner Productions, Inc., wrote:

I don't think I've ever written a fan letter to another producer, but I must compliment you on *Time Tunnel*. I think it is one of the best television shows on the air today and not only uniquely done but beautifully done in every respect.

After its premiere on September 9, 1966, the show earned equally enthusiastic notices from professional television critics. "The glossiest, most splendiferous of the new season's TV shows so far was last night's premiere of *Time Tunnel*, a science fiction adventure with production values which wouldn't quit," said the *Indianapolis News* review.

*Box Office* had some reservations, but was otherwise impressed:

It is a solid idea which appears to be getting the right treatment and which should pull the same audience as Allen's other two shows....it is a little more difficult to believe the young, handsome Darren as an electronics genius with a doctor's degree and years of experience on the Tunnel project than it is to believe in the tunnel itself. But Darren should draw in the femmes. The special effects department contributed greatly to the product's success.

Noting that he was a "rabid science fiction fan, which is more of a disease than a hobby," Bob MacKenzie in his Oakland Tribune column *Bob Mackenzie on Television* contrasted *The Time Tunnel* with *Star Trek*:

Judging by their first episodes, *Star Trek* and *Time Tunnel* are going to be preposterous, unbelievable, hammy and repetitious. But I am hooked already, of course, and will continue to tune them in, hating myself every minute. ... both series are lavish with what is called "production values," and contain some marvelous junk.

MacKenzie zeroed in on a potential logical fallacy behind the idea that Phillips and Newman seem to arrive at exactly the right time and place to experience important historical events first hand:

Logically, since there is no way to control where or when they land, there is no more reason for them to arrive on the Titanic just before it sinks than, say, in the water a hundred yards behind it, or 24 hours after it has sunk. But we will just have to swallow that. Or rather, I will; you can switch channels.

Misspelling Allen's name as "Irving Allen" (interestingly, the producer of the somewhat Irwin Allen-ish Matt Helm spy spoof movies), TV editor Fairfax Nisbet of *The Dallas Morning News* noted:

Admittedly Allen has grabbed off quite a premise with endless possibilities. The young people are handsome and attractive and if they do not fall into the Gielgud or Olivier class, in this case...everything will depend on the quality of the stories, and Allen has quite a track record for coming up with winners.

*The Time Tunnel* debuted one day after NBC's *Star Trek*. TV critic Russell Shaw directly compared the two shows, and Allen's show came out firmly on top:

**OPPOSITE**
Time Tunnel personnel Admiral Kirk (Whit Bissell), Dr. Ann McGregor (Lee Meriwether), and Dr. Swain (John Zaremba)—the trio who stay behind in the Time Tunnel complex and worry about Doug and Tony week after week.

The former is about a huge spaceship from earth touring the planets at some point in the future and running into the customary outer-space problems. The first show is about a murderous creature which could assume any shape at will; unfortunately the pace was plodding and the production values were none too good. On the other hand the first episode of *Time Tunnel* was quite expertly done. The gimmick here is an unpredictable time machine which keeps two young scientists bouncing about in the past and future but can't get them back into the present. If you enjoy science fiction (and I do) this one looks like a pretty respectable representative of the genre.

*The Time Tunnel* opened with a number of strong episodes that demonstrated the flexibility of the premise, immediately impressing with the promise that this was a concept that could not be reduced to *Voyage to the Bottom of the Sea*'s monster-of-the-week formula or the constantly reinforced Dr. Smith-Will Robinson-Robot character dynamic of *Lost in Space*. While the moon rocket sci-fi story "One Way to the Moon" bogged down in its claustrophobic space capsule and moon installation settings, "The End of the World" immediately broadcast Allen's genius at bringing the cosmic directly into viewers' living rooms. The Time Tunnel personnel (including an easily panicked technician named Jerry, played by handsome young Sam Groom) are terrified by the effects of a looming Halley's Comet, viewed inside the Time Tunnel from its unnerving approach near Earth in 1910. It turns out that an effect of the Time Tunnel brings in the gravitational and heat effects from the comet directly into the Tunnel and allows it to affect the control complex, unleashing a distinctly Irwin Allen-esque Hell (in apocalyptic action overseen personally by the producer).

The following episode, "The Day the Sky Fell In," had Tony Newman meeting up with his father—fated to die in the attack on Pearl Harbor in December, 1941. Actor James Darren not only had to perform his character meeting his own father—and himself as a young boy—but also his father's death, which Tony Newman can see coming. This moment, with Newman openly weeping and sobbing over the body of his father, is easily the most deeply and honestly emotional moment in the entire history of Allen's television work, more provocative than anything on *Star Trek* in depicting a handsome series lead breaking down in tears. It's an even more remarkable achievement given Allen's discomfort and impatience with the presentation of deep human emotions onscreen, either in his own or in others' work. Allen had pushed aside the realities of family relationships on *Lost in Space* and largely avoided the psychological stresses of a submarine environment on *Voyage to the Bottom of the Sea*, but *The Time Tunnel*, at least in its early episodes, seemed to offer possibilities for the producer to explore some genuine drama.

A Sept. 11, 1966, *Salt Lake Tribune* feature on "The Day the Sky Fell Down," noted that the production crew burst into applause after the emotional scene between James Darren and Linden Chiles, the actor playing Newman's father.

**ABOVE**
Tony Newman works with a 1950s Russian time machine under the auspices of Michael Ansara in "Secret Weapon."

Darren said in the piece:

> That was one of the most difficult scenes I've ever played, and I wasn't at all sure how well it would go. I've looked forward to this episode for some time because of the acting challenge it presented. Newman, whose father was reported missing in action, not only meets the man before his death, but he even sees and talks to himself at the age of seven. How many actors get a chance to play situations like that?

The sequence was a stressful one due to the schedule as well, since it was shot at the end of the day and would have been, had it not been filmed satisfactorily, split into work continuing the next week, breaking valuable focus for the actors.

"The Last Patrol," dealing with a less well-known battle during the U.S. War of Independence, showcased an equally intriguing dilemma, with Carroll O'Connor giving a superb double performance as a modern military man and history expert who takes the opportunity to meet with—and attempt to redeem—a despised ancestor of his.

*The Time Tunnel* also demonstrated very early on an ability to embrace some of the most eye-popping implications of its concept, as in the William Read Woodfield and Allan Balter-penned "Revenge of the Gods," with Doug and Tony trapped in a battle with the Spartans in ancient Greece. With their heroes about to be hacked to pieces, the Time Tunnel staff do what any red-blooded American time machine personnel would, and send an M.P. (the complex's dutiful security chief, Jiggs) armed with a submachine gun back in time to mow down a few dozen Spartans. They then pull the military officer back into the Tunnel, where he reappears as an old man, along with a furiously hacking Spartan soldier. It's Irwin Allen at his finest—a brilliant, 10 year-old's conception of what the coolest thing to do with a time machine would be.

A feature in *The New York/World Journal Tribune* by Harriet Van Horne seemed to home in on moments like this: "The show is one of the slickest, most suspenseful and imaginative of the new season, but it is also, sometimes, the funniest," Van Horne said, noting the use of time travel in the sitcom *It's About Time* and in *Star Trek* ("Tomorrow Is Yesterday"). "It is wholly inadvertent humor, however, and not accessible to the simple folk who swallow every word."

If *The Time Tunnel* could be ridiculous, it could also be ingenious, transporting Italian politician and philosopher Niccolò Machiavelli (Malachi Throne at his grandest) into the midst of the American Civil War in "The Death Merchant," or sending a shifty Robert Duvall from the present (setting a nuclear bomb in the time tunnel complex) to the far future (acting alongside gold-faced Vitina Marcus as citizens of a hive-like future society), and then to the prehistoric past (threatened by rubber-finned dinosaurs and the inevitable quicksand in one million B.C.) in "Chase Through Time." Another intriguing story, "Secret Weapon," had Doug and Tony discover a doomed Russian time machine in the 1950s, with a cruel Soviet

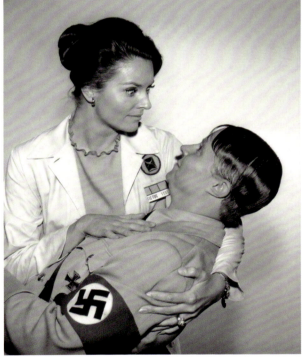

**RIGHT**
Lee Meriwether as the relatively deglamorized Ann MacGregor—and a joke publicity photo of the character seducing Adolf Hitler (Bob May) a character cut out of "The Kidnappers."

colonel (Michael Ansara) forcing the two Americans to help in their ill-fated experiments.

Despite the early publicity that showcased Allen's staff of historical researchers and the producer's insistence on accuracy, by the time the series had broadcast a dozen or so episodes, some critics zeroed in on the *The Time Tunnel*'s historical bona fides, or lack thereof.

In a December 13, 1966 column for *The Fort Worth Star-Telegram*, critic Jerry Coffey wrote:

> I could fill up the rest of this column—an entire week of columns, in fact—just listing the errors and distortions of fact and well-documented presumption in *The Time Tunnel* version of the climactic events at the Alamo… it really wasn't any worse than most of the other stories in the series which were based on specific historic or legendary events and personalities. Nearly all the scripts have taken liberties that should distress any well-read eighth grader. The show makes no claims at being anything more than fictional melodrama, which traditionally has been allowed to play pretty fast and loose with actuality. What bothers me isn't so much that history is distorted for entertainment purposes, but that it doesn't have to be in this series. When *Time Tunnel* started I thought it had more promise than any other entertainment series that had come along in years. The format seemed to offer limitless opportunities and an irresistible challenge for scriptwriters. Alas, virtually none of the possibilities have been realized. Instead, the series has depended almost entirely on ridiculously contrived plots that nullified the drama of the historic situation and on the increasingly repetitious use of the time tunnel's scientific gimmickry, while the historical characters have been played as conventional, one-dimensional heavies or heroes.

Coffey went on to note that the Alamo's Col. Travis was depicted by *The Time Tunnel* as "a brave blustery boob who didn't realize what was about to hit him."

While *The Time Tunnel* followed Irwin Allen form with its handsome leading men and the scientists and military men played by Whit Bissell and John Zaremba, the show was forward-thinking in another respect, casting former Miss America Lee Meriwether as a scientist and technician prominently featured week after week, tensely eyeing the computer monitors in front of her in the Time Tunnel complex. While *Star Trek* had also featured women in its cast, none were prominent regular characters and none were featured in the way Meriwether was—relatively deglamorized and shown more as a scientist than eye candy.

At least one newspaper columnist, Walter Saunders, complained about this development, saying that the show's "producers neglected girl-watchers" by dressing Meriwether in "stern-looking scientific outfits… her hair…combed on top of her head like an office stenographer who's been working for 50 years."

Interviewed by Saunders, Meriwether brushed off his concerns ("Most of my performing on *The Time Tunnel* has been limited to turning scientific dials and wringing my hands in front of the time tunnel.") But Meriwether

also revealed that her character was indeed intended to fulfill a more traditional function in the series—as a love interest for Colbert's Doug Phillips:

> In this series I'm supposedly in love with Doug, but it's quite a long-distance affair with him way out there somewhere. Hand-wringing kind of limits my role a bit. I've even suggested a story whereby I could enter the time tunnel and end up in a dangerous situation where Doug would have to rescue me. At least we'd be together for a while.

The writer agreed and went further, suggesting the producers "find a period of time where disaster strikes a bathing beach or a famous ballroom."

Meriwether herself, in 1995, downplayed the idea of her character being particularly progressive while acknowledging MacGregor's effect on young female viewers. "I was just so grateful to have a job and I was so happy to be acting and to be doing something that I thought was worthwhile. I loved the idea of them going back into history. And, I thought it was a wonderful teaching tool; I could see teachers using it all the time. At least three young girls wrote to me at different times [to tell me that my character had inspired them to] go

**ABOVE**
Caricature art by artist Bob Bentovoja, who created similar artwork for Allen's other TV shows and numerous other series, often for *TV Guide*.

**OPPOSITE**
Irwin Allen (right) crosses swords with James Darren on the set.

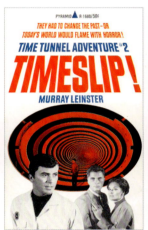
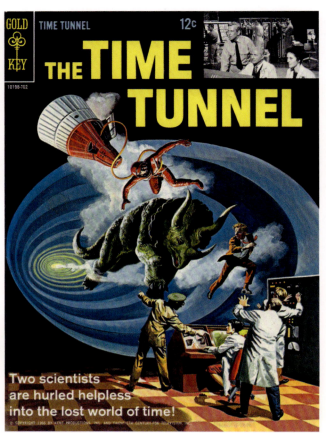

**LEFT**

*Time Tunnel* merchandise including a card game, comic book, paperback novels, a Japanese model kit, View-Master reel, board game and coloring book.

**OPPOSITE & FOLLOWING**

Interior artwork from Issue 1 of Gold Key's *Time Tunnel* comic book.

**RIGHT & OPPOSITE**
Cover and interior artwork from an obscure and ambitious Japanese *Time Tunnel* record adventure album.

into scientific fields—[one became a] microbiologist, and two became nuclear physicists."

Meriwether, John Zaremba and Whit Bissell had to do some real acting, since they were never privy to the images television viewers saw composited into the Time Tunnel, which the three characters had to react to. "We never saw any of the special effects," Meriwether said. "We acted a lot to little sticks with little round circles and faces drawn on them—one would be Jimmy and one would be Bob. And we would pretend that they were in some sort of peril usually and that was what we did most of the time, and played with a lot of fun dials, and made squiggly noises and squiggly lines, and it was a wonderful place to play."

For James Darren there was a strange time element just to working with Irwin Allen, because to the actor, Allen seemed like a character from a different time period. "He was a throwback to old Hollywood. There was something very eccentric about Irwin. He was a joy to watch. As an actor, when I wasn't in a scene, I would love to watch him direct. He was like something from the past, yet dealing in a contemporary situation. He was interesting as a director too because he would take the time to really explain everything to you as thoroughly as you needed. In fact, he preferred that because then if you ever made a mistake, it was totally your fault and not his 'cause he gave you the way to go."

ABC had *The Time Tunnel* airing at 8 pm on Friday nights, a tough time slot for a show designed to appeal to younger viewers. Nevertheless, *The Time Tunnel* debuted, like most of Allen's shows, with strong ratings. "Rendezvous With Yesterday"'s National Nielsens started at 23.8, handily beating *The Wild Wild West* and *Hogan's Heroes* on CBS and even football on NBC with a 46 share. But the following week the aggregate dropped to 16.4, losing out to *Hogan's Heroes* in the second half hour and to NBC, which placed first with *Tarzan* and Allen's perennial TV series competition, *The Man from UNCLE*.

*The Time Tunnel* also debuted at a time when new programs overall weren't exactly lighting the networks on fire. Fox television executive William Self commented on the situation in an *On All Channels* column by Dave Kaufman in November:

> I guess it has been called a bad season—everybody is calling it that. There haven't been any breakthrough shows. Maybe it's because we failed to come up with an exciting show. There isn't a show on the air you look at and say—that's a fresh approach.

Self cited the "relatively short commitment" networks offered to series as one problem.

> If you're going to invest in a unique concept, which might also involve unique sets or any unusual element, and that project is cancelled in 13 weeks, you're murdered. Our *Time Tunnel* is an example. Had this show been cancelled at midseason, it would have been a big loss for 20th. Therefore, I think too many production companies are aiming at the wrong target, in that sometimes we are more concerned about not being cancelled than we are in having a hit. The economic gamble is so great that we all

**ABOVE**
Allen on the *Time Tunnel* set with one of Paul Zastupnevich's monsters—which by 1966–67 could shamelessly make appearances on *Voyage to the Bottom of the Sea*, *Lost in Space* and *The Time Tunnel*.

**OPPOSITE**
Doug Philips (Robert Colbert) and Tony Newman (James Darren) arrive just in time for the attack on Pearl Harbor in *The Time Tunnel*.

play it a little too safe—we have relatively safe product. It's not exciting, but safe, and the public is getting bored with it. *Felony Squad* and *Tunnel* are good new shows. *The Green Hornet* is well done, but hasn't been as bizarre as the initial episode, and we are trying to go in that direction.

In a piece in *The Youngstown Vindicator,* Richard K. Shull expounded on the show's ratings challenges:

> [*The Time Tunnel* is] a good, honest adventure show... unfortunately, it's sandwiched between the sub-moronic *Green Hornet* and Uncle Miltie Berle's moribund variety show on ABC...and the gallows humor of *Hogan's Heroes* on CBS and the snickering sadism of *The Man from UNCLE* on NBC. The odds against its success...are monumental.

Praising its historical accuracy, Shull continued:

> *Time Tunnel* is doing a first-rate job of making history palatable to the small fry, perhaps a true reflection of the modern child's mind in which history, space research, and futuristic fantasy all commingle in one welter of events and places past and future.

A November 17, 1966 newspaper piece by Sandra Robinson rounded up Omaha viewers favorite TV shows in a survey. *Family Affair* was the favorite new show and *The Time Tunnel* tied with *Star Trek* for second place. In a ranking of the 10 most popular programs, October 20 through 26, *The Time Tunnel* placed at number 10 out of 10.

Actor John Zaremba acknowledged that the show was having ratings problems as early as November 20, 1966, in an article in *The Grand Rapids Press* by Dave Nicolette. Noting that the show had gotten up to 20th place and been climbing in the ratings:

> We're apparently not going to be TV casualties, not this season ...The public isn't exactly helpless on the borderline shows. Letters to the network and producers carry some weight, when the ratings indicate the show might die.

UPI's Vernon Scott, in a January 24, 1967 piece for *The Tennessee News Journal*, questioned what the audience for *The Time Tunnel* was, and cited the Friday night time slot as a factor in his concerns:

> Tots are in bed by that time. Teen-agers are too hep or out on dates. And any adult who watches it has got to be suspect. In the beginning the show might have been based on a good idea—but the idea is too costly for execution, for one thing. If you are going to put a couple of guys back in early Rome or in the War of the Roses you'd better have the money to make it look authentic. On this show it never does. The concept is handled clumsily, the acting poor, the scripts unbelievably bad.

Scott went on to specifically target the episode "The Ghost of Nero" (one of the show's lowest-rated outings):

> A spoof, you ask? No. A bit of satire, perhaps? No. It was pure tedium. A mature mind must ask itself why on earth this particular hour-long episode was filmed and aired,

and for whom it was intended.

Nevertheless, in a February 21, 1967 letter from Herman Rush to Allen, Rush cited the series as a success—considering the obstacles it was up against:

> All research evidence points to the fact that *Time Tunnel* in its first season has overcome less-than-ideal time period and station clearance problems. *Time Tunnel* is in rare and unfortunate position of being bridged by both other networks. It's telecast in only 170 markets and delayed in 56 markets, yet the show has maintained its appropriate lead-in, cut into the audience of the two competing shows that do not bridge it (*Man from UNCLE* and *Hogan's Heroes*), appeals to younger viewers, and rated a Q score of 35, 30% better than the average of all evening programs and higher than any other show on ABC.

The show's highest-rated outings in the 30-City Nielsens were:

| | |
|---|---|
| Massacre (pilot) | 21.0 |
| Devil's Island | 18.7 |
| One Way to the Moon | 17.8 |
| Secret Weapon | 17.1 |
| The Last Patrol | 17.0 |
| Crack of Doom | 17.0 |
| Revenge of the Gods | 16.8 |
| Visitor from the Stars | 16.8 |

Most of the higher-rated shows were from the earliest broadcast episodes, and ratings showed a steady decline over the season, with the lowest-rated shows being:

| | |
|---|---|
| Raiders from Outer Space | 14.2 |
| Merlin the Magician | 13.9 |
| The Kidnappers | 13.9 |
| Attack of the Barbarians | 13.6 |
| Billy the Kid | 13.6 |
| Town of Terror | 12.9 |
| The Death Merchant | 12.2 |
| The Ghost of Nero | 11.4 |
| Invasion | 11.3 |

The March 19 Nielsen National Rankings had *Lost in Space* as #51 out of 100 network series, *Voyage to the Bottom of the Sea* at #68, and *The Time Tunnel* in the bottom 10 at #91, an extremely rapid decline for a series that launched so strongly.

*The Time Tunnel* wasn't the only Irwin Allen series suffering from ratings problems: *Voyage to the Bottom of the Sea* was beginning a downhill slide in its third year; and, in its first color season, *Lost in Space* was suffering in competition with Fox's own *Batman*.

But the shows were all making their own pop culture impact, and Allen had made numerous merchandising deals to promote them. A January 12, 1967 Fox memo on merchandise included a *Voyage to the Bottom of the Sea* and *Time Tunnel* comic book series, a *Lost in Space* game, *Voyage* and *Lost in Space* bubble gum cards, *Voyage* Seaview and Flying Sub models by Aurora Plastics, a *Voyage* coloring book and paperback novel, a toy Seaview from Remco toys, and a *Time Tunnel* "desk gimmick."

**ABOVE**
Darren, Allen, and Colbert confer over a script on the set in this P.R. photo.

Allen was running three different television series, and attempting to launch more. *Land of the Giants* was on the drawing board, and Allen and Fox were considering a TV version of *Journey to the Center of the Earth* based on the Fox film. Whether or not Allen and his writers were stretched too thin, *The Time Tunnel* was suffering from the strain, and unlike *Lost in Space* and *Voyage to the Bottom of the Sea*, it couldn't lean on money-saving character dynamics or one-man "bottle" shows to speed up production and save on costs.

March 1, 1967 production notes from unit production manager Bob Anderson to Allen noted a recurrent problem with getting scripts in late:

> The art director and set decorator have been confused all year because they do not know who to take production problems to. After the sets are OK'd by either associate producer Jerry Briskin or Mr. Allen himself, the production manager should be responsible in laying out the work between director, art director and back lot operation. The communication on this between Bob Anderson and Jerry Briskin is bad, therefore [art directors] Rodger Maus and Norman Rockett have had production problems in getting ready on time.

Anderson recommended that Winton Hoch, the veteran cinematographer who had overseen all three Allen shows as they launched, alternate with another DP every other week, as the aging Hoch was beginning to work too slowly to keep up with the pace of production. Anderson also believed, "Paul Z is overworked now that there are three shows and possibly four shows next season."

Associate producer Jerry Briskin provided his own overview of the first season's production challenges after filming wrapped. Briskin cited the problem of not having shooting scripts available far enough in advance, leading to lack of preparation, last minute decisions, as well as unnecessary production problems and expenditures. Because of the delays and script changes:

> Allen and others did not have sufficient time to read and make notes on scripts. Budget meetings were held without final scripts; budgets were often received too late in production to make necessary changes to prevent overages and overtime. Sets were often not completed on schedule, leaving insufficient time for set dressing; overtime was spent on prop construction because they were started too late and not finished on time for filming. Cast budgets were affected with actors working

fewer days than they were brought in for or longer than expected; directors had insufficient time to prepare, actors received script pages at the last moment, office assistants had to work weekends getting typing and delivering script changes. Writers often created scenes that were outside the production's budget and production capabilities, requiring last minute changes to bring the stories within reason.

Whether these issues could be traced directly back to Allen is debatable. It would be natural for Allen, or any producer, to lavish more time and attention on a newly-launched series than on two already well into production, and Allen would cite *The Time Tunnel* as his favorite of the four science fiction series he had on the air in the 1960s. *Star Trek*'s Gene Roddenberry was known to have been happy to delegate creative responsibility as his series went on, but if anything, Irwin Allen may have stretched himself too thin by trying to maintain too much control over three highly complex, technically ambitious TV series.

"We hardly ever had a vacation," Sheila Mathews said of the period. "We took one to Hawaii in 1965 I think, it was or 1966. He brought along bags full of scripts because at that time I think there were three or four shows on—*Time Tunnel* was one of them. And he brought along all these scripts to sit on the beach in Maui, and work. I was having fun. That wasn't my idea of fun but he loved it—that was Irwin. I never could get him to go on vacations, at all."

Al Gail recalled at least one other Hawaiian outing Allen took with a different partner:

One of the only vacations I recall he took was with Groucho and he took the boat to Hawaii, and, I think they spent a week on the island. And of course I remember he was calling the office every twenty minutes. So he didn't enjoy the vacation at all, and, came back. And I think, that was probably his last vacation. His vacation was work. He loved it. He'd go home every night with these big, yellow, pads, and he'd come back the next morning and it'd be full of notes. So he ate, slept, motion pictures, television. But he loved what he was doing so, he didn't resent it. There was no strain. And he had a remarkable memory and, inasmuch as you're doing... at one time we were doing I think four series at the same time, and that took a lot of notes and a lot of attention. And he read every script. He'd take the script home with him at night, make his

**LEFT**
James Darren and Robert Colbert on the *Time Tunnel* set.

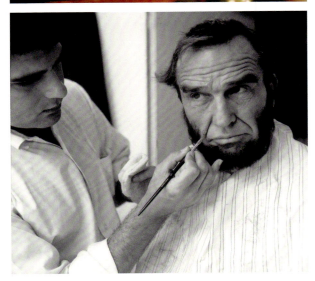

**RIGHT**

One of Admiral Kirk's ancestors (also portrayed by series regular Whit Bissell) winds up in the Time Tunnel facility.

John Crawford in one of many guest star turns on Irwin Allen's TV shows, this time playing King John in "The Revenge of Robin Hood"

Actor Ford Rainey being made up as Abraham Lincoln for the episode "The Death Trap"—Rainey was cast as Lincoln at least five times over the course of his career.

suggestions, write his notes on the border. And, we just went along and did the films.

Robert Colbert did believe that Allen may have spread himself too thin:

> He had [*The Time Tunnel*] going and believe me, while he had those three shows going, he had *Land of the Giants* in preparation. He had the storyboards going. He was into other projects. I don't know how hands-on Irwin was after he got things going—I'm sure he observed everything but he did delegate authority, and to a lot of good people and he kept a family around him—it was very tight. But we're all tired. He had an enormous energy. Paul Z. would get in there about five o'clock every morning and he'd probably be the first one on the set and the last one to leave, and then he'd be over doing other shows. I don't think Paul had four hours sleep in five years. But, you know that zwas just all part of it. You ran a horserace and if you weren't looking to see who was chasing you, you were just going flat out.

Allen's infectious enthusiasm, and his love of the technological toys of film and television production, was never in doubt. If there was a need to control, and oversee every conceivable detail of the works that bore his name, writer Shimon Wincelberg traced that back to his impression of Allen's upbringing, noting in 1995:

> I think it probably goes together, the need to control your environment, especially if as a child you felt very helpless, and picked on, and you felt you were funny looking, and wore thick glasses, and get beaten up by other kids, and you have these dreams of glory, and I think we all go through that.

Pressed on the question of whether that portrait of Allen was factual, Wincelberg admitted it was merely his impression, but that Allen always seemed child-like to him:

> ...At least emotionally at that time. And, of course you know he had this wonderful toy store to play in. In fact, he had a real toy store in his home. He had me come over to his house on Sunday morning a couple of times to work on a script, which was quite unnecessary, but he had nothing else to do, and I asked if I could bring my little daughter with me. He was delighted, and she had the run of the pool, and then you'd turn her loose in this room he had, which was like the inside of a circus tent, with a soda fountain, and she could have anything she wanted. He really loved children, in a perfectly wholesome way. What was interesting was, I always thought of him as sort of childlike, and once he took my wife and me to lunch, and his personality was totally different—he was suddenly Cary Grant. He had a wonderful, debonair, adult charm, and my wife thought he was just a terrific guy.

Fans were already aware of the possibility that *The Time Tunnel* could be cancelled in March, 1967. Viewer Ken Holley of Los Angeles wrote:

> I have heard rumors that *The Time Tunnel* has stopped filming and will not return next season. Please keep *The Time Tunnel* on the air.

Adding an unintentionally ironic suggestion, Holley asked, "Why don't you just transfer it to a different time?"

From Denis Crawford of Santa Susana, California:

> I can't begin to explain to you in so many words how much I enjoy watching *The Time Tunnel*. The acting and the set-up (The Time Tunnel itself, equipment, etc.) is tremendous. I also might add that *The Time Tunnel* has even helped me somewhat straighten out my history, you just can't forget something that's so exciting.

But Crawford went on to say:

> ...Why all of a sudden some of these crazy episodes lately, such as "Merlin the Magician," "Nero the Ghost," and a brain drain machine? I really like the show...but what has become of the show recently? I sincerely hope and wish this could be corrected.

ABC announced cancellation of the series, but at least one TV editor, Bob Hull, indicated the ax hadn't fallen all the way:

> When the word went out last week that the science fiction and history series would be axed after this season, youths all over the country started loading ABC's mailbag with protestations. As a result, we learned today, the network will announce tomorrow the return of the popular escapist drama. The Irwin Allen series, out of the same studio producing *Lost in Space* and *Voyage to the Bottom of the Sea*, probably will become another futuristic thing, with monsters and all, starting next year. The network reportedly balked at continuing the show as another historical *You Are There*. From now on, it'll be far out and beyond the history books.

While *The Time Tunnel*'s precipitous fall in the ratings and its great expense, along with consistent talk of it being on the edge of cancellation, made the show's ultimate cancellation by ABC seem to be a matter of course, in reality the network had apparently planned to keep *The Time Tunnel* on the air, just as Hull had stated. But changes in network upper management ultimately caused the show to be cancelled after all, and Allen and his team were left hanging while the show's fate was being decided.

On April 5, 1967, ABC's Leonard Goldberg confirmed the show's cancellation to Allen:

> Thank you for your telegram of March 30 to Tom Moore advising us of your plans to hold the cast and stages of *The Time Tunnel* under lock and key until May 15. We sincerely appreciate your courtesy in this matter, but then your actions in this case are typical of the cooperative and productive relationship we have shared with you over the years. I know that you and Fox are fully aware of our decision not to continue with *The Time Tunnel*. In all fairness and honesty to you, I must say that the decision remains firm and that we can foresee no possible opportunity for any reversal or alternative. As you know, we are looking forward to receiving the revised script from you on *Land of the Giants* and to the exciting plans we know you have for this project.

Robert Colbert ruminated on the show's cancellation in a Bob Brock newspaper column in 1968:

> Our ratings had been good, and I honestly thought we were set for three to five years. When I asked Allen what had gone wrong, he said the president of ABC had told him that he just had a feeling that *Time Tunnel* should be pulled out of the lineup. Of course, it cheered us to hear that ABC got over 600,000 letters of protest after canceling *Time Tunnel*, but it didn't bring the series back. It's now playing in syndication all over the world and the fan mail still comes in.

Allen himself discussed the show's cancellation in a piece in *The Oakland Tribune* in July, 1968:

> *Time Tunnel* was a good show. It was one of the best things I've ever done. I'm proud of it. You want to know how to bury a show: I'll show you. First you take the competition, *Tarzan* and *Wild Wild West*, both at 7:30. You stick *Time Tunnel* in at 8, with *Green Hornet* as a lead-in, which is no lead-in at all. Is a kid going to switch over in the middle of *Tarzan* to see *Time Tunnel*? It was unfair.

In a strange way, *The Time Tunnel* stands as one of Irwin Allen's great success stories. Cancelled after a single season, with only 30 episodes to its name (an unusually high, but not unheard of, number at the time), *The Time Tunnel* did indeed become a hit in strip syndication, running five days a week on local TV stations, in absolute defiance of the ordinary rules of syndicated broadcasting, which normally demanded a run of four or five years' worth of episodes in order to make for a profitable package.

*The Time Tunnel*'s varied stories made it seem almost an anthology show, and in repeats it actually boasted more variety than four years of a show like *Voyage to the Bottom of the Sea*, which began hitting a formula a little more than halfway through its run. *The Time Tunnel* also laid the groundwork for everything from *Quantum Leap* to *Terra Nova*, *DC's Legends of Tomorrow*, *Timeless*, and dozens of shorter-lived programs in between.

There's a bittersweet, even poetic element to the idea that, with the series never finished, Doug and Tony are still out there somewhere, lost along the infinite corridors of time. And Irwin Allen seemed never to quite accept the idea that the show had been cancelled—he would unsuccessfully attempt to revive the concept in one form or another for the rest of his career.

**OPPOSITE**
James Darren and Robert Colbert on the *Time Tunnel* set.

# "

## I HAVE THE MOST COMMERCIAL SUBCONSCIOUS IN TOWN. EVEN MY DREAMS HAVE COMMERCIALS.

**IRWIN ALLEN**

# UNDERFOOT

*Allen's last major hit TV series before returning to movies:* **LAND OF THE GIANTS**

**OPPOSITE**
The cast of *Land of the Giants*: (L to R) Gary Conway, Deanna Lund, Don Matheson, Kurt Kasznar, Barry Lockridge, Heather Young, Don Marshall—and a scene-stealing giant hand.

By fall, 1968, all three of Irwin Allen's science fiction series—*Voyage to the Bottom of the Sea*, *Lost in Space*, and *The Time Tunnel*—had been cancelled. Allen had a final show waiting in the wings, one that would have debuted months earlier, in January, as a mid-season replacement on ABC—except that at the time, ABC didn't need any mid-season replacements.

The final entry in Allen's famed quartet of sci-fi/action-adventure programs was *Land of the Giants*, a show Allen had in development as early as 1966. The format was similar to that of *Lost in Space*—a group of space travelers wind up stranded, and fighting for survival, on an alien planet. Instead of a tight-knit American family, the characters of *Land of the Giants* were a group of futuristic jet-setters, passengers on a "suborbital transport" called the Spindrift. After flying through a space phenomenon over Earth, the ship crashes in a strange wilderness, and the passengers quickly discover they are on a planet much like Earth—except that it is inhabited by 70-foot-tall giants.

Working with Anthony Wilson, Allen worked out a format for *Land of the Giants* that hinged on interaction between a sizable cast of adult characters. The Spindrift was commanded by Captain Steve Burton (Gary Conway), the show's nominal star and moral compass as the passengers are forced to make life-or-death decisions on the new planet. Burton's co-pilot was Dan Erickson (Don Marshall), a reliable second-in-command, while plucky stewardess Betty Hamilton (Heather Young) worked as an intermediary between the ship's crew and its passengers and worked to keep up morale.

The passengers were disparate individuals with their own agendas—Don Matheson played self-centered and cynical businessman and engineer Mark Wilson, and Deanna Lund was the even more selfish and smart-alecky heiress Valerie Scott. The final two passengers more or less intentionally reproduced the successful

Dr. Smith/Will Robinson dynamic from *Lost in Space*. Austria-Hungarian character actor Kurt Kasznar played a blustery and cowardly con man named Alexander Fitzhugh, who boards the Spindrift disguised as a military officer and somehow smuggles both a suitcase full of cash and a loaded revolver aboard the spacecraft. Fitzhugh's foil was young Barry Lockridge, played by child actor Stefan Arngrim—a shy little boy with a pet dog, "Chipper." Barry quickly sees through Fitzhugh's falsehoods but nevertheless develops an affectionate father/son relationship with the con man.

Irwin Allen had publicly forsworn science fiction during the launch of his movie *Five Weeks in a Balloon* in 1962. But after almost a decade producing sci-fi TV shows on the Fox lot, Allen had grown a lot more comfortable with the label of science fiction producer.

Speaking to a reporter from *The Dallas Morning News* in August, 1968, Allen said:

> There's no movie in the world today over-grossing *Planet of the Apes* and *2001: A Space Odyssey*. That must mean people want it and are willing to pay for it. I think *Giants* will feed that same interest. The peculiar shock of this show is that the world is just like everybody else's, only 12 times larger. I've been a science-fiction buff since the age of 10. I still haven't got it out of my system.

In another article by journalist Vernon Scott, Scott noted that Allen as a youngster loved Jules Verne, H.G. Wells and Edgar Rice Burroughs:

> I enjoy producing my shows because they are successful. You can really go wild in a science fiction series and get paid for it. And there's satisfaction in knowing the Navy department asked for plans of the Flying Submarine we used in *Voyage to the Bottom of the Sea*. It's satisfying work.

Allen also hadn't gotten his love of promotion out of his system, and *Land of the Giants* gave him an unusual opportunity to publicize the series long before it went on the air. In fact, the show went before the cameras a year before its broadcast, in September, 1967, just a few months after production had wrapped on *The Time Tunnel*. 17 episodes were filmed before ABC decided that the show would launch during the fall 1968 season rather than as a January mid-season replacement, so production on the remaining nine episodes was halted, and Gary Conway and some of the show's other actors were sent on a tour of the country to promote the series with media kits and gimmicks like buttons and bumper stickers.

Considering that Conway and Don Matheson were not exactly household names, that proved to be challenging—but the results underscored Allen's keen understanding of local television station management, gleaned from years of interacting with them while producing and promoting his earlier shows.

"We hadn't been on [the air yet], nobody knew who we were," Matheson recalled in 1995. "We'd go to these cities and ABC would beat the drum for us, at Irwin's urging and we'd go to these station managers and give

**LEFT & OPPOSITE**

*Land of the Giants* presentation artwork for the show's characters: Pilot Steve Barton, co-pilot Dan Erickson (in cockpit), stewardess Betty Hamilton, heiress Valerie Scott, Colonel Fitzhugh, and industrialist Mark Wilson (shown with Betty).

**FOLLOWING**

Some of the striking artwork used to sell *Land of the Giants* to ABC. Since the Spindrift spacecraft was not yet designed, Allen's artists painted *Lost in Space*'s Jupiter 2 into the presentation as a stand-in. While some of the concepts were too ambitious even for the show's record-breaking budget, many of these images did make it into the show.

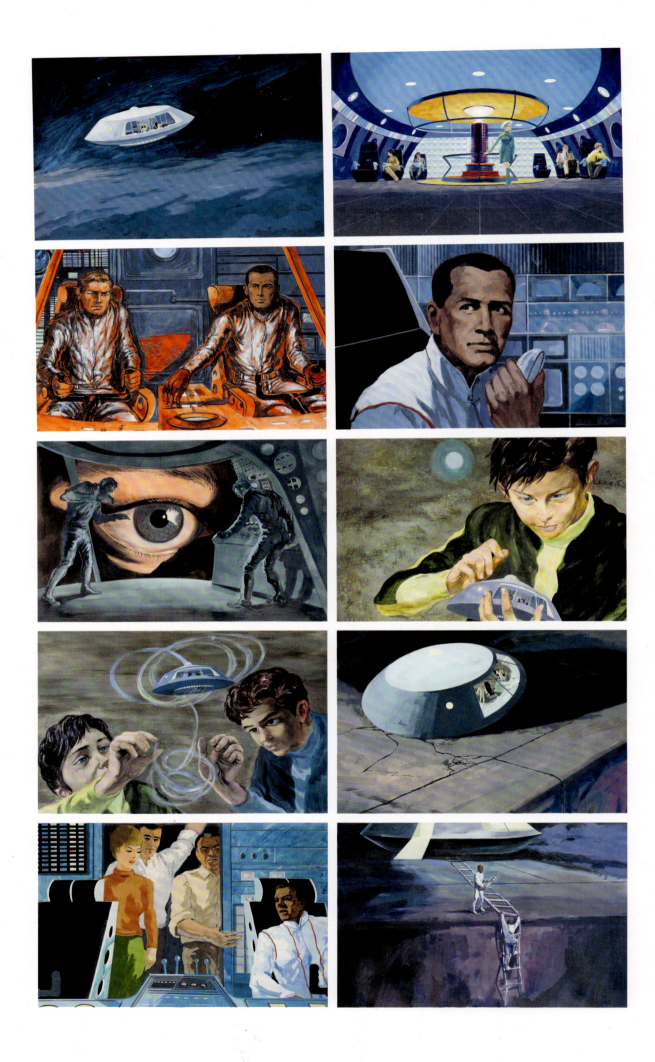

them this kit and they loved it. I said, 'You know, I'm not gonna give them this stuff.' And they said, 'Trust me, they'll love it.' And they did. They loved all these gimmicks he sent out. They were fighting over them. There was a lot of interest in this show and I think Irwin, wisely, in his Barnum and Bailey kind of way, knew that sending us all out like that was going to make for good numbers when we did get on the air. And he was right. It helped a lot."

By April 15, 1968—seven months before its debut—the show was already being described as "a merchandising success" in an issue of *Toy & Hobby World*. Ten manufacturers of toys, games, books, and candy had signed on for lines of merchandise for the series. William F. Dennis, VP of AB Merchandising, Inc., called *Giants* "the most important property in the merchandise licensing arena since *Batman*." Companies producing merchandise based on the show included Aladdin Industries, Inc. (lunch boxes), Aurora Plastics (models of the Spindrift and a diorama of a giant snake attacking the show's characters), Colorforms, Ben Cooper, Inc. (Halloween masks), Pyramid Publications, Remco Industries (which planned a battery-operated space ship, a play set, Walkie-Talkie, "space rifle and pistol," and other items); Sawyers, Inc. for View-master and Tru-View slide stories, Topps Chewing Gum, Inc., and Western Publishing Co. (story and comic books).

In a column for *The Los Angeles Herald-Examiner*, Allen told reporter Morton Ross:

> It's not enough to make a product. You must have some ability to sell your product, too. You need exposure. Nothing offers you more of it than these merchandising tie-ups. They're manufactured and printed in the millions. More than one child handles each one bought. They leave millions of impressions.

In terms of its concept, *Land of the Giants* was hardly the most sophisticated of Allen's series. Allen had continued to push the envelope over the years in terms of the technical challenges his shows pursued, however, and *Giants* would be the most expensive of his programs in terms of props, sets and visual effects. Two sound stages at Fox held the show's sets, and virtually every set shown on the program had to be built twice—one a normal-scaled set for the actors playing the giants, and another, far more vast set that was built to be inhabited by the Spindrift passengers, who would be shown interacting with, hiding, or fleeing from the giant characters in the same space.

To create the interaction between the human and giant characters, giant-size props—everything from a revolver and scissors to a spool of thread (used for rappelling off a table), a phone, and a giant camera— were constructed for the show. In a Sept. 8, 1968 interview in *The Buffalo Courier Express*, Kurt Kasznar described the show's environment as "a chamber of horrors with thyroid problems."

One of the most elaborate—and often-used—giant props was an articulated hand that could menace and (theoretically) grab and hold the "little people," as the Spindrift passengers would soon be called by the giants.

**ABOVE & OPPOSITE**
Part of the giant-sized mound of *Land of the Giants* merchandise, including coloring books, colored pencil sets, View-Master sets, a giant snake model kit, board games, Spindrift toothpick model kits, Colorform sets and comic books.

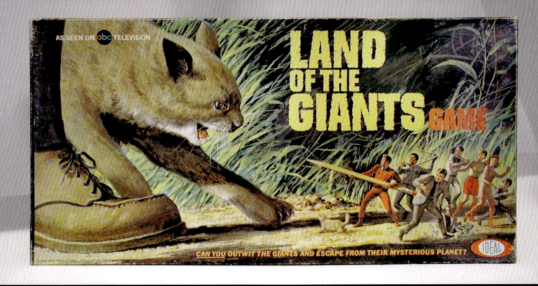

An *Oakland Tribune* feature in late July, 1968, had Allen teasing the appearance of the giant hand:

> Just imagine a hand as big as this room. If I told you what it cost you wouldn't believe it. It has hair, fingernails, everything. Inside it's a huge piece of machinery. The fingers are worked by cables, and each finger can move independently. It's run by a man 20 feet away, who plays on an electronic keyboard. In the pilot it picks up Gary Conway and lifts him high in the air. If it dropped him or squeezed him too hard, that would be the end of him.

The *Tribune* reporter painted a vivid portrait of the producer:

> Allen is a beefy, ebullient sort with a busy air, heavy black-rimmed spectacles and a mop of hair combed forward to conceal a receding hairline. He talks fast, giving the impression that he is sparing you precious minutes between important matters, and proves it by exchanging brusque remarks with aides who pop their heads in the door with questions and reminders about meetings.

Allen was at pains to point out that, despite its potentially childish premise, *Land of the Giants* was made for adults:

> You couldn't keep kids from watching this show. But if only kids watched, the show would be a failure. *Batman* had a high rating, but it was dropped because the viewers were all kids. The sponsors don't just want high ratings anymore; they want demographics. They want adult viewers. Kids don't buy any automobiles. So what we do is write adult problems into a spectacle show. That's family appeal.

Vernon Scott reported that each episode of *Giants* would cost a quarter of a million dollars, and that $700,000 had been spent on sets and props alone (the giant revolver built for the show cost $9,200). Many of the props were stored on the sprawling *Hello, Dolly* sets on the Fox Lot, but eventually had to be moved to the 25-acre Fox Ranch in Malibu for storage. "This is the biggest single thing I've ever done," Scott quoted Allen as saying. "Twenty percent of every hour show is involved with split screen, composites, matte and process shots. It's very tricky and time consuming."

Art directors Stan Jolley and Rodger Maus, veterans of Allen's previous productions, designed the show's sets and its giant props. Paul Zastupnevich, in addition to designing costumes for the series and serving as Allen's personal assistant, also wrangled the production's team of sketch artists that included Lois Green Cohen (who'd been an assistant art director on Mike Todd's *Around the World in 80 Days*), Tom Cranham (who would work on Allen's disaster movies *The Poseidon Adventure* and *The Towering Inferno*, *Viva Knievel!* and *The Swarm*, as well as *Star Trek: The Motion Picture*, *Jurassic Park*, and *True Lies* among numerous other movies), George Jenson (who later worked on *Close Encounters of the Third Kind*, *1941*, *Dune*, *The Rocketeer*, *Terminator 2: Judgement Day*, *The Perfect Storm*, and *Master and Commander: The Far Side of the World*) and Irma Rosien, who after *Land of the Giants* worked primarily in animation on shows like *Fat Albert and the Cosby Kids*, *He-Man and the Masters of the Universe*, *Ghostbusters*, and *Bravestarr*.

**ABOVE**
The cast works with the giant hand prop.

**OPPOSITE**
Box packaging and painted box art for the Aurora model kit of the Spindrift ship from *Land of the Giants* and packaging for a *Land of the Giants* target shooting play set.

**FOLLOWING**
Storyboard art for "The Deadly Lodestone," including visual effects setups.

# DEADLY LODESTONE

6 MED. CLOSE SHOT - MARK AND KOBICK (NORMAL SC.) KOBICK LOOKS TOWARD THE ENTRANCE TO THE AREA-WAY AND THEY MOVE IN THAT DIRECTION WHEN THE SERGEANT INDICATES THIS IS THE DIRECTION TO TAKE.

ZOOM IN

7 BACK TO MARK AND STEVE (OVERSC.) THEY START TO MOVE TO THE O.S. MARKET REAR. STEVE GLANCES OFF TOWARD AREAWAY ENTRANCE, AND FREEZES. MARK LOOKS ALSO, STEPS BACK SLIGHTLY IN REACTION.

COMP. MATTE

8 EXT. AREAWAY - NIGHT (COMPOSITE MATTE) STEVE AND MARK ARE IN THE F.G. OF THE SHOT, LOOKING OFF AT KOBICK AND THE SERGEANT. ONLY THE LOWER EXTREMITIES OF THE LATTER ARE VISIBLE, AND EVEN THOSE ONLY TO THE KNEES. MARK AND STEVE RAISE THEIR HEADS TO LOOK UP.

9 P.O.V. SHOT OF KOBICK AND SERGEANT - NIGHT (NORMAL SCALE) THEIR UPPER BODIES AND HEAD ONLY. KOBICK, HOLDING FLASHLIGHT, AND SERGEANT LOOM HIGH ABOVE THE CAMERA...

9-A ...AS THE POWERFUL FLASH-LIGHT HELD BY KOBICK STABS DIRECTLY AT THE CAMERA, WHILE THE SERGEANT STARTS HIS MOVE.

SUGGEST THE SEQUENCE BE 9-10-9-A-10-A

10 ANGLE ON STEVE AND MARK (OVERSC.) THEY LOOK AROUND WILDLY, PINNED IN THE BEAM OF THE POWER-FUL LIGHT. THE GREAT PIECE OF CRUMPLED WRAPPING PAPER LIES NEAR THE WALL DIRECTLY BEHIND THEM....

10-A ...TOGETHER, THEY LEAP FOR IT, AND SCRAMBLE UNDERNEATH. THE EYE OF THE FLASHLIGHT MOVES SWIFTLY TO FOCUS ON THE CRUMP-LED PAPER, ENCOMPASSING ITSO THAT EITHER OF OUR PEOPLE WOULD BE SEEN TRYING TO ESCAPE.

49 EXT. FOREST (CUL DE SAC TREE ROOT AREA) - DAY (NORMAL SC.) SHOT - KOBICK AND SERGEANT - THEY ARE NOW MOVING CAUTIOUSLY BUT PURPOSEFULLY.

50 BACK TO CUL DE SAC TREE ROOT (OVERSC.) MARK, VALERIE AND FITZHUGH HEAR FOOTSTEPS - LOUD AND MEASURED. THEY LOOK AHEAD, MESMERIZED BY WHAT THEY ARE OBSERVING.

COMP. MATTE

51 EXT. CUL DE SAC TREE ROOT AND FOREST - DAY (COMP. MATTE) OUR PEOPLE AND GIANTS - VALERIE, MARK, AND FITZHUGH ARE CROUCHED IN F.G., LOOKING THROUGH TREE ROOTS. MOVING TOWARD THEM ARE KOBICK AND THE SERGEANT WHO IS HOLDING THE DETECTOR AND AIMING IT ALMOST DIRECTLY AT OUR PEOPLE, AS WE: FADE OUT

COMPOSITE MATTE

52 (FADE IN) EXT. CUL DE SAC TREE ROOT AND FOREST - DAY (CONT. SC. 51 - COMP. MATTE) OUR PEOPLE ARE HUDDLED BEHIND THE TREE ROOT. KOBICK AND THE SERGEANT MOVE IN SO CLOSELY THAT THEIR UPPER BODIES ARE NO LONGER VISIBLE TO OUR PEOPLE. WE HEAR THE LOW HUM AND STEADY PINGING OF THE DETECTOR. OUR THREE PEOPLE EXCHANGE STARTLED GLANCES.

53 EXT. FOREST (CUL DE SAC TREE ROOT AREA) - DAY (NORMAL SC) MED. SHOT - KOBICK AND SERGEANT. THE TREE ROOTS AMONG WHICH OUR PEOPLE ARE HIDDEN, ARE VIRTUALLY AT THE GIANTS' FEET, BUT THE SERGEANT HAS TURNED THE DETECTOR TO SOME LOW UNDER-BRUSH A FEW FEET BACK OF THEM. KOBICK MOVES TO IT.

54 CLOSER ANGLE - KOBICK CROUCHES AT THE POINT WHICH THE DETECTOR IS INDICATING. HE PEERS INTO THE BRUSH, REACHES IN CAUTIOUSLY, EXTRACTS SOMETHING...

# DEADLY LODESTONE

**54-A** (CLOSER ANGLE CONT)... THEN KOBICK RISES INTO MED. CLOSE TWO SHOT WITH SERGEANT. HE SHOWS THE SERGEANT WHAT HE HOLDS IN THE PALM OF HIS HAND.

**55 INSERT** - KOBICK'S HAND - VALERIE'S BROOCH - DAY - THE BROOCH THAT VALERIE HAD BEEN WEARING IS BUT A TINY BIT OF METAL IN KOBICK'S ENORMOUS PALM.

## "DEADLY LODESTONE"

**SKETCHES IN RELATION TO USE OF SNORKEL**

CLIMBING UP TO DESK TOP

AS STEVE AND MARK ENTER SHOT ON TOP OF KOBICK'S DESK
OVER-SCALE HUMIDOR

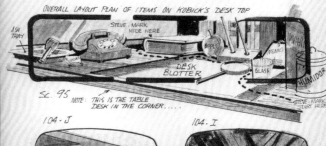

**Sc. 95** NOTE: THIS IS THE TABLE DESK IN THE CORNER.....
OVERALL LAYOUT PLAN OF ITEMS ON KOBICK'S DESK TOP

**104-J** CROUCHED BEHIND BOOK... HOPING THE PHONE WON'T RING...

**104-I** KOBICK ENTERS FRAME AND IS ABOUT TO UNLOCK DRAWER OF HIS DESK

## "DEADLY LODESTONE"

**GIANT SPIDER SEQUENCE RELATING TO SNORKEL**

**85 EXT. SWAMP - NIGHT - (OVER-SCALE)**
STEVE IN F.G. AS DAN MOVES OUT INTO SWAMP

CLOSE ON DAN
LOOKING UP - FROZEN IN HORROR....

**85-A** SPIDER COMPOSITE MATTE

**85-B** CLOSE SHOT - DAN
REVERSE...!

**85-C** CLOSE ON TARANTULA

**85-D** CONTINUE COMPOSITE MATTE
AS DAN TRIES TO FREE HIS LEG....

**85-E** ANGLE ON STEVE
SMALL LIMB OF TREE
STEVE HURLS LIMB AT SPIDER - O.S.

## "DEADLY LODESTONE"

**GIANT SPIDER SEQUENCE RELATING TO SNORKEL**

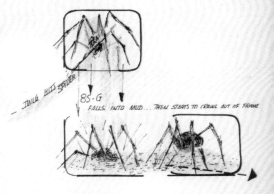

**85-F**
TWIG HITS SPIDER

**85-G**
FALLS INTO MUD... THEN STARTS TO CRAWL OUT OF FRAME

**85-H** CLOSE ON DAN
HIS EYES LOOK UP AT THE TARANTULA - AS IT PASSES CLOSE BY

**85-I** CLOSE ON TARANTULA

**85-J**
AS DAN STARTS BACK TO STEVE'S POSITION....

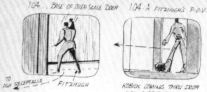

**ABOVE**
Color set design paintings for the interior of the Spindrift. The cockpit was originally intended as a reuse of the Flying Sub interior set from *Voyage to the Bottom of the Sea*—the red girder paint job would subsequently be used for the aquafoils in Allen's TV-movie *City Beneath the Sea*.

**OPPOSITE**
"Deadly Lodestone" storyboards continued.

**FOLLOWING**
Construction blueprints for the Spindrift miniature.

Zastupnevich described his work with the show's sketch artists:

> We used to make the books, the binders, the artwork, the ideas. Like *Land of the Giants*, when we were preparing for it, [Irwin] put me in charge of the art room. They would come to me and they'd say, "Well, what are we gonna do?" and I'd say, "Why don't we have a big foot—draw a big foot, and have a little grate, and a little figure running around the bottom and the foot coming down." So, the painting would be made and Irwin would see the painting and then he'd write a little episode around it. He loved that. So half the time we never knew what we were writing. So then I would say, "Well, we need a rope and we need a table, we have someone climbing up. Get me a little figure." And I would assign it to one of the artists. We had five to six people working, just doing the continuity sketches. So then a little continuity book would be made out of it.

George Jenson recalled one incident that showcased both Irwin Allen's pride in his art department and his sometimes cavalier attitude toward his employees:

> One time with Lois [Cohen], she stayed and had a sandwich at her desk at lunch and the rest of us left. Irwin had some people at the network and he rarely came into the art department but he wanted to show the executives the art department. They were at the door and Lois was inside and she heard the executives say, "Irwin, how do you afford all this? How do you afford to have all these artists?" And Irwin said, "Oh, they work for peanuts." I do think he had respect for us—he was good at Christmas time and we always got a nice package or gift and he was a thoughtful man in a way. He was very loyal and he would put up with things that maybe other people wouldn't out of loyalty, but he knew what he was getting with those people. But you did have to be very subservient to work with him and he didn't put up with any insubordination.

Illustrator Dan Goozee:

> People didn't want to go work for Irwin, because if you went over there you'd be held prisoner. Irwin liked to have his own art department so he could walk down the hall any time and see what was developing and he could just feed ideas directly into the system rather than waiting for a meeting with the [studio] art department. And I think Irwin also didn't think he was getting his money's worth if we were over in the [studio] art department because we might be over there working on someone else's project. In retrospect I have to say that Irwin was actually right—when 20th Century Fox reached a point, Darryl F. Zanuck went over to a meeting with stockholders in Century City and he came back and they had changed the locks on his doors, and he was out at Fox. And what used to be the art department ended up being just a two-story accounting office, filled with desk after desk of guys with little adding machines. So all the production companies ended up, like Irwin, setting up their own little mini design departments scattered around the lot and there was no central art department.

*Land of the Giants*' biggest prop and base camp was the spacecraft Spindrift, one of the most unusual vehicles in the Irwin Allen pantheon—and one of the least-used, at

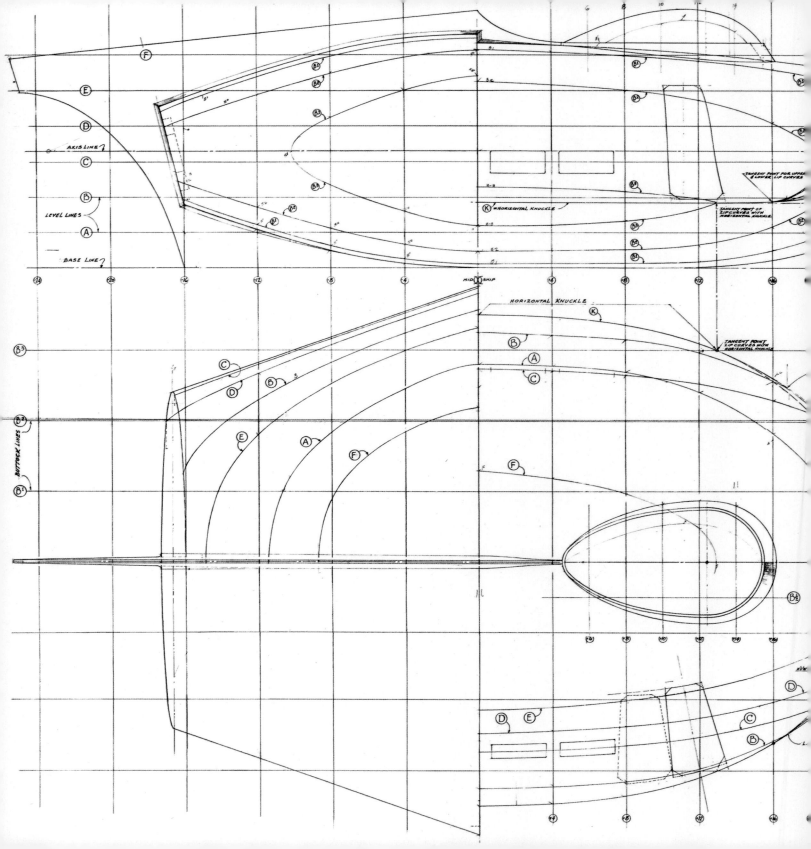

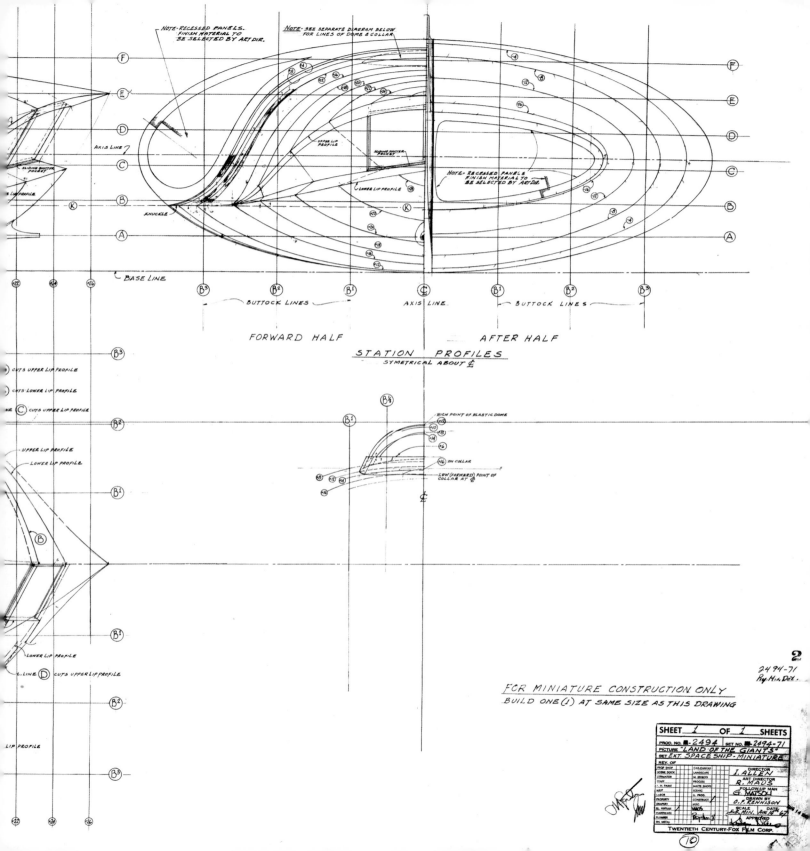

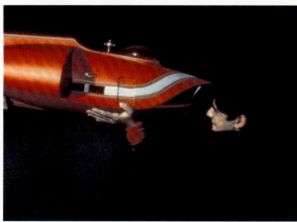

least in terms of action. The Spindrift was designed by production designer Rodger Maus, under the direction of art director Stan Jolley, who had supervised the look of *Voyage to the Bottom of the Sea* from its third season onward. Maus brought a certain influence from *Voyage*'s Flying Sub to the Spindrift, giving it a downward-curving prow and an "Irwin Orange" color scheme that gave the ship the look of a cooked Chinook salmon. The ship's flowing compound curves (which provided forced perspective from many angles, making the 52-foot, full-size set piece look even larger) and teardrop-shaped upper dome must have been a nightmare for the Fox construction department, particularly after the relatively simple and angular shapes of the Jupiter 2 and Space Pod props on *Lost in Space*.

Two miniatures of the vehicle, around three feet in length, were constructed, but unlike *Voyage to the Bottom of the Sea* and *Lost in Space*, *Land of the Giants* featured relatively little in the way of miniature photography. The opening journey through space, the space phenomenon encounter, and the crash on the giant planet were handled with a few brief and simple shots, with the Spindrift smashing into dark and foggy jungle greenery rather than a sunlit ocean or rock formation. Other than a later episode that had the ship interacting with a convict trapped in quicksand ("Manhunt") and another in which the spacecraft is stolen by a young boy giant ("Shell Game"), the Spindrift was depicted almost entirely by the impressive, life-sized standing set of the craft ensconced in a tangle of giant plant life, its engines and upper dome quietly throbbing with illuminated power.

According to a 1995 interview with Stefan Arngrim, the name "Spindrift" was coined by actor Kurt Kasznar:

> The ship had a number, which I don't recall, when we did the first episode, and it was about midway through the second show we shot which was the 'Weird World' episode with Glen Corbett. We were sitting around on the set one afternoon and Kurt said the ship should have a name, and, we got very silly and came up with all sorts of ridiculous names. But Kurt actually suggested Spindrift—which of course is the foam that is cast in the in the wake of a ship as it cuts through the water, and it stuck. We just started calling it that until the writers started putting it in the script.

The story doesn't quite jibe with the show's pilot episode, "The Crash," in which Gary Conway and other characters clearly refer to the craft as the Spindrift, and it's unlikely these moments were added to the episode after the fact, but not impossible.

If the show's special effects involving the Spindrift were minimal, the shots incorporating the giants were anything but. Supervised by L.B. Abbott, Art Cruickshank (a former animation cameraman at Disney who had worked on visual effects for *Lost in Space*, *Mary Poppins*, *Fantastic Voyage*, *Dr. Doolittle* and *Planet of the Apes*), and matte painting specialist Emil Kosa, Jr., the effects shots for *Land of the Giants* involved an enormous amount of compositing, sometimes smoothed over by matte painting work by Kosa, who finessed the shots of giant props, storm drains, and other environments

**LEFT**
The final Spindrift miniature design, with an influence from the Flying Sub's nose but quiet different overall.

the little people had to negotiate so that they fit in seamlessly with the normal-scaled sets inhabited by the giant characters.

Each show had to be meticulously planned to employ the expensive special effects shots of the giants in the most efficient manner possible.

Production illustrator George Jenson remembers:

> On *Land of the Giants* which I spent quite a bit of time on, we had two split screen shots per episode—I think that's how many we were allowed. L.B. Abbott would be the special effects guy, so if it was the people in the set responding to a giant crow, they would shoot the crow on the stage at the special effects department and they would splice the two together and it would look terribly corny sometimes.

In a March 5, 1969 interview, Allen described the financial challenged posed by the production:

> We do, in *Land of the Giants*, all the things everybody told us were impossible. But in the technical effects, there has never been anything that has been this involved. And that makes *Giants* the most expensive one-hour filmed show ever made—more than $200,000 per show. The series took a year and a half of preparation. And we spend 10 to 11 days on each segment—as compared to six on most shows. That's the way to bankruptcy as far as the front office is concerned.

In fact, the show averaged $267,000 per episode (versus an average $150,000 for an hour-long drama).

Allen broke down the costs of all his series in November, 1967, while filming the first episodes of *Land of the Giants*. *Voyage to the Bottom of the Sea* cost by far the most in terms of miniature effects and second unit shooting (mostly the former)—$100,000 versus $19,000 for *Lost in Space* and $30,000 for *Giants*. Allen projected that *Voyage* and *Lost in Space* would wind up running beneath their series budget, each by around $152,000, due to the ability on both shows to do cost-cutting "bottle" episodes with few performers or additional set construction. *Giants*, which was just launching, was projected to be over budget by $130,403—but with the previous two series running below their expected budgets, the production company was still $176,000 in the black.

With its heavy-duty optical effects and giant sets and props, the early *Land of the Giants* episodes dwarfed the other two series in terms of costs. *Voyage to the Bottom of the Sea* episodes ran from $188,305 ("Fires of Death") to $140,732 ("Sealed Orders").

*Lost in Space* costs were similar—$180,861 for the third season opener "Condemned of Space" with its space station effects, $144,081 for "The Space Creature" and its money-saving invisible monster.

*Land of the Giants*' pilot episode, "The Crash," was typically expensive at $330,757—but none of the ensuing five episodes came in for less than $195,000, and episodes two and three cost $246,683 and $205,175 respectively.

**RIGHT**
Some of the show's ambitious, finished composites that put the actors in the shot with giant humans and other creatures.

What exactly this money was buying in science fiction terms was never quite cleared up over the course of the series. *Land of the Giants* had an obvious inspiration in Jonathan Swift's *Gulliver's Travels*, albeit without the satirical thrust. It also looked back to movies like *Dr. Cyclops* and *The Incredible Shrinking Man*.

But the question of just what the giant world was remained open to interpretation. Did the Spindrift passengers go through a wormhole that put them on an alien planet? Or was the spacial phenomenon one that shrank the passengers down to a few inches in size and crash-landed them on Earth? "It's a mirror world," Allen explained in an early PR interview. "They have telephones, television sets, everything we have. In fact, in the first adventure the travelers are run over by an automobile. Only the auto is 90 feet high and passes 40 feet over their heads."

Stefan Arngrim recalled that the series format changed, from a somewhat alien world for the giants in early episodes to one that more specifically resembled Earth—an evolution that was muddied when ABC elected to air the original episodes out of production order, an odd decision considering that the first 17 episodes of the series had finished post production months before the show first aired.

> Initially, in the first few episodes, it was really a different world. There was a different written language. There was this whole series of arguments about physics that went on for several episodes. The Giants initially moved slowly. Their voices were muffled and bellowed and you couldn't understand them. It appeared to be a very different world, a different planet. It almost had a Fifties look to it initially—very low tech. That changed, though, because it was awkward. First of all, it was very difficult to interact with the Giants, which it became clear we had to do. If they spoke a different language or if they couldn't be understood that wasn't going to play. So, with very little explanation, it just changed. My assumption always was is that it was some kind of parallel world.

Instead of science fiction extrapolation, early publicity interviews for the show indicated that *Land of the Giants* would focus on character and drama. "There are no ray guns and no weird monsters on the show," said Gary Conway. "The stories will center around our relationship with the giants and with the conflicts in our own group. Kurt Kasznar, for instance, plays one of the characters. He's a con man who is always stirring up trouble."

**RIGHT**
Giant props and set pieces allowed the series to create some wild imagery completely in-camera.

**OPPOSITE**
The cast on the Fox sound stages, being filmed from a giant's point of view. Much of the environment is blackened out, to be completed by special effects work later.

Don Marshall, astronaut Gordon Cooper, Allen, and Deanna Lund on the set.

Conway seemed to be referencing Allen's earlier series, particularly *Lost in Space*—so the mention of a character who was "always stirring up trouble" must have sounded familiar. Script supervisor and producer Anthony Wilson had come up with the idea for the character of Dr. Smith on *Lost in Space*, so it was logical to bring a similar dynamic to *Land of the Giants*. Stefan Arngrim pointed out that the cast was well aware that the Barry Lockridge/Fitzhugh relationship was walking in the footsteps of Will Robinson and Zachary Smith.

> It was glaringly obvious. I mean we knew that. We knew that these were the archetypes that [Irwin had] chosen

here and there was Dr. Smith and Will and there was Mr. Fitzhugh and Barry. But the relationships I think were very different. Kurt and I developed a whole other thing. But we knew that those characters served a specific purpose. They'd been designed that way because they had worked before.

Arngrim's character was severely impacted by the decision to halt production midway through season one. 11 years-old when shooting began in September, 1967, Arngrim was 12-and-a-half when production resumed, and he was visibly different between the first episodes shot and the final nine shows in season one. By season two the young actor was entering puberty, and the character tended to be sidelined.

For Gary Conway, the series was a mixed blessing, as he had to address the concerns that *Land of the Giants* would be a show primarily aimed at children as the show was about to launch. In a profile by Nancy Sparks in *The Cincinnati Beacon* in early September, 1968, Conway said:

> I never think for a moment that I'm performing for children. This show is a sincere adventure on a dramatic level. It's not like, say, *Batman*, which became tongue-in-cheek. *Land of the Giants* has a Swiftian air about it.

Conway was a painter who earned his way through college by painting portraits, and he wasn't afraid to contrast his painting with the mass medium of TV:

> I think television is the lowest form of art. When people ask me, "How long have you been in the business," I get a funny feeling and I feel like gagging. I don't think of myself as being in a business. Television has a non-selective audience, unlike art, which seems to me has a certain kind of audience. That's why I feel TV doesn't qualify as art.

In the interview, Conway seemed to cast his TV show as an unpleasant rite of passage that every actor had to deal with:

> I feel every actor has to have a place where he can make mistakes. Take someone like Dustin Hoffman (of *The Graduate*). He's not going to have much of a chance because he can't afford to do a lousy film now. The great screen actor, I believe, is one who's gone through many, many years of horrible films, because his final works have a greater impact in the long run.

Although his prediction about Hoffman wasn't quite on the mark, Conway was quick to cast his TV show as something requiring tremendous acting skills:

> *Land of the Giants* is by far the most difficult job I have ever had to play because I have to play it with people who aren't even there (the giants). That's an incredible challenge. The material, in *Land of the Giants* or any other show, might be the worst but the job I do is what makes it art or doesn't make it art.

In a piece in *The New York Post* in August, Deanna Lund deflected a question about the acting challenges on *Land of the Giants*: "To be honest, this isn't really an actors' show. It's a producers' show." In 1995, when asked about

**RIGHT**
Allen directs Deanna Lund (reclining) and Heather Young on the Spindrift set

Conway at home—an artist trapped in a Lilliputian's body.

**OPPOSITE**
Deanna Lund poses for a publicity photo with the Spindrift miniature.

the "actors' motivation" for performing in the scenes with the giants on the series, Lund recalled:

> I remember asking that. I think it was Irwin. And I think [his] reply was a very abrupt: "Your paycheck." They didn't give you a lot of motivation. It was do the job, you know, hit the marks. I think the stars of the show actually were the special effects. Once in a while they would have a star in to do a Giant and they would try to give him as much to do as possible, but it was an ensemble group. I started out [trying to keep] my character as unlikable as I could, and as much of a rebel as I could. But as time went on she became I think part of the system, part of the group. But there was always that little rebellious streak. But that was more for interest.

Don Marshall, who had given a strong performance on *Star Trek* in the episode "The Galileo Seven," found his co-pilot character particularly ill-served:

> It was a disappointment. Because I didn't feel that they dealt with the characters enough. I think that if they'd gotten in there and saw some of the humor in the characters, some of the real fear—I mean, you saw the fear because there were giants or large cats or dogs or whatever, but you didn't see the person-to-person fear, or the anxieties, and we had some. They just didn't play them, and if they'd played them, the show would have been much stronger and I think they wouldn't have minded putting the money into the show. And that was the reason they took it off the air. It became more expensive than any other show they were doing and it was eating at the profits of other shows.

If the actors weren't exactly called upon to plumb the deepest emotional depths of their performing abilities, they were tested in another way. *Land of the Giants* became known as one of the most physically demanding programs for actors ever put on television, as the show's stars were required to do more rope climbing and rappelling than most Olympic athletes. "The cast does its own stunts," Allen bragged. "Even Kurt Kasznar. He's a fat man and not athletically inclined, but he wasn't about to let anybody get ahead of him. The others, fortunately, are good athletes."

Don Matheson recalled in 1995:

> When you saw us climbing those ropes, that was us most of the time, and sometimes all the way to the top. Sometimes we'd get a break and we'd climb out of frame and they'd pick us up later on, climbing over whatever we're supposed to have reached. But a lot of the times, we went all the way up. And they started taking it for granted,

**LEFT**
Allen on the *Land of the Giants* Spindrift set with Don Marshall and Gary Conway.

**RIGHT**
Actor Gary Conway in the cockpit of the Spindrift.

In camera miniature effects shot of the Spindrift approaching the space anomaly that will propel them to the giants' planet.

they said, "Hey, lookit, these guys are in great shape." Not just the guys, Heather and Deanna too. I don't know if you ever climbed a rope. It's tough. The stuntman showed us the easier way to do it. But it's still tough, to the point where, by the second or third episode, you came on the stage one day and looked around, and no stuntmen. I said, "Hey, wait a minute, what's going on?" They said: "You don't need a stuntman, you do this all the time."

Matheson said that eventually the cast refused to do the stunt work for long shots simply because they didn't want to be known for putting professional stunt personnel out of work.

Gary Conway said that another debilitating element of doing the show was the fact that the action was by necessity confined, day after grueling day, to the Fox sound stages :

In the previous series I had done, we could get out more and be outside. I remember that started to weigh on me. The other thing about the series is the fact that we really had to do it [everything] twice, because of the special effects, and so we had to do the show as it was and come back and, play it for the [blue] screen—for Abbott and Cruikshank, who were the special effects masters.

319

Despite the amount of work and strain, Conway admitted that the final effects were worth achieving:

> I think that the film *Honey I Shrunk the Kids* had marvelous effects, but there were some effects that were not that much better than we were doing on *Land of the Giants*. And just to think that they went on for eight or nine months or longer—to do that one show, and we were doing these once every seven days, and we were crowded with effects.

With its abundance of stunts, and its diverse group of mostly civilian characters plucked from differing segments of society, constantly trapped in situations that were variously claustrophobic and vertiginous, *Land of the Giants* showed Irwin Allen beginning to move toward the disaster movie formula for which he would soon become famous.

Despite the fact that *Voyage to the Bottom of the Sea*, *Lost in Space* and *The Time Tunnel* had all been cancelled, the debut of *Land of the Giants* on ABC seemed to prove that audiences had not tired of the Irwin Allen touch. An October 27, 1968 piece in *The Dallas Morning News* noted that the show debuted (in the Sunday time slot originally occupied by *Voyage to the Bottom of the Sea*) with the highest rating of the year. "Just think, out of the millions of television sets, more than half were tuned in on *Giants*. That's really gigantic," Allen was quoted as saying.

Reviews of the show focused on its impressive technical effects. Lawrence Laurent wrote in *The Washington Post*:

> To fans of space opera, *Land of the Giants* is worth watching. The special photographic effects by L.B. Abbott, Art Cruikshank, and Emil Kosa, Jr. are rather convincing. Anthony Wilson's script for last night's premiere had me thinking that a viewer might get more pleasure if he turned off the sound. Still, the technical effects are so dazzling that, with any luck, the battle between the earthlings and the giants ought to run for at least three television seasons.

George Gent in *The New York Times*:

> The youngsters appear to have a winner in ABC's new adventure series *Land of the Giants*, seen here on Channel 7 Sundays at 7 PM. There's nothing quite like seeing our world from the vantage point of the ants or as Lilliputians in a land of Gullivers to give us the tingles. Irwin Allen, who created the series and wrote, produced and directed the premier episode, has discovered the secret of far out adventure in the commonplace.

ABC immediately recognized show's impressive ratings and announced in November that the show was being picked up for a second season, which *Variety* noted was one of the earliest show pickups on record. "The remarkable thing about this order for nine additional segments is that ABC is so impressed with the impact of *Land of the Giants* that the order for the new segments came after only three segments had been broadcast," *The New Bedford Standard-Times* noted on November 10th.

ABC VP Leonard Goldberg, in an article in *The Jackson Tennessee Sun*, said:

> We are very pleased with the performance of the show. It completely dominates its time period Sunday evening, and in addition to quickly establishing itself as one of the most popular shows of the season, it has received considerable critical acclaim.

The show won 38 percent of the audience against 29 for CBS and 23 for NBC, increasing the 6-7 pm audience by 52 percent over *Voyage to the Bottom of the Sea*. And, as with *Voyage*, a considerable number of the show's fans were women. Actually, more than a considerable amount. "According to demographics, the biggest audience for *LOTG* is among women over 35, followed by the 18-to-35 age group, then kids," one newspaper article noted.

Morton Ross, in a column for *The Los Angeles Herald-Examiner*, stated, "*Land of the Giants* attracted a great deal of women over 35. Asked why, Allen shrugged and said, 'Women over 35 are fond of giants.'"

The show's emphasis on physical action and its concept of pitting normal-sized human characters against giants had another advantage: it translated very easily in foreign markets. "Do you know *Giants* acquired the biggest foreign gross in TV history?" Allen bragged in one newspaper piece. "This show can be run silently abroad, and viewers understand what is going on. That's why we are in 42 countries the first year."

Gary Conway acknowledged in 1995 that Allen's dismissal of his actors' yearning for more interpersonal stories was probably correct in the long run:

> We thought he was making a huge mistake by not doing that. But I think in some ways that was the secret of the success of the show and the fact that the show became more visual, and more action oriented. And that's why the show translated so well overseas. And I think that's why it's lived on, because it was it wasn't trapped into just the idiosyncrasies of characters and their inner relationships but it had a kind of a long view of things.

In fact, *Land of the Giants* quickly developed a following in Eastern Europe, which was at the time aligned with and controlled by the Soviet Union, two decades before the collapse of the USSR and the fall of the Berlin Wall. The show had carefully unveiled the idea that the giants' society was a totalitarian government, with a "Special Investigations Department" assigned to track down the "little people." Although the deliberate revelation of this plot-line was muddled when ABC elected to air the filmed episodes out of production order, the idea of a powerful, all-controlling government oppressing the "little people" was not lost on citizens of Communist governments in Eastern Bloc countries.

Gary Conway noted in 1995:

> There was an episode called "Manhunt" that dealt with a friendship that we had with a convict that was on the underground. What it pointed out was that the show really was about a very authoritarian society—the Giant society, and we were the Little People, really surviving that. And even within that society, there were people in rebellion. And that's why *Land of the Giants* became a

**OPPOSITE**
The impressive, full-size Spindrift exterior set and environment, and a look through the cockpit into the fogbound world of the giants.

phenomenal hit in many countries that had what we would call totalitarian societies.

Conway recounted a story of his mother visiting Romania in 1975 and finding the family she was staying with riveted by a *Land of the Giants* episode on a Sunday night:

> A couple years after that I got a letter from this woman who lived now in the United States, and she was a Romanian, and she mentioned the fact that when they took *Land of the Giants* off the air, there was the biggest protest that had ever been in Romania—something like two, three hundred thousand people had come to protest the fact that they were taking it off. I think they saw a lot of that symbolism to the concept…so that it did have an interesting impact.

Stefan Arngrim also made note of the political parallels in another 1995 interview:

> It got quite paranoid actually. The little people were sought almost like political criminals and captured to use against this sort of corrupt, dictatorial, government and it got quite political in an odd way. I mean we were playing that. I always thought that was rather odd too. That never quite struck me as something that Irwin would do. I was always a little curious about why he went in that direction.

Whether Allen drove the show's subtle anti-Communist undercurrents, or simply enjoyed the fact that he could sell *Land of the Giants* into heretofore unexplored markets, isn't clear. But the show's *Gulliver's Travels* inspiration certainly lent itself to allegory.

Conway continued:

> There was an episode called ["A Small War"] that stood out in my mind. The series was being done almost at the height of the Vietnam war and there was a lot of concern at that time about war toys. And this episode was about a little kid with his toy soldiers [who] comes across our group, and thinks it's his friend's war toys, and of course he goes to war with us. And I felt that it had a lot of great symbolism. Those are the kind of things that I think that Jonathan Swift would have liked had he been able to see his concept on television.

*Land of the Giants* may not have had the inherent flexibility and scope that a series like *The Time Tunnel* had, but it was nonetheless challenging for its writers, particularly after story editor Anthony Wilson departed to work on the western series *Lancer* early in the show's production. The strong characterizations Wilson had designed quickly fell by the wayside, and the show's attempts to portray the giants first as bellowing creatures with poor eyesight also gave way to much more straightforward actor interpretations as it became necessary for the little people to interact and relate to the giants as characters. With its group of castaways stumbling through endless sound stages full of fake greenery, the show sometimes resembled a straight-faced *Gilligan's Island* (*Gilligan*'s Skipper, Alan Hale, Jr., even appeared in one episode, "Our Man O'Reilly"), while other episodes often followed the formula of *The Fugitive*, with the little people briefly

**LEFT**
Publicity photo of Deanna Lund and Don Matheson, who married while the show was in production.

Celeste Yarnall as a woman used by the giants to lure other "Little People" into a trap in "The Golden Cage."

**OPPOSITE**
Deanna Lund and Gary Conway in a *TV Guide* cover portrait as photographed by Gene Trindl.

becoming involved with giant characters and their plights, which they help solve before moving on.

In an interview in *Starlog* magazine by Mark Phillips, writers Robert and Wanda Duncan (who wrote the episodes "Panic," "Collector's Item" and "Seven Little Indians") described Irwin Allen:

> …The most complex, exasperating, confusing man for whom we ever worked. He would call us on a Friday evening and say he needed a script for the following Tuesday. We had four hours to come up with a story outline, which Irwin would approve over the phone. Then, Wanda and I worked day and night over the weekend to get the final draft done and it would be sent to his office early Tuesday by messenger. Irwin didn't need the script that urgently, but it pleased him when writers demonstrated their willingness to go all out for his shows. That's how he tested their dedication. His moods were mercurial. He would appear out of nowhere late at night for a story meeting, maul a script, often unfairly, and disappear. Moments later, he would be back with an armful of toys for us to take home to our children.

In the same article, writer Esther Mitchell, who wrote a dozen episodes for the series including the excellent "The Clones" (in which cloned duplicates of the Spindrift passengers eventually break down in madness and paranoia), "The Lost Ones" and "Night of Thrombeldinbar," said:

> Irwin was an intelligent, curious and creative producer, but he was also a perfectionist. Since he demanded perfection of himself, that extended to the people he surrounded himself with, and when something went awry, they all suffered.

"I'm not married, and I work here in the office until midnight every night," Allen said in a newspaper piece on the series by Aldine Bird. "I'm up at 4 a.m., read scripts for an hour and a half, then arrive at the studio at 7 a.m."

Don Matheson was one of many Allen players who could back that statement up. Matheson described Allen:

> Mysterious. He was very hard to know. I mean I tried with humor, I tried sharing a problem, that something was going on in my life and I tried to pull him in. [Allen] wouldn't have any of it. But he could surprise you. I went to a screening at Fox one night and I got out at like nine or ten o'clock—and I parked right in front of Irwin's building. And he was coming out of his building with two bulging briefcases, I mean bulging. They wouldn't close, there was stuff sticking out. And we stopped and talked, the longest I've ever just shot the breeze with him about how he takes home this work every night. It was like I was a confidante or something and I certainly wasn't. Never had been. But like I was a real person, not an employee or an actor or whatever. And it was very strange. Never happened again.

As season two of *Land of the Giants* began, Allen once again switched up the show's title sequence, just as he had done with *Voyage* and *Lost in Space*, employing John Williams to write a more propulsive piece of music to accompany new split screen photography of the lead

**ABOVE**
Publicity photo of the *Land of the Giants* cast.

**RIGHT**
The animated title sequence from *Land of the Giants*.

characters to replace the animated title sequence of year one. The show maintained the storyline of its totalitarian government, even introducing the idea of a different region of the giant planet under the heel of an all-out dictator played by Nehemiah Persoff in "Land of the Lost." Kevin Hagen continued to play the semi-regular character of S.I.D. Inspector Kobick, a reliable nemesis for the little people, but the focus remained on physical action, and, while TV critics acknowledged the show's production gloss, the novelty of watching normal-sized people vs. giants was beginning to wear off. *The Hollywood Reporter*'s review of the season opener was as vanilla as they come:

> Special photographic effects men L.B. Abbott and Art Cruickshank consistently keep a high level in their department. The regulars keep their performances under good control throughout...

*Variety* reviewer J. Walter Thompson, in a September 24, 1969 piece also praised the show's high concept but acknowledged that strain was beginning to show:

> The little earthlings in *Land of the Giants* do a good job of making the viewer realize what it must feel like to be a cockroach—always on the run from overwhelmingly superior enemies. But this one basic situation wears a bit thin after endless repetition over the course of one one-hour episode, not to mention yet another season of one-hour episodes little different from the last.

Thompson still had praise for the show's cast, particularly Kurt Kasznar:

> This preem outing, however, had a couple of things going for it beyond the basic series plot, the best being the acting of Kurt Kasznar, portraying a desperate man caught in a series of highly charged situations, from being a caged mouse threatened by a cat to putting on a drunk set while supposedly informing on his buddies.

*Land of the Giants* maintained strong ratings throughout season two, but like *Lost in Space*, the show became a victim of demographic and budget concerns. It remained the most expensive show on television, and plans were still being made for a third season, including a storyline that would have aliens (giant aliens) invading the giant planet in an attempt to enslave the population, putting the little people in the odd position of helping the giants fight off the invasion. But the network wanted the show's budget reduced, something Allen balked at.

Stephan Arngrim recalled in 1995:

> We were told, as I remember it, fairly well in advance, before we wrapped [up the [second] season that the likelihood was that we were not coming back. We were in a very good position in the first year, we were in like the top ten and then we dropped down in [into the] top twenty and that's when the network said we'd like to cut this back. We'd like to bring the budgets down a little bit, and I don't think Irwin wanted to do that. So I suspect there may have been sort of a cancellation by mutual agreement.

Don Matheson and Deanna Lund had actually gotten married over the course of the show's production (although as with Allen's other programs, no hint of romance between the two characters was ever depicted on the show). Lund said she was at an ABC party and overheard Fox publicist Bay Ashley telling an executive that Matheson and Lund's characters would be married on the show "by a giant preacher..."—but the publicist was only joking. The two actors later got the news that the show would not go on.

Matheson recalled in 1995:

> Deanna and I were married at the time and home together that afternoon when somebody called and let us know. And we wound up having a cancellation party. Everybody that called to give us their sympathy or whatever, their condolences, we'd invite them over and it wound up one of the biggest parties we ever had. It was great. Our agents came. Called Irwin and invited him. He didn't show up. It was either that or just sit down and cry like babies, you know. 'Cause I was sad, I wanted to see it go on.

Like *Voyage, Lost in Space* and *The Time Tunnel, Land of the Giants* became a staple in local television syndication packages throughout the 1970s. However, with the show's cancellation in 1970, for the first time since 1964, there were no Irwin Allen television series on the air.

**OPPOSITE**
The end of an era: A lineup of full size props on the Fox lot after the cancellation of *Land of the Giants*, Irwin Allen's last 20th Century Fox television series. On view are the *Lost in Space* Space Pod (left, obscured by a tarp), the giant sea snail from *Dr. Dolittle* (center, background), the *Lost in Space* Chariot (center, foreground), and the *Land of the Giants* Spindrift

I BELIEVE THAT MAN HAS ALWAYS WANTED TO RETURN TO THE SEA.

**IRWIN ALLEN**

# THE SHOWS THAT NEVER WERE

*Allen's ambitious TV concepts:*
*from* **THE MAN FROM THE 25TH CENTURY**
*to* **CITY BENEATH THE SEA**

**OPPOSITE**
Makeup tests for aliens from Allen's
*The Man from the 25th Century.*

## THE MAN FROM THE 25TH CENTURY

By summer 1968, Irwin Allen was reaching a crossroads in his television career. The coup of launching three high-profile, technically spectacular science fiction shows in prime time had marked a pinnacle for Allen, but the abrupt cancellation of *The Time Tunnel*, his personal favorite of all his TV shows, had to have been a sobering blow in the middle of unprecedented success. Now Allen's remaining shows, *Voyage to the Bottom of the Sea* and *Lost in Space*, were wrapping up their final seasons on the air. Allen had *Land of the Giants* in production, he had produced 250 hours of television and earned six Emmy awards, and he was eager to continue his winning streak.

With the deactivated *Lost in Space* Robot standing guard in his office, Allen was trying to get network attention for his *Rodney the Robot* sitcom pilot but having little luck. With writer Arthur Weiss, Allen had also proposed a fanciful adventure show to feature Jonathan Harris called *Jumbalina and the Teeners*, with Harris' character traveling the world in a balloon with "four irresistible teeners."

A year earlier, in August, 1967, Richard Zanuck and William Self had authorized a deal to pay Allen for a pilot script for a potential TV show based on *The Lost World*, to be written by Anthony Wilson with a story, format and characterization created by Allen. Allen had also proposed a *Buck Rogers* TV series and Fox was looking at a potential *Journey to the Center of the Earth* series. With Allen's abundant use of footage from his *The Lost World* movie in all of his television series, Fox may have had second thoughts about wringing any further mileage out

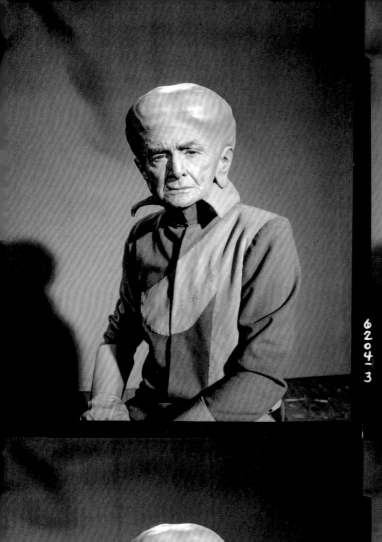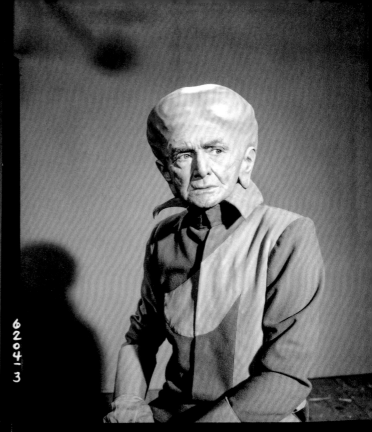

of *The Lost World*, and *Journey to the Center of the Earth*, with its own magnified lizard dinosaurs, would seem to have been a very similar prospect.

Allen also pitched a variation of *The Lost World* called *The Lost Island*—a TV series concept fascinatingly predictive of what would become J.J. Abrams' 2004 series *Lost*. Intended as a 2-hour pilot, it featured the survivors of an airliner that crashes in the Bermuda Triangle, who become caught between two warring, primitive tribes. The characters include the plane's pilot and navigator; a stewardess; "Agatha Blessings," a well-known mystery writer; a middle-aged business executive; a coddled housewife who loses her husband in the crash and now must learn to stand on her own two feet; a western rodeo star; and a retired high school science teacher "whose scientific knowledge proves extremely useful."

*The Lost Island* didn't go anywhere, and Allen's *Land of the Giants* was ready to explore the idea of airline passengers thrust into a strange new world. It's fascinating to ponder whether *The Lost Island* endured as a concept in ABC's vaults for years and eventually mutated into *Lost*, since *Lost* reportedly began as a notion (inspired by the reality show *Survivor*) being kicked around by ABC executives before J.J. Abrams developed it.

Allen had an idea for a futuristic anthology show called *Tales of Tomorrow* that never got beyond the presentation phase. He had also proposed three potential projects

**ABOVE & OPPOSITE**
Pitch artwork by Ron Croci for Allen's proposed *Tales of Tomorrow* TV series.

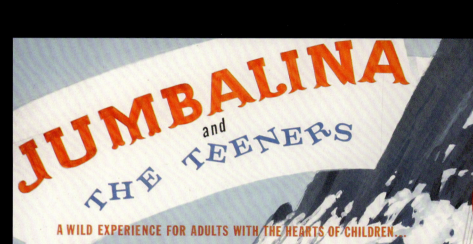

**OPPOSITE & RIGHT**
Pitch artwork for Allen's
*Jumbalina and the Teeners* and
*Safari* TV show concepts.

**FOLLOWING**
Pitch artwork for *The Man from
the 25th Century*.

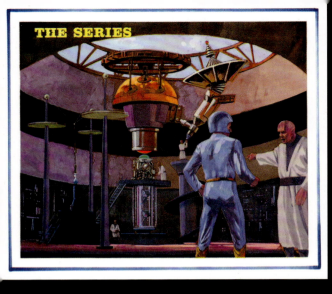

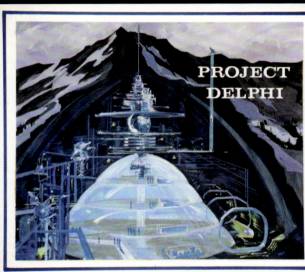

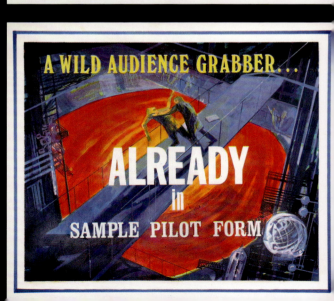

# THE MAN FROM THE 25TH CENTURY

to CBS in 1967, at least two of which were more off the beaten path for the producer. One was a modern day take on Aladdin: a young boy who appears from inside a sarcophagus at the Museum of Modern Art in Manhattan, having slept for 10,000 years, and still equipped with his magic lamp, "this wandering minstrel who spread good in the world of yesterday now starts his series of modern adventures..."

The second concept was called *Safari*. Big game hunter Richard Hamilton and his companion Yogi Britton operated "Safari Ltd.," and the pair loan themselves out for hire for different adventures every week.

The third concept was called *The Man from the 25th Century*—a science fiction series that was simultaneously forward-thinking and a throwback, described as follows in early development materials:

> The planet Andro, fading towards extinction because its source of power is waning, plans to replenish its ebbing life force by ruthlessly attacking and destroying Earth. To that end, an infant male Earthling is captured, transported to Andro for brainwashing and indoctrination during his growth to maturity, then sent back as a one-man fifth column to sabotage Earth's defenses...

Tomo is the Man from the 25th Century—he turns on the "Andromedians" and works with humans to save the Earth from destruction:

> Tomo...a young, good-looking identifiable hero...will be the basic focal point of the series. Adult stories will take us into his fantastic world of the future while others will take him with his unbelievable powers into our world of today.

Project Delphi, the central location and operating organization shown in the potential series, was a massive underground installation located in Glacier National Park (the location Allen had explored in 3-D in his RKO thriller *Dangerous Mission*)...and an apparent chance to reuse a lot of visual effects shots from *The Time Tunnel*. The Delphi project was designed to "fathom the mystery of Unidentified Flying Objects that come from outer space" and for "the development and perfection of a 'radial umbrella' designed to prevent penetration of Earth's atmosphere by missiles or hostile spaceships. Each week the non-humans from Andros arrive in flying saucers and create havoc with Earth."

The concept was similar to Gerry Anderson's TV series *UFO* (which went into production in the U.K. in 1969 and debuted in syndication in the U.S. in 1971), about a secret government organization that defends the Earth from attacking alien spacecraft, and the Larry Cohen/Quinn Martin series *The Invaders*, about a man who discovers a secret infiltration of Earth by aliens. Storyboard art even shows the Delphi organization using tank-like vehicles similar to the Mobiles (and even referred to as mobiles in the artwork) in *UFO*. To be fair, the Chariot from Allen's *Lost in Space* was likely the inspiration, and perhaps even an influence on the later *UFO*.

The Andromedians share the one "Achilles Heel" suffered by H.G. Wells' Martians from *The War of the Worlds*: they're vulnerable to Earth's bacteria. The idea of Andro being snatched from Earth as a child and trained by superior aliens was similar to the *Star Trek* episode "Assignment: Earth," a "backdoor pilot" for a potential series with Robert Lansing as a human trained by aliens to protect the course of human development on Earth. *The Man from the 25th Century* had also been planned as a backdoor pilot, with Tomo to be introduced on an episode of *Lost in Space*—an idea that never got to fruition.

Allen presented story concepts for the first 10 episodes of the series, including one that had Tomo returning to Andro to rescue his alien tutor from the planet's oppressive leaders, a story where Tomo's loyalties to his human allies are tested; another where an alien saucer makes its way through Earth's defenses and lands in a small town; and a story in which Tomo is hunted (through U.S. landmarks like Yellowstone National Park, the Grand Canyon, etc.) by an alien assassin.

Interestingly enough, Anthony Wilson (Allen's story editor on *Lost in Space*) had also written the pilot episode for Quinn Martin's *The Invaders*.

Wilson turned in a treatment for *The Man from the 25th Century* on June 20, 1967, in which Tomo is shown on Andro receiving his final training for his trip to Earth. While most of Earth's population is unaware of Andro or

**ABOVE**
Diagram of the Project Delphi installation, built around an energy-projecting "radial umbrella," looking like a predecessor to the Death Star cannon in *Star Wars*.

59 PAINTING #21
EXPLODED MOBILE UNIT BURNS IN B.G.

SMALL FIRE SUPERED

61. LIVE

EXT. GAS STATION - NIGHT

64 PAINTING #23
TOMO'S P.O.V. OF ALIEN SHIP

PLUS CUT-OUT GLOW

71. PAINTING #25

PLUS ANIMATED BEAM AND EXPLOSION.

**RIGHT**
Storyboard art showing the tank-like Project Delphi "mobiles" and alien spaceships with an influence from George Pal's *War of the Worlds*.

of Tomo's arrival, it has seemingly all been prearranged with Atwood and Project Delphi, and after landing on Earth, Tomo arrives at the underground installation and meets his human contacts, only to sneak out later and infiltrate secret parts of the compound. Caught by a guard, Tomo engages in combat, but at the last second refuses to kill the man—a fatal flaw in his training that Atwood and his Delphi crew plan to exploit in order to combat the Andromedians. When four Andromedians manage to penetrate Earth's defenses and land their saucer in a small town, Tomo agrees to help the Earth men deal with the threat. Once Tomo has assisted Atwood and the people of Project Delphi, it's agreed that returning him to Andro would be a death sentence, and Tomo appears to switch his loyalties to his native Earth—but we soon see that this is all part of Bonti's plan to infiltrate Earth's defenses. He still maintains some control over Tomo and hopes to lure other earthmen to Andro to create more human spies.

Allen planned *The Man from the 25th Century* as a vehicle for James Darren, one of the costars of *The Time Tunnel*, and an actor Allen had very much enjoyed working with.

Darren recalled in 1995:

> Irwin had called me and asked me if I would be interested in doing it, and I told him yes. I wasn't under contract at all. I loved working with Irwin and I assume he loved working with me, and he wanted to put me in a show right away. I wish it had been a better project because I would love to have worked with him more.

Allen mounted *The Man from the 25th Century* as a 16-minute pilot presentation, with John Crawford as Tomo's villainous overseer, Bonti, and Ford Rainey as General Atwood, head of Project Delphi. Bonti and his fellow Andromedians were standard "giant head" aliens in robes and high collars, while Tomo wears a futuristic gold lamé outfit on Andromeda and switches to a suit and tie on Earth.

Stock footage of the Jupiter 2 landing from *Lost in Space* depicts Tomo's landing on Earth, and in the pilot's

**ABOVE & OPPOSITE**
Production artwork of Tomo on the planet Andro, and his arrival at the hidden Project Delphi base—in his alien-constructed sports car.

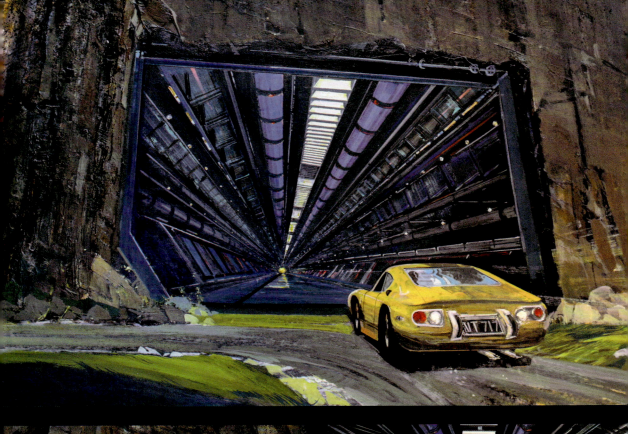

most dazzling moment, Darren drives a sports car out of the full-sized mockup of the Jupiter 2 and the hatch constructed—but never used—to launch the earlier show's Chariot vehicle from the Jupiter. The reuse of the Jupiter 2 wasn't entirely coincidental, since the show concept originated as a potential spin-off of *Lost in Space*. When Allen was presented with the potential cost of constructing a newly-designed spacecraft for the Tomo character, the producer reportedly bellowed, "He can walk!"

*Fantastic Voyage*'s art director Dale Hennesy worked on the show's design concepts, but most were rendered as flat, backlit artwork rather than sets (although a good-sized Delphi control room was built). After the comparatively sophisticated look and concept of *The Time Tunnel*, *The Man from the 25th Century* seemed like a throwback. Darren. for one, was underwhelmed:

> Looking at that pilot presentation now, I don't like the presentation myself. I think it was done inexpensively, which is not an excuse for it not being good. I think that there wasn't much imagination in that—it just looked corny to me. I think had that been done with more thought that it might've been able to be a possible series.

Compared to *UFO* and *The Invaders* (a very well-executed, adult series that would later influence *The X-Files*), *The Man from the 25th Century* came off as unsophisticated indeed. Although some lip service was given the Tomo character's reluctance to kill, the show's borrowed trappings and silly aliens didn't make for an impressive pilot concept, as Darren explained:

> There were lots of things that were missing, and I think that was the fault with the show. The fact that they used those same costumes again, and I think the network probably knew it at that point, that these were the same aliens with the same rubber heads that we had in so many episodes of *Lost in Space* and so many episodes of *The Time Tunnel,* that they were a little tired of it. I think *Man From the 25th Century* could've been like *Six Million Man*, a potentially interesting premise for a show instead of trying to incorporate all this other hokey stuff into it.

**LEFT**
James Darren in his silver costume as Tomo and Irwin Allen standby John Crawford as alien leader Bonti.

**OPPOSITE**
Footage from the network presentation reel for *The Man from the 25th Century*, created using minimal sets and actors composited into painted, backlit artwork.

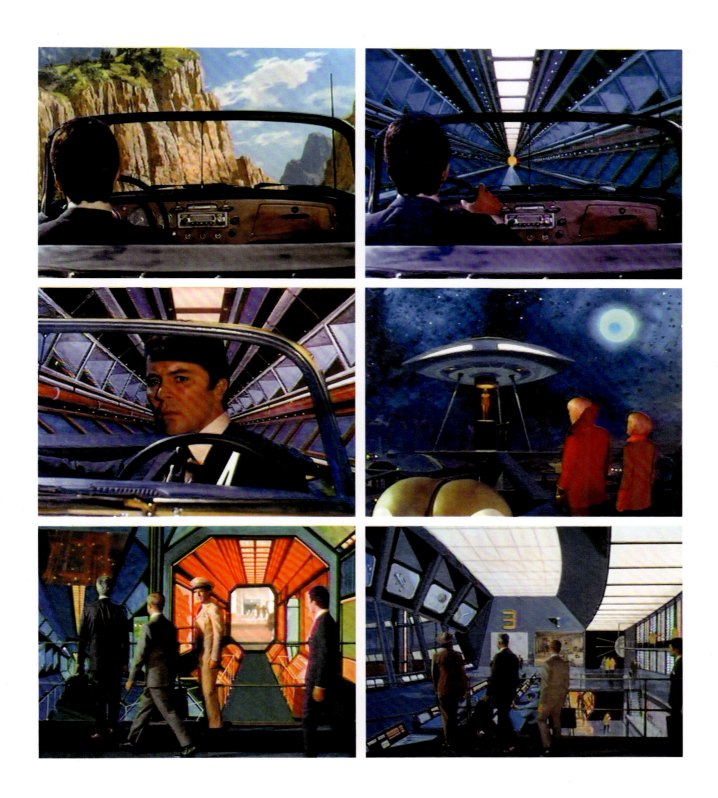

# CITY BENEATH THE SEA

*The Man from the 25th Century* never developed beyond its short pilot presentation. But, late in 1967, Richard Zanuck and William Self authorized a "Fox-Kent Joint Venture Development Project" with NBC for what would become arguably Irwin Allen's most ambitious TV series idea ever: *City Beneath the Sea*, set in a sprawling underwater metropolis, ten thousand feet below the surface of the Pacific Ocean. Allen would ultimately put himself in the director's chair for the project, both for its original, short presentation and eventually for a spectacular, 90-minute TV-movie.

Allen had been researching the idea for some time and had corresponded with Thomas M. Garber of Navy Project Neptune (Allen had originally chosen this name for the show's title, but NBC eventually requested it be changed to "something more exotic"): Garber had done two years of research on an underwater city concept conceived as a military installation "which acted as an underwater SAC base against submarines." But the base would also have been used by private industry and civilians for "underwater farming, mining, oil drilling, fishing, etc." Garber supplied Allen with designs for underwater vehicles; renderings of the exterior and interior of the base; schematic plans for a central control center, air purification, and compression building; emergency shelters; a reactor building; a garage for underwater vehicles; laboratories; cafeteria; hospital and recreation center—even a logo for the operation. Garber approached Allen with the idea of offering himself as a technical advisor on the series, although he was never appointed to this position.

Allen's story involved a sprawling underwater metropolis and a classic Irwin Allen "misunderstood hero"—General (later Admiral) Kevin Matthews, the former commander of Pacifica who returns under a cloud of suspicion during a critical point in the underwater city's development. In the original, short pilot presentation, Matthews' cohorts in Pacifica included a cool-headed, female security chief, a hot-headed Texan engineer in charge of a massive geothermal operation called Project Mole,

**ABOVE & OPPOSITE**
Early concept art of the underwater metropolis Pacifica in *City Beneath the Sea*.

344

and a half-amphibian scientist named Aguila. Allen's "misunderstood hero" plot-line entailed Matthews reluctantly returning to Pacifica after being involved in an underwater accident that resulted in the death of one of the city's founding builders and beloved heroes, Jessup (later named Bill Holmes). Matthews takes over Jessup's position and bulldozes his way over all opposition in order to solve Pacifica's problems, while his associates increasingly hold Matthews responsible for the death of Jessup and resent him for attempting to take the man's place. The first draft of the script also included a villain: Harmon Temple III, a turncoat with plans to sabotage Project Mole.

Early promotional tag-lines for the concept outlined the show's setting and characters:

> The year is 2068 A.D., and you are diving beneath the surface of the Pacific...Ten thousand feet down to Pacifica!

> The fabulous City Beneath the Sea, ultimate symbol of man's victory over the sea...The City's heart - Triton Complex, nerve center of the gigantic operation and headquarters of its newly appointed Administrator-General, Kevin Matthews.

> Project Mole, ambitious and elaborate...built to tap the Earth's core, unleashing the unbelievable energy from the center of the Earth...

> Presentation shows Matthews as a no-nonsense commander, constantly pushing his people and in conflict with many of them.

> Dr. Raymond Aquila, 32, is the first of his kind, a true son of the sea. Artificial gills, grafted at birth, give him the ability to live as easily undersea as on land.

> Harmon Temple III, the most successful financial villain of the 21st Century...so far, a respected citizen of Pacifica.

> Tim Matthews, widower Kevin's 10-year-old son, found stowing away inside the city.

> Choo Choo Kino...six-feet-two of Japanese-Polynesian-American-Irish beauty...

Allen was tasked with creating a short-format pilot presentation of the concept, very much in the manner of *The Man from the 25th Century*, that needed to be put together in little over a month from the original agreement, by early February, 1968, with options for a TV series to air on NBC in fall 1968.

NBC, of course, already had a high-profile science fiction series on the air—Gene Roddenberry's *Star Trek*. But *Star Trek* had been a frustration to the network since its 1966 launch—critically well-received, it faltered in nationwide ratings, and Roddenberry frequently butted heads with the network. *City Beneath the Sea* was conceivably a replacement for *Star Trek*, something that might draw in *Trek*'s demographically desirable audience but potentially reach the broader national viewing audience that Allen's shows had, and provide the added benefit of Allen's always smooth and cooperative relationship with the networks. The NBC slot had an extra appeal to

**LEFT**
Early concept artwork for *City Beneath the Sea*.

**RIGHT**

The cast of the short presentation for *City Beneath the Sea*: (l to r) Lawrence Montaigne as Dr. Aguila, Cecile Ozorio as Choo Choo Kino, Glenn Corbett as Kevin Matthews, Francine York as Lia Holmes, and Lloyd Bochner as Harmon Temple III.

Allen—he had placed shows on CBS and ABC, and an NBC series would give him programs on all three networks.

Two of the characters in Allen's early outlines were of particular interest in light of the show's potential relationship to *Star Trek*. As an artificially-augmented, water-breathing human, Raymond Aquila was an exotic character who would be a constant reminder of the show's futuristic, ocean-based society, just as *Star Trek*'s alien, Mr. Spock, symbolized *Trek*'s future world of alien planets and civilizations. Meanwhile the character of Choo Choo Kino was originally designated as the underwater city's tough and efficient, female chief of security—which would have made Allen's show far more progressive in its sexual politics than *Star Trek*, which had eliminated a female first officer for its starship captain after its initial pilot.

Early casting ideas for Matthews included Steve Forrest, Barry Nelson, Jeffrey Hunter, J.D. Cannon, Robert Lansing, Robert Stack, James Daly, Forrest Tucker, Leslie Nielsen, Bradford Dillman, and even Allen's old standby, Victor Mature. For Raymond Aguila: Vincent Beck, Bruce Dern, John Saxon, Skip Homier, Hampton Fancher (who would later work on the script for *Blade Runner*), Victor Lundin, Lee Bergere, Robert Duvall, Mark Lenard, and Michael Forrest were under consideration.

The character of Kevin Matthews would remain a challenge throughout development of the concept, as Allen fought to retain the character's combative nature

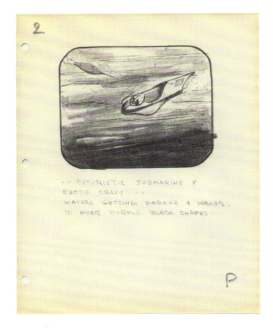

**ABOVE & OPPOSITE**
Storyboard and set concept art for the short *City Beneath the Sea* presentation, indicating the use of stock footage from *Voyage to the Bottom of the Sea* and *The Time Tunnel*.

Ⓐ **STOCK** A

① CONT. PLUS SUPER "JUNE 12, 2068"

② A **LIVE** (PLUS BLUE BACKING FOR TEXAS TOWER BURN-IN AND AND STOCK OCEAN) INT AQUAFOIL - NIGHT

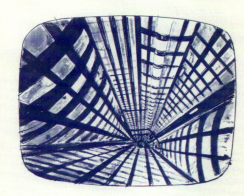
⑪ **STOCK** (MINIATURE SHOWING MOVING ELEVATORS)

and his conflict with the established administrative staff and citizenry of the underwater city. Production supervisor Hal Herman's notes on the first draft of the script indicated concerns about Deep Core engineer Tyler coming off as too strong as he accuses Matthews of being a liar and of trying to "rob a dead man of credit." Even Aguila "shows animosity against Matthews because of his friendship to Jessup. All these people seem a little childish about the Jessup situation." In later drafts Aguila becomes a more understanding ally to Matthews while others remain suspicious and resentful of his appointment. The notes question a number of interconnected threats to the city that are not clearly explained, but the primary questions relate to character:

> Why did Temple become a traitor? Did he kill Jessup in order to win command of Pacifica? Why does everyone resent Matthews...a well-qualified man who has been appointed to fill the shoes of a dead man?

Herman also suggested changing the character "Choo-Choo" name to "Luana, to avoid being cutesy."

In an August 22, 1967 meeting between Allen, NBC Vice President Herb Schlosser, John Hinsey, Herman Rush, and Harold Graham, Jr. the participants discussed NBC's response to the short pilot presentation outline. The network's position:

> The setting of the series should be in a futuristic city already past the experimental point; normal life and industry are going on. The stories in the series should not be limited to scientific and natural disasters or problems, but the conflict should come out of human relationships and antagonisms. Our heroes must be fighting other human elements (villains).

Regarding the presentation film, the network noted:

> Elements to be considered for inclusion in this film should be actual underwater footage, models of the City Beneath the Sea and its components, miniatures hopefully secured from GM, paintings a la LAND OF THE GIANTS, and cast.

A week later, on August 31, 1967, Allen met with Herb Schlosser, John Hinsey, Ross Donaldson of NBC, screenwriter Harold Jack Bloom (who had worked with Allen on his *Time Tunnel* pilot), David Gerber and Herman Rush. This time the network stressed:

> There must be a general feeling of believability, realism, and seriousness both in story and with the people. There must be continuous conflict among the people, not just threat from natural disasters. There should be the establishment of a relationship between the City Beneath the Sea and the Earth Above, that is, to the United States, to the rest of the world, and to people.

Allen cast Glenn Corbett as Kevin Matthews for the potential series' short pilot presentation. Corbett had been a regular on several TV series including *Route 66* and *The Road West*; he had played Zefram Cochrane in a 1967 *Star Trek* episode and appeared in the second filmed episode of Allen's *Land of the Giants* (which wouldn't air until fall 1968).

Lawrence Montaigne was cast as Aguila. Montaigne had played Spock's Vulcan rival, Stonn, in *Star Trek*'s famed "Amok Time" episode, but he had an even more intriguing connection to *Star Trek*, considering that Aguila could be *City Beneath the Sea*'s answer to Mr. Spock: Montaigne had been contemplated as a replacement for Leonard Nimoy as Spock midway through the series' run as a contingency should Nimoy's salary demands become problematic.

James Brolin, who was under contract to Fox at the time, was cast as engineer Bill Tyler, Cicile Ozorio became Choo Choo Kino, Francine York (who'd appeared on *Lost in Space*, *Batman* and *The Wild Wild West*) played Lia Holmes (now widow of the renamed Bill Holmes), and reliably oily heavy Lloyd Bochner played Harmon Temple III.

Live action for the 11-minute pilot presentation was shot between January 9th and 17th on Stage 14 and the Green Tank at 20th Century Fox, for a total cost of $228,543, including almost $20,000 in miniature work and $12,000 in photographic effects. Visual effects and materials were shot and created between December 27, 1967 and January 8, 1968 under the direction of L.B. Abbott and Art Cruikshank.

The pilot presentation is similar to *Man from the 25th Century* in its brevity and its reliance on flat, backlit artwork in place of certain sets and miniature shots. The underwater city itself is a painting with pinpoint lights projected from behind to represent windows, and the Triton complex command center is half set, half artwork. Stock footage of the Flying Sub from *Voyage to the Bottom of the Sea* was used to represent the city's "aquafoils," the shuttles between the city and the mainland. Abbott and Cruikshank did, however, build and destroy an elaborate miniature of the plot's "Project Mole" drill platform.

The story's conflicts are necessarily blunt—Glenn Corbett gives a shouty, one-note performance as Matthews, and just about everyone else in the short, especially James Brolin's Bill Tyler, spends their screen time shouting back at him. Laurence Montaigne appears in a wig and goatee as Aguila, conjuring up memories of the bearded, "evil" Spock from *Star Trek*'s "Mirror, Mirror," episode.

Explaining himself to Matthews, at one point Aquila says, "As an amphibian, my physical attributes might differ from yours, but my mental processes are just as clear and logical."

Like the *Man from the 25th Century* pilot presentation (as well as most episodes of *Star Trek* and other "action/adventure" TV shows of the period), the *City Beneath the Sea* presentation ends with a fistfight, this one between Matthews and the traitor, Harmon Temple. But Allen went *Star Trek* one better by staging the stunt man action against a raging inferno as the sabotaged Project Mole mining platform explodes and burns, finally toppling over, with the victorious Matthews apparently still on top of it—a cliffhanger ending that Allen hoped would help inspire NBC to green light a series.

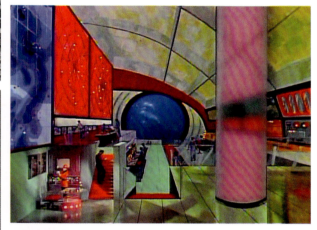

**ABOVE**
Norman Grabowski and James Brolin in the 1969 *City Beneath the Sea* pilot presentation.

**RIGHT**
Susana Miranda as Elena, a character demoted from tough security chief in the short pilot presentation to Admiral Matthews' secretary in the TV-movie.

**FAR RIGHT**
Images from the 1969 pilot presentation, with Glenn Corbett performing largely against blue screen and composited into painted, backlit artwork representing the film's locations.

A January 23, 1968 legal memo noted that "NBC has the right to order this series for a Fall 1969 start by ordering on or before April 1, 1969." *Star Trek* had been on the brink of cancellation since its first season on the air, but a combination of fan letter campaigns and NBC's ownership of RCA, the primary maker of color televisions (which used *Star Trek* to promote its TV sets) kept the show on the air through the summer of 1969.

But the possibility of Allen's project replacing *Star Trek*, or even finding its way on the network schedule as a regular series, was complicated by its ambitions. Allen reached out to writer and director John Meredith Lucas, a producer on *Star Trek*'s second and third season, to work with him on a new script for the project that Allen had retitled *Deep Quest*. The new storyline expanded on the idea of Commander Matthews' past, making him a city leader of a coastal megalopolis who is called back to the underwater city to address a series of crises, including a doomsday asteroid on a collision course with Earth. The asteroid threat forces the United States to begin moving all its gold—as well as its supply of a volatile new energy source—to Pacifica to ride out the impact. The gold shipments inspire a group of thieves to plan a heist of the gold using a cargo submarine, taking advantage of the chaos caused by the evacuation of the underwater metropolis during the emergency.

The new script also introduced a new character and foil for Admiral Matthews: Commander Patterson, a close friend of the dead Bill Holmes and the leader of Pacifica before he's forced to step down when Matthews returns. And, instead of the scheming Harmon Temple III, the new script introduced Matthews' black sheep brother Brett as the mastermind behind the gold heist plot. Allen also had the amphibian Aguila character sporting ESP powers, another similarity to *Star Trek*'s Mr. Spock.

The idea of Matthews' son stowing away inside the city was dropped and this character wouldn't appear in either iteration of the concept. Another casualty of the rewrite was "Choo Choo Kino" and her "six-feet-two of Japanese-Polynesian-American-Irish beauty." Pacifica's female security chief was reduced to the lowly station of Matthews' leggy secretary, Elena.

Allen worked out the new storyline between February, 1968 and January, 1969, while design work and further research were undertaken for the concept. Hal Herman's script notes on the new draft on Jan. 9, 1969, detailed that the idea of transporting gold to the city had been incorporated but had not been given enough screen time:

> The intensity of the impending doom of the rushing planetoid is not built to as big a climax as it should be... The highly technical flow of language becomes overwhelming throughout and washes out the story line which becomes more and more difficult to follow.

Also recommended was the deletion of an early scene of Matthews entertaining a girl at dinner, and more focus on the "marvelous basic story of the great gold caper against the onrushing planetoid."

Allen's script called for expansive sequences of the underwater city as well as scenes of underwater vehicle

**LEFT**
Storyboard art for the opening of *City Beneath the Sea*, closely matching the actual set photography and including likenesses of actor Stuart Whitman. (Note the repurposed Jupiter 2 miniatures used in the set background.)

**OPPOSITE**
Storyboard art for Matthews' trip with Patterson to Pacifica by "aquafoil." The aquafoil was realized via stock footage of the Flying Sub from *Voyage to the Bottom of the Sea*, but the latter illustrations show potential modifications to the miniature including additional rudders and control surfaces, outrigger engines, and even a top-to-bottom redesign of the ship. Ultimately the design was not modified so that the production could use the Flying Sub stock footage, even though the ship's paint scheme was intended to be white with red trim, unlike the Flying Sub's yellow with blue trim.

A-12

SC. 7  DISSOLVE TO  EXT. COASTLINE DAY

STOCK - PLUS MINIATURE COMP. MATTE.

SURF BEATING AGAINST EDGE OF MEGALOPOLIS. AQUA FOIL RISES FROM DISTANCE, SWELLING FROM DOT TO ALMOST FILL SCREEN.

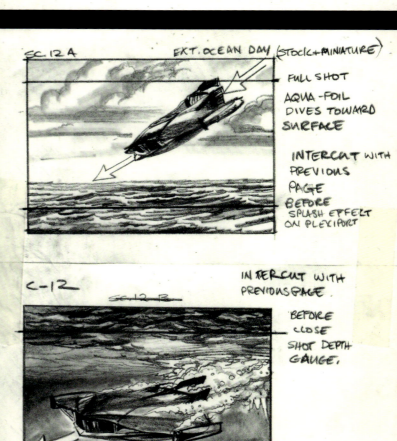

SC. 12A  EXT. OCEAN DAY (STOCK + MINIATURE)

FULL SHOT
AQUA-FOIL DIVES TOWARD SURFACE

INTERCUT WITH PREVIOUS PAGE BEFORE SPLASH EFFECT ON PLEXIPORT

C-12  SC. 12B

INTERCUT WITH PREVIOUS PAGE. BEFORE CLOSE SHOT DEPTH GAUGE.

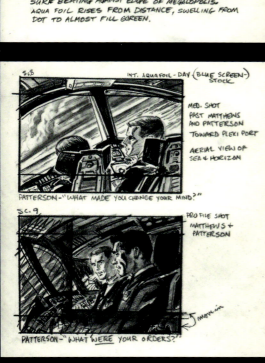

SC. 8  INT. AQUAFOIL - DAY (BLUE SCREEN) STOCK

MED. SHOT PAST MATTHEWS AND PATTERSON TOWARD PLEXI PORT

AERIAL VIEW OF SEA & HORIZON

PATTERSON - "WHAT MADE YOU CHANGE YOUR MIND?"

SC. 9  PROFILE SHOT MATTHEWS + PATTERSON

PATTERSON - "WHAT WERE YOUR ORDERS?"

SC. 14 — FULL SHOT - PLEXIPORT PAST M.O.P. (BLUE SCR. - MIN. & PTG.)

ESTABLISH PACIFICA.
CONTROLLER'S VOICE — "RED TWO SEVEN, TRITON CONTROL..."

SC. 15

LOW ANGLE - UPSHOT
- DEFENSE RING
MINIATURE
AQUA FOIL STREAKS
BY ROW OF
VULCAN FIVE
MISSLES.

SC. 20
P.O.V. - THROUGH PLEXIPORT
PROTEIN PROCESSING PLANT
(BURN-IN-MINATURE)

PATTERSON: "LAST MONTH THE PROTEIN PROCESSING PLANT SHIPPED EIGHT HUNDRED TONS"

SC. 21
INT. AQUA-FOIL
REVERSE

MATTHEWS: "WHAT'S THE STATUS OF THE HYDROPONIC NURSERY."

SC. 21 CONT'D
NEW ANGLE

MATTHEWS: "WOODIE, YOU'RE DOING AN EXCELLENT JOB."
PATTERSON REMAINS IMPASSIVE.

**OPPOSITE & ABOVE**
Storyboards for the aquafoil approach down to Pacifica and its protective ring of ballistic missiles, and the final miniature view of the city and its weapons.

accidents, the mass evacuation of the Pacifica, and the oncoming asteroid and its destruction by missiles. Compared to Allen's previous TV projects, even the technically challenging and expensive *Land of the Giants, Deep Quest* was in an entirely different league.

Allen's February 26, 1969 production script notes indicated that the high cost of special effects was already casting a shadow over preproduction:

> In all interior scenes of Full Scale aquafoils, minisubs, aquadozers, etc., indicate all shots as REVERSE FROM VIEWPORT unless absolutely necessary to include the viewport. All these numerous references, as now written, as to what can be seen through the viewports are extremely costly, time-consuming underwater Miniature shots plus Blue Screen or Process. I have already suggested (in my Interior Set Recommendations) that all script references to "plexibubbles" on minisubs, aquafoils, aquadozers, etc. be deleted in favor of enclosed "cockpits" with a front viewport only.

Allen also objected to the excessive use of two-way viewscreen connections between characters that would involve "costly Burn-Ins," recommending that intercom radio or phones be used for less important conversations.

Allen and his staff met with NBC executives on July 16, 1969. Notes from the meeting outlined network concerns:

> A need for greater in-depth development of principal characters. We should know their backgrounds, emotional conflicts, attitudes, inter-personal relationships. Emotional conflicts should be developed and emphasized in dramatic playing scenes, one against one, two against two, rather than "earthquake" scenes which allow little room for anything but the urgencies of command. Clarify the functions of the principal characters re: their work at Pacifica. There seems to be an overlap and lack of clarity as to specifics.

NBC had specific notes on the characters too. Matthews was "cold, shallow, much too 'snappish,' a man with physical problems to resolve but no emotional one."

At this stage Lia Holmes was another Pacifica Triton Complex worker, and the network recommended changing her position to that of a civilian to avoid confusing her with the other Triton personnel. They suggested that she might be married to Patterson, an idea that wasn't pursued. At this point Brett was going to rudely flirt with her, something the network said would be "even more obnoxious" should Lia be married. The network also found Brett's character too transparent ("Believe he now has 'heavy' written all over him.") and suggested he be made more likable and pleasant to throw audiences off the scent. The network also considered Aguila's characterization problematic ("Seems to be a complainer, selfishly covetous of own area with no regard for others.") and suggested that his ESP should be established earlier.

Allen objected to the idea of making Lia a civilian and of having her be married to Patterson ("This eliminates the relationship with MATTHEWS and the now-existing triangular inter-personal conflicts involving two brothers and one woman," he insisted). He suggested that Matthews, Patterson, Bill Holmes, Aguila, Elena and Brett were all involved in the creation and establishment of Pacifica, and that Matthews and Holmes were both in love with Lia, with Lia eventually marrying Holmes despite her interest in Matthews. When Holmes is killed in an emergency, Matthews is dogged by rumors that he is somehow responsible and Matthews ultimately resigns his commission and leaves Pacifica. Years later Matthews is ordered back to Pacifica by the President, where he faces the resentments of the others who have all become comfortable in their positions in the absence of Matthews. NBC approved of this setup for the show's drama.

The script at this stage opened with an earthquake, resulting in the orders to move gold from Fort Knox, which is being threatened by a seismic fault. The idea of "a highly fusionable element" is added to the transfer of gold. NBC suggested that Matthews transport a VIP to Pacifica at the beginning of the story and give the dignitary a tour of Pacifica, another suggestion Allen objected to:

> Too expositional and documentary in flavor. We will get the same effect upon Matthews' return to Pacifica as he encounters the abrasions and conflicts with the other characters.

Allen also suggested that opening the story with Matthews as a civilian would be "another plus factor" that would provide "a view of the WORLD OF TOMORROW outside his office windows."

Following implementation of NBC's and Allen's suggestions, another meeting was held with the network on August 1, 1969. NBC was enthusiastic about the latest draft with two exceptions: they nixed the idea of a prior romantic involvement between Matthews and Lia, insisting that Matthews, Lia and Bill Holmes be portrayed as just close friends. They also rejected the idea of Aguila possessing ESP, suggesting instead that he should simply have a kind of instinctive "intuitive sense." NBC also suggested that, "Conflict between Matthews and Patterson should be on a mature, 'clenched teeth' basis, rather than a 'yelling' scene.'"

By this point Allen had coined the term H-128 for the "fusionable material"—it would ultimately be called "fissionable H-128."

With the script approved, preproduction and casting moved on through the fall of 1969 and into the spring of 1970. By now *Star Trek* had been off the air for the better part of a year and any thoughts of *City Beneath the Sea* replacing Gene Roddenberry's show had been forgotten. Allen's concept was now positioned as a special movie for television—with a 98-minute running time, it would fill a two-hour time slot with commercials and possibly generate enough interest to develop it as a series. Allen's production company co-produced the movie with 20th Century Fox and Steve Broidy's Motion Pictures International—Allen had worked with Broidy as early as 1959 on *The Big Circus*, and fate would hook him up with

**LEFT**
Storyboard artwork showing the actor likeness of Stewart Whitman as Admiral Matthews, but with Aguila depicted as bald with very visible gills on his neck—quite different from the final casting of Burr DeBenning, gill-less and sporting a full head of 1970s hair.

**OPPOSITE**
Storyboard art showing a much more elaborate Pacifica loading bay.

SC. 48 — INT. LOADING DOCK TWO — EST. SHOT

BRETT ON EMERGENCY PHONE. WATER SPURTS FROM DAMAGED BULKHEAD - MINI-TRACTOR AND MEN ATTEMPT SEAL BRETT - "PATTERSON'S TRAPPED IN A MINI-SUB OUTSIDE."

SC. 50 — FADE-IN — INT. LOADING DOCK TWO

FULL SHOT CREW IN AIR LOCK

MINI-TRACTOR HAS PLATE AGAINST WALL BRETT WELDS IT WITH LASER BEAM. (STAGE EFX) HISS OF LASER

←ADD-MATT-EN

SC. 50 CONT. — PULL BACK MATTHEWS ENTERS FROM ELEVATOR AS REPAIR IS COMPLE[TE]

HE RUSHES OVER

SC. 80

INT. MATTHEW'S MINI-SUB
(BURN-IN-MIN.)
FULL SHOT MATTHEWS IN F.G.
THROUGH PORT WE SEE APPROACH OF WRECK.

MATTHEWS — "I'M GOING TO USE MYSELF AS A WEDGE."

SC. 82

CLOSE SHOT - VIEW SCREEN
(BURN-IN-MIN)
MATTHEW'S SUB PUSHES IN UNDER THE OVERTURNED AQUA-DOZER.

#97 AQUADOZER

**RIGHT**
Full size set sections of the aquafoil showing a white, red and gold color scheme quite different from the Flying Sub stock footage.

**OPPOSITE**
Storyboard art showing a much more elaborate aquadozer design, one with a multipart fuselage including a spherical pressure hull—and the final miniature design used in the production.

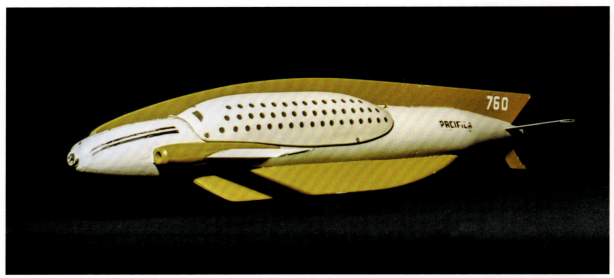

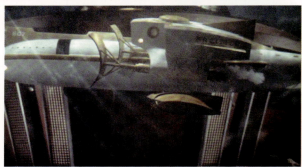

**ABOVE**
The mini-sub miniature from *Voyage to the Bottom of the Sea*, modified and repainted to make a passenger submarine for *City Beneath the Sea*. Photo courtesy of Greg Jein.

**LEFT**
Storyboard of the aquadozer accident and the final miniature sequence, filmed utilizing two commercially available Aurora Flying Sub model kits.

**OPPOSITE LEFT**
One of the miniature cargo subs used in filming. Designed by Rodger Maus, they feature the distinctive white and gold, Pacifica paint scheme. Photos courtesy of Greg Jein.

Production photo of the cargo subs leaving Pacifica during the movie's climactic evacuation scenes.

**OPPOSITE RIGHT**
Storyboard images of the cargo subs.

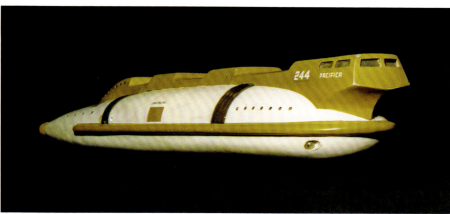

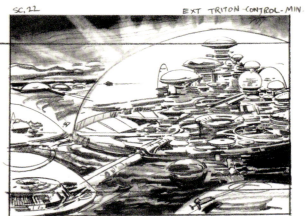

SC. 22 — EXT TRITON CONTROL - MIN.
LONG MOVING SHOT

SC. 23. — MOVING P.O.V. - THROUGH PLEXIPORT CARGO SUB (BURN-IN-MIN.) AT DOCK AT BASE OF TRITON CONTROL ADJOINING VAULT AREA.
PATTERSON: "ONE OF THE CARGO SUBS TRANSFERRING GOLD FROM FORT KNOX."

SC. 24 — INT. AQUAFOIL REVERSE MED SHOT.
MATTHEWS (SURPRISED): "THAT STARTED BEFORE I LEFT PACIFICA."

SC. 25. — EXT. TRITON CONTROL (MINATURE) FULL SHOT
CARGO SUB AT LOADING DOCK - AQUAFOIL MOVES INTO AIR LOCK.

**LEFT**

Storyboard images depicting "Lunderson's sub"—a cargo sub involved in the plot to steal the Fort Knox gold and H-128 supplies from Pacifica—as one of the standard, Rodger Maus-designed sub miniatures. In order to clarify the submarine as a nefarious "bad guy" vehicle, it was decided to redress the enemy "Vulcan" sub miniature from *Voyage to the Bottom of the Sea*'s episode "The Lost Bomb" to become Lunderson's cargo submarine.

A production photo of the sub emerging from a cave to approach a Pacifica cargo bay, and a shot of the Vulcan miniature as it appears today.

Broidy again shortly after *City Beneath the Sea*.

Allen detailed the production's progress in a May 13, 1970 Fox memo to NBC's Herb Schlosser and Peter Robinson. Delivery of an answer print was scheduled between December 1 and 15th. Set concept was finished and design work had started, with construction scheduled to begin by the end of May:

> The project has taken on great size and importance. We will be shooting on not less than three stages (Stages 21, 22 and B) here at Fox. Additionally we will be shooting in two huge underwater areas (the Green Tank and Moat). The shooting schedule has been laid out and is intended to shoot in 25 days, plus 10 days of miniature shooting and an additional day for second unit.

Allen was in discussion with both Stuart Whitman and Gary Collins to play Matthews. Up until this point Ben Gazarra, Richard Chamberlain, Robert Culp, James Franciscus, Rod Taylor, James Coburn, Don Murray, Tony Perkins, Harry Guardino, and Alex Cord had all been under consideration to play Matthews (Alex Cord would play the lead in another ambitious sci-fi pilot for NBC, Gene Roddenberry's *Genesis II*).

Candidates for Aguila included Michael Ansara, Cesare Danova, Henry Silva, Rudy Solari, Fernando Lamas, and Ed Ames—all familiar Hollywood "exotic" actors used to playing unusual roles, indicative of Aguila's position in the script as a kind of alien character. Many of these actors had portrayed Native Americans in westerns (Solari played an extraterrestrial "Amerind" on *Star Trek* while Ed Ames was Daniel Botone's Native American sidekick Mingo on Fox's *Daniel Boone* TV series).

Burr DeBenning's casting was considerably less outré—DeBenning was more in line with the youthful appeal of James Darren (who would also cameo on the movie as an astrophysicist) and he may have been cast because of his ability to perform the character's strenuous underwater scenes, something that might have been difficult for many of the older actors under consideration for the role.

On July 10, 1970, Allen approved plans for miniature construction of the City of Pacifica, which involved hanging a backing on Stage B, building a ground profile, assembling building units as they were completed in the miniature shop, with the final set to be checked by L.B. Abbott before final completion. Allen also approved "Special Flicker Devices to be built for effect lighting" to give the effect of shimmering underwater light coming from the surface.

Allen's television shooting sets had filled sound stages before, but he had never filled a sound stage with a miniature set. Art director Stan Jolley (of *Voyage to the Bottom of the Sea*) and Rodger Maus designed Pacifica as a series of underwater towers topped by mushroom-shaped, acrylic pressure domes, with numerous lit structures and interconnecting tubes linking everything to a central, rotating hub, the Triton Complex. L.B. Abbott and John C. Caldwell worked with the Fox prop department to manufacture the structures that would make up the city, using props from previous Irwin Allen productions (the Triton Complex was

**ABOVE**

Miniature of Pacifica dominated by the "Triton Control Complex," which was constructed around the remnants of the Jupiter 2 astrogator console from *Lost in Space*.

Robert Wagner (left) as Matthews' shady brother Brett, *Time Tunnel* veteran Robert Colbert as Patterson (middle), and Stuart Whitman (right) as Kevin Matthews, *City Beneath the Sea*'s "misunderstood hero."

Flood on the Pacifica loading dock.

363

**ABOVE & OPPOSITE**
Storyboard art of Triton Control, filming on the massive control room set, and establishing shot with a look through the room's main viewport at Pacifica.

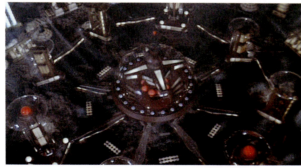 

**OPPOSITE**
Irwin Allen oversees the rigging of the special lighting effect for the cellophane and fiberglas "fissionable H-128" prop.

**RIGHT**
The H-128 as it appears in the TV-movie, and a series of shots of the many elaborate miniature effects in the TV-movie.

built on the Jupiter 2's central astrogation station) and everything from Ford Galaxy automobile grills to kitchen appliances. The final result was spectacular, colorful, and—in 1970—convincing.

The project retained the cost-saving measure from the original pilot presentation of reusing footage of the Flying Sub from *Voyage to the Bottom of the Sea* for Pacifica's all-purpose "aquafoils." The aquafoils were supposed to be white with red trim, as opposed to the Flying Sub's original yellow with blue trim paint job. Set pieces left over from *Voyage to the Bottom of the Sea* of the Flying Sub's exterior, forward windows (with its pilots and interior sets visible within) and its lower hatch were repainted with this look, and there was some consideration of augmenting the original Flying Sub design with additional, outboard engines or even altering the original prop's overall shape, but ultimately the temptation to reuse footage of the vehicle from *Voyage to the Bottom of the Sea* overrode any ideas of changing the Flying Sub miniature's design or paint job.

Other submarine vehicles from *Voyage* were repurposed for the TV-movie as well: a small, two-foot Seaview model was modified and appears in the background of at least two shots; the Seaview's two-man minisub (rarely utilized after *Voyage*'s first season) miniature was modified into a larger passenger submarine; and the show's enemy "Vulcan" submarine from "The Lost Bomb" was modified to become the nefarious cargo sub used by Brett's associates for the gold heist plot.

Even the Jupiter 2 made appearances when the original "Gemini 12" and Jupiter 2 miniatures had windows carved into them so that it could function as futuristic buildings outside Matthews' New York office and as Pacifica buildings in the large Pacifica miniature.

Rodger Maus designed several new vehicles for the story, particularly the show's most distinctive (and ridiculous) vehicle, the "aquadozer"—an underwater bulldozer with two huge bulldozer blades and dual, underslung water-jet propulsion units. The aquadozer had a touch of Spindrift influence with its central, vertical stabilizer fin and box-like rear power plant housing. Two miniatures around 18″ long (employing some interior cockpit details from Aurora's Flying Sub model) were constructed to interact with Flying Sub in two scenes of an aquadozer crashing down on top of an aquafoil. The production likely employed the commercially available Aurora Flying Sub model kits, which were around 8″ in diameter, for these sequences, rigged with headlights and red engine exhaust lighting.

While footage from *Voyage to the Bottom of the Sea* (including the impressive crash into the ocean seen at the beginning of the film) was used for most of the other aquafoil sequences, the 9″ Flying Sub miniature (built to interact with the 8-foot Seaview model) was employed in the early sequence of Patterson piloting his aquafoil with Matthews aboard into Pacifica and the Triton control center. Maus also designed some passenger and transport submarines with the same distinctive, fluted rear propulsion jets as the aquadozer.

**ABOVE**

Robert Colbert filming inside the waterlogged "aquafoil" set—actually the repainted Flying Sub interior set left over from *Voyage to the Bottom of the Sea*.

(l to r) Actors Robert Wagner, Paul Stewart and Rosemary Forsyth (seated) being directed by Irwin Allen.

Allen was determined to get the highest possible rating for *City Beneath the Sea*, which was shooting for a January, 1971 airdate—early enough that a TV series could potentially go into production and make it on the air by fall, 1971. A July 15th memo had a list of potential cameos for the project including Vincent Price, Edward G. Robinson, Henry Fonda, Sugar Ray Robinson, Tony Randall, Richard Basehart, James Darren, Robert Stack, Don Murray, James Franciscus, Walter Pidgeon, Joseph Cotton, Maurice Evans, David Frost, David Janssen, and Keenan Wynn. Of these, Sugar Ray Robinson, Edward G. Robinson, Basehart, and Joseph Cotton wound up in the film.

Interestingly, Richard Basehart was under consideration to play Admiral Matthews, which would have made *City Beneath the Sea* tie in even more closely to *Voyage to the Bottom of the Sea*. Allen was particularly interested in signing Robert Wagner for the role of Matthews' brother Brett—Wagner had just wrapped production on his popular show *It Takes A Thief* and, after years of supporting roles in film and television, was becoming a popular television star. Wagner wound up being one of the highest-paid cast members of the TV-movie—he spent his down time during production shopping for a 50-foot yacht, eventually purchasing the 58-foot Splendour, infamously involved in the death of Wagner's wife Natalie Wood in 1981.

Don Murray was under consideration to play Matthews along with Whitman, James Coburn, Anthony Perkins, Harry Guardino, and Alex Cord. Ultimately Stuart Whitman, the rugged star of the western series *Cimarron Strip* and the movie *Those Magnificent Men in Their Flying Machines*, played Matthews—although according to Robert Colbert (who would play Matthews' grumpy foil, Commander Patterson), Whitman still needed a little convincing:

> We started out shooting *City Beneath the Sea* and Stu came to me one day, we had been friends before, and he was very concerned about working for Irwin. He didn't know who he was or what he represented or anything. So he came to me and says, "What's it like?" I said, "Come onboard, Stu, you'll love it." So he went ahead and he signed for the part. And about two days before we started filming *City Beneath the Sea,* Stu was out on the beach playing volleyball, darned if he doesn't pull a major muscle in his arm and he's crippled. I mean that arm would not move, and we had to start shooting this action-packed adventure, with our lead, our star, a cripple. But we got through it somehow. You never knew it. But Irwin just went right on around it. He couldn't replace Stuart right at that time, but, "No, no problem, we'll work it out." And they did. And Stu, he always enjoyed having worked with him and, he thanked me later on.

Shooting for the TV-movie began on August 10, 1970 on the Fox stages. The massive Triton Control set (with a forced perspective look reminiscent of *The Time Tunnel*) was constructed on Stage 22, with most of the other sets (including the cavernous loading dock and gold vault sets) constructed and filmed on Stage 21.

The scene of a Pacifica loading dock flooding after being struck by an aquadozer was shot on August 26th.

"I was on the soundstage the day they shot the scene where the bulkhead is supposed to rupture and water comes shooting in, but it just trickled in," production illustrator Dan Goozee says. "George Swink, the production manager, told them not to tell Irwin because he didn't want to shoot it again. Irwin came on the set and asked how the shot went and everybody said, 'Great!' Irwin looked at the footage and said, 'Bullshit, we're shooting it again.'" Burr DeBenning's underwater scenes were shot at the Green Tank on September 17th—the last live action sequences shot for the production.

Miniature shooting commenced on September 23rd on stage B, with views of Pacifica and the city's lights going off (as power is shut off to route to the missile defense systems toward the climax) and the lights coming on again for the grand finale after the planetoid has been deflected. On September 28th, shots for Matthews and Patterson's initial underwater flight into the city were filmed, with more shots for the characters' "tour" of the city shot on the following day. Shots of "Lunderson's Sub"—the modified Vulcan submarine miniature from *Voyage to the Bottom of the Sea*—were done on September 30th.

All of these scenes were shot "dry for wet," with miniatures on wires shot against the huge Pacifica miniature set that had been constructed on the stage. An optical effect of shimmering water was overlaid on most of the footage to complete the underwater illusion; this effect is given away in one scene when what is supposed to be underwater camera footage of an aquadozer accident is frozen to make a still image—and the underwater "flickering" effect continues to play over the still.

The accident sequences involving the aquafoils and aquadozer miniatures were shot on October 5th and 6th. These were also scheduled to be shot on stage B, but these shots were done "wet for wet" in a small tank. Paul Stader was stunt coordinator, with Tom Sutton doubling for Whitman and Howard Curtis doubling Robert Wagner in their climactic fight scene in the gold vault.

Total costs for *City Beneath of the Sea* ran up to $1,600,000. While promoting the TV-movie in *Variety*, Allen expounded on his love of the sea—with reservations:

> I spent my earliest childhood on the beach. I also believe that man has always wanted to return to the sea. As for my brilliant sea background—I get seasick and need Dramamine to get on a boat. I'm a lousy sailor.

Allen told one columnist the movie was filmed off the island of Maui, with his cameramen "going down 70 to 80 feet":

> The film involved the longest preparation of any that I have ever done. It was preceded by a year and a half of heavy research and entailed a grim, risk job for some 14 to 16 stunt men we had down there.

However apart from a few magnified images of sea life seen in the windows of Dr. Aguila's underwater lab, all of *City Beneath the Sea*'s underwater action was filmed on

**PREVIOUS**
Caricature advertising art by Bob Bentovoja for NBC premiere of *City Beneath the Sea*.

**ABOVE**
The gold vault set and the climactic set-to between the Matthews brothers in *City Beneath the Sea*.

the lot at Fox. Allen had particular praise for his longtime visual effects supervisor, L.B. Abbott. "All I have to do is show him a rough diagram of what I want and it's as good as done." He was also still bullish on science fiction, insisting that, "People never grow up to not like sci-fi."

*City Beneath the Sea* aired on January 25, 1971, running against *Mayberry RFD, The Doris Day Show,* and *The Carol Burnett Show* on CBS and ABC's *Monday Night Movie* broadcast of *In Harm's Way. City Beneath the Sea* came in a strong second with a 31 overall share, and actually beat the ABC movie in its final half hour. *The Hollywood Reporter* pronounced the production "Good Enough For Theaters." Reviewer John Goff said the TV movie "makes one thankful for color TV sets."

Allen's staff passed around an equally enthusiastic *Variety* review proclaiming that "Irwin Allen's sci-fi special effects and sets are an art form of the fantastic unto themselves, and *City Beneath the Sea* is no exception." While taking note of the story's "contrived" situations, the review noted that, "It is the imaginative invention, the constant change of situations, the crackling pace, and ultimately the total showmanship in the utilization of special effects that is the ace here that captures audiences."

Underlined by staff was:

> With the large investment already committed in special effects and settings, "City" would certainly be a promising situation for a continuing TV series, now that the stalwart Whitman has saved Pacifica from destruction.

Pointedly *not* underlined was the last line:

> However, it will take more intelligent scripts and characterizations.

Richard K. Shull, in *The Indianapolis News*, was more cynical, likening the show to "a family reunion of Allen's past TV series, where the most apocalyptic challenge always boils down to a climactic fistfight between hero and villain." Taking note of the show's production design, Shull said:

> One thing never explained in any of Allen's shows is how the characters, who appear to be normal human beings, can survive in the architecturally sterile surroundings of Allen's future. Life in an Allen show is one morass of blinking lights and rotating computer drums, with the air polluted with the noise of hundreds of blinking and squeaking futuristic devices.

In *The L.A. Times*, Kevin Thomas, always friendly to genre projects, pronounced *City* "tremendous fun—and frequently tremendously funny...despite all the hokey dialogue handled by the actors...they play it absolutely straight, which, of course, is far more hilarious than if they camped it up."

*City Beneath the Sea* had the same potential for scope and story variety that *Star Trek* had—with a city of 20,000 people to explore, character, conflict, and story potential was almost limitless. For a series with such rich story potential, however, little in the way of possible script ideas for a *City Beneath the Sea* series were developed. The TV-movie broadcast was well-received, but not enough for NBC to exercise its option and continue the concept's development as a weekly series. Warner Bros. distributed the movie theatrically overseas, marking Allen's return to the big screen, albeit not the way he had probably intended.

Very early on NBC had expressed concern about the idea's budgetary risks—risks that Allen acknowledged. The show would require extensive miniature photography week after week. To portray the populace of Pacifica, large groups of supporting players and extras would be required. New sets would have to be manufactured to show different areas of the city. The "man alone" plots that had saved the production money on *Voyage to the Bottom of the Sea* would be unworkable on *City Beneath the Sea*; it was hard to imagine a plot that would have Commander Matthews isolated alone on Pacifica even once, let alone in multiple episodes, and in any case the mammoth Pacifica sets would still have to be lit and dressed for the occasion.

High costs had been part of *Star Trek*'s problems during its run on NBC, and *City Beneath the Sea* raised an issue that Roddenberry had intentionally avoided on his show: he dictated that the Enterprise would never journey back to Earth of the 23rd Century during the show because of the costs and challenges of depicting human civilization hundreds of years in the future. For *City Beneath the Sea*, Allen leaped from his usual settings of a decade or two in the future to the year 2053, and as the TV-movie showed, on top of the challenge of simply depicting the 10-mile-wide city of Pacifica, an above-water, coastal "Megalopolis" was just an aquafoil launch away.

Herman Rush reflected in 2016:

> It was too expensive to do as a television pilot and everyone recognized that. Irwin suggested let's do it as a television movie because you're approving more money and higher budgets, and it can be either 90 minutes or two hours. That's how *City Beneath the Sea* came about and it played as an on-air movie which was in a way a test as a pilot. It didn't rate that well that they felt it would make a series at the higher cost that they would have to justify.

*City Beneath the Sea* was thus limited to a couple of network showings and its theatrical run overseas, and networks avoided ambitious futuristic and space-oriented science fiction programs going forward (even the much ballyhooed and highly rated, original *Battlestar Galactica* was cancelled after its 1978-79 first season because the show was too expensive to produce). But the project remains a favorite of Irwin Allen fans for its spectacular production values, imaginative concept, and for the way it repackaged so many of the familiar props, miniatures, and set pieces from Allen's television productions.

And somewhere in an alternate universe, maybe Admiral Matthews had a few years of adventures managing Pacifica and its challenges.

**ABOVE**
Promotional buttons—one of Allen's favorite gimmicks—and a newspaper print ad for *City Beneath the Sea*.

**OPPOSITE**
The overseas theatrical release poster of *City Beneath the Sea* featuring art by Reynold Brown.

# EVERYONE WHO'S GOING TO GET KILLED, RAISE YOUR HANDS.

**IRWIN ALLEN**

on the set of *The Poseidon Adventure*

# VOYAGE TO THE TOP OF THE BOX OFFICE

*Allen gambles and wins with* **THE POSEIDON ADVENTURE**

Irwin Allen's run as the king of science fiction television was over by 1971. For anyone familiar with his name, Allen was the guy that made *Lost in Space* and *Voyage to the Bottom of the Sea*. His early theatrical movies were largely forgotten and TV viewers were often unaware that the *Voyage to the Bottom of the Sea* series had been based on a theatrical feature.

Allen, however, had been plotting his return to movie screens as early as 1968. "My film, *Circus World* [sic], is still running on the late show," he said in a July 15, 1968 interview in *The Chicago Tribune*, referring to 1959's *The Big Circus*. "So I may as well be producing them again." The same day, in *Variety*, Allen noted that he had closed a deal with Avco Embassy and Joe Levine for three movies, only one of them science fiction: "I have to start thinking in other terms now. Reality is stranger than fiction."

Allen had in fact stumbled on a property that fit in perfectly with his movie ambitions—one that played to his strengths as a producer of technically spectacular action and fulfilled his desire to tackle a story that had more dramatic power than the high tech adventures he had become known for. And it had the added advantage of stemming from the pen of one of Allen's favorite authors.

In a *The Saturday Evening Post* feature, Allen said:

> Paul Gallico was kind of a boyhood hero of mine. He wrote the best sports column in the country for *The New York Daily News*, and the most literate. And after a while he said a farewell to sports and went on to his great novels. We had both gone to Columbia University in New York and we had played on practically the same streets as schoolboys in Manhattan. It was just about two and a half years ago I heard a little bit of a rumor that a new Gallico book was coming along. I knew his agent here on the Coast, and so I put in an urgent request to see the galleys.

**OPPOSITE**
Mort Kunstler's vivid Style B poster art painting for *The Poseidon Adventure*.

**FOLLOWING**
A diagram of the action as it moves through the S.S. Poseidon in *The Poseidon Adventure*, similar to a schematic requested by screenwriter Wendell Mayes early in preproduction for Irwin Allen's movie.

Gallico had written short stories and novels that had been made into films—his story "The Man Who Hated People" was made into the musical *Lili* in 1953, and his book *Thomasina: The Cat Who Thought She Was a God* was adapted by Disney into *The Three Lives of Thomasina*. Gallico had been on the ocean liner Queen Mary on a voyage in 1937 when the ship was hit by a series of large waves and listed over to its side, and appeared close to overturning. The event lasted for just a few seconds but seemed "an eternity" to the young Gallico.

30 years later Gallico was looking for an idea for an adventure novel—frustrated that all the possible settings for such a tale, from faraway jungles to outer space, had already been exploited—when he remembered his experience onboard the ocean liner and thought up the concept for what would become *The Poseidon Adventure*. Gallico discussed the idea with an architect who told the author he thought an ocean liner could be capsized "under certain conditions." Later he scoured through the records of the library of Lloyds of London to see if anything like such an event had ever occurred, and found the tale of a 34,000 ton iron-ore cargo ship, Jakob Verolm, that capsized in the South Atlantic in a storm. The hull remained floating with its keel up for 40 days. It took Gallico 18 months to write the novel, and at one point he and a friend built models of rooms inside the Queen Mary and turned them upside down in order to properly visualize the world that his characters would be traversing.

In Gallico's story, an underwater earthquake capsizes the ocean liner SS Poseidon during a voyage in the North Atlantic ocean, and a group of trapped passengers led by Reverend Frank Scott struggle to make their way up toward the keel of the vessel where they might be rescued. With a young brother and sister and their estranged parents, a bickering pair of newlyweds (including a tough New York cop, Mike Rogo, and his former prostitute wife Linda), an aging Jewish couple, Manny and Belle Rosen, and others involved in the grueling and terrifying trek through the overturned vessel, conflicts and attractions brew among the passengers as they fight to survive.

Allen recalled in the *Saturday Evening Post* piece:

> When I read *The Poseidon Adventure*, I said, "Hell, I want to make money with this." I'm a very commercial-minded guy and there is a unique combination in the Gallico book. Most pictures, for better or worse, are either intimate stories with no hardware, or enormous hardware stories that have no foreground focus on people, I think here we have a story of very unique people...to begin with it almost sounds like soap opera. If you are able to tell a highly commercialized story that has great emotion, great conflicts, great heart tugs, great interplay between characters, and then set it in a scene of unusual hardware for background, the chances are that you have better than a fighting chance for success in the picture business.

In 1995 Al Gail recalled that Allen had movie rights to *The Poseidon Adventure* before the book went on sale:

> After *Voyage*, I took a year off and my wife and I spent the year traveling around Europe. I needed the rest. And I spoke to [Irwin] on the phone, as I did almost every other week. He said, "I just bought a book, called *Poseidon Adventure*, by Paul Gallico." And I was walking past a bookstore and I saw a whole window display of it. I said, "How did he get that book?" But he did. And, that was the start of *Poseidon*.

James Darren recalled Allen working on *Poseidon* as early as 1967, although records show Allen purchasing the rights to the novel in March, 1969 for $100,000:

> Irwin's thing was the sell. That's what he did, that's what he did really well. He was a great salesperson. He could sell anything. I remember when he was storyboarding *The Poseidon Adventure* when we were doing *The Time Tunnel*. So he was already in the sales process for those things. Selling them via storyboard.

Certainly Allen could have been in preproduction on *Poseidon* during production of *Land of the Giants* and he would surely have been at work on the movie while Darren was working on the set of *City Beneath the Sea* in 1970:

Allen wrote Don Kopaloff of Avco Embassy Pictures, Corp. on June 3, 1969, announcing they were in business. But Allen's mind was already on promotion:

> I am, however, terribly concerned about the fact that no publicity has been issued announcing this, other than one or two line leaks which now threaten to kill any kind of a big story.

Allen enclosed a press release announcing *Poseidon* and the purchase of Martin Caidin's science fiction novel *No Man's World*, which was to have been filmed before *Poseidon*. The story involved American astronauts exploring the moon for 24 hours, who discover that Russian astronauts have landed on the opposite side of the satellite. Caidin's novel *Marooned* was being shot with Gregory Peck as Allen made his announcement, and it's possible that the lackluster box office of that project deep-sixed *No Man's World*. A third project was *Almost Midnight*, which had the mob stealing four atomic bombs to terrorize the country. Of these, only *Poseidon* would be produced.

Allen hired Wendell Mayes (*Anatomy of a Murder*, *Advise and Consent*) to tackle the screenplay for *The Poseidon Adventure*, and Mayes went to work by June 9th. Mayes wanted to start the story earlier than the book in order to introduce the audience to the characters more thoroughly before the disaster, and to lay some foreshadowing about the oncoming capsizing. The screenwriter requested a cross section of the ocean liner with a schematic trail of the trek and blow-ups of the obstructions facing the characters, and Allen set his team of artists and designers, including Tom Cranham and Dan Goozee, to work on the enormous challenge of visualizing the movie.

By mid-July, Mayes had delivered 41 pages of screenplay, moving from the opening of the film through the first horrifying moments after the ship capsizes. Allen was satisfied with the work, but had some reservations. He was concerned with the amount of sex in the script—Gallico's book had contained an

**OPPOSITE**

Storyboards showing a final pullback from the trapped passengers emerging onto the hull of the Poseidon to a view of the entire overturned hull of the ocean liner surrounded by rescue vessels, and its eventual submersion—action eliminated early on by Irwin Allen to reduce costs.

early rape scene in which a young sailor, panicking in the darkness after the turnover, rapes the teenaged girl Susan Shelby. The novel also included a scene in which New York cop Mike Rogo's wife (and former prostitute) Linda attempts to seduce the obsessive Reverend Scott, leading to an ugly confrontation. Mayes felt that the sex was "important to keep the story together," but this was unexplored territory as far as any of Allen's projects were concerned.

Nevertheless by mid-September Allen had approved Mayes' suggestion that a passenger named Richard, who Allen found weak (describing him as "a gray shadow") be revealed as homosexual to explain his "unusual interest" in Reverend Scott (Scott, the story's lead character, was described in a memo as "an ordained minister and concealed religious fanatic").

Allen was already working to keep the costs down by micromanaging every possible detail on what he realized would be an unprecedented, mammoth production. On October 7, he suggested ending the film the moment naval engineers break through the hull and the passengers realize they're rescued, instead of telling the story of all the surrounding rescue vessels as originally planned. Artwork for a sweeping sequence of rescue ships surrounding the overturned Poseidon had been prepared, but Allen's instincts told him that such a sequence would not only be challenging and expensive to film, but would actually drain the film's finale of dramatic power.

Allen's detailed concerns were over the descriptions of physical action—he wanted them to be as complete as possible in order to illustrate the unique elements of the project for Avco Embassy's perusal. For the early, post-capsizing scenes in which the passengers climb a Christmas tree and a companionway to escape the ship's flooding dining salon, Allen felt that Mayes hadn't emphasized the near impossibility of navigating each obstacle, instead illustrating the journeys through a series of dissolves that made the climbs seem easily accomplished. In his notes, Allen demonstrated an intricate knowledge of the physical details of the production, exactly where the characters were in relationship with the ship, and of character details and beats he wanted to emphasize or eliminate.

Allen was particularly fascinated by the character of Reverend Scott, another classic "misunderstood hero," whose seemingly tyrannical, maniacal drive to reach the keel of the Poseidon pushes the survivors to their limits and alienates many of them.

Allen said in an August 19 memo to Mayes:

> Obviously the driving, motivational force and prime mover in our play, as well as the most complex and difficult character to understand from a psychological viewpoint. We feel, however, that the revelation of his paranoia, the obsessive lengths to which he'll go in his own private, psychotic, religioso-maze of a world, come on too soon and too strongly. We suggest, rather, that his actions and dialogue as now constituted speak for themselves without the necessity for the above-mentioned, almost melo touch.

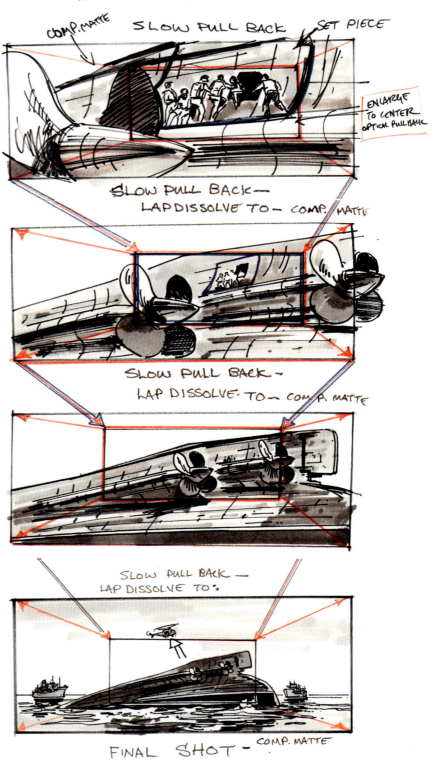

SC. 91 BLUE SCREEN?

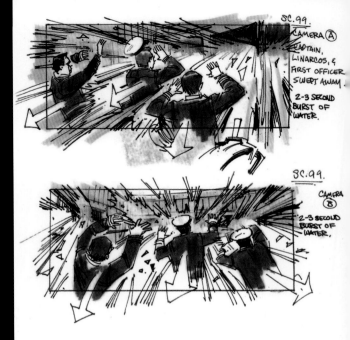

SC. 99 CAMERA Ⓐ
CAPTAIN, LINARCOS, & FIRST OFFICER SWEPT AWAY.
2-3 SECOND BURST OF WATER.

SC. 99 CAMERA Ⓑ
2-3 SECOND BURST OF WATER.

WATER MORTARS THROW WATER AGAINST WINDOWS

SC. 99 INT. BRIDGE NIGHT. WINDOWS SMASHED BY WATER.

LINARCOS
CAPT.
1ST OFFICER
CAMERA Ⓐ
CAMERA Ⓑ

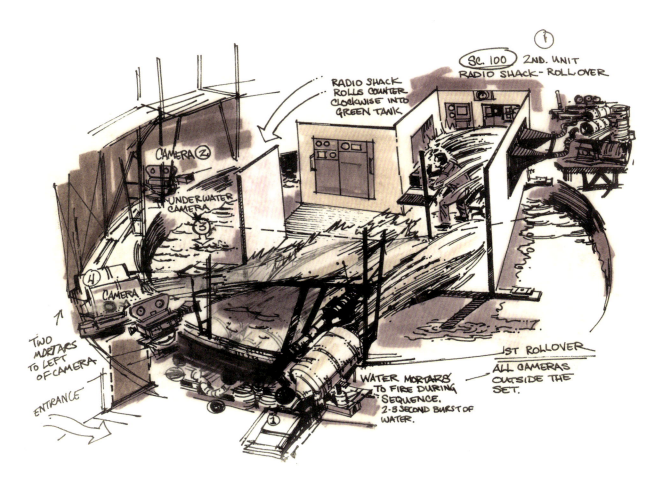

**LEFT**
Storyboard art for the Poseidon's rollover after being struck by the tidal wave.

Allen was referring to a moment in which Scott would have kicked the Christmas tree back down into the flooding dining salon after he and his chosen group of survivors climbs it, preventing the remaining passengers from joining his group—a demonstration of paranoia that Allen was eager to avoid showing as "sadistic."

Mayes, meanwhile, had expanded on the story's rape scene by having a major character, a shy tailor named Martin (who would eventually be played by Red Buttons), instigate the rape. Allen objected to the idea in a memo:

> MARTIN: Once again, we have a shocking, unexpected action, (i.e., the rape of Susan) for which we are totally unprepared. Martin has been almost completely lost up to now, and although we realize that as a participant in what is going on, he is almost constantly in the background, we really haven't seen him or heard from him as a reacting human being since his horror at the scene in the deckwell when the officer is drowned. We feel we need to know something more about this man, at least as to his reactions, overt or hidden, concerning the events that are submerging him.

Mayes' script also had Linda Rogo—depicted as an unpleasant individual throughout much of the action—referring to Belle Rosen variously as a "kike" and "Jew," lines that Allen preferred to soften to remove the anti-Semitism. Mayes had also invented a different character named "Jane Kinsale" to attempt the seduction of Reverend Scott, which was undertaken by Linda Rogo in the novel. Mayes had Scott react cruelly and sadistically to suggest what the script described as "a de-balled man"—making the basis for Scott's ultimate suicide a "Gothic horror" element with Scott described as "hermaphroditic."

Allen found this too much and went back to the missed opportunity of Scott's lack of a reaction to the deaths of Linda and Belle, and suggested that the deaths of these characters should motivate Scott's suicide—which in the film, ultimately played more as self-sacrifice for the good of the surviving characters.

Allen also reiterated that Mayes needed to take the time to sum up the characters' journey and the enormity of their final challenge to reach the propeller shaft above them in the burning engine room, bringing the characters' arcs to a final point. In particular, Allen wanted to emphasize Rogo's reaction to the death of his wife Linda, which became one of the most powerful and iconic moments in the film.

Allen had been in the empowering position of directing his previous theatrical films—*The Lost World, Voyage to the Bottom of the Sea,* and *Five Weeks in a Balloon.* He had directed all of his television series pilots and the elaborate, feature-length TV-movie *City Beneath the Sea.* Now he had secured the rights to what he was certain would be his most important and successful motion picture project yet, but Avco Embassy executives seemed to see Allen as a producer, not a director. A Sept. 15, 1969 letter from Alan Riche of CMA suggested possibilities such as John Boorman, George Roy Hill, Ralph Nelson, Sydney Pollack, Martin Ritt, Mark Rydell, Franklin Schaffner, Peter Yates, and Anthony Harvey to direct the film.

On December 4, the production completed its official script delivery to Don Kopaloff of Avco Embassy. The next day in a meeting with Kopaloff, Ken Rotcop, and Sidney Marshall, Rotcop objected to the sexual incidents in the script but Kopaloff had no issues with them. Later Kopaloff reported that Lennie Lightstone objected to the abrupt ending Allen had suggested, saying it lacked "cinematic value." By Christmas, the beginnings of a falling out between Allen and Mayes over the script ensued. Allen told Erwin Gelsey of the Gersh office that Mayes was seven weeks late delivering his first draft. In the first week of January, Mayes began complaining about how he was being treated, but he continued to work to address the studio's issues with the screenplay. By February 27th, Mayes was told his assignment was completed.

On January 14, 1970, Allen received comments on the script from Avco Embassy's New York office. The rape of Susan was first in line:

> It is felt that her initial reaction is not a realistic one; that she is much too quick to understand and forgive Martin. This traumatic experience added to the other emotional and physical ones she'd undergone, would result in outraged shock, anger and stunned disbelief. Then, after recovering from this beat, she would gradually become aware of Martin's own reactions, and her understanding of this pitiful little man would come to the fore.

Siding with Allen regarding Scott's "hermaphroditic" revelation, the studio preferred that he be "a psychological eunuch rather than physically abnormal."

Avco Embassy had expressed some concerns over Paul Gallico's title—*The Poseidon Adventure* might not be on-the-nose enough to get the picture's concept across to a potential audience. Noting that they still preferred *The Poseidon Adventure*, Allen and his staff churned out a laundry list of alternate titles, many of them laughable: *A Day to Remember, Scott's Children, The Upside-Down Hell* (which ultimately inspired the film's memorable tag line "Hell—Upside Down!"), *The Trek, The Endless Night, The Brave & The Foolish, Night of Disaster, The Condemned Flock, Nightmare of Death, The Sinking Ship and Surviving Souls, A Sea of Trouble, The Great Adventure, The Waves of Destiny, The Unholy Alliance, Cry Danger, ...And Not A Drop To Drink..., Once Upon A Crow's Nest, Roll-Over!, How Long Can You Tread Water, Give Your Wife A Cruise for Christmas, The Poseidon Maze,* and *We'll Never Forget You, Reverend Scott.*

Avco Embassy's concerns were beginning to weigh on Allen as the company's executives vacillated over the challenges that *The Poseidon Adventure* would pose as a production. The company had hits like *The Graduate* and *The Lion in Winter* as late as 1968, but it had never mounted anything on the scale of *The Poseidon Adventure*—in fact, since *Easy Rider* had become a shock success in 1969, all the major Hollywood film studios were looking at smaller, counter-culture projects to reach contemporary audiences, and Avco Embassy needed to look no farther than their own *The Graduate* for an example. Allen was still comfortable in the familiar confines of 20th Century Fox, and he knew Fox

**OPPOSITE**
Early production painting for the overturned Poseidon's engine room.

The final engine room set.

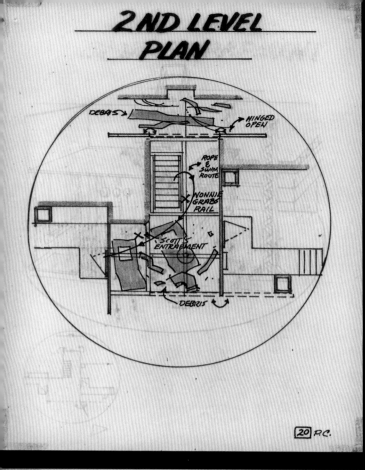
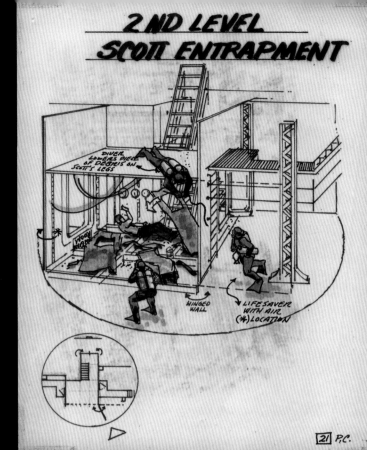

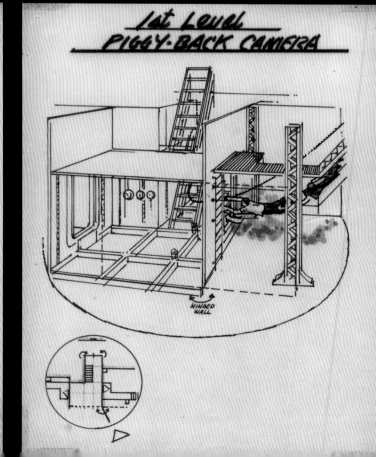

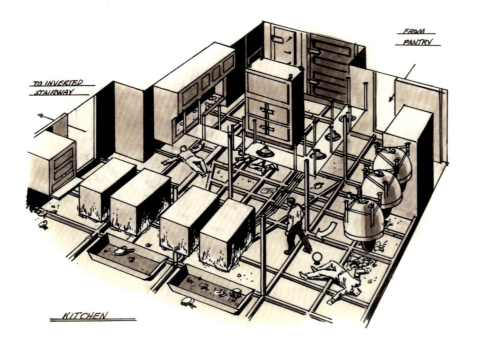
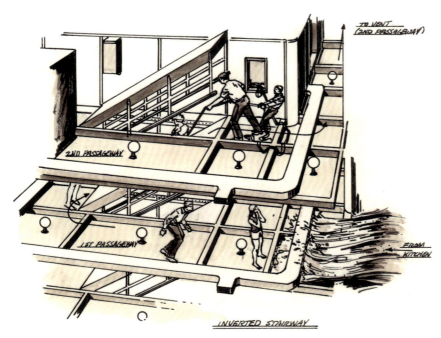
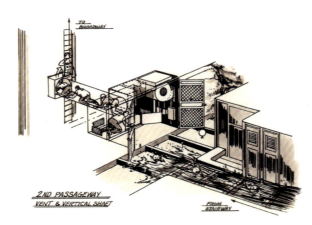

**ABOVE AND LEFT**
Storyboard art depicting key sets in the movie, created to facilitate construction and action blocking.

had the facilities, the staff and the production facilities necessary to make his movie.

By 1970 Allen had convinced Fox executives to take on *The Poseidon Adventure*. He would quickly discover, however, that his home studio of the past decade wouldn't give him any more largesse than Avco Embassy had. The studio had lost money from a string of unsuccessful and expensive musicals including *Hello, Dolly!*, Fox's attempts to duplicate the success of 1965's *The Sound of Music*.

"At the time Fox was reeling and really back on its heels," illustrator Dan Goozee recalls. "They had too many Roadshows going on—they were competing with themselves because they had all these big movies out at the same time, so they were cutting into their own profits."

Longtime Fox chairman Darryl Zanuck was removed from his perch and Gordon T. Stulberg came in as president with an eye toward controlling costs and connecting with contemporary audiences. Fox was no more eager to have Allen as director of *The Poseidon Adventure* than Avco Embassy had been, and the studio's list of possible directors included Gordon Douglas, Sidney J. Furie, George Seton, John Boorman, Ralph Nelson, John Guillermin, Richard Zarafian, and Bud Yorkin.

By the beginning of March, Allen had approval to start budgeting the movie; Bill Creber was hired as production designer three weeks later, and David Negron was hired to make three paintings illustrating the script for budgeting purposes.

Casting *The Poseidon Adventure* would be crucial. Allen's love of old time movie stars was well known, and *Poseidon* would ultimately showcase a mix of veterans and at least one cutting edge talent who would help raise the film's artistic and box office prospects to a new level. Initial casting ideas for Reverend Frank Scott included Burt Lancaster (who had played a memorably sleazy evangelical preacher in *Elmer Gantry*), Paul Newman, George C. Scott, Rock Hudson, Stuart Whitman, Charlton Heston, James Garner, Kirk Douglas, Robert Redford, and Robert Culp. For the story's tough New York cop: Mike Rogo, Richard Widmark, Robert Ryan, Ernest Borgnine, Eli Wallach, Jack Klugman, and Jack Warden were considered. Susan Hayward, Kim Stanley, Janice Rule, Lee Grant, Lee Remick, and Lainie Kazan were looked at for Linda Rogo; Lou Jacobi, Ned Glass, Lou Gilbert, and Edward G. Robinson were considered for Mannie Rosen, and Shirley Booth, Maureen Stapleton, and Coleen Dewhurst for his wife Belle. Sally Field was considered for young Susan Shelby, while the smaller but commercially important role of a singer named Nonnie had real singers Judy Geesen, Judy Carne, and Lulu up for the part.

Allen spent the next year working to make the film's story and costs amenable to Fox executives, and he continued to champ at the bit to be *The Poseidon Adventure*'s director. In an April 19, 1971 memo to Fox chief of production Elmo Williams, Allen noted that he had trimmed 22 pages from the script, eliminating three shooting sets and "several gratuitous sex scenes and two affairs—and one abnormality (Scott's physical problem) and still leaves us with enough sexual excitement to keep the most sophisticated audience titillated." The Martin-Susan rape and the character Jane's attempted seduction of Scott remained.

The same day Allen wrote Dick Shepherd of CMA about a meeting with Elmo Williams, Stan Hough (VP of Production at Fox) and Allen's staff:

> Despite the "in depth" probe of the meeting, not one word was said as to the director. (You know how anxious I am to do the job.) During the session [Williams] kept questioning the budget—"Could I do it for the price, etc."—I told him once we were agreed on the budget, I would freeze it—offer completion above that figure. What I didn't say was that this offered protection on my part would prevail *only* if I were the director (and therefore could control the cost) and only if they offered the usual additional percentage of profits (above a 50-50 split) to Steve Broidy for providing such completion.

Allen would have cause to revisit this promise to Fox of completion money for the project later.

By July, 1971, Allen's name was still nowhere to be seen on a list of potential directors for *Poseidon* that included Gordon Douglas, George Seaton, and Ralph Nelson.

On July 2, 1971, Allen consulted Williams about Fox's Foreign Department's "request to put at least three foreign stars in the picture." The characters of Richard and Jane Shelby were slated to be changed from an American to an Italian couple to be played by Rossano Brazzi and Gina Lollobrigida. A "young, beautiful, Italian-accented girl" would be sought to play the daughter, and the character of Robin—the movie's kid appeal—would be dropped. Ultimately the kid would stay in the picture and the parents would be dropped as key characters.

By the end of July, 1971, Fox reached a decision as to who would direct *The Poseidon Adventure*. They went with Gordon Douglas, a reliable hired hand whose work went back to the 1930s. Douglas had done a number of pictures for Fox—the westerns *Rio Conchos* and *Stagecoach* and the spy spoof *In Like Flint*, and Fox had also distributed three movies Douglas made with Frank Sinatra—*Tony Rome*, *The Detective*, and *Lady in Cement*. Douglas also had experience with big special effects pictures, having made the classic giant bug movie *Them!*, which featured an army of full-size, 20-foot-long mechanical ants, in 1954. Allen was disappointed in the choice, but he had to accept it in order to keep the production in play.

Gene Hackman was now on a list of possible actors to play Scott that included Kirk Douglas, Rod Steiger, Michael Caine, and Lloyd Bridges. Ernest Borgnine, Telly Savalas and Warren Oates were under consideration for Rogo; Ann-Margaret, Barbara Parkins, Sally Kellerman, and Connie Stevens for Mrs. Rogo; Jack Weston, Zero Mostel, and Burgess Meredith for Mannie Rosen; Ruth Gordon and Estelle Parsons for Mrs. Rosen. Allen had the brilliant idea of casting a young Gene Wilder (who'd made *The Producers, Start the Revolution Without Me* and

**ABOVE**

Irwin Allen on the Queen Mary, looking very much like he's in the director's chair.

Irwin Allen apparently toasting director Ronald Neame (right) on set.

**OPPOSITE**

*The Poseidon Adventure* cast in a publicity photo with an important costar—the Queen Mary, docked in Long Beach, California.

Shot of the Poseidon miniature showing the detergent suds used to help scale the water cascading off the vessel's bow.

Stella Stevens (center) with Ernest Borgnine and Gene Hackman, in one of her gravity-defying dresses designed for the movie by Paul Zastupnevich (shown with Stevens in the black and white publicity photo).

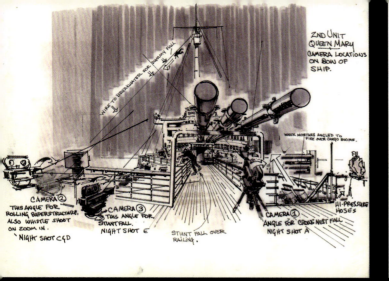

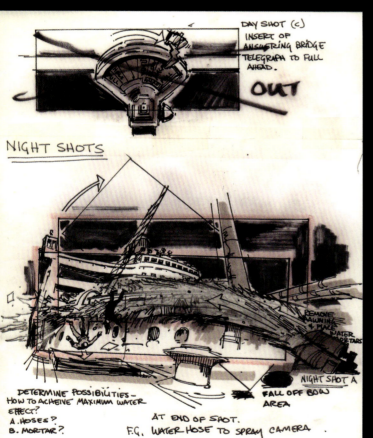
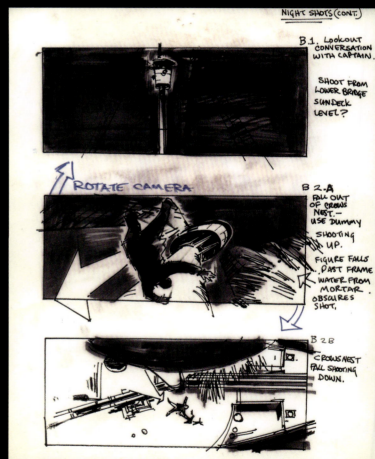

*Willy Wonka and the Chocolate Factory*) as Martin, but when Wilder's schedule prevented him from taking the role Allen looked at Roddy McDowall (who would ultimately play the ship's steward, Acres) and Peter Lawford before settling on his old standby and friend, Red Buttons.

In August, 1971, Allen secured another important star for the picture—one that *The Poseidon Adventure* couldn't be made without: the ocean liner Queen Mary. Paul Gallico had had the venerable cruise ship in mind when he wrote his novel, and since the Queen Mary had been permanently moored at the port of Long Beach since 1967, it would provide a critical filming location for the film's exterior sequences as well as research for the film's miniatures and full-size sets.

Gordon Douglas' tenure as director of the movie was short-lived. Although accounts vary as to why, he and Allen parted company by October, and Gordon Stulberg called British director Ronald Neame into the unenviable position of being Irwin Allen's second unwanted director. In his autobiography, *Straight from the Horse's Mouth*, Neame quoted production designer Bill Creber as saying, "We were all a little miffed because Gordon Douglas was a friend, and we said, 'Why do we need this new guy?'"

Unlike Douglas, who was more or less a Fox staff director, Neame had a more rarified career making British dramas and comedies, and had just come off the Oscar-winning *The Prime of Miss Jean Brodie*. He was an experienced actors' director who had helped Maggie Smith win Best Actress for her role as Jean Brodie and he would help get the most out of *The Poseidon Adventure*'s cast. Allen accepted Neame's presence grudgingly, as evidenced in a memo:

> ...The Producer is pleased and honored to extend to the Director (but only in accordance with those very special conditions and in that special manner listed below) that privileged credit reserved for those few Senior Directors who have reached the pinnacle of their profession; such credit to read: A RONALD NEAME FILM.

Allen's agreement stipulated that Neame's credit was to appear exactly the same size as Allen's and that, "it shall appear directly after the last cast credit but never preceding the main title." The agreement further stated that Neame and Allen would have equal say over the writing of the script, casting, the shooting schedule and the choice of cameraman, editor, and composer among other primary crew members. Allen reserved for himself authority in administrative and budget matters, the hiring and firing of personnel, and all matters of promotion, publicity, and advertising.

Allen was also determined to have Neame recognize his standard procedure of completely storyboarding his films.

Production illustrator Dan Goozee recalls:

> Some of the people at the Fox art department were award-winning artists in their own right in the fine arts field, but they worked there because they liked the steady paycheck. Irwin pretty much invented the term "movie magic," which was basically showing how the shot was done from behind, over the shoulder of the cameraman, showing where the camera was, where the explosives were going to come out of...he did that, particularly on *Poseidon* and the rollover sequence where he had a lot of special effects and stunts, so he could have some kind of control. We'd have a big production meeting and he'd hand out these sketches so each group would know what their role would be in the scene, and that saved a lot of confusion and a lot of extra takes. But he determined early on that even though Ronald Neame was going to be the director, he was going to be the second unit director, meaning that Irwin would get to do all the fun shots with the explosions and effects. In fact at one point Ronald Neame whispered to someone that he was afraid to have someone light a cigarette in a shot for fear that Irwin will say it should be second unit."

Neame himself did not work from storyboards and felt they restricted the acting process, and the two men reached a compromise that allowed Allen to plan and storyboard the film's elaborate action sequences, but not the dramatic scenes involving the actors. In his autobiography, Neame claimed that Allen liked to have complete storyboards on the walls of his office during production for visitors to see, and that in the case of *Poseidon* Allen had his artists work off of production stills of the dramatic scenes after the fact to create the artwork instead of filming sequences using storyboards as a guide. This explains the fidelity of some of Allen's production artwork, much of which contains authentic actors' likenesses and other details that wouldn't have been accessible to the artists had they been at work early in the preproduction process when storyboards are normally generated.

When submitting his set budget to Allen, Bill Creber suggested the idea of building the Dining Salon in a "squirrel cage" that would roll completely over to do capsizing shot live in camera rather than by cutting to the miniature of the Poseidon. At this point the script indicated a shot of an underwater volcano erupting and causing the tidal wave that swamps the ship; Creber noted, "an arbitrary point of view of a miniature is very dangerous, especially in a realistic kind of picture. I would rather see an instrument reading—how about just letting a storm capsize ship?"

With Fox insisting *Poseidon*'s screenplay still needed work, Neame and Allen agreed to hire writer Stirling Silliphant to rewrite Wendell Mayes' script. Silliphant had done abundant work for television as well as the 1960 theatrical chiller *The Village of the Damned*, and he had won an Oscar for his screenplay to 1967's *In the Heat of the Night*.

Mayes found out his script was being rewritten after reading about it in a newspaper column in mid-November, and Silliphant quickly wrote his fellow screenwriter a lengthy letter to apologize for the embarrassment. Silliphant would become invaluable to Allen on the producer's disaster movie cycle.

Despite Silliphant's efforts, on January, 1972, Stulberg called Neame and Allen into his office to tell him that his readers had reacted quite negatively to the screenplay. Budget estimates for the project added up to $4,315,185,

**OPPOSITE**
Storyboards for a sequence of a lookout plummeting from the Poseidon's crow's nest during the rollover—to be achieved through a combination of miniatures and a dummy being tossed from the Queen Mary's crow's nest.

with $2,211.170 worth of added financing needed to complete the picture. "They think it would be a disaster to proceed," Ronald Neame quoted Stulberg as saying in his autobiography. Stulberg explained that the studio couldn't afford to spend $5 million on "such a risky project" and that he had decided to cancel Fox's funding of *The Poseidon Adventure*.

Stunned, Neame and Allen asked to revisit the subject later in the day, although Stulberg told them it was very unlikely he would change his mind.

Now Irwin Allen's long years in Hollywood and the immense daisy chain of connections, partnerships, and friendships he had established over the years were about to bear fruit in a potentially desperate situation. Unknown to Neame, who was mulling over the idea of returning to the U.K., Allen had walked across the street with production manager Hal Herman to the Hillcrest Country Club, where he found his friends Steve Broidy of Motion Pictures International and Sherrill Corwin of Metropolitan Theatres Corporation. Allen had already convinced the two men to guarantee two and a half million dollars against Fox's two and a half million to provide the necessary five million dollars in financing—and a surprised Stulberg quickly agreed to the deal when he met with Neame and Allen later that day. Allen's connections and tenacity had saved *Poseidon* from a fate far worse than a marauding tidal wave.

On January 22, 1972, Allen met with Neame, Fox Vice President of Production Jere Henshaw and Silliphant on the following points: the movie had to be rated G, which would affect some of the sexual incidents in Mayes' draft; Mayes had the characters arrive at the skin of the ship at the exact time the rescuers cut through, and all agreed this was too coincidental and additional story material should be added—this turned into the climb through the burning, upside-down stairway and the death of Linda Rogo at the climax of the film; the group elected to drop a character named Kemal, who would have been an expert on the ship, adding to the uncertainty of the civilian characters groping their way through the Poseidon; and, finally, Robin and Susan's parents, the Shelbys, were dropped from the script, which then depicted the teenaged older sister and her younger brother traveling alone on the Poseidon.

Silliphant added the idea of Susan developing a crush on Scott, a "hero-worship" relationship that would cause her to be hysterical when Scott sacrifices himself. The group agreed that Scott "should be a genuine rebel and non-comformist, not a traditional drill-instructor or brow-beater, but inspirational..." They also agreed that there should be a "time lock"—the idea that the ship might sink at any moment, killing them all.

Silliphant submitted his completed revised shooting script on February 9, 1972. After two years of struggle, *The Poseidon Adventure* was nearing the shooting stage.

Another important element fell into place on March 27, when Lionel Newman recorded the song "There's Got To Be A Morning After" on Stage 1. Written by songwriters Al Kasha and Joel Hirschhorn in one night, the song was performed by Renée Armand so that actress Carol Lynley (playing the singer Nonnie) could lip-synch to Armand's recording during filming.

By now the rest of the cast was set. Gene Hackman nabbed the starring role of Reverend Scott. A reliable character actor throughout the 1960s, Hackman had a breakthrough performance in 1967's *Bonnie and Clyde* and just prior to his work on *The Poseidon Adventure*, he had taken on the role of Detective Popeye Doyle in William Friedkin's *The French Connection*, a blockbuster hit that would make Hackman a box office superstar and win him an Oscar while *Poseidon* was in production.

Hackman was on the cutting edge of movie audience tastes, but for the rest of the cast Allen hired familiar, reliable movie stars: Ernest Borgnine as the blustery Mike Rogo; talented and sexy comic actress Stella Stevens as his wife Linda; Jack Albertson as Manny Rosen; the difficult but very convincing Shelley Winters as Belle Rosen (Stevens had worked with Winters in 1969's *The Mad Room* and swore never to work with her again, but broke her vow to do *Poseidon*); Red Buttons as shy haberdasher Martin; Pamela Sue Martin as young Susan Shelby; and Eric Shea as her younger brother Robin. Roddy McDowall—fresh off the *Planet of the Apes* films and probably happy to have his face visible onscreen again, joined the cast as the ship's steward, Acres, Leslie Nielsen played the Poseidon's ill-fated captain, and Arthur O'Connell played a humble Catholic priest frustrated with Reverend Scott's take-no-prisoners attitude.

Filming started April 3, 1972 and ran for 70 days, with the first three weeks consisting of scenes taking place before the ship capsizes and the last 55 days spent on the surviving passengers' odyssey through the overturned ship. Some sets were built on tracks so that they could slide into the Fox studio moat to create the illusion that they were filling up with water. The film's sets filled five sound stages at 20th Century Fox.

*Poseidon*'s first major action scene involved the ocean liner's ballroom, where a tidal wave interrupts a New Year's Eve celebration. The set had to be designed around a massive, stained glass skylight that a stunt man would fall through after the ocean liner overturns.

"The ballroom was based on the scale and roughly the art deco style of the Queen Mary," Bill Creber says. "You also have to remember that we started out having no money, so everything you'd do, you'd figure out how to reuse and find stuff that you can repaint and rescale. The murals at the end of the ballroom, the big Egyptian figures, were drawn in a very art deco style and they were quite large, 15 feet high, and they were from *Cleopatra*. The skylights on the ceiling and eventually the floor were from *Hello, Dolly!*, the Harmonia Gardens."

Creber and his crew took the upper, curved part of two *Hello, Dolly!* arches together to form an oval into which fake, breakable glass could be inserted. "We did that because they still had the molds that they made that glass in, so it wasn't an architectural reason, we just did it because we had the molds large enough—and nobody has ever recognized it."

**OPPOSITE**

P.R. photos of the final *Poseidon Adventure* cast, from top left to bottom right: Gene Hackman, Ernest Borgnine, Carol Lynley, Roddy McDowall, Stella Stevens, Shelley Winters, Jack Albertson, Pamela Sue Martin, Arthur O'Connell, Eric Shea, Leslie Nielsen, and Red Buttons.

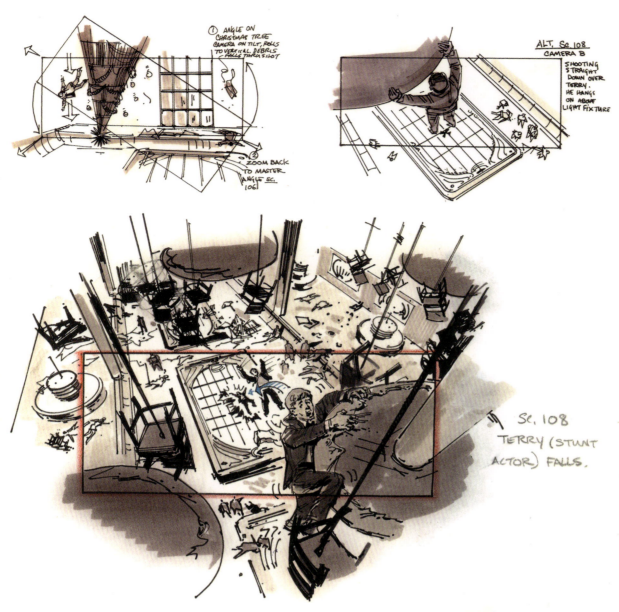

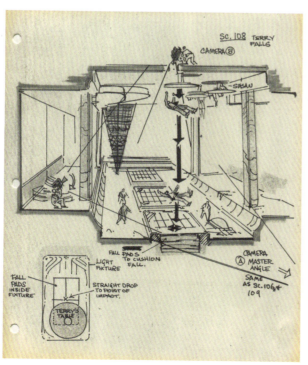
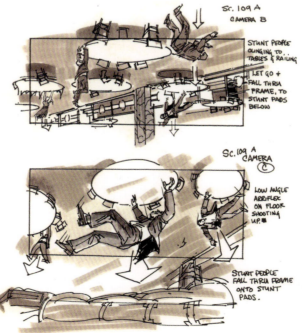

**LEFT & OPPOSITE**
Movie Magic diagrams for shooting scenes of passengers hanging and dropping from the bolted down banquet tables after the Poseidon overturns.

Ernie Orsatti performed the iconic shot of a survivor of the rollover hanging by his fingernails from a table bolted to the floor—now ceiling—of the dining salon where the New Year's Eve party is taking place. The character loses his grip and falls through a skylight, where he is electrocuted to death.

Bill Creber recalled, "In the production meetings, I told Irwin, 'Why don't we find a stunt man who can act a little bit and fit the part and take the fall, so for once in a movie you can see the guy's face who does the stunt?'" Allen thought that was a great idea and he had Ernie Orsatti, Jr., the son of Allen's old boss at the Orsatti Agency, in mind. Stunt coordinator Paul Stader trained Orsatti, Jr., to take the 32-foot fall by having the actor dive off a billboard off of Main Street in Santa Monica, next door to Stader's gym.

"We got to the day or two before shooting and we did the fall a dozen times with a real stuntman so we knew it would work," Creber says. "It was all laid out just right and the hole cut in the stage floor and eight feet of cardboard boxes and air fall pads, plus, to make it look like ceiling, we stretched some muslim, so you could drop an egg on it and it wouldn't break."

By this point, Orsatti had been filmed interacting with the movie's stars in the New Year's Eve party scenes, and according to Creber, the experience started to change Orsatti's perspective. "Ernie comes to me and says, 'You think they can get a stuntman to make that fall? I'm an actor now and I don't want to get hurt.' I said, 'Ernie, if you don't want to get you fired and me fired, you're going to do that fall.'"

Allen provided Orsatti with some extra incentive—in keeping with Creber's suggestion, he would have a camera pointing straight down from directly above Orsatti to give the budding actor a dramatic closeup as he grimaces in terror before letting go of the table he's hanging from and falls away from the camera, down into the skylight. Allen had four other cameras set up to record the action, and there was tremendous pressure to get the spectacular sequence in one take so that the skylight wouldn't have to be rebuilt. Orsatti created one delay in filming when he wore the wrong color socks to match his tuxedo, meaning he had to hang for six minutes while a costumer grabbed another pair for him—all adding to the risk that the actor would be too exhausted to fall at the right moment and hit the skylight correctly.

A careless crew member caused another potential problem. "The prop man for some reason was wearing a lab coat," Creber says. "In the pocket of the lab coat he has a little screwdriver, and the little screwdriver falls out and falls down and goes through the candy glass." Creber climbed down from his perch next to camera five, the one positioned for the close-up on Orsatti, and discovered a quarter inch hole in the skylight glass from the screwdriver. "I look at it and I figure, I'm not telling anybody," Creber says.

There was an audience for the fall—people from all over the lot had come to see Ernie Orsatti plummet into the skylight. At the proper moment Allen had all five cameras up to speed, and for this shot it was Allen himself who'd be calling "Action!"

Orsatti performed the stunt perfectly, with lighting effects technicians adding a spectacular strobing effect from the underlying lights the performer had landed on to create the illusion of a deadly electrical short caused by the fall. Creber managed to punk his producer in the aftermath: "After it was all over Irwin shouts out, 'How's that for camera number five?' and I yelled down, 'We're ready whenever you are, Irwin!' He said, 'Creber, the next person down off that table is you!'"

Allen also directed the subsequent action sequence of explosions ripping through the glass ceiling and the panic of the Poseidon passengers who had made the unfortunate choice to remain behind while Reverend Scott and the other primary characters climb out of the dining salon. "Irwin was up there in a big Chapman crane with a cameraman directing all this stuff with a bullhorn, and he was a good director," production illustrator Dan Goozee says. "He knew exactly what he wanted and he was one of the first guys who'd set up with five cameras. He'd film an explosion from five different angles and it would wind up looking like one gigantic explosion."

The production used over three million gallons of water at Fox Studios, including having the cast swim through a 63,000 gallon tank while cameramen wearing scuba gear filmed them. The waterproof lights used in the sequence heated the water so much that 6,000 pounds of ice had to be dumped into the tank to keep the water clear enough for filming. 125 stunt men were used in the production, and six water "howitzers" were activated by compressed air and held 300 gallons of water each to shoot onto the set to simulate the impact of the tidal wave.

**ABOVE**
Iconic images from the film of Orsatti's plunge into the skylight.

**OPPOSITE**
Lobby card photo of the explosion and water cannon effects of the ballroom flooding with water after the initial rollover.

Belle Rosen (Shelley Winters, with Jack Albertson, left) prepares to take her fateful swim to rescue Gene Hackman's Reverend Scott in this Japanese Souvenir book photograph.

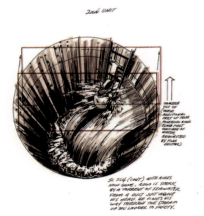

**ABOVE**
Gene Hackman and Ernest Borgnine in a lobby card photo of the shaft sequence prior to the Roddy McDowall character's fall.

**LEFT**
Storyboard artwork for the shaft stunt sequence.

**OPPOSITE**
Scott (Gene Hackman) grieves over Belle, who dies of a heart attack after saving Scott's life.

**FOLLOWING**
Filming the shaft sequence.

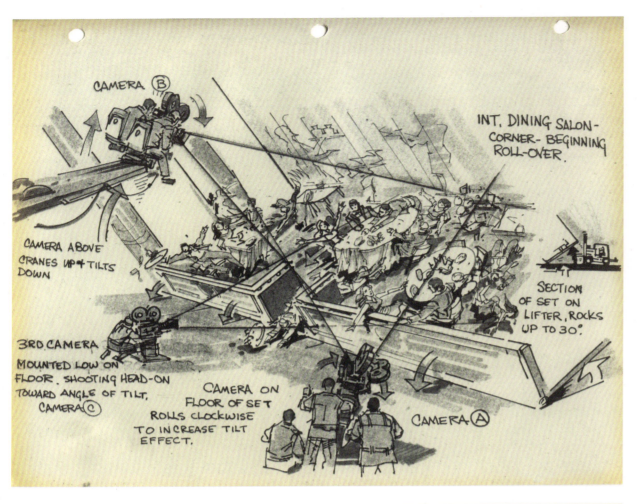

**BOTH PAGES**
"Movie Magic" artwork, Allen's term for storyboard art that depicted how shots would be accomplished, including camera placement and special effects rigging—and artwork of the overturned ballroom with tables now suspended from the ceiling.

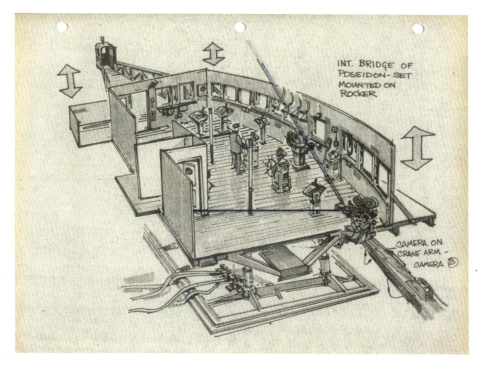

Ronald Neame wanted the actors to perform as many of their own stunts as possible in order to create realism. That included Shelley Winters, who had to swim by herself underwater through obstacles for a number of yards. Gail recalled in 1995:

> She had never done any underwater swimming. We had a stuntman, our head stuntman [Paul Stader] who worked with us for many years, come to her hotel, and give her lessons in the pool, and she did that by herself. She insisted on doing it. She would not take a stuntwoman. She did that swimming and she deserved a lot of credit, cause it was a tough, tough scene.

But there were still 353 man-days of work for stunt men and women. Allen shot the explosion and death of Roddy McDowall's Acres character in one of the Poseidon's central access shafts, and all the underwater scenes of characters swimming from the boiler room to the engine room. Doubling for Roddy McDowall, stunt man Larry Holt, 26, fell backwards 40 feet down a ventilating shaft into water—the shaft was only seven feet in diameter, leaving very little room for error. Holt did the fall once, actually breaking a three inch plank with his head but suffering only a small bump from the impact. When Allen wasn't certain the cameras had captured the stunt, Holt agreed to perform it again, but eventually cooler heads prevailed.

Allen trumpeted the incident in publicity materials:

> I've had long experience in the action genre. And have never had anyone suffer a major injury. This was the most dangerous stunt I'd ever seen. I just didn't want Larry to do it again.

Fortunately, the scene photographed perfectly.

For film publicity, Director Ronald Neame spoke highly of Allen:

> When you have such a producer, who is a friend and whose opinions you can trust, it is most helpful to a director. Sometimes when one is as close to a film as a director usually is, he can't always maintain complete perspective. It helps greatly to have someone a step apart watching over things.

A.D. Flowers, who had destroyed dozens of full-size reproductions of WWII fighter planes in Fox's *Tora! Tora! Tora!*, supervised *Poseidon*'s challenging physical effects:

> We had a sequence in which the sea bursts the wall of the grand salon of the ship and drowns 100 persons. I estimated that it would take about 200,000 gallons to achieve the effect the director wanted. That amount of water would have taken the whole sound stage with it, so we had to devise a way to give it the desired look without actually delivering the necessary quantity. We set up a system of water mortars, which hurl 300 gallons each with great force, and special pumps delivering 3500 gallons a minute through an intricate web of pipes. The shot was made with 8,000 gallons.

Week three of filming was spent on location on the Queen Mary—*Poseidon Adventure* was the first theatrical film shot on the vessel. In 1936 the ocean liner actually experienced something like the catastrophe seen in the movie—in October of that year she navigated a 55-knot gale while traveling from New York to Southampton. At one point the ship rolled so much that passengers becamze hysterical and quite a few were injured. Afterwards the chairs in the dining saloon and elsewhere on the ship were rigged so that they could be anchored in place, a detail that inspired the look of the upside dining saloon in the film. Stabilizers capable of preventing such pitching weren't added to the ship until 1957.

Miniature shots were scheduled for June 6th at the Sersen Tank at Fox Ranch. The Poseidon miniature was built for a cost of $60,000. Special effects supervisor L.B. Abbott had essentially retired from Fox after Allen's TV series went off the air, and the venerable Fox Special Effects department had been shut down. *The Poseidon Adventure* marked the first of many occasions when Abbott would emerge from "retirement" to work for Allen.

Abbott had obtained blueprints of the actual Queen Mary on which to base the miniature, but in order to fit the ship into the Sersen Lake tank, Abbott had to build the model at 1:48 actual size, drastically smaller than the 1:16 scale most miniature on-screen marine models used to achieve a convincing effect. (By comparison, the 8-1/2 foot Seaview model produced for Voyage to the Bottom of the Sea, with a fictional length of only ~400 feet, was also constructed at the same 1:48 scale as the ~1,000-foot Poseidon.)

A 1:16 scale Poseidon would have been 63 feet long, far too large to be accommodated in the Sersen tank. Even at 1:48 scale, the model was an impressive 21 feet long, which required Abbot to crank his cameras at seven times normal speed to film a realistic Poseidon at sea.

He was also limited by the dilapidated Sersen Lake sky backing, which had fallen into disrepair, forcing Abbott to shoot the Poseidon miniature from overhead angles so as not to show the horizon and tattered sky backing (some night shots were achieved with a horizon in view, since the light was low enough to not catch the warped sky painting panels behind the ship).

Abbott and his crew used large dump tanks holding 1,750,000 gallons of water to create the unforgettable shot of the tidal wave swamping the Poseidon. Over a period of 30 minutes, Abbott shot three takes—one in which the wave turned out much too large, obscuring the miniature; one in which the wave wasn't large enough; and a final take that perfectly achieved the desired effect. A.D. Flowers rigged the miniature's smoke stacks to explode underwater for several shots paced through the film's running time to show the overturned ship in danger of breaking up.

Gene Hackman's onscreen conflict with Ernest Borgnine's character became the grounding dramatic through-line of the movie. Costume designer Paul Zastupnevich ingeniously helped to establish Hackman's rabble-rousing character by fitting him in a sports coat and one of Zastupnevich's beloved turtleneck sweaters— the cutting edge equivalent to the standard priest's collar

**ABOVE**
The miniature of the S.S. Poseidon operating in the Sersen tank at the Fox Ranch in Malibu, California. Visual effects supervisor L.B. Abbott had to keep to overhead, "helicopter shot" perspectives of the model in order to avoid showing the damaged sky backdrop painting of the tank.

The iconic footage of the Poseidon being struck by a tidal wave—created by dump tanks holding 1,750,000 gallons of water.

**OPPOSITE**
Storyboard artwork for the Poseidon capsizing sequence.

worn by the traditional cleric played by Arthur O'Connell opposite Hackman.

But Zastupnevich felt that Allen undercut some of the other drama in order to focus on suspense and action. He noted in 1995:

> In *Poseidon Adventure*, you have Carol Linley and Red Buttons, in a little love scene, after her brother has been killed with the ship turning over, and it was the most heartrending scene I've ever sat through. In fact the crew, when Carol and Red finished the scene, they applauded. When Irwin got it in the cutting room, he cut the scene in pieces. He would go up to Gene Hackman climbing a ladder with water coming down, fire coming, then he'd cut back to the scene, you'd get a few more lines then he'd go back to the hero. Back and forth, back and forth. And I said, "What are you doing? You're destroying, a tender moment." "Oh no," he says, "the audience will get impatient." *He* got impatient. I was so upset at the time because I felt he destroyed an Oscar performance for both Red and Carol.

Allen wrote Paul Gallico to update him on the status of the film being made of his book:

> It took a full two and a half years of lunatic agonizing from the day I read the galleys until the first day of principal photography. Then, at the eleventh hour, after making the deal with the studio, having a brilliant script written, casting the winners of eleven Academy Awards, I found the studio willing to invest only one-half the money needed (two and a half million instead of five million), and then found myself involved in a frantic seventy-two-hour chase to dig up that other two and a half million.

Allen had another scare during a wrap party for the cast and crew shortly after completion of the main shoot. "They had the wrap party in the upside down engine room set on a soundstage," illustrator Dan Goozee recalls, "and Ernie Borgnine just absolutely gave Irwin a heart attack by deciding to run all the way up the upside down stairs all the way up to the roof of the soundstage and wave at everybody, and everyone was convinced the whole thing was going to collapse and Ernie was going to get killed at the wrap party."

With shooting completed, *The Poseidon Adventure* went into postproduction, and in mid-July Lionel Newman and Allen discussed possible composers for the project with Elmo Williams. In order of preference they were John Williams, Dominic Frontiere, Jerry Goldsmith, Lawrence Rosenthal, and Jerry Fielding (Fielding would later score *Beyond the Poseidon Adventure*). Elmo Williams wrote back noting that the studio's order of preference was John Williams, Rosenthal, Goldsmith, and Fielding: "We know that Gordon [Stulberg] is very high on Johnny Williams so I am hoping you can make a deal with him. Certainly he's proven his talents many, many times."

Allen was more than happy to use John Williams—Williams had long been a favorite of Allen's dating back to the composer's scoring on *Lost in Space*, and he had called on Williams to set the musical tone for all of his subsequent television shows. Williams, meanwhile, had

**ABOVE**

Storyboard artwork for the Poseidon capsizing sequence.

Divers at work on the overturned Poseidon miniature.

Ernest Borgnine and Gene Hackman face off as Red Buttons (center), Stella Stevens (left) and Jack Albertson's (right) characters attempt to intervene in this lobby card shot from the movie.

**OPPOSITE**

The Poseidon miniature between takes in the Sersen tank.

**RIGHT**
The completed engine room set, a nightmare vision of fire, water, and dizzying heights.

**OPPOSITE**
Storyboard art for the climactic engine room sequence.

409

embarked on the beginnings of a prestigious career in theatrical films after years of scoring television and theatrical comedies—his scores for *Goodbye, Mr. Chips, The Reivers,* and *The Cowboys,* and his Oscar-winning adaptation of *Fiddler on the Roof* had placed him at the first rank of film composers, and *The Poseidon Adventure* would mark the first of many box office blockbusters that would bear Williams' music.

A few days later Elmo Williams wrote Steve Broidy of Motion Picture International to assure him that Broidy's investment in the film, which had bailed the project out of cancellation, had been a wise one:

> This is going to be the big one this year. It is a film that I am sure will win honors, make money, and a product all of us can be proud of. Irwin has really pulled this one off. You will always be glad you got into this one—that I promise.

Broidy wrote Williams back:

> I am elated to get your personal reaction, which I value very highly. As you know, Sherrill and I have always had a great deal of faith in Irwin. We realize he is not only an outstanding executive as well as a great picture maker, but he is a showman of unusual proportion and there are very few if any in the industry today.

Allen himself enthusiastically wrote Broidy on September 20 about John Williams' score:

> There are 59 pieces in the orchestra, the largest used here at Fox in many years. John Williams' score is magnificent and he is brilliant as a conductor. I think the music will be responsible for yet another great improvement in the overall finished product.

**TOP LEFT**
Irwin Allen clowning with composer John Williams, a veteran of Allen's TV shows who would score *The Poseidon Adventure* and *The Towering Inferno* before moving on to *Jaws* and *Star Wars*.

**TOP RIGHT**
Original "Hell, Upside-Down" one-sheet poster featuring the Mort Kunstler painting.

**OPPOSITE**
The original key art by Mort Kunstler used in posters and promotional materials for *The Poseidon Adventure*.

**LEFT**
Lobby card photo of Eric Shea's and Gene Hackman's harrowing run through a flooding passageway, achieved by sliding the set down a track into a tank of water.

Carol Lynley, Red Buttons and Stella Stevens deal with rising water in another lobby card shot.

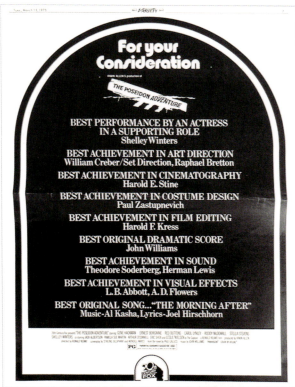

**RIGHT**
Trade ads touting the movie for Oscar consideration—and bidding patrons to give it a second viewing. Many took Allen's promotional department up on the offer.

Despite Allen's confidence, Fox executives were still nervous about the movie's prospects. The film's first test screening in Minneapolis, however, quickly indicated that the studio potentially had a big hit on their hands. Out of 190 total cards, 174 (97%) enjoyed the picture; 153 out of 190 rated it "Excellent," 32 "Good," and only 4 "Fair." 175 out of the 190 said they would recommend the movie to their friends; 110 said they would see it more than once.

At a second test screening in San Francisco, out of 425 cards completed, 388 rated the movie either "Excellent" (272) or "Good" (116). Comments included:

- It was emotionally draining.
- Fantastic. One of the best pictures I've seen.
- I'll see it again if my stomach can take it.
- This has been by far one of the best movies I have ever seen.
- I have never enjoyed any pictures as much as I've enjoyed THE POSEIDON ADVENTURE.
- I found this the most emotionally moving picture ever. Thank you for a great picture.
- Triple excellent. But I wouldn't see the movie again because I couldn't go through an experience like that again.

Allen's stars were equally impressed once they saw the finished production.

Roddy McDowall said in 1995:

> With *Poseidon* it just was such a gigantic spectacle. I was always astonished that *Poseidon* was so difficult to get going, but I think that's because I've always had a visceral reaction to sea disasters. Any natural disaster has such huge audience identification. It's something bigger than all of us, and it seems very gripping. It was the first big movie on such a gigantic level—a very, very stylish, production.

Red Buttons recalled that he had a choice at the time to do a different, potential blockbuster—Ross Hunter's musical adaption of *Lost Horizon*:

> I had a choice at that time to play the tap dancer in *Lost Horizon*, or to do the haberdasher in *The Poseidon Adventure*, and that was one of the best choices I ever made, to choose *The Poseidon Adventure*. I think that's a picture that's gonna be around for many, many years. Irwin was just at his best in that picture. Everything clicked in for Irwin on that picture. He was really, the captain of the ship, of the Poseidon.

In a Nov. 22, 1972 interview in T*he Atlanta Journal,* Allen predicted that Gene Hackman, Ernest Borgnine, Jack Albertson, and Red Buttons would be nominated for Oscars. "We made the picture to be released in time to qualify for the Oscars. And we are going to actively try to win as many as possible."

*The Poseidon Adventure* was released on December 13, 1972, and became an immediate box office sensation. Even critics recognized the winning ingredients Allen had brought to the screen. *The Hollywood Reporter* review read:

Irwin Allen's production of *The Poseidon Adventure*... gives its audience the kind of imaginative experience that makes Hollywood movies famous. It's difficult to recall a movie as physically exciting since the earth opened up in *San Francisco*, the 1936 classic.

*The Reporter* incorrectly credited Ronald Neame both for the direction of actors and for the film's action sequences ("Neame's action work is as good as the performances…"). Promotional shorts released for the movie, however, showed Allen at the center of the action and Allen kept himself center stage as the movie became the focus of newspaper and magazine features. *The Hollywood Reporter*'s comparison of *Poseidon* to the prototypical disaster movie *San Francisco* was apt—*The Poseidon Adventure* had reintroduced and reinvented a genre that Hollywood had never really taken full advantage of.

Vincent Canby wrote an essay entitled "What Makes *Poseidon* Fun?" comparing the movie favorably to George Seaton's and Ross Hunter's *Airport,* which "thoroughly bored" the critic. *Airport* had been the first big budget attempt at a disaster movie, but it boasted very little disaster—a brief explosion and decompression on an airliner, which then lands safely—after lengthy and interminable scenes of glossy drama between familiar actors. *Poseidon*, on the other hand, within its first 30 minutes threw audiences into a harrowing situation they'd never experienced before, playing on primal fears of the water, of drowning, of dark, enclosed spaces and fire. The entire film in fact is a play on Poe's "The Premature Burial," with the Poseidon, once capsized, a thousand-foot-long coffin trapping its passengers.

With Hackman and Borgnine generating incredible sparks of tension as they butt heads throughout the odyssey, and the three-hanky death of Shelley Winters' character, who saves the trapped Reverend Scott from an underwater grave only to die of a heart attack from the strain in the moments afterward, the movie kept audiences in white-knuckled suspense throughout its 117-minute running time. Neame's—and Allen's—insistence on the film's stars performing their own stunts produced what was at the time a shocking realism, particularly in a key sequence in which Hackman and child actor Eric Shea scramble down a corridor that is filling rapidly with water. Hackman actually stumbled during the action (the rising water was achieved by lowering the set on rails into a tank on the lot) and with the water rising up to the waists of Hackman and Shea, the appearance that they are within inches of falling and drowning is electrifying.

*The Poseidon Adventure* was a grand, old fashioned entertainment, an antidote to the socially conscious, gritty and often depressing realism dominating movie screens at the time. Just as Allen predicted, *Poseidon* racked up Oscar nominations—13 of them, winning awards for Best Original Song and for Visual Effects. But only Shelley Winters was nominated for her acting (the movie also earned nominations for Harold Stine's cinematography, Best Art Direction-Set Decoration, Best Costume Design, Best Sound, Best Film Editing, and Best Original Dramatic Score). The film made $93,300,000 in the U.S. alone, making it one of the biggest box

office grossing movies of all time, and earning Allen a Producer of the Year award from the National Association of Theater Owners.

After struggling for so long to get the movie made, and particularly after having to rescue the project from cancellation at the hands of Fox executives, Allen's best revenge was watching *The Poseidon Adventure* right the listing ship of 20th Century Fox after its years of misbegotten, over-budgeted musicals.

"After it was done, Gordon Stulberg told him, 'Irwin, you saved the studio,'" Dan Goozee recalls.

Irwin Allen's gamble had paid off in spades—with one movie production, he had become one of the most powerful players in Hollywood.

**ABOVE AND OPPOSITE**
The signed menu—and dollar bills—from Irwin Allen's celebration dinner with the investors who saved his bacon on *The Poseidon Adventure*.

# Chasen's

**THURSDAY, MAY 31, 1973**

*TWA*

*To Steve & Irwin (not necessarily) in that order!*
*This has been a memorable evening — the distribution of "our" money — oh that wonderful, beautiful*

## Hors d'Oeuvres

**No Credit Cards Honored**

| | | |
|---|---|---|
| Whole Guaymas Shrimp Cocktail 3.50 | Beluga Caviar (per ounce) 10.25 | Terrine de Foie Gras de Strasbourg 6.50 |
| Prosciutto Ham and Melon 3.50 | Lobster Cocktail 4.00 | Escargots Bourguignonne 3.75 |
| Crab Legs or Shrimp Remoulade 3.50 | Imported French White Asparagus Vinaigrette 2.85 | Marinated Herring 1.75 |
| Sea Food and Avocado Cocktail 3.50 | | Matjes Herring in White Wine 1.50 |
| Nova Scotia Smoked Salmon 3.75 | | Pate of Chicken Liver Maison per Person 1.75 |

*Ship "Poseidon" — — — now we can afford to raise it and have a party!*

## Soups

| | | |
|---|---|---|
| Chicken Broth 1.25 | Boula Boula 1.75 | French Onion au Gratin 1.75 |
| Consomme Bellevue 1.25 | Creme de Sorrel Sante 1.50 | Consomme en Tasse 1.25 | Creme of Fresh Tomato 1.00 |
| COLD: Vichyssoise 1.25 | Creme Senegalaise 1.25 | Madrilene 1.25 | Jellied Consomme 1.25 | Petite Marmite Henry IV 1.75 |

## Fish

| | | |
|---|---|---|
| Shrimp Newburg 7.25 | English Dover Sole 7.25 | Fresh Cape Cod Scallops 6.75 |
| Lobster Newburg 7.75 | Lowestoft Plaice 7.25 | Filet of Rex Sole 6.25 |
| Lake Superior Whitefish 7.75 | Assorted Sea Food Poulette 6.50 | Colorado Mountain Trout 6.50 |

## Specialties

| | |
|---|---|
| Breast of Chicken Charlemagne Rice Saffron 6.25 | Roast Eastern Prime Rib of Beef Parsley Potatoes 7.50 |
| | Chopped Sirloin, Chasen 5.50 |
| Breaded Veal Cutlet, Milanaise 7.75 | Chicken Livers with Rice Pilaff, Maison 6.00 |
| Sweetbreads, Financiere, Rice Pilaff 8.00 | Tenderloin of Beef, Champignons 7.00 |
| Roast Chicken Parisienne (for Two) 12.50 | Veal Cutlet, Viennoise 7.50 |
| Stuffed Boneless Squab, Wild Rice, Montmorency 8.00 | Chicken Curry with Rice, Chutney 6.25 |
| Rack of Lamb, Bouquetiere 19.00 (for Two) | Breast of Chicken, Smitane, Wild Rice 6.75 |
| Grenadine of Beef, Bearnaise 8.25 | Deviled Beef Bones, Baked Potato 5.50 |
| Breast of Chicken Madras, Wild Rice, Pineapple 6.75 | Veal Scallopine a la Marsala, French Peas 7.50 |
| Minute Steak Saute, O'Brien Potatoes 8.50 | Schnitzel Holstein 7.50 | Chicken Tetrazzini 5.25 |
| Chicken Kiev, Rice Saffron 6.50 | Brizzola Steak, Maison 8.50 |

## Today's Suggestions

*Congratulations to all of us!*

SOUP: SCOTCH LAMB BROTH BARLEY .85

| | |
|---|---|
| Beef Stew in Casserole Bourguignonne, Mushroom, Carrots, Onion, Potatoes | 7.50 |
| Medaillon Veal Saute Mascotte, Artichoke, Mushroom, Tomate | 8.50 |
| Fricassee Chicken a l'Ancienne, Buttered Noodles | 7.00 |
| Filet Rex Sole Saute Dine, Almonds, Grapes, Batonnet Potatoes | 7.00 |
| Broiled Lake Superior Whitefish Sardoise, Eggplant, Tomate, Allumette Potatoes | 7.95 |

*Samuel 5/31/73*

*Irwin — our accomplishments were not without*

## From the Grill

| | |
|---|---|
| Eastern Prime New York Tidbit Steak, Sauce Diablo 9.25 | Eastern Prime New York Cut Steak 9.25 |
| Butterfly Steak, Mustard Sauce 8.25 | Filet Mignon 9.25 | Mixed Grill, Chasen 6.75 |
| Spring Lamb Chops, Mint Sauce 7.75 | Half Spring Chicken, Julienne Potatoes 6.00 |
| Calf's Liver Steak and Bacon 7.00 | Calf's Liver and Bacon or Onions 7.00 |

SAUCES: BEARNAISE 75 MUSHROOM 60 HOLLANDAISE SAUCE 65

*your uncle*
*make and enjoy picture that makes us reflect your creat*

## Cold Buffet

| | | |
|---|---|---|
| Tartar Steak, Yolk of Egg, Anchovies, Capers, Onions 7.75 | Chicken Salad 4.50 | Lobster, Crab or Shrimp Salad 6.25 |
| Breast of Chicken, Quartered Tomato 4.50 | | Roast Prime Ribs of Beef, Potato Salad 6.00 |

*athletic skill*

## Salads

| | | | |
|---|---|---|---|
| Bill Grady (Square Deal) 1.50 | French Endives (in Season) 2.25 | Maude's Salad 1.85 | Caesar Salad (per Person) 1.85 |
| Avocado 1.35 | Heart of Palm Salad 1.85 | Sliced Tomatoes 1.25 | Green Goddess Salad 1.50 | Spinach Salad 1.85 |
| Mixed Green 1.25 | Kentucky Limestone Lettuce 2.25 | Fruit Salad 2.50 | | Kay's String Bean Salad 1.85 |

DRESSINGS-IMPORTED ROQUEFORT 60 VINAIGRETTE 60 LORENZO 60

*To Sherrill and Steve*

## Potatoes and Vegetables

| | | | |
|---|---|---|---|
| Au Gratin 1.00 | Parsley 1.00 | Hashed Brown 1.00 | Baked Idaho 1.00 | Hashed in Cream 1.00 |
| Cottage Fried (For Two) 2.50 | | Saute 1.00 | Lyonnaise 1.00 | French Fried 1.00 |
| Stewed Tomatoes 1.00 | Succotash 1.00 | | Lima Beans 1.00 | Wild Rice 1.50 |
| String Beans 1.00 | Heart of Palm 1.50 | Broccoli 1.00 | Zucchini Florentine 1.00 | Garden Peas 1.00 |
| Plain or Creamed Spinach 1.00 | | Corn Saute Mexicaine 1.00 | Carrots Vichy 1.00 | French Peas 1.00 |

*It couldn't have been done without*

## Cheese

| | | | |
|---|---|---|---|
| Swiss Gruyere 85 | Bel Paese 85 | Imported Swiss 85 | Imported Roquefort 85 |

*the both of you. No one*

## Desserts

| | | | |
|---|---|---|---|
| Coupe Alexander with Anisette 1.50 | Fresh Pineapple 1.25 | Crepes Suzette (for Two) 5.50 | Chocolate Parfait 1.25 |
| Marrons Parfait 1.50 | Melons in Season 1.00 | Peach Melba 1.50 | Cup Custard Caramel 1.00 | Sabayon (for Two) 3.50 |
| Cherries Jubilee (for Two) 5.00 | | Profiteroles au Chocolate 1.25 | | Baba au Rhum, Flambe 1.75 |
| Banana Shortcake 1.25 | Strawberry Shortcake 1.00 | Pineapple Eureka with Creme de Menthe 1.50 | Frozen Eclair 1.25 |
| | Cheese Cake 1.00 | Grapefruit Maraschino 1.35 | Ice Cream or Sherbet 85 |

*had better partners to begin with*

## Beverages

| | | | |
|---|---|---|---|
| Postum 75 | Iced Coffee 75 | Irish Coffee 1.75 | Sanka 75 | Coffee Expresso 1.00 |
| Pot of Coffee 75 | Cafe Diable (for Two) 4.25 | Tea 75 | Cappucino 1.75 | Iced Tea | Demi Tasse 75 | Milk 75 |

MICHELOB ON DRAFT — SINGLE PORTIONS SERVED TO ONE PERSON ONLY — Imported Parmesan Cheese Toast 75c per Order

Available for Private Parties - THE CHESTNUT ROOM - THE NEW YORKER ROOM Open to 1:00 a.m. — Closed Mondays

State and Local Sales and Use Taxes will be Added to the Above Prices.

*now richer mes to*

### Catering Service of Quality and Distinction

*finish with — Warmest — Irwin*

# MINIATURE GALLERY
## THE POSEIDON ADVENTURE

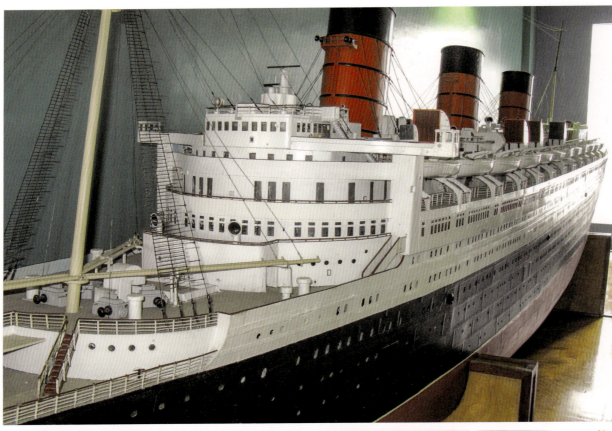

The 21-foot long miniature of the *S.S. Poseidon*, a detailed reproduction of the ocean liner *RMS Queen Mary*, is displayed at the Los Angeles Maritime Museum in San Pedro, California. Photos by Gene Kozicki

> **WE'RE ALL HERE TO PROVE TO THE WORLD THAT POSEIDON ADVENTURE WAS NO MISTAKE, AND THAT WE CAN DO IT AGAIN.**
>
> **IRWIN ALLEN**

# NOVEL SOLUTION

*Allen gets his biggest hit and a career pinnacle with* **THE TOWERING INFERNO**

In the wake of *The Poseidon Adventure*, Irwin Allen was a kingpin. He had been successful in his years making television, but making one of the biggest blockbusters in movie history put the producer in an entirely new league. The other studios were rushing to get their own disaster movies into production—Universal had *Earthquake* with Charlton Heston, *Airport 1975*, and *The Hindenburg*, and Warner Bros. and Fox were actively on the lookout for disaster-style properties. All eyes were on Irwin Allen and his next project—whatever it would be.

Allen, who had mentioned his 1959 movie *The Big Circus* when discussing his eventual return to theatrical projects in the late 1960s, still had the big top on his mind. Now in the position where he could count on a major studio to enthusiastically support just about any project he could think of, he returned to the idea of another movie set inside a three-ring circus—one that would again involve secret plots and sabotage, this time in the service of an audacious heist. Allen sought out the cooperation of the world's most famous operating circus, Ringling Brothers and Barnum and Bailey, who had last cooperated with a movie production on Cecil B. DeMille's *The Greatest Show on Earth*. Allen planned for a movie with a running time of almost three hours, to be shot in two different 70mm processes and potentially in 3-D.

3-D—and movies about circuses—hadn't been a thing since the 1950s. But Allen's love for the big top remained strong in the past decade, and he exulted in his newfound connections to the Ringling Brothers' high court.

Allen hired author Alistair MacLean to write *Circus* (which Allen, perhaps with a mind to the big top's three rings, would eventually call *Circus, Circus, Circus!*). MacLean had written a series of best-selling novels in the thriller genre, starting with *The Guns of Navarone*, which had been made into a hit movie in 1961. A second WWII adventure, *Where Eagles Dare*, had been written for the screen by MacLean in 1969 and adapted by the author into another best-selling novel, and his Cold War thriller *Ice Station Zebra* became billionaire Howard Hughes' favorite movie in 1968. Allen intended for MacLean to write *Circus* as a novel which would then be adapted into a screenplay for the movie.

**OPPOSITE**
Detail of John Berkey's spectacular painting for *The Towering Inferno*'s theatrical movie poster.

20th Century Fox agreed to produce *Circus* for a Christmas, 1975 release—but it's unclear how enthusiastic studio executives were about the idea. *Circus* had action and suspense ingredients, but movies like *The Poseidon Adventure* and earlier spectacles had already pushed the big top off most adults' radar by the early 1970s. Nonetheless, Allen was planning to travel to Chicago with MacLean to spend a week with the Ringling Brothers circus to work on the project when the possibility for the producer's next movie unexpectedly solidified.

Fox and Allen had been pursuing a book property called *The Tower* by Richard Martin Stern. The story involved a massive, 125-story skyscraper located next to the World Trade Center in New York City, and a deadly fire that rages through its upper floors, trapping and threatening the lives of hundreds of people.

The characters include Will Giddings, one of the building supervisors who receives an anonymous letter notifying him that the electrical and general contractors behind the building's construction have conspired to use substandard materials to finish the skyscraper's electrical wiring and circuitry. Paul Simmons is the electrical contractor and Bert McGraw is the general contractor in charge of the building's construction—and Simmons' father-in-law. Giddings works to track down the conspirators with the help of fire commissioner Tim Brown while the building's opening ceremonies are beginning. Meanwhile a mentally unstable metal worker detonates a bomb, causing a chain reaction fire that rages through the building, shutting down elevators, blocking stairwells, and consequently trapping important guests near the top of the building. The story involves a "breeches buoy" cable strung between the Tower and the World Trade Center to allow people to be lowered one by one off the burning building—a rescue attempt that is only partially successful.

*The Tower* was a perfect follow-up to *The Poseidon Adventure*—essentially taking the SS Poseidon, standing it up so that it loomed a thousand feet tall, and setting it on fire. But Fox and Allen weren't the only ones to take notice of the property.

"Jerre Henshaw of Fox and I bid up to $340,000 for it, but Warner Bros. outbid us," Allen said in a Sept. 22, 1973 article in *The San Francisco Chronicle*.

Incredibly, a second manuscript showed up with essentially the same storyline—Tom Scortia and Frank Robinson's *The Glass Inferno*. The skyscraper in question wasn't as impressive as the one in *The Tower*—"The Glass House" is only 66 stories tall. The story has the building's architect, Craig Barton, meeting its owner, Wyndom Leroux, and questioning him after discovering that some of his original plans for the building had been changed. They quickly discover that a fire has broken out in the lower floors beneath them, and Barton heads down to assist fire division chief Mario Infantino, a high-rise fire expert, and fire chief Karl Fuchs, in fighting the blaze, which is the result of the building's owners bribing local officials to change building codes so that they could construct the Glass House more cheaply. The action has some people being rescued from the roof of the building by helicopter, and in the climax,

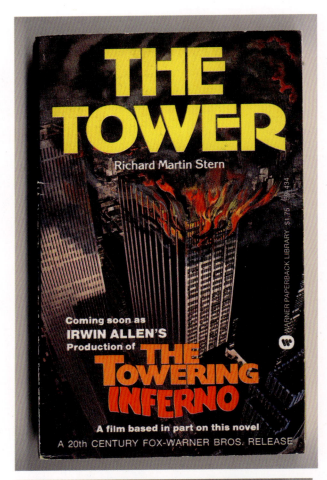

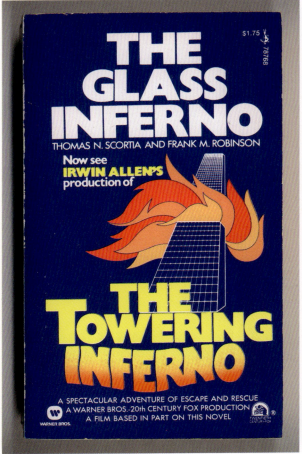

**LEFT**

*The Tower* and *The Glass Inferno*—two novels about skyscrapers on fire, and a coincidence that gave Irwin Allen the perfect follow-up to *The Poseidon Adventure*.

**ABOVE**
Early Joe Musso artwork of a fight scene from *The Tower*—from a storyline that never found its way into the screenplay of *The Towering Inferno*.

water tanks on top of the building are exploded to unleash enough water to douse the fire.

A stunned Allen initially assumed Scortia and Robinson had plagiarized Stern's novel—but Stern was an East Coast author and no one but his publisher knew about *The Tower*. Scortia and Robinson were located on the West Coast. Somehow the two virtually identical ideas had been generated independently.

Allen and Fox pounced, purchasing *The Glass Inferno* for $400,000. Allen had his team of artists storyboard the entire novel, with the intention of getting Fox's production one step ahead of Warner Bros.

"I'll never forget our first production meeting," Joe Musso said in 2016. "Irwin sat down and said, 'We're all here to prove to the world that *Poseidon Adventure* was no mistake, and that we can do it again.'" While the production was being visualized, writer Stirling Silliphant was working to develop a screenplay.

Now the two gargantuan studios were at a standoff, both ready to go into production on expensive, high-stakes movie concepts with the distinct possibility that the two movies might cancel out each other's profits at the box office.

Just as he had done when Fox had planned to cancel *The Poseidon Adventure*, Allen used his connections and negotiating skills to solve the problem, approaching Warner Bros. head of production Dick Shepherd with the idea of making the movie a co-production between the two studios—an unprecedented arrangement in which Fox and Warner Bros. would split the production costs (of around $14 million) and the profits from the movie.

At a pivotal meeting at Allen's offices on July 13, 1973, Allen and Fox's Jere Henshaw showed off Fox's progress to Shepherd and pitched his concept for a co-production.

Joe Musso recalls:

Irwin's offices at the time were on the second floor of the producers' building. He had about one half of the second floor, and if you went up the stairs there was a big, wide gold leaf door with a gold doorknob and that was Irwin's office. They had this celotext fabric on the hallway walls and you could pin stuff on it. They knew they were going to put the deal together to have two studios team up to do the movie and some of the things that were in the initial book, like the girl going out the window on fire and things like that. The building wasn't designed but we knew what the San Francisco firemen would look like, so we had things we could work with. We were coming up with looks for the Promenade room and [illustrator] Nikita [Knatz] and I were designing some of the stuff with Bill Creber looking over our shoulders. Somewhere along the way they were going to combine studios so Irwin had us put all the artwork up along the hallway, and Bill Creber and I are hanging up sketches with Nikita and [assistant art director] Steve Sardanis and [art director] Ward Preston. Irwin comes along and says, "Now Bill, before the folks from Warners get here you're going to have to explain what some of this shit is so I know what the hell I'm talking about!"

Allen went into the July 13th meeting loaded for bear as seen in his notes for the conference:

The fire and the building are the obvious stars. Explore the possibility of giving the fire a soul—a human sound—a musical note—something that gives it a third dimension. The fires get underway too fast and get too big, too soon. A gradual development would be better. Specify at one point that the fire is out or virtually contained before it erupts again.

The script would turn on a theme of corruption—similar to that suggested in *The Poseidon Adventure* with the ship's owner urging the captain to push the Poseidon

CLOSE ON WINDOW LIROUX LOGO...
PAN UP TO LIROUX...

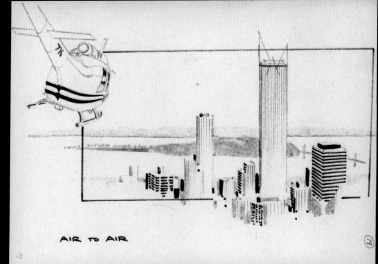

AIR TO AIR

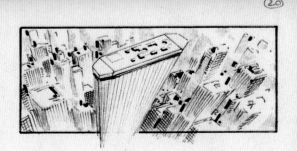

...POVs FROM LIROUX'S COPTER AS IT CIRCLES THE GLASS TOWER...

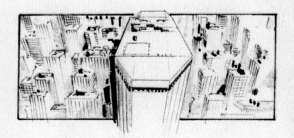

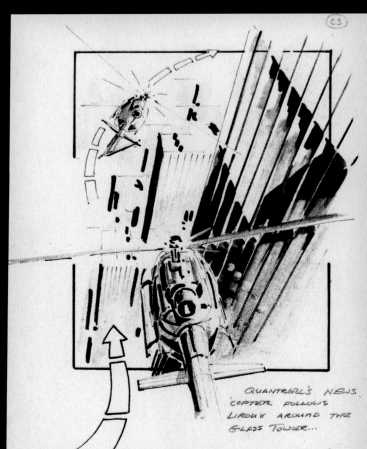

QUANTRELL'S NEWS COPTER FOLLOWS LIROUX AROUND THE GLASS TOWER...

too hard to complete its journey—but more developed, with the callow villainy of the building's electrical contractor and his enabling father-figure, the owner.

Corruption was a constant theme in post-Watergate pictures, one that would figure in Peter Benchley's novel and Steven Spielberg's film of *Jaws* a year after *The Towering Inferno*. The treatment noted:

> The theme will be more explicit, involving man's sins of omission under the umbrella of expediency, and an insight into one of the new villains of modern society, bigness.

Nevertheless, some of the story's ideas of societal corruption were downplayed:

> Following the theme of the picture, building and fire inspectors will not have been paid off: but intelligent, amoral men like Leroux and Bigelow have found loopholes in the building codes. Their attitudes and actions will clearly convey that part of the picture's philosophy—things can be too big for anyone to really care.
>
> The first scene will introduce the most important character, actually the star of the picture...THE GLASS TOWER. Included in the introduction will be tenants of differing social strata as well as VIPs so there is audience identification with people on varied social levels. Once the fire starts, the GLASS TOWER must be personalized almost as a human being. It battles against its enemy, does not take its seemingly hopeless cause lying down. The audience must be rooting for it and the gallant efforts to help save itself.

Shepherd and the executives at Warner Bros. came away convinced: Allen was the man to make the movie, and the idea of two of Hollywood's biggest studios collaborating would be an unbeatable promotional angle: *The Towering Inferno*, as it would come to be called, would be billed as a project so spectacular that it required two mammoth movie studios to pull it off. With Fox and Warner Bros. agreeing to the combination of forces, Allen deployed his art team do a shot break-down list from both novels, and had Stirling Silliphant work with Sidney Marshall to begin combining the characters and situations from both works to create one screenplay.

Allen's brokering of the Fox/Warner Bros. team-up might have been his greatest triumph. But it came with another dose of frustration when he once again broached the idea of directing to Fox. With *The Poseidon Adventure's* enormous success under his belt, Allen was confident that this time, his home studio would relent—but the mega-producer had inadvertently given Fox executives the perfect excuse for keeping him out of the director's chair. With two studios and two novels being combined into what would become a three-hour blockbuster, *The Towering Inferno*, in Fox's view, had simply become too big for any one man to manage. Fox executives preferred that Allen, the logistical mastermind, supervise the production as a whole and leave directing chores to someone more established.

The studio chose British director John Guillermin, who had made the WWI aerial adventure *The Blue Max* for Fox in 1966. Guillermin had made a series of taut

**RIGHT**
Production artwork paintings for the Glass Tower Promenade and the climactic fire and flooding of the set.

**OPPOSITE**
Early storyboards for the film's opening sequence had a news team shooting the arrival of building contractor Liroux's helicopter at the Glass Tower.

425

dramas and thrillers in England before demonstrating a facility for action films, first with two unusually good Tarzan movies (1959's *Tarzan's Greatest Adventure* and 1962's *Tarzan Goes To India*), then with war movies like *The Blue Max* and *The Bridge at Remagen* in 1969. More formulaic movies like the blaxploitation sequel *Shaft in Africa* and the Charlton Heston hijacking thriller *Skyjacked* proved Guillermin a reliable, if sometimes ornery, Hollywood commodity.

Guillermin and Allen couldn't have been more different on set—the soft-spoken Guillermin directed quietly while smoking a pipe, while the flamboyant Allen would arrive with a full entourage of personnel backing him up, often to browbeat Guillermin into adjusting his shooting style to match Allen's expectations.

While he wasn't given the director reins for the movie, Allen insured that he would have a director's credit on *The Towering Inferno*, insisting that he direct—and receive credit for—the film's complex action sequences, around half of the movie, himself.

Just as he had on *The Poseidon Adventure*, Allen made himself the centerpiece of the film's publicity materials—if there was an auteur behind *The Towering Inferno*, it was Allen, not Guillermin. Allen filmed (and staged) production meetings, showing him arriving on the lot in his Rolls Royce, phoning from his car to alert his staff to prepare for a production meeting, and sweeping into the office to take control of the situation.

"One-point-one million, just for miniature effects?" he's shown demanding as he looms over a meeting table, just before shrugging to the camera: "Well, it's only money!"

Allen had rehired *Poseidon Adventure* production designer Bill Creber to work on *Inferno*. In addition to a record-breaking 57 sets (the most ever built for a Fox production), Creber had to design the exterior of the Glass Tower itself. Unlike the Poseidon, which was really a venerable, well-known ocean liner albeit with a different name, the Glass Tower was a fanciful, thoroughly designed, semi-science-fiction invention, as unique and memorable as the Seaview, the Jupiter II, or the Spindrift. Creber realized it as a 138-story obelisk with geometric, angular slabs cut out of the shape, and finished the structure in gold, making it a 1300 foot gold ingot, a visual stand-in for the two studios' box office hopes.

"We tried a few things—everybody took a shot at it, and we had five illustrators," Creber recalled. "I said, 'Let's come up with a giant prism,' and I had a prism somewhere and I brought that and showed it to them and Dan Goozee, a very fine illustrator."

Goozee remembers:

> We talked about it looking like a tall quartz crystal. I said why don't you let me take some blocks of balsa wood down to the construction shop and cut facets off the wood so we could get some kind of shape that looks dynamic? After a couple of days of that we got some really weird looking building blocks and pinned them together from different angles and that's

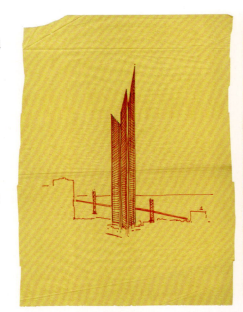
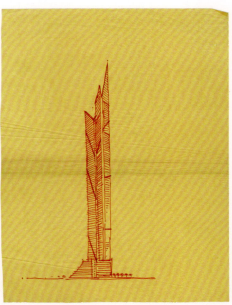
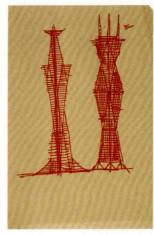

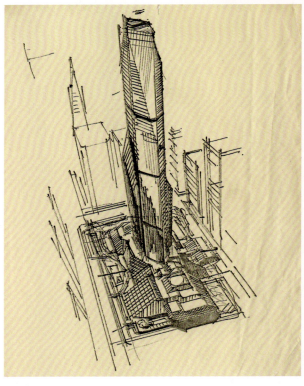

**ABOVE**

Early design concept sketches for the Glass Tower, drawn by illustrator Dan Goozee under the direction of production designer William Creber.

**RIGHT**
Early color studies for the Glass Inferno as seen against the San Francisco skyline, both in daylight and engulfed in flames at night.

427

how we arrived at the overall structure. They wanted the thing to be polygonal, not just a straight rectangular building.

Creber picks up the tale:

> The next day [Goozee] brings in the sketch he did and I said, "That's it." We showed it to Irwin and that's the way it happened.

Creber and Goozee had worked out the building's shape, but the Glass Tower's color and detail were more problematic, as Creber relates:

> Irwin always wanted a gold tower. Making it gold is not easy. You do a mirrored gold object at night and it's black. It just reflects sky so there is no building. So we invented a horizontal ledge that sticks out from [each window on the] building about 18 inches, so you're really looking at the mullions [vertical, often decorative, edged dividers] of the window, not the glass. When you look up, it's like looking up at venetian blinds; all you see is the horizontal part and it doesn't reflect any of the black sky, so that's how we got it to work.

The interior sets, particularly the office complex that Robert Wagner's character would eventually stumble through in his slow-motion death scene, were designed with the same angular look that made *The Towering Inferno* fit in seamlessly with Allen's sci-fi projects while still appearing convincingly realistic. Creber also had to design a second, more prosaic structure, the Peerless Building, to tie the outlandish Glass Tower into the San Francisco skyline in long distance shots and to serve as the mooring site for the "breeches buoy" chair cable that would be strung between the two buildings.

Irwin Allen also needed a filming location to represent the ground floor exterior and lobby of the Glass Tower, and he found one in San Francisco's Bank of America Center. On April 11, 1974, Allen and Fox reached a deal with the Bank of America Center to film the ground floor scenes of the movie there. Allen assured the owners:

> There will be no identification with the Bank of America whatsoever. Ours is a mythical building called "The Glass Tower" whose mall and lobby happen to have a vague similarity to yours. Additionally, in several instances throughout the picture, when any of our cast enters your building and looks up, the screen will show not the Bank of America building but our mythical building.

The production also used the Hyatt Regency Hotel for some ground floor interior shots and views of the building's lantern-like scenic elevators, which were recreated for the production in miniature and full-size to depict scenes of one elevator full of trapped passengers that was pulled away from the Tower and lowered safely to the ground via helicopter.

In a December 5, 1973 memo, Creber noted that the production planned to build miniature buildings at 1:48, 1:32, 1:16, and 1:8 scale. However, only a 1:24 scale tower was fully constructed.

A March 25, 1974 budget for exterior miniature sets included $80,000 for the exterior of the 1:24 scale tower,

**ABOVE**

Production designer William J. Creber atop the Golden Gate Bridge during second unit shooting of plates for shots of the Glass Tower incorporated into the San Francisco skyline.

Joe Musso's production illustration of the Glass Tower's lobby, designed under the supervision of William Creber.

**OPPOSITE**

The final Glass Tower design worked out by production designer William Creber and illustrator Dan Goozee, in a study for the establishing shot of the building against the San Francisco skyline, and in an unused overhead shot next to the fictional Peerless Building.

$125,000 for the exterior ground-floor Embarcadero area, $50,000 for the 1:8 scale upper exterior section of the building (built at this larger scale for helicopter interaction and explosions), and $35,000 for the 1:24 scale adjacent Peerless Building. $16,000 was spent on the miniature storage tank area that would be exploded—and flush out water—at the climax of the film.

Other interior miniatures cost $33,000, plus $18,000 more for lighting and physical effects that included gas jets which could emit controlled flames. The total budget for miniatures added up to $385,000.

Just as he had with Gene Hackman on *The Poseidon Adventure*, Allen wanted a contemporary box office superstar to lead the cast of *The Towering Inferno*.

Allen went after Steve McQueen, the "king of cool" who had parlayed his lead role on the 1958 TV western *Wanted: Dead or Alive* into a supporting role in John Sturges' *The Magnificent Seven* and *The Great Escape* in the early 1960s, before taking on starring roles in Fox's epic *The Sand Pebbles* (which earned him an Oscar nomination for Best Actor) and the prototypical San Francisco cop movie *Bullitt* in 1968. McQueen had just come off another highly touted dramatic adventure, Franklin Schaffner's *Papillon* (which also boasted an appearance by Bill Mumy), that put the laconic McQueen up against Dustin Hoffman, and McQueen was now at the pinnacle of his career as a movie star.

Allen offered McQueen a million dollar salary for *The Towering Inferno*—an unprecedented fee at the time.

Director Harry Harris recalled in 1995:

> I wasn't involved in it but I was working for [Allen] at the time he was doing it. He came up with this movie, *Towering Inferno*. And at that time it was unheard of to hire an actor for a movie and pay 'em one million dollars, and Irwin went to Steve McQueen and said, you come and do my movie I'll pay ya one million. In those days it was an ego trip for the actors. Today you see Bruce Willis getting 12–20 million. Then he'd put so much attention to the publicity of it. He had a way of doing the showmanship that made people want to come into these things.

Allen's original plan had McQueen playing the movie's architect, Craig Wilson, and *Poseidon Adventure* alum Ernest Borgnine playing the blue collar role of the fire chief in charge of fighting the blaze.

Allen's dealings with McQueen soon developed into a master class for handling fragile movie star egos. In a June 15, 1974 meeting between Allen, agent Freddie Fields, Jere Henshaw, Stirling Silliphant, and Sidney Marshall regarding Steve McQueen's reactions to Silliphant's script, the men discussed a script addition, "the Idaho Project," that had been created entirely to give McQueen's character the socio-political relevance that the actor felt had to be incorporated into Barton. "The Idaho Project" would have been an eco-friendly development which Barton would be called away from in order to travel to the opening ceremonies of the Glass Tower—a commercial project that Wilson would be much more ambivalent about.

**ABOVE**

Allen with Steve McQueen (right)—originally to star in the film with Ernest Borgnine in the supporting role of the Fire Chief.

Early storyboard image showing Steve McQueen as architect Craig Wilson.

McQueen in one of his early scenes from the film.

**RIGHT**
Early storyboards depicting McQueen in the architect role, Ernest Borgnine as the fire chief, and Burt Lancaster in the role eventually played by William Holden.

McQueen's "negatives" included his feelings that the "Idaho Project must have a great deal more import for Craig Wilson. Much more deeply rooted in the man and his life drive. Possibly involving his feelings toward the masses of underprivileged e.g. the American Indian. It should be something 'for the people.'"

At this point in the screenplay's development, Craig's wife/girlfriend "Zib" would have been having an affair with Paul Simmons, the shady contractor that ultimately would be played by Richard Chamberlain. McQueen disliked this development and the report stated that McQueen:

> ...Does not believe Craig's relationship with Zib nor does he understand it. Particularly the area of her having an affair with Paul Simmons. There seems no true motivation for it, nor could there be any if Craig Wilson is the man he should be.

McQueen also noted that Craig never gets off the ground as a character—"He has a middle, no beginning or end. We don't know what the 'Tower' means to him." McQueen felt that anyone could play the role of Craig and questioned why the production wanted him for the role—"Merely to 'hype the picture?'"

Allen and his team suggested the film open with Craig supervising the "Idaho Project":

> We see Craig Wilson—Levis, half-boots, sweaty work shirt, unshaven, dirty hands and nails, supervising the job. "Bert" [an early version of the character played by William Holden] arrives on the scene and pulls the plug on the Idaho Project, leading to a fight with Craig that reveals the architect's character and dedication.

McQueen's concerns seemed less about the quality of the character and situation and more about his own vanity, insisting that Wilson take on wildly noble ambitions and also be the kind of man who couldn't possibly ever have a woman tempted away from him. But McQueen's next decision seemed surprisingly self-effacing: he told Allen that he wanted to withdraw from the character of the architect—the film's starring role—and instead play the supporting role of the fire chief. McQueen in fact suspected that the blue collar fire chief was closer to his own taciturn sensibilities as an actor, and that the chief would be more involved in action than the architect.

McQueen than made another surprising suggestion: that Allen hire Paul Newman to play the architect character.

Allen now had to switch gears—but the idea of fronting *The Towering Inferno* with not one but two box office superstars (oddly appropriate given that the movie was based on two books and was being made by two studios) had an undeniable appeal to Allen the showman. Along with Robert Redford and Dustin Hoffman, Paul Newman was one of the only actors who could rival McQueen's star power. Newman had been a leading man since the late 1950s, and with Robert Redford he had headlined two of the biggest box office hits of the past decade, 1969's *Butch Cassidy and the Sundance Kid* and 1973's Best Picture Winner, *The Sting*. *Butch Cassidy* and *The Sting* had created a new genre—the "buddy movie," in which two star actors squabbled and joked their way through an adventure, a formula that would be adapted into mostly cop movies over the next few decades. Newman and McQueen would each be paid $1 million plus 7.5% of the film's potential grosses.

Newman was less high-maintenance than McQueen, but Stirling Silliphant nevertheless had to tailor his script so that the two stars had the same number of speaking lines.

Burt Lancaster had originally been under consideration to play the building's unscrupulous owner, now named Jim Duncan. Lancaster was a powerful screen personality who had proven his ability to play both heroes and heels over the years, but adding Paul Newman—and another million dollars—to the casting budget put Lancaster out of the film's price range. William Holden, now beginning the twilight of his career and consigned to grizzled character parts in films like The Wild Bunch and The Wild Rovers, came onboard as Duncan. It was a role that Holden chafed in, embittered about his diminished star status and convinced that the part of the corrupt building owner was "one dimensional."

Allen wanted another old time star, David Niven, to play a con artist preying on a widowed art dealer who was to have been played by Olivia de Havilland. When Niven proved unavailable and de Havilland turned down the role, Allen turned to Peter Ustinov, and finally to legendary dancer Fred Astaire to play con man Harlee Claiborne. There was brief consideration of teaming Astaire with his old dance partner Ginger Rogers, but instead Allen cast legendary screen beauty Jennifer Jones as the widowed Lisolette.

Allen had a love of stunt casting going back to Groucho Marx in The Story of Mankind and Steve Allen in The Big Circus. He had cast retired boxer Sugar Ray Robinson in City Beneath the Sea and for The Towering Inferno he made a show of casting football player O.J. Simpson in one of his first major movie roles. Simpson followed that up with two disaster-type thrillers, The Cassandra Crossing and Capricorn One, eventually spoofing himself in the Naked Gun movies before his infamous 1995 murder trial.

With two directors and four camera crews at work, Allen's predilection for meticulous planning and storyboarding became critically important.

Illustrator Joe Musso:

> I was working with four different camera crews. Guillermin was doing the first unit so I had to get his blocking the way he was doing his shots, because Irwin would pick it up with the action unit. And Irwin worked with complete camera units where Fred Koenekamp was DOP of the first unit, Joe Biroc was director of the second unit, Irwin had his own first AD Matt Carding, Guillerman had Newt Arnold and Wes MacAffey, so it was completely different units. I had to meet with John and John did his homework. I'd get his blocking with stick figures, then go back and do storyboards, and the studio wanted to see this stuff particularly since Warners was looking over their shoulders also. I had to lay out what Guillermin was doing

**ABOVE**

Paul Newman and Steve McQueen—two superstar actors anchoring a movie made by two gargantuan movie studios.

Faye Dunaway and Paul Newman, as seen near the end of the film.

**OPPOSITE**

Publicity shot of The Towering Inferno's cast: (l to r) Steve McQueen, Robert Wagner, Faye Dunaway, William Holden, Jennifer Jones, Fred Astaire, Paul Newman, Richard Chamberlain, Robert Vaughn, and O.J. Simpson.

(l to r) Director John Guillermin, screenwriter Stirling Silliphant, and producer Irwin Allen in a script meeting with actor Paul Newman.

433

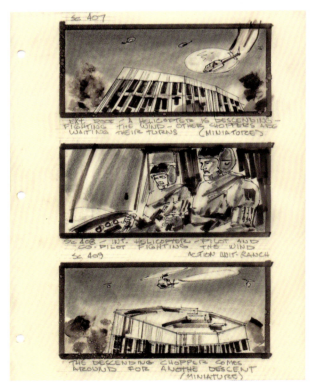

**LEFT & OPPOSITE**
Storyboard art for the rooftop helicopter explosion sequence.

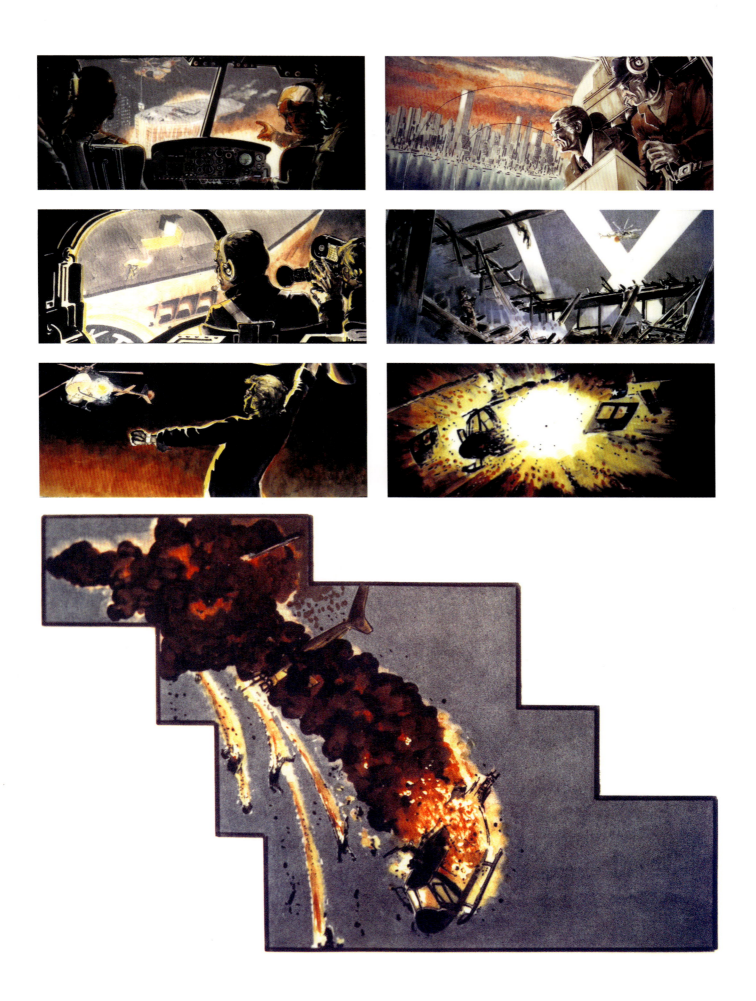

and then go into the action scene that Irwin was doing, and some of it had to cut in with miniature helicopter footage and the aerial unit that was shooting in San Francisco, and some of that would be background plates that we were using.

While Allen was the guiding creative force behind the entire production, Musso says that Guillermin's contribution was also vital to the ultimate success of the finished product, and the director had his own strategy for insuring that the film's dramatic sequences would come out the way he intended:

> The one thing I remember Guillermin saying is, "This is Irwin's movie." But Guillermin was enough of a director, like John Ford, that he cut in the camera. He did it in such a way so that, when you have a master shot, he'd tell the actors to leave out a key line of dialogue and they'd pick it up in the closeup, so you were forced to cut. Or when he wanted to cut he'd have an actor walk in front of the camera. Irwin would look at the dailies and go, "Why'd he do that?" But he did it because it would force Irwin to cut in a certain way. When he was on the set, they assigned [writer] Bill [William] Welch to him for any dialogue changes, and I remember Guillermin saying, "At least they got rid of a lot of that dialogue." The guy was good.

L.B. Abbott once again emerged from retirement to handle visual effects for *The Towering Inferno*. As with *The Poseidon Adventure*, Abbott faced the challenge of photographing natural elements (fire and water) interacting with a miniature that was smaller in scale than desirable. While sections of the Glass Tower were built in 1:8 scale for closeups, the complete structure was constructed in 1:24 scale (making human figures around three inches tall) and stood over 70 foot tall, making it probably the largest miniature building ever constructed for a motion picture. This was not an ideal size to depict flames, but Abbott was constrained by the necessity of filming angles looking downward from the top of the burning Glass Tower, and 70 feet was the highest that camera cranes were able to reach.

The huge miniature was rigged with hundreds of gas jets, with each window containing an acetylene emitter (which created yellow, smoking flames), a butane emitter (which made blue, smokeless flames), and an air feed as well as a spark ignitor, all of which allowed the effects crew to control the color and intensity of the fire. Because of the dangerous height and the fact that hot gas and flame from the combustion and explosions being filmed would be traveling upward, Abbott decided that it would be too dangerous for camera operators to work on the crane, so he rigged the crane and cameras so that camera operation, focus and other elements for the shots could be achieved via remote control.

The miniature work was filmed at the drained Sersen Lake tank in Malibu, starting with camera tests in late July and continuing through August and into September of 1974. Van der Veer Photo Effects handled the work of compositing the Glass Tower and Peerless Building into the San Francisco skyline. The tank room explosion was filmed in the moat at Fox with A.D. Flowers supervising the pyrotechnic work on September 20th. Miniature photography was completed on September 30th.

**ABOVE**
Director John Guillermin (left) on the set with Irwin Allen and Paul Newman.

The massive miniature set-up of the Glass Tower and Peerless Building (on the right) at the Sersen Lake facility in Malibu, California. The Glass Tower, built at 1:24 scale to represent a building 130 stories tall, itself stood over seven stories (70 feet) in height.

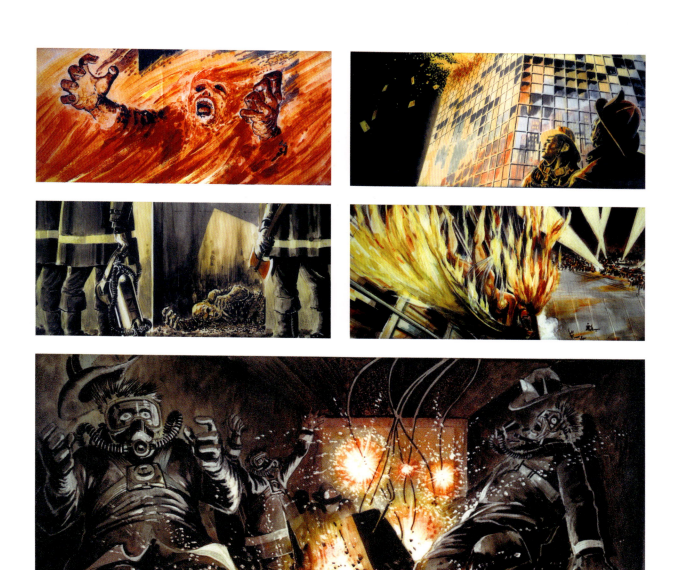

**RIGHT & FOLLOWING**
Conceptual and storyboard art as well as "movie magic" set planning schematics for a number of the film's complex fire scenes.

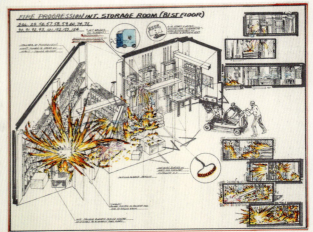
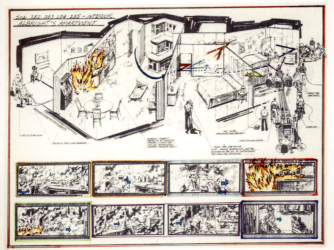
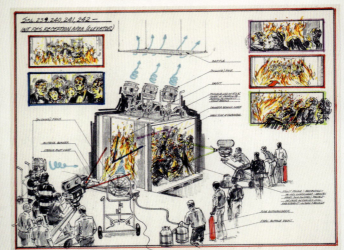

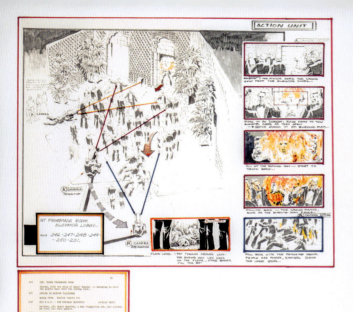
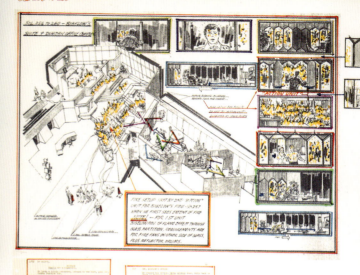
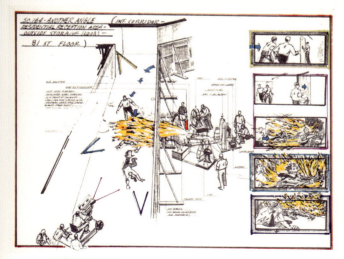
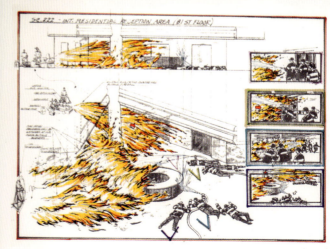

**LEFT**
Several of the movie's harrowing "fire gags" being filmed.

**OPPOSITE**
Scenes of Steve McQueen's character shot so that he could deliver dialogue resting against a wall after the actor injured his leg during the shoot, and some of the film's highly convincing exterior miniature shots of the burning Glass Tower.

The live action shoot directed by Allen featured numerous dangerous "fire gags" that had stunt men and women (often wearing sculpted, fireproof face masks that seriously limited their ability to see and breathe) staggering through sets after glue and other flammable liquids had been applied to their costumes and ignited. The stunt performers normally could perform for only around 15 seconds before they were in danger of being burned, and supporting stunt and safety personnel had to rush in and douse the flames within that time frame. Often this activity happened on camera, with stunt performers standing in for characters in the scene desperately trying to extinguish the flames engulfing their fellow characters.

A large number of real fire fighters were involved in the production, both as technical advisors and even as performers. Joe Musso recalls:

> They had off-duty firemen playing the firemen. They would start the fires with these gas jets, and these guys were so good, they would go right into action and put the fire out in like a second. Irwin would say, "Guys, that was great, but we have to do it again. So this time for heaven's sake, don't make it look so easy!"

Musso related how some important sequences were developed late in production, including a stairwell scene in which Newman, Jennifer Jones and child actor Mike Lookinland are imperiled by an explosion, forcing the trio to climb four floors down on a bent metal stair railing:

> In the original script it was a firehose. Irwin was very upset and said, "Look, we just did that in *Poseidon*, we can't do that again." I said, "What happens if the explosion goes off and a couple of the stairwells collapse?" Irwin said, "Do you have a picture of how that would look in your mind? How do they get down?" And Bill Welch said, "Well, you have the twisted stairwell rail." Irwin got all excited—"Oh yeah, the stairwell is all twisted, that sounds great! Joe, lay it out and we'll film it." [Stunt coordinator] Paul Stader was in the meetings too and we had to work with him because we had to make the stairwell look twisted, but it had to be twisted in such a way that the stunt people could work with it.

While filming the scene in question, Paul Newman insisted that he could perform the stunt himself, but Allen assured him that the production's insurance would not allow for it and stuntman Larry Holt, who strongly resembled Newman, did the shots of Newman descending down the railing.

Both Paul Newman and Steve McQueen suffered minor injuries while on set, and one late sequence was rewritten to allow McQueen to deliver his dialogue while sitting against a wall in exhaustion after the actor suffered a leg injury that kept him off his feet for a few days.

Production illustrator Joe Musso recalled that Allen would often use his understanding of movie star vanity to manipulate his actors, particularly when Steve McQueen had to play some scenes on top of a mockup of the movie's scenic elevator, hanging over a parking lot in downtown Los Angeles:

Steve McQueen was afraid of heights. He's always very macho but he didn't want to do the bit with the scenic elevator and we needed the piece of film where the helicopter lands and picks Steve up and takes off to fly back up to the building. At first he didn't want to do it and Mike Johnson looked enough like Steve to do it as his stuntman. But the genius of Irwin was, he goes up to the helicopter pilots and he says, "I'm going to introduce you to Steve McQueen. When I do, start talking about his movies. Talk about which ones you like and really get into it with him." So Steve chatted with them and the pilots really got into talking about his films, and then after a while Irwin said, "Okay guys, we need to shoot the scene of Steve's stunt man getting into the helicopter." And McQueen just says, "That's okay, Irwin, I'll do it." He was scared out of his wits, but he didn't want to show these guys that he didn't want to do it. And they only had to fly him up about ten feet.

Musso also recalled how some other characters in the elevator sequence called for unusual stunt performer casting:

When they had to land the scenic elevator, it was shot in downtown Los Angeles late at night and there was no way Child Services would let the little girl in the elevator work

**LEFT**
Storyboard art of a terrifying, unfilmed sequence in which a character unsuccessfully attempts to ride a mattress through the windows of the Glass Tower to the ground.

**ABOVE**
Paul Newman on the set between takes.

**OPPOSITE**
Storyboards and set planning schematics for the stairwell sequence, and a publicity shot of Allen directing the movie.

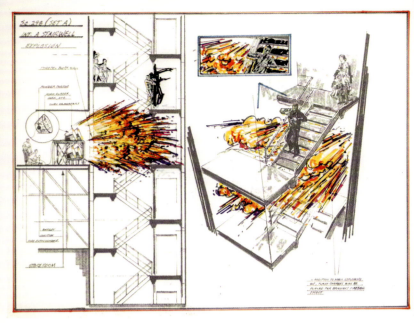

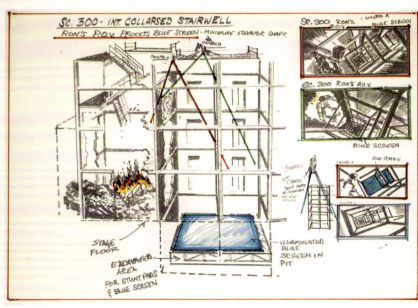

that late. So they had Felix Silla, who was a little person, play her. Felix had grown a mustache so you'd look at the character from the back and it's this cute little girl in a blue dress and a wig, and turn her around and it's this guy with a mustache and a cigarette in his mouth. Irwin is like, "Can't you at least get him to shave the mustache off? I don't know how Faye Dunaway is going to keep a straight face!" Faye Dunaway had to hand this guy with a mustache off to somebody.

The biggest moment for Allen and the cast—and one preserved on film to show Allen's control of the action scene filming processes—was the movie's climactic explosion of water tanks located underneath the roof of the Glass Tower to douse the fire. All of the film's stars were required to be tied down on the film's Promenade set, representing the top floor of the building and the scene of the grand opening party where many dignitaries and guests are trapped. The expensive set was constructed 10 feet off the ground and surrounded by an immense, 340-foot cyclorama representing the San Francisco skyline. The raised set allowed both for a sensation of height, as camera angles could look downward onto the cyclorama outside, and to allow for the drainage of water for the climactic explosion and flooding, which involved dumping 7000 gallons of water on the actors.

One of the legends about Irwin Allen regarded his use of a starting pistol as a directing tool—stars often recalled that Allen would fire off his pistol as his own way of calling "Action!" But he may have simply used it on a few occasions to get a strong reaction out of an actor. He certainly employed the sidearm in the climactic water tank explosion sequence—when Fred Astaire is visibly jolted by an explosion behind him, he's reacting to the sound of Allen's starter pistol at close range.

Dan Goozee also recalls Allen using the gun on one other occasion:

> In a production meeting once he pulled out a starter pistol and fired a couple of .22 blanks into the ceiling and said, "Now that I have your full attention...." But Irwin would also give out huge amounts of gift baskets, wine and cheese, to everybody—secretaries, production designers, probably the guy that came in and swept up at night got one too. And he also kept a huge supply of models of the Seaview and these little toys in his office and any time a kid came through to visit Irwin made sure he didn't leave without taking some of those with him.

Allen immersed himself in research on fire fighting and the vulnerabilities of high-rise buildings during the run-up to production on the film, and he dedicated *The Towering Inferno* to the world's firefighters. He became a crusader about the dangers of high-rise fires after the movie was released. In a 1974 *Los Angeles Times* interview, he said:

> I spent two and a half years researching this film, and I learned that if you are in a building above the eighth floor and a fire breaks out, you are in trouble. A lot of us who worked on the picture feel this way now. Paul Newman used to go to a dentist on the 14th floor of a building. Now he goes to one on the third floor. Listen, I don't make message movies. But as it turns out, I've got the hottest

### Martine Franck, Paris, 1979
NEGATIVE: 24×36 MM _ 200/1137
— 318

December 1979. The magazine *Photo Journal* was to publish an article by Jean-Claude Gautrand about me and assigned Martine Franck to take my portrait (the article and portrait appear in issue 4 of the magazine, published in February 1980). We went to the Tuileries gardens where I would suffer what I usually inflict upon others. As I had my camera slung over my shoulder, I took advantage of a moment when Martine had just reloaded her Leica to steal an image of her with my Foca 50-mm. The backlight is not chosen but imposed, since I was the subject. To obtain detail in the background and, naturally, in the figure, printing from my negative is a nice laboratory challenge. Cropping to the left and top.

### Dennis Stock, L'Isle-sur-la-Sorgue, Vaucluse, 1980
NEGATIVE: 24×36 MM _ 201/0521
— 319

My friend and colleague Dennis Stock, who owns a home in the Vaucluse, came to see me in L'Isle-sur-la-Sorgue on March 14, 1980. He had recently told me that the photograph so often published as *The Reporter*, a work by Andreas Feininger, was actually a portrait of him taken when he had just joined the Magnum agency as a young reporter (the date of the portrait is actually 1951 and not 1955). I then offered to photograph him, making almost the same gesture while holding up the photograph in question. It had been reproduced on page 61 of *L'Appareil photographique* (Photographic Equipment), published by Life, which I had taken out of my library. This took place on our small kitchen terrace. The camera Dennis held is an Olympus equipped with a 250-mm Minolta mirror lens. 50-mm. Sun a little veiled. Simple to print, except for the need to push the photograph in the book, which is slightly clouded by a reflection. Full frame.

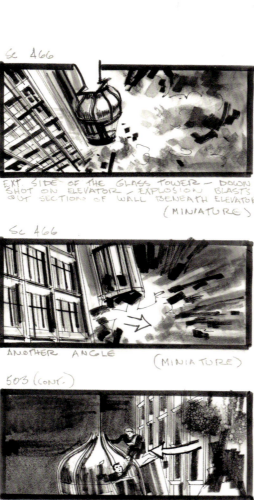

**OPPOSITE & RIGHT**
Production artwork and storyboards for the elevator rescue sequence

**FAR RIGHT**
Publicity photos taken during shooting of the elevator explosion sequence, and below, final images from the film from the sequence.

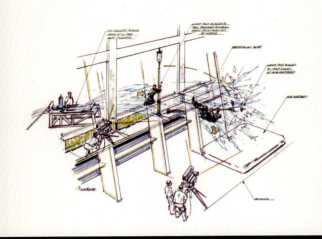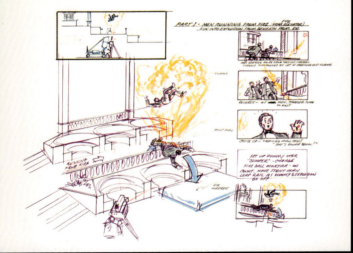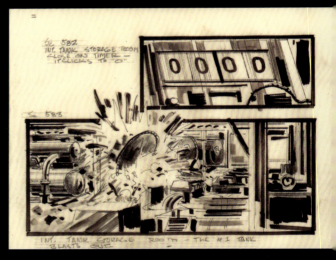

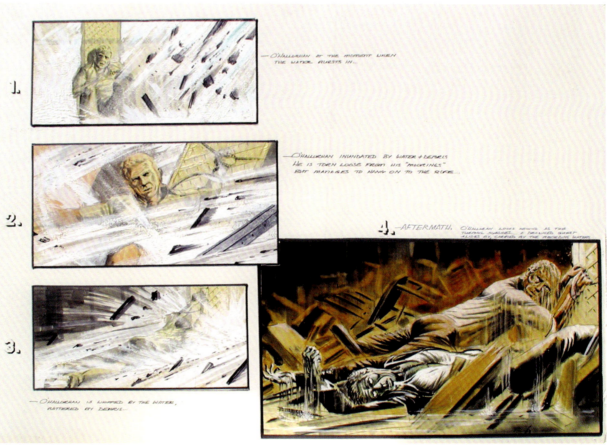

**LEFT & OPPOSITE**
Black and white and color storyboard art and set planning schematics for the climactic explosion of the Glass Tower's rooftop water tanks, and a photo from the scene as it was shot.

447

message in the world in *The Towering Inferno*. That there can be a terrible fire disaster in tall buildings. Did you know that until last week, when a fireproof government building was opened in Seattle, there were no really fireproof buildings in the United States? It's because of our antiquated fire codes.

Allen also explained his philosophy behind the disaster movie formula:

One reason audiences flock [to my disaster films], is that I take ordinary people—your butcher, your baker, your fireman—and put them in extraordinary circumstances that require superhuman effort and great heroism to overcome. The moviegoer sees it happen on the screen, and when he exits, he believes he could have done it, too. He is happy. I don't make films about astronauts or brain surgeons, because there aren't enough of them to fill a theater. But there are 2,600,000 firemen in the country, and they have wives and friends, and they'll all come to see my picture. Another reason, and I don't like to say it, is that people are observers of the macabre. It is a trait of all of us, to one degree or another. People are drawn to chasing a firetruck, or to seeing who's being put in an ambulance. It doesn't speak too well of us...but it's good for the box office.

Allen also was asked what his idea of the ultimate disaster movie would be:

Doomsday. What a disaster! It would be the end of the world. And maybe I could get Charlton Heston to play Mr. Doom.

While the producer was doing special previews in Hartford, Dallas, St. Louis and San Jose, he continued to champion a national fire code in a Nov. 24, 1974 *Dallas Times Herald* profile:

The only codes are local or state ones and they are antiquated, based on the tensile strength of steel. I only hope this picture...will stir up enough interest to establish a national fire code.

Allen also reiterated his faith in "his" stars:

I am a total, absolute believer in the star system. A star will not save a bad movie, but if you have a star in a good picture it will double or triple its value. There is no question that Steve McQueen and Paul Newman and Faye Dunaway are bankable names.

Allen put together a TV special for the film's highly anticipated premiere, broad-ast from the Avco Center in Westwood. Stars from the film as well as friends of Allen and veterans of his previous productions made appearances, including Groucho Marx and Henry Fonda; Rhonda Fleming of *The Big Circus* (noting that she had just purchased an apartment building); William Holden in a tuxedo and looking virtually identical to his appearance in the movie; Gregory Peck (who somehow managed to avoid acting in any disaster pictures throughout his career); Martin Milner; Adam West; Robert Wagner (who was reminded that he was in Fox's 1953 *Titanic*, the proto-disaster movie); Susan Flannery, who had appeared in two episodes of *Voyage to the Bottom of the Sea* and was working on the soap opera *The Bold and the Beautiful* at the time; Groucho Marx ("If the picture makes as much money as they think it will, I'm going to burn my house down."); Mary Tyler Moore; and Gene Hackman ("Everybody likes pain, don't they?"). Also appearing was Sheila Mathews, who announced her engagement to Irwin Allen on camera.

In 1995, Robert Wagner recalled Allen's dedication to the project:

I went up to San Francisco on a junket with Sheila and Irwin and a group of us, to open the picture there. Now I would think he probably had seen the picture, conservatively, fifty times. Every time they went to a showing he'd sit through the whole thing, in a theatre. I had seen it twice. I got up and left. I mean I, I went out to dinner, and so did most of the actors—we all kind of trickled out, but he sat there right to the very end. He wanted to see what the audience was thinking. Every place he went he sat through the whole picture. Now can you imagine? I mean he sat through all the pre-production, post-production, directed it, got the actors, got the script, put everybody together—but he loved it. He loved it. He did it. But he sat there and he watched it.

*The Towering Inferno* opened on December 20, 1974 to disaster-movie-sized business. By now the genre was an established and not particularly beloved one by critics—*The Poseidon Adventure* had been a surprise outlier after several years of smaller, more realistic movies; *The Towering Inferno* had all the expectations heaped on Allen as the newly crowned "Master of Disaster," a moniker he would proudly embrace over the ensuing few years.

Reviews for the movie were sometimes savage, but Roger Ebert, in a Jan. 12, 1975 column, argued that many of his compatriots were judging *Inferno* against prestigious dramas when it really needed to be considered for what it was—a superbly made genre picture:

*The Towering Inferno* is...a disaster picture...the latest in an occasionally honorable list of movies that recently has included *The Poseidon Adventure, Juggernaut, Earthquake* and *Airport 1975*. It is also, in terms of its special effects and its spectacular stunts, the best.

While noting that critics were attacking the film for its cliched dialogue and predictable plot, Ebert pointed out:

One of the good things about *The Towering Inferno*, however, is that it was so well made, the large part because of the technical standards of Irwin Allen, who produced it and directed its action scenes and was also producer of *Poseidon*. When whole city blocks of skyscrapers come apart and fall over in *Earthquake*, we can enjoy the illusion, but we know it is an illusion. In the case of *The Towering Inferno*, however, the special effects are for the most part pretty realistic. The flames look like flames, the heights look like heights, and when Paul Newman and Steve McQueen take turns hovering above utility shafts dozens of stories high, we almost can hear the echo and feel the vertigo.

Noting that the acting in *Towering Inferno* was "of a high quality too," Ebert stated that critics attacking

**OPPOSITE (LEFT)**
Footage from the climactic water tank explosion done in miniature and the subsequent full scale flooding of the Promenade deck

**OPPOSITE (RIGHT)**
Color production concept artwork of the flooding sequence.

SC 535 EXT. THE SIDE OF THE GLASS TOWER — PARKER FALLS

REVERSE ANGLE

**OPPOSITE**
Storyboards for the breech's buoy sequence.

**RIGHT**
The breeches buoy sequence and actress Elizabeth Rogers in the hot seat.

the movie for not being a great drama were missing the point:

> We do not get art but we do get craftsmanship. To expect more from a genre picture is to ask it to transcend its genre, and when that happy event happens, as it sometimes does, then we are in another league anyway.

Critic Rolf Rykken in *The Cincinnati Enquirer* managed to trash Allen while praising his movie:

> Irwin Allen has finally delivered. Through television junk like *Voyage to the Bottom of the Sea* and *Land of the Giants* and feature film embarrassments like *Poseidon Adventure*, Allen has offered us impressive—but predictable—special effects and little else. Now, due primarily to believable and impressive special effects, plus highly identifiable actors, *Towering Inferno* is the best movie Allen has ever produced.

While Rykken took potshots at "hack screenwriter" Stirling Silliphant, critic Robert Marks praised Silliphant as essential to *The Towering Inferno's* success:

> He fashioned the screenplay from two similar novels...the good fortune is that Silliphant was left alone in writing the screenplay. An old hand at this sort of thing, he etches the characterizations quickly, the dialogue is superficial; the fighting of the fire is the focus.

Reviews were still filing in in March, after the film had earned its 8 Academy Award nominations, and while even the most grudging critics praised the performances of Paul Newman, Steve McQueen and Faye Dunaway, the lions' share agreed that Fred Astaire's acting nomination for his role as an aging con man was more sentimental than deserved.

Virginia critic Edward Jones wrote:

> His performance is all right, but hardly Oscar material. Astaire ought to be getting the "Red Buttons Lonely Old Man of the Year" award...

Jones still praised the film:

> It is a fine motion picture that exploits all the spectacle-producing advantages film has over other art forms, and produces some of the most breath-taking thrills the near-capacity audiences here will ever see on a theater screen.

Michael J. Tanney, an associate professor of film history at the Anne Arundel Community College, took a stab at Allen's penchant to not look too closely into the human condition—in effect justifying Allen's impatience with heavy-duty dramatics. After pointing out the similarities between many of the scenes in *The Poseidon Adventure* and ones in *The Towering Inferno*, Tanney noted:

> The human element is not dwelled upon to the extent that it was in the earlier film, and perhaps, we can be grateful for that. Allen must have realized this time that peo-ple who dig this kind of movie want nothing more than pure sensation. They can identify with the characters just enough in *Inferno* so that when a body falls in flames from the building, they can work up a smidgen of concern and

not feel too guilty about their real interest in such scenes.

*The Towering Inferno* made over $200 million during an incredibly long theatrical run that lasted over a year—a figure that's even more impressive given the fact that Allen's film was almost three hours long, which limited the number of times it could be shown in theaters on any given day. Local theaters, used to running films for a couple of weeks at best, kept *Inferno* on tap sometimes for a month or more. "HELD OVER!" marquees trumpeted. Paul Newman and Steve McQueen each pocketed around $12 million based on their 7.5% participation in the film's box office grosses.

The film was nominated for eight Academy Awards, including Best Cinematography (since John Guillermin's dramatic and Irwin Allen's action units were shooting simultaneously, the movie earned nominations for two cinematographers, Fred J. Koenekamp and Joseph Biroc), Best Editing (Harold F. Kress and Carl Kress), Best Original Song, Best Supporting Actor (Fred Astaire), Best Art Direction-Set Decoration (William J. Creber, Ward Preston and Raphael Bretton), Best Sound (Theodore Soderberg and Herman Lewis), Best Music (John Williams), and a Best Picture nod.

There was. however, no nomination for direction or writing, the standard sops for artistic achievement necessary for a movie to be taken seriously as a Best Picture contender. Ultimately, the film won for editing, cinematography, and song. In a *United Feature Syndicate Hollywood Hotline* column by James Bacon in May 4, 1975, Allen said he was not disappointed in losing the Oscar for *The Towering Inferno*, saying, "I treasure the Bank of America award it won."

*The Towering Inferno* still holds up remarkably well as an example of screen spectacle and suspense. Allen took the fool-proof phobias of water, enclosed spaces, and fire from *Poseidon Adventure* and added acrophobia to the mix, a concept perfectly encapsulated by sci-fi book cover artist John Berkey's incredible movie poster painting over the rooftop of the Glass Tower, looking down 135 floors of glass and fire to the streets of San Francisco below, while rescue helicopters hover over the burning roof and a hapless civilian rides the terrifying "breeches buoy" to the Peerless Building. Particularly in a movie theater, Inferno was an absolute nightmare for acrophobes.

John Guillermin got effectively understated performances from both McQueen and Newman—you believe them and their quiet masculinity as a counterpoint to the raging fire and the panicking denizens of the building around them.

Some of the most effective and horrifying moments involve supporting characters or borderline extras and stunt performers. At one point, frightened Promenade guests jam into the last elevator on the top floor, only to have it stop and open on the very floor where the fire is raging, leaving a horrified McQueen to briefly—and uselessly—direct fire hoses directly at the elevator passengers as they are engulfed in flames. A few moments later the elevator arrives back on the top floor and opens to release one staggering male victim on

**ABOVE**

A Irwin Allen on the set with Robert Wagner.

Promotional button and "Survival Certificate" for the movie, and one of Irwin Allen's many real-life honors granted from fire departments and officials from across the country for raising awareness of fire safety with *The Towering Inferno*.

**OPPOSITE**

Photos from the San Francisco and Tokyo premieres of *The Towering Inferno*.

fire, who falls to the floor as Fred Astaire's character makes a futile attempt to snuff out the flames with his jacket. Almost ignored behind that spectacle is the open elevator in the background, packed with the bodies of the other passengers who have all been burned to death.

Jennifer Jones' sympathetic character Lisolette winds up on another terrifying ride down the side of the building in one of the Tower's glass scenic elevators. When an explosion tears the elevator loose from its moorings, she staggers backward, briefly tries to save an infant being held by another woman, then falls through the elevator glass, and in a long shot we see her body, still in her evening gown, plummet and bounce down the side of the building to her death.

One of the most riveting performances in the film comes from Elizabeth Rogers, a friend of Allen's and Sheila Mathews, who had played Lt. Uhura's sometimes relief communications officer, Lt. Palmer, on *Star Trek* and made appearances on several of Allen's TV shows. Rogers played the first person lowered down in the "breeches buoy," a metal chair that hangs from a cable strung between the Tower and the nearby Peerless Building that lowers passengers one by one across a thousand foot drop in high winds. Rogers has just a few seconds to be strapped into the chair and register her terror at the idea of the upcoming ride, but she is so convincing that anyone with acrophobia would have to be gripping their seats in white-knuckled horror at the prospect of getting into that chair.

All the other elements in the movie fall into place—Richard Chamberlain is a perfect, sullen and vicious villain; Holden manages to make his "one-dimensional" character sport at least two dimensions as he turns from enabling Chamberlain's cost-cutting to taking responsibility for his actions; and John Williams' score ratchets up incredible tension as the film builds up to its explosive climax.

Despite missing out on an Academy Award himself, Allen basked in tributes from firefighters and a key to the city of San Francisco in the aftermath of the movie.

Paul Zastupnevich said in 1995:

> I think the most important thing that he ever did was *Towering Inferno*. The fact that he made everyone aware that skyscrapers were inaccessible, and smoke alarms, and he made everyone really aware of how important it is that we have more stringent fire rules [regulations]. In traveling with him through France and Italy and England, and all the accolades and honors that he got really made me aware of how he had really affected the whole world.

**ABOVE**
The final domestic poster art for the movie.

**OPPOSITE**
John Berkey's stunning poster art for *The Towering Inferno*.

> "
> # THE WHOLE WORLD HAS IRWIN ALLEN. WHO HAVE I GOT?
>
> **IRWIN ALLEN**

# THE MASTER OF DISASTER

*Theme parks, marriage, a building at Warners— and Evel Knievel*

**OPPOSITE**
Irwin Allen in the mid-1970s, ready to launch into the stratosphere after the success of *The Poseidon Adventure* and *The Towering Inferno*.

By the early months of 1975, it was clear that *The Towering Inferno* would be one of the biggest box office successes in movie history—a fitting follow-up to *The Poseidon Adventure,* and Irwin Allen's crowning achievement in the genre he had practically invented. Other studios offered competition, but movies like *Earthquake* and *The Hindenburg* seemed to be half-hearted imitations of the blockbusters that Allen made with so much enthusiasm and glee.

1975 would be one of the most important in Allen's career—in effect a year-long celebration of the producer's power and success. But it would also contain a few harbingers that the Master of Disaster's days of bestriding Hollywood like a colossus would be unexpectedly brief.

One such warning sign was Allen's ill-fated attempt to add his brand of Hollywood magic to Palos Verdes' long-standing Marineland of the Pacific, an oceanarium established in 1954 and one of the predecessors of the Sea World tourist parks. 20th Century Fox had acquired the park in 1973, after two decades of plummeting fortunes for the marine attraction, and in December of 1974, just before the premiere of *The Towering Inferno* and at the height of hype for the movie, Fox announced that Irwin Allen (with his own financial stake in the park) would convert Marineland into a "winter extravaganza" for the holidays, at a cost of $500,000. On the face of things, Allen seemed an inspired choice for a makeover of the park—he had beaten Jacques Cousteau himself to the big screen with his Oscar-winning documentary *The Sea Around Us*, and his *Voyage to the Bottom of the Sea* TV series was probably second only to Cousteau's ABC documentary specials and possibly *Flipper* in terms of popularizing sea life and the oceans on network television. Add *The Poseidon Adventure*, certainly one of the most successful maritime adventure films ever made, and it was easy to see why Fox wanted to assign the Master of Disaster to sprucing up the beleaguered aquatic park.

Marineland's talent at the time included Glenn Yarbrough and the Limelighters, a great American high-diving team, a company of repertory actors in residence, The Marineland Players, who performed daily with killer whales, pilot whales and dolphins—the company counted Richard Dean Anderson among other budding actors. Attractions also included a Sea Arena for high divers, The Aquamaniacs, and Dawn and her Dolphins; the Killer Whale Coliseum; Seaside Stadium with pilot whales, dolphins and human performers; a Comedy Bowl with California sea lions, clowns, and "world-famous aqua comic" Johnny Edwards; a South Seas Pearl Diving Pavilion; and the Marineland Diver; Pirate's Cove; Shopper's Paradise; Sky Tower; Giant Alpine Slide; a Clown Bounce as well as a baby walrus and mother, penguins, elephant seals, and sea lions.

Allen's first assignment for the park was to mount the "Winter Wonderland" show that would transform Marineland into an icy, snow-covered Christmas environment from December through January. A thousand tons of snow was purportedly imported for the occasion, two frozen lakes for ice skating were created, and "the world's largest Christmas tree," designed to loom at a Glass Tower-sized 403 feet in height, was included along with a "Giant Alpine snow slide." Press for the park claimed that the new attraction pulled in 100,000 people over 16 days, and indeed attendance was up over normal levels for the park, but not enough to make up for the enormous cost of the makeover.

Patrons, in fact, were less than impressed. Children encouraged to "dress warmly" were actually overdressed for the 70-degree weather; the "world's largest Christmas tree" turned out to be a water slide decorated with Christmas lights; and the purported "thousand tons of snow" was barely adequate to add melting slush to a few key play areas for kids. "They brought in all that shaved ice to create snow and it turned out to be one of the hottest days of the year, and as fast as they could lay it down, it was melting," Joe Musso recalled. At least one letter to the *Los Angeles Times* described Allen's inspiration as a "Marineland Disaster" and claimed that commercials misrepresented the attraction.

In a March issue of *Coast* magazine, Allen defended the makeover and expounded on his further plans for the park:

> The problem is that Marineland was a one-time attraction. You'd go, feed the seals, and then go back home and tell everybody that you'd fed the seals. What we're creating now is the kind of park that demands return visits.

Allen explained that the oceanographic aspect of the park would remain:

> We'll keep it as exciting and modern as possible. But we are also planning on bringing in four seasonal festivals each year, plus constructing a number of permanent rides. Ultimately we plan on making Marineland a motion picture theme park.

Allen had a record label involved that would ostensibly put out recordings of the live entertainment performances planned for the park, and he planned a $2.5 million *Voyage to the Bottom of the Sea* ride for spring 1975.

**LEFT**
Irwin Allen joins a few Rose Bowl Parade veterans to open his "Winter Wonderland" attraction at Marineland.

Marineland had always been in competition with Anaheim's Disneyland (it had opened a year before Disney's famed attraction), and it also now faced competition from the Universal Studios tour, which had its own motion picture-based rides and attractions. When asked about similarities to Disneyland and the Universal Studios tour, Allen, with more than a touch of hubris, retorted, "I don't know what's going on at Universal. I don't copy people, people copy me."

A 1975 studio bio for Allen indicated that he had plans far beyond a simple renovation of Marineland: a proposed $400 million, 475 acre resort and recreation complex in Long Beach, to be named Irwin Allen's Pleasure Island, adjacent to the Queen Mary. But the poor reception to the Marineland makeover ultimately scuttled those plans. In a civil suit filed by Deputy Attorney General Michael Botwin in Los Angeles Superior Court, Marineland was charged with false advertising in a detailed suit that described numerous ways in which the park's winter wonderland had been misrepresented to disappointed kids, with plastic, fiberglass, and cotton standing in for much of the promised snow. Marineland ultimately settled the suit, paying $15,000 in civil penalties and $5,000 in attorney's fees, along with a promise to never promise kids tons of fake snow again.

In the meantime, Allen engineered a much happier event that had been in preproduction for almost a decade and a half. Allen had started dating actress and singer Sheila Mathews while working on his *Voyage to the Bottom of the Sea* feature film in 1961. Since then Allen had cast Matthews in *Five Weeks in a Balloon*, in an episode of *Voyage to the Bottom of the Sea*, in three episodes of *Lost in Space* (including as one of "The Space Vikings," a valkyrie named Brynhilda, in 1967), two *Land of the Giants*, in *City Beneath the Sea* (as a woman trying to smuggle her robotic dress-maker out of Pacifica during a mass evacuation), as a nurse in *The Poseidon Adventure*, and as the mayor's wife in *The Towering Inferno*. Allen had pledged to marry Matthews after *The Towering Inferno* was released, and the nuptials were planned for February 15, 1975. Vernon Scott wrote a piece on Allen's pre-nuptial "stag party," wherein a banquet room in a Beverly Hills hotel was rented for 200 guests, with Steve Allen the master of ceremonies and attendees including George Jessel, Jack Carter, Jim Backus, George Burns, Bill Dana and, reportedly, a bearded lady and an albino sword swallower representing Allen's "old girlfriends."

Allen staged the wedding proper with all the showmanship he lent to his movie productions. He rented the Grand Ballroom of the Beverly Hills Wilshire Hotel, and production designer Bill Creber remade the ballroom with a circus theme, removing the central chandelier to create the center of the Big Top. A 35-piece mariachi band was hired and Paul Zastupnevich himself designed Sheila Mathews' wedding gown.

An article in *The L.A. Herald Examiner* stated that the event sported "enough flower arrangements for a Tournament of Roses float." The wedding party included Steve and Jane Allen, Ernest and Tovah Borgnine, Red and Alicia Buttons, Jerre Henshaw and his wife Michelle, Allen's agent Herman Rush and his wife Joan, and Allen's attorney (and best man) Eddie Rubin, as

**RIGHT**
Irwin Allen with wife Sheila Mathews, and Allen's friend and agent Herman Rush (right) and his wife Joan at Allen's wedding in February, 1975.

well as Allen's ever-present best friend Groucho Marx. According to Rush, Allen directed the ceremony himself and arranged the members of the wedding party by height. Columnist James Bacon noted that, "Irwin has been a bachelor so long that the orchestra kept repeating 'Stranger in Paradise' all through the ceremony."

In a 1995 interview, Sheila Allen explained the reason for the couple's extended. 13-year-long courtship:

> We had two different religions going here. I was Catholic and he was Jewish. I had my little Irish mother who kept saying, "I love Irwin—when are you two going to get married?" And then in the next breath she'd say, "You're going to get married in the Catholic church, aren't you?" And of course I knew that was never gonna happen. So that made it a little difficult. These are entirely different times we're talking about. Were it today [it would] be very different.

Despite that challenge, friends of the couple said that Allen found the perfect match in Sheila. Red Buttons noted in 1995:

> Sheila complemented Irwin, and Irwin, in all his gruffness, just treated her like a doll on a shelf. You could tell the affection. And that made us all feel good, because, Irwin was not like that. Irwin would not wear his heart on his sleeve.

A couple of weeks before the wedding, Allen participated in another unprecedented media event—a taping of the variety program *The Merv Griffin Show*, 90 minutes devoted entirely to "the Master of Disaster." Griffin was a singer and former bit actor who parlayed game shows and his variety program into a financial empire.

Allen wasn't exactly a stranger to TV appearances, going back to his own game show and appearances on Groucho Marx's *You Bet Your Life*. But never before had anyone devoted a 90-minute program solely to the producer and his work. In fact, it was extremely rare for any behind-the-scenes talent to be featured on a variety program like Griffin's, normally showcasing actors and other performers. Allen was being accorded an honor normally reserved for someone like Alfred Hitchcock—but by now Allen had, in fact, become a household name, a motion picture and television creator who had attained star status. He was joined on *The Merv Griffin Show* by *Poseidon* star Gene Hackman, Walter Pidgeon of the *Voyage to the Bottom of the Sea* movie, and Henry Fonda—a longtime neighbor and friend.

Introducing Allen, Griffin noted that the Master of Disaster had created the first celebrity panel game show—an accomplishment the host must have greatly appreciated, since it helped lay the groundwork for Griffin's own immensely lucrative career in television.

Hackman, who could be dismissive and testy about commercial filmmaking in general, was a surprisingly warm and engaging booster for Allen as he recalled working on *Poseidon*:

> I read the script and thought it was kind of an interesting idea because I'd never done a big Hollywood film and I thought it would be fun to work on the lot. And it was fun but it wasn't the old Hollywood; the fun was in the intricacies that Irwin was able to put together. He's more than a showman; he's really a kind of entrepreneur of this kind of entertainment film, and technically he knows everything there is to know about water and fire. It changed the whole economy of films because back then it cost a big chunk of change and at that time a lot of people were still worried about it because they'd lost money on a lot of big films. So he is a tremendous gambler. It's fun being involved with that kind of energy.

Pidgeon reflected on *Voyage* more wryly:

> He upset me terribly. His doggone energy just drove me nuts. You'd come on the set at 8:30 and this guy had been in his office since 5:30.

In his own act of showmanship, Griffin delayed Allen's entrance on the program until almost half of its 90-minute running time was over. Dressed in a bright yellow jacket that made Allen look a little like a human Flying Sub, the producer jogged around the set on his entrance to demonstrate his energy. But despite his larger-than-life persona on set, Allen came off as a somewhat subdued, perhaps even slightly ill-at-ease talk show guest, not the kind of natural raconteur—or provocateur—that made Alfred Hitchcock and Orson Welles oft-requested presences on similar programs.

Griffin showed a lengthy making-of segment on *The Towering Inferno*, which was still burning up theaters in February. Allen pointed out that *Inferno* would be the

**LEFT**
Irwin Allen's 1975 appearance on *The Merv Griffin Show*—an entire 90-minute episode devoted entirely to the Master of Disaster.

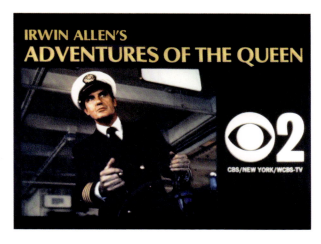

**ABOVE**
Robert Stack in a CBS promotional image for *Adventures of the Queen*.

first movie to gross $400 million worldwide, and that it had made $34 million in the U.S. after seven weeks in release, more than any other film. When Griffin mentioned that Allen's friend Henry Fonda hadn't yet been in any of his movies, Allen turned to Fonda and asked if the actor was available. Fonda was, and he and Allen made a handshake agreement then and there for Fonda to appear in Allen's upcoming *The Swarm*—an agreement Fonda held to. Fonda himself wrapped up the program on an odd note, reading a lengthy poem Benjamin Franklin had written about marriage, in honor of Allen's upcoming nuptials.

Allen's honeymoon with Sheila took the form of a London publicity tour for *The Towering Inferno*, one that was attended by some of the film's stars and Allen's staff, including Paul Zastupnevich:

> I went along on the pretext that I was going to do radio shows, and interviews, about the costumes and whatnot, but at the same time, I was there to follow through and handle things for him. I would have breakfast with them in the morning and [Irwin] would go up the wall because I would say to Sheila, "Oh, there's a cute little church down on the corner that you might like to see," or, "There's an antique shop around..." And so all of a sudden he'd turn to me and he'd say, "What do you tell her that for? She's gonna get very upset with me because I haven't done anything with her!" And I said, "Well, that's your fault. It's your honeymoon not mine."

Allen still had a production deal with 20th Century Fox after working with both Fox and Warner Bros. on *The Towering Inferno*. But his long and comfortable relationship with Fox was beginning to show signs of wear after the studio had denied him directing gigs on his two disaster projects. Allen had ambitious motion picture plans to follow up *The Towering Inferno*, and Warner Bros. executives, ecstatic over their participation in *Inferno*, were eyeing the Irwin Allen hit machine jealously.

Allen had whipped up a kind of television follow-up to *The Poseidon Adventure* at Fox, that would use *Poseidon's* familiar setting of the Queen Mary ocean liner. Filmed in the fall of 1974 while *The Towering Inferno* was in post production, *Adventures of the Queen* was a potential pilot for a new series starring Robert Stack and David Hedison, about an ocean liner that is hijacked for ransom.

Allen told Bob Thomas in a February 11, 1975 piece in *The Los Angeles Times*:

> I agreed to come back to television only if I could make the biggest pilots in the history of the medium and could score a "home" run by putting them on all three networks, That was my mountain to climb, because it was there. After all, how many mountains are left?

Included in Allen's "home run" deal were *Adventures of the Queen* and another adaptation of *The Swiss Family Robinson* (this time done as a straight period piece, the way he'd originally pitched it to CBS before updating it to what became *Lost in Space* in 1964), both budgeted at $1 million. Asked what would happen if both pilots sold, Allen said, "No problem. I've got great staffs, and three series at once would be easy to handle."

He pointed out that he'd already had four series on the air at once, though *Voyage to the Bottom of the Sea*, *Lost in Space* and *The Time Tunnel* had all left the air prior to the debut of *Land of the Giants* in 1969. But since *Giants* had gone into production a year before it debuted on ABC, Allen did in fact have four TV shows in production at the same time in 1967. Allen's third entry in the "home run" pilot sweepstakes was called *Time Travelers*, but it wouldn't go into production until much later.

In an interview by Don Freeman for *The San Diego Union*, Allen continued to insist that he wasn't taking a step down from features by doing television again:

> Why television? This is why television: the medium has an immediacy. In pictures, you work and work and it's two years before you see the results in a theater. TV is fast— bang bang, pop pop, and you're on the air. Besides, I'll tell you the truth—I need a nervous breakdown every day to keep my blood moving.

For *Adventures of the Queen*, Allen tried to maintain the same level of spectacle and glamour that had made *The Poseidon Adventure* so successful. Art director Stan Jolley recreated parts of the Queen Mary for the TV-movie, including a simulation of the ship's cargo hold that had to hold thousands of gallons of water in an explosion sequence supervised by special effects man Logan Frazee. Allen once again cast Sheila Mathews (nee Allen), this time as a "blonde opera singer." Also onboard was veteran actress Gloria Stuart, who would regain her prior fame a couple of decades later in yet another ocean liner-based disaster epic, James Cameron's *Titanic*.

Allen maintained that his position at 20th Century Fox was in no danger of disappearing any time soon:

> I have a lavish suite of offices at Fox, and I have a full-time staff that includes a dozen illustrators constantly on the boards, creating new disasters. I received a million to make this pilot movie, probably more than has been spent on any similar project, and I will receive $250,000 for each show in the series that will come from this movie.

That same month, Allen explained his new take on *The Swiss Family Robinson*: "It will be entirely different from the Disney version," he said, "but I don't want to disparage [Disney] because I love the man and his work."

Allen's adaptation of the Johann David Wyss novel followed all the familiar elements: a family shipwrecked by a storm on a tropical island, struggling to survive the elements and a gang of pirates while building a treehouse dwelling that would probably fetch six figures in the current California real estate market. Easygoing Martin Milner (of the long-running Jack Webb cop show *Adam-12*) played the Robinson paterfamilias, Karl; Pat Delaney played his feisty wife Lottie, and a young Helen Hunt played one of the Robinson teenaged daughters. Having developed this property once before with *Lost in Space*, Allen added an element that Wyss had neglected: a regular foil for the Robinson family, in the person of a scurvy pirate named Jeremiah Worth, played by veteran heavy Cameron Mitchell.

Allen hired Harry Harris to direct the pilot, and in 1995 the director didn't recall the assignment too fondly:

> I personally felt it should have more of an adult tone to it, and it was written that way, and I made it that way. One of his producers was a guy named Arthur Weiss who was an intelligent man, but he didn't like what I was doing, and he said, "They're not gonna buy this show," and I said, "Why not?" He said, "It's a little too mature. We're doing a 'spunky show for kids.'" I said, "Well, it's a mature story and the people are people, and I'm playin' 'em for real people." I didn't want to go with the pirates were coming and all that crap. So, I shot it my way and they sold it, and I think he was wrong.

There had always been an unspoken understanding among the networks that programs airing in the seven and eight p.m. time slots should be viewable by younger audiences, but in 1975 the Federal Communications Commission actually mandated the idea, establishing a "Family Viewing Hour" from eight to nine p.m. The mandate would be declared unconstitutional two years later, but by the time *The Swiss Family Robinson* pilot aired in late April, television producers and critics were already railing against the idea. In the April 23 review of the pilot, *Variety* noted that the program was an example of what could be expected from the network's new "family hour" programming, describing it as:

> ...Lower-case action-adventure that in its narrative form and special effects retrogresses to the days of the Saturday matinee serials...made on the cheap and devoid of character development or narrative force that could sustain on anything but gunpowder, gunfights, blowups, volcanoes and other dismal special disaster effects.

Despite the reviews, ABC was happy with the pilot movie's ratings, and for the first time since *Land of the Giants*, Irwin Allen would gear up to produce a weekly television series at 20th Century Fox. Around the same time, Allen was presented with an opportunity to revisit his earlier Robinson family when Bill Mumy, then acting on a half-hour "dramedy" series called *Sunshine*, came to Allen with an idea for a *Lost in Space* reunion.

Mumy remembered in 1995:

> I co-wrote a screenplay that I took to Andy Siegel, who at that point in time was head of the movie for television at CBS, the network that *Lost In Space* was originally on. He was very enthusiastic about the project. We took it to Twentieth Century Fox, where we filmed the show. And at that point in time they still had our props, and a lot of our costumes and things. And the studio was very receptive to making it. I got copies of the screenplay to the cast members, who definitely helped me make it better.

**LEFT**
Concept art for Allen's *The Swiss Family Robinson*.

**RIGHT**
Promotional announcement and footage from Allen's *The Swiss Family Robinson*.

**FOLLOWING**
Color storyboard artwork by Joe Musso for Allen's long-gestating, never-made 70mm action epic *Circus, Circus, Circus!*, which was to have starred Steve McQueen.

Jonathan [Harris] had some very strong thoughts on it. We went and did a re-write—made it better. Everyone was ready to go. I mean I had the studio, I had the cast, and I had the network, ready to make a movie of the week.

Mumy in fact had everything but *Lost in Space*'s creator, Irwin Allen. Mumy was 22 and had already written an episode of the *Sunshine* TV series, so with the cast, a studio, and an executive at CBS behind him, he had every reason to believe that Allen would greet the idea of a *Lost in Space* reunion enthusiastically.

Not so:

He wouldn't read it. He wouldn't discuss it with me. He didn't want to hear about any of his old projects at that time. He said, "I'm not looking back—I'm only looking forwards. But if at any point in time I want to go back to *Lost In Space*, I'll have someone write the script and it won't be you. And if I want you to be in it, I'll call your agent." And that was the last bit of my conversation with Irwin. I said, "I'm not doing this as a way to make money—I'm doing this to resolve the show."

Allen had every reason to be looking forward—*The Towering Inferno* was still a sensation, and the disaster movie genre was the new recipe for box office blockbusters. But just out of Irwin Allen's line of sight, another blockbuster production was about to remix that recipe.

During the making of *Inferno*, stunt coordinator Paul Stader had given the crew updates on a troubled production being shot on the other side of the country, on the East Coast. Fox diving expert Fred Zendar, who had been a technical advisor on Allen's *Voyage to the Bottom of the Sea* movie and had worked on the Fox lot doing stunt work and scuba supervision on *Fantastic Voyage* and the *Voyage to the Bottom of the Sea* TV show, had been toiling on the movie, which involved an inexperienced young director, a massive amount of shooting on the open ocean, and a temperamental mechanical shark.

"It was a big disaster," Joe Musso recalled. *Jaws* had been a best-selling novel, but its production, in the midst of the disaster movie cycle, had been treated as merely another entry in the genre, and little was expected of it. Director Steven Spielberg had made one electrifying TV movie success, the suspense thriller *Duel*, about a driver terrorized by a hulking semi truck on the desert freeways outside Los Angeles. His track record as a theatrical director, however, was minimal, and the technical challenges of filming *Jaws* off the coast of Martha's Vineyard seemed to be defeating him.

Then *Jaws* opened. Spielberg had ingeniously shot around the malfunctioning mechanical shark (built by special effects veteran Robert A. Mattey, who had made the mechanical giant squid for Disney's *20,000 Leagues Under the Sea*)—while the shark was being repaired, Spielberg would simply shoot the surface of the water, or yellow flotation barrels towed by a boat off-camera, supposedly attached to the giant shark that lurked just beneath the surface. The approach turned *Jaws* into a Hitchcock movie, an exercise in unbearable tension and suspense that sent beachgoers fleeing from the ocean and became

SC 201A EXT. CIRCUS SITE – LOS ANGELES – (DAY)
WE HOLD ON ELEPHANTS PULLING LINES – THE PARKED CIRCUS CARAVAN IS IN THE BACKGROUND.

SC 202A (CONT.)
WE THEN MOVE TO REVEAL THAT THE ELEPHANTS ARE RAISING THE CANVAS OF THE HUGE CIRCUS TENT.

SC 201A (CONT.)
ANGLE TO SHOW THE NOW-ERECT TENT – ONCE ESTABLISHED THE CAMERA BEGINS TO PAN OVER TO ONE SIDE ––––

SC 204 – EXT. MACE'S MOTOR HOME
– CAMERA CONTINUES TO PAN OVER TO PARKING AREA WITH CIRCUS VEHICLES – CAMERA ZOOMS IN ON MACE'S TRAILER

SC 211 – EXT PARKING AREA
MACE EXITS FROM HIS MOTOR HOME – CAMERA TRACKS HIM AS HE STRIDES TOWARD JACK REEVES' TRAILER

SC 217A – MACE'S P.O.V.
ANIMAL WAGON & MENAGERIE BEING PLACED IN MENAGERIE TENT.

SC 217 (CONT.)
JACK REEVES IN FG WATCHING MACE'S DIRECTION – REEVES BEGINS TO FOLLOW MACE AT A DISTANCE.

SC 218
MACE WALKS DOWN THE NARROW AISLE OF ANIMAL CAGES – SUDDENLY REEVES APPEARS AT THE FAR END AND TURNS HIS CYCLE IN MACE'S DIRECTION.

SC-219 — REEVES ROARS HIS CYCLE DOWN THE NARROW AISLE OF CAGES TOWARD MACE (CAMERA STAYS WITH REEVES AS BACKGROUND BLURS PAST)

SC-220 — CAMERA LOW, ANGLED UP AT MACE AS HE LEAPS UP GRABBING THE BARS OF CAGES ON EITHER SIDE AS REEVES ROARS TOWARD HIM — MACE THEN SWINGS HIS LEGS FORWARD AND UP.

SC 220 A — SIDE VIEW AS MACE SWINGS UP AND OUT OF PICTURE IN ACROBATIC FLIP.
SC 220 B — LION LUNGES TOWARD MACE'S HAND ON BARS OF CAGE — SIMULTANEOUSLY AS REEVES STARTS TO GO BY — CUT TO A QUICK

SC 220 C — HIGH ANGLE LOOKING DOWN ON MACE AS HE FLIPS HIS FEET OVER HIS HEAD AS REEVES GOES BY UNDERNEATH —

SC 220 D — REEVES BLASTS HARMLESSLY PAST AS MACE DROPS TO THE GROUND —

SC 221 — MACE HOLDS HIS GRAZED HAND AS WATCHES REEVES DISAPPEAR FROM VIEW — MACE THEN STARTS TO TURN TOWARD CAMERA —

SC 222 — CAMERA FOLLOWS MACE AS HE RUNS INTO ANIMAL TENT AND OVER TO THE PARKED GYMKHANA BIKES —

SC 223 — MACE BLASTS OUT OF TENT AND DOWN THE PATH BETWEEN CAGES —

the kind of box office hit that no one had ever seen before. It quickly eclipsed *The Towering Inferno* and became a new yardstick by which action movies would be measured.

A month after *Jaws* hit theaters, the fallout from *The Towering Inferno* and its unprecedented collaboration between 20th Century Fox and Warner Bros. came to a head in the form of a major transition for Irwin Allen and his staff. On July 18th, *The Hollywood Reporter* announced a feature production affiliation agreement between Allen and Fox. Allen's old deal with the studio had expired on April 10th, and the new deal called for Allen's services as a producer and/or director on a non-exclusive basis for three major theatrical films, including *The Day the World Ended,* a period epic about a volcanic eruption, *Circus, Circus, Circus!* (now being scripted by Edward Arnhalt), and a sequel to *The Poseidon Adventure.* Allen was considering the new IMAX process for *Circus*, or possibly 70mm 3D, which had not been developed at the time. "The physics for it exist," Allen said.

Allen also had a star in mind for the circus movie: Steve McQueen. McQueen would have played the daredevil head of a mammoth, traveling circus—a character halfway between Victor Mature's character in *The Big Circus* and Evel Knievel.

"*Circus* was a big heist," Joe Musso recalled. "McQueen has this jet pack and flies around the circus as part of his act and at the end there's this whole thing down at the Port of Los Angeles where the ships are docked and there's this big fight with cranes that McQueen gets involved in."

Fox had passed on a fourth project, *The Walter Syndrome*, based on Richard Neely's novel about a serial killer in 1938. Allen was still working on his *Swiss Family Robinson* TV series for the studio as well as the Marineland theme park.

The *Reporter* article brought up the major bone of contention in Allen's relationship with Fox, noting that, "among [Allen's] desires under a new contract was the privilege of directing. At one point that was being resisted by 20th which took the position that his large-scale films required his full attention as producer." Also noted was "trade buzz a few months ago that Allen might go to Warner Bros. never materialized in any formal announcement, but of course since his new 20th deal is nonexclusive, anything elsewhere is possible."

Just 24 hours later, that conclusion was borne out when Allen signed a two-year, non-exclusive, multiple picture contract with Warner Bros., representing $100 million in production money. *Hollywood Reporter* writer Ron Pennington noted that Warners Chairman of the Board and CEO Frank Wells said that this was the biggest contract ever awarded a producer-director in the history of the company. The deal called for Allen to make two big budget pictures a year (similar in scope to the $14 million *The Towering Inferno*) plus smaller features budgeted at around $5 million a piece.

Allen said that the two features he had completed screenplays for—*The Walter Syndrome* and a movie about killer bees called *The Swarm*—were not included in the

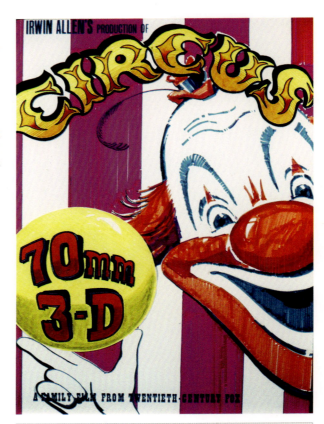

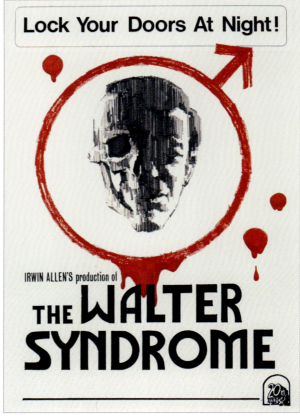

**LEFT**
Preliminary poster art concept for *Circus, Circus, Circus!*

Pitch artwork for *The Walter Syndrome*, a period serial killer story that was never made.

**OPPOSITE**
More Joe Musso storyboard art for *Circus, Circus, Circus!*

SC 397  INSERT TV SET - CIRCUS ARENA
WE SEE TWO GIANT CANNONS TILT UPWARD —

SC 397 B
TUBE IMAGE CUTS TO THE RINGMASTER — AS HE INTRODUCES THE FLYING ZACCHINIS —

SC 401  DELANEY & TV SET
WE SEE THE RINGMASTER ON THE TUBE AGAIN

SC 403  INT. TENT. ROLPH & CANNON
ROLPH PRETENDS TO MAKE SOME ADJUSTMENT ON THE CONTROL PANEL —

SC 404  MACE & LINDA
MACE COMPLAINS TO LINDA ABOUT ROLPH —

SC 406  SPLIT SCREEN
ON LEFT — CIRCUS ACTION ON RIGHT — ROLPH PREPARES TO FIRE — DELANEY WATCHES CIRCUS ACTION ON TV & CUES WILSON & JOHNSON — JOHNSON THRUSTS DETONATOR INTO DELANY'S HANDS AS THEY RUN PAST —

SC 406 CONT —
ROLPH BLASTS THE ZACHINIS FROM THE CANNONS SIMULTANEOUSLY AS DELANEY DETONATES THE DOOR

SC 407. INT. TENT
THE ZACHINIS FLY PAST EACH OTHER ACROSS THE TENT INTO NETS SAFELY —

deal, and that the two projects were now in limbo and could ultimately go forward at Warner Bros., Fox, or some other studio.

Interestingly, Allen in 1974 had written actor, comedian and director Woody Allen to discuss the lead role in *The Walter Syndrome*. Allen was between his comedies *Sleeper* and *Love and Death* at the time and didn't take Irwin up on his offer. Irwin Allen was never able to attach a commercially viable lead actor to *The Walter Syndrome*, which ultimately doomed the project.

Unlike Fox, which was still reluctant to allow Allen to direct, Warner Bros.' Frank Wells and president John Calley were eager to have the Master of Disaster sitting in the directors' chair. Al Gail recalled in 1995 another little item they threw in to sweeten the pot:

> Because it was a co-production deal with Warners, Warners said come over here. We'll build you your own building—which they did—and roll out the red carpet. And they had the facilities that we needed.

Allen would be leaving 20th Century Fox after almost a decade on the venerable lot. But he still had projects in production at the studio. His *Swiss Family Robinson* series would premiere on NBC in September, and Allen's earlier statements about Walt Disney would come back to haunt him. Television reporter Lee Winfrey noted in a July 11, 1975 piece for *The Philadelphia Inquirer* that Allen's TV show would be going head to head with NBC's *The Wonderful World of Disney*. Although the Disney program had slipped from 11th place to 18th place during the 1974-1975 season, it was still a powerhouse.

Working to develop the show for ABC's Family Hour, Allen noted that he was figuring out how to entertain viewers in "a non-violent violent method." But regardless of how strong Allen's show would be as a competitor, Winfrey noted that Disney's position with NBC was such that there was virtually no chance of *The Wonderful World of Disney* being cancelled, since the show's place on the network also came with broadcast rights for all the Walt Disney movies, a higher per-hour rate paid by the network than it paid for similar shows, and a guarantee of 30-second ad space within the programmed hour to advertise Disney movies. "So storm your strongest, Irwin Allen," Winfrey challenged: "You're hammering on a mighty rock."

Allen, however, wasn't intimidated, and by the time *The Swiss Family Robinson* launched in September, he was already boasting about a spin-off from the show to star Frank Langella as pirate Jean Lafitte. An October 24, 1975 *Hollywood Reporter* article quoted Allen as saying that the Lafitte program "will be a big, expensive kind of show with lots of scenes on the water and major battle sequences."

Unfortunately neither *The Swiss Family Robinson*, nor the back door pilot episode featuring Lafitte, was very well-received. A January 31, 1976 review in *The Los Angeles Times* dismissed both ideas with the headline "Robinsons Spawn Second Disaster."

In February, Allen announced his production of *The Last Ride West* at Fox—from a script that had been sitting in his office for almost a decade. An article in *The Los Angeles Herald-Examiner* noted that the movie, about the last ride of the Pony Express, would be the "biggest western ever made" with Annie Oakley and "every famous character of the old West"—69 speaking parts, to be made at a cost of $22 million.

Production illustrator Joe Musso described the plot:

> *Last Ride West* has the government realizing they're heading toward the Civil War, and the Confederacy is going to break away and seize the base in San Francisco and cut off the West from the East. So they have to send a pony express rider west to warn everyone and get there in time to beat the ship that's going to dock there and seize the base, and it's about the pony express rider's adventures. It was very well written, but one script had him meeting all these famous people—George Custer, Wyatt Earp, Buffalo Bill, and I told Irwin these people didn't all exist at the same time. But the studio got wind of it and at some point all the famous people got written out.

John Wayne was momentarily considered for the lead with the project positioned as a possible television sale, but *The Last Ride West* was never made.

In fact, Allen's deal with Warner Bros., and the lack of enthusiasm over the reception of *The Swiss Family Robinson*, which looked unlikely to be brought back for a second season by ABC, was adding to a soured relationship between Allen and Fox. Allen had shot a pilot based on a script by Rod Serling (one of Serling's last works before he died in June, 1975) called *Time Travelers*. A more modestly-produced update of *The Time Tunnel*, *Time Travelers* was shot at Fox on the studio's *Hello, Dolly!* sets, which Allen's team had

**ABOVE**
Allen at the groundbreaking ceremony for the Irwin Allen Building on the lot at Warner Bros.

been able to set aflame in order to reproduce the great Chicago Fire that the plot revolved around. Allen cast Sam Groom, an early regular on *The Time Tunnel* (then a soap opera star), along with co-star Tom Hallick and Tricia Stewart. In a March 14 piece in *The Herald-Examiner*, Allen claimed that after showing the *Time Travelers* pilot to ABC, an executive said, "I've just seen the best pilot in the history of television." That accolade wasn't enough to get the program picked up by the network, however.

At Warner Bros., ground was broken for the new Irwin Allen Building on March 29, 1976, three weeks after Allen and his staff pulled up stakes and moved from Fox to the Warner Bros. Burbank Studios. Allen still had projects in production at Fox—*The Day the World Ended* was supposedly a year away from shooting, and Allen also had *The Swarm*—the movie about a marauding mass of killer bees that would be the Master of Disaster's answer to *Jaws*—on the boards.

Allen called an April 22 press conference to mark his takeover of an entire 52-office building on the Warner Bros. lot in Burbank. WB President Frank Wells was present, saying Allen's move was "the beginning and the end of a dream that started two years ago when we first previewed *The Towering Inferno*."

However, on April 23, 1976, Fox passed on Allen's beloved *Circus, Circus, Circus!*, balking at the production's $15 million budget, and pushed back production on *The Swarm*. Ten days later, on May 3, 1976, *The Los Angeles Herald-Examiner* announced that Allen was officially splitting with 20th Century Fox, his home studio for almost a decade. The producer also sold his interest in Marineland as his much-ballyhooed makeover of the amusement park, and his plans for an "Irwin Allen Land" resort, had come to nothing:

> Allen insists his split with Fox and his sell-out of his interest in Marineland is totally amicable, although he hedged some specifics on projects which were already under development at Fox and were to be bought by Warners. *The Day The World Ended* is apparently back to the blank paper stage, but is set for Warner's shooting next year at a $15-million budget. The *Poseidon* sequel remains at Fox.

Allen was quick to reconfigure most of his major projects in production as Warner Bros. efforts. He still planned *The Last Ride West* as "the biggest western ever made." *The Day the World Ended* was budgeted at $15 million, putting it in the same league as the mammoth *The Towering Inferno*, while *Circus, Circus, Circus!* was planned at a more modest but still huge $10 million. *The Swarm* was slated as a smaller picture at $5 million—the killer bee idea in fact was already being exploited by some low budget film and television productions.

The move to Warner Bros., and the dissolution of Allen's relationship with Fox, at least temporarily hobbled production for Allen and his team. The script for *The Swarm* was still being worked on, as was *The Day the World Ended*, as the studio vacillated between making it a fact-based period movie or a modern-day thriller in the vein of *The Towering Inferno*. With nothing ready to film, one of the production company's smaller projects now took center stage—and it inadvertently gave Irwin Allen his first chance to direct a domestic feature film (given the release of *City Beneath the Sea* as a theatrical overseas) since *Five Weeks in a Balloon*.

Exhibitor Sherrill Corwin, once president of the Motion Picture Theater Exhibitors Association and with Steve Broidy one of the men who'd pulled Irwin Allen's fat out of the fire by putting up production money for *The Poseidon Adventure*, had a script about motorcycle daredevil Evel Knievel—and he had gotten Knievel himself to agree to star in the movie.

Allen's idling production team, with its superstar lineup of stunt talent and technical personnel, was the ideal force to get *Viva Knievel!* rolling, and Allen owed Corwin more than a few favors—not only had Corwin jumped in to help Allen save *The Poseidon Adventure*, but his greenlighting of *The Sea Around Us* at RKO had won Allen an Oscar and put Allen on the map in Hollywood as a producer.

Evel Knievel had become a famed, even notorious, public figure by 1976, with a line of toys and a history of feverishly promoted motorcycle stunts, not to mention a youthful life of misbehavior and lawlessness behind him (on one of his first jobs he had somehow managed to pop a wheelie in a mammoth earth mover, an accomplishment worthy of movie treatment on its own). Knievel might have seemed to be the perfect subject for an action-packed movie. In fact, there had already been at least two movies about Evel Knievel—a well-received, 1971 comedy starring George Hamilton, and a 1974 TV-movie starring Sam Elliott. Knievel had arguably reached the height of his popularity two years earlier, attempting to jump Snake River Canyon in a steam-powered "skycycle" in September, 1974 (Knievel had always bragged about the idea of jumping the Grand Canyon on his motorcycle—an impossible but undeniably poetic idea).

The Snake River Canyon jump had been a notorious disaster—Knievel's highly promoted, futuristic "X-2 Skycycle" had malfunctioned and crashed well short of the opposite side of the canyon, embarrassing the daredevil and adding more injuries to his well-publicized legacy of broken bones. But, as *Viva Knievel!* geared up for production, Irwin Allen had no qualms about his real-life star.

in a June 12, 1976, *Los Angeles Times* interview, he gushed:

> We think Evel Knievel is second only to Muhammad Ali in the sports world. He's got more charisma than any other figure in sports. We tested Knievel and he tested like a dream.

*Viva Knievel!* would be Allen's first theatrical film production since *The Towering Inferno*. Ironically, Sherrill Corwin had hired Gordon Douglas, the man who was to have directed *The Poseidon Adventure*, to helm the movie. Health problems quickly sidelined Douglas during the production's first, ambitious day of shooting, however.

Joe Musso recalls:

> The first day that we were shooting was at Long Beach stadium. They had the stadium filled and Evel was going to take his motorcycle and leap over these cages of lions and tigers. We only had so many extras but we locked off the cameras and moved them around to make it look like a full stadium. And they had some 40-foot scaffolding they put up so we could get some angles looking down on everything. Gordon got up there and he'd been having trouble with his ulcers, and about halfway through the day he got so sick they had to take him to the hospital. Irwin stepped in and directed for the rest of the day—and Irwin was looking for a chance to direct anyway, and it was his production team and the studio was fine with it because they sort of wanted Irwin anyway. By the end of the day, by the time we got to shoot the leap, the lions and tigers were all asleep—they had to get fire hoses and hose them down to get them moving around and looking dangerous.

*Viva Knievel!* was now Irwin Allen's opportunity to show he could still direct a theatrical motion picture from top to bottom—if he decided to take credit for it.

In an August 1, 1976 interview in *The Baltimore Sun*, Allen continued to be bullish on his star. "Evel hits that screen like a John Wayne—bigger than life. He comes at you like this," Allen said, imitating a cannonball. The article noted that Sherrill Corwin of Metropolitan Theaters productions convinced Knievel to make the movie. Knievel had told Corwin that he wanted to make a movie that could be seen by the whole family and make a strong statement against drug abuse.

But Knievel's anti-drug stance was just this side of counter-intuitive. While he was eager to get the word out to kids about the dangers of drugs, the daredevil was also completely at ease about extolling the virtues of good, clean booze. After delivering a line in the movie about being tired, Knievel admitted, "I really was. Those actors can fake that stuff. I stayed up until 6 a.m. drinking tequila. That's my method acting."

Meanwhile, Knievel seemed impatient with the drudgery of movie-making, and declared in the *Baltimore Sun* piece:

> If I had to do this for a living, I couldn't take it more than once every two or three years. I can't stand all this waiting around. I'm a man of action. I usually make a million dollars in two or three seconds. This way, it's taking three months.

Joe Musso recalled that Knievel was an unpredictable presence on the set:

> Evel was kind of crazy at times; he would do these interviews and if it was a female reporter he would go, "What are you doing tonight?" Irwin said, "I've got a G-rated movie and an X-rated star."

Although Knievel was married and had three children in real life, the movie presented him as single and on the prowl, with model-turned-actress Lauren Hutton, playing a photographer, as a potential love interest. In 1995, Paul Zastupnevich recalled that Hutton's famous

**LEFT**
A promotional button for *Viva Knievel!*

Allen confers with Lauren Hutton on location.

Trim and fit screen legend Gene Kelly, ready for his role as a broken down alcoholic—with Lauren Hutton on location on *Viva Knievel!*

**ABOVE**
Allen lures Knievel out of his trailer.

A battle-damaged Evel Knievel endures an interview on the set of *Viva Knievel!*

gap-toothed look rankled Allen, who sometimes judged actors on their dental work. When Hutton showed up for work on the picture, Allen insisted that she wear a dental insert to obscure the gap between her front teeth:

> He says, you're a model—that's what I bought. He said "I want you as a model, and I want you to dress like a model." She wanted to dress in sloppy, GI clothes and be a Margaret Whitney, war type of photographer. And he says, "I hired Lauren Hutton, not a photographer." So, she had to accede to his wishes.

Allen had brought in his usual group of actors, including Red Buttons as a shady promoter, Leslie Nielsen as a white collar drug lord plotting to use Knievel's transport truck to ship drugs across the border from Mexico, as well as Marjoe Gortner as a jealous and corrupted protege of Knievel's who's conspiring with Nielsen's character. Leslie Nielsen would begin lampooning his straight roles in movies like this just a few years later starting in *Airplane!* and later the *Police Squad!* TV series and *Naked Gun* movies. Marjoe Gortner was a short-lived 1970s phenomenon, a former televangelist who made a name for himself playing psychopaths, notably in 1974's *Earthquake*.

The movie's biggest casting coup was famed movie star and dancer Gene Kelly, playing former motorcycle jumper and now washed up mechanic Will Atkins, who the ever-loyal Evel Knievel keeps gainfully employed out of the sheer goodness of his heart. Knievel was only 38 years old when he starred in *Viva Knievel!,* while Gene Kelly was 64. Knievel might have been almost half Kelly's age, but as Indiana Jones once said, "It's not the years, it's the mileage." Stiff and immobile from years of injuries, his face swollen and red from alcohol abuse, Knievel made Kelly—who was supposed to be *playing* an old alcoholic—look tanned and healthy by comparison.

Allen brought his "A" game to *Viva Knievel!* in terms of its technical execution. Gary Charles Davis doubled for Knievel on the film's abundant motorcycle stunts, and even in early scenes in a parking lot with Knievel horsing around with Marjoe Gortner's character or trying to impress Hutton's "women's lib" photographer, the stunt work is daring and Fred Jackman, Jr.'s cinematography is slick. Production designer Ward Preston (who had done *The Towering Inferno* and would later work on *Airplane!*) designed a special, eagle-winged motorcycle for Knievel that was tailor-made to be marketed as a toy. And while the drug smuggling plot-line is cartoonish, the climax features a lot of ambitious stunt work, with Knievel jumping a motorcycle off a mountainside onto a transport truck as it emerges from a tunnel and then taking on the drivers hand-to-hand years before *Raiders of the Lost Ark*'s famed truck chase.

With the film finished, Allen potentially had a high-profile movie release, one on which he had directed almost every scene.

"The film came together and when it was in postproduction Irwin came into the office and started sounding everybody out, asking if he should take the director credit, and we all said he shouldn't," Joe Musso recalls. "It just wasn't an Irwin Allen movie."

**ABOVE**
Allen happily calling "Action!" on the set of *Viva Knievel!*—his first theatrical directing work since *Five Weeks in a Balloon*. Allen would nevertheless decline to take a directing credit on the picture.

**LEFT**
The specially designed motorcycle built for *Viva Knievel!*

Allen working with stunt supervisors on location.

Allen with Knievel preparing for a motorcycle sequence.

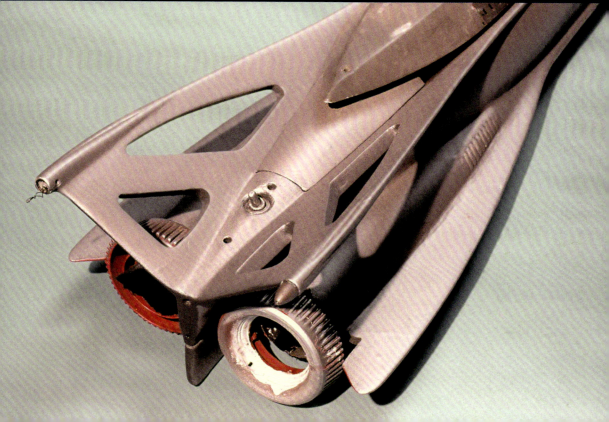

instead settled on facilities at the Columbia ranch, which were close to the Warner Bros. lot in Burbank. Columbia had its own "green tank" and a tank with a 50-foot sky backing—smaller than Sersen Lake but well-maintained. Abbott moved bubble machines, optical ports and a filming bathysphere to the ranch, but he also inquired about a possible "dry-for-wet" miniature underwater set, a cost-saving measure that had been used successfully on *City Beneath the Sea*.

Allen continued to mine his associates from his years at Fox, hiring prop man Herb Cheek, who had supervised the construction of the Seaview for *Voyage ot the Bottom of the Sea*, to construct the project's miniatures. He also hired veteran art director and filmmaker Eugène Lourié, a protege of director Jean Renoir, as Nemo's art director.

Lourié had worked on Allen's *Time Travelers* TV-movie and his work went back to the early 1930s. On *Captain Nemo*, Lourié was busy with activities like meeting with L.B. Abbott and production manager Donald Klune at the Palm Restaurant to discuss the upcoming giant lobster sequences with a lobster supplier. According to Joe Musso, Lourié's office contained a large "thank you for not smoking" sign that stood on display while Lourié himself indulged in his longtime pipe smoking habit. He would explain to visitors that he wanted *them* to abstain from smoking, not him.

Allen wanted Christopher Lee to play Captain Nemo, with Richard Basehart, Cornel Wilde, Ian Bannon, Richard Kiley, Lloyd Bridges, and Robert Vaughn as possible backups. For Nemo's nemesis, Professor Cunningham, Burgess Meredith's name appeared first, followed by Donald Pleasance, and Jose Ferrer. The story's female lead, Kate, had Tyne Daly, Lynda Day George, Joan Collins, and Shirley Knight under consideration, while Mel Ferrer was set for supporting character Dr. Robert Cook, and Horst Bucholtz was cast as the King of Atlantis.

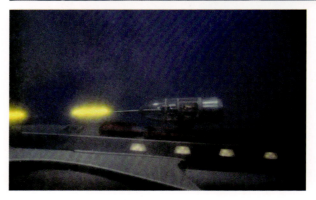

Allen had set Alex March as *Nemo*'s director, noting in a memo:

> Cooperation to the fullest from all hands must be given to him since he is a key man in the operation. However, Alex must understand that we are a company devoted to quality but religiously adhering to budgets and schedules. There can be no deviating from these two points.

March had directed two episodes of *Voyage to the Bottom of the Sea* and other episodic television for Fox including *Custer* and *Judd for the Defense*. But he had also made several quirky feature films including 1968's *Paper Lion* with Alan Alda, 1969's *The Big Bounce* with Ryan O'Neal, and the strange, satirical comedy *Mastermind* with Zero Mostel, which was released in 1976 after sitting on the shelf for several years. By 1977 March was cranking out episodes of cop shows like *Serpico* and *Baretta*, but he still had an independent streak and he quickly began butting heads with Allen.

Over the years the design of Nemo's Nautilus for the project has been the subject of much speculation, particularly where its relationship to Allen's earlier Seaview from *Voyage to the Bottom of the Sea* is concerned. It had been reported on more than one

**ABOVE**
The Raven submarine as it appeared in the TV miniseries, cobbled together from a Mattel *Space: 1999* Eagle toy.

A diminutive android fires the Raven's deadly "delta ray" cannon.

occasion that the 8-foot Seaview miniature had been modified, its nose chopped off and other changes made in order to create an early version of the Nemo Nautilus—and that Allen had hated the new design and ordered his designers to create a new Nautilus from scratch. In fact, the modified Seaview had a distinctive "bad guy" look and was always intended to be the show's enemy sub, the Raven.

Allen wanted to give his Nautilus the same kind of ornate, Victorian look that Disney's Harper Goff had given the famous fictional submarine in the 1954 *20,000 Leagues Under the Sea*. The script describes the discovery of the submarine as follows:

> We are looking at a masterpiece: a scientific marvel that is also a magnificent work of art. Nautilus is a flawless airfoil. Its bronzed titanium hull, sleek and slim and gleaming in the underwater shadows, is a triumph of engineering technically superior to anything of current design. Nautilus is splendid, its utilitarian function no less awesome than the aesthetic reaction it evokes.

Eugène Lourié had designed a shark-like Nautilus, and a 2-foot-long miniature of the sub had been constructed between mid-June and the first week of July by Herb Cheek's prop department. An 8-foot plaster mold had also been completed to make a larger miniature of the sub, on a par with the 8-foot Seaview that had been made for *Voyage*.

Cheek was also working on cleaning, painting, and re-rigging Columbia's Green Underwater Tank for the show's underwater scenes. The production had planned to use the 6-foot miniature Tigerfish submarine from *Ice Station Zebra* for Professor Cunningham's submarine, the Raven. But on June 24, Donald Klune wrote Allen to inform him that the idea of using the MGM sub model would likely be scrapped:

> MGM's Polaris which is at Universal smells like trouble. There is a new estimated date in finishing with the above of August 1, 1977. Therefore, L.B. Abbott has contacted 20th Century Fox and there is an 8-foot miniature of your Seaview still in existence. We are checking on the condition and availability. Eugène Lourié and L.B. Abbott both feel by using this miniature they would have total control and its design is better than the Polaris. L.B. Abbott just notified me that the Seaview is in good condition. Ivan indicated that the rental would be $600 per month.

Allen approved the idea and Lourié and Herb Cheek began the process of modifying the Seaview into the Raven. This explains the brutalist, angular look of the Seaview modifications, which replaced the TV sub's familiar manta ray nose with something like the head of a screwdriver, with bat-like fins extending off the superstructure behind the nose, a pair of antenna-like periscopes, sections carved out of the large rear fins and beefed up engine cylinders. This design, and the 8-foot Seaview miniature, was ultimately never used on the show, but the model was photographed by *Starlog* magazine contributors Bill Cotter and Mike Clark and it appeared in the magazine in the 1980s with little explanation.

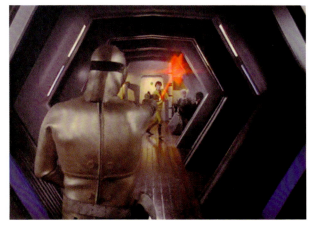

**RIGHT**
The Raven corridor "*Star Wars* fight"—complete with *Star Wars* music quotations from composer Richard LaSalle.

As to why the modified Seaview wasn't used, it's possible that Allen disliked the design, but it's more likely that budget considerations prevented the large Seaview miniature, and the proposed and under-construction, 8-foot model of the Nautilus, from being utilized. Most of the effects shots in the TV-movie, apart from closeup shots of laser weapons on the two subs being fired, utilized the 2-foot model of the Nautilus.

For the Raven, Herb Cheek settled on an even more modest, low-budget tactic—he used parts from a commercially available, 2-foot-long Mattel toy of the Eagle spacecraft from the Gerry Anderson TV series *Space: 1999*. Given the easy construction of the 2-foot Raven model, it's very unlikely that Cheek ever made or even considered making an 8-foot version of the Raven, for which custom-made enlargements of the *Space: 1999* toy's components would have had to have been constructed. Costs and the lack of large-scale studio tanks ultimately kept the miniature work for *Nemo* cut down to size, with most shots utilizing two-foot models shot dry-for-wet with a spinning "bubble vortex" overlaid on the footage to sell the idea that the submarines were cruising beneath the ocean surface.

Meanwhile Christopher Lee proved unavailable to play Captain Nemo. On June 17, 1977, Allen wrote actor Cornel Wilde:

> It's been years since we both said, "Let's make a movie together"—the time has now come. I should be most pleased if this would work so that you would play Captain Nemo. I do think the role is ideally suited.

By now, *Star Wars* was dominating the conversation nationwide and George Lucas' space fantasy would soon begin to influence every science fiction property in production at the time. When Wilde turned down the role of Nemo, Allen wrote Jose Ferrer, who had originally been under consideration for the film's villain, and explicitly mentioned the idea of going after the *Star Wars* audience with Nemo:

> The intent here is to embody the same excitement and bigger than life feeling inherent in STAR WARS and to show in formidable style a submarine of the Victorian era versus a futuristic one of 100 years from now. It's cloak and dagger; it's cowboy; it's camp; it's wild; it's wonderful! The network and the studio are enormously enthusiastic, and, needless to say, it has my total excitement, attention and love (I always respond this way when I smell lots of money)...as you already know, I am an old hand at this, and I have rarely been so enthusiastic about such a combination.

To play the show's two younger stars, Allen hired Tom Hallick, who had starred in his *Time Travelers* TV-movie, and Burr DeBenning of *City Beneath the Sea*. With Lynda Day George as their leading lady, the trio formed a very standard, photogenic but dull anchor for the series around which Jose Ferrer and Burgess Meredith could chew Eugène Lourié's scenery unimpeded.

With shooting set for August 28, Allen screened *City Beneath the Sea* and *Voyage to the Bottom of the Sea* for his team at Warner Bros. to give them an idea of what he was aiming for. By now the overall budget had inched up to $2,550,000, and the network's enthusiasm was no doubt fueled by the idea of being one of the earliest productions to capitalize on *Star Wars*.

But, as Allen would soon discover, reproducing the style and energy of the Lucas space fantasy was no easy task. The challenge would defeat a number of mega-budget theatrical movie productions over the next few years, and network television shows would have an even harder time of it. In a "production critique" memo from Arthur Weiss to Sidney Marshall (cc'ing Allen) sent on July 11, Weiss complained:

> There is no Irwin Allen-*Star Wars* kind of action until more than halfway through the script (the Professor destroys a nondescript reconnaissance submarine on page 39). There is no *Star Wars* conflict between Nemo and the Professor until page 44 which is almost two-thirds through the script.

Weiss suggested that the Raven should be spying on naval exercises earlier in the story and that Act 1 should end with the "*Star Wars* fight between the Raven and the Nautilus." The term "*Star Wars* fight" quickly became a buzzword in production memos. Discussing the meeting between Nemo and his nemesis, Cunningham, on page 47, Weiss suggested:

> First they should have a helluva *Star Wars* fight up and down the Raven corridor (which is now not used at all) ending with Nemo and Jim's capture as in the current script...there is not enough quantity and variety of *Star Wars* kind of special effects action which is the life-blood of Nemo just as it was of *Star Wars*. Must have more.

Allen did add more—and the budget went up accordingly. By September 7, 1977 it had ballooned to $3,267,567, and while Allen and the network executives were happier, CBS Standards and Practices were not. An October 11 memo to Allen read:

> With these two new underwater battle sequences, we are once again forced to confront the question of what constitutes an acceptable quantity of action in this series...the continued packing-in of more and more action material...threatens to make the whole unacceptable.

The network censors complained about the amount of laser beam fireworks over the course of the series:

> As usual, there should be no apparent injuries...Our essential concern remains that the level of violence in this series not continue to creep upward as the material is augmented or reworked.

Allen's references to *Star Wars* in his communications with stars and CBS executives were understandable, but while Allen fully understood the impact of the space fantasy in terms of box office dollars, the pacing and feel that had made the George Lucas movie so unique and groundbreaking were elusive to him. He saddled Burgess Meredith's character with an iron-plated, hulking robot servant named Tor, clearly looking for a Darth Vader effect (Tor would bellow lines like, "Enemies must be destroyed!"), as well as a contingent of gold-plated

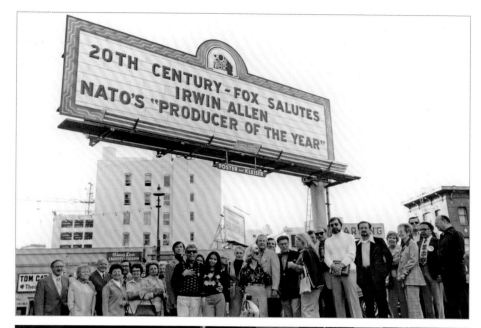

**ABOVE**

Allen and his staff from *The Towering Inferno* gather under a Fox sign honoring him as NATO's Producer of the Year.

Seated at the celebration at Fox (with Sheila Allen just barely visible in the background at the next table) is *American Graffiti* producer Gary Kurtz (foreground, second from left) and Marcia and George Lucas (foreground, right side of table), *Graffiti*'s editor and director—who had just signed their deal to make *Star Wars* with Fox. Within two years, *Star Wars* would shake up the world of Hollywood blockbusters and begin to overshadow Allen's work.

Allen let *Viva Knievel!* go out with Gordon Douglas' name on it, and when the movie went up for review at the end of 1976, his decision seemed well-founded. *Variety*'s review on December 31 singled out Evel Knievel for faint praise:

> Actually, Evel the actor emerges from the wreck in better shape than the bent careers of his veteran co-stars, Gene Kelly, Marjoe Gortner, Red Buttons, Lauren Hutton and Leslie Nielsen. For him, it's a chance to show he can be fairly natural in front of the camera when the demands are minimal; for them, it's a credit best forgotten.

*Viva Knievel!* is today notable for its stunt work, the stunt casting of Knievel playing himself, and for a few wildly over-the-top sequences, particularly the opening, with the saintly Knievel sneaking into an orphanage late at night to deliver toys—Evel Knievel toys, of course—to underprivileged boys. When one Tiny Tim-like urchin is exposed to Knievel's benedictions, he throws away his crutches and miraculously regains the ability to walk, inspired by Knievel's history of limping away from horrific motorcycle crashes.

Allen gave his wife Sheila perhaps her most memorable role as tough-talking nun Sister Charity, who busts in on Knievel's late-night visitation with a withering "Knievel!" before dragging the motorcycle stunt hero out into the hallway, where the two old warriors for decency share some flirtatious compliments before Knievel disappears into the night.

Just as unforgettable was a later sequence in which Gene Kelly's long-suffering character gets thrown into a corrupt drug treatment facility (overseen by a slimy Dabney Coleman) and stoked up on LSD, leading to the legendary Kelly finally getting his chance to play a balls-to-the-wall narcotic freakout scene.

Evel Knievel's star power was not enough to get audiences to watch *Viva Knievel!* The motorcycle daredevil's popularity had never recovered from the Snake Canyon jump, and audiences looking for earthbound stunts were already flocking to Burt Reynolds' movie *Smokey and the Bandit,* which had opened a month before *Viva Knievel*'s June, 1977 premiere.

Knievel himself would put the final nails in the coffin of his career a few months later when he took a baseball bat to promoter Shelly Saltman, who had authored an unflattering book on Knievel and the Snake Canyon jump after working with Knievel to publicize the jump in 1974. In the outcry and legal fallout from the assault (which took place outside the commissary on the 20th Century Fox lot), Knievel lost his lucrative marketing deals, did a few months of jail time and eventually declared bankruptcy.

Instead, *Star Wars* became a sensation. Audiences lined up around the block for the movie, many returning to see it five, ten times or more. In Dale Pollock's book *Skywalking: The Life and Films of George Lucas*, the author describes Irwin Allen viewing the long lines for *Star Wars* at the Mann's Chinese Theater in Hollywood from a restaurant across the street. Allen couldn't understand how a movie with "no stars" was attracting such enthusiastic audiences.

Allen, in fact, had had an unwitting close encounter with George Lucas, his wife (and *Star Wars* editor) Marcia, and the movie's producer Gary Kurtz three years before *Star Wars* opened, in the fall of 1975 when Fox, still in the afterglow of grosses from *The Towering Inferno*, declared Allen Fox's Showman of the Year and threw a dinner event celebrating Allen and a number of Fox productions and personnel. Seated a table away from Allen and his group was the Lucases and Kurtz, ensconced with Peter Fonda and Susan George of Fox's *Dirty Mary and Crazy Larry* (which was being released overseas at the time). Lucas and Kurtz were coming off their hit *American Graffiti* and had just started working with Fox on *Star Wars*.

It's mystifying how Allen was unable to see the appeal—or his own influence—on *Star Wars*. The film boasted a brassy, symphonic score from composer John Williams that at times riffed on Williams' brilliant brass triplet effects from Allen's *Lost in Space* series—Williams in fact acknowledged years later in an interview with author Jon Burlingame that *Lost in Space*, with its "robots and strange characters," was a warm-up for his work on *Star Wars*. The film's robotic comic relief, C-3PO and R2-D2, bore more than a passing resemblance to the dynamic of Dr. Smith (whose fussy, faux British accent and cowardice seemed transferred to Anthony Daniels' interpretation of C-3PO) and the Robot (whose squat, blue collar look and smart-mouthed sarcasm—even if it's never quite translated—inhabited R2-D2).

Allen's explosive, special-effects-filled television series had helped lay the groundwork for future science fiction universes, and his two disaster movies had laid the foundations of the special effects blockbusters that would completely dominate Hollywood's production cycle post-*Star Wars*. Even Allen's emphasis on action and adventure in his science fiction projects, as opposed to the thoughtful, allegory-rich sci-fi of Kubrick's *2001: A Space Odyssey*, proved prescient. Yet Allen, at least in June, 1977, was unable to stare into the face of *Star Wars* and see himself.

That would start to change as Allen elected to once again return to science fiction—and to the direct inspiration for his earliest stab at sci-fi, *Voyage to the Bottom of the Sea*. Allen had continued to work to develop TV series ideas for ABC, and in September, 1975, ABC's George C. Reeves wrote Allen's agent Herman Rush about three potential television projects that Allen would develop and deliver:

> ...A Circus project, a Swashbuckler project and a third project TBA. It is understood that Irwin Allen is going to lay-off the Circus project (if it goes forward) at Twentieth Century Fox...

The Circus project was Allen's attempt to keep his *Circus, Circus, Circus!* idea viable in the event that Fox elected not to back it as a motion picture. One of the other concepts turned into the pilot *Time Travelers*. And, by the end of October, 1975, Rush and Allen had hired writer Robert Malcolm Young to write something called *The Further Adventures of Captain Nemo*, "based on material developed by Irwin Allen, deliverable by December 1, 1975." On November 24, Allen alerted the

**ABOVE**

Promotional art for Allen's "mini-disaster movie" for television, *Flood!*

Writers Guild that he had created the "format, theme, characters, characterizations and settings" for *The Further Adventures of Captain Nemo*.

Nemo, of course, was the anti-hero of Jules Verne's novel *20,000 Leagues Under the Sea*, the chief inspiration—along with Walt Disney's 1954 live action movie adaptation—for Allen's *Voyage to the Bottom of the Sea* feature film and television series. Allen had been toying with the idea of transplanting Nemo's submarine Nautilus into the 20th century, and in June, 1976, he had an outline for a potential series—but one quite different from what would eventually develop out of the concept.

Allen's outline concerns Peter Nemo, "a 38-year-old oceanographer, expert engineer, and Captain in the United States Naval Reserve" with a wife and three children, and a fellow naval engineer at Groton named Franklin Jarvis. Nemo is summoned to a will reading where he learns he has inherited a secret island in the South Pacific, as well as a fortune, and the hidden submarine Nautilus, all from the legendary 19th century figure Captain Nemo. Peter Nemo learns that Captain Nemo was searching for Atlantis and takes the Nautilus out to complete his ancestor's search—with his family along for the voyage. ABC had purchased Allen's *Time Travelers* and aired it as a 90-minute TV movie in March of that year, and this fulfilled Allen's commitments to the network and allowed him to shop *Captain Nemo* to another network, CBS.

Allen had good reason to head to CBS to try to sell his *Captain Nemo* show. William Self had returned to the network after working for 15 years at 20th Century Fox, and after a year of co-producing feature films including John Wayne's last movie *The Shootist* and Charles Bronson's *From Noon Til Three*. Self, of course, had given Allen the original go-ahead to make *Voyage to the Bottom of the Sea* into a weekly TV series at Fox in 1964, and Allen gleefully reminded the CBS executive of that fact in his October 6, 1976 cover letter while sending over the *Captain Nemo* script ideas:

> Dear Bill: Shades of VOYAGE TO THE BOTTOM OF THE SEA! Enclosed herewith please find six episodes of the propose Irwin Allen-CBS project on "CAPTAIN NEMO." We have six writers anxiously standing by to move forward on completed screenplays.

The *Captain Nemo* concept had changed quite a bit since June. The idea of a family inheriting the Nautilus had been tossed, and Allen now returned to more traditional character models for the series: military men and scientists. The potential series' first script outline, entitled "Deadly Blackmail," opened during U.S. Navy exercises and had Cmdr. Tom Porter and Lt. Jim Franklin in a diving bell descending to the ocean bottom. They encounter a wrecked submarine, the Nautilus, and find onboard the relic a frozen Captain Nemo, who had been searching for the lost continent of Atlantis. The two men are assigned by the U.S. government to remain with Nemo onboard the Nautilus; meanwhile, a nuclear bomb has been assembled from stolen government ordnance and a warhead is aimed at Los Angeles, ransoming the city for $500 million.

Porter and Franklin discover that Nemo cannot leave his submarine for more than six hours or he will die. Using the Nautilus, Nemo, Porter, and Franklin intercept the battleship carrying the nuclear warhead and overpower the blackmailers, and Nemo uses a laser onboard the Nautilus to intercept the nuclear warhead and the battleship.

Other story ideas included "Monster of the Deep"—in which the Nautilus encounters a giant lobster—and "Terror in the Sea," in which Nemo and the Nautilus discover Atlantis after engaging an enemy submarine from a Middle Eastern country. The conflict in the show boiled down to a duel of wits between Nemo, a 19th-century genius thrust into the 20th century, and Waldo Cunningham, a ruthless, renegade scientific genius with his own super-submarine, the Raven.

In November, Allen saw the first project he'd begun for Warner Bros. after moving to the studio from Fox air on NBC. *Flood!* was a mini-disaster movie with a cast of Irwin Allen regulars: Martin Milner and Cameron Mitchell from *Swiss Family Robinson*, Richard Basehart from *Voyage to the Bottom of the Sea*, Carol Lynley and Roddy McDowall from *The Poseidon Adventure*, Whit Bissell, Francine York, and Elizabeth Rogers from his various other television productions, in a story that had a small town in Oregon threatened with a major flood after a dam bursts. *Flood!* didn't make much of a splash, although the *Los Angeles Times* review on November 24th was sympathetic:

> Dialogue and characterizations are at best standard, but the actual flood sequences are reasonably impressive for a movie-for-TV's small-scale image.

A month after *Flood!* aired, Allen had delivered the script for the second episode of *Captain Nemo* to CBS, and on January 12, 1977, the script for the third episode was finished and delivered. At this point *Star Wars* was only a worrisome blip on 20th Century Fox's accounting ledgers. As far as television was concerned, the only successful science fiction properties were two action-adventure shows based on the novel *Cyborg* by author Martin Caidin: *The Six Million Dollar Man* and *The Bionic Woman*. The first program had started as a series of TV-movies starring Lee Majors that ran on ABC in 1973 and launched as a weekly series in 1974; the spin-off *The Bionic Woman* debuted in 1976.

In early 1977, Irwin Allen's best way to gin up network excitement about a *Captain Nemo* series was to make it sound like his answer to *The Six Million Dollar Man*. Allen sent producer Paul Monash one of the *Captain Nemo* scripts with a cover letter saying:

> It's bigger than life and twice as exciting! As you read it, please be aware that it's intended to outdo *The Six Million Dollar Man* and *The Bionic Woman*—in short, it's the fourteen million dollar CAPTAIN NEMO.

By late February, however, production executive Arthur Weiss (who had a wealth of writing experience on underwater adventures including episodes of *Sea Hunt*, *Flipper*, *Voyage to the Bottom of the Sea* and the movie *Around the World Under the Sea*) questioned whether

Allen's rendering of Captain Nemo could really go head to head with Colonel Steve Austin. In a Warner Bros. memo, Weiss wrote Allen that the character of Nemo:

> ...Lacks the 'Nemo factor' which would give him the distinguished equivalent of the attributes of Superman or the Bionic Man, Batman, et al. I expect from Nemo: Mental genius, super-scientific techniques, heroic personality. I don't get this from him or what he does. In fact, Waldo [the story's villain] has the more formidable character and super-scientific techniques.

Weiss also noted that the teleplay's style "seems to waver, sometimes toward Batman (parody) or Bionic Man (bigger than life extension of science fact)." Weiss preferred the latter approach, but his concerns would highlight problems that would stick with the production until its ultimate network airing.

*The Return of Captain Nemo* (as the project came to be known) showed Irwin Allen struggling with a changing production landscape and changing tastes in Hollywood. Had he made the show in the 1960s at Fox, the production would have looked more spectacular and been far easier to put together. But, having left Fox for Warner Bros., Allen was now figuratively at sea, without the production facilities that had allowed him to put out 30-odd episodes of *Voyage to the Bottom of the Sea* a year for four years.

Allen began by reaching out to MGM about using their sets and the miniature submarine from 1968's *Ice Station Zebra*. According to the studio, a torpedo room and enlisted men's quarters, engine room and control room, plus a six foot miniature "Nautilus" (actually called the USS Tigerfish in the film and portrayed by the real-life sub USS Ronquil, which was quite similar to the U.S. Navy's nuclear submarine Nautilus) were all built for $225,000 in 1968 and rentable for $30,000.

By May 13, 1977, this idea quickly became the shooting plan for much of *The Return of Captain Nemo*. Production coordinator Art Volpert wrote Richard Kobritz:

> Heads up that the MGM Polaris sub sets will be used for a Polaris sub in the miniseries and redressed as the Nautilus, shooting as Polaris for seven days and Nautilus for four, suggest shooting at MGM to save costs of packing and moving sets. Another big factor is the availability of the tank at MGM to shoot thirteen days of miniatures at a minimal charge, eliminating costly construction of a tank or going to CBS Studio Center to rent theirs. MGM will also give us miniature subs scaled to their tanks.

By May, CBS had agreed to three 2-hour *Captain Nemo* segments at $600,000 per segment for a total of $1,800,000, positioning the show as a special miniseries. Allen's special effects supervisor L.B. Abbott discussed the idea of using a water tank in Malta that was one of the largest in the world and had been constructed and used on major film productions since 1964. Abbott was also looking into rehabilitating the facilities at Fox, but they had deteriorated considerably—the sky backing at the Sersen tank at Fox ranch had been in disrepair even during the filming of *The Poseidon Adventure,* and by this point the huge tank had been drained and was largely inoperable. Abbott

**ABOVE**
Jose Ferrer as Captain Nemo, with costars Burr DeBenning (right) and Tom Hallick (background).

The shark-like Nautilus—a two-foot-long miniature designed for *The Return of Captain Nemo* by Eugène Lourié.

**OPPOSITE**
The 8-1/2 foot Seaview miniature from *Voyage to the Bottom of the Sea*, severely modified—but never used—for *The Return of Captain Nemo*'s "bad guy" submarine, the Raven.

"stormtrooper" androids which were virtually identical to the golden "Raddion" android from the *Lost in Space* episode "The Dream Monster." The most audacious touch, worked out by Allen and Eugène Lourié, was a hull-mounted "delta ray" turret on the Raven that was operated by a gold-faced midget android who took firing orders from Tor.

Despite these touches, Meredith's comical performance, straight out of his Penguin persona from the 1966 *Batman* series, undermined any attempt to get at the *Star Wars* mystique. Director Alex March labored for a more grounded tone, but Allen wouldn't have it.

Noting that Allen and much of his team were focused on preparing *The Day the World Ended* and were coming off work on *The Swarm* (Jose Ferrer even shot a small part for *The Swarm* during an on-set break from his work as Nemo), Joe Musso said:

> Alex was trying to do *Star Wars* and Irwin wasn't letting him—Irwin was doing *Voyage to the Bottom of the Sea* gone wrong. Irwin and Alex March got into a big fight at the end and they weren't even talking, because Alex wanted final cut. He said, "My name's going on it." They were buddies from way back but by the end they weren't talking and Irwin was picking takes that Alex didn't like. Alec would try to cut it a certain way and Irwin would go in and change it.

Interviewed by *The Oregon Journal* the day before *Captain Nemo*'s March 8, 1978 premiere on CBS, Allen was almost defiant, bridling at comparisons between the show and *Star Wars*—all while describing Nemo as "*Star Wars* under the sea":

> I'm the fellow who did all of the *Star Wars* tricks—the laser beams and the gadgetry—as long as 15 years ago. I take great pride to do it again and I don't have to take my hat off to anyone else!

The next day he continued the argument with journalist Dennis Washburn:

> I was doing this sort of thing for a lot of years before *Star Wars* was ever an idea. And what has happened over the years is that the optical effects and trick photography have advanced so far that we can do a lot of things now that we couldn't back in the days of *Voyage to the Bottom of the Sea*.

*The Return of Captain Nemo* aired over three weeks, on March 8, 15th and 22nd on CBS, and television reviewers in the spring doldrums largely recognized the series as unreformed pulp.

Dave Montoro stated in *The Florida Times-Union*:

> ...A slick and entertaining piece aimed at viewers with a taste for escapist entertainment...Has a grand presence that is perfect for the part. When the veteran actor says that he has been in suspended animation for a century, you can't help but take him seriously. Meredith, though, almost is recreating the comic book character of Penguin he developed in the *Batman* series. That's not really bad since this show is designed to have two-dimensional bad guys, but it's still

**LEFT**
Burgess Meredith holds court with the mighty Tor on the elaborate bridge of the Raven in *The Return of Captain Nemo*.

amusing. Tor could be taken straight out of a Boris Karloff movie. It's so reminiscent of those B-grade horror flicks that it's funny.

Having said that, Montoro added:

> Cliches aside, "Nemo" is decent early evening fare with a big enough budget to allow for fine special effects and a striking musical score. Congratulations, Mr. Allen, it's not a disaster after all."

Ruth Koch of *The Florida Sun-Tattler* largely agreed:

> ...Not a great show. But it is a lot of fun, especially with Ferrer in the lead. ...great television escapist fun in the true tradition of Irwin Allen.

Joe Musso remembers not all the notices being so kind:

> One of the reviews he got for *Captain Nemo* said, "If you like *20,000 Leagues Under the Sea* you're probably going to hate *Captain Nemo*. In fact if you liked anything in any kind of movie you're probably going to hate *Captain Nemo*." Irwin brought that in and said, "Why don't they like me anymore?"

*The Return of Captain Nemo* was tough viewing even for fans of Allen's original TV shows—by 1978 the kids who had been thrilled by Allen's earlier shows were nearly out of high school, and Nemo's campy villain, robot sidekick, and risible dialogue (at one point one of the heroes blurts, "We're headed lickety split in the opposite direction of heaven!") made *Voyage to the Bottom of the Sea* and its relatively sober acting performances seem sophisticated by comparison. Jose Ferrer played Nemo as a man well aware of his own legend, brimming with self-confidence and bravado along with a cool intelligence. One has to wonder whether Allen saw a bit of himself in the character—Nemo comes off as a combination of Irwin Allen and Mr. Spock, and seen from the perspective of modern Hollywood age-ism, it's exciting to watch the still-trim Ferrer taking the lead in the show's action scenes, even taking on the younger Mel Ferrer in a sword-fight (Allen pointed out in one publicity interview that *Captain Nemo* marked the first time Jose Ferrer and Mel Ferrer had worked together onscreen—but in fact the two actors weren't related).

Ferrer's charisma, however, was undercut by Burgess Meredith's comical vamping, and two male leads so handsome and uninteresting that they all but disappeared into the show's set design.

Composer Richard LaSalle (who had worked on *Lost in Space* and *Land of the Giants*) had often been encouraged by Allen to imitate music from other, familiar movie scores—he recycled his *City Beneath the Sea* theme for *Captain Nemo*, along with snippets from Jerry Goldsmith's *Planet of the Apes* score (which he had also referenced in *City Beneath the Sea*), and even Bernard Herrmann's *Vertigo*.

At one point the show presented a wholesale pastiche of the prison cell corridor shootout from *Star Wars*, with the actors firing lasers on a similarly-designed corridor set and LaSalle's score blatantly quoting John Williams' *Star Wars* rebel fanfare. *Star Wars*, in fact, was still in theaters when *Captain Nemo* aired, making the show's attempt to be "*Star Wars* underwater" even more transparent.

Frank Van der Veer (the veteran photographic effects supervisor who had done many of the effects for the original *Star Trek* and handled the composites and laser beams on *Nemo*) and L.B. Abbott were nominated for an Emmy Award for *The Return of Captain Nemo*. But with the submarine miniatures limited to an unimpressive two feet in length and often shot dry-for-wet, the special effects couldn't match the scope and grandeur of the best work on *Voyage to the Bottom of the Sea* from a decade earlier, and Van der Veer's optical overlays of swirling underwater silt made a lot of the action difficult to make out. For a sequence of the Nautilus becoming trapped in a minefield, L.B. Abbott and Allen simply reused the 17-year-old footage of the minefield from the *Voyage to the Bottom of the Sea* movie, compositing the Nautilus miniature over it. Much more impressive were the underwater diving sequences supervised by Paul Stader and shot off the coast of Catalina—with scuba divers chasing each other and firing laser beams back and forth.

CBS seemed satisfied with the miniseries' ratings and suggested an addition to the cast in a March 15th memo from writer Norman Katlov to Allen. CBS wanted:

> ...A girl aboard the Nautilus. She is an Annapolis graduate, a Lieutenant (equal with Jim). She's bright. Her presence creates a little animosity from Tom and Jim, a mild resentment over her "privileges" as a woman, i.e., she gets a cabin to herself; Tom and Jim must share a cabin; some competition over her between Tom and Jim. She should be introduced in story #1 when we go into a series. A girl in jeopardy is more dramatic.

By the time *Nemo* had finished its three-episode run, however, the network's enthusiasm had dimmed, and the show never went forward as a network series. It would be the last science fiction program that Irwin Allen would ever get on television.

Allen did have one last science fiction project in his quiver—but this one would bring new meaning to the phrase "Master of Disaster."

**OPPOSITE**
Poster art for an overseas theatrical release of *The Return of Captain Nemo*, repackaged as *The Amazing Captain Nemo*.

> **"**
> ### WHEN WE ARE DISMISSED BY THE CRITICS WE FEEL BADLY. NO ONE KNOWS ALL THE WORK THAT GOES INTO ONE OF THESE MOVIES.
>
> IRWIN ALLEN

# BAD BUZZ

*Allen finally wins back the director's chair—but* **THE SWARM** *becomes a real disaster*

**OPPOSITE**
Irwin Allen directing a bee-covered stunt player in his ill-fated disaster movie *The Swarm*.

Irwin Allen's celebrated move from 20th Century Fox to Warner Bros. had been made with a single goal in mind: to give Allen the opportunity, finally, to put his name as a director on his blockbuster theatrical movies. With projects like *The Day the World Ended* and *Circus, Circus, Circus!* still in development, Allen geared up a movie idea that had been intended as a lower-budgeted side project and shifted it into production as his next major motion picture.

Allen had been intrigued by newspaper stories about the migration of aggressive, "Africanized" bees from South America toward the United States since the early 1960s. Africanized bees were hybrids of western honey bees and African honey bees, introduced in Brazil in the 1950s with the intent of increasing honey production. But, after some of the bee hybrids escaped in 1957, they began to breed with and dominate local bee hive populations and move inexorably northward toward the U.S.

Because of the aggressive nature of the Africanized bees and the way their easily-disturbed hives unleashed swarms of stinging "warrior" bees, these bees became known as "killer bees," and by the early 1970s there was a sense of urgency and even a little panic, particularly in regions like the Southwest and California, which would be on the vanguard of the killer bee invasion when the species reached the United States. In 1974, author Arthur Herzog wrote a book called *The Swarm*, and Allen quickly pursued the rights. If novels had inspired *The Poseidon Adventure* and *The Towering Inferno*, why not a movie about killer bees invading the U.S.?

20th Century Fox purchased rights to Herzog's novel in May of 1974, announcing that it was to be made by Irwin Allen Productions. Allen had a treatment for *The Swarm* from Stirling Silliphant by July 5, 1974—while *The Towering Inferno* was still in production. The normally critical Arthur Weiss responded enthusiastically in a July 9th memo to Allen: "Treatment indicates the

hair-raising, gripping shocking potential of picture." Weiss's memo indicated that the film would contain scenes of "mass death" in Pittsburgh, Marysville, and New York, adding, "Nobody follows scientific explanations and theory: cut them to bone where they are absolutely necessary."

Herzog's novel had opened with an attack by a swarm of bees on a family picnicking outside New York City, but its focus thereafter had been somewhat technical and scientific—Herzog even introduced graphs, medical charts and computer readouts. This was an approach used to incredible success by author Michael Crichton in his novel *The Andromeda Strain*, which had become a sensational best-seller in 1969, and was made into an absorbing suspense film by Robert Wise in 1971. Crichton's novel—and Wise's film—were plausible and realistic, which made the story of government attempts to investigate and control a space-born virus all the more terrifying. With the threat of the Africanized honey bees earthbound and very real, *The Swarm* had the potential to be even more gripping, and Allen's keen sense of promotion told him that he would be able to use news headlines about the approaching, real-life bee invasion to promote his movie.

Allen reached out to Arthur Herzog to get the author's feedback on Silliphant's screenplay as it developed. By September 30, 1975, Herzog had begun a lengthy and detailed correspondence with Allen, which the producer initially welcomed, incorporating many of the author's suggestions—but as production went on, Allen increasingly ignored the author's input. In his Sept. 30 letter, Herzog praised Silliphant's script while noting that it had "some serious flaws":

> My basic objection to Stirling's work has to do with what I and the reviewers found strong about *Swarm*, that is, realism. There are places where the story in your version lacks credibility.

In the book, the character that would become Michael Caine's Brad Crane was an environmental scientist with the National Academy of Sciences. The screenplay described Crane as "an industrial reformer."

Herzog was unimpressed:

> I don't know what that is and neither will anyone else. And why should an industrial reformer—use say Ralph Nader as a model—know anything about bees? How does he support himself? Why would scientists accept him? The audience has to cope with a credibility problem right away and it's distracting.

Herzog objected to Allen's opening the film at the military outpost ("I keep thinking that *Andromeda Strain* opened like this"), thought Crane's appearance at the military base was unbelievable, and that Allen should open the film with civilians and Herzog's scene of the bee attack on the picnic:

> Let me say parenthetically that credibility would be increased by saying a little more clearly that bees *live* somewhere. They just don't fly around as the script suggests.

Nevertheless, after four pages of detailed criticism in this vein, Herzog said:

> I think it'll be a great film even if you use the present script.

Then he added something that had to be music to Allen's ears:

> ...and I hope you direct it as I've heard you will.

After Allen relocated to Warner Bros. in the summer of 1975, Warners announced that *The Swarm* would be Allen's first multi-million dollar project for the studio.

"Only Irwin Allen could undertake a picture of this type," Frank Wells said in a press release. "It is not only a classic Irwin Allen disaster film, but it's also a giant spectacle about survival with awesome scope."

*Variety* reported that the movie would be filming in South America, Mexico, Houston, Washington and Alaska, but apart from some shots obtained in Houston, all of *The Swarm* would be shot in and around the Warner Bros. studios in Burbank.

As the production moved forward, Allen brought writer David Zelag Goodman onboard to rewrite Silliphant's script. Goodman had written the hyper-violent *Straw Dogs* for director Sam Peckinpah as well as the period gumshoe movie *Farewell, My Lovely*. He had also worked on adapting the science fiction adventure *Logan's Run* for MGM and seemed suitable for a sci-fi project like *The Swarm*. Goodman's initial rewrite was received well by Allen, but Allen was now ensconced at Warner Bros., and at least two of the studio's production executives, Paula Weinstein and Tina Nides, had serious concerns about the screenplay, which they related to David Geffen and Frank Wells in a June 8, 1976 memo:

> The basic problem with THE SWARM is that unlike all the successful disaster pictures to date, it is so removed from reality as to be neither frightening nor exciting. The problem with the David Z. Goodman script is that it ignores reality: we are never convinced that the situation he has set up could happen to us. There are no characters for us to care about...it would be far better to return to the Silliphant script which, at the very least, gives us fuller characters but most of all explains the reason the bees attack and lays the responsibility fully on our shoulders.

In keeping with his work on *Logan's Run*, Goodman had developed a fanciful sci-fi/fantasy concept in which "bees have evolved to a higher level and can differentiate between good and evil." This was an idea that had been toyed with in a couple of other insect-focused science fiction films, Saul Bass's directorial debut *Phase IV*, about intelligent ant colonies experimenting on humankind, and *The Hellstrom Chronicle*, a documentary-like feature implying that insects all around the world were intelligent societies preparing to engage in direct competition with human civilization.

The memo suggested that the movie open with the bee attack on the missile base instead of its aftermath, and to turn the Brad Crane character into more of a "maverick,

**OPPOSITE**
Production paintings by Joe Musso indicating some of the potential intensity and scope of *The Swarm*.

take-charge character" who butts heads with the establishment and military leaders and leads the way to solving the bee problem.

The readers went on to damn Allen's project with faint praise:

> We have detailed some ways in which to improve what we basically believe is an exploitation film. Let's have this be a picture where we can care about our central characters as we did in TOWERING INFERNO and JAWS.

Allen's associate Al Gail also chimed in on the script, agreeing that the Brad Crane character, while "well-drawn" needed to be responsible for the vanquishing of the bees at the film's climax, noting that in the book Henry Fonda's character of Dr. Krim is the man most responsible for solving the problem.

The reference to *Jaws* in the Weinstein/Nides memo is telling. It had been a year since *Jaws* had become an unprecedented box office phenomenon, and *The Swarm* was now part of a wave of "nature strikes back" imitators that included *Grizzly, Day of the Animals, Orca,* and a veritable swarm of killer bee projects. Allen in fact had already been beaten to the punch by *The Deadly Bees*, a horror film from Amicus Productions released in 1966. Gloria Swanson had starred in 1974's *Killer Bees* (a casting that Allen himself would have surely approved of), Ben Johnson had starred in a TV movie called *The Savage Bees* that would be broadcast in November, and John Saxon would soon be cast in *The Bees* for a 1978 release. NBC's late night sketch show *Saturday Night Live* had been lampooning the idea since at least early 1975 in a series of comedy sketches with John Belushi wearing a black and yellow bee costume with comic, dangling antenna, crying "we are…THE KILLER BEES!" in an exaggerated Mexican accent. The onus was on Allen to make *The Swarm* the kind of spectacular production that would bury its imitators and critics.

Stirling Silliphant returned to the project in late June and wrote Sidney Marshall and Al Gail on July 1st. One of the biggest issues with *The Swarm* thus far had been the story's characters. Irwin Allen had wrestled with the appeal of science fiction since his first work in the genre, swearing off the genre briefly after 1961's *Voyage to the Bottom of the Sea* feature, then spending the better part of the next decade at 20th Century Fox defining himself as a sci-fi producer as he cranked out the *Voyage* TV series, *Lost in Space, The Time Tunnel, Land of the Giants,* and *City Beneath the Sea*. With *The Poseidon Adventure* and *The Towering Inferno,* he had finally found the formula to combine spectacle and special effects with strong, relatable characters—everyday people thrown into outsized, terrifying situations. But *The Swarm*'s characters hewed back to Allen's old standbys, the archetypes that had populated his science fiction shows: scientists and military men. The challenge for *The Swarm* was to find a way to get ordinary people into the narrative.

To solve part of the problem, Silliphant suggested a septuagenarian love triangle involving a school teacher, a town pharmacist, and a rancher. The script described what would become Olivia de Havilland's teacher character as a "Maureen Stapleton-Shelley Winters type" and suggested Red Buttons for the role of the town pharmacist who would be played eventually by Fred MacMurray (Ben Johnson, already a veteran of at least one killer bee movie, would play the rancher). Silliphant also outlined 14 other townspeople characters to round out the story, and suggested cameo roles for Robert Wagner and Natalie Wood as a couple driving through the county who come under attack. By focusing on the townspeople, Silliphant hoped to make "our main characters less austere, less coldly scientific and more human in their own right."

In the meantime, Allen was faced with the enormous technical challenge of realizing the film's most important characters: the bees.

He had determined early on that the bee swarms would have to be realized via a combination of real bees, practical effects created on set and on location by Howard Jensen, and photographic effects by L.B. Abbott and his team. Of course today, *The Swarm*'s visual effects would be easily accomplished using computer generated imagery—software programs designed to generate swarms of visible, moving particles, and even elaborate CGI characters, have been in use now for years. But in 1976, techniques like this hadn't even been imagined. Allen and his crew would have to find a way to

**ABOVE**

Fred MacMurray, Olivia de Havilland, and Ben Johnson, the old-time stars in *The Swarm*'s small-town love triangle—an attempt to get some relatable characters into a story dominated by scientists and soldiers.

**ABOVE**
Storyboards for a dropped scene that pits the African bees against American honeybees.

control the movement of live bees, recreate the look of swarming bees by blowing large particles through the air with fans, and create some kind of visual overlay that would recreate the look of massive, airborne swarms of bees for long shots.

Allen's production schedule from mid-1976 through early 1977 included writing and polishing the screenplay; meetings with bee experts; viewing insect films; surveying bee farms; positioning bees and equipment; hiring sketch artists for the action sequences; having L.B. Abbott position specialized photographic equipment in London to do bee macrophotography; determining how the bee sequences would be shot and composited and what special equipment would need to be built to do so; doing tests with bees and people to find ways of filming the bee attacks; creating latex masks for bee attack victims; doing photographic testing of real bees, simulated bees, and artificial bees; building models of the more elaborate sets; doing location surveys—and all of this was merely preproduction before principal photography and the special photography of live bees.

A February 10, 1977 memo from Allen to Charles Greenlaw stated that Allen had had his first "Method-Concept Meetings" with key personnel to "determine and refine all production problems as they related to each sequence."

One of the effects Allen and his art department had worked out was the idea that victims suffering from stings from the marauding bees would experience hallucinations of giant bees looming in front of them. In February the production approached George D. Dodge and Dale R. Thompson of Dodge-Thompson Photography "regarding macro-photography to shoot macro closeups of 'bee's eye and head,' Giant size bee in room (part of hallucination sequence)" at $200/day and a total of $2,100.00. Dodge and Thompson added Ariflex and Mark II camera and film and developing costs for a total of $4,100.00.

On April 15, 1977, Allen offered the lead role of Brad Crane to Burt Reynolds, who had just opened *Smokey and the Bandit* and was at the height of his box office star status. However, in Allen's view (at least according to the tone of his letter), he was doing Reynolds a favor:

> All good things come to those who wait and deserve—you and I waited long enough and we sure as hell deserve each other. You are our unanimous and only choice to play the lead. I do believe that you, together with an all-star cast, will make THE SWARM another TOWERING INFERNO or POSEIDON ADVENTURE—and that's not half bad. ... warmly looking forward to making millions of dollars with you!

The same day Allen wrote Warner Bros.' Frank Wells to assure him that, "Burt is ready and willing subject only to script approval" to make sure that Wells would be okay with any salary request from Reynolds.

Two Southern California beekeepers, Gary and Bob Varney, had written production manager Norman Cook to offer their services in wrangling the enormous

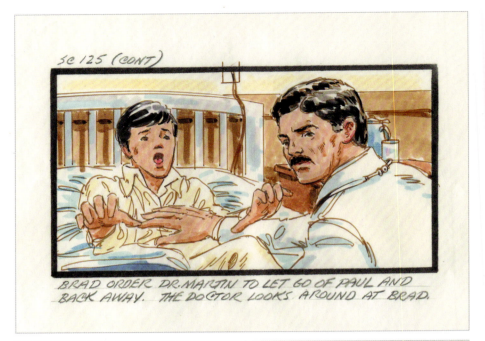

**ABOVE**
Storyboards for the giant bee hallucinations to be suffered by bee-stung characters in the movie.

**ABOVE**
Production illustrator Joe Musso (right) on the Warner Bros. lot with a container of live bees ready to be released for the picnic sequence.

**FOLLOWING**
Storyboard art for the movie's opening helicopter sequence and the "bee picnic," complete with sexy, bee-stung mom.

amount of live bees necessary to shoot the movie's attack scenes. Their letter, dated April 22, 1977, noted that exact cost and schedule estimates could not be provided because there was not a shot breakdown at the time the letter was written:

> We must purchase and make extensive use of pheromones which will be used in the handling of the bees during photography, and will be the single most important clue to the amount of time each shot will take.

Second:

> If the picture is to commence photography in August of this year, we need to begin immediately building colony population and preparing for all other production needs. This is a multi-month process and must start immediately…

Varney indicated that the pheromone tests and colony growth would cost $30,000.00 and take four to six weeks for the population of 600 colonies, requiring the purchase of 600 queen bees and other bees as needed. Ultimately, the production had to pay the two men enough to cover the income they would have made over two years of operation of their business, due to the amount of time and resources building the bee colonies for *The Swarm* would eat up.

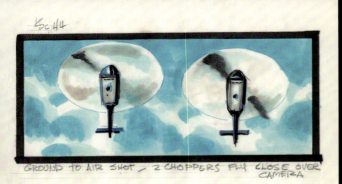

Sc 44 — GROUND TO AIR SHOT — 2 CHOPPERS FLY CLOSE OVER CAMERA

Sc 42 — SAME SET UP AS Sc 39 — TWO CHOPPERS HEAD SOUTH

Sc. 44 INT HELICOPTER #1   CLOSE ON THE LEAD PILOT

PILOT'S STUNNING SHOCK REACTION TO........

Sc 45   COMPOSITE — MOVING WITH THE FLIGHT OF BEES OVER THE TEXAS COUNTRYSIDE —

Sc. 46   COMPOSITE WITH PELLETS — BLUE SCREEN — AIR TO GROUND PLATE
INT. HELICOPTER #1 — ANGLED OVER PILOT — LOOK OUT AT THE SWARM BELOW HIM —

Sc. 47 — BEES COME FROM BEHIND CAMERA AND SMASH INTO WINDSHIELD — DISORIENTING PILOT

Sc 48   COMPOSITE WITH PELLETS — CAMERA FOLLOWS THE #1 CHOPPER AS IT COMES DOWN & CRASHES INTO THE MOUNTAIN SIDE —

Sc. 50   INT. HELICOPTER #2   ANGLE ON THE SECOND PILOT.
THE PILOT REACTS TO SOMETHING O.S. HE ALMOST WHISPERS INTO HIS HELMUT MIKE: "OH MY GOD!... BEES! MILLIONS OF BEES!"

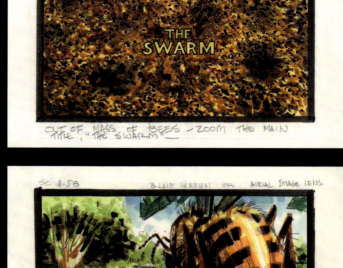

A May 12, 1977 memo from Arlyn Irving to Norman Cook discussed "possible useful effects" included:

> Robbing Bees—Large amounts of feed put out daily in shallow trays...will attract hundreds of thousands of bees, resulting in a struggling, fighting nearly berserk mass of bees [that would] follow a direct path from their hive to the food supply. A swarm (a mass hanging on a limb) can be made artificially by hand shaking the bees from a hive onto a branch placed on the ground. It can be picked up and used where wanted. When ready the mass of bees can be shook on the ground in front of the hive and they will walk to the hive and enter in a mass like a flock of sheep.

On July 19, Allen alerted his staff that he needed *The Swarm*'s cast locked up by the end of the week, with photography scheduled to begin on August 10th. Locations had been approved with the exception of one at Redlands for shooting of full-sized trains (a subsequent train wreck would be shot in miniature).

Allen told *The Los Angeles Times*:

> This will be a survival movie, not a disaster movie. The sense of survival is one of the strongest senses in man— stronger than mother love, hunger or sex. This story is going to be about how the world survives when nature goes crazy. I have set out to make the most terrifying survival picture of all time.

Fred Koenekamp, Oscar-winner for *The Towering Inferno*, was onboard as cinematographer. A company had been chosen to supply miniature trains and helicopters in the same way that miniature helicopters had been rented for *The Towering Inferno*. But Allen had lost at least one key collaborator, production designer Bill Creber. Among Allen's staff, Creber was known as one of the few men who could say, "no" to Irwin Allen, and after *The Towering Inferno*, Creber had found himself at odds with the Master of Disaster.

40 years later, Creber recalled:

> In his eyes he was invincible. After the success of *The Poseidon Adventure* and the success of *The Towering Inferno*, he had a syndrome—this is my opinion—but he had an ego, that's for sure, and so did I. You don't do that kind of work without one. There are times when you just have to say, "Wait a minute, that's the wrong way." I worked with directors who were very positive and directors who were negative but most of the time I was lucky and guys respected what I had to say.

Creber's final falling out with Allen occurred over a simple request that, to Creber, demonstrated that the mega-producer now viewed the experienced production designer as little more than an assistant:

> We were in quite a sizable meeting and he was very proud of his office, and he said, "Excuse me guys... Bill, would you go straighten that picture?" And that did it. It was as simple as that.

Stan Jolley, a veteran of Allen's TV shows with feature experience on the films *Walking Tall* and *Drum*, would design *The Swarm*, utilizing the Warner Bros. backlot for

**ABOVE**
Production designer Stan Jolley's futuristic, underground military compound set—with actor Bradford Dillman (left) outfitted in what looks like one of the old Seaview crewmens' jumpsuits—opposite Richard Widmark (center) and Michael Caine.

Olivia de Havilland and Fred MacMurray with Allen.

**LEFT**
Early sequence of an unfortunate helicopter pilot encountering "Bees! Bees! Millions of bees!" The sequence featured a seamless cut from full scale helicopter footage to a miniature radio controlled helicopter diving in a long trajectory straight into a mountainside and exploding.

**OPPOSITE**
Storyboard art for a sequence of boys goading the bees and hiding under garbage cans from the swarm.

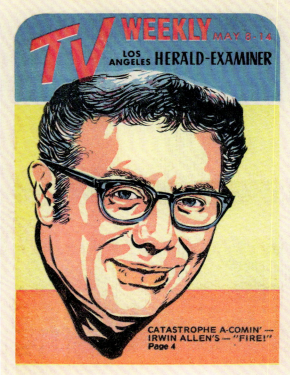

the village square of the small town under assault by the bees, and bringing the distinctive "Irwin Allen Look" to an underground military instillation that forms the location for much of the action and dialogue in the first half of the film. The military base would boast rows of computer screens, blinking lights, and two-way TV screens that would raise and lower their way into the shot for conversations between the main characters and Washington.

Artists Tom Cranham and Joe Musso were assigned to create a concept for the story's nuclear plant under the direction of Jolley and L.B. Abbott—this would ultimately take a fanciful, *Time Tunnel*-like approach—one year after the eventual release of *The Swarm*, *The China Syndrome*'s realistic depiction of a nuclear reactor would make *The Swarm*'s look ridiculous.

By August 7, Stirling Silliphant had turned in his final script polish, and Arthur Herzog continued to write Irwin Allen with inquiries and comments about the production. Herzog was eager to be invited to the set. Overall he was happy with the changes he had seen in Silliphant's later script drafts:

> It is a terrific script. Infinitely better than the first one I saw. Great action, colorful effects, good characters, etc.

Herzog's criticisms still turned on "the issue of credibility" and he reminded Allen that, while working on the novelization of *Orca* for Dino de Laurentiis, he had warned the writer and producer that the film would have problems because of its lack of credibility, and that his criticism was born out by the failure of the film.

Herzog zeroed in on one of the most risible early scenes in the movie, when a helicopter pilot, getting his first sight of the Swarm, blurts out "Oh my God! Bees! Bees! Millions of bees!"—the author suggested some more believable lines of dialogue needed to lead up to this moment. Herzog also, across four pages of suggestions, continued to criticize the character of Crane, how he reaches his conclusions, and how he is granted authority throughout the story.

The author ended the lengthy list of suggestions with one more: "I could, of course, write this additional stuff myself and very quickly."

Having gotten no response to this suggestion, a week later Herzog wrote to assure Allen that he could use any material he wanted from the previous letter without obligation and again asked when Allen planned to shoot the film in Los Angles. Allen wrote back on August 19, assuring Herzog that his suggestions were helpful and enclosing the latest version of the script, noting that shooting was to commence on August 22nd and that Herzog was welcome to attend.

On the first day of shooting, Jeffrey Berg wrote Warner Bros.' Jack Freedman to complain after seeing a trade ad in Variety crediting the screenplay to Silliphant before the credits had gone to Writers Guild arbitration: "David Z. Goodman wrote three drafts of this script and I think it is improper to indicate 'screenplay by 'credits at this time."

**ABOVE**

Promotional art for Allen's 1977 TV-movie *Fire*.

Allen's face graces the cover of the *L.A. Herald-Examiner's TV Weekly*.

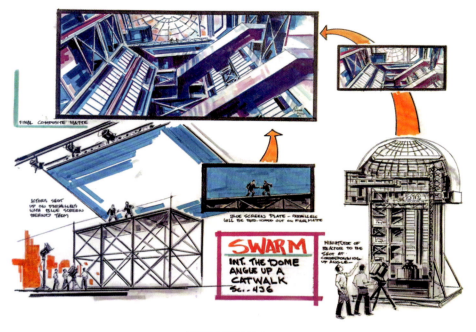

Even worse for Allen, Burt Reynolds sent a telegram to the producer after bowing out of the film. The telegram read, "Sorry I can't be with you. Happy Swarm!"

Herzog was trying to make arrangements to join the shoot, but after not hearing from Allen for a couple of weeks, on Oct. 10, he wrote again noting that he was under a tight schedule on a new book and wanted a detailed indication from Allen of his shooting schedule and when the best time would be to visit. Herzog's growing impatience with Allen was hinted at in his wrap-up:

> I don't much like the idea of landing blind in LA, going to Burbank and hammering at the door. So, in view of our mutually beneficial cooperation, I do hope you'll get right back to me.

It's questionable whether Allen was losing patience with Herzog or whether he was just too busy with other matters to respond to the author. In addition to the complex production of *The Swarm*, Allen was also shepherding a series of television projects to completion. His TV-movie *Fire!* had aired in May, with *The Los Angeles Times* review noting, "By now, producer Irwin Allen's disaster formula is pretty predictable." Nevertheless, the newspaper declared that *Fire!* was an improvement on the previous TV-movie, *Flood!* (with *Flood!* and *Fire!* out, one had to wonder if there was an "Irwin Allen's production of *Famine!*" waiting in the wings). The review noted that *Fire!* "benefits from its brisk pacing and sense of scope."

Herman Rush and Allen had also worked out a deal to make a movie called *Cable Car*, which would eventually be titled *Hanging By A Thread*, as the first film in a second group of projects for NBC. After the cable car movie, Allen and Rush had *Cave-In* and something called *Gambler's Special* in the works. Allen and Rush also had three two-hour movies planned for CBS at $1.3 million each, with Warner Bros. investing $650,000 in them for foreign theatrical distribution.

Paul Monash of CBS had suggested optioning the book *Twister* (a treatment had been done by Herman Groves) but Herman Rush suggested dispensing with the commitment by finding a single subject for a six-hour miniseries. Added to all of this was production on *The Return of Captain Nemo*, which coincided with work on *The Swarm*.

Nevertheless, by December 22, Allen still hadn't written Herzog, and the author's letters were becoming increasingly passive-aggressive:

> I hope I have better luck with this letter than the last, which wasn't answered. I confess to being vaguely surprised in view of my attempts to help. Anyway, I hope you will mention the novel in your future ads—the recent ones didn't.

Herzog apparently never got to watch his novel being filmed as *The Swarm* was well into postproduction by this point. Allen had delivered his director's cut on December 12th—it was this version, 156 minutes in length, that would be scored by composer Jerry Goldsmith. Previews for the film were to be held on March 24.

**ABOVE**
Joe Musso's "movie magic" artwork for *The Swarm*'s nuclear power plant—done very much in the style of the futuristic power plant for Allen's *The Time Tunnel*, and a concept that would be dated by the movie *The China Syndrome* a year later.

**RIGHT**
The nuclear power plant explosion sequence as it appears in the film.

**FOLLOWING**
Storyboards for the nuclear power plant explosion sequence.

SC. 435 SECOND UNIT - MINIATURE MATTE

EXT. NUCLEAR POWER STATION - DAY

SC. 436

INT. THE DOME - ANGLE UP A CATWALK  (STAGE)
(ABBOTT & 1ST UNIT)
(BLUE SCREEN - PLUS PLATE)

spanning the huge area. HUBBARD and ANDREWS, a top executive
of Southern Power and Energy Corporation, are walking.

SC A. 436

INT. THE DOME - ANGLE UP A CATWALK  (STAGE)
(ABBOTT & 1ST UNIT)
(BLUE SCREEN -
PLUS PLATE)

Hubbard and ANDREWS, a top executive of Southern Power
and Energy Corporation, are walking. They come to a
stop near an observation balcony, look down,

SC. 441

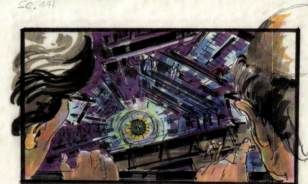

HIGH DOWN ANGLE - PAST HUBBARD AND ANDREWS  (STAGE)
(ABBOTT & 1ST UNIT)
(BLUE SCREEN)

A stunning monolithic structure that houses the
atomic reactor. Pulsating red globes encased in
circular strands of gleaming titanium reflect the
throbbing heart of the atomic pile.

SC. 458  BLUE SCREEN WITH MINIATURE PLATE

TECHNICIANS TRYING TO ESCAPE -
TOWARD CAMERA WHEN CATWALK
FALLS OUT OF SCENE - MAN RUNS
GIVES WAY -

SC. 458-A  BLUE SCREEN WITH MINIATURE PLATE

TECHNICIAN ON FIRE AND PIECE OF CATWALK FALLS IN B.G.
(DOLL IN MINIATURE SET) - FIGURES CATCHING ON FIRE
RUN IN F.G.

Sc 459 — MINIATURE
MOLTEN FUEL BEGINS TO SPLASH UP TOWARDS THE CONTAINMENT DOME —

Sc 461 — F.G. PEOPLE & BLUE SCREEN PLUS MINIATURE PLATE
GEYSERS OF STEAM BLASTS OUT THE GAPS IN THE DOME

Sc 461-A — MINIATURE
A GIANT FIREBALL BLASTS UP AS THE BREEDER REACTOR GOES

LAP DISSOLVE TO:

Sc 461-B
THE FIREBALL EXPLOSION FILLS THE SCREEN

Sc 462 — MINIATURE
THE NUCLEAR POWER PLANT — LONG SHOT — EXPLOSIONS START BLASTING THE BUILDINGS APART
LAP DISSOLVE TO:

Sc 462 B
A HIDEOUS MUSHROOM SHAPE CLOUD BEGINS TO TAKE SHAPE — CAMERA FOLLOWS IT UP —

**ABOVE**
(l to r) Bradford Dillman, Henry Fonda, Michael Caine, Katherine Ross, Allen, Olivia de Havilland, Fred MacMurray, Richard Widmark, and Richard Chamberlain—duplicating the walking PR cast photo from The Towering Inferno, but with less happy results for Allen.

**OPPOSITE**
Michael Caine and Katherine Ross on the set with Allen, and Allen at work directing.

**FOLLOWING**
Storyboard artwork depicting the bees entry into Houston—imagery left out of the film.

Allen finally wrote Herzog back a week later on December 29:

> THE SWARM goes well!! At the moment it looks bigger than THE TOWERING INFERNO.

If *Jaws* had cast its shadow over *The Swarm*, upping the ante for thrills and horror, *Star Wars* had raised the stakes for the movie's visual effects. Musso had worked with pyrotechnic expert Joe Viskocil (who had done the miniature explosions for *Star Wars*, including the climactic Death Star explosion) on the low budget spoof *Flesh Gordon*, and when Allen tasked L.B. Abbott with creating a nuclear mushroom cloud in miniature for the film's atomic power plant explosion, Musso recommended Viskocil.

Musso said of Viskocil:

> He was a master of miniature explosions—he knew exactly the right powder to use to make you swear it was the real thing. When we were doing *The Swarm*, I brought him in because everyone was trying to figure out how to blow up the nuclear power plant. Before, what they would do for nuclear explosions is they would get a clear tank of water and pour dye into it and it would funnel down and mushroom out, and then they would flip the footage and since it was clear water they'd have whatever background on the other side of the mushroom cloud. But Irwin had this miniature set he wanted to blow up and he wanted the mushroom cloud to emanate from the set.

SC 479 COMPOSITE WITH PELLETS

ANGLED ON THE SWARM AS IT FLIES TOWARD THE CITY OF HOUSTON

SC 481 SECOND UNIT COMPOSITE WITH PELLETS

6 CROP/DUSTING PLANES DROP INSECTICIDE OVER THE SWARM TO THE OUTSKIRTS OF HOUSTON (DISSOLVE OUT PELLET PLATE AS ...)

SC 482

TV MONITOR SHOWING A THICK WHITE CURTAIN JUST OUTSIDE THE MAIN SUBURBAN AREA

SC B-488

TROOPS MOVE FORWARD ON LINE & THEN FLANK BUILDINGS ON ONE SIDE OF THE STREET

SC C-488

ANOTHER ANGLE FROM BEHIND TROOPS AS THEY MOVE FORWARD OPENING FIRE ON BUILDINGS (ALREADY SHOT)

Sc D-488

ANOTHER ANGLE OF TROOPS FIRING (ALREADY SHOT)

Sc E-488

VIEW FROM INSIDE A WINDOW WITH BEES CLUSTERED ON OUTSIDE OF IT / TROOPS FIRING TOWARDS WINDOW

Sc E-488 (CONT.)

FIRE FROM FLAME THROWER HITS WINDOW

Sc H-488

L.S. OF SOLDIERS FIGHTING BEES — REVEALS OIL TANKER PARKED IN F.G.

Sc I-488

FIREBALL BLASTS OUT OF BUILDING —

SC 536 — COMPOSITE SHOTS WITH PELLETS, SMOKE

BEES BEGIN TO RISE INTO THE SKY —

SC 537

FOUR CHOPPERS FLYING OVER HOUSTON SKYLINE — COMPOSITE PELLETS FOLLOW CHOPPERS ACCROSS HOUSTON SMOKING — MAKE TWO PASSES WITH 2 CHOPPERS ENTERING & EXITING SCREEN — CHOPPERS FLY SAME PATTERN ON BOTH PASSES — SHOOT AT MAGIC MOUNTAIN — MAKE 50 FOOT HANDLES, HEAD & TAIL, I.E. BEFORE & AFTER EXIT — SHOOT AT MAGIC MOUNTAIN —

SC 540 — COMPOSITE WITH PELLETS

4 HELICOPTERS TRAVEL ACCROSS HOUSTON SKYLINE — SWARM FOLLOWS — HOUSTON SMOKING — SAME AS SC 537 — BUT MORE UP ANGLE —

SC 540 — COMPOSITE SHOT WITH PELLETS

THE SWARM IN FORMATION BEING CALLED OUT OF THE SMOKING CITY BY THE SOUND —

SC 550

CONTINUATION OF SWARM LANDING ON OCEAN — BY SOUND SPEAKERS — USE SC 546 WATER —

SC 556

ROCKETS EXPLODE ON OIL SLICK STARTING FIRES.

**OPPOSITE**
Storyboard artwork depicting aircraft luring the bees out into the Gulf of Mexico to be burned at the film's finale.

**RIGHT**
More "fire gags" as flame thrower-wielding soldiers battle the bees—action that mirrored sequences from *The Towering Inferno* but without *Inferno*'s scope and tension.

Viskocil met with Allen, L.B. Abbott, and members of Abbott's special effects team at the sound stage at Warner Bros. where the miniature nuclear power plant was to be constructed. Told that the production needed an explosion twelve feet in height with a mushroom cloud, Viskocil set up two demo explosions, telling Abbott and Allen that one would be realistic and the second one would be "flashier."

"He'd figured out exactly where gravity would fold it over to make a perfect, twelve foot mushroom cloud," Musso recalls. "Bill [Abbott] said, 'Boy, is that a relief,' and Irwin was astonished."

After the nuclear plant miniature was constructed a few weeks later, Allen asked Abbott if he had Viskocil lined up to do the explosion. Abbott replied that his own powder men had studied what Viskocil did during the demo and that they were confident they could duplicate the explosion, so Viskocil wasn't needed.

Musso related:

> Irwin said, "No Bill. We don't do that on an Irwin Allen film." He said, "That guy could do the cloud when you said it couldn't be done. If your effects guys want to do it they can do it, but you're bringing that man in, you're paying him for the day and you're giving him credit."

Viskocil was brought in to observe the miniature explosion, and he told Musso that he thought Abbott's men were using too much powder. The resulting explosion was, in fact, too bright and powerful, obliterating the miniature and its scenic background. Only Allen's insistence that the detonation be filmed by three cameras salvaged the shot—Allen had all three angles cut together to create one explosion, but the mushroom cloud he had hoped for wasn't visible and there was no money or time to rebuild the expensive power plant miniature.

Despite Allen's insistence, Viskocil's name didn't appear in the film's credits—this was before the current age of 10-to-15-minute credit sequences to include hundreds of visual effects artists, and only supervisor L.B. Abbott, Howard Jensen and Van Der Veer Photo Effects received credit for the movie's visual effects.

Despite these problems, Allen was bullish on *The Swarm*—finally, six years after *The Poseidon Adventure*, an Irwin Allen Production would be opening with Allen's name on it as a director. Allen had pulled together another all-star cast: he'd had Henry Fonda locked in since their handshake agreement on *The Merv Griffin Show*, and he'd found a replacement for Burt Reynolds in the form of British actor Michael Caine. Old veterans like Richard Widmark (as the chief military officer in the film), Fred MacMurray, Ben Johnson, Slim Pickens, and Olivia DeHavilland were sharing the screen with younger talents like Bradford Dillman and Katherine Ross.

The painstaking planning and control of live bee colonies had paid off with convincing shots of bees swarming the family killed off early in the film and in a later attack when the swarm fights back against a group of young boys who make the mistake of angering the hive.

Not everyone was happy with Allen's decisions as a director, however. Joe Musso recalled that a lot of the methodical planning and design that had helped make *Poseidon* and *Towering Inferno* so effective seemed to be forgotten on *The Swarm*:

> On *The Towering Inferno*, Irwin said that every sequence had to top the previous sequence, had to be more exciting and more spectacular. When we were doing *The Swarm* I kept thinking, "When did we forget that?" I think after *Towering Inferno* it was almost like Irwin wasn't listening to anybody. He would take this spectacular raking shot of men with fire extinguishers and put it on the monitors in the background so you really couldn't see it. And they had another scene where the bees attack the square in Marysville, and they had a guy crash through this window with bees on it and it scares everyone and everyone falls back. But Irwin fell in love with the slow motion and he shows it that way so there's no scare, no shock value.

The movie, particularly in its 158-minute version, was turning out extremely talky, but without the intelligent suspense of something like *The Andromeda Strain*. And the action component seemed to meander, particularly as the film headed toward a conflagration in Houston (prompting Richard Widmark's infamous line: "Houston on fire. Will history blame me...or the bees?").

Musso continued:

> We'd actually laid out the shots of the bees coming in to Houston so they're coming in from infinity, so there's great perspective. But Irwin decided to just cut to Houston and the bees are just there. The original script had [the film's main characters] going up the stairwell fighting the bees, trying to reach the roof to get out on a helicopter, and that's where the Richard Widmark's character dies. It's really harrowing, and that was cut out.

Allen also reduced the impact of the film's finale by cutting out a sequence of helicopters luring the bees through Houston's skyscrapers toward the ocean where they would ultimately be burnt to death. Instead, he simply cut to Caine's character arriving at an airport to board a helicopter and view the resulting conflagration from the coast, with the bees being lured into the trap already a *fait accompli*.

Allen also had his geriatric love triangle of Fred MacMurray, Olivia de Havilland, and Ben Johnson end in the service of a spectacular miniature train crash. The original sequence had been filmed to show bees attacking and killing Olivia de Havilland, with the camera panning down to show her hand touching Ben Johnson's hat to indicate that she had chosen him over Fred MacMurray's character. Instead, Allen cut out de Havilland's death scene, after the aging actress had endured a swarm of live bees covering her during the shoot. According to Joe Musso, de Havilland was livid:

> She went to Irwin and said, "You mean you put me through all that and made me put those bees all over my face and you cut the scene out? How can you do that to me?"

Pre-release publicity on the movie was going strong enough that some scientists publicly worried that the

**LEFT**

A visibly happy Irwin Allen on set, at last directing an Irwin Allen disaster movie—and a less happy bee swarm victim.

Olivia de Havilland and Ben Johnson prepare to meet their doom in a miniature train crash.

Star Michael Caine (right) in one of his many shouty confrontations with costar Richard Widmark (left).

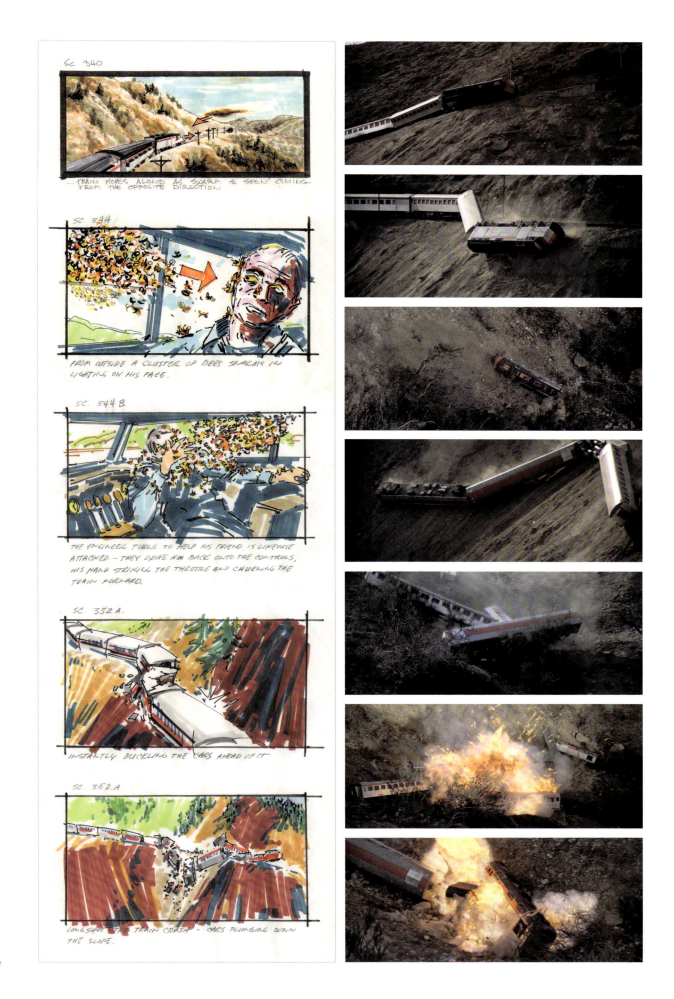

RIGHT
Storyboard art for the train crash, and the crash as it appeared in the final film.

movie would give bees a bad name, doing for them what *Jaws* had done for sharks. A February 21 piece in *The Hollywood Reporter* noted that the American Bee Association was threatening a class action lawsuit against the movie for defaming the name of the American Honey Bee. "Of course, we encourage these sidebar oppositions," Allen said happily. "Because the hysteria of each group has proven very good in promoting motion picture attendance."

Nevertheless, Allen eventually placed a disclaimer in *The Swarm*, declaring that its Africanized bees were not to be confused with the "industrious hard-working American honey bee to which we are indebted for pollinating vital crops that feed our nation."

On March 17, 1978, Allen wrote Warner Records' Mo Austin, delivering what he described as "Jerry Goldsmith's spectacular score on THE SWARM":

> THE SWARM opens in more than 1300 first run theaters on July 14th. It is the largest number of theaters for an opening ever to be enjoyed by any motion picture in all of motion picture history. The exploitation and promotion on the picture itself will be gigantic.

A March 29, 1978, status memo noted that post production was on schedule and under budget, that a "short version (2 hours and 15 minutes)" was being prepared at the request of Terry Semel and a longer version of 2 hours and 38 minutes was being prepared for television.

What Allen wasn't noting in public was that the screening of *The Swarm* that had been prepared for Warner Bros. executives and the movie's crew had gone poorly. Very poorly. Allen retreated to his office after the screening to await what he may have assumed would be congratulatory phone calls.

Joe Musso recalls returning, disillusioned, to his own office at the art department only to have his boss show up at the door:

> Irwin says, "My entire staff saw the screening, all the vice presidents at Warners, and not one person to pick up the phone." So he had to call his staff together. And everyone was saying, this is really bad.

Despite its budget and running time, *The Swarm* was seriously lacking in action and scope. Spectacular footage had been shot, but much of it had been relegated to background monitor screens or left on the cutting room floor altogether. "I said to George Swink, 'Can't we get some of those scenes back up?'" Musso says. Swink explained that Allen had finished mixing music and the other, final aspects of post production, and that it would be too expensive at this late date to reconfigure the film.

*The Swarm* was awaiting release in March, and production on Allen's *Circus, Circus, Circus!* was planned to begin in August—contingent upon the reception of *The Swarm*, of course.

In early June, Allen sent a memo to Terry Semel regarding a preview of *The Swarm* in Tucson:

**ABOVE**
Child actors and extras in some of *The Swarm*'s underwhelming action.

**ABOVE**

Katherine Ross and Michael Caine with Allen (right) on the beach in Santa Monica, standing in for the Texas coastline and the Gulf of Mexico for the film's finale.

Helicopters lure the bees out of Houston and into the Gulf of Mexico in the film's finale.

Excellent audience reaction. Solid commercial picture. Totally suspenseful. Audience sat on edge of seats throughout.

In July, Allen told *The New York Times* that a theater manager in Albuquerque had said to him, "Listen, the best proof you've got a hit is that everyone who went to the toilet ran up the aisle and ran back, and the popcorn business was the worst in the history of the theater."

Despite the previews, Warner Bros.' faith in *The Swarm* had been crippled, and with Allen's cooperation they determined to put the film out with no advance reviews, flooding the market with the biggest release in the history of the industry, opening *The Swarm* in 1400 theaters simultaneously, and gambling that the movie would make money during its first week in release before word of mouth killed it.

Allen continued to tout the film in publicity interviews, assuring *The New York Times*:

> Laugh if you want to, but those bees have been moving northward at the rate of 270 miles a year. They're in Venezuela now, and nobody knows how to stop them. People and cattle are dropping like flies down there. The African killer bee is the single most serious threat to our way of life. At one point we had 22 million bees and more than 100 men taking care of them. Not killer bees, of course. You think I'd imperil the country for the sake of a movie? We used ordinary honeybees, which are very similar in appearance, not that I guess it matters much to the audience. We had $100 million in special bee insurance. Everyone got stung at least once.

Publicity and marketing for *The Swarm* were omnipresent, ginning up excitement for a movie that sounded like it would make *The Poseidon Adventure* and *The Towering Inferno* look like small-scale comedies by comparison. On July 10, 1978, Herzog wrote Allen from New York about PR for *The Swarm*: "Everybody talks about it here; I can't wait to see it."

Allen put together a half-hour television special for CBS that treated the movie as a documentary-like suspense thriller based in reality. "It is, in fact, a prediction," the special's narrator intoned, later explaining that a mere four stings from the Africanized bees were capable of killing a grown man.

The film's cast heaped praise on Allen. "He's the most organized man I've ever seen in my life," Michael Caine insisted, while Richard Chamberlain enthused, "He's an extraordinary director; he's like a little kid with a new toy and it's a wonderful atmosphere he creates." The special unspooled Chamberlain's scene inside a nuclear reactor plant with Jose Ferrer, with Ferrer bellowing:

"No, no, no, Doctor—see this! Billions of dollars have been spent to make these nuclear plants safe—fail safe! The odds against anything going wrong are astronomical, Doctor!"

"I appreciate that, Doctor," Chamberlain replies as both actors attempt to put the most condescending spin on the word 'doctor.' "But let me ask you—in all your fail-

**LEFT**
*The Swarm* B poster art by C.W. Taylor

**OPPOSITE**
Allen casts a critical eye on one of his bee victims.

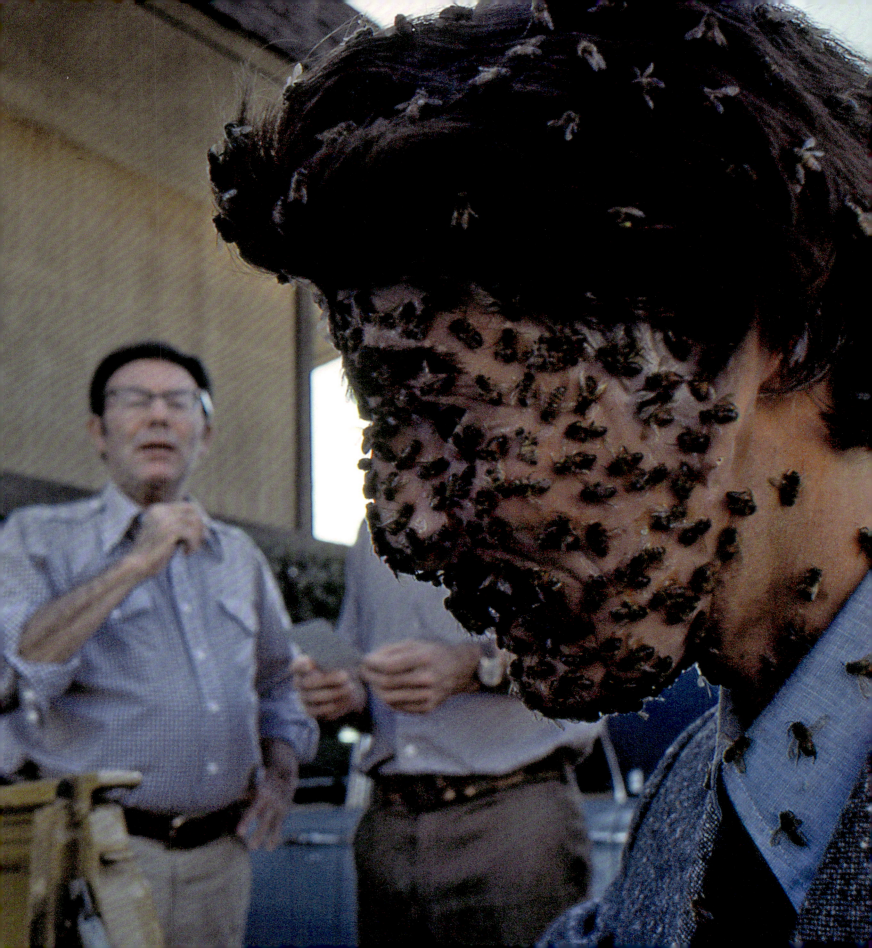

safe techniques, is there any provision against an attack by killer bees?"

At one point in the special, an interviewer asks Allen about the iffy potential for a movie about bees, to which Allen brusquely replies, "Perhaps you've heard of a little movie called *The Towering Inferno*?" It wasn't wise to question the Master of Disaster.

Talking about the special in a June, 27, 1978 piece for *The Hollywood Reporter,* Allen said, "We are in the same genre as *Jaws 2*. It is a terror film."

*The Swarm* opened on July 14, 1978. Three days later, in a show of solidarity with Allen, Ted Ashley, chairman of the board of Warner Bros., announced three films to be made over the next 15 months—"the most substantial production commitment in the history of the company." First would be *Beyond the Poseidon Adventure,* to begin production Aug. 29th and be directed by Allen. Second was *The Day the World Ended,* to start January 21, 1979, with Allen to announce a director shortly. The third was *Circus, Circus, Circus!*, to be directed by Allen and to start filming August 1979.

"These production commitments speak for themselves," Ashley said. "Irwin Allen is unique as a filmmaker whose pictures consistently have reached the broadest possible worldwide audiences. We are proud indeed of our association with him."

Even as Warner Bros. circled the wagons, reviews for the movie were rolling in—reviews that had been delayed by the fact that most critics had to pay to attend commercial screenings on opening day or later in order to see the movie. *The New York Times* confidently declared *The Swarm* to be "the surprise comedy hit of the season"; *Newsweek* called it the worst film of the year—in August.

Critic Richard Corliss, writing in *New Times:*

> The whole movie could have come out of a fifties time capsule—the kind we used to bury in our fallout shelters.

Corliss noted the irrelevance of much of Allen's cast of grand old movie stars, pointing out that *The Exorcist, Jaws, Star Wars,* and *Close Encounters* became massive hits without using old time movie stars as box office bait:

> ...We can't help wondering why Allen spends so much of his money on fading stars in advanced middle age. Will they bring people into the theater? No. The story, the gimmick, the effects, the display's the thing.

On a July 17, 1978 radio show, "Rambling With Gambling," host John Gambling discussed the entertainment scene with film critic Walter Spencer, touching what would become a recurrent theme in reviews of *The Swarm*:

> It's always a bad feeling when a movie company will not screen a picture for the critics until the very day it opened. I could really say he brings new meaning to the phrase disaster movie, because *The Swarm* certainly is the biggest disaster of the year...it's just a total wipeout, and unfortunately it traps a lot of very good people along the way...the bees are really pretty crummy. They get up there in big swarms in the sky and they look like somebody got a little bit of dirt on the lens of the projector. Apparently they wiped out a quarter of a million bees for this movie and it's a waste of time. It's just laughable. I mean, it's the *inadvertent* comedy of the year. I saw this in a movie theatre over the weekend and people were rolling on the floor laughing at the dumb lines in the movie.

Critic David Sheehan:

> An all-star cast turns a ridiculous script into a laughable burlesque with outlandish over-acting.

KFWB radio critic Chuck Walsh noted:

> Irwin Allen has this time not so much depicted a disaster as created one. It's amazing that a script by respected screenwriter Stirling Silliphant, produced and directed by Irwin Allen, and featuring performances by some of Hollywood's major and proven stars could possibly be so just plain god-awful, possibly one of the all-time worst.

Critic Jim Wright even took the film to task for some unintended racism:

> Even more amusing is the way all of the characters begin to refer to the killer bees as "Africans" after the film's first 15 minutes. Obviously no racial overtones were intended, but it's ironic that with the exception of Jose Ferrer, the entire cast is decidedly WASPish.

Wright noted that Allen had already been beaten to the killer insect punch by movies like *Bug,* Fox's *Damnation Alley* (with its "killer cockroaches"), *Empire of the Ants,* and the TV-movie *The Killer Bees.*

One of the most devastating reviews of *The Swarm* came on *Good Morning America* from Rona Barrett. Barrett was better known as a gossip and entertainment columnist than a critic—she in effect did the same work that Irwin Allen had been doing at the beginning of his career 30 years earlier. But her takedown of *The Swarm*—and of Allen—on *GMA* must rank as one of the harshest burns ever laid down onto a Hollywood creative talent:

> [Allen] boasts this movie about a killer bee attack cost fifteen million dollars, and if that's the case he should be sued by Warner Bros. stockholders for misappropriation of funds. The movie is a laughable, horrendous disaster from start to finish with cardboard characters and stilted dialogue worthy of a *Saturday Night Live* parody. Every stock situation in the book is presented here with the depth of a cartoon, including a love interest for Caine and a stupid subplot with Lee Grant as a television newscaster who drew special laughs when she dropped a microphone in mid broadcast to help [Patty Duke] Astin into a car. Irwin Allen, who knows how to produce, doesn't know a thing about directing. *The Swarm* has all the thrills of beeswax.

Allen's seemingly foolproof formula for successful disaster movies seemed to break down with *The Swarm,* with most of the filmmaker's hard-learned lessons ignored by the Master of Disaster himself. Gone were the

**ABOVE**
Years after *The Swarm*, Allen and Shiela, still friends with Michael Caine (left) and his wife Shakira Baksh (right).

ragtag group of socially mismatched characters banding together to survive—the characters driving the action in *The Swarm* are all scientists and military men, the heroes of standard, old-fashioned sci-fi films (Bradford Dillman, playing an aide to Richard Widmark's general, spends the first part of the film looking ridiculous in what appears to be a leftover, futuristic orange jumpsuit from *Voyage to the Bottom of the Sea*). *Poseidon* and *Inferno* had been built on primal, universal fears—of drowning, claustrophobia, hydrophobia, and fire. *The Swarm* hinged entirely on a horror of insects in general and bees in particular. Instead of confining the characters inside a situation in which there was no escape, Allen has them wandering around a sunlit countryside, with the film's central menace nowhere in sight throughout much of the film's running time. The logistics of controlling and eliminating the menace of the bees are confounding, all leading up to a climax that's lacking in tension or satisfaction as it seems difficult to believe that setting fire to the bee swarm over the ocean would completely eliminate the threat.

Within the first few minutes of the film, a bit actor playing a helicopter pilot (actually Allen's assistant and dialogue coach, Steve Marlo) unleashes one of the worst line readings in film history as he yells, "Oh my god—bees, bees, millions of bees!" But under Allen's direction, the film's cast of Oscar-winning movie stars don't fare much better. Michael Caine gives one of the strangest performances of his career as heroic scientist Brad Crane, whose primary character trait is his insistence on handing out healthy sunflower seeds for everyone to munch on. Crane is the nominal hero and Richard Widmark, as a grumpy general suspicious of the bee expert, seems to be intended to be the film's heavy—but in scene after scene, Widmark's general seems to make far more sense than Caine's character. Allen engineers one heated dialogue scene between a shouty Caine and Widmark, with the camera nervously circling, Crane yelling about the threat of the bees and Widmark insisting that they wouldn't enter the U.S. mainland for years.

"On whose timetable, General?" Caine demands. "Yours or theirs?"

Later a philosophical Crane ponders the irony of bees threatening civilization: "I never dreamed it would be the bees. They've always been our friends."

This type of disaster movie dialogue had already been the subject of parody in the Zucker Brothers' early film *Kentucky Fried Movie*, in a segment entitled "That's Armageddon!"

Stirling Silliphant's stab at relatable characters via the love triangle between Fred MacMurray, Ben Johnson, and Olivia DeHavilland is sabotaged by the deaths of all three characters via train crash two-thirds of the way through the film—but the real problem was that these characters were too old (it would be MacMurray's final film appearance) and too cliched to carry the burden of being the only major "civilian" characters in the movie.

Slim Pickens, as a local rancher angrily grieving over his soldier son's death early in the film, has the strongest dramatic scene in the movie, but he too was too old for the film's target audience, leaving Michael Caine and Katherine Ross (great in artier fare like *Butch Cassidy and the Sundance Kid, The Graduate,* and even *The Stepford Wives* but at sea in purely commercial movies like John Wayne's *The Hellfighters* or *The Swarm*) to struggle with holding on to the mainstream audience.

L.B. Abbott's special effects are actually impressive for the era, but again, Allen elected to place the technically spectacular and vivid shots of Houston aflame behind venetian blinds and on television screens, robbing the movie of the scope that *Poseidon* and *The Towering Inferno* had in spades.

Only Jerry Goldsmith's exciting score manages to emerge unscathed. When Goldsmith's agent Richard Kraft brought up *The Swarm* to the composer years later, mentioning John Williams' work on *The Poseidon Adventure* and *The Towering Inferno*, Goldsmith ruefully replied, "Yeah, John got the good versions and I got the stinker." In fact, Williams had originally been attached to score *The Swarm*, but at some point had removed himself from the project, leaving Irwin Allen's orbit forever.

The scathing reviews for *The Swarm* no doubt hit Allen hard, but even worse for a man with his reputation was the financial hit Warner Bros. took on the movie. With a budget and promotional costs that had ballooned to $21 million, the movie took in only $10 million at the box office. The golden touch of the Master of Disaster had disappeared, and his dream of directing a Hollywood blockbuster had soured.

Adding insult to injury was a lawsuit filed by Texas theater owners attacking Warner Bros. distribution of the movie, accusing the studio of "blind bidding":

> The practice of requiring motion picture exhibitors...to submit bids on a given motion picture months prior to its release and without any prior screening of the picture... it takes advantage of the exhibitor's lack of knowledge and ability concerning the motion picture in question to a grossly unfair degree and...resulted...in a gross disparity between the consideration paid by Plaintiffs for *Swarm* and the value Plaintiffs received.

According to *Variety* coverage, Presidio Enterprises of Austin, Texas invoked a state consumer deception law (the Texas Deceptive Trade Practices & Consumer Protection Act) in order to sue the studio for $187,841 in damages plus costs. A Federal court jury found in favor of Presidio on March 24, 1983, awarding Presidio $56,000 in damages (which was tripled under the Texas consumer protection law with the addition of attorneys' fees and court costs) after which Warner Bros. appealed. A U.S. District court jury then overturned the decision in March, 1985.

Over his years as a producer, Irwin Allen had his staff scour newspapers and magazines for mentions of Allen and his productions, eventually hiring newspaper clippings services to do the job. These organizations would send envelopes full of newspaper and magazine articles to Allen's offices, where Allen and his staff would go through them to gauge public and critical reaction to his productions. Consequently, for each of Allen's projects there are piles of hundreds of newspaper clippings filling boxes. *The Swarm* is the sole project of Allen's on which Allen and his staff stopped reading the clippings, and to this day there is at least a full box full of unopened and unread clippings still sealed into their envelopes just as they had arrived from the clipping services. At some point Allen simply no longer wanted to hear the bad news.

Allen had described *The Swarm* as "a survival picture." Now the question was whether Allen himself could survive its fallout.

**OPPOSITE**
Key art for *The Swarm* by C.W. Taylor.

A HUNDRED THOUSAND DOLLARS A DAY THIS IS COSTING US!

I'M NOT WORRIED; I'M SUICIDAL!

**IRWIN ALLEN**

# SEQUELS AND VOLCANOES

*Allen's time as a feature film producer finally runs out*

**OPPOSITE**
*When Time Ran Out* poster art by Robert Tanenbaum.

## BEYOND THE POSEIDON ADVENTURE

The reception for *The Swarm* had all but decimated the Irwin Allen brand; the movie had become a brief, national joke and then had largely disappeared from public view.

A more volatile filmmaker might have retreated into seclusion or worse, but Irwin Allen's most central character trait now became his saving grace: Allen was nothing if not a workaholic, and rather than pausing to lick his wounds, he simply dived back into shepherding other projects toward completion, hoping that his next project would wash away the bitter taste of *The Swarm*.

Allen had two projects that had been in development for several years: *The Day the World Ended* and a sequel to *The Poseidon Adventure*. Of the two, *The Day the World Ended* was by far the most ambitious and the movie Allen was itching to direct, but just as *The Swarm* neared the end of postproduction, Allen announced to his staff that their next movie would be *Beyond the Poseidon Adventure*.

*Poseidon 2* had been on Allen's plate since production on *The Towering Inferno*, but finding a story worthy of the project had proven challenging. Allen's initial approach had been to take the original *Poseidon* characters and involve them in a train tunnel disaster in the Swiss Alps. That concept earned a letter of protest from author Paul Gallico in June, 1975:

> There is, of course, no doubt that POSEIDON initiated the run of disaster pictures and the only thing that has puzzled me was that having made a great success through POSEIDON ADVENTURE and contemplating a sequel

you never came to the writer who initiated this success, namely me. [The Swiss Alps idea] doesn't seem to me worthy of your original smash hit.

Meanwhile Gallico insisted he had a "$50 billion idea for a sequel" and urged Allen to contact him.

Almost a year later, in March of 1976, Gallico sent Allen a treatment for the sequel. By this point Allen had come to the realization that abandoning the setting of the Poseidon from the original film would be a mistake. The name "Poseidon" had to be in the movie's title for marketing reasons; otherwise there would be little awareness that this was a sequel to one of the most successful movies of all time. With the ship name in the title, it made no sense to take the action to an entirely different location and situation, and in any case moviegoers drawn to a *Poseidon* sequel would expect something in the vein of the first movie.

Nevertheless, while Allen agreed with Gallico about where the sequel should be set, he did not agree with the author's approach and he wrote Gallico with suggestions for changes. The fragile Gallico pronounced himself "shattered" at Allen's criticisms. Gallico's contract for a novel to be based on the treatment indicated that he was to give Allen's suggestions due consideration, and he agreed to some of Allen's changes but elected not to incorporate other major ideas, indicating that his novel would likely be different from the finished film. This wasn't uncommon even for novelizations, since they are often based on early screenplay drafts in order to get books out in conjunction with movie's theatrical releases.

Gallico went ahead with his plan, writing a sequel to Allen's movie rather than one to his book (since the higher-profile movie had made changes to Gallico's characters and plot). Gallico had characters from the movie (including Ernest Borgnine's Mike Rogo) and a number of new characters heading back inside the overturned Poseidon immediately after the closing moments of the original film.

Allen continued to go in his own direction, ultimately hiring Nelson Gidding (who had written screenplays for *The Andromeda Strain* and *The Hindenburg*) to work on a script that at one point had the twin brother of Gene Hackman's Reverend Scott, a helicopter pilot, arriving at the wreck of the Poseidon, and at another had a tiger and other dangerous animals loose on the overturned ocean liner.

Before his falling out with Allen, production designer Bill Creber registered his disapproval of Allen's ideas for the sequel:

> I said, "That's the wrong story, Irwin. There's more there than that." I wanted him to make a treasure hunt, and he didn't like the idea. He liked his idea better because he had become an invincible movie maker.

An early treatment of the script actually began moving in the "treasure hunt" direction, introducing the character of Captain Bela, "a suicidal and ruthless terrorist, and a member of a revolutionary group in urgent need of

**ABOVE**
Early promotional image for *Beyond the Poseidon Adventure* created around the time of *The Towering Inferno*, while the project was still at Fox—and indicating a considerable departure from what the film would eventually become.

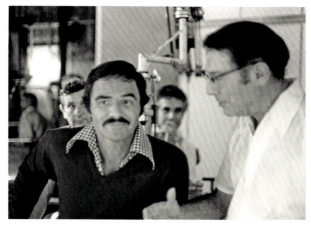

**ABOVE**

Actor Burt Reynolds (left), a movie star Allen had pursued since *The Swarm* and almost landed for the lead of *Beyond the Poseidon Adventure*—instead Allen settled for his *Swarm* star Michael Caine.

Allen on the set of *Beyond the Poseidon Adventure* with star Michael Caine (left) and Shirley Knight (middle).

Michael Caine on the set with Sally Field.

arms and ammunition." The plotline introduced some shocking, hidden motivations for some of the original *Poseidon* characters: a bank arranges to smuggle arms for Bela's group onboard the Poseidon, with Leslie Nielsen's captain character revealed to be in on the plot, and Ernest Borgnine's cop character assigned to guard a shipment of gold onboard the ocean liner. Bela and his ship planned to intercept the Poseidon at sea during the height of the New Year's festivities and remove the arms, making it look like a hijack. A woman named Hely is traveling as one of the passengers but is a plant, ordered to destroy the radio room as Bela's ship comes alongside the Poseidon—but the freak tidal wave seen in the first film ruins the plan.

Entering the fray is a Dutch salvage boat owned by a character named Klaas (who would become Michael Caine's Captain Mike Turner in the film), his partner, and a female passenger. The plot had Bela's helicopter landing on the Poseidon and offloading survivors, including two children and Nonnie. But Rogo becomes suspicious at the sight of armed men on the chopper, pulls a gun on the pilot and orders the chopper back to the Poseidon. The trio from the salvage boat enter the ship after the helicopter departs and encounter Rogo. The action was to range throughout most of the ship interior and at this point the idea of animals loose on the ship was still being considered. Klaas was to question the Mediterranean tidal wave and eventually theorize that earthquake or other tectonic activity must have caused the wave, leading to the discovery that the Poseidon is capsized over an active volcano. Another note in the memo stated that, "The final battle must not be behind two stockades but a running battle through the ship."

Borgnine's Rogo would have acted as a "number two" to Klaas, and the memo suggested that he sacrifices his life to allow the others to get to safety at the end. Another suggestion: "Manny Rosen…should die fairly soon after BELA is discovered on board the POSEIDON. This should compare with his wife's death in first film." Nonnie and the children are held as hostages on Bela's ship, then brought onboard Poseidon so Bela can threaten to drown them as leverage over Klaas and the others. Martin (Red Buttons) is given responsibility for getting the kids off the Poseidon by Klaas, and in a suspense scene he has to outwit Klaas' guards to get the children past them.

Already Allen was well aware that getting Gene Hackman back to play Reverend Scott or his helicopter pilot twin brother would be difficult if not impossible. But the story retained a *Psycho*-like twist that would have had Scott's brother piloting the terrorist helicopter, which is destroyed in an explosion in the first moments of the movie.

*Beyond the Poseidon Adventure* was shaping up as a potentially compelling combination of familiar characters placed into unusual new situations, as well as new heroes and villains. But plans quickly changed over the availability (or interest) of Ernest Borgnine, Red Buttons, and the other original *Poseidon* cast members, and Allen then considered the idea of introducing the Poseidon survivors as cameos only—and having them killed off in the shocking opening moments of the film.

Giddings' original script had the Poseidon sinking over a volcano that explodes at the climax of the picture—an idea that Allen loved, but the studio expressed doubts about. By 1978, Allen's secretary, Margaret Reeves, was a trusted enough member of Allen's inner circle that Allen actually sought her opinion of the story.

Dan Goozee recalls Reeves as a unique presence in the Irwin Allen offices:

> Everyone called him Irwin; that's what he liked to be called; only Margaret called him Mr. Allen. Margaret had tremendous power; she was a gatekeeper and if you wanted to see Irwin you had to go through her. I once walked in there to ask Irwin for a raise and I sat down and Irwin started this tale of woe, saying, "This is the worst possible time you could ask; I'm just trying to keep all you people working and I would if I could but you put me in a terrible bind..." I walked out thinking I was lucky just to have a job. And Margaret asked me what he said, and when I told her, she said, "That's what he tells me, every time."

Reeves wrote a brutally honest memo to Allen on May 30, 1978. She took particular exception to the idea of killing off the original Poseidon survivors in the helicopter explosion on page 5 of the script. Reeves implored Allen not to include this development, insisting that, "It will alienate your audience totally."

Reeves also weighed in on the volcano idea:

> Having the Poseidon resting on a submerged volcano falls in the unlikely, incredible category and should be changed.

But Reeves' issues with the script involved more than simple pyrotechnics:

> The only characters I really believe in or have any empathy for are Celeste and Tex. The others don't ring true and I don't care about. The main problem of the script is the trek itself and the similarity to POSEIDON 1 and this may be an incurable problem. Too many people have seen the original (both theatrically and on television) and remember it too well and this is just a carbon copy. Perhaps another writer (someone who has not worked on the script before) could come up with a fresh approach that would make it different and startling. As it stands now, I feel you are just reshooting the original movie with a different (and less appealing) set of characters.

After losing Burt Reynolds on *The Swarm*, Allen wanted Reynolds to star in *Beyond the Poseidon Adventure*, playing the salvage boat captain.

Joe Musso recalls:

> The studio had just brought over Clint Eastwood and they wanted Clint to play the captain, and Clint came over and met with Irwin, and they gave Burt a chance to read the script. Then they get a call from John Wayne, and Wayne wanted to do it. The minute Irwin heard John Wayne, there was no talk about Burt or Clint. It was ironic because had he chosen to do it, it would have been the last thing he did.

Wayne, obviously, didn't make *Beyond the Poseidon Adventure*—nor did Burt Reynolds or Clint Eastwood. All three actors turned the movie down after reading the script.

Allen then called Michael Caine. *The Swarm* had not yet been released, and Caine hadn't yet been exposed to the extremely negative reactions that critics and audiences would have to the completed picture, so he was open to the idea of following up *The Swarm* with the *Poseidon* sequel. Allen was still finalizing the deal to get the *Poseidon* project confirmed as a Warner Bros. production, since 20th Century Fox still had some claim to rights to the project. Allen was also beholden to the backers that had bailed him out when *The Poseidon Adventure* had been on the verge of cancellation at Fox: Steve Broidy and Sherrill Corwin.

In a March 29, 1978 memo on the status of the production, Allen said he was:

> ...Working with Jack Freedman to clarify and help in resolving all the rights we required in the purchase from Twentieth Century-Fox. Also working with Ed Rubin in seeing what would be the absolute minimum acceptable to Steve Broidy and Sherrill Corwin on a possible purchase or settlement of some kind of their interest in POSEIDON. We are now talking about an early July start with an outside chance of delivering the picture for Christmas, certainly no later than Easter. This will surprise Terry Semel who is anxious to get the picture for next summer...

The budget for *The Day the World Ended* was near finalization at around $15 million, with a three-hour running time per a commitment of 10 million dollars from NBC for television airing and a theatrical length of 2 hours and 15 minutes. Allen's *Circus, Circus, Circus* was still being budgeted and the L.A. Sports Arena had been reserved from July 15th through September, 1979 for filming.

Michael Caine was considered the number one candidate to star in the *Poseidon* sequel, but the production was also looking into Robert Shaw of *Jaws* as a backup. Shaw had a plum role in Richard Lester's revisionist fairy tale *Robin and Marian* and had figured in two post-*Jaws* thrillers, *The Deep*, and *Black Sunday*, but neither had been well-received, and Shaw's other choices—*Swashbuckler* and *Force 10 from Navarone*, were outright bombs. Shaw would die just a few months after being mentioned as a casting possibility, in August, at the age of 51. Michael Caine would star in *Beyond the Poseidon Adventure*.

Meanwhile, Burt Reynolds, after turning down the sequel, called Allen regarding his paramour and costar in *Smokey and the Bandit*, Sally Field. Field was looking for another commercial project and Reynolds wanted to know if Allen would consider the actress—who ironically had been under consideration for a part in the original *Poseidon Adventure*—for the sequel.

For Allen, Sally Field was a steal—*Smokey and the Bandit* had been second only to *Star Wars* at the box office in 1977. Goldie Hawn, Natalie Wood, Sally Field, Genevieve Bujold, Jessica Lange, Katherine Deneuve, and Valerie Perrine had all been considered for the role of Celeste

**OPPOSITE**

Allen works with his cast and crew on and around the 200-foot section of the Poseidon's hull constructed for the film and towed to the ocean off Catalina Island.

Whitman, a reluctant passenger brought onboard Caine's salvage boat by his partner, Wilbur Hubbard, but Field turned out to be the perfect choice.

Allen considered Burgess Meredith and Karl Malden for Wilbur, eventually settling on Malden. Telly Savalas, who had once been under consideration to play tough cop Rogo in the original *Poseidon Adventure*, was now first in line to play the movie's villain, Stefan Svevo—but Allen looked at Christopher Plummer, Robert Vaughn, and Rod Steiger for Svevo as well. Steiger was also under consideration for the volatile war veteran Frank Mazzeti, along with Robert Preston and George Kennedy. Allen would eventually cast Peter Boyle, an actor very much in the vein of Gene Hackman, whose character combined the volatility of Hackman's Reverend Scott and the tough New Yorker feel of Borgnine's Mike Rogo in the original film. Ned Beatty and Slim Pickens vied for the role of Tex, a folksy Poseidon wine steward posing as a billionaire. Allen had been impressed by Pickens' dramatic turn in *The Swarm* and cast him as Tex. For blind passenger Harold Meredith, Allen had looked at James Stewart, Eddie Albert and even Alec Guinness before choosing Jack Warden.

At this point the budget for *Beyond the Poseidon Adventure* had been set at $12 million. Allen's idea to have the Poseidon sinking over a volcano was also torpedoed by the studio after Warner's Frank Wells called Allen to tell him that a survey of potential audiences rated the volcano idea poorly.

Allen's clout with the studio dropped dramatically after the critical and box office reception of *The Swarm*. His contract stipulated that he had to remain in place as the *Poseidon* sequel's director, but his grandiose notions for the movie were being quickly sidelined by pressures to keep the budget low.

This would affect the look of the sequel, as the careful attention to realism and detail that had made the original *Poseidon Adventure*'s upside down sets so effective was discarded for the sake of expediency.

In the first film, the threat to the passengers came in the form of an inexorably rising tide of water as the Poseidon settled in the water. But Allen and production manager Norman Cook quickly agreed for the sequel that fire was cheaper than water, so most of the story's action sequences would involve flames, leaving only a scuba diving swim sequence for the movie's climax.

A 200-foot section of the Poseidon hull built to scale, constructed in San Pedro and towed to Catalina Island, became the centerpiece for the film's climactic action, filmed over a month in November, 1978. One of Allen's strengths as a producer, and one of the characteristics that had kept him in good with both 20th Century Fox and Warner Brothers over the years, had been his ability to keep costs under control—he prided himself in bringing his projects in on schedule and often under budget. But, by now, Allen's famed way with a budget ledger was beginning to unravel. *Beyond the Poseidon Adventure* had already swollen from its $12 million budget to $17 million.

**ABOVE**
Karl Malden (background), Mark Harmon and Angela Cartwright (below) and Michael Caine (foreground) on the *Beyond the Poseidon Adventure* set.

**LEFT**
Promotional artwork for Allen's TV-movie *Hanging by a Thread*.

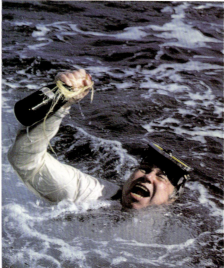

**ABOVE**

*Beyond Poseidon*'s female costars, Sally Field (left), Veronica Hamel (middle), and Shirley Jones (right).

Peter Boyle (left) and Karl Malden.

Slim Pickens trades his life for precious champagne at the movie's bullet-riddled conclusion.

**FOLLOWING**

Storyboards from *Beyond the Poseidon Adventure*.

To play the daughter of Boyle's character, Allen hired Angela Cartwright from *Lost in Space*. Cartwright hadn't done a great deal of work since *Lost in Space*, apart from one season on a sequel to the Danny Thomas sitcom *Make Room for Daddy* (called *Make Room for Granddaddy*) that aired from 1970 to 1971. Over the next eight years, Cartwright had gotten only four television roles. The chance to appear in such a high profile, theatrical movie sequel was a major career opportunity, she recalled:

> I was really kind of excited about it, because I was with Michael Caine and Sally Field and all these really, great people, and Mark Harmon played my love interest. The whole idea of working within that group of people was really exciting to me. And it wasn't that bad a script.

Unfortunately for Cartwright, Allen's disinterest in intimate, emotional moments meant that a key aspect of her role wound up on the cutting room floor.

Cartwright was supposed to be pregnant, and played the entire role as though she was "with child," noting that her onscreen relationship with her father (Peter Boyle) and with Harmon's character (a Poseidon elevator operator) were affected by the pregnancy. Cartwright didn't discover this primary motivation for her character had been cut until she attended a preview of the film:

> Mark and I are sitting at the preview of the movie, and he cut the line out, where I said I'm pregnant. I turned to Mark and I said, "Wait a minute—I didn't say I was pregnant," and he goes "I know that. What happened to the line?" And that really kind of ticked me off.

Sheila Allen had played a Poseidon nurse in the first film—in the sequel Shirley Jones played a nurse named Gina Rowe, who was theoretically the same character, and consequently the only character from the original movie to figure in the sequel. Unfortunately, the fact that the nurse had been quite a small role in the original movie, and that the character was now played by a different and quite different-looking actress, robbed whatever impact this callback might have had.

Sheila Allen was at the same preview where Cartwright discovered how her part had been edited, and she theorized that her husband's idealization of young Penny Robinson from *Lost in Space* made him uncomfortable with the idea of having her *Beyond* character shown as pregnant:

> With Angela, he had seen her in *The Danny Thomas Show*, growing up as a little girl, and he was quite taken with her. He thought she was darling and he put her in *Beyond the Poseidon*. I think when he came to see that scene in the cutting room, he didn't like the idea of her being pregnant and not being married. That's my interpretation. I saw it in the cutting room and I thought it was beautifully done. Angela and Mark Harmon were very sweet together. And when we showed the film, I don't know if it was a rough cut or what, and they saw that they weren't in it at the end of the film their faces just dropped. They just couldn't believe it.

Just prior to the release of *Beyond the Poseidon Adventure*, Allen's TV-movie *Hanging By A Thread* was broadcast

# INVERTED PASSAGEWAY SEQUENCE

## ELEVATION DIAGRAM OF ACTION

SUGGESTED POSITION OF CHARACTERS WHEN GIRDER COLUMN CRASHES THRU —

over two nights on NBC. Four hours might have seemed like a long time to spend with a small group of characters trapped inside a cable car dangling over a ravine, but the plot had the group (played by a gang of Irwin Allen veterans including Sam Groom, Patty Duke, Burr DeBenning, and Cameron Mitchell) reliving turning points in their lives via flashback. It was another pilot for a potential series that wouldn't sell.

*Beyond the Poseidon Adventure* had one advantage over *The Swarm*. Nelson Gidding's screenplay set up a number of sharply drawn characters and the film's plot gave them ample time—actually almost too much time—to play off one another. Freed up from his static, unnecessarily mysterious role in *The Swarm*, Michael Caine went into firm heroic mode to play the movie's gruff salvage boat captain. Slim Pickens chewed up the low-budget scenery in his role as a billionaire who turns out to be a lowly wine steward, although Peter Boyle delivers one of his more tentative performances as an angry war veteran desperate to find his daughter (and furious to discover she may have fooled around with the hunky Poseidon crewman played by Mark Harmon). Jack Warden played a thoughtful blind man, Shirley Knight his sympathetic wife.

The sequel also benefited from an all-out villain: Telly Savalas as an international criminal out to grab a stash of plutonium from the Poseidon. And a pre-*Hill Street Blues* Veronica Hamel added some glamorous intrigue as a vixenish passenger who's secretly one of Savalas' ill-fated contacts.

The biggest treat in the movie was Sally Field. Irwin Allen had provided comic relief characters in his films before, and Field's Celeste Whitman was the kind of self-aware, almost postmodern character that would be common in movies going forward (especially after *Airplane!* utterly deflated the disaster movie genre). But there had never been anyone like her in an Irwin Allen movie, and she managed to puncture so many of the script's cliches with her line deliveries that she almost comments on the film from outside. It's all the more amusing given the fact that Fields was clear in later years that she did *Beyond* purely for the money and did not have a great time making the movie. She even pulls off a crying scene that's one of the most convincing emotional breakdowns in any Irwin Allen production.

The potential of Fields and the other characters never quite takes off, unfortunately. Like *The Swarm*, *Beyond the Poseidon Adventure* is a talky movie, painfully lacking in the kind of tension and razzle-dazzle that the original *Poseidon* and *The Towering Inferno* had in spades. Working with a decent-sized but poorly spent budget, Allen was unable to match, let alone surpass, his groundbreaking effort of seven years earlier. He made use of abundant stock footage from the first film, not just the opening tidal wave and other miniature work of the Poseidon, but even footage of the first film's fiery engine room set, which veteran production designer E. Preston Ames couldn't duplicate.

The deadly, hellish atmosphere produced by Bill Creber's upside down sets and Harold E. Stine's dank cinematography is wholly lacking, particularly when

the characters enter the Poseidon's galley—a chamber of horrors full of burnt corpses in the original, but clean, brightly-lit and corpse-free in *Beyond*. In fact, the *Beyond* characters somehow get through their entire adventure without encountering a single dead casualty from the original disaster. With abundant scenes of people crawling around through rectangular air ducts, the action more and more resembled Allen's television work, and, despite the large, varied cast, people like Shirley Jones and Shirley Knight have very little to do. Even less occupied are Savalas' handful of machine-gun-toting minions, who are so faceless they might as well have been wearing stormtrooper gear.

Allen's earlier mandate of intensifying jeopardy fell by the wayside along with the movie's budget, so that there's a long, talky stretch of dead air before the film's climax, which involved the survivors scuba diving from inside the wreck to the surface, only to be set upon by Savalas and his remaining thugs in a violent shoot-out finale that results in the (unimpressive) explosion of the Poseidon.

After the nonstop promotional drumbeat that heralded the release of *The Swarm*, *Beyond the Poseidon Adventure* snuck into theaters with a stunning lack of publicity. A *Time* magazine review attempted to analyze the movie's supposed theme of "spiritual seasickness" with tongue very much in cheek.

Roger Ebert in his review, barely mentioned the movie, talking about a conversation he'd had with Allen years earlier in which Allen had told Ebert his idea of the Swiss Alps train tunnel version of a sequel, and Ebert had suggested simply having a second tidal wave turn the Poseidon over so that the passengers would have to start all over again from the bottom: "But what did we really, sincerely, expect anyway, from a movie in which Karl Malden plays a character named 'Wilbur,' and Slim Pickens plays a character named 'Tex'?" was about all Ebert had to say about the sequel.

**ABOVE**
Angela Cartwright and Mark Harmon on the set of *Beyond the Poseidon Adventure*.

**OPPOSITE**
With little in the way of miniature work or other special effects, the storyboards for the film focused on character blocking and action.

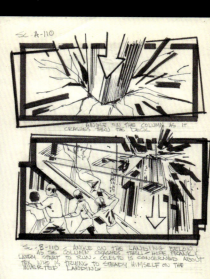

*Variety* noted, "*Beyond the Poseidon Adventure* comes off as a virtual remake of the 1972 original, without that film's mounting suspense and excitement."

The disaster movie genre had been all but dead even before the release of *The Swarm*, and the *Poseidon* sequel seemed like an afterthought—even fans of the original likely had little idea a sequel was even in production, let alone released. It wasn't the movie's sequel status that killed it—*Jaws 2* had been a huge hit the year before. But Warner Bros. had grown timid after *The Swarm*, and *Beyond the Poseidon Adventure* turned out as more a contractual obligation than a movie.

Ensconced in his own office building on the Warner Bros. lot, Allen insisted on moving forward. He had retained his loyal family of production personnel and worked to make Warners his home, just as Fox had been.

Used to keeping his staff employed and cared for, Joe Musso recalled Allen adopting an unusual new "family":

> When we were at Warners there were a lot of cats at the studio, and you'd never know it, but Irwin had a real affinity for cats. There was this one cat, Whitey, and you'd come in and see Irwin talking to Whitey, and he'd have his secretary Margaret leave cat food out for him, and the next thing you knew Whitey brought friends over, so we had all these cats, and Irwin gave them all names. He had this set designer, Harold Furman, his nickname was Snuffy, and he had him build them this cat house, like a dog house with boxes on top of each other loaded with carpeting, so it was "Irwin's Cathouse." At the far end of this building was the main entrance and off to the corner was this elegantly designed cathouse with cats hanging around it.

"Whitey" remained Allen's favorite and became the producer's unofficial mascot:

> One day Irwin came in and he was beside himself that Whitey was bloody—he'd got into a fight with something, so he had Margaret take him to the vet. We were in a production meeting and Irwin's on the phone: "How's Whitey doing? How's Whitey doing?" As soon as she came back she had to report on how Whitey was doing, and she said, "He's doing fine, resting comfortably after his surgery." Irwin said, "Surgery? What surgery?" And she said, "Well, the vet thought he'd have him neutered." Irwin said, "Neutered? What's neutered? I hope it's not what I think it is." And she said, "Well Irwin, he'll be better this way, he won't get into fights this way." He said, "Well, yeah, but how do you think Whitey's going to feel about it? You never asked him if he wanted to be neutered!"

After the sinking of *Beyond the Poseidon Adventure*, Allen still had *The Day the World Ended*, a movie project he had been talking about since just after the release of the original *The Poseidon Adventure* in 1973. *The Day the World Ended* was based on a book by Gordon Thomas and Max Morgan-Witts, about the explosion of Mount Pelee on the island of Martinique in 1902, and how concerns over an upcoming election caused political leaders to downplay the danger of the volcano to the citizens of the island town of St. Pierre. The volcano eventually killed 30,000 people, and in the book there are only three survivors from St. Pierre.

**ABOVE**
Allen with Sheila Allen, shooting *Beyond the Poseidon Adventure* off Catalina with Telly Savalas (left).

**LEFT**
Newspaper advertising art for the movie.

**OPPOSITE**
William Kuntsler's poster artwork for *Beyond the Poseidon Adventure*, seen on the movie's press kit.

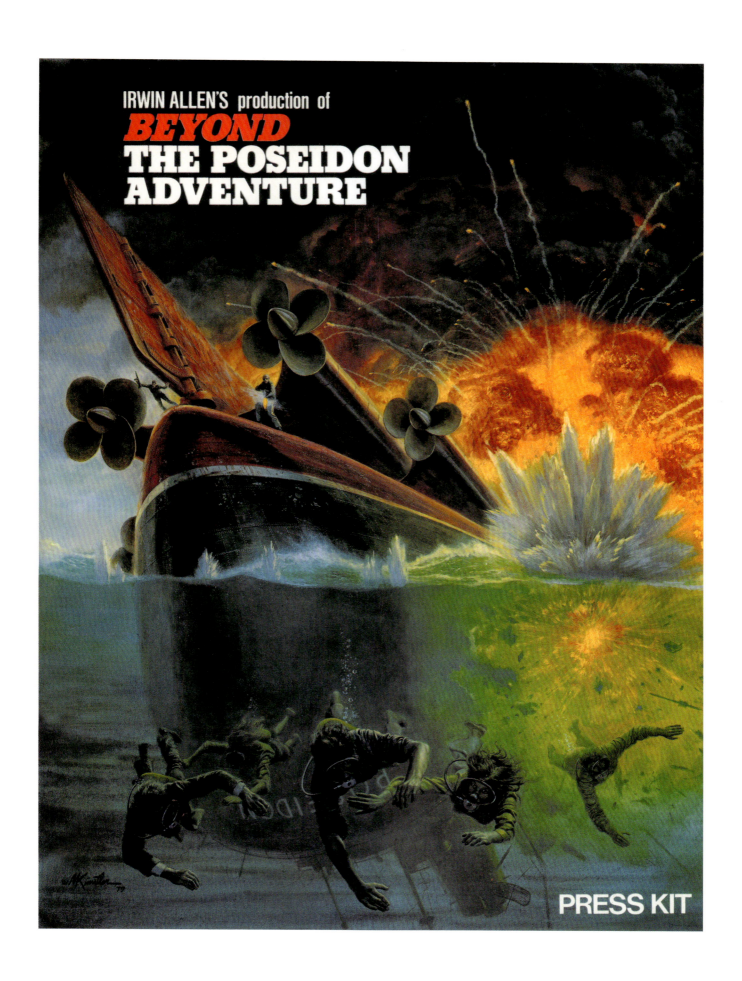

## WHEN TIME RAN OUT...

*Variety*'s Army Archerd reported in June, 1974 that Allen was pursuing Robert Redford for *The Day the World Ended.* After snagging Gene Hackman for the original *Poseidon* and Paul Newman and Steve McQueen for *Towering Inferno,* Redford seemed to be the last great American box office star that Allen hadn't conquered.

At that point *The Day the World Ended* was intended, like *The Swarm,* to be budgeted at $6-7 million. Screenwriter Edward Anhalt, who had written everything from comedies and Elvis pictures to historical subjects like *Becket* and *Luther,* worked on the script. Meanwhile Fox's Alan Ladd, Jr., had suggested (perhaps recalling the similarly-themed, and unsuccessful, period volcano movie *Krakatoa: East of Java*) that the movie should be done as a contemporary story.

"Fox developed it two ways, one as a period piece and one as a modern story," Joe Musso recalled. Nelson Giddings then produced a contemporary draft of the story that so displeased Fox executives that they took a pass on the project altogether (publicly the studio's stance was that the movie's budget had grown too large, a prophetic observation).

Allen then took *The Day the World Ended* with him when he moved to Warner Bros. in 1975 (Warners had to pay $1 million for the rights to the project). Warner Bros. budget estimates showed that making *The Day the World Ended* as a period movie would add $5 million to the budget. The studio was also leery of the movie's title. "Particularly with the way it ended, they felt the title *The Day the World Ended* promised too much, so they changed it to *When Time Ran Out*," Musso said.

By 1976, Allen had hired Carl Foreman to write the contemporary version of the story. Foreman had some big movies under his belt like *High Noon, The Bridge on the River Kwai,* and *The Guns of Navarone.* But, he had also been responsible for *MacKenna's Gold,* a star-studded but overblown western, and the underwhelming sequel to *The Guns of Navarone, Force 10 from Navarone,* which had

**ABOVE**
Early promotional artwork for *The Day the World Ended*, another project that originated during Allen's days at 20th Century Fox.

**ABOVE**

Paul Newman and Jacqueline Bisset have their "sucky" confrontation in *When Time Ran Out...*

Bisset with William Holden (right), like Newman, a holdover from Allen's *The Towering Inferno*.

Red Buttons and Ernest Borgnine—largely rehashing their character archetypes from *The Poseidon Adventure*.

attempted to grab the post-*Jaws*/*Star Wars* audience by casting Robert Shaw and Harrison Ford together.

Foreman had his own theory of why disaster movies were popular, which he recounted in a June 14, 1976 issue of *Variety*:

> Since the Russians developed the A-bomb, we've been living in a nightmare. I think that's where the disaster film started, It's a phenomenon of our times that we've learned to live on the edge of a volcano or an earthquake and manage to go on with our daily lives. All the bull is over when a disaster strikes. That's when the men are separated from the boys, so to speak. Sometimes people are capable of the most marvelous heroism, and others find that they have been coping behind a face for so long, they're like little animals.

In 1976, Allen told *Variety*'s Army Archerd that the characters would include:

> ...The mousy bookkeeper who arrives at the motel with $9 million in a valise and a young, beautiful society girl with terminal cancer. They all arrive at this hotel that's doomed because of the volcano eruption, and just to make sure they're doomed I plan to go wild with earthquakes and tidal waves as well.

The movie was originally planned to begin shooting in early 1977 and a December 1975 issue of *Boxoffice Magazine* had Yul Brynner, Henry Fonda, Charlton Heston and Jennifer Jones in the cast.

Robert Redford showed no interest in the project, period movie or not. If Brynner, Fonda, Heston and/or Jennifer Jones were ever seriously attached, production delays pushed them out. Both Paul Newman and Steve McQueen were under contract after *The Towering Inferno* to do one more project for Allen. McQueen had shown interest in both *The Last Ride West* and *Circus, Circus, Circus*, but as *When Time Ran Out...* moved forward at Warner Bros., Allen was eager to lock up McQueen for the volcano movie—but production kept being pushed back.

Allen wrote McQueen in March, 1977 and proved he still had a way of opening an inquiry letter: "The beer is still ice cold—the sauna is still red hot and you and Ali still have all my love." Allen invited McQueen to visit "my 'money machine,' the most sensational accommodations anyone ever had at a studio—two brand new giant buildings."

Allen had given McQueen a script for *The Day the World Ended* a year earlier but now wanted him to read Carl Foreman's version, noting that John Calley had dubbed it "the best motion picture material I have ever read in my life." Allen insisted that he and the studio believed the movie would be another "hundred million dollar profit maker." Allen also stated that he would be in New York the following week to close a deal with Ringling Bros.-Barnum & Bailey Circus for *Circus, Circus, Circus*—"the biggest circus movie of all time"—to be made in 1979.

McQueen had two other projects lined up—the western *Tom Horn* and a contemporary action movie, *The Hunter*. His commitments to them allowed him to slip out of his contractual obligation to Allen. *Tom Horn* and *Hunter* would be McQueen's last movies; he died of cancer in November, 1980. With McQueen off the hook, Allen turned again to Burt Reynolds, who had dodged the bullets of both *The Swarm* and *Beyond the Poseidon Adventure*. He wrote Reynolds in January, 1978, urging him to call the producer about *When Time Ran Out*. "Looking forward to finally talking to you about a disaster—worth a couple of million dollars." Reynolds politely declined the offer.

Allen still had Paul Newman under contract, and Newman didn't have any scheduling conflicts to save him. The paycheck on *When Time Ran Out...* was still enough to attract someone of Newman's stature, although the actor admitted in interviews years later that he took the project strictly for the money.

He was more diplomatic in a June 10, 1979 *Los Angeles Times* profile by Lee Grant, saying, "Irwin Allen films are great fun to make. And if you want to work, fun is what you might as well be having." Newman nevertheless noted that he was under no delusions that Allen's movie was going to be great art. "At this particular moment in my life—today, but maybe not tomorrow—I work to support my other habits."

Newman would play an oil drilling manager, Hank Anderson, who is warned that a volcano near the oil rig he is working is about to erupt. The other characters include the two owners of a luxury hotel near the site, played by William Holden and James Franciscus, and a trio of women (including Jacqueline Bisset, Veronica Hamel, and Barbara Carrera) who are involved in relationships or affairs with all three men.

Allen had brought Stirling Silliphant back to rework Carl Foreman's screenplay. "A great script isn't written," he told one reporter. "It's rewritten."

In a profile in *O'ahu* magazine, Allen explained that he felt right at home working on the screenplays for his films:

> Basically I'm a writer and I think a writer has a particular affinity to motion picture making, because basically what you're doing is writing with pictures. Being a writer is very helpful because I'm better able to understand the writers that have worked for me over the years and I am better able to help them edit their material. And as a writer you're better able to understand movement, motivation and development of any film."

Allen said of *When Time Ran Out...*:

> It's the most expensive picture I've ever made, the biggest picture I've ever made, and the one with the greatest number of stars I've ever made, so I would say I've enjoyed it thoroughly.

In April, 1978, Newman submitted a list of suggestions for changes. It's interesting to contrast Newman's suggestions with Steve McQueen's on *The Towering Inferno*. McQueen's were mainly tied up with his actor's ego, with the intent of making his character—and consequently Steve McQueen—look more appealing

by having the architect be involved in a grand, philosophical project that would aid "the American Indian" and to squash the idea that any woman involved with him could possibly drawn into an affair with another man.

Newman had some similar concerns—he wanted to change a line about his character observing pressure in the oil field for "the last 10 days, but only since last night—otherwise what kind of putz is Hank to hang around ten days doing nothing?" The screenplay also had Newman's character descending into the volcano core in a high-tech probe capsule—originally "on a dare." Newman wanted Hank "telling Bob [James Franciscus' character] that he wants to see for himself, that he does not believe the volcano is dormant, as Bob insists." Newman also suggested a dramatic scene between him and Jacqueline Bisset earlier in the film be "suckier," suggesting that it be established that the two characters had had an affair, that Bisset's chose Holden's "Conrad HIlton" character but now was throwing herself at Hank, who "is a little pissed by this and tells her he doesn't take other men's ladies."

But the bulk of Newman's suggestions related to other characters and action and were quite detailed, indicating a solid understanding of the story and its potential as well as its possible pitfalls. In all, Newman went over 22 different story points with Silliphant and helped eliminate problematic elements in a number of scenes.

After *Beyond the Poseidon Adventure*, Warner Bros. executives had firmly shifted to the same perspective that held sway at 20th Century Fox: they didn't want Irwin Allen in the directors' chair. A humbled Allen was looking into directors Arthur Hiller, Michael Crichton, Jerry Jameson (*Airport '77*), James Goldstone, and John Badham. The studio had hoped to get Ronald Neame

**ABOVE**

*When Time Ran Out...* heavy James Franciscus (left) with William Holden (second from right).

Paul Newman stares into the abyss.

or John Guillermin back, but Newman had director approval written into his contract, and he had found Guillermin's process on *The Towering Inferno* tiring. James Goldstone had directed Newman's 1969 racing movie *Winning*, a personal, if not vanity project for the actor. And he had one would-be disaster movie under his belt, 1977's *Rollercoaster*.

Newman wanted Goldstone, and got him. But Goldstone proved to be a high-maintenance experience for Irwin Allen. The director wrote Allen in October, 1978 to express his concerns about the project. He wanted a script rewrite done before December 1st to address "character motivations, relationships, dialogue and certain mechanical aspects." Goldstone also wanted to check out the locations in Hawaii and discuss casting decisions:

> If I cannot find the means to get myself all the way into the director's harness so that I feel prepared to fully contribute to the planning of the picture, then, in deference to you, Warner Bros. and myself, I feel it would be better if I removed myself as director at this juncture than wait until a later date when legitimate differences of opinion might severely hamper the creative and financial success of the film.

In late December, Allen wrote Frank Wells about the possibility of casting James Caan as Spangler (the role went to James Franciscus), and Goldstone wrote Allen about the possibility of utilizing Bronson Canyon in Los Angeles as a location for the film's climactic bridge crossing sequence. Bronson Canyon was a familiar location for countless low budget movies from *Robot Monster* to episodes of *Star Trek*; the bridge sequences would ultimately be shot on a soundstage at MGM. But after *Beyond the Poseidon Adventure* and *The Swarm*, Allen was determined to give *When Time Ran Out...* production value by shooting on location in Hawaii, and the Sheraton Keauhou Bay Resort and Spa in Kailua-Kona became the movie's pivotal hotel.

In January, 1979, Goldstone met with Paul Newman with more script notes. Newman objected to a number of scenes in which Hank was "thwarted." Newman also reiterated suggestions for a beach love scene between his character and Jacqueline Bissett's that a lot of "laughter" be involved—the final scene reflects this, with Hank sharing a recollection with Kay and both actors doing a lot of spontaneous laughter and teasing. Newman had a number of other suggestions and observations on ways to streamline and make the movie's action be more logical and suspenseful, and he had extensive notes on the relationship between James Franciscus' Spangler and his cheating wife Nikki (Veronica Hamel); Newman's suggestions were to soften the character of Spangler and make him less of a total villain, allowing him to move from someone more understanding of his wife's feelings to eventually shutting her out.

The production moved to O'ahu for a long and sometimes frustrating location shoot. *On Location* magazine's Sept. 1979 issue reported the plan to shoot from February to March at the Kona Surf Hotel, then to the Hilo side of the Big Island to the Naniloa Surf Hotel,

**RIGHT**
Storyboard artwork for a tidal wave sequence which was toned down considerably in the final movie over budget concerns.

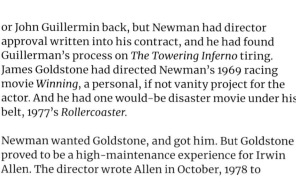

and filming around Mauna Kea volcanic crater. The Kona Surf Hotel was to be engulfed by a tidal wave, hit by hot lava balls and destroyed.

Allen's production office was quoted on the post-production effects as saying: "burn-ins and blue screens have not been charted yet and there's no way of telling how much it will cost."

Despite his early insistence on creative control and input, James Goldstone was easygoing where actors were concerned, which is exactly what Newman wanted. Others, like Veronica Hamel, were frustrated by the lack of direction they received during the production. Like Newman, Hamel, Ernest Borgnine, Red Buttons and William Holden were under contract to Irwin Allen and had little choice but to appear in the movie. What they didn't have was Paul Newman's clout and leverage. Just as he had on *The Towering Inferno*, William Holden was chafing at his casting as a supporting player, with Paul Newman as the production's star. Five years after *The Towering Inferno*, Holden had one last moment of glory under his belt, an Oscar nomination for his role in Paddy Chayefsky's *Network*. But he had little else to brag about other than a part in the horror movie sequel *Damien: Omen II*, and Holden's alcoholism was catching up to him on the set of *When Time Ran Out...* After several instances of Holden acting out on the set, James Goldstone insisted that his producer rectify the situation and a reluctant and saddened Allen allowed Holden to go into six days of treatment, adding delays to the production which was already being hampered by the island's abundant rain storms.

The film's glamorous cast earned it a lengthy feature in *Cosmopolitan* magazine by Richard Grenier in February of 1980—and Allen's frustrations in making the film were on full display.

"A hundred thousand dollars a day this is costing us!" Allen ranted during one downpour. "I feel as if I had a tube in my side and my life blood was running out! I'm not worried; I'm suicidal!" At one point, Allen turned to director James Goldstone and said, "Hey, Jimmy, come here. If it rains again tomorrow, why can't we shoot anyway? So it rains! We'll work it into the story! Big deal! We show a cloud! Why can't it rain on them just as it rains on us?" Goldstone patiently pointed out the issues in terms of continuity and cinematography Allen's suggestion would bring up, and Allen withdrew the half-serious idea.

Ruminating on the disaster genre later in the article, Allen said:

> You've got to give them hope. At the end. That they can succeed. That they can survive. At the end of a disaster movie, you've got to close on hope.

Allen was running short on hope himself, in fact, as the shoot ground along. For the film's expensive stars, however, *When Time Ran Out...* amounted to an all-expenses-paid Hawaiian vacation. Jacqueline Bissett's fee no doubt ate up a substantial amount of the budget, along with Paul Newman's—Bisset had become a sex symbol sensation after her wet T-shirt scuba diving scenes in 1977's *The Deep*, and she was at the height of her star power. She simply enjoyed the social aspects of the shoot, throwing parties and teasing Paul Newman (who had his wife Joanne Woodward along for the ride). Bissett commented:

> We all get together to make a movie, and we work together and eat together and get up early in the morning and have such fun. And then suddenly it's over, and everyone goes his separate way. For a while, this little world exists, and then it's gone.

**LEFT**
Allen in his element—on the set of his most expensive movie and surrounded by stars.

**OPPOSITE**
A fascinating diagram laying out how Allen planned to ratchet up tension during the lava pod sequence.

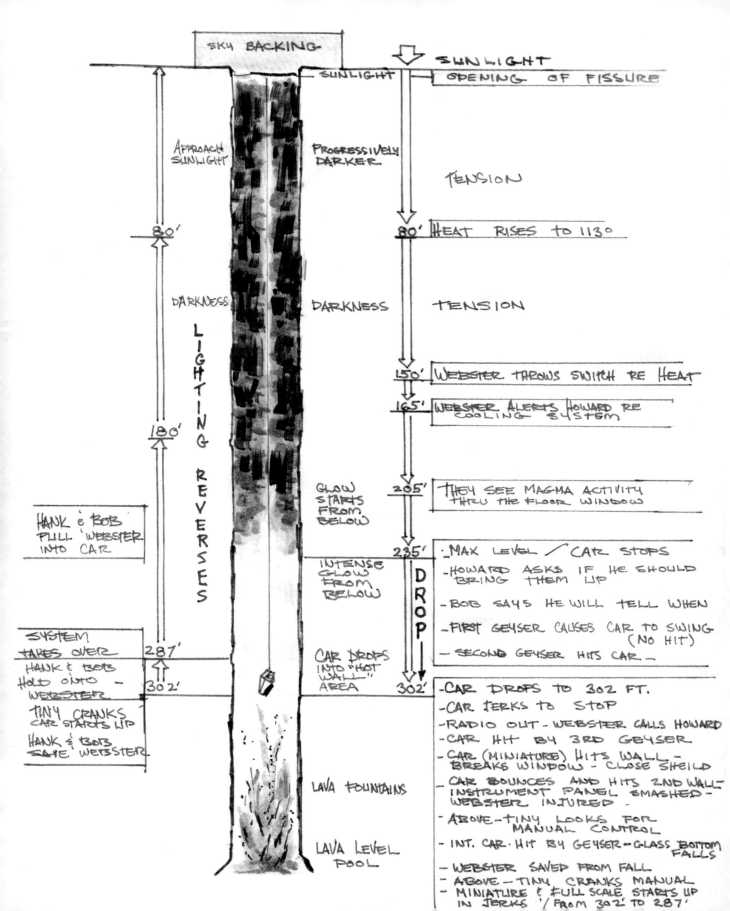

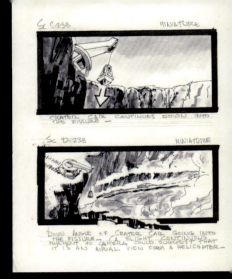

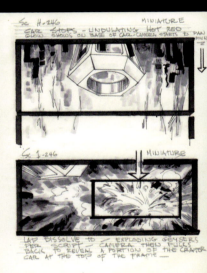
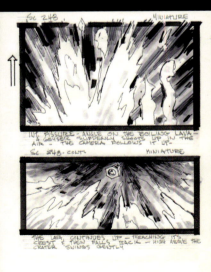

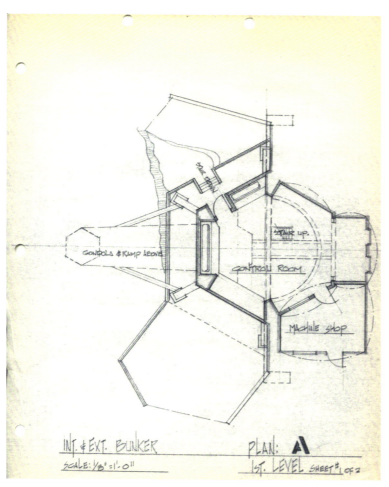

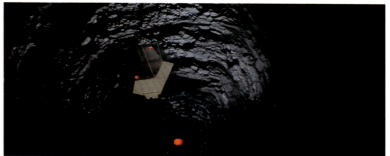
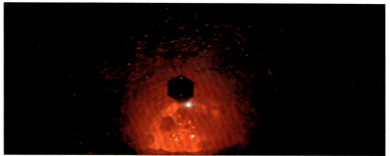

**OPPOSITE**
Storyboards for the film's early lava pod sequence.

**ABOVE**
Construction diagram for the lava crater research facility and lava pod berth.

**RIGHT**
The lava pod miniature sequence from the film.

Despite the bad weather, James Goldstone and cinematographer Fred Koenekamp were getting impressive footage out of the Hawaii locations, at least for the movie's first half. An early well blowout sequence with Paul Newman in which Newman and his crew are showered in oil is gritty, realistic, and convincing—compared to Allen's typically slick, Hollywood look, it almost belongs in another movie. The Sheraton Hotel setting and environs give the early sequences a lush, glamorous feel, perfectly accented by Paul Zastupnevich's costumes.

There's even a glossy, science fiction touch early on as Newman's character visits what seems to be an experimental observation station built directly over the story's volcano, and he and Franciscus descend into the volcano core in a probe capsule with a clear, circular floor that winds up shattering during an accident, leaving the characters dangling precariously over the bubbling lava below.

Again demonstrating his familiarity with Hollywood's grand old technicians, Allen hired legendary cinematographer Stanley Cortez, who had lensed Charles Laughton's incredible *Night of the Hunter*, to shoot the miniatures involved in the sequence (it would be Cortez's last screen credit). Allen had also hired Philip "Matt" Jefferies, production designer on the original *Star Trek*, to design the movie—Jefferies would work on most of Allen's major projects throughout the rest of the producer's career.

According to Joe Musso, Allen was less autocratic and more open to input on *When Time Ran Out...* However, the cast of A-list stars and the Hawaiian location photography and weather delays had taken a huge toll on the production's budget. The movie was to feature two climactic sequences—a dangerous crossing over a bridge with lava moving underneath it, and the final destruction of the grand hotel by volcanic fireballs at the end of the film. It had already been determined that the bridge crossing sequence would be filmed on a Hollywood soundstage in order to control the physical effects needed. MGM's Stage 30, the "Esther Williams stage," had a tank for water sequences beneath its floor, which allowed space for the lights and smoke effects to be rigged beneath the bridge, built 30 feet above the stage. Burgess Meredith played an aging circus performer who tests the bridge crossing by using his balancing skills to cross it—in a throwback to the Gilbert Roland Niagara Falls scene from *The Big Circus*.

"The bridge sequence was even in the original Martinique script," Joe Musso points out. "But it didn't have the circus performer doing the wire walk."

Pyrotechnic expert Joe Viskocil provided some consultation on the lava effects—again uncredited—and the look of the river of lava wound up being effective. But the studio-bound sets and the slow-paced, low stakes sequence ultimately proved too old-fashioned for an action movie that would be released the same year as George Lucas' *The Empire Strikes Back*. With the obvious studio sets, the sequence wound up looking like something out of Allen's 1960 *The Lost World* production.

**LEFT & OPPOSITE**
Storyboards for the film's bridge crossing sequence.

# BRIDGE SEQUENCE ~ PROGRESSION OF BRIDGE DESTRUCTION

Sc 547

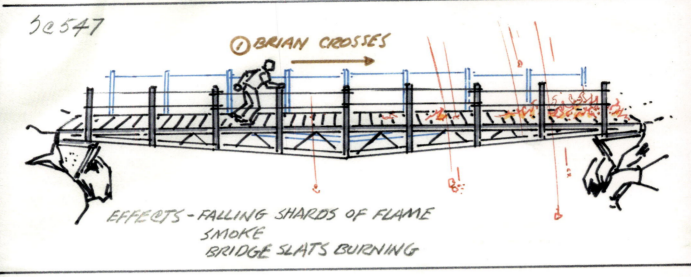

① BRIAN CROSSES

EFFECTS - FALLING SHARDS OF FLAME
SMOKE
BRIDGE SLATS BURNING

Sc 551

② FENDLY
③ GREENBERG

FIRE GAINING   BRIAN

SC 554 - ROSE & RENE SCENE ~ CAN BE INTERCUT IN COUNTERPOINT TO CROSSING OF SAM, SHELBY & MONA

Sc 536-37

⑤ SHELBY
⑥ MONA
④ SAM
① ② ③

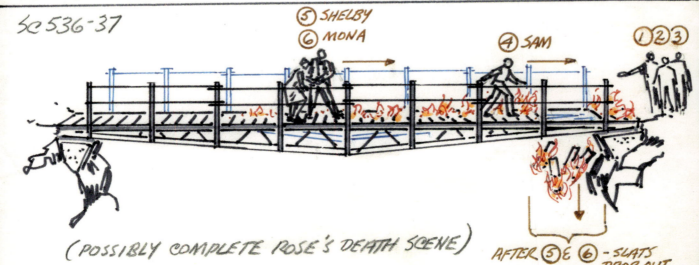

(POSSIBLY COMPLETE ROSE'S DEATH SCENE)

AFTER ⑤ & ⑥ - SLATS DROP OUT

Red Buttons said in 1995:

> It was a fiasco. It was just too late. Irwin was doing a story about people trying to get across a bridge, you know, when people were going to the moon and *Star Wars* and stuff like that. I mean it, it just passed him by, I felt.

The bridge crossing might have passed muster if Allen had been able to come up with something spectacular for the movie's final destruction of the hotel. But for whatever reason, Allen reportedly turned down additional money to add special effects to what would become an incredibly anticlimactic climax.

Joe Musso explains:

> They had footage of everybody standing around watching the volcano around the hotel. I read that prior to a volcanic eruption you get lightning in the sky, and I thought they could matte in the lightning bolts and people watching in awe. The studio got jazzed and they wanted to put their own money into building a miniature of the steel refinery by the hotel that would melt down and molten steel would destroy the hotel and then run into the ocean. Phil Jeffries had designed all these sets to be breakaway and we still had James Franciscus and Veronica Hamel at the hotel, and we were all ready to do this. We laid out all these shots of the hotel crumbling into the ocean. And then Irwin comes in one day and says, "You know, I changed my mind, we're just going to have a few fireballs come in and destroy the hotel." It looked ridiculous—the explosion looked like it was animation and it was just awful. It needed that powerful ending.

After filming was completed, Red Buttons dutifully went on *The Tonight Show* with Johnny Carson to promote the movie. But he too was disillusioned, recalling later:

> You couldn't shoot that picture and think at that point that you really had something. Why it was done I haven't any idea. But he had just come off some big ones, and he got all these people to do it and, who knows what the deal was.

Once again Warner Bros. gave the movie a subdued rollout in late March of 1980, the final demonstration of their lack of faith in Allen, so noted in the March 31, 1980 in *The Hollywood Reporter's* review:

> Warner Bros. seems to be doing its best to disguise the fact that *When Time Ran Out* is yet another disaster movie from Irwin Allen. The International Cinema Corp. presentation...was tossed into general release Friday without the benefit of any advance screenings...

The *Reporter* was predictably unenthusiastic about the movie:

> James Goldstone's direction is overly pedestrian and it just drags along under his guidance. It's a pretty dull disaster, and the special effects, credited to Robert MacDonald and Joe Unsinn, with special photographic effects by L.B. Abbott, are not particularly elaborate.

*The New York Times*' Janet Maslin described the movie as "...waxen even by Mr. Allen's standards."

**OPPOSITE**
"Movie magic" diagram of the bridge sequence.

**RIGHT**
The completed bridge crossing sequence.

Meanwhile David Ehrenstein in *The Los Angeles Herald-Examiner* pointed to an alternate career path for Allen—unaware that the producer had already tried his hand at the suggested line of work and failed:

> It's clear that disaster/adventure-film producer Irwin Allen has missed his real calling. His talents would be put to better use in another leisure industry—the theme park. This latest Allen opus, a horizontal replay of his *The Towering Inferno*, is a handy blueprint for what Irwin Allenland might be like.

Casting and location costs for *When Time Ran Out...* had ballooned the film's budget to over $20 million. Allen's earlier statement that the film was the most expensive he'd ever made had sounded like a boast, but now it seemed more an admission of guilt. Aside from some nice location photography, there was little to show for the money invested.

The movie might have gone down as one of Hollywood's great box office disasters, but it wasn't even allowed that distinction—Michael Cimino's *Heaven's Gate* was released in the fall of 1980 after a year of seething publicity about its cost overruns, its budget topped out at $44 million and it made only $3 million. *When Time Ran Out...* couldn't even break $2 million at the box office, meaning a loss of around $18 million for the studio, compared to *Heavens Gate*'s titanic $41 million worth of red ink.

Somehow, *When Time Ran Out...* still nabbed an Oscar nomination for Paul Zastupnevich's costume design, but when the title was read at the 1981 Oscar telecast, it seemed to be a movie few people knew even existed.

*When Time Ran Out...* seems a frustrating, missed opportunity today. The cast is strong and the opening scenes are lush and convincing. Red Buttons and Ernest Borgnine, almost repeating their roles from *The Poseidon Adventure*, are charming, and Paul Newman—who reportedly took the money and used it to set up his *Newman's Own* food company—is a charismatic lead as always. The actor has a lot of scenes in *Where Time Ran Out...* where he stares moodily off into the distance, and you can almost make out the gleam of salad dressing in his steel blue eyes.

But the movie offers diminishing returns once it hits the halfway point, and by the time it reaches the lengthy bridge-over-lava sequence, it begins to pale in comparison even to the old 1950s Frank Sinatra volcano movie *The Devil at 4 O'Clock*. The final destruction of the movie's hotel makes even the underwhelming explosion of the ocean liner in *Beyond the Poseidon Adventure* look impressive—once Allen could have counted at least on some impressive miniature destruction from L.B. Abbott and his crew, but those days were long gone. Instead, there's a brief and cheap-looking animation effect and the movie, and would-be spectacle, is over.

A little over a month after the release of *When Time Ran Out...*, CBS broadcast Allen's TV-movie, *The Memory of Eva Ryker,* over two nights. Allen had gone back to the location of The Queen Mary once again for the TV movie, with Natalie Wood in a dual role, playing a mentally

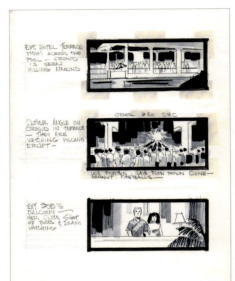

**OPPOSITE**
Storyboard art for the film's climax…

**ABOVE**
…and the final images from the film.

unbalanced woman in the present and her mother, who is murdered on an ocean liner that was torpedoed during World War II. Donald A. Stanwood's novel had been partially set aboard the Titanic, with the "present day" sequences set in 1961. Lew Grade's mammoth production of *Raise the Titanic* (which had some similarities to Stanwood's novel) may have forced Allen to change the story's setting, and with Wood and Morgan Fairchild onboard, *The Memory of Eva Ryker* became part period mystery, part 1980s nighttime soap opera.

Director Walter Grauman, in an interview for the Archive of American Television, recalled that star Natalie Wood told him she was terrified of drowning in dark water, and asked for a stunt performer to replace her in a scene where she was to be chased along a beach at night by the villain played by Bradford Dillman. She then had to play the drowning scene of Claire Ryker on a set designed to lower into a water tank to create the illusion of the ocean liner sinking. Only a few months later, Wood drowned in the midnight waters off of Catalina when she fell off her husband Robert Wagner's yacht (which Wagner had purchased while making Allen's *City Beneath the Sea*).

*The Memory of Eva Ryker* would be Irwin Allen's final project for Warner Bros. After the misfires of *The Swarm* and *Beyond the Poseidon Adventure*, the losses on *When Time Ran Out...* became the last straw for the studio— Warners was now out of the Irwin Allen business. They failed to renew Allen's momentous contract and in 1980 Allen was forced to vacate the building that had been built and named for him.

"Warners refused to renew his contract," Joe Musso recalls. "We were basically part of the company and he had to let his entire staff go, and it kind of broke his heart."

There was only one question remaining to be settled: what would become of Irwin's Cathouse? Musso explained:

> When it came time for him to move out, the question came up of what to do with the cats. The studio was going to call Animal Control and just get rid of them. Irwin had these big production offices, and right next to them was this little Spanish bungalow where Clint Eastwood's offices were. Clint had a Trans Am and we'd see him working on his car in an old dirty T-shirt. When Clint found out they were going to take the cats and maybe destroy them, he said, "You can't do that. They keep all the rodents off the lot." So he said, "I'll take care of them." So Irwin's Cathouse became Clint's cats. He paid to have them move everything down to the other end of the lot, and they had one of the caretakers on the lot feed the cats, and Irwin's cathouse went down there with them, and Clint took care of the cats.

**LEFT**
Domestic poster art for *When Time Ran Out...*, which played down the film's disaster movie aspects.

Promotional artwork for *The Memory of Eva Ryker*, Allen's last released project from his stint at Warner Bros.

**OPPOSITE**
Poster for the *When Time Ran Out...* release in Spain, which fully embraced the disaster angle.

552

> **YOU'VE GOT TO GIVE THEM HOPE. AT THE END. THAT THEY CAN SUCCEED. THAT THEY CAN SURVIVE.**
>
> **AT THE END OF A DISASTER MOVIE, YOU'VE GOT TO CLOSE ON HOPE.**
>
> — **IRWIN ALLEN**

# IRWIN IN WONDERLAND

With **ALICE IN WONDERLAND** and **PINOCCHIO**, Allen goes out on a song

**OPPOSITE**
Color caricature artwork for *Alice in Wonderland*, Allen's star-studded final production.

For several months after his ouster from Warner Bros., Irwin Allen led a nomadic existence, working out of the Universal Sheraton hotel. After decades of working on studio lots, Allen was, however briefly, a man without a country, and in a way, there were no studios to return to—not the self-contained cities he had flourished under at Fox and Warner Bros. Gone were the special effects, art, and craft departments that he had been able to depend on for consistency and efficiency in his movies and television productions, largely replaced by contract workers who moved from project to project rather than enjoying the stability of studio employment. Throughout the 1970s, Allen had at first triumphed, then floundered as the last bastion of Old Hollywood, hiring the movie stars that had inspired him as a younger man and the old guard technicians that had added spark to his best productions. But these same artists were now increasingly behind the curve in the wake of the *Star Wars* movies and *Alien*, productions that appeared to be in another universe compared to Allen's.

In late October, 1980, Allen signed a production deal with Columbia Pictures Television, facilitated by his old friend and former TV agent Herman Rush, who was head of Columbia Studios' television division at the time. The contract allowed him to move onto the lot (actually the far side of the same Burbank Studios lot inhabited by Warner Bros.) and continue to explore a number of television production ideas.

For the present at least, Allen's days as a movie producer, the "Master of Disaster"—were over. Allen still managed to enthuse over his deal with the studio, saying of Columbia in *Variety*, "They set no limits. I'm delighted with their general attitude."

Allen had plans for a TV show about firefighters called *Pumper 1*, and something called *Fantasy* for NBC, which a memo described as being about:

> ...A despot who decides that troubles ensue when people read books, especially fiction, and consequently bans books and holds a book-burning. Plot has all the characters from fictional novels meet in a darkened library to rally against the book burner.

Allen had another sci-fi concept called *The Hunters*, about a safari from another planet which comes to Earth to hunt humans in a small midwestern town.

Allen also made another attempt to return to his beloved *Time Tunnel* concept, which he had already revisited several years earlier in *Time Travelers*. Development of the concept went back to Allen's stint at Warner Bros. and extended into his stay at Columbia. In December, 1978, writer Norman Katkov (who had worked on *Viva Knievel!*, Allen's TV-movie *Fire!*, and *The Return of Captain Nemo*) was at work on something called *Time Travel Agency*. In Katkov's treatment, hero Jack Pollard is summoned during an emergency involving an American space flight. Pollard arrives at a 60th floor office identified as Worldwide Import-Export. Ltd. (a seeming nod to Ian Fleming's James Bond and his Universal Exports cover organization). There he meets Mr. Aquarius, the middle-aged man behind the time travel agency, and the Conductor, who operates the organization's time travel machinery and accompanies Pollard on his time travels—this time to 16th Century Rome to find Leonardo Da Vinci and a possible, mathematical solution to the astronauts' plight.

"Each week a desperate man or woman, driven by a matter of the most critical urgency including life or death, will come to Mr. Aquarius demanding to be taken back in time," the proposal read.

*Time Travel Agency* wasn't the only time travel project Allen had in the pipeline. In January, 1979, Robert Malcolm Young wrote an outline for a potential ABC series called *The Time Project*, based on Allen's concept. The story has historian (and widower, of course) Mike Berringer spending 12 years traveling all over the world, searching through references to time travel, and finally tracing them to a time machine called the Ovoid, which is hidden in a cave on the California coastline. Berringer buys the property and builds a house to hide his discovery. Berringer's daughter Dana is a tomboy maturing into a 16-year-old "foxy lady" who likes "boys, lots of boys." His 12-year-old son Casey is "an ingenious klutz," and the kids' surrogate mother is Jane, an elderly New England housekeeper.

The gimmick was a family team of time travelers. "At this very moment a single American family is traveling back in time!" was one of the tag-lines. The Berringers travel back in time:

> ...To solve the most desperate and critical problems of the present. Our time travelers are friendly, identifiable, real people. They are fallible, often uncertain, surprised by their own courage when it is called for. They are not cardboard cutouts, openly heroic or touched by omniscience.

**ABOVE**
Irwin Allen in his office in the early 1980s. (Photo by Mike Clark)

The time travel device itself would be an object of mystery rather than a human invention:

> The Ovoid is an object eight feet high that looks like a giant diamond with thousands of gleaming facets. Around the base of the giant Ovoid are six smaller Ovoids. Eons ago the Ovoid came to Earth from a distant galaxy.

There's also a 36-hour time limit for each time trip (later upped to 72 hours). In addition to the visual impact of the Ovoid, Allen's concept had the Berringer house itself as a special design concept ("It reminds visitors of an aircraft").

Berringer goes back in time to redress the Aaron Burr scandal, visits Leonardo Da Vinci in an attempt to save an American space mission, travels to China in 214 B.C. to recover a snake venom antidote to save a top ranking diplomat, and to France in 1431 to meet Joan of Arc. The Berringers are captured by Roman Centurions in Nazareth during the life of Christ, travel back to ancient Egypt to find the solution to a plague of locusts threatening the U.S., are held by slave owners in 1859 Appalachia, seek out art captured by the Nazis in 1940, and travel to 1836 to experience the battle of the Alamo. Dana Berringer falls in love with a patrician from Pompeii in 79 A.D. Unlike Doug and Tony in *The Time Tunnel*, Berringer and his family must be careful not to change anything in the past so as to not alter the timeline.

With its family "inheriting" and controlling a fantastic, technological object from the past, *The Time Project* was Allen's attempt to reconfigure his original concept for *The Return of Captain Nemo*, and the idea was similar to other short-lived sci-fi TV shows of the 70s like *Fantastic Journey*, with wholesome families getting mixed up with time travel, aliens, and the Bermuda Triangle.

Katkov outlined the reaction of Warner Bros. executive Cliff Alsberg in a January 18, 1979 memo to Allen:

> Cliff Alsberg's most repeated and strongly felt reaction to the presentation is: The Berringers do not react to their time travel with enough incredulity. When they find themselves in the past (or in the future), they must respond as the audience would respond: incredulous, astonished, spellbound, unbelieving, flabbergasted, wide-eyed, wide-mouthed, speechless. They must be almost helpless at first. The differences in their clothing, in their language, in the civilization around them must almost immobilize them....They have no easy—indeed, any—answers to their dilemma. They must find their situation incredible. They are in a constant state of disbelief. Alsberg suggests that, given the proper stimulus, Mike could even break down and cry.

The "incredulity" advice was ignored as recently as 2011's time travel show Terra Nova, where characters sent back to the Cretaceous Era seemed more interested in teenage dating issues than the momentous idea of being transported to another world millions of years before the dawn of human history.

Alsberg did like some of the story possibilities, but felt "smaller" stories would be preferable, "not yarns about

**RIGHT**
Concept rendering of the "Ovoid" time travel device from Allen's proposed *The Time Project* series.
Art by Tom Cranham.

major historical events." Alsberg also felt "the Ovoid is a poor TIME TRAVEL device." He suggested other concepts like a moving "rip" in the atmosphere close to the Berringer house or a "warped" tree into which people can disappear when they get close enough. But he did like the idea of a 72-hour "time lock" and found the Berringer family appealing. "Alsberg does not want: The President, the Alamo, or the Ovoid." But he liked the idea of Dana Berringer falling in love with someone in the past.

Robert Malcolm Young worked on a teleplay for the concept, part of which involved the Berringers encountering Jesus of Nazareth at the age of 12. In a February 23, 1979 memo from Katkov to Allen about Robert Malcolm Young's first draft. Katkov thought Young's draft was very good but he didn't think there was enough plot. He objected to a scene in which two Roman soldiers see the four Berringers wearing 20th Century clothing and ignore them—the sort of thing that happened often on *The Time Tunnel*.

A February 27, 1979 memo from Katkov outlined Al Gail's thoughts. Gail thought the script and both stories focused too much on Dana:

> The other people in our story are almost totally neglected. Our series lead is Mike. He is lost in this draft. His character is not developed.

Eventually the entire idea of a family team using their personal time machine to journey through time was dropped, and *The Time Project* developed into a completely different concept over the course of the next year. Writer Herman Miller presented a treatment on May 13, 1980 called "Windows of Time," and once again Allen had discarded the idea of an ordinary family and returned to his old staple of scientists and military men.

"Windows of Time" is set in 1988 in the midst of an energy crisis, as a nuclear meltdown has caused all reactors worldwide to be shut down and OPEC nations reveal their oil reservoirs are all but depleted, leaving industry and transportation in a state of near chaos. In order to deal with the problem, Project Timepiece is revealed: "an experimental project begun two decades ago in secrecy (making it potentially the same as *The Time Tunnel*'s Project Tic-Toc)," designed to send two men traveling in time.

Unlike *Time Tunnel*'s Doug and Tony, however, these two men, Lt. Colonel Casey Redman and Dr. Lucas Royce, are temperamentally mismatched. Intending to travel a few hundred years into the future to find the answer to the energy crisis, they wind up millions of years hence, when the earth is dying—the sun is a red giant but the earth is quickly cooling into an ice age. There they meet OMEGA, the last man on earth, who has been waiting for their predicted arrival with "the principle of a renewable and pollution-free energy source." They then wind up in 1888—"a world of no pollution, of faith in itself and faith in its future. It is something our own time has lost..."

By the time Miller finished his final draft script in October, 1980, Allen and his production team were at Columbia. Miller's version of *The Time Project* was more in line with a classic Irwin Allen program. Casey Redman was a very capable but somewhat unserious military man, while Lucas Royce was a brilliant but, as the teleplay later reveals, emotionally troubled scientist. After Warner executives objections to the crystalline, pyramid-shaped alien time travel device in the earlier *Time Project* concept, Allen went back to the idea of a "star" vehicle in the show, a time traveling ship called the Kronos 1.

Miller gives the vehicle all the verbal showmanship that we presume Allen would have provided in terms of the ship's design and special effects execution:

> This is the world of tomorrow. This is magic time. This is the stuff dreams are made of. It is almost impossible to take it all in at once—the surrounding gantries, support structures, massive in scale, graceful parabolas that surround and contain an ovoid bubble, glass-like, yet with a sheen that hints of something more than titanium and aluminum—a ship, a machine, a device, a structure, a dream, a piece of art, a sculpture of pure form, fragile, delicate, yet containing a hint of vast power...a Lady, a regal Queen, a fragile goddess—unique and wondrous.

With the character of Omega, the Earth's final inhabitant millions of years in the future, patiently waiting for the arrival of the two time travelers so he could hand over high technology and some cryptic words of advice, the teleplay suggests some time travel confluences to be revealed over the course of the series. Miller also borrowed ideas from *Star Trek*—Royce and Casey use devices called communicators and refer explicitly to a Prime Directive that restricts them from interfering in human history.

Once transported to the late 1800s, Casey falls for a female inventor, allowing for a lot of discussion about the equality of the sexes. More interestingly, Royce tracks down his own grandfather—an abusive ex-slave owner—and exacts some vengeance on the man for his future mistreatment of Royce's mother and father. And it is Royce the scientist who eventually becomes unhinged, taunting his grandfather and the locals with his knowledge of future history and becoming determined to remain behind in the past in order to ensure that future events will transpire favorably for humanity. Despite the temptation of taking his paramour from the past back inside the Kronos 1 to return to the present (the ship can only transport two people through time), Casey convinces Royce to board the ship so the two men can presumably have further adventures.

On December, 1980, Allen was the recipient of a particular honor that was the flip side of his feting on *The Merv Griffin Show* five years earlier. The late night, Canadian-bred satirical TV show *SCTV (Second City Television Network)* broadcast a sketch entitled "The Irwin Allen Show," with Rick Moranis (who also often portrayed Merv Griffin on the program) playing Allen as a mischievous talk show host who sets guests Robert Wagner (played by a stunt performer) and Shelley Winters (Robin Duke) on fire, unleashes an earthquake on Charlton Heston (Joe Flaherty), and besets Red Buttons (Dave Thomas) with giant killer bees, quipping, "That's what he gets for wearing too much makeup. There's nothing killer bees like more than a good Number 9 Pancake." Allen's public reputation had gone from household name in 1975 to joke fodder in 1980, and one had to wonder whether the *SCTV* writers were even aware that there had actually been a real Irwin Allen Show in the early days of television.

Allen soon got a small measure of revenge and some rare good news when ABC greenlighted his *Pumper 1* TV series idea in January, 1981. Allen still had T*he Time Project* (called "the godson of *The Time Tunnel*" in a January issue of *TV Guide*) as well as *The Hunters* alien safari idea plus *Fantasy*, which Allen now said would include characters like Robin Hood, Sherlock Holmes, and Little Miss Muffet.

None of these ideas, *The Time Project* included, would ever see the light of day, but *Pumper 1* quickly evolved into *Code Red*, with Lorne Greene as the patriarch of a family of firefighters that included Andrew Stevens, Sam Jones, and Julie Adams. *Code Red* was a labor of love for Allen, an outgrowth of his experience on *The Towering Inferno* and the numerous accolades he had received from firefighters in the years after the release of the blockbuster.

Family-oriented and educational, with lessons in safety in every episode, the show ran for 19 episodes—a single season—on ABC between September, 1981 and spring 1982. The show would be Allen's last weekly television series. Production illustrator George Jenson, who had worked on *Lost in Space, The Time Tunnel* and *Land of the Giants* and later on productions like *Close Encounters of the Third Kind* and *Romancing the Stone*, says that the Irwin Allen who made *Code Red* was not the man he knew at Fox in the late 1960s:

> We used to call him the Emperor. That was his persona. [Warner Bros. had] opened up the studio for him there

**OPPOSITE LEFT TOP**
Allen on the set of *Code Red*, 1981.

**OPPOSITE LEFT BOTTOM**
(L to R) Sam Jones, Martina Deignan, Andrew Stevens, and Lorne Greene, the stars of *Code Red*.

**OPPOSITE RIGHT**
Magazine cover and ad promoting *Code Red*, Irwin Allen's final weekly TV series, which ran for a single season between 1981 and 1982.

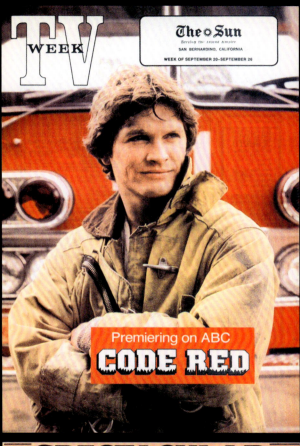

## SPECTACULAR
### ABC SUNDAY MOVIE DOUBLE FEATURE!
**NEW FOR FALL!** abc 8:00PM 7 42

FROM THE CREATOR OF
"THE POSEIDON ADVENTURE"
AND "THE TOWERING INFERNO"
COMES A NEW ADVENTURE
OF BLAZING ACTION
AND SUSPENSE!

IRWIN ALLEN'S
# CODE RED

**STARRING**

LORNE GREENE · JULIE ADAMS · ANDREW STEVENS · MARTINA DEIGNAN · SAM J. JONES

and he had a beautiful suite with a fireplace and it was really a beautiful setup, and then it all seemed to crumble. I worked for a week or two on a pilot about the fire department, *Code Red*, and he seemed for the first time since I'd met him, very humble and gracious and very nice, a different man in a way.

By September, 1982, with *Code Red* off the air, Irwin Allen began to explore an idea that he had dismissed a decade earlier when his career was at its height—a *Lost in Space* movie.

After the success of the *Star Trek* films, Warner Bros. was investigating the idea of a movie based on the Rod Serling TV series *The Twilight Zone* (that project would go ahead, leading to a well-made but extremely ill-fated movie production in 1983). At the same time, and at Allen's behest, Warner Bros. marketing research looked into the idea of a *Lost in Space* movie as compared to the prospects of *The Twilight Zone*. Their conclusion:

> Study results indicate that a movie based on *Lost in Space* would be a highly risky project. It would almost certainly not have the built-in appeal of the movie version of *Star Trek* nor our current *Twilight Zone* project, simply because the TV series does not currently have as large nor as satisfied a following. The results suggest that the potential for the success of this project would depend heavily on our ability to deliver a highly satisfying, action-filled movie with lots of special effects, and to create characters more interesting than those featured in the TV series.

Recovering from that rebuke, Allen announced a deal with Columbia in December that included something called *No Limits*, which Allen told *TV Guide* was "the best of Irwin Allen. It's under the water, on the shore and in outer space." The package also included a comedy called *No Way Out*.

Neither of these announced projects ever went into production. Allen still had two finished TV-movie "mini-disaster films," relics of his production deal at Warner Bros., languishing on the shelf, completed but unaired. In February, 1983, NBC broadcast *The Night the Bridge Fell Down*, about a group of character actors—sorry, *characters*—trapped on a collapsing bridge along with a crazed bank robber played by Dezi Arnaz, Jr.

*The Night the Bridge Fell Down* had the extreme misfortune of airing the same night as the final episode of CBS' *M*A*S*H*, "Goodbye, Farewell and Amen." As the last episode of one of the most popular and acclaimed television series ever put on the air, the *M*A*S*H* finale drew over 106 million viewers, one of the largest audiences in television history. It's no surprise that even among Irwin Allen's subset of TV disaster movies, *The Night the Bridge Fell Down* is one of the most forgotten.

*Cave In!*, which aired on NBC on June 9, didn't fare much better. Interestingly, both TV movies featured Leslie Nielsen, who had filmed them in 1979, back when he was still a perennial TV show guest star and utility player noted for his dour, dull seriousness. Just a year later Nielsen starred in *Airplane!*, and by 1983 he had already starred in the Zucker Bros. series *Police Squad!*, lampooning TV cop show conventions and himself to

brilliant effect. Viewers watching *The Night the Bridge Fell Down* and *Cave In!* likely had to stifle a chuckle every time Nielsen was on screen.

In the fall of 1983, Irwin Allen began looking into a genre that had barely been explored in movies and television, but which would seemingly have been right up Allen's alley—the comic book superhero adventure. At this point there were only a few relevant examples, led by the 1966 *Batman* series, which had been a huge but short-lived sensation and had established a mock-serious, "campy" style that later projects in the genre would struggle to overcome. The most successful attempt to do exactly that was Richard Donner's 1978 movie *Superman*, which took flight via a stupendously forthright and charming performance by Christopher Reeve as the Man of Steel to become a mammoth blockbuster. The movie had spawned two sequels and a wave of stillborn comic book superhero projects including Batman and Dick Tracy movies that would not see the light of day for over a decade.

Other attempts at superhero projects were all on television—a *Captain America* pilot that turned the Marvel Avenger into a helmeted, motorcycle-riding stunt man, and a *Wonder Woman* TV-movie with Cathy Lee Crosby an unrecognizable, platinum blonde Amazon. There was a technically ambitious attempt to do Marvel's linchpin hero *Spider-Man* with Nicholas Hammond that managed a 14-episode run on CBS between 1978 and 1979. More successful: a disco-driven, *Wonder Woman* TV series starring Lynda Carter on ABC, and an adaptation of Marvel's *The Incredible Hulk* that ran for five seasons between 1977 and 1982.

There were plenty of other popular characters in the Marvel Comics stable, and in October 5, 1983, Allen met with producer Carla Singer, writer Tony Kayden, Dick Kirschner, Bill Wells, and Marvel's Stan Lee about Kayden's script for a pilot movie based on *Daredevil*, about a blind lawyer who gains radar-like sight and super agility after being exposed to a bath of chemicals as a young man. Rights to *Daredevil* had been picked up by another producer as early as 1975, but nothing had come of the project. Of course, the Daredevil character was later made into a poorly-received Ben Affleck movie and has recently been adapted very successfully as a Netflix TV series, and it's interesting to see how Allen's project may have paralleled how the character would eventually be translated.

Allen clearly was interested not only in the idea of a blind action hero, but of the possibilities for gadgetry and visual impact that a *Daredevil* series would bring. A memo from the October 5 meeting had two elements that were certainly new to the *Daredevil* concept: one note suggested the elimination of a pet cat named Merlin for a more traditional seeing-eye dog—although in the comics, blind lawyer Matt Murdock has no pets of any kind:

> Matt Murdock does not use a cane but rather uses the dog for guidance, (This presents a problem because of the already agreed-upon, folded-up billy club which is contained within the structure of the cane itself. Perhaps the solution here is that Matt uses a cane and the dog whereas DAREDEVIL has no need for either.)

In addition to the billy club, a trademark weapon of the comic book character, the memo makes note of "sonic glasses" to aid Daredevil in seeing, a technological element of his super abilities rather than the superhuman senses that the dousing of industrial chemicals grants him in the comic book.

Of Murdock's lawyer partner Foggy Nelson, Allen noted:

> A younger version of John Houseman would be a proper prototype [*Producer and actor John Houseman had starred as a stuffy, tyrannical law professor on the TV series* The Paper Chase *in the late 1970s*]. ...he is old-school, a Harvard law graduate, slightly stuffy and a brilliant lawyer. He is not unkind but he is slightly annoyed that Matt spends so much time with the poor and/or non-paying clients in the clinic downstairs.

The teleplay had incorporated Murdock's classic origins, with his father a broken down boxer who runs a gym in Hell's Kitchen—but Allen suggested dumping that element. The network had its own suggestion about a tongue-in-cheek finale for the TV-movie:

> CBS recommends that we actually have a costume party at the end given by Karen [Page]. This will complete the rationale as to why Matt bought a costume which does become DAREDEVIL's permanent costume. Then, as a touch of irony, Matt goes to the party as the now famous DAREDEVIL. To top that touch—there are, in fact, five or six more guests who also come dressed as DAREDEVIL.

According to the book *Marvel Comics, The Untold Story*, Stirling Silliphant himself eventually produced the final draft of the *Daredevil* pilot. But after Columbia extended its one year option on the property in late July, 1984, CBS officially passed on the project that August. Through 1984 and 1985, 30 years before Netflix's *Defenders* series and the Marvel *Avengers* movies, Allen and Stan Lee had continued to pitch and develop show concepts for many of the Marvel characters, including *Power Man* (otherwise known as Luke Cage), *Iron Fist, The Fantastic Four,* and *Black Widow*—a comic book hero super-stable that anticipated just about everything dominating movie and TV screens today. Unfortunately, none of these projects came to fruition—Allen never made a comic book-based series, and eventually his professional correspondence with Stan Lee and Marvel ended.

Allen continued to conceive and pitch science fiction and fantasy projects to the networks, but he hadn't succeeded in getting one on the air in almost a decade, going back to *The Return of Captain Nemo* in 1977. The Irwin Allen brand—once the province of the flashiest shows on television, and then some of the most spectacular and explosive theatrical movies ever made—had now been diminished to a dwindling series of moribund TV-movies and one relatively realistic, short-lived TV series about a family of firefighters.

**OPPOSITE**
Production photos from Allen's 1983 *The Night the Bridge Fell Down* with Leslie Nielsen, Dezi Arnaz, Jr., and James MacArthur.

Advertisement for *The Night the Bridge Fell Down*.

# ALICE IN WONDERLAND

Allen was now approaching 70 years old, and four decades of functioning as a workaholic, Type-A personality had taken their toll. The unstoppable producer who furiously scribbled down ideas in the middle of the night on a notepad kept by his bed, the man who arrived at his office before everyone else on the lot and stayed there after most of his team had left, was now diminished and slowing down. Even worse, Hollywood production seemed to be leaving him behind. The studio system he had thrived in was now gone, and Allen had been leaping from lot to lot as the departments of artists and craftsmen that had helped him realize his vision died off and disappeared.

Just as he had done so often—and so successfully—in the past, Irwin Allen reached back into the childhood that he had never really left to find one more story that he hadn't yet explored: Lewis Carroll's *Alice in Wonderland*. Allen's interest in the story wasn't casual.

Television legend Steve Allen said in 1995:

> He loved to read. He really knew what was in his library, and he used it and he studied. He was aware of the world of culture, and he was not just a dilettante. He cared about ideas and history. He was very interested in history.

Carroll's story was a particular favorite of Irwin Allen, and when he approached Steve Allen with the idea of his writing songs for a musical treatment, he came prepared:

> Irwin came to me with at least a dozen books, some of them quite rare, long out of print books, editions of the *Alice in Wonderland* story by Lewis Carroll, and books about it, books analyzing its sub-texts and its hidden psychological meanings and that sort of thing. It was actually helpful in doing the work I did.

Allen's classic TV shows had always appealed to children, but he hadn't done anything aimed directly at kids. *Alice in Wonderland* would indeed be a musical, and Allen wanted to corral a bunch of big name stars to cameo as Carroll's famous characters, everyone from the Mad Hatter to the Cheshire Cat. Allen had jumpstarted his early movie career by adapting a

**LEFT**
Allen's longtime costume designer and assistant Paul Zastupnevich with his artwork for *Alice in Wonderland*, and with Allen in the project's production offices.

**OPPOSITE**
Storyboard artwork for Allen's production of *Alice in Wonderland*.

SC 28A, 29, 30, 31 CONTINUOUS SHOT 1
PULL BACK TO REVEAL RABBIT HOLE
WHITE RABBIT ENTERS HOLE...

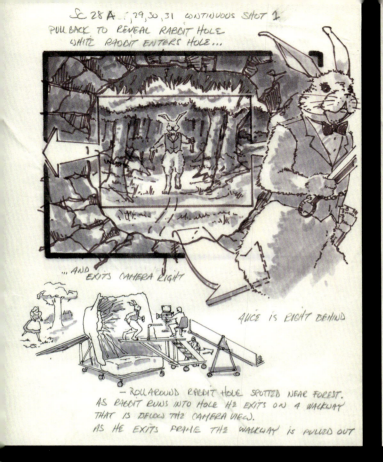

...AND EXITS CAMERA RIGHT

ALICE IS RIGHT BEHIND

— ROLLAROUND RABBIT HOLE SPOTTED NEAR FOREST.
AS RABBIT RUNS INTO HOLE HE EXITS ON A WALKWAY
THAT IS BELOW THE CAMERA VIEW.
AS HE EXITS FRAME THE WALKWAY IS PULLED OUT

SC 32 HIGH ANGLE, ALICE. BLUE SCREEN
ALICE FALLING AWAY FROM CAMERA
MOTION CONTROL ON ALICE —

BACKGROUND PLATE: PHOTOGRAPH
MODEL OF INT. RABBIT HOLE

ALICE FLYING IN FRONT OF
BLUESCREEN: SHOOT WITH
ZOOM LENS.
— SAME RIG AS SC 49.
SHOOT AS MUCH FOOTAGE
AS POSSIBLE OF ALICE
TUMBLING; ZOOMING AWAY,
ETC.

BLUE SCREEN
SC 239 G
OVER ALICE AS SHE WATCHES THE CAT
START TO DISAPPEAR, LEAVING ONLY ITS
GRINNING HEAD —

CAT ACTOR IS PHOTOGRAPHED
WITH HIS HEAD THRU A
HOLE IN A BLUE SCREEN
CARD

BLUE SCREEN PLATE OF CAT HEAD

BACKGROUND PLATE WITH
ALICE AGAINST THE FOREST —

CAT ACTOR IS PHOTOGRAPHED
WITH A BLUE HOOD ON AND
LEANING AGAINST A BLUE WALL

BLUE SCREEN PLATE OF CAT BODY

SC 793 G = ANGLE ON THE CREATURES

... A GROWING BELLYACHING DISCONTENT ON THE
PART OF THE GUESTS ...

bestseller in Rachel Carlson's *The Sea Around Us,* and he still knew the value of a famous book property. Allen told Stephen Farber of *The New York Times*:

> Over 100 million copies of Carroll's book have been sold. We're talking about one of the greatest pre-sold audiences of all time. That's why we want to put it on at Christmas, as a family special. This is a program that could play every year for the next 20 years. If we're half as fortunate as *The Wizard of Oz,* we'll be in gravy.

Allen was entering the territory of Rankin-Bass and Syd and Marty Krofft, but he was quick to point out that *Alice in Wonderland* fit in perfectly with his earlier output:

> Fairy tales are the most horrific of all stories. Carroll's book has fire, flood, earthquake, nightmares, goblins, ghosts. It is the kind of story I understand best.

Allen fought to reassemble some of his long-standing production team to tackle the new project. Costume designer and assistant Paul Zastupnevich was still with Allen after 35 years, and he would be tasked with creating the look of most of the movie's growing cast of characters. Cinematographer Fred J. Koenekamp, who had shot *The Towering Inferno, The Swarm,* and *When Time Ran Out...* for Allen was brought onboard, but a number of Allen's old hands had passed on or retired.

Sidney Marshall, who'd started as a story editor on *Voyage to the Bottom of the Sea,* worked as an associate producer on *The Poseidon Adventure* and *The Towering Inferno,* had died in 1977 while working as a production executive on *The Swarm.* Production manager Norman Cook had started working with Allen on *City Beneath the Sea* in 1971 and he had died of liver disease in 1981 while on location in Pennsylvania working on the Tom Cruise movie *Taps.* Allen's two closest associates were still his cousin Al Gail, now a production executive on *Alice,* and post production supervisor George Swink, whose work with Allen dated back to *The Sea Around Us.*

Swink had to find a replacement for one of Allen's most important old collaborators, special photographic effects supervisor L.B. Abbott. Abbott had unofficially retired—and come out of retirement—numerous times, but this time he really was retired. The visual effects master's last credit was on 1982's *Wrong Is Right,* and he died in September, 1985, just a few months before *Alice in Wonderland*'s December airing on CBS. Allen would turn to John Dykstra—the man behind the groundbreaking effects in *Star Wars*—and Dykstra's Apogee, Inc.

Allen had hired writer Paul Zindel to adapt Carroll's books. Zindel was an award-winning playwright ("The Effect of Gamma Rays on Man-in-the-Moon Marigolds") who had adapted the stage musical *Mame* for the big screen in 1974. Interestingly, the same year he worked on Allen's *Alice in Wonderland* Zindel also contributed to the screenplay to Andrei Konchalovsky's brutal thriller *Runaway Train.*

Allen had hired Steve Allen to write the project's songs—in what would become an increasingly challenging, even monumental task.

Allen said in a *USA Today* cover story on the production:

> Irwin doesn't consider himself especially knowledgeable about music. I told him, if you can get Stephen Sondheim to do your lyrics, I would rate him a better lyricist than myself. If you can get Michel Legrand to do your score, I think you should do that because Legrand is my favorite modern composer. Of course, I knew he couldn't get either one of them.

Steve Allen's ability to crank out the tunes, and Allen's determination to get as many big name stars on the project as possible, turned what might have been a 90-minute special into a two-part production that ate up four hours of prime time real estate.

Al Gail said in 1995:

> The musical aspect grew and grew. In the beginning there may have been a couple of songs, but then Steve Allen was involved in writing the tunes, and, he came up with some excellent tunes. And before we knew it we had ten to fifteen songs in the film. And that added to the budget and added to the time shooting.

Steve Allen saw the opportunity as a godsend coming from Irwin:

> Speaking just as a songwriter, even if we hadn't been close friends, which we were, I would have been eternally grateful to him, because never I think in the history of the musical theatre has any songwriter been presented with thirty-seven stars. Generally if you write the score for a musical, you're lucky if they get one important person to star in it, and then the others are supposed to be good but the world never heard of them. Whereas in this case, song after song comes by with nothing but stars and superstars performing them. So what more could a songwriter ask—nothing.

While Steve Allen said his producer largely left him to his own devices as far as the songwriting was concerned, Irwin Allen also had specific input on a few numbers:

> He wanted a song for the Cheshire Cat played by Telly Savalas, and he said he wanted something kind of sober and somber, so I wrote something, and he said, "That's a very good song but I don't think it's right for this spot." And I was annoyed, cause we all think whatever we wrote last Tuesday is great. On the other hand he's the boss so, write him another song. So I did and he said this is closer, but it's still not what I'm looking for. And again I was annoyed, I didn't say that to him but I was. So I said all right, he wants sober and somber and depressing, I'll give him depressing, and I wrote a song which the cat sings to little Alice and it's one of the most depressing songs ever written. It's called, "There's No Way Home," and what he's saying to her is "Honey, you ain't never gonna get out of this mess you're in—you're gonna be lost forever wandering through space."

At this point there was no question of Allen directing, even on a television production, and particularly not one as technically ambitious as this one. Allen initially offered the director's chair to Ronald Neame of *The*

SC 290 · WIDE SHOT AS ALICE JOYOUSLY JOINS THE PROCESSION INTO THE CROQUET FIELD CAMERA PULLS BACK AND UP (WITH SLIGHT TILT DOWN)

**ABOVE**
Storyboard artwork for Allen's production of *Alice in Wonderland*, framing Alice's entrance into The Queen of Heart's Croquet-Ground.

*Poseidon Adventure*. Neame had made four films in the considerable wake of *The Poseidon Adventure*, all high-profile productions: *The Odessa File*, the disaster movie *Meteor*, the Walter Matthau comic adventure *Hopscotch*, and Matthau's stint as a Supreme Court justice in *First Monday in October*. Neame was idle between 1981 and 1985, but he still turned down the job on *Alice in Wonderland*, perhaps noting that *The Poseidon Adventure* was still far more remembered as an Irwin Allen film than a Ronald Neame one.

Allen then turned to Harry Harris—"Midnight Harry," the director of 43 episodes of Allen's television shows (including 24 episodes of *Land of the Giants*, almost half the series' run). Harris had been busy since his last experience working with Allen on the pilot for *The Swiss Family Robinson* in 1975, making episodes of *Man from Atlantis*, *Hawaii Five-O*, *The Waltons*, *Eight Is Enough*, *Cagney and Lacey*, *Scarecrow and Mrs. King*, and *Remington Steele*. He'd even won an Emmy for an episode of *Fame* in 1982, so he went into negotiations with Allen over *Alice in Wonderland* in a position of strength—particularly since he didn't particularly want the job.

Allen had wrangled over 40 stars for cameos in the movie, and at $3.5 million an hour, *Alice in Wonderland* would become the most costly miniseries ever filmed, and boast the largest cast. Production had to be moved to MGM for stage space for the show's 72 sets and 500 costumes. Ironically, considering Allen's ambitions for the project, *Alice in Wonderland* was shot on the same stages where *The Wizard of Oz* had been filmed in 1939.

Allen even added choreographer Gillian Lynne, who'd worked on the Andrew Lloyd Webber musical *Cats*, to put the stars through their dancing paces.

Harris recalled in 1995:

> I knew it [would] really be a killer to do—four hours, with all of those people and all of those costumes and all of those sets and all of those musical numbers. [Irwin] offered it to me for not much money—okay money, not much—which was my out, not wanting to do it. I just was afraid to do it, cause I knew what I would be going through to get it done.

Harris then took a tongue-in-cheek but ultimately effective tactic to get out of the job. With a potential deal in place, Harris' agent told the director he needed "a deal breaker"—a demand so outrageous that Allen would balk and let Harris off the hook:

> I said, "Okay, tell him I'll work for his money, but I want a brand new Mercedes Benz four-door sedan, 500 SEL."

The luxury car cost 60 grand—and Harris' agent assured Harris that he'd just broken the deal. In fact, after relaying the stipulation to Allen, the agent called Harris back to say that Allen had replied with the ultimate showbiz threat—that Harris would never work in Hollywood again:

> About ten minutes later the phone rings, and I'll never forget that phone call. [Irwin] said, "I can't believe what I just heard—something about an automobile!" He said,

"I'm not in the automobile business. I'm in the movie business. I'm a movie producer. That's ridiculous!" I said, "Well, okay." He hung up on me. Well, I got that car, and I had to take him for a ride in it and, I don't know whether I was sorry I took the job or not. It was a very hard job.

Finding an Alice for *Alice in Wonderland* was every bit as important as nabbing a songwriter and director. Allen had originally had his eye on two child actresses who had broken out in 1982. One was Drew Barrymore of *E.T.: The Extraterrestrial*. "She had turned into a young lady and was really too big," Allen told Farber in the *Times*. Barrymore had starred as a preadolescent in *Firestarter* and would be featured in another Stephen King thriller, *Cat's Eye*, in 1985.

Allen was also interested in Heather O'Rourke of *Poltergeist*, but O'Rourke turned down the role and worked on a TV-Movie, *Surviving*, with Molly Ringwald in 1985 (O'Rourke would do two *Poltergeist* sequels and would die tragically in 1988 of complications from Crohn's Disease).

In a July 16, 1985 interview for the NEA's *Lively Arts* magazine, Allen claimed that he tested over 600 girls for the part of Alice before finding 9-year-old Natalie Gregory of Orange County:

> She's terrific. She's got a computer for a mind. Explain something to her once and she nods. It's in the computer.

According to Harris, speaking in *The Orange County Register*, a kid with the brain of a computer was exactly what the part required. Gregory would be tackling the largest speaking role ever written for a child. "She will be in every scene and play opposite 42 different stars. We needed someone who could handle that load without being rattled or burdened by personal problems." Gregory had appeared on *Magnum P.I., Cagney & Lacey* and *Matt Houston*, but nothing of the magnitude of *Alice in Wonderland*.

Allen's ability to wrangle boatloads of big name stars (a skill set that he had honed as far back as *The Story of Mankind*) paid off in spades as the cast of *Alice in Wonderland* began to swell to include Allen regulars like Red Buttons, Shelley Winters, Telly Savalas, Roddy McDowall, Jack Warden, Karl Malden, Ernest Borgnine, and Don Matheson (and even stunt performer Ernie Orsatti as a flying lizard), as well as showbiz vets like Donald O'Connor, Sammy Davis, Jr., Martha Raye, Imogene Coca, Carol Channing, Anthony Newley, Robert Morley, Sid Caesar, Harvey Korman, Merv Griffin, Pat Morita, George Gobel, Steve Lawrence and Edie Gorme, Louis Nye, Jonathan Winters, and Lloyd and Beau Bridges, as well as popular younger TV stars like Scott Baio, Patrick Duffy, Ann Jillian, Donna Mills, John Stamos—even Ringo Starr.

Allen told the NEA magazine:

> I've got 41 stars in this. Stars are important. If you make a product that is pretty good, stars will help. If you make a product that is great, they'll still help. We've caught lightning in a bottle. Suddenly, everyone is excited about this production. When I was casting it, everybody wanted

**ABOVE**
Sheila Allen (right) as Alice's mother, with Natalie Gregory in Allen's *Alice in Wonderland*.

**OPPOSITE**
Natalie Gregory (top left) anchored a cast of celebrities including Ann Jillian as the Red Queen, Telly Savalas as the Cheshire Cat, Red Buttons as the Rabbit, Karl Malden as a walrus and Sammy Davis, Jr. as the Caterpillar and Father William.

SC 399 FULL SHOT REVERSE...

ALICE TRAPPED AGAINST THE MANTEL AS THE
CREATURE REARS UP, JAWS HIGH, WINGS FLAPPING
CLAWS STRETCHING FORWARD

SC 821C REVERSE (OF SC 821)

AS THE WHITE KNIGHT VALIANTLY BATTLES THE
JABBERWOCK ALICE TURNS AND FLEES DOWN A CORRIDOR

to be in it. I got calls from everybody and his agent. I think this is going to be a big hit.

"Actors either want to work for lots of money, or they want to do something with lots of their friends," Jayne Meadows (actress and wife of Steve Allen) said in *The New York Times*. "That's how they get drawn into something like 'Night of 100 Stars.'" Veteran British comic actor Robert Morley added, "It's very amusing to be with a lot of old pros sitting around reminiscing about when they were famous." Allen also found a place for Sheila Allen, perfectly cast as Alice's kindly mother.

Even Harry Harris was impressed by the time the entire show got cast:

> He got a star-studded cast and he paid a fortune for 'em. I think we spent eight million dollars [on casting]. But he's got Steve Allen doing the music and he's got all these movie stars. He's got Sid Caesar and Imogene Coca and he's got Ringo Starr playing one of the characters. He's got people comin' from all over that wanted to do this. He paid 'em a lot of money for a days' work or two, but there's a lot of publicity involved, and it was a kind of a glitzy thing and they liked the way that he made it. He made it a Hollywood movie. He was kind of the last of the Hollywood guys around. He had that kind of knack, that showmanship quality.

The arduous production took its toll on everyone, including Allen, who couldn't spend as much time on set as he had in the old days. Costume designer Paul Zastupnevich actually pointed this out as an advantage, saying that without Allen's constant oversight on the sets and costumes, "I got to do whatever I wanted."

But in at least one case, Allen bent over backwards to accommodate a cast member with her own health concerns when actress Ann Jillian was diagnosed with breast cancer and underwent a double mastectomy while working on the special.

"If I were casting *Alice in Wonderland*, I'd cast Irwin Allen as the King of Hearts," Jillian said in an AP profile. "He's an incredibly compassionate man. He totally rearranged the shooting schedule. That enabled me to do what I had to do. I could not imagine not coming back to work and doing something I really wanted to do."

Anthony Newley was also hospitalized for minor surgery after two days of work on the mini-series. Throughout these difficulties, Allen maintained an even temperament and good humor that surprised some of his associates as well as newcomers who knew of his reputation. In the *USA Today* cover story, writer Paul Zindel pointed out that Allen, who "is capable of a temper that could easily wipe out an entire secretarial pool" had been surprisingly easy to work with.

One person not surprised by Allen's generosity on set was Steve Allen:

> He was a remarkably generous person. He would invite, oh, twelve of us to dinner at Chasen's, and even if you go to a dinner at a restaurant like that alone, you'd better bring along your credit cards. He would just pick up the check for the whole thing—he was talking sometimes about thousands of dollars, I'm sure, for a large dinner party, and he did that sort of thing again and again. Or he would invite ten or twelve or fifteen of us to some big public event and buy tickets, five hundred dollars a chair. So that's the word that comes to my mind—generosity.

Al Gail added:

> He gave literally, millions, to the hospital—Cedars Sinai, and, other projects as well. He was a very charitable man and a very loyal man. Underneath the so-called gruff exterior, he had a soft heart.

Allen's biggest conflicts on the production occurred off the set. One regime at CBS had happily given Allen the go-ahead on *Alice in Wonderland*, but when new management entered, they looked on the old regime's choices—and on Allen—with disdain, despite the fact that the production wasn't costing CBS a dime.

Harry Harris recalled:

> It was fully financed by Proctor and Gamble. [Irwin] had it all laid out, what he wanted and who he wanted, and he went to CBS and they said, "Great idea—go ahead with it." The guy at CBS bought it. But in the middle of it, while we were making it, they had a change of command at CBS, and a new guy came in, and he didn't want it. Too late. We're in the midst of it. He gave Irwin a bad time, and Irwin hated him cause he put everything we did down. Now it wasn't *Gone With the Wind*, but it was an entertaining show for kids, and the CBS guy didn't want to associate himself with this project.

One of the disagreements Allen had with CBS was over the makeup designs done for the movie's large cast of characters, who had to be costumed and made up to resemble tortoises, rabbits, walruses, lions, even Humpty-Dumpty. Allen had hired makeup artist Werner Keppler (*Battle for the Planet of the Apes, Star Trek II: The Wrath of Khan, The Last Starfighter*) and Leo Lotito, Jr. (*Planet of the Apes, When Time Ran Out..., V*) to provide prosthetic makeups that would give the characters the same imaginative, fairy tale look that had been given the characters in the original *The Wizard of Oz* and other productions. Allen had great experience with this kind of work in his prior television productions—in fact, makeup artist John Chambers had done some simian prosthetics to make actor Michael Conrad look like an ape-man for the *Lost in Space* episode months before the premiere of Chambers' Oscar-winning makeups for *Planet of the Apes*. But when CBS executives saw the first footage of the elaborate character makeups on *Alice*, they complained that the work obscured the faces of the famous actors Allen had hired and publicized for the program. Consequently a great deal of the imaginative makeup work was scrapped, and characters like Patrick Duffy's goat, Red Buttons' rabbit, and Telly Savalas' Cheshire Cat appear in whiteface or with just a few whiskers added to their famous features. Interestingly, Duffy and Buttons are less recognizable than the unmistakable mugs of Ernest Borgnine (as a lion) and Karl Malden (in the most elaborate makeup as a walrus), who were some of the few actors to retain their prosthetic makeup jobs.

**OPPOSITE RIGHT**
Test photography of the Jabberwocky on set, and images from the TV-movie, with the monster threatening Alice as she becomes trapped in a spider's web.

**OPPOSITE LEFT**
Storyboard artwork of the Jabberwocky.

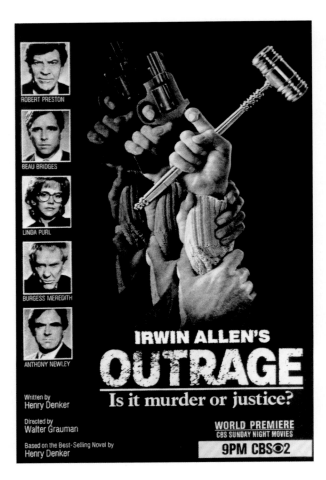

Another characteristic Allen touch was the Jabberwocky, a dragon-like monster created by Tim Turner and Adam Hill of Berman Studios. The Jabberwocky was a man in a suit (Berman artist Tom McLoughlin) in the manner of the dragon in *Lost in Space*'s "The Questing Beast," but with a more modern flare—and lots of slime—courtesy the Berman technicians.

Steve Allen recalled:

> It looked like something you'd get scared to death with at the Universal Tour, but it was very effective. Whether any other producer or director would have contrived to emphasize that element in the production I don't know, but it made sense that [Irwin would do] that because of his long experience with shocking audiences or scaring them.

The Jabberwocky appears throughout the production as a figment of Alice's imagination, but a nerve-wracking one that was probably relatively frightening for young children even in 1985, particularly when the creature briefly traps Alice against a spider web occupied by a large tarantula by moonlight.

After four decades of movie and TV production, Allen was still likely more comfortable scaring audiences than drawing them in with deep emotion, something Harry Harris acknowledged ivn 1995:

> In his television stuff there was never anything between the people—never. It was always man against the elements, man against the monsters, or the Little People against the Giants. It was always putting one against the other.

For Harris and others, the pattern fit in with Allen's demeanor on set, which was always approachable, but still officious, with co-workers kept at arms' length. But the crucible of *Alice in Wonderland,* perhaps combined with Allen's advancing years and declining health, had worn some of the edges off of Allen's emotional armor, leading to a remarkable scene between Allen and Harry Harris after production wrapped:

> The day that we wrapped the show, we were at MGM, he said, "I want you to come up to the office." I thought, "Oh God, now what's he gonna yell at me about?" [He] brought me in the office, he closed the door, and he came and he gave me a hug, and he sat down in his chair and he cried. I had never seen any emotion come from him, ever. But he was doing the thing he wanted to. We just completed one of the things he wanted to do. But I saw that emotion come out on him. This was something he wanted, and he got it completed and he got it done the way he wanted to, and it was over with and he broke, sat down and cried. And I felt really strange about it, but it was like a whole change of character for this guy. I knew he had a soft side to him, but that's the first time I saw that.

Allen still faced pushback from the network, which didn't grace *Alice in Wonderland* with the most advantageous time slot for its debut.

Alex Gail remembers:

> They didn't really give it an honest shot. They put it on Sunday night when a kid's gotta go to school. But it was a cute show. It was a darn good show, and it was really an achievement on everybody's part to make this thing. It was a great experience for everybody. That to me was probably one of the best things he's done in television.

*Alice in Wonderland* benefited from all the publicity Allen had drummed up over its casting and production—it won its time slot and wound up being one of the top ten shows for the year for CBS, according to Allen. The special was also nominated for five Primetime Emmy Awards, for Hairstyling, Makeup (Werner Keppler, Terry Smith, Leo Lotito Jr.), Art Direction (Philip M. Jeffries, Ross Bellah, Hub Braden, Audrey A. Blasdel, Robert De Vestel), Costume Design (Zastupnevich), and sound editing (Joe Melody).

Anyone who grew up watching television variety programs like *The Carol Burnett Show* or *The Sonny and Cher Comedy Hour,* or even episodes of *The Love Boat,* will find Irwin Allen's *Alice in Wonderland* familiar and even comforting territory. It's a simple and colorful cavalcade of celebrity guest stars and musical numbers tied together by Natalie Gregory's wholesome and charming performance as Alice. Gregory pulls off her epic role convincingly and even holds her own against famed hoofer Sammy Davis, Jr. in a soft shoe number (in the *NEA Lively Arts* magazine piece, Davis noted that when he was having difficulty with one of his dance steps, Gregory helpfully "showed me what I was supposed to do"). Composer Morton Stevens sets the stage with his opening main title music, which is pure showbiz razzle dazzle, and Steve Allen produces at least one touching song, "Alice, Can You Hear Us," which wraps up the production with a performance by the entire cast. While

**RIGHT**
Promotional artwork for *Outrage,* a courtroom drama that was a departure from Irwin Allen's more genre-based television work—and his last television production.

**ABOVE**
Irwin Allen near the end of his career, preparing for production on *Alice in Wonderland*.

it may seem off the beaten path for Irwin Allen's career, the parade of cameo performers in outlandish costumes and makeup, playing to a child performer, more than once recalls *Lost in Space* and Will Robinson's weekly encounters with villainous guest stars.

Allen had maintained his trademark optimism throughout the production, even looking hopefully back toward movie theater screens as he told a *USA Today* reporter, "A disaster cycle is out there somewhere ready to come around again."

The producer had at least some reason for hope. *Alice* had done well enough to attract the attention of the studio that had once named a building after Allen, and then cast him into the wilderness. "Once *Alice in Wonderland* happened, the ratings were pretty good, and once that hit, we were back at Warners and all was forgiven," Joe Musso recalled.

After *Alice in Wonderland* was completed, Allen's friend and cousin Al Gail, his collaborator and sounding board back to the very beginning of his career, elected to retire—a not unexpected but still sobering blow to Allen.

Sheila Allen said in 1995:

> He was kind of upset when Al decided to retire because they were the closest of confidantes all the years down. And you need somebody like that when you're in this business, I think. You need a sidekick that you can talk to and say things to that you don't say to anybody else. So that was hard on him then. He had his stock company of players, he was very faithful to people that he loved and worked with and he would hire them all the time. But he also had in his production area a group of wonderful people whom he was very close to. And as a lot of time went by they would retire, and that was kind of sad for him too. It wasn't that easy for him to pick up new people to have that rapport with that you build up over years.

Even without Gail and the many other members of his team who had died or retired, Irwin Allen pressed on. His last television production would be the TV-movie *Outrage!*, filmed just after *Alice in Wonderland* and broadcast on CBS in March of 1986.

*Outrage!* was something Allen hadn't done since the very beginning of his movie career at RKO—a straight crime drama about a father who kills the man accused of raping and murdering his daughter after the criminal gets off on a technicality. Allen took advantage of a standing courtroom set from another production to keep costs under control, and rehired director Walter Grauman (*The Memory of Eva Ryker*) to shoot the movie, which would feature veteran actor Robert Preston (*The Music Man*) in his last screen performance.

A month later, Allen would already be plotting another project in the mold of *Alice in Wonderland*: Australian-based UAA Films had partnered with Allen for a new production of *Pinocchio*, to be written by Paul Zindel of *Alice in Wonderland* and to feature 14 songs by Steve Allen.

# PINOCCHIO

Warner Bros.' enthusiasm over *Pinocchio* rekindled some of Allen's old energy, and he had his team of designers at work over a year between 1986 and 1987 creating sequences and designs for the project. In another bid to reclaim past glories, Allen even reached out to his alienated old production designer, Bill Creber—but not directly, as Creber remembers:

> He had Musso call me to do *Pinocchio*. He said Paul Z had a costume all made, and I said, "I knew it." I had just worked for some puppeteers on *Flight of the Navigator*. Those guys are geniuses, they are so good at what they do. So I thought, let me call my puppeteer buddies about this because it's right up their alley. I got them on the phone and I said Irwin Allen wants to make *Pinocchio*. He said, "A boy in a puppet suit." And I said, "Yeah." He said, "You can't do that. The audience is going to know it's a boy in a puppet suit." *Pinocchio* is all about the scene where the puppet turns into a boy. And if the audience perceives that it's a boy, you've blown this whole story. It's so wrong-headed. So I called Irwin back and said I didn't want to do it because it had gotten to me that Paul Z had made this wonderful costume for a boy.

Joe Musso recalls avoiding a beef with Disney:

> We had some wonderful things planned for *Pinocchio*. Disney said that they didn't have any problem as long as we didn't do what they did—they took liberties with the book. In their movie, Monstro's a big whale, and in the book it's a big fish, and they just sneak out while the whale's sleeping, and of course Disney had this big chase with the whale. In the books they had this giant and we were going to make him look maybe 20 feet tall, still big enough to get inside the belly of a whale, and I think they wanted Gene Hackman to play the giant. Somehow the whale swallows the giant and his wife and they're chasing Pinocchio inside the whale, and all this chasing around

**ABOVE**
Concept artwork for Allen's unproduced musical *Pinocchio* by Dick Lasley (top) and Joe Musso (bottom).

**OPPOSITE**
Costume design sketches for Pinocchio's attire.

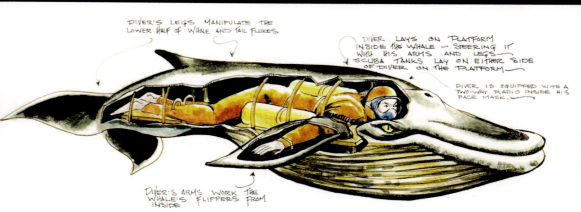

DIVER'S LEGS MANIPULATE THE LOWER HALF OF WHALE AND TAIL FLUKES

DIVER LAYS ON PLATFORM INSIDE THE WHALE — STEERING IT WITH HIS ARMS AND LEGS — SCUBA TANKS LAY ON EITHER SIDE OF DIVER ON THE PLATFORM

DIVER IS EQUIPPED WITH A TWO-WAY RADIO INSIDE HIS FACE MASK.

DIVER'S ARMS WORK THE WHALE'S FLIPPERS FROM INSIDE

BODY OF THE WHALE IS FORMED WITH LIGHT TUBING — COVERED WITH HARDWARE CLOTH OF CHICKEN WIRE — A FLEXIBLE RUBBER SKIN IS LAYED OVER THE WHALE FORM — A SCUBA DIVER OPERATES THE WHALE FROM INSIDE —

**ABOVE**
Concept artwork for the exterior, operating mechanics, and interior of *Pinocchio*'s whale.

**FOLLOWING**
Additional concept artwork by Joe Musso and Dick Lasley.

its heart and stuff gives the whale indigestion, so all this mayhem is going on inside the whale and the whale is reacting to that until Pinocchio and his father get away.

Allen was prohibited from using a sperm whale because Disney's version had featured one. When Musso suggested a blue whale Allen, producer of *The Sea Around Us*, asked, "What's a blue whale?" When Musso explained that it was the largest whale species, twice as big as a sperm whale, Allen immediately got the president of Warner Bros. on the phone. "He said, 'We're gonna use a blue whale, it's twice as big as a sperm whale!' And he got the studio jazzed about that," Musso laughed.

Steve Allen worked on songs for the project, and had also completed a book, music and lyrics for a treatment of Charles Dickens' *A Christmas Carol*.

By late March, 1987, Allen was also writing CBS' Bud Grant about another TV series idea, *101 Grove Street*:

> This is a hard-hitting, modern day story that takes place in San Francisco involving the San Francisco Health Department. I have approval to shoot in and around the building and, should we go to series, I have access to over two hundred thousand available true life stories. This show would be perfect timing. The subject of health is the biggest topic in the U.S. today.

Allen was also still trying to keep the ball rolling on *Pinocchio*:

> Finally, I proposed to you the possibility of converting *Pinocchio*, which I'm still preparing as a theatrical feature with Warner Bros., into a three or four hour miniseries for TV done on the same grand scale that we did *Alice in Wonderland*. As you remember, *Alice* took its time period and was in the Top 10 for the year. *Pinocchio* would also be a musical with some ten songs written and performed by the likes of Lionel Richie, Stevie Wonder, etc. It would be filled with even more special effects than was *Alice* and be done on even a grander scale. The preproduction on *Pinocchio* is virtually finished and the artwork and concepts are quite marvelous and available to be seen at any time. I am enclosing herewith a copy of the script by Paul Zindel who, as you know, is a Pulitzer Prize winner and the writer of the *Alice* script.

Allen also inquired about a second rerun of *Alice* on CBS which would allow domestic release of the film on videocassette, indicating that foreign videocassette sales had done very well.

By this point Allen's health—and his luck—were beginning to fail. The producer had to begin slowing down as cardiovascular disease hobbled him.

Steve Allen remembered:

> It must have been particularly galling because he was a doer. He loved to have two projects on the rails and planning six more and, therefore when his health no longer permitted, that in his last few years, I can only guess what it must have felt like. But he still maintained his friendships and those of us who loved him would go down to his lovely home and visit with Irwin and Sheila at their house in Malibu.

**LEFT**
*Pinocchio* concept artwork by Dick Lasley (top) and Joe Musso.

**OPPOSITE**
Concept art depicting Pinocchio narrowly escaping the green fisherman's frying pan.

Allen's longtime assistant and costume designer, Paul Zastupnevich, had his own health concerns and took note of Allen's:

> We drifted apart in '87, '88. I had a slight stroke but fortunately I bounced right out of it. And he was the kind of an individual, he was private—he didn't want anyone to know how sick he was so he hid himself. He made excuses with himself. He had meetings and things like that so we were not in constant touch with one another.

Soon even Allen's socializing suffered. Red Buttons added:

> He became more a recluse. Nobody knew what was wrong with Irwin. Irwin was an inside kind of a guy. When he became ill nobody knew the nature of the illness. We knew he was ill, but, he was not a crybaby. There was no whining. There was no looking for sympathy. Irwin was tough. He had a veneer, a toughness about him, and, he didn't want anybody to feel sorry for him. We started seeing less of Irwin and the word got around that Irwin wasn't feeling well, and I think most of us who knew him were hoping for the best.

Allen's hopes for *Pinocchio* were dashed when the project fell victim to unforeseen financing problems, as Joe Musso related:

> *Pinocchio* we were getting ready to film and Warner Bros. put up half the money and this Australian production company put up the other half, and somehow they defaulted just when we were getting ready to start filming. They went bankrupt and we had all these stars lined up, and to even try to get it started up again would have broken the window of some of the people they wanted to use.

Allen had another unusual project, *Oh, God! 4*, in the works. The original *Oh, God!* had been a surprise star turn for veteran comedian George Burns in 1977, and had been followed by two sequels, *Oh, God! Book II* in 1980 and *Oh, God! You Devil* in 1984.

Burns had been 81 when he'd filmed the first movie, and in 1990 he was 94. As Musso explains, Burns' age—his comedy trademark for the past couple of decades—ultimately derailed the project:

> They had this great script for *Oh, God! 4* and they were ready to start filming, and suddenly they couldn't get insurance on George Burns for more than two weeks and he was the star of the movie—there was just no way we could film all his scenes in two weeks.

Allen had one more possible ace in the hole. The first blush had gone off the *Star Trek* movie franchise since Allen had first approached Warner Bros. about making a *Lost in Space* movie in the early 1980s—now the *Trek* franchise had spawned a new slate of syndicated TV shows as well as the movies, and producers were turning to other old television properties to revive them for the big screen. "Irwin wanted to do a big *Lost in Space* movie on the scale of *Star Wars* and *Star Trek* and bring it into the modern era," Musso says.

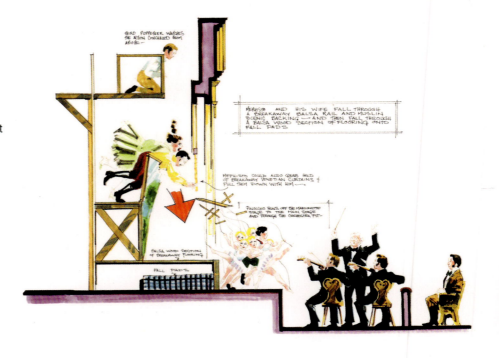

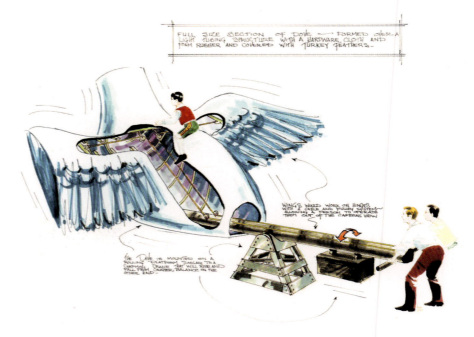

**ABOVE & OPPOSITE**
More production concept artwork by Joe Musso for Allen's *Pinocchio*.

THE DOVE AND MINIATURE DUMMY OF PINOCCHIO FLY OVER A MEDIEVAL WALLED VILLAGE (CARCASSONNE, FRANCE). THE DOVE IS SHOT IN SLOW MOTION FLYING IN FRONT OF A FRONT PROJECTION SCREEN OF THE BACKGROUND.

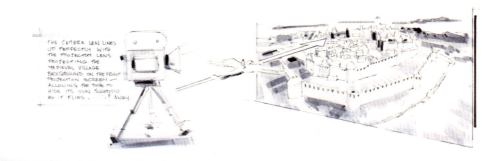

THE CAMERA LENS LINES UP PERFECTLY WITH THE PROJECTOR LENS PROJECTING THE MEDIEVAL VILLAGE BACKGROUND ON THE FRONT PROJECTION SCREEN — ALLOWING THE DOVE TO HIDE ITS OWN SHADOW AS IT FLIES AWAY.

LONG SHOT OF THE REAL DOVE WITH THE MINIATURE DUMMY OF PINOCCHIO FLYING PAST A FRONT PROJECTION SCREEN OF NEUSCHWANSTEIN CASTLE, GERMANY. SHOT IN SLOW MOTION.

THE CAMERA LENS LINES UP PERFECTLY WITH THE PROJECTOR LENS PROJECTING THE CASTLE BACKGROUND ON THE FRONT PROJECTION SCREEN — ALLOWING THE DOVE TO HIDE ITS OWN SHADOW AS IT FLIES PAST.

TREE BRANCH IN FRONT OF THE FRONT PROJECTION SCREEN

THE REAL DOVE WITH THE MINIATURE PINOCCHIO FLYING PAST THE FRONT PROJECTION SCREEN

To that end, Allen approached what he considered to be the one indispensable element in any *Lost in Space* revival—Jonathan Harris:

> I got a telephone call one morning—this is Irwin Allen's secretary, and I must say, I was taken aback. It's been sixteen or seventeen years and I said, "What does he want?"

Allen summoned Harris for a meeting at his offices at Warner Bros. "I must say I was interested and curious," Harris said. The veteran actor was also unprepared for what he would see when he met Allen face to face again after so many years:

> He had changed considerably, he really had. And I was taken aback at the appearance because [he was] very very, very thin. So we shook hands. I was afraid of cracking a bone for the fragility, you see.

Harris, Allen, and Allen's production manager went to a Cantonese restaurant for lunch where Allen put his cards on the table.

"I am thinking about *Lost In Space*," Allen said. "I think I want to do something about it."

"Like what?" Harris asked.

"Haven't decided yet. Either another series, or a motion picture, or a special. What do you think about that?"

"Irwin, I think that boat has sailed. You should have looked into that ten years ago."

"I've been busy," Allen growled.

"Doing what? *Alice in Wonderland*?"

Now it was Allen who was taken aback. "I spent thousands of dollars on market research. The interest is out there."

After several moments enjoying putting Allen on the defensive, Harris now asked if Allen had a script for the project, and Allen assured him a "wonderful" script was being written as the two men were speaking. Harris politely assured him that he would love to read the screenplay when it was finished:

> And then he said something that was so un-Irwin, totally. He said, "Of course I can't do it without you." He had never mentioned that I was in the show to anybody, when we were doing it, you see. And I thought that was very surprising. I said, "Well, that's very nice." And he said they have the Robot. I said that'll be a good idea.

Armed with the knowledge that Harris was going to appear at a convention in New Jersey the following week, Allen told the actor that as far as any revival of *Lost in Space* was concerned, "Now you can say, possibility. Nothing definitive."

Harris recalled that Allen called the very next day to reinforce the narrative.

**OPPOSITE**
A larger than life figure deserves a larger than life desk: Allen in his palatial office at Warner Bros.

**ABOVE**
A late-in-life photo of Irwin Allen, flanked by Sheila Allen and Michael Caine.

"What are you gonna say at the convention in New Jersey?" Allen asked.

"Possibility. Nothing definitive," Harris replied.

Allen said, "That's right," and hung up.

So ended Jonathan Harris' last discussion with Irwin Allen.

Joe Musso recalls that Allen's health really started to decline precipitously around the time he tried to get the *Lost in Space* revival going:

> He went and had bypass surgery, but he didn't want the studio to know. He was at home and he would have his secretary take the call and transfer it to his home. One day Sheila called me and asked me to come out to the house, that Irwin wanted to see me. I went down there, they were in Malibu, and Al Gail was there and Irwin had been sick and he was suddenly coming out of it and it was like he wanted to see his family again. Sheila had lunch made and it was like old times with Irwin.

Musso remembers that Allen pointed to a stack of fan letters in the room—the producer was still getting them from people who'd grown up on *Voyage to the Bottom of the Sea, Lost in Space, The Time Tunnel, Land of the Giants*—from people who had thrilled to his disaster movies and knew Allen as a personality, a star in his own right, worthy of his own circle of fans:

> Now that he was feeling good he said, "Sheila, I got all those requests—get the letters out and I'll sign them." Sheila said no, that's too much work, and Irwin said, "Sheila, they took the trouble to write, the least I can do is sign them." But it was like he wanted to get back at it. And it was two weeks later he had the heart attack and died. Al Gail said later, "I'll bet you didn't realize how sick he was." His heart just gave out. Because of the heart problem, it made him diabetic a little bit, and it gave him a hernia, and they were going to have an operation for the hernia, and suddenly he woke up about six o'clock in the morning and he had a heart attack.

Irwin Allen died on November 2, 1991 at age 75.

Ironically, his death occurred little over a week after *Star Trek*'s Gene Roddenberry's demise on October 24th—the two men had produced the most memorable science fiction TV shows of the 1960s.

Like his movies, and even his wedding, Allen's funeral at Forest Lawn was a star-studded affair, largely organized by actor Red Buttons at the request of Sheila Allen.

Red Buttons recalled:

> I got the rabbi. I was like the master of ceremonies and people spoke, with adoration and kindness, for Irwin. Wonderful turnout. Wonderful. I remember even saying, "You know Irwin, it's standing room only." It was a strange dichotomy, Irwin's funeral. We tried to make it a bit joyous, just a celebration of his life. There was great affection in what was said about him.

Paul Zastupnevich, who had helped Allen organize and decorate countless social events, tried to bring a little Irwin Allen zing to the funeral by ordering balloons for the wreath that would temporarily decorate Allen's gravesite at Forest Lawn. Even with the legendary producer dead, Zastupnevich still felt the same pressure to knock it out of the park that he had been under on a daily basis in decades of work for Allen.

"I said to the florist, 'Please, I want at least fifty balloons on the thing.' Because I knew that [if Irwin were alive] he would be saying it wasn't big enough—make it larger."

Hoping for a *Towering Inferno*-sized effect, Zastupnevich arrived to find something more akin to *Beyond the Poseidon Adventure*. The florist had misunderstood his directions and provided a meager 15 balloons rather than 50. When exhibitor Sherrill Corwin's wife Dorothy approached him to ask who'd sent the balloons, a chagrined Zastupnevich admitted, "I did, Mrs. Corwin."

"I thought you did," the woman smiled. "It made me think of all the parties we attended; he always had balloons."

Zastupnevich, speaking only a couple of years before he too would die at the age of 75, recalled the moment as one of mutual understanding about the man so many had worked and played with over the years. For Irwin Allen, every workday was a parade under his own personal big top, alive with balloons, fireworks, and the biggest toys anyone ever played with.

"I still say he was a boy at heart."

**OPPOSITE**
The many faces of Irwin Allen: writer, producer, director, Hollywood personality, and brand name—the mogul late in his storied career.

HE LOVED HIS LIFE, AND WHAT MORE CAN YOU SAY ABOUT SOMEBODY THAN THAT THEY GOT TO DO EXACTLY WHAT THEY LOVED TO DO.

HE LOVED BEING IRWIN ALLEN.

**SHEILA ALLEN**

# LIFE AFTER DEATH

*Irwin Allen's legacy lives on as his concepts evolve and continue to influence other creators*

In the decades after Irwin Allen's death in 1991, his name continued to define a style of lavish, colorful entertainment. His best-known works, from *Lost in Space* to *The Poseidon Adventure* and *The Towering Inferno*, have become iconic touchstones. They helped define science fiction television in the 1960s and the advent of the motion picture blockbuster in the 1970s. If anything, his work inspired generations of young filmmakers—from Steven Spielberg and George Lucas to Roland Emmerich and James Cameron. Filmmakers who, in turn, continue that tradition—armed with bigger budgets and more special effects resources than Irwin Allen ever dreamed possible.

In 1994, Kevin Burns, a young television executive at Twentieth Century Fox, set out to prove to Sheila Allen that there were still people at the studio who remembered and cared about Irwin's legacy. With that in mind, he produced an ambitious feature length tribute to Irwin for the Sci-fi Channel, entitled *The Fantasy Worlds of Irwin Allen*. It featured interviews with most of the surviving cast members of Allen's television shows and movies, behind-the-scenes footage of the special effects shoots from the series, and a recreation of the iconic Jupiter 2 "landing site" set that had once occupied a soundstage at 20th Century Fox.

Although modestly budgeted, the cable TV special forged a friendship between Burns and Allen which led to Burns—along with his friend and former Fox feature film executive, Jon Jashni—being entrusted with the development and management of all the Allen properties under the name Synthesis Entertainment in 1999.

By this time New Line Cinema was already well into the development and production of a big budget theatrical

**OPPOSITE**
One of the Robinson family's Chariots on an alien planet in Netflix's 2018 *Lost in Space* series.

**LEFT**

Bill Mumy, June Lockhart and Jonathan Harris with the Robot on the set of 1995's *The Fantasy Worlds of Irwin Allen*.

Sheila Allen with the Robot on the set of *Fantasy Worlds*.

Jonathan Harris, Bill Mumy and Bob May (inside the Robot) suit up on the flight deck of the Jupiter 2 in *Lost in Space Forever* (1998).

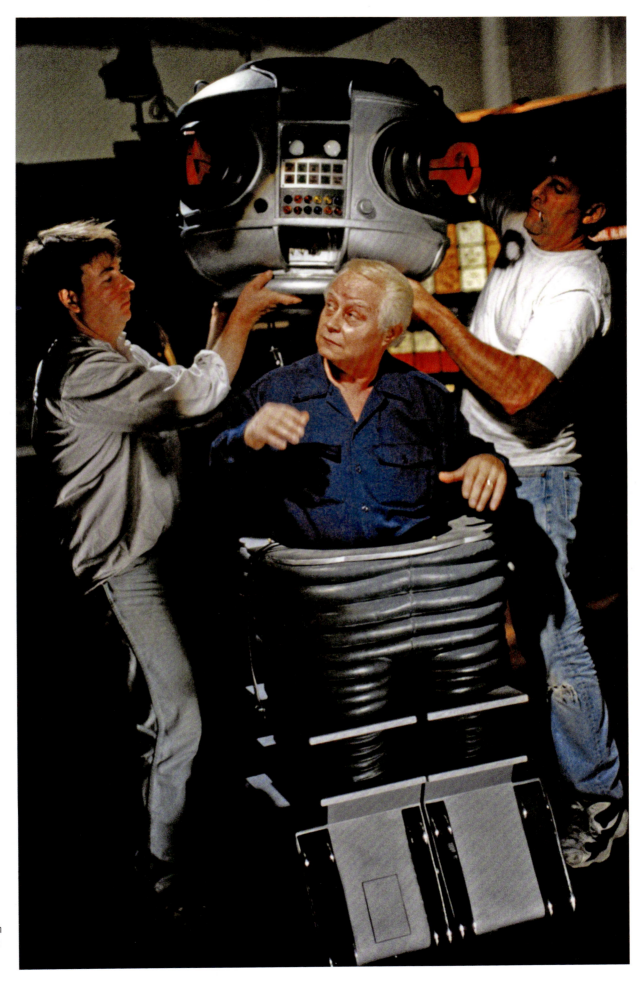

**RIGHT**
Bob May gets into the robot suit one last time for *Lost in Space Forever* with the help of Steve Buscaino (L) and Ron Hamill (R).

film version of *Lost in Space* that hit theaters in 1998, without the involvement of Burns and Jashni. Starring William Hurt, Mimi Rogers, Matt LeBlanc, Heather Graham, and Gary Oldman as Dr. Smith, the movie reunited the original show's surviving cast members, Mark Goddard, Marta Kristen, June Lockhart, and Angela Cartwright in cameo roles—with Dick Tufeld providing the voice for the newly-designed Robot.

Although the film earned praise for its production design and special effects, it failed to recapture the innocence and charm of the TV show. Kevin Burns produced a syndicated TV special, *Lost in Space Forever*, that allowed viewers to revisit the series and judge the difference for themselves. Designed to promote both the classic series and the New Line movie on DVD, *Lost in Space Forever* was hosted by John Larroquette and assembled Bill Mumy, Jonathan Harris, and Bob May on a mock-up of the flight deck of the Jupiter 2. Back in costume and in character, Harris, Mumy, and May (along with Dick Tufeld) brought the classic characters back to life in what would be the final on-screen reunion of Will Robinson, Dr. Smith, and the Robot.

In 2001, Burns and Jashni inked a deal with Twentieth Century Fox Television to develop all of Irwin Allen's TV properties with Synthesis. The first project was intended to be an NBC TV movie/back door pilot entitled, *Lost in Space: The Journey Home*. As written by Brent Maddock and Steve Wilson (*Short Circuit, Tremors*), the program would have featured a new group of space colonists who rescue the original TV Robinson party, who have been frozen aboard the Jupiter 2 for seventy years. Unfortunately, the death of Jonathan Harris—who had agreed to reprise his signature role of Dr. Smith—brought the project to a halt.

Similiarly ill-fated was a 2002 attempt by Synthesis to re-boot *The Time Tunnel*. As written by Rand Ravich and directed by Todd Holland, the plot involved a cold fusion experiment done by the Department of Energy which accidentally creates a "time storm" that lasts 240 minutes.

Dubbed "The 240," the storm creates a number of anomalies that alter history for everyone but the personnel at the experimental facility—who must then use the equipment to travel back in time to repair the anomalies without creating further alterations to the time stream. David Conrad played Doug Philips, who was reluctantly recruited for the assignment due to his knowledge of a crucial battle in WWII Germany. The original show's Tony Newman became "Toni" Newman, played by Andrea Roth. With its open-ended, mission-oriented plotline and a willingness to address the kind of mind-bending paradoxes created by time travel that the original series often chose to ignore, the pilot was thought by many Fox network executives to have tremendous potential. Nevertheless, the project was shelved in order to make room in the schedule for Joss Whedon's epic, *Firefly*—which, ironically, was cancelled after only eleven weeks.

In 2004, Synthesis and Fox took another run at *Lost in Space*—this time as a remake. Written by Doug Petrie and directed by John Woo, *The Robinsons: Lost in Space*

**ABOVE**

The stars of the 2002 *Time Tunnel* pilot: (left to right) Kavan Smith as Flynn, David Conrad as Doug Philips, and Andrea Roth as Toni Newman.

The Robinson family, Major West, and the Robot onboard the Jupiter 2 in this promotional photo for the 2004 *The Robinsons: Lost in Space* pilot directed by John Woo.

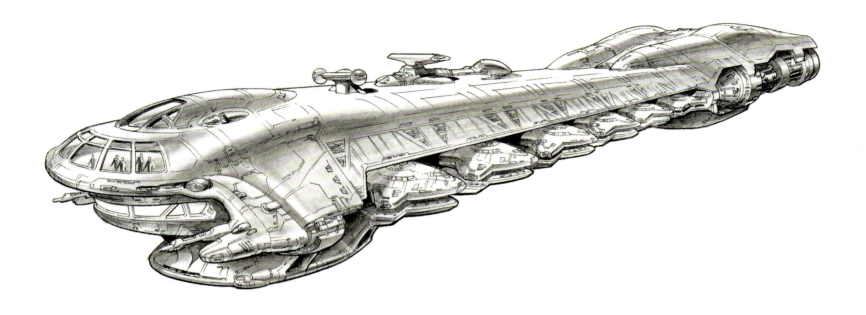

**ABOVE & RIGHT**
Design for the Jupiter 2 colony ship for John Woo's 2004 *The Robinsons: Lost in Space* pilot.

Daren Dochterman's study for a Seaview-like observation deck for the new Jupiter 2.

Brad Johnson as John Robinson and Jayne Brook as Maureen Robinson.

Director John Woo with Adrianne Palicki as Judy Robinson.

was set in the year 2082 and took place after an alien invasion of Earth has been repelled with the help of military commander John Robinson (Brad Johnson). John's ongoing wartime exploits helped to alienate him from his family, including wife Maureen (Jayne Brook), sons Will (Ryan Malgarini) and David (Gil McKinney), and daughter Judy (Adrianne Palicki). The show's humanoid-looking Robot was constructed by Will (and voiced by Dick Tufeld).

As produced for the now-defunct WB network, *The Robinsons: Lost in Space* was beset with behind-the-scenes production problems and ultimately was not picked up by the network as a series. Nevertheless, this third attempt to re-launch the Jupiter 2 offered some interesting connections to other science fiction TV shows: the Jupiter 2 set was later used by the 2004 *Battlestar Galactica* TV series as the set for the battlestar Pegasus; actress Jayne Brook went on to play the recurring Admiral Cornwell in *Star Trek: Discovery*; and Adrianne Palicki got her own space show when she played the first officer of the starship on Seth McFarlane's series, *The Orville* in 2017.

In 2006, filmmaker Wolfgang Petersen remade *The Poseidon Adventure* as simply *Poseidon*. Petersen had made the ultimate WWII U-boat movie with *Das Boot* in 1981, and had helped pioneer digital water simulation technology with his adaptation of Sebastian Junger's book, *The Perfect Storm*, a disaster movie about fishing trawlers trapped in a killer storm in the Atlantic Ocean. Petersen cast Kurt Russell and Richard Dreyfuss, two of Hollywood's most reliable, everyman actors—but the film failed to recapture the impact and drama of the original movie, despite more than thirty years of advancements in moviemaking technology. Allen's once-derided formula of filling his projects with old time movie stars found its true validation in the *Poseidon* remake. For many critics, the absence of outsized personalities like Ernest Borgnine, Gene Hackman, Shelley Winters, and Stella Stevens, turned Paul Gallico's high-concept blockbuster into just another forgettable action movie.

But the film did demonstrate how visual effects and set construction techniques had advanced. The new Poseidon ocean liner, designed by concept artist Daren R. Dochterman under the supervision of production designer William Sandell, was an entirely digital creation in its exterior views, as was the massive tidal wave that swamps it. ILM and other vendors took advantage of the water simulation capabilities of software developed for movies like Petersen's *The Perfect Storm*, and digital set extensions allowed for the interior of the new Poseidon to boast massive atriums, providing the kind of epic scope that the miniature work and soundstage photography of the original could only suggest.

On November 13, 2013, Sheila Allen died at the Malibu beach house she had occupied with Irwin since the 1970s. For decades, she had scrupulously preserved her husband's papers and production materials (much of which provided the research and imagery for this book), and worked with Kevin Burns and Jon Jashni to keep Irwin Allen's projects in the public eye.

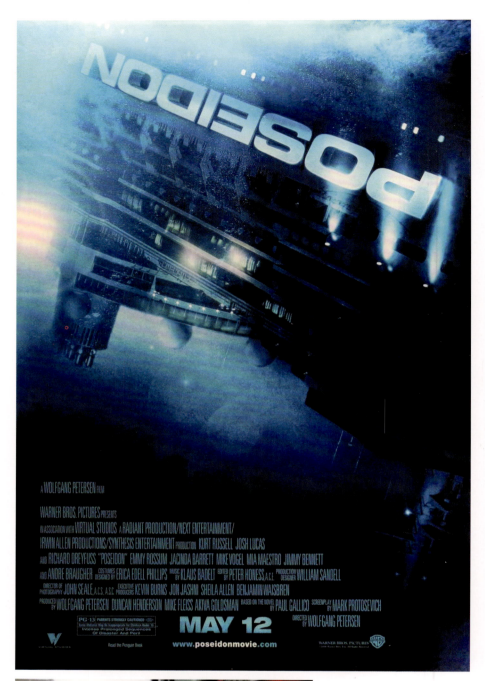

**ABOVE**

Poster art for the 2006 remake of *The Poseidon Adventure*.

Jon Jashni and Kevin Burns of Synthesis Entertainment at the premiere of *Poseidon* in 2006.

**RIGHT**
Daren Dochterman's design concept artwork for the oceanliner Poseidon for the 2006 film including an image of the tidal wave about to strike.

Concept artwork of passengers falling inside the Poseidon's atrium as the ocean liner capsizes. (Art by Daren Dochterman)

Shortly before her death, Sheila expanded Synthesis' role in managing the Irwin Allen properties. She authorized the restoration and re-mastering of the original *Lost in Space* television series to 2K HD—just in time for the show's 50th Anniversary in 2015. She also gave Burns and Jashni her blessing to arrange for what would become the sale of all the Allen properties to Legend Pictures in 2014. This sale allowed Synthesis to have unprecedented creative input—which, in turn, would affect the fate of everything from *Lost in Space* and *The Time Tunnel* to *Voyage to the Bottom of the Sea* and *Land of the Giants*.

Shortly after the deal was made with Legendary, Burns and Jashni brought in writers Matt Sazama and Burk Sharpless (*Dracula Untold*) and development executive Peter Johnson to work with them in developing a new *Lost in Space* for television which would ultimately stream on Netflix. They also invited director Neil Marshall (*Game of Thrones*) and his partner Marc Helwig to join the creative team as executive producers, with Marshall, an experienced hand at action and genre filmmaking, slated to direct the show's initial two episodes. In January 2016, veteran writer and showrunner Zack Estrin (*Prison Break*) set about prepping what would be ten one-hour episodes at a total budget of $95 million dollars—enough for a decent-sized Hollywood action film and nearly more than Irwin Allen was given to produce all 83 episodes of the original series.

Playing John Robinson (now a former Navy Seal) is Toby Stephens. John's wife Maureen is now an accomplished aerospace engineer, played by Molly Parker. As in the original, the Robinsons have three children, Will (Maxwell Jenkins), Penny (Mina Sundwall), and Judy (Taylor Russell)—but this time Judy is the child of Maureen's first marriage. Ignacio Serricchio plays Don West (now a roguish smuggler) and Parker Posey takes on the gender-swapped incarnation of Dr. Smith.

All ten episodes of the Netflix *Lost in Space* were available for streaming on April 13, 2018. Although it received mixed to positive reviews, it quickly became an audience favorite—particularly with families. In many ways it was an antidote to the sophisticated but often violent and determinedly adult-oriented approach taken by contemporary science fiction programming, from HBO's *Westworld* to CBS All Access's *Star Trek: Discovery*. With an approach that managed to please fans of the original program and attract new viewers, the show earned a pickup for a second season that was announced on May 14th, 2018.

The landscape for television has altered radically since 1965 when *Lost in Space* originally went on the air, and it has in fact altered just as radically since *The Time Tunnel* and *Lost in Space* were rebooted as TV pilots in 2002 and 2004. In the 1960s, one-hour science fiction adventures were rare and risky propositions for network television. While there might have been dozens of westerns, doctor, and lawyer shows on the air, the presence of any one science fiction show set in outer space was often a good argument against the purchase of another for a network (as Gene Roddenberry famously told and retold the tale of how *Star Trek* was rejected by executives at

**ABOVE**
Toby Stephens and Maxwell Jenkins as John and Will Robinson in 2018's *Lost in Space*.

Jon Jashni, Neil Marshall, Kevin Burns and Bill Mumy (as "the real" Dr. Smith) on set.

**OPPOSITE**
Images from Netflix's *Lost in Space* depict the Jupiter 2 and debris from its colony ship plummeting toward an alien planet; The Robinsons (Molly Parker and Toby Stephens, front; Maxwell Jenkins and Mina Sundwall, rear left) and Dr. Smith (rear right) in the Chariot; The Jupiter 2 trapped in ice; Dr. Smith (Parker Posey) and the Robot.

CBS because, "we already have *Lost in Space*"). That situation remained intact through the 1970s and 1980s until *Star Trek: The Next Generation* became a success in syndication and *The X-Files* staked a claim for years on the Fox network. Since then, countless science fiction and fantasy shows have had successful runs on television, everything from a remake of *Battlestar Galactica* to *Buffy the Vampire Slayer*—not to mention numerous iterations of *Star Trek*.

The presence of streaming television services has also changed the equation since *The Robinsons: Lost in Space* and *The Time Tunnel* pilots failed to sell in the early 2000s. Streaming services like Netflix not only provide a home for always-available rerun viewing of popular TV shows, but also a platform for new programs that might be a hard sell to the flagging major broadcast networks. Netflix's *Lost in Space* is a lavish production that, in a way, fulfills the promise of the original *Lost in Space* and Irwin Allen's experiment with cliffhanger endings. The opening episodes of the original *Lost in Space* became serialized by default when Allen chose to break apart his expensive and imaginative pilot and stretch out the story of the Robinson family's exploration of a new planet across five episodes. Now serialization is expected of any dramatic television series, and the Netflix platform has allowed for a movie-quality production of *Lost in Space* that still conjures up the childhood thrills of the original—the crash of the Jupiter 2, the journey across alien landscapes by the Chariot, the early threat of the menacing Robot—while adding a level of adult sophistication to the character relationships and deepening the nefarious Dr. Smith by casting the character as a woman who may be lying about everything, including her own identity.

Loaded with cliffhanger perils, the Netflix *Lost in Space* reinvents the concept for modern audiences while adding countless "Easter eggs" for fans: a chicken named Debbie in homage to the original show's Bloop; an alien derelict ship with an overhead map of the galaxy, a nod to "The Derelict;" a planet with a deadly, elliptical orbit; Maureen Robinson launching herself in a weather balloon a la John Robinson's rocket belt; a climactic battle between the Robinson's Robot and an alien automaton as in "War of the Robots"—and the list goes on. Parker Posey's Smith—legitimately frightening in some moments, theatrically comic in others—is a reinvention of the character that perhaps only this quirky actress (a self-admitted fan of the original show herself) could have pulled off, while the space and planetary action and visual effects have a classic science fiction look and realism that recreates the excitement and wonder of the original series in a way that adult fans can completely buy into.

It's anyone's guess how successful future adaptations of Allen's works will be. Allen's TV shows are products of the 1960s, with all the charm and naiveté that most television programming of the period boasted. They came along when children and younger viewers had never before seen anything as colorful, action-packed, and imaginative before on their TV sets—just as adult moviegoers had never experienced a movie as immersive and harrowing as *The Poseidon Adventure* or as vertiginous and gripping as *The Towering Inferno*.

When Allen said in 1985 that, "there's another disaster wave out there" waiting to be ridden, he was correct—since Allen's death we've had *Dante's Peak, Volcano, Deep Impact, Armageddon, The Day After Tomorrow, Titanic, San Andreas* and many others. But the Allen formula has never quite been matched—we no longer have movie stars of the caliber of Paul Newman, Steve McQueen, or Gene Hackman, so most of these films are lucky to boast a single interesting character—the stars are the special effects.

That idea too—special effects driving productions—was almost an Irwin Allen invention; and, like the *Poseidon* tidal wave, once it was launched it raged out of control, leaving Allen's first and best, more character-based disaster movies foundering in its wake.

Over the course of his long career, Irwin Allen shifted back and forth between innovator and imitator. He started out beating Walt Disney to the punch of long-form nature documentaries, then chased the giant footprints of movie impresarios like DeMille (with *The Big Circus*), Disney (with *Voyage to the Bottom of the Sea*), and Mike Todd (with *Five Weeks in a Balloon*). In his tenure at Fox in the 1960s, Allen brought movie spectacle, futuristic visuals and high tech visual effects to TV science fiction, then made the disaster movie wholly his own with *The Poseidon Adventure* and *The Towering Inferno*. Before Steven Spielberg and George Lucas, Allen had audiences lining up to watch action-packed, special effects-driven blockbusters—for two years between the release of *Poseidon* and *Inferno*, Irwin Allen *was* the Steven Spielberg of the era—until Steven Spielberg became the Steven Spielberg of the era when *Jaws* was released a year after *The Towering Inferno*.

In his days at Warner Bros. throughout the remainder of the 1970s, Allen found himself chasing Lucas and Spielberg on projects like *The Return of Captain Nemo*. Yet in 1985, with his career in its twilight, Allen was pitching projects that today are the multi-billion-dollar province of Marvel Comics, Kevin Fiege, Netflix, and Disney—Luke Cage, Daredevil, The Fantastic Four, Black Widow. It's doubtful, perhaps impossible, that those comic book properties would have been developed by Allen with anything like the sophistication that the Marvel superheroes are portrayed with now—but Allen would have done them first.

Irwin Allen never quite got back the artistic validation that he earned with his Academy Award for *The Sea Around Us* in 1953. But he outdid that acclaim in adulation from audiences, from the devoted fan bases for his TV shows, and, where Allen always felt it counted most—in pure box office. A show business fan since childhood, Allen lived his life surrounded by movie stars, hard working studio craftsmen, and the multi-million dollar toy box only motion picture production could provide.

An eternal man-child himself, he will probably always be remembered best by the children who grew up on his work: children who grew up to be film directors, special effects artists, and producers themselves.

Bill Mumy—Will Robinson himself—probably said it best:

I worked for Steven Spielberg in 1983 on the *Twilight Zone* movie, and Steven Spielberg walked up to me, thanked me—I was doing a little cameo, reprising an episode that I had been on as a kid. And Spielberg walked up to me and he shook my hand and he said, "Thank you for doing this. You know, your work on *The Twilight Zone* and *Lost In Space* was a huge inspiration to me when I was a kid."

And if Irwin Allen was responsible for inspiring Steven Spielberg and George Lucas and that type, then he should be smiling.

**OPPOSITE**
Concept art of Will Robinson and the Robot from 2018's *Lost in Space*: a contemporary interpretation of the most familiar relationship from Irwin Allen's *Lost in Space*, characters and situations created by Allen half a century ago that will continue to inspire filmmakers and audiences well into the 21st Century.

# ABOUT THE AUTHOR

**JEFF BOND** is a freelance writer and magazine editor currently living in Los Angeles. He's the author of books on Star Trek, Seth McFarlane's *The Orville*, and Danny Elfman as well as a book on the Netflix series *Narcos*. He grew up watching Irwin Allen's television shows and movies, and this book represents the one he always wanted to see dedicated to Allen's works.

**ABOVE**
The author poses with one of the 36" Flying Sub miniatures from *Voyage to the Bottom of the Sea*. Photo by Lou Zutavern.